collection marabout service

Afin de vous informer de toutes ses publications, **marabout** édite des catalogues et prospectus où sont annoncés, régulièrement, les nombreux ouvrages qui vous intéressent. Pour les obtenir gracieusement, il suffit de nous envoyer votre carte de visite ou une simple carte postale mentionnant vos nom et adresse, aux Nouvelles Editions Marabout, 65, rue de Limbourg - B-4800 Verviers (Belgique).

Du même auteur :

Dictionnaire commercial et financier, français-allemand / allemand-français.
(Marabout Service n° 21).

Dictionnaire commercial et financier en 4 langues.
(Standaard Uitgeverij — Editions Erasme).

nouvelle édition, entièrement revue, à paraître en 1981.

J.-V. Servotte

dictionnaire commercial et financier

français-anglais
anglais-français

marabout

© N.V. Scriptoria, Anvers, Antwerpen/Amsterdam 1978.

Toute reproduction d'un extrait quelconque de ce livre par quelque procédé que ce soit, et notamment par photocopie ou microfilm, est interdite sans autorisation écrite de l'éditeur.

Les collections **marabout** sont éditées par la s.a. Les Nouvelles Éditions Marabout, 65, rue de Limbourg, B-4800 Verviers (Belgique). — Le label **marabout**, les titres des collections et la présentation des volumes sont déposés conformément à la loi. — Distributeurs en **France** : HACHETTE s.a., Avenue Gutenberg, Z.A. de Coignères- Maurepas, 78310 Maurepas, B.P. 154 — pour le **Canada** et les **Etats-Unis** : A.D.P. Inc, 955, rue Amherst, Montréal 132, P.Q. Canada — en **Suisse** : Office du Livre, 101, route de Villars, 1701 Fribourg.

TABLE DES MATIERES
CONTENTS

Comment utiliser le dictionnaire :	5
How to use the dictionary	6
Dictionnaire français-anglais	7
Supplément	392
Index	459
Address, salutation, complimentary close	501
Abbreviations	505
Weights and measures — metric	510
— british & U.S.	511

COMMENT UTILISER LE DICTIONNAIRE

Le dictionnaire comprend une série de locutions et termes commerciaux, financiers et économiques, classés alphabétiquement en langue française, avec, en regard, les équivalents anglais.

En dehors des termes précités, l'ouvrage contient un choix d'expressions d'usage courant dans la correspondance commerciale.

Ordre des locutions : 1. le mot suivi d'un complément ; 2. le mot suivi d'un verbe ; 3. le mot comme complément d'un substantif ; 4. le mot comme complément d'un verbe.

Exemple : **prix** *m.*
        1. — d'avant-guerre
        2. les — montent
        3. chute *f.* des —
        4. augmenter les —

Genre des mots : Le genre est indiqué pour chaque substantif français *(m., f., pl.)*. Le genre d'un mot n'est pas spécifié lorsqu'il ressort clairement de l'adjectif qui l'accompagne.

Index : Le dictionnaire proprement dit est suivi d'un index alphabétique pour l'anglais. Le numéro en regard des mots renvoie à la page où figure la traduction.

Là où il y a plusieurs numéros, celui en caractères gras indique la page où la traduction est complétée par un choix d'expressions.

Principales abréviations :

adj.	adjectif	*jur.*	terme de droit
adv.	adverbe	*m.*	masculin
Amer.	Amérique	*mar.*	maritime
assur.	assurance	*pl.*	pluriel
compt.	comptabilité	*qqch.*	quelque chose
f.	féminin	*qqn.*	quelqu'un
Gr. Br.	Grande-Bretagne	*tel.*	téléphone

HOW TO USE THE DICTIONARY

This dictionary contains commercial, financial, economic and legal terms and phrases. The French terms are arranged in alphabetical order, with their English equivalents opposite them.

Phrases of common occurrence in commercial correspondence are also given.

Order of phrases : 1. word followed by a complement ; 2. word followed by a verb ; 3. word as a complement to a substantive ; 4. word as a complement to a verb.

Example : **prix** *m.*
       1. — d'avant-guerre
       2. les — montent
       3. chute *f.* des —
       4. augmenter les —

Gender of words : The gender is indicated for each french substantive, unless it can be inferred from a concord *(m., f., pl.)*.

Indices : The dictionary itself is followed by reverse indices for the english. The number shown against each word refers to the page on which the translation can be found.
Where more than one number is given, that in bold type indicates the page on which the translation is accompanied by a series of phrases.

List of abbreviations :

adj.	adjective	*jur.*	law
adv.	adverb	*m.*	masculine
Amer.	America	*mar.*	maritime
assur.	insurance	*pl.*	plural
compt.	bookkeeping	*qqch.*	something
f.	feminine	*qqn*	somebody
Gr. Br.	Great Britain	*tel.*	telephone

A

à
1 – 30 francs
2 – 3 heures
3 – 3 pour cent
4 – l'usine
5 – quai
6 – la douzaine
7 – Paris
8 aller – Paris
abaisser (*le prix*)
abandon *m.*
1 – du navire et du fret

2 – du navire et des facultés (voir *délaissement*)
3 – de la prime
4 droit *m.* d'–
abandonner
– une prime
abattement *m.* (*impôts*)

abondance *f.*
abondant
abonné *m.*
1 – à un journal
2 – au chemin de fer
3 – au téléphone
abonnement *m.*
1 – à un journal
2 (carte d')–
3 conditions *f. pl.* d'–
4 souscrire un –
abonner, s'– à
abordage *m.*
aborder (*un navire*)
abréviation *f.*
abrogation *f.*
abroger
abscisse *f.*
absence *f.*
pendant son –
absentéisme *m.*
absorber (*pouvoir d'achat*)
abus *m.*
– de confiance
accablé
1 – de commandes
2 – de dettes
accalmie *f.*
accaparement *m.*

at, in
1 at 30 francs
2 at 3 o'clock
3 at 3 per cent
4 ex works
5 ex quay
6 by the dozen
7 in Paris
8 to go to Paris
to reduce, to lower
abandonment
1 – of the ship and freight

3 – of the option
4 right of –
to abandon
– an option
abatement, tax rebate

abundance
abundant
subscriber
1 – to a newspaper
2 season ticket holder
3 telephone –
subscription
1 – to a newspaper
2 season ticket
3 terms of –
4 to take out a – to
to subscribe to
collision
to collide with
abbreviation
abrogation
to abrogate
absciss(a)
absence
during (in) his –
absenteeism
to skim off
abuse, misuse
breach of trust, abuse of confidence
overwhelmed
1 – with orders
2 deep in dept, heavily indebted
lull
buying up, hoarding

accaparer / 8

accaparer	to buy up
accapareur *m.*	buyer up
accélération *f.*	acceleration
acceptation *f.*	acceptance
1 – (*lettre de change acceptée*)	1 –
2 – à découvert	2 uncovered –
3 – commerciale	3 trade –
4 – conditionnelle,	4 qualified –
5 – de banque	5 bank –
6 – de cautionnement	6 collateral –
7 – de complaisance	7 accommodation –
8 – en blanc	8 blank –
9 – par honneur	9 – for hono(u)r
10 – par intervention	10 – by intervention
11 – partielle	11 partial –
12 – sans réserves	12 general (clean) –
13 faute d'–	13 in default of –
14 commission *f.* d'–	14 commission for –
15 compte *m.* d'–	15 – account
16 crédit *m.* par –	16 – credit
17 débiteurs *pl.* par –	17 liabilities of customers for –
18 délai *m.* d'–	18 term of –
19 maison *f.* d'–s (*Gr. Br.*)	19 – house, accepting house
20 marché *m.* d'–s	20 – market
21 refus *m.* d'–	21 refusal to accept, non acceptance
22 envoyer à l'–	22 to send out for –
23 munir de l'–	23 to accept
24 présenter à l'–	24 to present for –
25 refuser l'–	25 to refuse to accept
26 revêtir de l'–	26 to accept
27 soigner l'–	27 to procure –
accepter (v. *aussi agréer*)	to accept
1 – à présentation	1 – on presentation
2 – des documents	2 – documents
3 – une lettre de change	3 – a bill
4 – une offre	4 – an offer
5 faire –	5 to get accepted
6 traite *f.* acceptée	6 accepted bill, acceptance
accepteur *m.*	acceptor
– par honneur, par intervention	– for hono(u)r, supra protest
accès *m.* (à)	access (to)
accessoire	accessory, subsidiary
1 frais *pl.* –s.	1 attendant expenses
2 occupation *f.* –	2 subsidiary occupation
3 revenus *m. pl.* –s	3 subsidiary earnings, income
accident *m.*	accident
1 – d'auto	1 motor car –
2 – de route, de circulation	2 traffic (road) – [juries
3 – du travail	3 injuries to workmen, industrial in-
accise *f.*	excise
1 exempt d'–	1 free from –
2 soumis (sujet) aux droits d'–	2 liable to –
acclamation *f.*, par –	acclamation, by (with) –

accommodement m.
  en venir à un –
accompagné
  –des documents suivants
accompagnement m.
  feuille f. d'–
accompli
  1 32 ans –s
  2 un fait –
accord m.
  1 – commercial
  2 – de clearing
  3 – financier
  4 – monétaire
  5 – Monétaire Européen

  6 d'– avec
  7 d'un commun –

  8 un – prend fin
  9 terminaison f. d'un –
  10 adhérer à un –
  11 conclure (passer) un –
  12 être d'–
  13 tomber d'–
accorder
accrédité, l'–

  banque –e
accréditer
  – auprès d'une banque

accréditeur m.
accréditif m. (v. aussi *crédit docum.*)
  1 – à ouvrir chez la banque ...
  2 – rotatif
  3 – rotatif cumulatif
  4 en vertu d'un –
  5 l'– expire
accroissement m.

  1 – de fortune
  2 rythme m. d'–
  3 taux m. d'–

accueil m.
  1 brochure f. d'– (voir *brochure*)
  2 faire bon – à une traite

  3 remercier pour l'aimable – réservé
    à...
accueillir

arrangement
  to come to terms
accompanied
  – by the following documents
accompaniment
  covering (accompanying) letter
accomplished
  1 full 32 years
  2 an – fact
agreement
  1 trade –
  2 clearing –
  3 financial –
  4 monetary –
  5 European Monetary –

  6 in concert (–) with
  7 by mutual –, by common consent

  8 an – terminates
  9 termination of an –
  10 to accede to an –
  11 to conclude an –
  12 to be at one, to agree
  13 to come to terms
to grant
the accredited person

  accredited bank
to raise the credit
  to open a credit for... with a bank

guarantor
credit
  1 letter of – to be opened at...
  2 revolving –
  3 cumulative revolving –
  4 under a –
  5 the – expires
increase

  1 – of fortune
  2 tempo (pace) of –
  3 rate of –, growth ratio

reception

  2 to hono(u)r (meet) a draft

  3 to thank for the welcome which you
    gave (for the courtesy shown) to
to receive

accumulation / 10

accumulation *f.*
accumuler
accusé *m.*
  1 – de bien trouvé de notre extrait de compte
  2 – de réception

  3 le présent envoi n'appelle pas d'– de réception
accuser
  1 – une hausse
  2 nous (vous) accusons bonne réception
achalander
  bien achalandé

achat *m.* (v. aussi *tempérament*)
  1 – à découvert (*bourse*)
  2 – à terme (*à crédit*)
  3 – à terme

  4 – à terme ferme

  5 – au comptant

  6 –s de placement

  7 –s de soutien

  8 –s en vue d'obtenir la majorité

  9 – ferme
  10 –s spéculatifs
  11 – sur échantillon
  12 – sur livraison
  13 contrat *m.* d'–
  14 note *f.* d'– (*courtier*)
  15 pouvoir *m.* d'– (voir *pouvoir*)
  16 prix *m.* d'–
  17 faire des –s
acheter
  1 – à crédit
  2 – à découvert
  3 – à la baisse
  4 – à la hausse
  5 – à tempérament

  6 – à terme

  7 – (au) comptant
  8 – ferme
  9 – dont

accumulation
to accumulate

1 confirmation of our statement of account
2 acknowledgment (receipt) of...

3 no acknowledgment expected

to accuse
1 to show a rise, an advance
2 we acknowledge (receipt of)

to procure (provide with) custom
well connected, well attended, with a large custom

purchase, buying
  1 bull purchase
  2 purchase on credit
  3 (*valeurs*) buying for the account, for the settlement
  4 purchase for future delivery during specified periods
  5 purchase for cash

  6 investment buying, buying for investment purposes
  7 supporting purchases

  8 buying with a view to securing a majority
  9 fixed purchase
  10 speculative buying
  11 purchase by sample
  12 purchase for delivery
  13 purchasing contract
  14 bought note, broker's note

  16 purchase price
  17 to make purchases, to go shopping
to buy, to purchase
  1 to buy on credit
  2 to buy for a rise
  3 to buy on a fall
  4 to buy for a rise
  5 to buy on the instalment plan

  6 (*march.*) to buy forward ; (*valeurs*) to buy for the account, for the settlement
  7 to buy for cash
  8 to buy firm   [option
  9 to give for the call, to buy a call

10 – ou

acheteur *m.*
1 – de bonne foi
2 – d'un dont, d'une prime directe

3 – d'un ou, d'une prime indirecte
4 au gré de l'–
5 marché *m.* des –s
6 position *f.* –
acompte *m.*

1 – mensuel
2 – minimum (*vente à tempérament*)
3 – sur dividende
4 donner un –

5 payer par –s
6 verser un –
acquéreur *m.*
1 – de bonne foi
2 trouver –s
acquêt *m.* (v. aussi *communauté*)
acquisition *f.* (v. aussi *action*)
1 –, possession et aliénation

2 prix *m.* d'–
acquit *m.*
1 – à caution
2 – de douane
3 – de payement
4 – de transit

5 donner –
6 ,,pour –''

acquitté
1 marchandises –es
2 vendre à l'–
acquitter
1 – une dette

2 – une facture

acte *m.* (*action*)
1 – d'administration
2 – de commerce
3 – de disposition
acte *m.* (*document;* v. aussi *certificat*)
1 – authentique
2 – constitutif
3 – de cautionnement

10 to take for the put, to sell a put option
buyer, purchaser
1 bona fide purchaser
2 giver for a call, buyer of a call option
3 taker for a put, seller of a put option
4 at buyer's option
5 buyers' market
6 bull position
instalment, payment of account down-payment
1 monthly instalment
2 minimum down-payment
3 interim dividend
4 to pay (a sum) on account

5 to pay by instalments
6 to pay... on account
purchaser, buyer
1 bona fide –
2 to find buyers
property acquired (in common)
acquisition, purchase
1 acquisition, possession and alienation
2 purchase price

1 bond note, transhipment note
2 custom house receipt
3 receipt for payment
4 transit bond

5 to give a receipt
6 received (with thanks)

1 duty-paid goods
2 to sell duty paid
to pay
1 to pay (off) a debt

2 to receipt a bill

act
1 – of administration
2 – of merchant, commercial –
3 – of disposal
deed, instrument
1 deed, public instrument
2 deed of partnership
3 surety bond

actif / 12

4 – de cession
5 – d'échange
6 – de décès
7 – de mariage
8 – de naissance
9 – de notoriété (*héritier*)
10 – de protêt
11 – de société
12 – de vente
13 – notarié
14 – récognitif
15 – sous seing privé
16 – translatif de propriété
17 suivant – reçu par le notaire...

18 passer un –
actif (*marché*)
actif *m.*
  1 – et passif
  2 – disponible
  3 –s donnés en garantie
  4 – immobilisé

  5 – liquide
  6 – net
  7 – réalisable
  8 apport *m.* de l'– à la nouvelle société
  9 côté *m.* de l'–
  10 passer à l'–
action *f.*
  1 – à la souche
  2 – au porteur
  3 – ancienne
  4 – à vote plural
  5 – bénéficiaire
  6 – d'apport
  7 – de banque
  8 – de capital
  9 – de chemins de fer
  10 – de dividende
  11 – de fondateur
  12 – de jouissance
      [gestion]
  13 – de garantie (en garantie de
  14 – de numéraire
  15 – de priorité
  16 – de priorité cumulative
  17 – différée
  18 – entièrement libérée
  19 – gratuite

4 deed of conveyance, deed of transfer
5 barter arrangement
6 death certificate
7 marriage certificate
8 birth certificate
9 identity certificate
10 deed of protest
11 deed of partnership
12 sale contract
13 notarial deed
14 act of acknowledgment
15 deed under private seal
16 deed of transfer
17 in accordance with the deed passed before Mr... notary public

18 to draw up a deed
brisk, active
assets
  1 – and liabilities
  2 available –
  3 – pledged as collateral
  4 fixed –

  5 liquid (available) –
  6 net –
  7 realizable –
  8 contribution of the – to the new company
  9 assets side
  10 to put on the assets side
share (*plur.* shares, stock(s)), **equities**
  1 unissued –
  2 bearer –
  3 old –
  4 – with plural voting right
  5 participating –
  6 vendor's –
  7 bank –
  8 capital –
  9 railway –
  10 participating –
  11 founder's –
  12 profit-sharing certificate (to holders of redeemed shares)
  13 qualification –
  14 cash –
  15 preference –
  16 cumulative preference –
  17 deferred –
  18 fully paid –
  19 bonus –

13 / action

20 – minière	20 mining –
21 – nominative	21 personal (registered) –
22 – nouvelle	22 new –
23 – ordinaire	23 common (ordinary) –
24 – populaire (*Allem.*)	24 people's share
25 – privilégiée	25 preference –
26 – privilégiée participante	26 participating preferred –
27 – rachetée	27 amortized –
28 – sans valeur nominale	28 – without par value
29 – souscrite	29 – applied for, – subscribed
30 à raison d'une nouvelle – pour 2 anciennes	30 in the proportion of one new – for two old ones (for every two ones)
31 acquisition *f.* de ses propres –s	31 buying in (repurchase) of –
32 capital–s *m.*	32 – capital
33 certificat *m.* d'–	33 – certificate
34 coupure *f.* d'–	34 subshare
35 cours *pl.* des –s	35 – prices
36 échange *m.* d'–s	36 exchange of –s
37 émission *f.* d'–s	37 issue of –s
38 estampillage *m.* d'–s	38 stamping of –s
39 indice *m.* des –s	39 – index
40 libération *f.* d'–s	40 paying up of –s
41 lot (paquet) *m.* d'–s	41 block of stocks
42 marché *m.* des –s	42 – (stock) market
43 porteur *m.* d'–s	43 shareholder
44 promesse *f.* d'–s	44 promise of –
45 rachat (retrait) *m.* d'–s	45 paying off of –s
46 répartition *f.* d'–s	46 allotment of –s
47 société *f.* par –s	47 joint stock company
48 souscripteur *m.* à des –s	48 (subscriber) applicant for –s
49 souscription *f.* à des –s	49 application for –s
50 transfert *m.* d'–s	50 transfer of –s
51 attribuer des –s	51 to allot –s
52 créer des –s	52 to issue –s
53 détenir des –s	53 to hold –s
54 diviser des –s	54 to split –s
55 échanger des anciennes –s contre des –s nouvelles	55 to exchange old –s for new ones
56 émettre des –s	56 to issue –s
57 libérer des –s	57 to pay up –s
58 libérer des –s entièrement	58 to pay up –s in full
59 nourrir des –s	59 to pay up –s
60 placer des –s	60 to issue –s
61 placer des –s dans le public	61 to place –s with the public
62 racheter (retirer) des –s	62 to pay off –s
63 répartir des –s	63 to allot –s
64 souscrire à des –s	64 to apply (subscribe) for –s
65 transférer des –s	65 to transfer –s

action / 14

action *f. (jur.)*
1 – de change, cambiale
2 – en ...
3 – en dommages-intérêts

4 – en résolution, – résolutoire
5 – personnelle
6 – revendicatoire
7 intenter une – en justice

actionnaire *m.*
activité *f. (marché)*
 1 en pleine –

 2 déployer une grande –
actuaire *m.*

actuel
 1 malaise –
 2 prix –s
addition *f.*
additionnel, centimes -s
additionner
adiré
adjudicataire *m. (fournitures, travaux)*
 – *(vente)*
adjudicateur *m.*
adjudication *f. (fournitures, travaux)*
 1 – *(vente)*
 2 – (attribution) au plus bas soumissionnaire,
 3 l'– aura lieu le ...
 4 par –, par voie d'–

 5 mettre en –
adjugé
adjuger
admettre
 1 il est généralement admis que
 2 nous n'admettons pas que
 3 n'– aucun retard *(affaire)*
administrateur *m.*
 – délégué

administratif
 par voie administrative
administration *f.*
 1 – centrale *(entreprise)*
 2 – communale
 3 – des contributions
administrer

action
1 action on a bill of exchange
2 ... –
3 – for damages

4 – for rescission
5 personal –
6 – for recovery
7 to bring an – against, to sue

shareholder
animation, briskness
 1 at work, going, in full activity

 2 to show great activity
actuary

present
 1 prevailing depression
 2 ruling prices
addition, casting
additional percentage
to add up, to cast, to total
lost
contractor

successful bidder
adjudicator, awarder
invitation for tenders
 1 sale by auction
 2 allocation to the lowest tender (er)

 3 the allotment will take place on...
 4 by contract, by tender

 5 to invite tenders for
gone
to knock down
to accept
 1 it is generally accepted that
 2 we cannot assume that
 3 to admit no delay
director
managing –

administrative
 administratively
management
 1 general management
 2 municipal administration
 3 taxation authorities
to manage, to administer

admission *f.* (v. aussi *cote*)
 – temporaire (*douane*)

adopter
 1 – une position d'attente

 2 – une résolution
adressé *m.* au besoin
adresse *f.* (v. aussi *inconnu*)
 1 – au besoin
 2 – commerciale
 3 – complète
 4 – privée
 5 – télégraphique

 6 – et profession (voir *profession, qualité*)
 7 à l'– indiquée
 8 bureau *m.* d'–s
 9 changement *m.* d'–
 10 côté réservé à l'–, côté de l'–
 11 liste *f.* d'–s
 12 livre *m.* d'–s (*bottin*)
 13 machine *f.* à –s
 14 parti sans laisser d'– (voir *partir*)
 15 nous devons votre – à...

 16 envoyer à l'– de
 17 prendre le nom et l'–
adresser
 1 – une lettre à
 2 nous vous adressons sous ce pli

 3 s'– à
adultération *f.* (*monnaie*)
aérien
 1 compagnie *f.* de navigation –ne
 2 ligne –ne
 3 récépissé –

 4 récépissé de poste –ne
 5 service –
 6 trafic –
 7 trafic postal –
aérogare *f.*, **aéroport** *m.*
affaire *f.*
 1 avoir – à
 2 commencer une –
 3 donner de l'extension à une –
affaires *f. pl.*
 1 – à la gomme
 2 – à prime
 3 – à terme

admission
 temporary –

to adopt
 1 to assume a waiting attitude

 2 to pass (carry) a resolution
address in case of need
address
 1 – in case of need
 2 business –
 3 full –
 4 private –
 5 telegraphic –

 7 to the stated –
 8 inquiry office
 9 change of –
 10 – side
 11 mailing list (*pour envois réguliers*)
 12 directory
 13 addressing machine

 15 we owe your – to, we are indebted to... for your –
 16 to send to the – of
 17 to take name and –
to address
 1 to – a letter to
 2 enclosed we are handing you, we are enclosing herewith
 3 to apply to
debasement
aerial
 1 aerial navigation (air line) company
 2 airline
 3 Air Receipt

 4 Air Mail Receipt
 5 air service
 6 – traffic
 7 air mail traffic
airport
business
 1 to have to do with
 2 to start a –
 3 to extend a –
business
 1 bogus transactions
 2 option dealings
 3 time bargain

affection / 16

4 – au comptant	4 cash transactions
5 – courantes	5 current matters
6 – d'arbitrage	6 arbitrage transactions
7 – de bourse	7 exchange business
8 pour –	8 on –
9 les – ralentissent	9 – declines
10 les – reprennent	10 – is recovering, has become more lively
11 les – sont à peu près nulles	11 there is almost nothing to do in –
12 les – vont bien	12 – is thriving
13 les – vont mal	13 trade is bad
14 accroissement *m.* des –	14 increase of –
15 chiffre *m.* d'–	15 turnover
16 connaissance *f.* des –s	16 knowledge of affairs, – knowledge
17 développement *m.* des –	17 development of –
18 diminution *f.* des –	18 diminution (decrease) of –
19 essor *m.* des –	19 development of –
20 expérience *f.* des –	20 – experience
21 extension *f.* des –	21 – expansion
22 gens *f.* d'–	22 – men
23 homme *m.* d'–	23 – man
24 lettre *f.* d'–	24 – letter
25 marche *f.* des –	25 trend of –
26 monde *m.* des –	26 – world
27 mouvement *m.* des –	27 – movement
28 ralentissement *m.* des –	28 decline of –
29 relations *f. pl.* d'–	29 – relations
30 stagnation *f.* des –	30 stagnation of –
31 volume *m.* des –	31 volume of –
32 voyage *m.* d'–	32 – travel, – tour
33 entrer en –	33 to enter into –
34 être dans les –	34 to be in –
35 faire de bonnes –	35 to carry on (to do) a large –
36 se retirer des –	36 to retire (withdraw) from –
37 traiter des –	37 to carry on –
38 voyager en –	38 to travel on –
affectation *f.* (*somme*)	**appropriation, earmarking**
– hypothécaire	mortgage charge
affecter	**to earmark**
1 – une somme à	1 to charge (–) an amount to
2 – une somme à la réserve	2 to put an amount to the reserve
3 être affecté par	3 to be affected by
affermage *m.*	**leasing**
affermer	**to lease**
affichage *m.*	**billsticking, placarding**
panneau *m.* d'–	billboard
affiche *f.*	**bill, poster**
1 colonne *f.* –s	1 advertising (poster) pillar
2 annoncer par voie d'–s	2 to placard, to bill, to post up

afficher
  1 – les prix
  2 défense *f.* d'– (voir *défense*)
affidavit *m.*
affluer
afflux *m.* d'or
affranchir (v. aussi *port*)
  1 insuffisamment affranchi
  2 non affranchi
affranchissement *m.*
affrètement *m.*
  1 – à (en) cueillette

  2 – au poids
  3 – au voyage
  4 – à temps, à terme
  5 contrat *m.* d'–

affréter
affréteur *m.*
  fréteur et –
afin de
afin que
âge *m.*
  à l'– de 30 ans
agence *f.*
  1 – de placement
  2 – de publicité
  3 – de renseignements
  4 – de voyages
  5 – en douane

  6 – immobilière
  7 avoir des –s dans les principales villes de...
  8 confier une – à
  9 supprimer une –
agenda *m.*
agent *m.*
  1 – d'affaires
  2 – d'assurances
  3 – commercial
  4 – consulaire
  5 – de change
  6 – de douane
  7 – en douane
  8 – exclusif
  9 – général

agio *m.*
  les –s (*frais d'escompte*)
agiotage *m.*

---

to post (up), to stick
  1 to mark up prices

affidavit
to flow to
inflow (influx) of gold
to stamp
  1 insufficiently stamped
  2 unstamped
stamping, prepayment
chartering, freighting, loading
  1 berth(liner) freighting, loading on the berth
  2 freighting on weight
  3 voyage charter
  4 time charter
  5 contract of affreightment, chartering agreement
to charter
charterer
  owner and –
in order to
in order that
age
  at the – of 30
agency
  1 employment –
  2 advertising –
  3 inquiry –
  4 travel –
  5 customs –

  6 estate –
  7 to have branches in all the principal towns of...
  8 to entrust... with an –
  9 to discontinue an –
pocket diary
agent
  1 business –
  2 insurance –
  3 commercial –
  4 consular –
  5 stockbroker
  6 customs officer
  7 customs –, custom house broker
  8 sole –
  9 general –

agio, exchange premium
  discount charges
stock gambling, agiotage

agioleur / 18

agioteur *m.* — stock gambler
agrafage *m.* — stapling
agrafe *f.* — staple
agrafeuse *f.* — stapler
agréer — to accept
  agréez, Monsieur, mes sentiments respectueux etc. — yours faithfully, (*Amer.*) yours (very) truly, very truly yours
agricole — agricultural
  1 banque *f.* – — 1 – bank
  2 crédit *m.* – — 2 – credit
  3 exposition *f.* – — 3 – show, – exhibition
  4 industrie *f.* – — 4 – farming
  5 prix –s — 5 – prices
  6 région *f.* – — 6 – district
agriculture *f.* — agriculture
aide *f.* — help, assistance
  – Marshall — Marshall aid
aide-comptable *m.* — assistant accountant
aisance *f.* sur le marché monétaire — easiness on the money market
aisé, les gens -s — the well-to-do people
ajournement *m.* — postponement, adjournment
ajourner — to postpone, to adjourn
ajouter — to add
ajustement *m.* — adjustment
  – des salaires — wage –
ajuster — to adjust
  1 - un compte — 1 – an account
  2 - un différend — 2 – a difference
aliénable — alienable
aliénation *f.* — alienation
aliéner — to alienate
alignement *m.* — adjustment
  1 – des prix — 1 – of prices
  2 – (*de rue*) — 2 building line
  3 – monétaire — 3 – of exchange rates
alimenter (*caisse*) — to supply, to maintain
  – un fonds par ... — to maintain a fund by...
alinéa *m.* — paragraph
  –! — new –
aliquote
  partie – — aliquot part
allège *f.* — lighter, barge
  transborder sur des –s — to transship into –s
allègement *m.* — lightening
  – des impôts, – fiscal — – of taxation
aller — to go
  1 – et retour — 1 out and home
  2 l'– et le retour — 2 the out and the home voyage
  3 billet *m.* d'– et retour — 3 return ticket
  4 assurer pour l'– et le retour — 4 to insure out and home
  5 – jusqu'à (100 frs) — 5 – as high as...
  6 – par le train — 6 – by train
  7 fret *m.* d'– — 7 outward freight

allocation *f.*
 1 – de chômage
 2 – de la mère au foyer (*Belg.*)
 3 – de naissance
 4 – familiale
allonge *f.*

allouer
almanach *m.*
alphabétique
 par ordre –
amarrage *m.*
amarrer
ambassade *f.*
ambassadeur *m.*
amélioration *f.*
 légère –; sensible –
aménager
 bien aménagé
amendement *m.*

 1 – (*de terres*)
 2 proposer un – à...
amiable, à l'-
 1 arrangement *m.* –

 2 vente *f.* –
 3 vendre –

amortir
 1 – une dette

 2 – un emprunt
 3 – des obligations
 4 – sur immeubles
amortissable
amortissement *m.*
 1 – d'une dette

 2 – d'un emprunt
 3 – pour usure
 4 – sur les bâtiments

 5 caisse *f.* d'–

 6 date *f.* d'–
 7 emprunt *m.* d'–
 8 plan *m.* d'–
 9 tableau *m.* d'–
ample (v. aussi *informé*)
 pour de plus –s renseignements
 s'adresser à ...
ampleur *f.* (voir *marché*)

allowance
 1 unemployment benefit, dole
 2 – for mothers in the home
 3 birth allowance
 4 family –
rider

to allow, to grant
almanac
alphabetical
 in – order
mooring
to moor
embassy
ambassador
improvement
 slight –; marked –
to fit up
 well equipped
amendment

 1 land improvement
 2 to propose (to move) an – to...
amicable
 1 – settlement

 2 – sale, private sale
 3 to sell privately

to amortize, to sink
 1 to amortize (pay off) a debt

 2 to redeem a loan
 3 to pay off bonds
 4 to write off on buildings, on pre- [mises
amortizable, redeemable
redemption, amortization
 1 discharge of a debt

 2 redemption of a loan
 3 depreciation for wear and tear
 4 writing off (depreciation) on premises
 5 sinking fund

 6 date of redemption
 7 amortization loan
 8 terms of redemption
 9 amortization table
wide
 for further particulars apply to...

ampliation *f.*
 pour −
amputer (*un crédit*)
an *m.*
 1 dans un −
 2 par −
 3 il y a un −
 4 le jour de l'−
 5 renouvellement *m.* de l'−
analyse *f.*
 1 − du marché
 2 − des ventes
 3 − marginaliste
 4 certificat *m.* d'−
analyste financier *m.*

anatocisme *m.*

ancienneté *f.*
 par rang d'−
ancre *m.*
 1 être à l'−
 2 jeter l'−
 3 lever l'−
animation *f.*
animé
 1 marché −
 2 rue −e
année *f.*
 1 − bissextile
 2 − budgétaire
 3 − civile
 4 − commerciale
 5 − de base
 6 − financière
 7 l'− passée
 8 l'− précédente
 9 l'− prochaine
 10 − sociale
 11 − sous revue
 12 d'− en −
 13 pendant toute l'−
 14 ouvert toute l'−
annexe *f.*
 1 avec 3 −s
 2 en −
annonce *f.* (v. aussi *insérer*)
 1 − à la radio
 2 − de rappel
annonceur *m.*
annuaire *m.*
 1 − de publicité
 2 − du commerce

certified copy
 true copy
to curtail, to reduce
year
 1 a − hence
 2 a −
 3 a − ago
 4 New Year's day
 5 turn of the −
analysis
 1 market −
 2 sales −
 3 marginal −
 4 certificate of −
security (investment) analyst

anatocism, the taking of compound interest
seniority
 by (according to) −
anchor
 1 to ride (lie) at −
 2 to cast −, to drop −
 3 to weigh −
liveliness
brisk
 1 − market
 2 busy (lively) street
year
 1 leap −
 2 financial (fiscal) −
 3 calendar (civil) −
 4 commercial −
 5 basic −
 6 financial −
 7 last −
 8 the previous −
 9 next −
 10 company's −
 11 − under review
 12 from − to −
 13 throughout the −
 14 open all the − round
enclosure
 1 with 3 −s
 2 herewith
advertisement
 1 radio announcement
 2 reminder −
advertiser
year book
 1 advertising directory
 2 trade directory

21 / annuité

3 – du téléphone | 3 telephone directory

annuité *f.* | **annuity**
1 – à vie | 1 life –
2 – contingente | 2 contingent –
3 – différée | 3 deferred –
annulation *f.* | **cancellation, cancelling**
– d'un crédit | cancellation of a credit
annuler | **to cancel, to annul**
1 ...et annule toute liste antérieure que vous pourriez posséder de nous | 1 ... and supersedes any former list you may have from us
2 – un chèque | 2 to cancel a cheque (check)
3 – un crédit | 3 to cancel a credit
4 – un ordre | 4 to cancel an order
5 – un timbre | 5 to cancel a stamp

antichrèse *f.* | **antichresis, pledging of the revenue of real estate**

anticipé | **anticipated, in advance**
1 payement – | 1 prepayment, payment in advance
2 remboursement – | 2 accelerated redemption
anticipation, par - | **in advance**
anticiper |
– un payement | to anticipate a payment
anticyclique | **anticyclical**
antidate *f.* | **antedating**
antidater | **to antedate, to date back**
anti-inflation *f.* | **anti-inflation**
anti-inflationniste | **anti-inflationary**
politique *f.* – | anti-inflation policy
apériteur *m.* | **leading underwriter**
appareil *m.* | **apparatus**
1 – administratif | 1 administrative machinery
2 – de production | 2 production machinery
3 – financier | 3 financial machinery
appartenir | **to belong**
1 à qui il appartiendra | 1 to whom it may concern
2 pour le compte de qui il appartient (voir *compte*) |
appel *m.* |
1 – au marché des capitaux | 1 recourse to the capital market
2 – de fonds | 2 calling, call
3 faire un – de fonds de... | 3 to make a call of...
4 verser un – de fonds | 4 to pay a call
5 – téléphonique | 5 telephone call

appelé (*jur.*) (voir *fidéicommis*) |
appeler | **to call**
1 – l'attention sur | 1 – attention to

application / 22

2 – un versement sur... | 2 – an instalment of... on...

application *f.*
en – de
appliquer
s'– à...

appoint *m.*
1 faire l'–
2 prière de faire l'–   [*salaire*]
appointements *m. pl.* (voir aussi
1 – fixes
2 les – importent peu (*annonce*)
3 toucher ses –
4 avec indication des – demandés
apport *m.* (v. aussi *actif*)
1 – en nature
2 – en société
3 action *f.* d'–
apposer
1 – les scellés

2 – sa signature
apprentissage *m.*
1 contrat *m.* d'–
2 être en –
approbation *f.*
– des comptes
approuvé *m.* de compte

retourner l'– dûment signé

approuver
approvisionnement *m.*
1 ... (*action*)
2 – (*provisions*)
3 – en matières premières
4 source *f.* d'–
approvisionner de
s'–
approximatif
1 estimation approximative
2 calcul –
approximativement
appui *m.* (*aide*)
1 à l'– de...

2 pièces *f. pl.* à l'–
après bourse
marché *m.* –
apurer
1 – un compte

application
in pursuance of
to apply
to be applicable on

bill
1 to make up the even money
2 no change given
salary
1 fixed –
2 – no object
3 to draw one's –
4 stating – required
assets brought into business
1 assets in kind brought in
2 assets transferred to company
3 vendor's share

1 to affix the seals to

2 to put (affix, set) one's signature
apprenticeship
1 articles of –
2 to be apprenticed
approbation
approval of the accounts
acknowledgment, reconciliation

to return the signed reconciliation

to approve

1 supplying
2 stock, supply
3 supply of raw materials
4 source of supply
to supply (with)
to lay in a stock of...
approximate
1 rough estimate
2 – calculation
approximately
support
1 in – of...

2 vouchers
after hours (in the street)
street market, (*Amer.*) curb market

1 to audit and agree an account

2 – une dette
3 – un solde déficitaire
arbitrage *m.*
  1 – direct, simple
  2 – indirect, composé
  3 – du (de) change

  4 – sur titres
  5 opérations *f. pl.* d'–
arbitrage (*jugement*)
  1 soumettre à un –
  2 trancher par –
arbitragiste *m.*
arbitral
  sentence –e
arbitre *m.*
arbitrer
archives *f. pl.*
argent *m.*
argent *m.* (*monnaie*)
  1 – à bon marché
  2 – au jour le jour
  3 – à vue
  4 – comptable
  5 – comptant
  6 – courant
  7 – de poche
  8 – en barres
  9 – en caisse
  10 – frais

  11 – liquide
  12 – monnayé
  13 – mort
  14 – remboursable fin du mois
  15 – remboursable le 15 du mois
  16 cours *m.* – (A.)
  17 loyer *m.* de l'–
  18 marché *m.* de l'–
  19 rareté *f.* de l'–
  20 somme *f.* d'–
  21 taux *m.* de l'–
  22 coter... –
  23 placer de l'–
arithmétique *f.*
  – commerciale

armateur *m.*
  – affréteur
armement *m.*
armer (*un navire*)
arrangement *m.*
  1 – à l'amiable

2 to wipe off a debt
3 to wipe off a debit balance
arbitrage
  1 simple –
  2 compound –
  3 – in exchange, arbitration of exchange
  4 stock –, – in securities
  5 arbitrage transactions
arbitration
  1 to refer to –
  2 to settle by –
arbitrageur, arbitragist
arbitral
  arbitration award
arbitrator
to arbitrate
archives
silver
money
  1 cheap –
  2 day-to-day –
  3 call –, – on (at) call
  4 hard cash
  5 ready –
  6 current –
  7 pocket –
  8 bar silver
  9 cash in hand
  10 fresh –

  11 available cash, ready –
  12 species
  13 dead –
  14 end of month settlement loan
  15 fortnightly settlement loan
  16 buyers, prices bid
  17 price of –
  18 – market
  19 scarcity of –
  20 sum of –
  21 – rate
  22 to be bid for at...
  23 to invest funds
arithmetic
  commercial –

(ship)owner
  owner charterer
shipping company, the owners
to man and supply
arrangement
  1 amicable settlement

arrérages / 24

2 – avec les créanciers
3 faire un –
arrérages *m. pl.*
arrêt *m.*
  1 – de payement
  2 faire – sur
arrêté *m.*
  1 – d'assurance (provisoire)
  2 – de caisse
  3 – de compte
  4 – ministériel
  5 approuvé par – royal
arrêter
  1 – un compte au...
  2 – un marché
  3 – le payement d'un chèque

arrhes *f. pl.*

arriéré *m.*
  1 faire rentrer des –s

  2 régler (solder) un –

arriéré (*adj.*)
  1 dividende –
  2 intérêts –s
  3 payement –
arrière-caution *f.*
arrimage *m.*
arrimer
arrimeur *m.*
arrivage *m.* (*de marchandises*)
  nouvel –
arrivée *f.* (v. aussi *assurance. bon,*
  1 à l'–   [*heureux*])
  2 gare *f.* d'–
arriver
  1 – à bon port
  2 – à un compromis
arrondir
  1 – à
  2 – au franc supérieur

  3 – en moins
  4 – en plus
  5 en nombres arrondis
article *m.* (*compt.*) (v. aussi *écriture, poste*)
  1 – collectif
  2 – de dépense
  3 – de redressement, – rectificatif
  4 – de virement

2 composition with the creditors
3 to make an –
arrears
stop, stoppage
  1 stopping of payment
  2 to attach, to seize

  1 cover note
  2 making up the cash
  3 settlement of account
  4 departmental (ministerial) order
  5 approved by Royal Decree
to stop
  1 to make up (close) an account on...
  2 to conclude a bargain
  3 – a cheque (check)

earnest, deposit

arrear
  1 to collect (recover) outstanding debts
  2 to pay off –, to make up back payments
overdue, in arrear, outstanding
  1 overdue dividend
  2 arrears of interest
  3 overdue payment
countersurety
stowage, stevedoring
to stow, to stevedore
stower, stevedore
arrival
  fresh –
arrival
  1 on –
  2 – station
to arrive
  1 – safely
  2 to come to a compromise
to round off
  1 – to
  2 – to the next higher franc

  3 – downwards to
  4 – upwards to
  5 in round numbers
item, entry

  1 combined (compound) entry
  2 item of expense
  3 correcting entry
  4 transfer entry

25 / article

5 – inverse, – de contrepassement
6 inscrire un – sur
7 pointer des –s
8 radier un –
article *m.* (voir aussi *produit*)
 1 –s de bureau
 2 –s de consommation
 3 – de fond (*journal*)
 4 –s de grande consommation
 5 – de journal
 6 – cinq de la loi
 7 – de luxe
 8 –s de première nécessité

 9 – de réclame
 10 – de série
 11 –s de voyage
 12 – saisonnier
 13 le présent –
 14 au sens de l'–...
 15 en vertu de l'–

 16 tenir un –
artisan *m.*
artisanal
 coopérative –e
artisanat *m.*
ascensionnel
 1 mouvement –
 2 tendance –le
assainir
assainissement *m.*

 1 – monétaire

 2 programme *m.* d'–

assemblée *f.*
 1 – des créanciers
 2 – extraordinaire
 3 à l'– générale des actionnaires

 4 assister à une –
 5 convoquer une –
 6 déposer des titres en vue de l'–

 7 tenir une – générale
asseoir
 1 – une hypothèque
 2 – un impôt sur...
 3 réputation bien assise
 4 voter par assis et levé

5 contra entry
6 to make an entry in
7 to check off items
8 to strike out an item
article
 1 stationery
 2 commodities
 3 leading –
 4 staple products
 5 newspaper –
 6 section five of the Act
 7 – of luxury
 8 – of prime necessity

 9 leading line
 10 mass produced –
 11 travel requisites
 12 seasonal goods
 13 the present –
 14 within the meaning of –...
 15 in pursuance (by virtue) of section...
 16 to deal in (to keep) an –
craftsman
handicrafts
 – co-operative
handicraft, craft
rising
 1 upward movement
 2 – (upward) tendency
to reorganize
reorganization, (financial) reconstruction
 1 re-establishment of currency, financial rehabilitation
 2 programme of (financial) reconstruction
meeting
 1 – of creditors
 2 extraordinary –
 3 at the general – of shareholders

 4 to attend a –
 5 to convoke (call, convene) a –
 6 to deposit securities with a view to attending the –
 7 to hold a general –

 1 to raise a mortgage
 2 to establish a tax on
 3 well-established reputation
 4 to give one's vote by rising or remaining seated

assermenté
traducteur –
assiette *f.* **des impôts**
assistante sociale

assister à
association *f.*
1 – des banques
2 – des employeurs, – patronale
3 – des pays et territoires d'outre-mer
4 – en participation

5 – Européenne de libre Échange
6 – générale
7 – ouvrière
8 – professionnelle
9 – sans but lucratif

associé *m.*
1 – commanditaire
2 – commandité
3 – gérant
associer, s'- avec
assortiment *m.*
un ample –
assortir
assujetti
1 – à l'impôt
2 – au droit de timbre
assumer
1 – tous les risques
2 n'– aucune responsabilité
assurable
1 intérêt *m.* –
2 valeur *f.* –
assurance *f.* (voir aussi *police*)
1 – à capital différé
2 – au premier risque
3 – automobiles
4 – avec participation aux bénéfices

5 – contre la casse
6 – contre la grêle
7 – contre la maladie
8 – contre la maladie et l'invalidité

9 – contre la perte des loyers
10 – contre la vieillesse
11 – contre le bris des glaces
12 – contre le chômage
13 – contre les accidents
14 – contre les accidents du travail

sworn
– translator
basis of assessment
social aid, social worker

to attend
association
1 bankers' association
2 employers' –
3 – of the overseas countries and territories
4 special (particular) partnership

5 European Free Trade Association
6 general –
7 labour –
8 professional –
9 non-profit –

partner
1 silent (sleeping) –
2 active –
3 managing –
to associate oneself with
assortment
a large (rich) – of
to assort
liable
1 – for tax
2 – to stamp duty
to assume
1 – all risks
2 – no responsibility
insurable
1 – interest
2 – value
assurance, insurance
1 endowment insurance
2 first loss –
3 motor car insurance
4 profit sharing (participating) insurance

5 – against breakage
6 hailstorm insurance
7 sickness insurance
8 sickness and disablement insurance

9 rent insurance
10 old-age insurance
11 plate glass insurance
12 unemployment insurance
13 accident insurance
14 employers' liability insurance

27 / assurance

15 – contre les risques de guerre
16 – contre les risques de remboursement au pair
17 – contre les risques du crédit
18 – contre le vol
19 – contre l'incendie
20 – contre tous risques

21 – contre tous risques d'auto (voir police), (*Belg.*) – omnium
22 – de crédit
23 – crédit à l'exportation
24 – de cautionnement
25 – de responsabilité civile

26 – des bagages
27 – dotale
28 – du bétail
29 – du fret
30 – en cas de décès

31 – en cas de vie
32 – fluviale

33 – maritime
34 – mixte
35 – mutuelle
36 – obligatoire

37 – pluie (vacances)
38 – pour le compte de qui il appartiendra [valeur
39 – pour une somme supérieure à la
40 –s sociales
41 organisme *m.* d'–s sociales
42 – supplémentaire

43 – sur bonne arrivée [les
44 – sur bonnes ou mauvaises nouvelles
45 – sur corps, sur navire
46 – sur facultés, sur marchandises
47 – (sur la) vie
48 – terrestre
49 – vieillesse
50 l'– court
51 agent *m.* d'–s
52 certificat *m.* d'–
53 compagnie *f.* d'–
54 contrat *m.* d'–
55 courtier *m.* d'–

15 war risk insurance
16 insurance against risks of redemption at par
17 credit insurance
18 burglary insurance, theft insurance
19 fire insurance
20 all risk insurance, insurance against all risks
21 motor vehicle comprehensive –

22 credit insurance
23 export credit insurance
24 guarantee insurance
25 public liability insurance, third party insurance
26 luggage insurance
27 dowry insurance
28 livestock insurance
29 freight insurance
30 whole-life insurance

31 (pure) endowment assurance
32 river insurance

33 marine (maritime) insurance
34 endowment assurance
35 mutual insurance
36 compulsory insurance

37 weather insurance
38 insurance for account of whom it may concern
39 overinsurance
40 social insurances
41 social insurance institution
42 additional insurance

43 insurance on (subject to) safe arrival
44 insurance made lost or not lost
45 hull insurance
46 cargo insurance
47 life insurance
48 non-marine insurance
49 old-age insurance
50 the insurance runs
51 insurance agent
52 insurance certificate
53 insurance company
54 insurance contract
55 insurance broker

assuré / 28

56 fonds *m.* d'–
57 police *f.* d'–
58 preneur *m.* d'–
59 prime *f.* d'–
60 timbre *m.* d'–
61 valeur *f.* d'–
62 couvrir l'–
63 contracter une –
64 donner l'– que

65 effectuer, soigner l'–
assuré *m.*
assurer
 1 – pour...
 2 s'– contre
 3 s'– de
 4 je vous assure que

 5 vous pouvez être assuré que ...

assureur *m.*
 – conseil
atermoyer

atomique
 1 énergie *f.* –
 2 application pacifique de l'énergie atomique
attache *f.* de bureau
attaché commercial
attacher
 1 coupon attaché
 2 avec documents attachés
attendre
 1 en attendant votre réponse

 2 s'– à
attendus *m. pl.* (*jugement*)
attente *f.*
 1 contre toute –
 2 dans l'– de
 3 garder (observer) une attitude d'– (d'expectative)
 4 liste *f.* d' –
attention *f.*
 1 – (*emballage*)
 2 à l'– de monsieur
 3 votre lettre a eu notre meilleure –

 4 dont le contenu a eu toute notre –

 5 attirer l'–

56 insurance fund
57 insurance policy
58 insurance taker
59 insurance premium
60 insurance stamp
61 insurance value
62 to cover the insurance
63 to take out an insurance
64 to assure that

65 to effect the insurance
insured, insurant
to insure
 1 – for...
 2 – against
 3 to ascertain, to make sure of
 4 I assure you that

 5 you may rest (be) assured that

insurer, underwriter
 insurance consultant
to defer payment, to grant a respite
atomic
 1 atomic (nuclear) energy
 2 peaceful use of – energy

paper clip
commercial attaché
to attach
 1 with (cum) coupon
 2 with attached documents
to wait
 1 looking forward to receiving your reply
 2 to expect
the reasons adduced
expectation
 1 contrary to all –s
 2 awaiting
 3 to assume a waiting attitude

 4 waiting list
attention
 1 (handle) with care!
 2 – of Mr...
 3 your letter had our careful (best) –
 4 we duly noted contents of your letter

 5 to attract –

6 attirer spécialement l'– sur
7 faire – à
attirer
– des capitaux
attribuer
1 – des actions
2 – intégralement
attribution *f.* (v. aussi *avis*)
1 – d'actions
2 – partielle
au fur et à mesure
– des besoins
augmentation *f.*
1 – de 10 %
2 – de capital
3 – de prix
4 – de salaire
5 – de valeur
6 accuser une –
7 subir une –
augmenter
1 – les prix de
2 les prix augmentent
aujourd'hui
1 d'– en huit
2 cours *m.* d'–
autarcie *f.*

authenticité *f.*
– des documents
authentiquer
auto(mobile) *f.* (v. *voiture*)
1 en –
2 industrie automobile
3 marché automobile
autobus *m.*
auto-camion *m.*
autocar *m.*
autofinancement *m.*

automation *f.*
autorisation *f.*
  1 – d'accepter
  2 – d'acheter
  3 – de négocier
  4 – de payer
  5 – de transfert
  6 – d'exportation
  7 – d'importation
  8 – maritale

  9 – préalable
10 soumis à une –

---

6 to draw specially the – to
7 to pay – to
to attract
– capital
to allot
1 – shares to…
2 – in full
allotment
1 – of shares
2 partial –
as, in proportion as
as and when required, wanted
rise, increase
1 10 % rise, rise of 10 %
2 increase of capital
3 increase of price
4 rise in (of) wages
5 increase in value
6 to show a rise
7 to undergo (experience) a rise
to increase
1 – prices by
2 prices are rising
to-day
1 this day week
2 –'s price
autarchy, autarky, self-sufficiency

authenticity
– of the documents
to authenticate, to legalize
motor car, auto
1 by car
2 automobile industry
3 auto market
motor bus, bus
motor van, motor lorry, truck
motor coach
self-financing

automation
authorization
  1 authority to accept
  2 authority to purchase
  3 authority to negotiate
  4 authority to pay
  5 authority to transfer
  6 export permit
  7 import permit
  8 husband's –

  9 prior –
10 subject to –

autorisé / 30

autorisé
1 milieux –s
2 personnes –es à signer
3 signatures –es

autoriser
autorité *f.*
1 la Haute Autorité

2 les –s compétentes
3 –s financières
4 –s fiscales
5 –s monétaires
autrement
1 – (*sinon*)
2 ou –
aval *m.*
1 – de banque
2 bon pour –
3 commission *f.* pour –
4 donneur *m.* d'–

5 signé pour –
avaliser

avaliseur, avaliste *m.*

avance *f.*
1 – à découvert
2 – contre nantissement
3 –s de caisse
4 –s en clearing
5 – en compte courant
6 – garantie (contre garantie)
7 – gratuite
8 – sur marchandises
9 – sur nantissement
10 – sur titres
11 à l'–, d'–
12 payable d'–
13 consentir des –s
avancer (*argent*)

avantage *m.*
1 à notre – mutuel
2 à votre –
3 cela présente beaucoup d'–s
4 nous avons l'– de vous faire savoir

5 –s accessoires (*salaire*)
avantageux
à des conditions avantageuses

authorized
1 influential circles
2 those – to sign
3 – signatures

to authorize
authority
1 the High Authority

2 the competent authorities
3 financial authorities
4 taxation authorities
5 monetary authorities
otherwise, differently
1 otherwise, or else
2 or otherwise
guarantee, guaranty, backing
1 bank guaranty
2 guaranteed by
3 commission on bank guaranty
4 guarantor, backer

5 guaranteed
to guarantee, to back

guarantor

advance
1 unsecured –
2 – against security
3 cash –s
4 clearing –s
5 – on current account
6 secured –
7 – free of interest
8 – on (against) goods
9 – against security
10 – on (against) securities
11 in –
12 payable in –
13 to make –s
to advance

advantage
1 to our mutual benefit
2 to your –
3 it offers many –s
4 we have the pleasure to inform (of informing) you, we have (take) pleasure in informing you

5 fringes, fringe benefits
advantageous
on – terms

avant-bourse
avant-guerre m.
  prix m. d'–
avant-hier
avaries pl.
  1 – communes, grosses
  2 – particulières, simples
  3 franc d'–
  4 menues –
  5 dépôt m. d'–
  6 calculer l'étendue des –
avarié
  1 – par l'eau de mer
  2 – par l'étalage
avenant m. (*police*)

avenir m.
  dans un proche –, – rapproché
avenu, considérer comme nul et non –

avers m. (*monnaie*)
avilir
  s'–
avilissement m.
  – de la monnaie
avion m.
  „par –", (*lettre*)
avis m.
  1 – d'arrivée
  2 – d'attribution
  3 – de convocation
  4 – de crédit

  5 – de débit

  6 – de débit (du virement)

  7 – de disposition
  8 – d'embarquement
  9 – de non-répartition
  10 – d'encaissement

  11 – de réception
  12 – de répartition
  13 – de retour de souscription
  14 – de traite
  15 – de virement (*au bénéficiaire*)

  16 – d'expédition
  17 – d'opéré
  18 jusqu'à nouvel –

before hours
prewar period
  prewar price
the day before yersterday
average
  1 general –
  2 particular –
  3 free from (of) average
  4 petty –
  5 – deposit
  6 to state (adjust) the amount of the –
damaged
  1 sea-damaged
  2 window-soiled, shopworn
endorsement

future
  in the near –
  to consider null and void

face side, obverse
to depreciate, to lower
  to depreciate, to fall in price
depreciation
  – of currency
airplane, aircraft
  by air mail
advice
  1 – of arrival
  2 letter of allotment
  3 notice of meeting
  4 credit –

  5 debit –

  6 notification of debiting

  7 draft –, – of draft
  8 – of shipment
  9 letter of regret
  10 collection –

  11 acknowledgment of receipt
  12 letter of allotment
  13 letter of regret
  14 – of draft
  15 notification of crediting

  16 – of dispatch
  17 – of deal (execution)
  18 until further –

aviser / 32

19 sans (autre) –
20 sans – préalable
21 sauf – contraire

22 sous – (immédiat)

23 suivant –
24 donner un – de (*tirages*)

25 être d'–
aviser
  – une traite
avocat *m.*
  1 – conseil
  2 consulter un –
  3 remettre entre les mains d'un –
avoir *m.* (*côté du crédit*)
  1 doit et –
  2 inscrire à l'– d'un compte

avoir (*biens*) *m.*
  1 – bloqué
  2 – de compte-chèque
  3 – en banque

  4 – en caisse
  5 – en compte courant
  6 – en compte nostro
  7 – en devises
  8 tout son –
ayant cause *m.*
ayant compte *m.*
ayants droit *pl.*

19 without further notice
20 without notice
21 unless advised to the contrary

22 under (immediate) –

23 as per –
24 to give (send) an – of..., to advise

25 to be of opinion
to inform, to notify
  to advise a bill of exchange
lawyer, counsel, barrister
  1 counsel, consulting barrister
  2 to take legal advice
  3 to place in the hands of a solicitor
credit side
  1 debit and credit
  2 to enter to the credit of an account

property, possessions
  1 blocked assets
  2 drawing account
  3 credit balance at the bank

  4 cash in hand
  5 assets on current account
  6 credit balance of nostro account
  7 assets in foreign currency
  8 the whole of one's fortune
assign
customer
parties entitled, assigns

B

bâbord *m.*
bâche *f.*
bagages *m. pl.*
  1 – à (la) main
  2 – en franchise
  3 – enregistrés
  4 assurance *f.* de –
  5 bulletin *m.* de –

  6 excédent *m.* de –
bague fiscale
bail *m.*
  1 – à cheptel
  2 – à ferme
  3 – à loyer

port (side)
sheet
luggage, (*Amer.***) baggage**
  1 hand luggage
  2 free luggage
  3 registered luggage
  4 luggage insurance
  5 luggage ticket

  6 excess luggage
fiscal band, revenue band
lease
  1 – of livestock
  2 farming –
  3 house-letting –

4 - emphythéotique
5 donner à -
6 prendre à -
7 renouveler le -
8 résilier un -
9 tenir à -
bailleur m.
1 - de fonds
2 - de fonds (*société*)
3 - de gage
4 - et preneur

baisse f.
1 - des prix
2 mouvement m. de -
3 opération f. à la -
4 tendance f. à la -

5 acheter en -
6 être à la -
7 être à la (en) - (*valeurs*)

8 spéculer à la -
baisser
1 - (*diminuer*)
2 - de... à...
3 faire - (*cours*)
baissier m.
-s et haussiers
balance f.
1 - commerciale, - du commerce
2 - commerciale active
3 - commerciale passive
4 - de caisse
5 - des paiements
6 équilibre m. de la - des paiements
7 excédent m. de la - des paiements
8 - de vérification
9 - déficitaire
10 - d'un compte
11 - flattée
12 - par soldes

balancer
1 - un compte

2 - les livres
3 se -
4 se - par
balayures f. pl.
bancable
1 effets m. pl. -s
2 place f. -

4 long -, ninety-nine year -
5 to -, to let on -
6 to take on -
7 to renew the -
8 to cancel (terminate) a -
9 to hold on (by) -
lessor
1 money lender
2 silent (sleeping) partner
3 pawnbroker
4 - and lessee

fall, decline
1 fall of prices
2 downward movement
3 bear operation
4 downward tendency

5 to buy on a falling market
6 to go for a fall
7 to be falling, to be down

8 to speculate (go) for a fall
to fall, to decline
1 to lower
2 to fall (drop) from... to...
3 to bear (force) down
bear
bears and bulls
balance
1 trade -, - of trade
2 favo(u)rable - of trade
3 unfavo(u)rable (adverse) - of trade
4 cash -
5 - of payments
6 - of payments equilibrium
7 - of payments surplus
8 trial -
9 adverse -
10 - of an account
11 cooked -
12 trial - showing differences of the postings

1 to balance an account

2 to balance (up) the books
3 to balance
4 to show a balance of...
sweepings
bankable, bank...
1 bankable bills
2 bank(ing) place

bancaire / 34

bancaire
1 commission *f.* – (*Belg.*)
2 concentration *f.* –
3 établissement *m.* –
4 milieux *m. pl.* –s
5 opérations *f. pl.* –s
6 réforme *f.* –
bande *f.*
1 sous –
2 largeur *f.* de –
banque *f.*
1 (*sur lettre*) – :
2 la – (*système, branche*)
3 – et finances
4 – agricole
5 – coloniale
6 – commerciale, – de commerce
7 – de circulation
8 – de compensation
9 – de crédit
10 – d'émission
11 – de dépôt
12 – de recouvrement
13 – des Règlements Internationaux
14 – d'escompte
15 – d'État
16 – de virements
17 – d'outre-mer
18 – encaissante
19 – foncière
20 – hypothécaire
21 – industrielle
22 – mixte
23 – mondiale
24 – nationale
25 – qui avise, – notificatrice
26 – qui confirme (*le crédit*)
27 – qui ouvre le crédit, – émettrice
28 action *f.* de –
29 avoir *m.* en –
30 carnet *m.* de –
31 chèque *m.* de –
32 commission *f.* de –
33 comptabilité *f.* de –
34 compte *m.* de (en) –
35 consortium *m.* de –s
36 crédit *m.* de –
37 dépôt *m.* en –
38 directeur *m.* de –
39 employé *m.* de –
40 garantie *f.* de –

banking, bank...
1 banking commission
2 concentration in banking
3 banking establishment
4 banking circles
5 banking business, operations
6 banking reform
wrapper
1 in a –, by bookpost
2 spread
bank
1 – account :
2 banking
3 banking and finance
4 agricultural (rural) –
5 colonial –
6 – of commerce, commercial –, trade –
7 – of issue
8 clearing –
9 credit –
10 – of issue, central –
11 deposit –
12 collecting agency
13 – of International Settlements
14 discount –
15 State –
16 transfer –
17 overseas –
18 collecting –
19 land –
20 mortgage –
21 industrial –
22 mixed-type –
23 World –
24 national –
25 advising –
26 confirming –
27 (credit) opening –, issuing –
28 – share
29 cash in –s, – balance
30 – pass book
31 – cheque (check)
32 banking commission
33 – bookkeeping
34 banking account
35 banking syndicate
36 – credit
37 – deposit
38 – manager
39 – clerk
40 – guarantee

35 / banqueroute

41 guichets *m. pl.* de la –
42 maison *f.* de –
43 mandat *m.* de –
44 opérations *f. pl.* de –

45 toutes –

46 papier *m.* de –
47 rapport *m.* de –
48 réserve *f.* de –
49 ruée *f.* sur les guichets d'une –
50 situation *f.* de la –
51 succursale *f.* de –
52 avoir de l'argent en –
53 avoir un compte en –
54 déposer de l'argent en –

55 fonder une –
56 verser à la –
banqueroute *f.*
1 – frauduleuse
2 – simple
3 faire –
banqueroutier *m.*
banquier *m.*
1 –s (*bilan*)
2 référence *f.* de –
baraterie *f.*
barème, barrême *m.* (*comptes faits*)
barème, barrême *m.* (*tarifs*)
1 – des salaires
2 – de transports
3 reviser les –s
barrement *m.*
1 – général
2 – spécial
barrer (v. aussi *biffer*)
– un chèque
barrières *f. pl.* de douane (douanières)
1 réduction *f.* des –
2 abaisser les –
bas
1 au – de la page
2 – (*emballage*)
bas *m.* de laine
faire un –
base *f.*
1 –s d'un contrat
2 sur la – de
3 sur une – solide, saine
4 prix *m.* de –

41 – counters
42 banking house
43 – post bill
44 banking operations, business, transactions
45 every description of banking business, banking business of every description transacted
46 – paper, – bills
47 – report
48 – reserve
49 run on a –, – run
50 – statement, – return
51 branch –
52 to keep money at the –
53 to have an account with a –
54 to place money at the –

55 to establish a –
56 to pay into the –
bankruptcy
1 fraudulent –
2 –
3 to go bankrupt
bankrupt
banker
1 money at –s
2 –'s reference
barratry
ready reckoner
scale
1 – of salaries
2 – of charges for carriage
3 to revise tariffs
crossing
1 general –
2 special –
to strike out
to cross a cheque
customs barriers, customs walls, tariff walls
1 lowering (reduction) of –
2 to lower customs barriers
low
1 at the bottom of the page
2 bottom
hoard, stocking
to hoard
base, basis
1 bases of a contract
2 on the basis of
3 on a lasting (sound) basis
4 basis (base) price

baser sur / 36

baser sur

les prix sont basés sur
bassin *m.*
1 – à flot
2 – à marée
3 – à sec
4 – flottant
5 – houiller
6 passer au –
bateau *m.*
1 – charbonnier
2 – citerne
3 – de navigation intérieure
4 – pétrolier
5 – pilote
6 – remorqueur
batelier *m.*
batellerie *f.*
bâtiment *m.*
1 – commercial
2 – d'usine
3 activité *f.* dans le –
4 industrie *f.* du –, le –
bâtir (voir aussi *propriété, terrain*)
battre
1 – monnaie
2 – pavillon belge
3 – un record
bénéfice *m.*
1 –s bruts
2 – de discussion

3 – de division

4 – d'exploitation
5 – distribué
6 – du doute
7 – espéré
8 –s exceptionnels
9 – net
10 – non distribué
11 – reporté
12 – sur le change
13 avec part aux –s
14 sous – d'inventaire

15 diminution *f.* du –
16 marge *f.* de –

17 part *f.* de –
18 perte *f.* de –

to base on

prices are based on...
dock, basin
1 wet dock
2 tidal dock, tidal basin
3 dry dock
4 floating dock
5 coal basin
6 to dock
boat
1 coal ship, collier
2 tanker
3 vessel of inland navigation
4 oiler, oil ship
5 pilot –
6 tug, tug –
lighterman
inland navigation
building
1 commercial –
2 factory –
3 – activity
4 building industry
to build

1 to coin money
2 to fly the Belgian flag
3 to beat (break) a record
profit
1 gross –(s)
2 benefit of discussion, beneficium excussionis
3 beneficium divisionis, benefit of division
4 working –s
5 distributed –
6 benefit of the doubt
7 imaginary (anticipated) –
8 excess –s
9 clear –s
10 undistributed (unappropriated) –
11 balance brought forward (from)
12 exchange –s
13 with share in the –s
14 under beneficium of inventory

15 profit shrinkage
16 margin of –

17 share of the –s
18 loss of –

19 prise *f.* de –s	19 – taking
20 répartition *f.* de –	20 distribution of –s ; appropriation of –s
21 surplus *m.* de –	21 surplus –s
22 avoir part aux –s	22 to share in the –s
23 rapporter des –s	23 to yield (leave) a –
24 réaliser des –s	24 to make –s
bénéficiaire *m.*	**beneficiary**
1 – d'une lettre de crédit	1 – of a letter of credit
2 – d'une lettre de change	2 payee
3 – d'une licence	3 licensee
4 – d'un mandat-poste	4 payee of a money order
5 – d'une police d'assurance	5 – of an insurance policy
bénéficiaire (*adj.*)	
1 être –	1 to show profit
2 marge *f.* –	2 margin of profit
3 solde *m.* –	3 profit balance
4 solde *m.* – non réparti	4 undivided profits
bénéficier	
1 – de	1 to profit by
2 – sur...	2 to make a profit on
besoin *m.*	**need**
1 –s en capital	1 capital –s, capital requirements
2 –s en marchandises	2 requirements in goods
3 – urgent	3 urgent –
4 au –	4 if necessary, if required, if – be
5 en tant que de –	5 as far as necessary
6 pour les –s de notre service de...	6 for the requirements of our... department
7 avoir – de	7 to want
8 créer de nouveaux –s	8 to create new wants
9 être dans le –	9 to be in want
10 pourvoir à un –	10 to meet the needs, a want
besoin *m.* (*lettre de change*)	**(a referee in) case of need**
au – chez...	in case of need apply to
bétail *m.*	**cattle**
bien-fondé *m.*	**soundness**
bien-trouvé *m.*	
1 certificat *m.* de –	1 proof of agreement
2 formule *f.* de –	2 form of acknowledgment
3 reconnaître le – d'un compte	3 to approve an account
biens *pl.*	**goods**
1 – corporels	1 corporeal (tangible) property
2 – de consommation (voir *consommation*)	2 consumer(s') –
3 – de production	3 producer(s') –
4 – d'investissement	4 capital –, investment –

biens-fonds / 38

    5 – économiques
    6 – et avoirs
    7 – immeubles, immobiliers
    8 – incorporels
    9 – libres
    10 – meubles, mobiliers
biens-fonds *pl.*
biffer
    – les mentions inutiles

bilan *m.*
    1 – au (31 déc.)
    2 – consolidé
    3 – déficitaire
    4 – de fin d'année
    5 – d'ensemble
    6 – d'entrée, d'ouverture
    7 – d'essai
    8 – flatté, maquillé, truqué
    9 – intérimaire
    10 – résumé
    11 analyse *f.* de –
    12 article *m.* de –
    13 commentaire *m.* du –

    14 contrôle *m.* de –
    15 date *f.* du –
    16 extrait *m.* de –
    17 établissement *m.*,(formation *f.*)du –
    18 maquillage *m.*, (truquage *m.*) de –

    19 approuver le –
    20 camoufler le –
    21 déposer son –
    22 dresser (établir, former) le –
    23 porter au –
    24 truquer (maquiller) le –
billet *m.*
    1 – à ordre
    2 – au porteur

    3 – circulaire
    4 – d'aller et retour
    5 – de banque
    6 – de bord, d'embarquement
    7 – de chemins de fer
    8 – de complaisance
    9 – de correspondance
    10 – de loterie
    11 – d'entrée
    12 – gagnant
    13 – simple

---

    5 economic –
    6 property and assets
    7 real property, real estate
    8 incorporeal (intangible) property
    9 free –
    10 movables, personal estate
landed property
to strike (rule, cross) out
    to strike out words not applicable, what is not wanted

balance sheet
    1 – as of (as at) ...
    2 consolidated –
    3 debit balance
    4 annual –
    5 general –
    6 opening –
    7 trial balance
    8 veiled (cooked, doctored) –
    9 provisional (interim) –
    10 condensed statement of condition
    11 statement analysis
    12 – item
    13 explanatory statement to the –

    14 control of the –
    15 date of –
    16 summarized –
    17 drawing up of a –
    18 window dressing of the –

    19 to adopt (approve) the –
    20 to fake the –
    21 to file one's petition in bankruptcy
    22 to draw (strike, form) the –
    23 to put into the balance
    24 to cook (fake) the –
ticket
    1 promissory note
    2 bill payable to bearer

    3 circular –
    4 return –
    5 bank note
    6 mate's receipt
    7 railway –
    8 accommodation bill
    9 transfer (–)
    10 lottery –
    11 admission –
    12 winning –
    13 single –

14 planche *f.* à –s	14 note printing press
15 couper (diviser) des –s (de banque)	15 to halve bank notes
16 émettre des –s (de banque)	16 to issue bank notes
17 retirer des –s (de banque)	17 to withdraw bank notes
billion *m.* (million de millions)	(*Gr. Br.*) **billion**, (*Amer.*) **trillion**
bimensuel	**fortnightly**
bimestriel	**bimonthly**
bimétallisme *m.*	**bimetal(l)ism**
blanc *m.*	**blank**
1 en –	1 in –
2 endosser en –	2 to endorse in –
3 ,,laisser en –''	3 to leave –
blanc-seing *m.*	**blank signature**
bloc, en bloc	**en bloc, the whole lot, in one lot**
bloc-notes *m.*	**memorandum (writing) pad**
bloquage, blocage *m.*	**stoppage**
1 – des dividendes	1 dividend limitation [freeze
2 – des prix	2 price stop, price freezing, price
3 – des salaires	3 wage stop
bloquer (*compte*)	**to block, to stop**
obligation *f.* de –	obligation to hold
boîte *f.*	**box**
1 – à suggestions	1 idea –
2 – aux lettres	2 letter –
3 – postale	3 post office –
bon	**good**
1 – pour	1 – for
2 – pour aval	2 guaranteed by
3 – pour pouvoir	3 procuration conferred by
4 –ne arrivée	4 safe arrival
5 –ne qualité moyenne	5 – average quality
6 à – marché, à – compte	6 cheap(ly)
7 de –ne foi	7 in – faith [of a bill
8 assurer la –ne fin d'un effet	8 to assure the protection (meeting)
bon *m.*	**note**
1 – à tirer, donner le –	1 to pass for press, O. K. good for printing
2 – à tirer après corrections	2 good for printing with corrections
3 – de caisse (*banques*)	3 (bank) cash certificate
4 – de commande	4 order form
5 – de livraison	5 delivery order
6 – du Trésor	6 Treasury Bond
boni *m.*	**surplus, over**
bonification *f.*	**allowance**
1 – (*amélioration*)	1 improvement
2 – (*bourse*)	2 backwardation, back
3 – d'intérêt	3 payment of interest
bonifier	
1 – des intérêts sur... au taux de...	1 to allow an interest on... at the rate of...'

bonus / 40

2 – qqn d'une remise
3 – une perte
bonus *m.*
bord *m.*
  1 à – de...
  2 livre *m.* de –
bordereau *m.*
  1 – d'achat (*courtier*)
  2 – de caisse
  3 – de chargement
  4 – de compte
  5 – de courtier
  6 – de crédit
  7 – d'encaissement
  8 – d'escompte
  9 – de salaires
  10 – des espèces
  11 – de vente (*courtier*)
  12 – de versement
  13 – numérique (*titres*)
  14 suivant – ci-inclus
bottin *m.*
boule *f.* de neige, système –
bourse *f.*
  1 – de commerce, – de marchandises
  2 – des grains
  3 – des valeurs (mobilières)
  4 – du travail
  5 – maritime, – des frets
  6 la Bourse de Londres
  7 après –
  8 avant –
  9 première –
  10 sur la –, en –, à la –
  11 dans (sur) les –s étrangères
  12 admission *f.* à la – (*titres*)
  13 bulletin *m.* de la –
  14 chômage *m.* de la – (boursier)
  15 clôture *f.* de la –
  16 comité *m.* de la –

  17 cours *m.* de la –
  18 cote *f.* de la –
  19 heures *f. pl.* de la –

  20 impôt *m.* sur les opérations de –
  21 jour *m.* de –
  22 journal *m.* de la –
  23 manœuvres *f. pl.* de –
  24 marché *m.* en –
  25 membre *m.* de la –
  26 opérations *f. pl.* de –
  27 ordre *m.* de –

2 to allow someone a discount
3 to make good a loss
bonus
board
  1 on –, aboard
  2 log book
list, statement, bordereau
  1 bought note
  2 cash statement
  3 cargo list
  4 statement of account
  5 broker's note, contract note
  6 credit note
  7 list of bills for collection
  8 list of bills for discount
  9 wage(s) sheet, (*Amer.*) payroll
  10 specification
  11 sold note
  12 paying in slip, credit slip
  13 specification of numbers
  14 as per enclosed statement
directory
snowball system
exchange
  1 produce –
  2 corn –
  3 stock –
  4 labour –
  5 shipping –
  6 the London Stock –
  7 after hours –
  8 before hours
  9 opening of the –
  10 on the stock –
  11 on foreign stock –s
  12 admission to the stock – list
  13 – gazette
  14 bank holiday
  15 closing of the –
  16 – committee

  17 stock – price, market price
  18 – quotations
  19 – hours, official hours, the session
  20 – tax
  21 – day
  22 – gazette
  23 – manœuvres
  24 stock market
  25 member of the –
  26 stock – transactions
  27 – order

28 panique *f.* en –
29 prix coté en –
30 règlement *m.* de la –
31 tendance *f.* de la –
32 tenue *f.* de la –
33 usages *m. pl.* de la –
34 valeurs *f. pl.* de –
35 aller à la –
boursicoter

boursicoteur, boursicotier *m.*
boursier *m.*
boursier
  1 langage –

  2 milieux –s
boycottage *m.*
boycotter
branche *f.*
  1 – d'affaires, – de commerce

  2 – d'industrie
  3 au courant de la –
  4 ce n'est pas de notre –

brasserie *f.*
brevet *m.* (*d'invention*)
  1 bureau *m.* des –s
  2 demande *f.* de –
  3 frais *m. pl.* du –
  4 titulaire *m.* d'un –
  5 demander un –
  6 obtenir un –
  7 prendre un –
breveté
breveter
briqueterie *f.*
bris *m.*
broché (*livre*)
brochure *f.*
  1 – d'accueil

  2 – de propagande
brosserie *f.*
brouillard *m.*
brouillon *m.*
  faire un –
bruit *m.*
  1 le – court que
  2 –s de dévaluation
brut
  1 – (*marchandises*)

---

28 panic on the –
29 market price, market value
30 – rules and regulations
31 – tendency, tendency on stock –
32 tone
33 – customs, usage
34 stock – securities
35 to go to 'Change
to dabble, to scalp

dabbler, scalper
stock exchange operator
market..., stock exchange...
  1 stock exchange terminology, parlance
  2 stock exchange circles
boycot(ting)
to boycott
branch
  1 – of trade, of business

  2 – of industry
  3 well up in the trade
  4 this is not in our line (of business)

brewery
patent
  1 – office
  2 application for a patent
  3 – charges
  4 patentee
  5 to apply for a –
  6 to obtain (secure) a –
  7 to take out a –
patented
to patent
brick works
breakage
sewn, paper-bound
brochure, booklet
  1 welcome booklet, employee (works) handbook

  2 advertising brochure
brush manufactory
waste book
rough draft
  to make a –
rumo(u)r
  1 it is –ed that
  2 –s of devaluation
gross
  1 raw

budget / 42

2 – pour net
3 bénéfice –
4 montant –
budget *m.*
  1 – annexe, – complémentaire
  2 – de fonctionnement
  3 – en équilibre, équilibré
  4 – extraordinaire
  5 – couvrant la période de...
  6 – familial
  7 – ordinaire
  8 discussion *f.* du –
  9 exposé *m.* du –

  10 approuver un –
  11 dresser le –
  12 inscrire (porter) au –

budgétaire
  1 année *f.* –
  2 compressions *f. pl.* –s

  3 dépenses *f. pl.* –s
  4 déficit *m.* –
  5 équilibre *m.* –
  6 politique –
  7 prévisions *f. pl.* –s
  8 recettes *f. pl.* –s
bulletin *m.*
  1 – de bagages
  2 – de commande
  3 – de cours, – de la cote
  4 – de souscription

  5 – de versement
  6 – d'expédition (*poste*)
bureau *m.* (*meuble*)
  1 – américain
  2 – ministre
  3 – pour dactylographe
bureau *m.* (*comité*)
réunion *f.* du –
bureau *m.* (*office*)
  1 –x (*bâtiments*)
  2 – central
  3 – de change
  4 – de (la) douane
  5 – de l'état civil
  6 – d'enregistrement
  7 – de placement
  8 – de poste
  9 – de publicité

2 – weight for nett
3 – profit
4 – amount
budget
  1 supplementary –
  2 operational –
  3 balanced –
  4 extraordinary –
  5 – for the period...
  6 family budget
  7 ordinary –
  8 debates on the –
  9 budget speech

  10 to pass a –
  11 to draw up the –
  12 to – for, to provide in the –

budgetary
  1 financial year
  2 retrenchment in budgeted expenditure
  3 budget(ary) expenditure
  4 budgetary deficit
  5 budget equilibrium
  6 – policy
  7 budget estimate, the Estimates
  8 budget(ary) receipts
form
  1 luggage ticket
  2 order –
  3 list of prices, list of quotations
  4 application –

  5 paying in slip, deposit slip
  6 dispatch note
desk
  1 roll top –
  2 kneehole (pedestal) –
  3 typewriter table
board
meeting of the –
office
  1 – buildings
  2 head –
  3 exchange –
  4 custom house
  5 registry –
  6 registration –
  7 employment agency
  8 post –
  9 advertising agency

10 – de renseignements	10 inquiry (information) –
11 – des hypothèques	11 mortgage registry
12 – de tourisme	12 tourist –
13 – de vente	13 selling –, sales –
14 – du contentieux	14 law bureau, law department
15 – d'un journal	15 newspaper –
16 – du télégraphe	16 telegraph –
17 – (central) du téléphone	17 (telephone) exchange
18 – du timbre	18 stamp –
19 – principal	19 head –
20 – privé	20 private –
21 – restant	21 to be called for
22 à – ouvert	22 on demand, on presentation
23 après les heures de –	23 after – hours
24 aux –x de...	24 at the – of...
25 pendant les heures de –	25 during business (–) hours
26 nos –x seront fermés du... à...	26 our – will be closed from... to...
27 employés m. pl. de –	27 – staff
28 fournitures f. pl. de –	28 stationery
29 frais m. pl. de –	29 – expenses
30 heures f. pl. de –	30 business hours, – hours
31 locaux m. pl. pour –x (à louer)	31 – premises, – room, (–s to let)
32 machines f. pl. de –	32 – machines
33 meubles m. pl. de –	33 – furniture
34 travaux m. pl. de –	34 – work
35 au courant de tous travaux de –	35 familiar with – routine (work)
36 travailler dans un –	36 to work at an –

but m. (voir aussi *association*)	**aim, objects**
1 –s d'utilité publique	1 public purposes
2 le – d'une société	2 the objects of a company
3 le – de la présente est	3 the object of (in writing) the present is
buvard m.	**blotting paper, blotting book**
tampon m. –	hand blotter

C

cabine f. téléphonique	**telephone call box,** (*Amer.*) **tele-**
câble m.	**cable** [**phone booth**
1 – (*télégramme*)	1 –, cablegram

câbler / 44

2 – (*transfert*)	2 telegraphic (–) transfer
3 – (*sur*) Londres	3 London –, – on London
4 par –	4 by –
câbler	**to cable**
cablogramme *m.*	**cable, cablegram**
cabotage *m.*	**coasting**
caboteur, cabotier *m.*	**coaster**
cachet *m.*	**seal**
1 5 –s (*lettre*)	1 5 –s
2 apposer un –	2 to affix a –
cacheter	**to seal up**
cire *f.* à –	sealing wax
cadastral	**cadastral**
1 extrait –	1 land registry certificate
2 plan –	2 – plan
cadastre *m.*	**cadastral register**
1 bureau *m.* du –	1 Land Registry (Office)
2 registre *m.* du –	2 land (cadastral) register
cadastrer	**to enter in the cadastral register**
cadre *m.*	**frame, framework**
1 dans le – de l'accord	1 within the framework of the agreement
2 dépasser le – de...	2 to be beyond the framework (scope) [of...
café *m.* (*boisson*)	**coffee**
– (*établissement*)	coffee house, café
cahier *m.*	**writing book, copy book**
1 – des charges	1 (building) specifications [fications
2 conditions du – des charges	2 conditions of the (building) speci-
caisse *f.* (*emballage*)	**case**
1 – à claire-voie	1 crate
2 – doublée de fer blanc	2 tin-lined –
3 – doublée de zinc	3 zinc-lined –
caisse *f.*	**cash,** (*tiroir*) **till**
– (*comptoir*)	cash desk
1 – et banque	1 cash in hand and at bankers
2 – d'amortissement [*tion*)	2 sinking fund
3 – de compensation (v. *compensa-*	
4 – des dépôts et consignations	4 Deposit and Consignment Office
5 – de grève	5 strike fund
6 – d'épargne	6 savings bank
7 – d'épargne postale	7 postal savings bank
8 – de prévoyance	8 relief fund, provident fund
9 – de retraite	9 pension fund
10 – de secours	10 relief fund
11 – (de secours en cas) de maladie	11 sick benefit fund
12 – enregistreuse	12 cash register

45 / caissier

13 payable à nos –s
14 compte *m.* de –
15 déficit *m.* de –
16 (département *m.* de) –
17 dépenses *f. pl.* de –

18 espèces ou billets en –
19 excédent *m.* de –
20 garçon *m.* de –
21 inspection *f.* de la –
22 livre *m.* de –
23 mouvement *m.* de –
24 recettes *f. pl.* de –
25 relevé *m.* de –
26 situation *f.* de la –
27 solde *m.* en –
28 sorties *f. pl.* de –
29 tare *f.* de –
30 vérification *f.* de la –
31 alimenter une –
32 consolider la –
33 faire la –

34 fournir sur les –s de…
35 payer à la –
36 tenir la –
37 vérifier la –
caissier *m.*
 – principal
caissière *f.*
calcul *m.*
1 – des intérêts
2 erreur *f.* de –
3 faire un –
calculateur *m.*
calculer
1 – un prix
2 machine *f.* à –
3 calculé en DM
cale *f.*
1 – flottante
2 – sèche
3 buée *f.* de –
calendrier *m.*
1 – à effeuiller
2 – perpétuel
calicot *m.*
call money *m.*
 taux *m.* du –
calquer
cambial
 droit –
cambiste *m.*

13 payable at our counters, offices
14 cash account
15 cash deficit
16 cash department
17 cash payments

18 cash or notes in hand
19 cash surplus
20 collecting clerk
21 cash revision
22 cash book
23 cash transactions
24 cash receipts
25 cash statement
26 cash position
27 the balance in hand
28 cash disbursements
29 shortage in the cash
30 verification of the cash
31 to maintain (supply) a fund
32 to strengthen the funds
33 to make up the cash

34 to draw on… (on the office of)
35 to pay at the desk
36 to keep the cash
37 to verify the cash
cashier
 chief cashier, head cashier
(lady)cashier
calculation
1 – of interest
2 error of –
3 to make a –
calculator
to calculate
1 – a price
2 calculating machine
3 expressed in DM
hold
1 floating dock
2 dry dock
3 ship's sweat
calendar
1 tear-off –
2 perpetual –
banner
call money
 – rate
to trace
exchange…
 exchange law
cambist

camelote f.
camion m.
– automobile [tage]
camionnage m. (transport; voir fac-
1 – (prix)
2 – (service)
camionnette f.
camionneur m.
camoufler (bilan)
campagne f.
1 – de publicité
2 – de vente
3 – sucrière
canal (de navigation) m.
candidat m.
1 examen m. de –s
2 liste f. de –s
candidature f.
poser sa –
caoutchouc m.
plantation f. de –
caoutchoutier
1 société caoutchoutière
2 valeurs caoutchoutières
capable
1 – (jur.)
2 – de gagner sa vie
capacité f.
1 – (jur.)
2 – annuelle
3 – d'absorption du marché
4 – d'achat
5 – de charge (navire)
6 – de production

7 – de travail (ouvrier)
8 –s (de production) excédentaires

9 taux m. d'utilisation de la –

capitaine m.
1 – de port
2 le – et l'équipage
3 copie f. du –
capital m.
1 – acceptant les risques, – à risques
2 – actions
3 – appelé
4 – circulant
5 – d'apport
6 – de réserve
7 – de roulement
8 – disponible

cheap goods
lorry, truck
  motor lorry, (motor) truck
cartage
1 –
2 – service
delivery van
carter, carman
to fake
campaign
1 advertising –
2 selling –, sales –
3 sugar –
ship canal
candidate
1 examination of –s
2 nomination
candidature
  to offer oneself as a candidate
rubber
  – estate, – plantation
rubber
1 – company
2 – shares
able
1 qualified; legally competent
2 capable of gainful employment
ability
1 legal competency, –
2 annual capacity
3 market's absorption capacity
4 purchasing capacity
5 carrying capacity
6 productive power

7 fitness for work
8 surplus of (productive) capacity, excess capacity
9 degree of capacity utilization

captain, master
1 harbour master
2 the captain and the crew
3 captain's copy
capital
1 risk (-bearing) –
2 share –, – stock
3 called up –
4 floating (circulating) –
5 initial –
6 reserve –
7 working –
8 available –

9 – engagé, investi	9 invested –
10 – en quête d'emploi	10 – seeking investment
11 – entièrement versé	11 fully paid up –
12 – espèces, – (en) numéraire	12 cash –
13 capitaux étrangers	13 foreign –
14 – fixe	14 fixed –
15 – flottant	15 floating –
16 – immobilisé	16 fixed –
17 – improductif, – mort	17 dead (idle) –
18 – initial	18 initial –
19 – libéré de 30 %	19 – of which 30 % is paid up
20 – minimum	20 minimum –
21 – mobile	21 floating –
22 – nominal	22 nominal –
23 – non appelé	23 uncalled –
24 – obligations	24 debenture –
25 – oisif	25 dead (unemployed) –
26 – productif	26 productive –
27 – représenté par (divisé en)... actions de... francs chacune	27 – divided into... shares of... francs each
28 – roulant	28 floating –
29 – social, – nominal	29 – stock, share –
30 – souscrit	30 subscribed –
31 – versé	31 paid up –
32 – et intérêts	32 principal and interest
33 accumulation *f.* de –	33 accumulation of –
34 afflux *m.* de capitaux	34 inflow (influx) of –
35 apport *m.* de capitaux	35 – produced
36 approvisionnement *m.* en capitaux	36 supply of –
37 augmentation *f.* de –	37 increase of –
38 besoins *m. pl.* en capitaux	38 – requirements
39 compte *m.* de –	39 – account
40 création *f.* de –	40 creation of –
41 dépense *f.* de –	41 expenditure of –
42 dilution *f.* de –	42 watering of stock
43 diminution *f.* de –	43 reduction of –
44 évasion *f.* (exode *m.*, fuite *f.*) de capitaux	44 flight of –
45 manque *m.* de capitaux	45 want of –
46 marché *m.* des capitaux	46 capital market
47 mouvement *m.* des capitaux	47 movement of –
48 pénurie *f.* de capitaux	48 scarcity of –
49 placement *m.* de capitaux	49 investment of –
50 prélèvement *m.* sur le –	50 – levy
51 rapatriement *m.* de capitaux	51 repatriation of –
52 réduction *f.* de –	52 reduction of –
53 reflux *m.* de capitaux	53 reflux of –

capitalisation / 48

54 transfert *m*. de capitaux
55 apporter des capitaux
56 attirer des capitaux
57 augmenter le –
58 diluer le –
59 emprunter des capitaux
60 engager des capitaux
61 entamer son –
62 fournir les capitaux
63 immobiliser un –
64 investir un –
65 joindre au –
66 mobiliser un –
67 placer son – dans
68 réunir les capitaux
69 verser des capitaux

capitalisation *f*.
  taux *m*. de – (*d'un titre*)
capitaliser
capitalisme *m*.
capitaliste *m*.
capitaliste *adj*.
capture (v. *franc*)

carburants *pl*.
carène *f*.
cargaison *f*.
 1 une – de bois
 2 – en vrac
 3 – flottante
 4 – mixte
 5 – sur le pont
 6 recevoir une –
cargo *m*.
carnet *m*.
 1 – à souche(s)
 2 – d'échéance(s)
 3 – de banque
 4 – de chèques
 5 – de commandes
 6 – de compte
 7 – de dépôt
 8 – de formules
 9 – de mariage
 10 – d'épargne   [*volet*]
 11 – de passages en douane (voir
 12 – de recettes
 13 – d'indication (*banque*)
carte *f*.
 1 – d'abonnement
 2 – d'échantillons
 3 – de visite
 4 – d'identité
 5 – guide

54 transfer of –
55 to bring in –
56 to attract –
57 to raise (increase) the –
58 to water the –
59 to raise (to borrow) –
60 to engage –
61 to break into one's –
62 to furnish (provide) –
63 to immobilize –
64 to invest –
65 to add to the –, to capitalize
66 to mobilize a –
67 to invest one's – in
68 to raise –
69 to pay up –

capitalization
  rate of –, yield
to capitalize
capitalism
capitalist, investor
capitalistic

fuels
bottom
cargo
 1 a wood –
 2 bulk –
 3 floating –
 4 mixed –
 5 deck –
 6 to book a –
cargo boat
note book
 1 counterfoil book, stub book
 2 bill diary, maturity tickler
 3 pass book
 4 cheque book, check book
 5 order book
 6 pass book
 7 deposit book
 8 book of forms   [and deaths
 9 booklet for registration of births
 10 savings bank book
 11 customs pass book
 12 receipt book
 13 list of correspondents
card
 1 season ticket
 2 sample –
 3 visiting –
 4 identity –
 5 tab (guide) –

6 – lettre
7 – perforée
8 – postale
9 – postale avec réponse payée
10 – routière
11 laisser sa – chez...
cartel *m.*
– de l'acier
cartellisation *f.*
carton *m.*
1 un – (*boîte*)
2 en –
cartothèque *f.*
cas *m.*
1 au – ou, en – que
2 en – de
3 en aucun –
4 en tout –
5 le – échéant

6 discussion *f.* (étude *f.*) de –
case *f.*
– réservée aux mentions de service
casier *m.*
– judiciaire
casse *f.* (v. aussi *assurance*)
catalogue *m.*
1 – illustré
2 demandez notre –
cataloguer
catégorie *f.*
se classer dans une –
cause *f.*
1 – (*d'un effet de commerce*)
2 à – de
3 pour – de décès
4 pour – de déménagement
5 pour – de santé
caution *f.* (*personne*)

1 – (*garantie*)
2 – (*bouteille*)
3 – de banque, bancaire
4 –s et garanties données
5 –s pour compte de tiers

6 – solidaire
7 – solvable
8 bonne et valable –
9 s'adresser aux –s
10 fournir –
11 fournir une –

6 letter –
7 punch(ed) –
8 postcard
9 reply paid postcard
10 route map, road map
11 to leave one's – on
cartel
steel –
formation of cartels
cardboard
1 a carton
2 cardboard
card index
case
1 in case
2 in – of
3 in no –
4 at any rate, anyhow
5 if there is occasion, should it so happen, should the occasion arise
6 case study
frame, space
space for service instructions
pigeon-hole cabinet, filing cabinet
police records
breakage
catalogue, list
1 illustrated catalogue
2 – on application
to catalogue
category
to fall into a –
cause
1 consideration
2 owing to
3 on account of death
4 on account of removal   [ill health
5 for reasons of health, on grounds of
surety, guarantor

1 surety, security, guarantee
2 deposit (on bottle)
3 bank guarantee
4 securities and guarantees given
5 guarantees given for account of others

6 joint security
7 good surety
8 good and valid security
9 to apply to one's sureties
10 to give security
11 to find (provide) a surety

cautionnement / 50

12 se porter – de

cautionnement *m.* (*action*)
1 – (*contrat*)
2 – (*de fonctionnaire*)
3 – (*somme*)
4 – en actions (*administrateur*)
5 – en numéraire
6 – personnel
7 – réel

8 acte *m.* de –
9 actions *f. pl.* de –

cautionner
cavalerie *f.*
cavalier *m.*
cédant *m.*
céder
1 – des actions
2 – un droit
3 – un effet
4 commerce *m.* à –

5 débiteur cédé

cédule *f.*
centime *m.*
–s additionnels
centre *m.*
1 – commercial
2 – commercial (*shopping*)

3 – industriel
certain
1 le –

2 donner le –

certificat *m.*
1 – (*d'employeurs*)
2 – d'action(s)
3 – d'analyse
4 – d'assurance
– de bonne conduite
6 – de capacité
7 – de constructeur
8 – de déchargement
9 – de dépôt
10 – de fonds de placement
11 – de franc bord
12 – de jauge, – de tonnage

12 to stand surety for...

securing, guaranteeing
1 security, bond
2 security
3 security
4 qualification in shares
5 security in cash
6 personal security
7 collateral security

8 surety bond
9 qualification shares

to become surety for, to secure
kite flying, kites
signal
transferor, grantor
to transfer
1 – shares
2 to cede a right
3 – a bill
4 business (offered) for sale

5 (obligor of an assigned debt; debitor cessus)
acknowledg(e)ment of a debt
centime
surtax, additional percentage
(*Amer.*) center, (*Gr. Br.*) centre
1 trading (commercial) –
2 shopping center

3 industrial –
certain
1 fixed (direct, –) exchange

2 to quote fixed (–) exchange, to quote in home currency
certificate
1 testimonial
2 share –
3 – of analysis
4 insurance –
5 good-conduct –
6 – of proficiency, of competency
7 builder's –
8 landing –
9 warehouse warrant
10 (investment)trust share (certificate)
11 free board –
12 – of (ad)measurement

13 – de navigabilité
14 – de poids
15 – de pureté
16 – de qualité
17 – de trésorerie, du Trésor
18 – d'expédition postale
19 – d'origine
20 – sanitaire

21 certificat-or
22 – provisoire (*titre*)
certificateur *m.*
 – de caution
certification *f.*
certifier
 copie certifiée conforme
cessation *f.*
 1 – d'entreprise
 2 – de commerce
 3 – de payement
cesser
 1 – les affaires
 2 – les payements
cessible
cession *f.*
 1 – d'actions
 2 – de biens (aux créanciers)
 3 – d'une créance

 4 acte *m.* de –
cessionnaire *m.*
 1 – (*d'une créance*)
 2 – (*d'actions*)
 3 – (*d'une lettre de change*)
chaîne *f.*
 –s volontaires
chambre *f.*
 1 – de commerce internationale
 2 – de compensation

change *m.* (voir aussi *devises*)
 1 – (*commerce*)

 2 – (*de monnaie*)
 3 – à vue
 4 – direct
 5 – du jour
 6 – étranger, extérieur
 7 – favorable
 8 – flottant
 9 à – déprécié
 10 à – élevé
 11 au – du jour

13 – of seaworthiness
14 – of weight
15 – of purety
16 – of quality
17 treasury –, (*Gr. Br.*), treasury bond
18 – of mailing
19 – of origin
20 – of soundness

21 gold –
22 scrip (–), provisional –
guarantor
 countersurety
certification
to certify
 certified true copy
ceasing
 1 stoppage of business
 2 closing of the business
 3 stoppage (suspension) of payments
to cease, to stop
 1 to stop business
 2 to stop payments
transferable
transfer
 1 – of shares
 2 cession of property to
 3 assignment of debts to...

 4 deed of –
transferee, assignee
 1 assignee
 2 transferee
 3 transferee
chain store
 voluntary chains
chamber
 1 International – of Commerce
 2 clearing house

exchange
 1 exchange

 2 change
 3 sight bill
 4 direct –
 5 – of the day
 6 foreign –
 7 favo(u)rable –
 8 floating (currency) rate
 9 with a low rate of –
 10 with a high rate of –
 11 at the – of the day

changement / 52

12 arbitrage *m.* de –
13 bénéfice *m.* sur le –
14 clearing *m.* des –s
15 compte *m.* de –
16 contrôle *m.* des –s

17 cours *m.* du –
18 cours *m.* de – flottant, fluctuant
19 fonds *m.* d'égalisation des –s
20 marché *m.* des –s
21 marché *m.* des –s à terme
22 office *m.* du –
23 opérations *f. pl.* de –

24 opérations *f. pl.* de – à terme
25 opérations *f. pl.* de – au comptant
26 pair *m.* du –
27 pays *m.* à – élevé

28 perte *f.* au –
29 politique *f.* du –
30 position *f.* de –
31 première de –, (voir *premier*)
32 prescriptions *f. pl.* en matière de –
33 régime *m.* des –s multiples
34 répartition *f.* des –s
35 restrictions *f. pl.* en matière de –
36 risque *m.* du –
37 service *m.* du – (*banque*)
38 seule de –, (voir *seul*)
39 spéculation *f.* sur le –
40 taux *m.* du –
changement *m.*
1 – d'adresse
2 – de domicile
3 – en mieux

4 – en pire, en mal

5 subir un –
changer
1 – de domicile
2 – de main
3 – de la monnaie
4 – (*de train*)
changeur *m.*
chantier *m.*
1 ,,–'' ! (*route*)
2 – de bois
3 – naval

12 arbitration of –, arbitrage in exchange
13 profit of –, – profits
14 foreign – clearing
15 foreign currency account
16 – control, control of exchange

17 rate of –, – rate   [rates
18 variable (flexible, fluctuating) –
19 – equalization fund
20 foreign – market
21 forward – market
22 foreign currency control office
23 foreign – transactions

24 forward – transactions
25 spot – transactions
26 par of –
27 country with a high rate of –

28 loss on foreign –
29 – policy
30 foreign – position

32 foreign – orders, currency laws
33 multiple rate system
34 allotment of foreign –
35 foreign – restrictions
36 – risks
37 foreign – department

39 speculation on foreign –
40 rates of –
change, alteration
1 change of address
2 change of domicile
3 change (turn) for the better

4 change (turn) for the worse

5 to undergo a change
to change, to alter
1 to change one's residence
2 to change hands
3 to change money
4 to change
money – changer
works
1 road up, road works
2 timber yard
3 ship (building) yard

53 / chapeau de capitaine

chapeau m. **du capitaine**
charbon m. (voir *stock*)
 1 –s de soute
 2 –s domestiques
 3 pénurie f. de –
 4 faire le –
charbonnage m.
charbonnage m. (*mine*)
charbonner
charbonnier m.
 – (*marchand*)
charge f. (*office*)
 en vertu de sa –
charge f. (*l'action*)
 1 – (*cargaison*)
 2 – à (en) cueillette
 3 – en vrac
 4 – complète
 5 – utile
 6 être en – (pour Anvers)
 7 prendre en –
 8 rompre –
charge f. (*frais*)
 1 –s d'exploitation
 2 –s financières
 3 –s fiscales
 4 –s fixes
 5 –s sociales
 6 alourdissement m. des –
 7 3 personnes à –
 8 à notre –
 9 sans –s de famille
 10 être à la – de...
chargé m.
 – sur le pont
chargement m. (*action*)
 1 – (*cargaison*)
 2 – en pontée, sur le pont [*charge*]
 3 – à (en) cueillette, – en vrac (voir
 4 – du pont
 5 délai m. de –
 6 frais m. pl. de –
charger
 1 – en (à) cueillette
 2 – en pontée, sur le pont
 3 – en vrac
 4 – une cargaison
 5 – sur un wagon
 6 – qqn de...

 7 – un compte de...
 8 se – des recouvrements

primage
coal
 1 bunker –s
 2 house coal
 3 coal shortage
 4 to –, to bunker
coaling
coal mine
to coal, to bunker
coaler, coal ship
 coal merchant
office
 in (by) virtue of his –
loading
 1 load, cargo
 2 general cargo
 3 bulk cargo
 4 truck load
 5 carrying capacity
 6 to be in – (for Antwerp)
 7 to take over, to take care of
 8 to break bulk
expenses
 1 working –
 2 financing –
 3 fiscal charges
 4 standing (fixed) charges, –
 5 social charges
 6 increase of charges
 7 3 dependent persons
 8 at our –
 9 without encumbrances [by
 10 to be chargeable to..., to be borne
cargo
 deck –
loading
 1 cargo, load
 2 shipment (stowage) on deck

 4 deck cargo
 5 time for –
 6 – (shipping) charges
to load
 1 – with general goods
 2 to ship on deck
 3 to ship in bulk
 4 – a cargo
 5 – on a waggon
 6 to charge (entrust) someone with

 7 to charge an account with
 8 to undertake the collections

chargeur / 54

chargeur *m.*
charte-partie *f.*
chauffage *m.*
  1 – central
  2 appareil *m.* de –
  3 tuyau *m.* de –
chauffe, surface *f.* **de –**
chauffeur *m.*
  – d'automobile
chavirer
chef *m.*
  1 – comptable
  2 – de bureau
  3 – de famille
  4 – de gare
  5 – d'entreprise
  6 – de publicité
  7 – d'équipe
  8 – de service
  9 – de vente
  10 – d'exploitation
  11 – du personnel
  12 femmes –s d'entreprises
  13 de ce –
  14 du – de

chemin de fer *m.*
  1 par –
  2 indicateur *m.* des chemins de fer
  3 réseau *m.* des chemins de fer
  4 (valeurs de) chemins de fer
chemise *f.* (*couverture*)
cheptel *m.*
chèque *m.*
  1 – de (se montant à)...
  2 – à barrement général
  3 – à barrement spécial
  4 – à ordre
  5 – à porter en compte

  6 – au porteur
  7 – avisé
  8 – barré, croisé
  9 – bloqué
  10 – certifié
  11 – compensé
  12 – de banque
  13 – en blanc
  14 – de voyage
  15 – dividende
  16 – égaré

  17 – (il)limité

shipper
charter party
heating
  1 central –
  2 – apparatus
  3 – pipe
heating surface
stoker, fireman
  driver
to capsize
head, chief
  1 chief accountant
  2 chief clerk, head clerk
  3 head of family
  4 stationmaster
  5 head of business
  6 advertising manager
  7 foreman
  8 head of department
  9 sales manager
  10 works manager
  11 staff manager
  12 women executives
  13 for that reason
  14 on account of

railway
  1 by rail
  2 – guide
  3 net of –s
  4 – shares
folder
livestock
(*Amer.*) check, (*Gr. Br.*) cheque
  1 – for..., amounting to...
  2 – crossed generally
  3 – crossed specially
  4 order –
  5 – only for account ("account payee")
  6 – to bearer
  7 advised –
  8 crossed –
  9 stopped –
  10 certified -
  11 cleared –
  12 bank –
  13 blank –   [check
  14 traveller's –, (*Amer.*) traveler's
  15 dividend warrant
  16 lost –

  17 (un)limited –

55 / chéquier

18 – nominatif
19 – non barré
20 – ouvert
21 – périmé
22 – postal
23 – retourné
24 – sans provision

25 – sur place
26 – visé
27 carnet *m.* de –s
28 compte *m.* de –s
29 cours *m.* du –
30 falsification *f.* de –
31 formule *f.* de –

32 loi *f.* sur les –s
33 opérations *f. pl.* par –
34 perforeuse *f.* de –
35 portefeuille *m.* –s
36 transmission *f.* d'un –
37 annuler un –
38 barrer un –
39 détacher un – du carnet

40 émettre (tirer) un – sur...

41 encaisser un –
42 endosser un – en blanc
43 envoyer un – à l'encaissement

44 fournir un – sur
45 payer un –
46 payer un – à présentation

47 refuser le payement d'un –
48 remettre un – à
49 toucher un –
chéquier *m.*
Cher Monsieur,
cher
  1 argent –
  2 indemnité *f.* de vie chère
  3 acheter –
  4 coûter –
  5 vendre –
  6 il fait – vivre à...
chercheur *m.*
cherté *f.*
  – de la vie
chevalier d'industrie *m.*
chiffre *m.*
  1 –s arabes

18 not negotiable –
19 uncrossed –
20 open –
21 stale –
22 post(al) –
23 returned –
24 – without sufficient funds (to meet it), dud –

25 town –
26 marked –
27 – book
28 – account
29 – rate
30 forgery of a –
31 – form

32 –s Act
33 – transactions
34 – perforator, – protector
35 –s in hand
36 transfer of a –
37 to cancel a –
38 to cross a –
39 to tear out a – from the book

40 to draw (write out) a – on

41 to collect (cash) a –
42 to endorse a – in blank
43 to send a – for collection

44 to draw a – on
45 to pay a –
46 to meet (pay) a – on presentation

47 to dishonour (reject) a –
48 to send a – to
49 to cash a –
cheque (check) book
Dear Mr...,
dear
  1 – money
  2 cost-of-living bonus
  3 to buy –, at a high price
  4 to be expensive
  5 to sell –
  6 the cost of living is high in...
researcher
dearness, high prices
  dearness (high cost) of living
swindler
figure
  1 Arabic numerals

chiffré / 56

2 –s comparatifs	2 comparative –s
3 – d'affaires annuel	3 annual turnover
4 – d'affaires important	4 large turnover
5 – de repère (*clé télégr.*)	5 test number
6 – indice	6 index number
7 en –s	7 in cipher
8 en –s ronds	8 in round –s
9 offre sous –...	9 persons interested are invited to apply under No...
10 écrire en –s	10 to write in cipher
11 énoncer en –s	11 to express in –s

chiffré
1 en –
2 télégramme –

cipher...
1 in –
2 – telegram

chiffrer
1 – un télégramme

to work out, to figure (cipher) out
1 to cipher a telegram

2 se –
3 se – par des milliers

2 to amount
3 to run into thousands

chimie *f.*
chimique

chemistry
chemical

chirographaire
1 créancier *m.* –

1 unsecured creditor

2 obligation *f.* –

2 simple (naked) debenture

choix *m.*
1 – de domicile
2 – de la profession
3 au –
4 au – de l'acheteur
5 de –
6 grand – de...
7 articles *m. pl.* de premier –
8 faire un –

choice
1 election of domicile
2 – of a profession
3 at –
4 at buyer's option
5 selected, –
6 large (varied) assortment of...
7 first-class articles
8 to make a –

chômage *m.*

unemployment

1 – conjoncturel
2 – frictionnel
3 – saisonnier
4 – structurel
5 – technologique
6 allocation *f.* (indemnité *f.*) de –

1 cyclical –
2 frictional –
3 seasonal –
4 structural –
5 technological –
6 dole, – benefit

7 assurance *f.* contre le –

7 – insurance

8 courbe *f.* du –
9 lutte *f.* contre le –
10 recrudescence *f.* du –

8 – curve
9 combating (fight against) –
10 recrudescence of –

11 régression *f.* du –
12 résorption *f.* du –
13 taux *m.* de –
14 lutter contre le –

11 decrease in –
12 absorption of –
13 – ratio
14 to combat –

chômage m. (*chem. de fer*)

– (*navire*)
chômer
– (*fabrique*)
chômeur m.
1 les –s
2 – complet
3 – partiel
chose corporelle (voir *corporel*)
chute f. des prix
ci
ci-après (voir aussi *mentionné*)
ci-contre
ci-dessous
ci-dessus
ci-inclus, ci-joint

1 veuillez trouver –

2 nous vous remettons –

3 les pièces –es

4 – copie de votre lettre

circonstance f.
1 –s aggravantes
2 –s atténuantes
3 –s indépendantes de notre volonté

4 dans les –s présentes

5 par suite de –s imprévues

6 selon les –s
7 concours m. de –s

circulaire f.

1 lettre f. de crédit –
2 distribuer (envoyer) des –s
circulation f. (voir aussi *échange, mouvement*)
1 – des capitaux
2 – des devises
3 – des effets de commerce
4 – des marchandises
5 – des personnes

6 – des valeurs mobilières
7 – des voyageurs

demurrage

laying up
to be unemployed, to be out of work
to be at a standstill, to stand idle
unemployed person
1 the unemployed
2 wholly unemployed
3 temporarily unemployed

collapse (heavy fall) of prices
say
hereafter, further on
opposite
hereunder, below
above
herewith, subjoined

1 enclosed please find

2 we hand you herewith, we are enclosing, we enclose herewith

3 the subjoined documents, the documents enclosed herewith
4 herewith copy of your letter

circumstance
1 aggravating –s
2 extenuating –s
3 –s outside (beyond) our control

4 under the present –s

5 on account of unexpected –s

6 according to –s
7 concurrence (concourse) of –s

circular

1 – letter of credit
2 to send out (issue) –s
circulation

1 – of capital
2 currency dealings
3 bill transactions
4 movement of goods
5 movement of workers (of labour), transfer of manpower
6 transactions in securities
7 passenger traffic

8 – fiduciaire
 9 – forcée
10 – monétaire [d'œuvre
11 libre – des travailleurs, de la main-
12 rapidité *f.* de –

13 mettre en –
14 retirer de la –

circuler
ne circule pas le dimanche (*train*)
cire *f.*
 – à cacheter
ciseaux *m. pl.*
1 –
2 mouvement *m.* en –
classe *f.*
1 – d'un navire
2 – moyenne
3 – ouvrière
4 de première –
5 billet *m.* de deuxième –
classement *m.*

1 – horizontal

2 – par fiches
3 – par ordre alphabétique

4 – par ordre numérique
5 – suspendu
6 – vertical

7 pour votre –, votre dossier
8 système *m.* de –
classer
1 – une lettre
2 – par ordre alphabétique
3 – par ordre chronologique
4 – par ordre numérique
5 – suivant ...
classeur *m.*
 – (*personne*)
meuble *m.* –
classification *f.*

classifier
clause *f.*
1 – à ordre
2 – au porteur
3 – avarie
4 – commissoire
5 – compromissoire

 8 fiduciary –
 9 forced –
10 currency –
11 free movement of labour
12 rapidity (velocity) of –

13 to put into –
14 to withdraw from –

to circulate
does not run on Sunday
wax
sealing –
scissors
1 price –
2 – movement
class
1 – of a ship
2 middle –
3 working –
4 first-rate, first- –
5 second – ticket
filing

1 horizontal (flat) –

2 card index system
3 – in alphabetical order

4 – in numerical order
5 suspension –
6 vertical –

7 for your files
8 – system
to file
1 – a letter
2 – in alphabetical order
3 – in order of date
4 – in numerical order
5 to classify according to...
file
filing clerk
filing cabinet
classification

to classify, to class
clause
1 order –
2 bearer –
3 average –
4 commissoria lex
5 arbitration –

6 – contraire
7 – conventionnelle
8 – d'annulation
9 – d'arbitrage
10 – de collision
11 – de concurrence
12 – de franchise
13 – de guerre
14 – de la nation la plus favorisée
15 – de négligence
16 – de recours et conservation

17 – dérogatoire
18 – de sauvegarde
19 – de valeur fournie
20 – de valuation (*assur.*)
21 – dollar
22 – échappatoire
23 clause-or   [(*sauvetage*)
24 – pas de résultats, pas de payement
25 – résolutoire
26 – sans (autre) avis
27 – suivant avis
28 insérer une –
clavier *m.*
clé, clef *f.*
  1 – de répartition

  2 – télégraphique
  3 industrie –
clearing *m.*
  1 – bilatéral
  2 – multilatéral
  3 par la voie du –

  4 accord *m.* de –

  5 avances *f. pl.* en –
  6 compte *m.* –
  7 office *m.* du –

  8 opérations *f. pl.* de –
  9 système *m.* de –

  10 versement *m.* au –
cliché *m.* (*imprim.*)
client *m.*
  1 – (*banque, notaire, avocat*)
  2 – de passage, – occasionnel
  3 – difficile
  4 – régulier
clientèle *f.*
  1 – (*fonds de commerce*)

6 stipulation to the contrary
7 agreement –
8 cancelling –
9 arbitration –
10 collision –, running down –
11 competition –
12 franchise –
13 war –
14 most-favoured-nation –
15 negligence –
16 suing and labouring –

17 derogatory –
18 saving –
19 value given –
20 valuation –
21 dollar –
22 escape –
23 gold –
24 – no cure no pay
25 avoidance –
26 – "without (other) advice"
27 – "as per advice"
28 to insert a –
keyboard
key
  1 distribution basis

  2 telegraphic –
  3 – industry
clearing
  1 bilateral –
  2 multilateral –
  3 through –

  4 – agreement

  5 – advances
  6 – account
  7 – house

  8 – transactions
  9 – system

  10 – payment
block
customer
  1 client
  2 chance (casual) –
  3 burdensome –
  4 regular (permanent) –
custom, customers, connection
  1 goodwill, custom

climat / 60

  2 – bancaire
  3 nombreuse –

  4 service *m.* à la –
  5 accroître la –
  6 attirer la –
  7 constituer une –
  8 détourner la –

  9 la – diminue
climat *m.*
  1 – de la bourse
  2 – de la conjoncture
  3 – économique
clôture *f.*
  1 – annuelle des livres
  2 – de la bourse
  3 – d'un compte (= *fermer*)
  4 – des magasins
  5 en – (*bourse*)
  6 être ferme en –
clôturer
  1 – à perte
  2 – les livres
  3 – un compte (*fermer*)
  4 – ferme à...
coassocié *m.*
coassurance *f.*
cocaution *f.*
cocréancier *m.*
code *m.*
  1 – chiffré
  2 – civil
  3 – commercial, – de commerce
  4 – privé
  5 – télégraphique
codébiteur *m.*
coder
codirecteur *m.*
coefficient *m.*
  1 – de couverture
  2 – de liquidité
  3 – de pondération
  4 – de solvabilité
  5 – d'exploitation
  6 – de trésorerie
coffre(-fort) *m.*
  1 – de nuit (*banque*)
  2 accès *m.* aux coffres-forts

  3 carte *f.* d'accès aux coffres-forts
  4 compartiment *m.* (de –)

  2 bank's clientele, customers
  3 wide connection, numerous customers
  4 service
  5 to extend the connection
  6 to attract custom
  7 to build up a connection
  8 to take away the custom

  9 custom is dropping off
climate
  1 – (tone) of the Stock Exchange
  2 cyclical –
  3 economic –
closing
  1 annual balancing of the books
  2 close of the exchange
  3 – of an account
  4 shop –
  5 at the close
  6 to close firm
to close
  1 – at a loss
  2 to balance the books
  3 – an account
  4 – at...
copartner
co-insurance
cosurety
joint creditor
code
  1 cipher –
  2 Civil –
  3 Commercial –, commercial law
  4 private –
  5 telegraphic –
joint debtor
to code, to put into code
joint manager
coefficient, ratio
  1 cover –
  2 liquidity ratio
  3 weighting –
  4 solvency coefficient
  5 working coefficient, ratio of working [expenses
  6 cash ratio
safe, strong box
  1 night safe
  2 access to safes

  3 admission card
  4 safe deposit box

5 contrat m. de location de –	5 safe deposit agreement
6 galerie f. de coffres-forts	6 safe deposit, vaults safe deposit vault
7 location f. de –	7 safe hiring
8 loyer m. d'un –	8 rent (charge) for a safe deposit box
cogestion f.	**joint management**
coin m. (*bourse*)	**section, market**
colis m.	**parcel**
1 – chargé, – de valeur déclarée	1 insured –
2 – grevé de (contre) remboursement	2 cash-on-delivery –
3 – postal	3 postal –
4 par –	4 by – post
colisage m., note f. de –	**packing list**
collationner	**to collate, to compare**
colle f. **de bureau**	**office paste**
collectif	**collective**
1 contrat –	1 – contract
2 liste collective	2 – list
3 procuration collective	3 joint procuration
collection f.	**collection**
collègue m.	**colleague**
collision f.	**collision**
1 clause f. de –	1 – clause
2 entrer en – avec...	2 to come into – with
collusion f.	**collusion**
colocataire m.	**cotenant**
colonial	**colonial**
denrées –es	– produce
colonie f.	**colony**
colonne f.	**column**
1 – créditrice	1 credit –
2 – débitrice	2 debit –
3 – du libellé	3 description (particulars) –
4 – du montant	4 amount –
5 la plus forte –	5 the stronger side
6 en-tête m. de –	6 headline
7 livre m. à –s	7 columnar book
8 remplir une –	8 to fill up a –
colportage m.	**hawking**
colporter	**to hawk**
colporteur m.	**hawker**
combler	**to fill**
1 – un déficit	1 to make up a shortage
2 – une perte	2 to make up a loss
3 – une vacance	3 – a vacancy
comité m. (voir aussi *bureau*)	**committee**
1 – consultatif	1 advisory board, advisory –

commande / 62

2 – de direction, – directeur | 2 managing –, board of management
commande *f.* (voir aussi *ordre*) | **order**
  1 – de... | 1 – of...'
  2 – de l'étranger | 2 – from abroad
  3 –s en carnet, en cours | 3 –s on (in) hand
  4 –s non exécutées | 4 backlog of unfilled –s
  5 – supplémentaire | 5 additional –
  6 par – de... | 6 for an – of
  7 sur – | 7 to –
  8 bulletin *m.* de – | 8 order form
  9 carnet *m.* de –s | 9 order book
  10 confirmation *f.* de – | 10 confirmation of –
  11 entrées de –s | 11 new –s booked
  12 numéro *m.* de – | 12 order number
  13 annuler une – | 13 to cancel an –
  14 enregistrer une – | 14 to book an –
  15 exécuter une – | 15 to execute (fulfil) an –
  16 faire (passer) une – | 16 to give an –, place an – with
  17 obtenir une – | 17 to obtain an –
commander | **to order**
commanditaire *m.* | **silent partner, sleeping partner**
commandité *m.* | **acting partner**
commandite *f.* (société en – simple) | **limited partnership, silent (sleeping) partnership**
  société *f.* en – par actions | partnership limited by shares
commanditer | **to finance**
commerçable (*papier*) | **negotiable**
commerçant *m.* | **trader, merchant**
commerçant *adj.* | **business...**
  1 quartier – | 1 – quarter
  2 rue –e | 2 shopping street
commerce *m.* | **commerce, trade, trading**
  1 le – avec le Japon | 1 the trade with Japan
  2 un – de... | 2 a... business
  3 – ambulant | 3 hawking
  4 – de cabotage | 4 coasting trade
  5 – d'échange | 5 barter
  6 – de contrebande | 6 contraband trade [quantities
  7 – de demi-gros | 7 wholesale dealing in small
  8 – de denrées coloniales | 8 produce trade
  9 – de détail | 9 retail trade
  10 – de (en) gros | 10 wholesale trade
  11 – de (en) transit | 11 transit trade
  12 – d'exportation | 12 export trade
  13 – d'importation | 13 import trade
  14 – d'outre-mer | 14 oversea(s)trade
  15 – extérieur | 15 foreign trade
  16 office *m.* du – extérieur | 16 foreign trade agency

17 – intérieur
18 – intermédiaire
19 – local
20 – maritime
21 – avec les colonies
22 le – va mal (voir aussi *affaires*)

23 actes *m. pl.* de –
24 balance *f.* de –
25 chambre *f.* de –
26 code *m.* de –
27 école *f.* de –
28 effets *m. pl.* de –

29 fonds *m.* de –
30 institut supérieur de –
31 liberté *f.* de –
32 livre *m.* de –
33 maison *f.* de –
34 registre *m.* du –
35 tribunal *m.* de –
36 usage *m.* du –
37 aller dans le –

38 être dans le –
39 faire le – de
40 ouvrir un –
commercer

commercial
1 agence –e
2 agent –
3 aviation –e
4 bottin –
5 centre –

6 école –e
7 entreprise –e

8 langue –e
9 mouvement –
10 opération –e

11 politique –e
12 relations –es

13 société –e
14 style –
15 terme –

16 valeur –e
commercialiser
commettant *m.*

17 home trade
18 intermediate trade
19 local trade
20 maritime trade
21 colonial trade
22 trade is bad

23 acts of merchant, commercial acts
24 balance of trade
25 chamber of commerce
26 commercial code, law
27 commercial school
28 trade bills

29 business
30 commercial college (university)
31 freedom of trade
32 account book
33 business house
34 trade register
35 commercial court
36 trade custom
37 to go into business

38 to be in trade
39 to deal in
40 to start a business
to trade, to deal

commercial
1 – agency
2 – agent
3 – aviation
4 – directory
5 – center

6 – school
7 – undertaking, enterprise, trading concern

8 business (commercial) language
9 – traffic
10 business transaction

11 – policy
12 business relations

13 trading company
14 business style
15 – (business) term

16 – value
to commercialize
principal

commis m.

1 – de banque
2 – expéditionnaire
3 – principal
4 – principal (*boursier*)
5 – voyageur

commissaire m.

1 – aux (des) comptes

2 – de police

3 – priseur
4 collège m. des –s
5 rapport m. des –s (voir *rapport*)

commission f. (*comité*)

1 – bancaire
2 – centrale
3 – d'arbitrage
4 – d'enquête
5 – paritaire
6 – permanente
7 être membre d'une –

commission f. (*rémunération*)

1 – de... %

2 – d'acceptation
3 – d'achat, sur les achats
4 – de banque
5 – de colonne, – sur la plus forte colonne

6 – de compte
7 – de confirmation
8 – de découvert

9 – (de) ducroire

10 – de garantie, – syndicale (*émission*)
11 – de guichet (*émission*)
12 – d'encaissement
13 – de payement
14 – d'escompte
15 – de vente, sur les ventes
16 – spéciale
17 franc de –
18 passible d'une –, sujet à une –

19 commerce m. de –
20 compte m. de –
21 livre m. de –
22 maison f. de –

clerk

1 bank –
2 forwarding –
3 chief –
4 authorized –
5 commercial traveller

commissioner, commissary

1 auditor

2 commissioner of police

3 auctioneer
4 auditors

commission, committee

1 banking commission
2 central committee
3 arbitration committee
4 committee of inquiry
5 wages council
6 standing committee
7 to be on a committee

commission

1 –, charge of ... %

2 – for acceptance
3 buying –
4 banker's –
5 – on the stronger side

6 turnover –
7 confirmation –
8 overdraft –

9 del credere –

10 underwriting –

11 selling agent's –
12 – for collection
13 payment –
14 discount
15 – on sales
16 extra charge
17 free of –
18 subject to a –

19 – business
20 – account
21 – book
22 – house

23 taux *m.* de –	23 rate of –
24 faire la –	24 to do – business
25 prélever une –	25 to charge a –
commissionnaire *m.*	**commission agent**
1 – ducroire	1 del credere agent
2 – en douane	2 customs agent
3 – expéditeur	3 shipping agent
commodat *m.*	**free loan**
commun	**common**
1 – diviseur	1 – divisor
2 droit –	2 – law
3 échéance –e	3 average due date
4 fonds –	4 – fund
5 pour compte –	5 on joint account
communauté *f.* (v. aussi *régime*)	**community**
1 – d'(réduite aux) acquêts	1 – of goods acquired during marriage
2 – d'intérêts	2 – of interest
3 – Européenne du Charbon et de l'Acier	3 European Coal and Steel –
4 – Économique Européenne	4 European Economic –
5 – Européenne de l'Energie Atomique	5 European Atomic Energy –
6 – des Six	6 – of the Six
7 en – de biens	7 in – of goods
communication *f.* (*téléphone*)	
1 – interurbaine	1 trunk call
2 – locale	2 local call
3 – téléphonique	3 call
4 fausse –	4 wrong connection
5 la – est mauvaise	5 the line is bad
6 couper la –	6 to cut off connection
7 demander une –	7 to book a call
8 mettre en – avec...	8 to put through to...
9 prendre la –	9 to take the call
communication *f.* (*de pièces*)	**production**
communiquer	
1 – des pièces	1 to produce documents
2 – des renseignements	2 to communicate information
compagnie *f.* (voir aussi *société*)	**company**
– des chemins de fer	railway company
comparaison *f.*	**comparison**
1 en – de	1 as compared with, in (by) – with
2 par –	2 by –
3 soutenir la – avec	3 to stand (bear) – with
comparaître devant...	**to appear before**
comparant *m.*	party
1 le – d'une (de première) part	1 – of the first
2 le – d'autre (de deuxième) part	2 – of the second

comparer / 66

comparer à — to compare with
compartiment *m.* (*bourse*) — section
  1 – (*ch. de fer*) — 1 compartment
  2 – de coffre-fort (voir *coffre-fort*)
compensation *f.* — compensation
  1 – de dettes — 1 settlement (of debts) per contra
  2 – (*bourse*) — 2 making up
  3 par la voie de la – — 3 by –
  4 caisse *f.* de – (*allocat. famil.*) — 4 equalization fund
  5 chambre *f.* de – — 5 clearing house
  6 cours *m.* de – — 6 making up price

  7 jour *m.* de – — 7 contango day, making up day
compenser — to compensate
  1 – une perte par — 1 to make good a loss by
  2 – un chèque — 2 to clear a cheque (check)
  3 se – — 3 – each other, to be compensated
  4 valeur compensée — 4 value –d, value here and there
compétence *f.* — competency, authority
compétent — competent
compétitif — competitive
  1 position compétitive — 1 – position
  2 prix –s — 2 – prices
complémentaire, produits –s — complementary goods
compléter — to complete, to make up (a sum)
comportement *m.* — behavio(u)r
  1 – du consommateur — 1 consumer –
  2 – de la bourse — 2 – of the Exchange
  3 – économique — 3 economic –
compression *f.* — retrenchment, curtailment
comprimer — to retrench, to curtail, to cut down
compromis *m.* — bond, compromise
  – d'avarie (grosse) — (general) average bond
compromissoire, clause *f.* **–** — arbitration clause
comptabilisation *f.* — recording in books
comptabiliser — to record, to enter (in)
comptabilité *f.* — bookkeeping
  1 – commerciale — 1 commercial –
  2 – de banque — 2 bank –
  3 – de sociétés — 3 company –
  4 – en partie double — 4 – by double entry
  5 – en partie simple — 5 – by single entry
  6 – industrielle — 6 industrial –

  7 méthode *f.* de – — 7 – method
  8 service *m.* de la – — 8 accountant's (–) department
  9 tenir la – de... — 9 to keep the books of...
comptable *adj.* — accountable, bookkeeping...
  1 machine *f.* – — 1 bookkeeping machine
  2 période *f.* – — 2 accounting period
  3 pièce *f.* – — 3 bookkeeping voucher
  4 quittance *f.* – — 4 accountable receipt
  5 valeur *f.* – — 5 book value

67 / comptable

comptable *m.*	bookkeeper
expert – *m.*	chartered accountant
comptant	cash
1 – *m.*	1 –
2 – avec 2% d'escompte	2 – less 2% discount
3 – compté	3 – down
4 – contre documents	4 – against documents
5 – contre remboursement	5 – on delivery
6 – sans escompte (net)	6 net –
7 au –	7 in –, for –
8 achat *m.* au –	8 – purchase
9 affaires *f. pl.* au –	9 – transactions
10 argent *m.* –	10 ready money
11 cours *m.* du – (*change*)	11 – price, spot price
12 marché *m.* au –	12 spot market
13 opérations *f. pl.* de change au –	13 spot exchange transactions
14 payement *m.* au –	14 – payment
15 valeurs *f. pl.* au –	15 securities quoted on the spot [market
16 vente *f.* au –	16 – sale
17 acheter (au) –	17 to buy for –
18 payer –	18 to pay –
19 vendre (au) –	19 to sell for –
compte *m.* (v. aussi *ouverture*)	account
1 – à découvert	1 overdrawn –
2 – à demi (de – à demi)	2 (on) joint –
3 – à échéance fixe	3 fixed deposit –
4 – à préavis	4 deposit – at notice
5 – à vue	5 demand deposit –, call deposit –
6 – annuel	6 annual –
7 – bloqué	7 blocked –
8 – capital	8 capital –
9 – courant (voir *compte courant*)	
10 – de chèques	10 cheque –, drawing –, checking –
11 – (de) chèques postaux	11 postal cheque –, postal transfer –
12 – collectif	12 summary –
13 – créditeur	13 creditor –
14 – d'acceptation	14 acceptance –
15 – d'achat	15 – of goods purchased
16 – d'attente	16 suspense –
17 – d'avances	17 loan –
18 – de banque	18 bank –
19 – débiteur	19 debtor –
20 – de caisse	20 cash –
21 – de capital	21 capital –
22 – (de) chèques	22 cheque –, drawing –, checking –
23 – de choses, – titres	23 impersonal –, stock –
24 – de clearing	24 clearing –

compte / 68

25 – de commission	25 commission –
26 – de consignation	26 consignment –
27 – de contre-partie	27 contra –
28 – de dépôt(s)	28 deposit –
29 – de dépôts à préavis	29 deposit – at notice
30 – de dépôts à terme	30 fixed deposit –
31 – de dépôts à vue	31 demand deposit –, call deposit –
32 – de divers	32 sundries –
33 – d'effets à payer	33 bills payable –
34 – d'effets à recevoir	34 bills receivable –
35 – de fret	35 freight –
36 – de liquidation	36 liquidating –
37 – (de) marchandises	37 goods –
38 – de méthode	38 suspense –
39 – en participation	39 joint –
40 – de personnes (de déposants) (voir aussi *titres*)	40 personal –
41 – de quinzaine	41 fortnightly –
42 – de réserve	42 reserve –
43 – de retour	43 – of re-exchange
44 – de profits et pertes	44 profit and loss –
45 – des résultats	45 profit and loss –
46 – de vente	46 – sales
47 – d'exploitation	47 trading (working) –
48 – d'intérêts	48 interest –
49 – d'ordre	49 suspense –, contingent –
50 – du grand livre	50 ledger –
51 – effets	51 bills –
52 – en banque	52 banking –
53 – (tenu) en francs	53 franc –
54 – (tenu) en monnaies étrangères	54 currency –
55 – espèces	55 cash –
56 – joint	56 joint –
57 – loro	57 loro –
58 – nostro	58 nostro –
59 – ouvert	59 open (unsettled) –
60 – particulier	60 private –
61 – titres (voir aussi *de personnes*)	61 stock –, impersonal –
62 – vostro	62 vostro –
63 à – (*à crédit*)	63 on –, on credit
64 en règlement de votre –	64 in settlement of your –
65 pour – commun	65 for joint –
66 pour – de	66 for – of, on behalf of
67 pour le – de qui il appartiendra	67 for – of whom it may concern

68 pour son propre –
69 arrêté m. de –
70 commission f. de –
71 état m. d'un –
72 extrait m. de votre – chez nous

73 extrait journalier (d'un –)
74 relevé m. de –
75 la tenue de votre – chez nous
76 titulaire m. d'un –

77 valeur f. en –
78 apurer un –

79 arrêter un –
80 avoir (posséder) un – auprès d'une banque

81 charger un –
82 décharger un –
83 dresser, établir un –

84 être établi à son –
85 fermer, liquider un – de banque
86 ouvrir un – auprès de...
87 passer, porter en –

88 porter les frais en –

89 régler un –
90 rendre – de (*se justifier*) à...

91 rendre ses –s
92 repasser un –
93 solder un –
94 tenir – de

95 tenir les –s

96 vérifier un –
compte courant m.

1 en –
2 avance f. en –
3 extrait m. de votre –

4 titulaire m. de –
5 avoir un – auprès de

6 entretenir un – chez

7 ouvrir un – à... dans nos livres

68 for one's own –
69 settlement of –
70 turnover commission
71 state of an –
72 statement (abstract) of your – with us

73 daily statement of –
74 statement of –
75 the conduct of your – with us
76 – holder

77 value in –
78 to audit and agree an –

79 to close (make up) an –
80 to have (keep) an – at (with) a bank

81 to charge an –
82 to discharge an –
83 to make out an –

84 to be in business for one's own –
85 to close (wind up) an – with a bank
86 to open an – with...
87 to pass to –

88 to charge someone for the expense

89 to settle (pay) an –
90 to render – to...

91 to render –
92 to re-examine an –
93 to balance an –
94 to take – of

95 to keep the –s

96 to check an –
account current, current account

1 on current account
2 advance on current account
3 statement (abstract) of your current account
4 current account holder
5 to have an account current with

6 to keep a current account with

7 to open a current account in our books

compter
 1 – en trop
 2 – pour
comptes faits *pl.*

comptoir *m.*
 1 – *(caisse)*
 2 – *(étranger)*
 3 – *(succursale)*
 4 – de vente
concentration *f.*
 1 – bancaire
 2 – horizontale
 3 – verticale
concern *m.*
concernant
concerne : *(lettre)*
concession *f.*
 1 – minière
 2 demande *f.* de –
 3 accorder une –
 4 demander (solliciter) une –
 5 faire des –s
 6 obtenir une –
 7 prolonger une –
 8 retirer une –
concessionnaire *m.*

concessionnaire *adj.*
concevoir
 conçu en ces termes

conclure
 1 – un contrat
 2 – un marché
 3 nous en concluons
conclusion *f.*
 1 la – d'un contrat
 2 tirer une –
concordat *m.*
 1 – judiciaire
 2 – de 50 %

 3 projet *m.* de –
 4 proposition *f.* de –
 5 accorder (adopter) le –
 6 homologuer le –
 7 offrir (présenter) un –
concordataire
 1 débiteur *m.* –

 2 procédure *f.* –
 3 proposition *f.* –

---

to reckon, to count
 1 to overcharge
 2 to count as
ready reckoner

counter
 1 cash desk
 2 factory, agency
 3 branch
 4 selling office
concentration
 1 – in banking
 2 horizontal –
 3 vertical –
concern
concerning, as regards, relative to
re, subject :
concession
 1 mining –
 2 application for a –
 3 to grant a –
 4 to apply for a –
 5 to make –s
 6 to acquire a –
 7 to extend a –
 8 to cancel a –
concessionary, grantee

concessionary
to draft
 running as follows

to conclude
 1 – (enter into) a contract
 2 to strike a bargain
 3 we conclude from this
conclusion
 1 the – of a contract
 2 to draw a –
composition
 1 –
 2 a – of 10 s. in the £, of 50 cents on the dollar
 3 draft –
 4 proposal for a –
 5 to accept the –
 6 to sanction the –
 7 to offer a –
composition...
 1 bankrupt who has made a composition with his creditors
 2 composition proceedings
 3 proposal for a composition

concorder (avec)
- avec ses créanciers

concours *m.*
- d'étalages

concurrence *f.*
1. - déloyale
2. - (im)parfaite
3. - monopolistique
4. - pure
5. - vive (âpre, acharnée)
6. à - de
7. jusqu'à - de
8. clause *f.* de -
9. prix *m. pl.* défiant toute -
10. battre la -
11. éliminer la -
12. faire - à
13. tenir tête à la -

concurrencer

concurrent *m.*
concurrentiel
1. capacité (force) -le

2. position -le

condamner (v. aussi *dépens*)
condamné à des dommages-intérêts

condition *f.*
1. -s climatiques
2. -s de livraison
3. -s de payement
4. -s de vente
5. -s d'usage
6. -s générales
7. -s régissant votre compte

8. à - (*envoi*)
9. à - que
10. aux -s les plus avantageuses
11. aux (dans les) -s suivantes
12. dans ces -s
13. en bonne - (voir aussi, *état*)
14. envoyer à -
15. être soumis à des -s
16. imposer des -s
17. poser des -s

conditionné, bien -

conditionnel
conducteur *m.*
- de travaux

---

to agree with
to compound with one's creditors

competition
window dressing -

competition
1. unfair -
2. (im)perfect -
3. monopolistic -
4. pure -
5. brisk (fierce, severe) -
6. amounting to, to the amount of
7. to the extent of...
8. - clause
9. competitive prices
10. to beat (crush) -
11. to eliminate -
12. to compete with
13. to meet (face) -

to compete with

competitor
competitive
1. competitive capacity

2. - position

to condemn
condemned (cast) in damages

condition
1. weather -s, climatic -s
2. terms of delivery
3. terms of payment
4. terms of sale
5. usual terms
6. general -s
7. terms for the conduct of your account
8. on approval, on sale or return
9. on - that, provided that
10. on the most advantageous terms
11. on the following terms
12. under these -s
13. in good -
14. to send on approval
15. to be subject to -s
16. to impose -s
17. to establish (to make) -s

well-conditioned

conditional
overseer
works foreman

condoléance *f.*
  1 lettre *f.* de −

  2 exprimer ses (sincères) −s

conduite *f.* (voir aussi *certificat*)
conduite *f.* (*direction*)
  − des affaires
conduite *f.* (*tuyau etc.*)
  1 − aérienne (*câble*)
  2 − d'eau
  3 − de gaz
confection *f.*
  1 − (*titres*)

  2 − pour dames
  3 frais *m. pl.* de − (*titres*)

  4 magasin *m.* de −
confectionner (*titres*)
conférence *f.*
  faire une − sur
conférence *f.* (*réunion*)
  tenir −
confiance *f.*
  1 − réciproque
  2 digne de −
  3 en toute −
  4 abus *m.* de −

  5 homme *m.* de −
  6 l'homme de − de...
  7 maison *f.* de −

  8 poste *m.* de −

  9 abuser de la −
  10 ébranler la −
  11 gagner la −
  12 inspirer de la −
  13 jouir de l'entière −
  14 justifier la −
  15 regagner la −
  16 retirer la −
confidentiel
  1 à titre −
  2 strictement −
  3 lettre −le
confier à...
  − une agence à...
confirmation *f.*
  1 en − de
  2 dans l'attente de votre −

condolence
  1 letter of −

  2 to express one's (heartfelt) sympathy
behaviou(u)r
conduct
  − of affairs
piping
  1 overhead cable
  2 water pipe, water system
  3 gas pipe
ready-made clothing
  1 printing

  2 confection
  3 cost of printing

  4 ready-made (clothes) shop
to print
lecture
  to deliver a − on
conference
  to hold a −
confidence
  1 mutual −
  2 trustworthy, reliable
  3 in entire −
  4 breach (abuse) of −

  5 reliable person
  6 the confidential agent
  7 trustworthy house, reliable firm

  8 position of trust

  9 to abuse −
  10 to shake (shatter) the −
  11 to gain −
  12 to inspire −
  13 to enjoy full −
  14 to justify the −
  15 to recover −
  16 to withdraw the −
confidential
  1 in confidence, confidentially
  2 strictly −, private and −
  3 − letter
to entrust... to...
  to entrust someone with the agency
confirmation
  1 in − of
  2 awaiting your −

confirmer
 1 – un télégramme par lettre
 2 crédit confirmé
confiscation *f.*
confisquer
conflit *m.*
 1 – d'intérêts
 2 –s de lois
 3 – de salaire
 4 – du travail
 5 entrer en – avec...
conforme
 1 – au contrat
 2 être – à
conformément (à)
 1 – aux dispositions du contrat

 2 – à vos instructions
 3 – aux statuts
conformer, se – à
conformité *f.*
 en – de...
congé *m.* (v. aussi *vacances*)
 1 – de maladie
 2 – payé
 3 en –
 4 – supplémentaire
 5 rappeler de –
congé *m.* (*démission*)
 1 donner – (*locataire*)
 2 donner son – à
congédiement *m.*
congédier
conjoint
conjointement
 – et solidairement
conjoncture *f.*

 1 – d'armement
 2 – favorable
 3 – surchauffée
 4 basse –
 5 haute –
 6 dans la – actuelle, présente
 7 amélioration *f.* de la –

 8 analyse (étude) *f.* de la –

 9 chômage dû à la –
 10 déroulement *m.* (évolution *f.*) de la –
 11 fluctuations *f. pl.* de la –

to confirm
 1 – a telegram by letter
 2 confirmed credit
confiscation
to confiscate
conflict
 1 – of interests
 2 –s of laws
 3 wages –
 4 labo(u)r –, labo(u)r disputes
 5 to come into – with...
according to
 1 in accordance with the contract
 2 to agree (correspond) with
according to
 1 in accordance with the terms of the contract [structions
 2 – (in accordance with) your in-
 3 – the articles
to comply with...
conformity
 in – with
leave (of absence), holiday
 1 sick leave
 2 paid holidays, holidays with pay
 3 on leave
 4 extra leave
 5 to call back from –
dismissal
 1 to give notice (of removal)
 2 to dismiss, to discharge
dismissal
to dismiss, to discharge
joint
jointly
 – and severally
economic cycle, (*situation*) market condition, state of the market
 1 armaments boom
 2 favo(u)rable situation, market
 3 overheated boom
 4 slump
 5 boom
 6 in the present (economic) situation
 7 improving in the economic conditions
 8 analysis of business conditions, cyclical research
 9 cyclical unemployment
 10 trend of the economic cycle

 11 fluctuations on the market, cyclical fluctuations

conjoncturel / 74

12 ralentissement *m.* de la –
13 redressement *m.* de la –
14 renversement *m.* (repli *m.*, retournement *m.*) de la –
15 sensible à la –
16 surchauffe *f.* de la –
conjoncturel
1 chômage –
2 fluctuations *pl.* –les
3 prévisions *pl.* –les
4 reprise – le
connaissance *f.*
1 –s approfondies de...
2 il est venu à notre –
3 porter à la – de
4 prendre – de (*lettre*)
connaissement *m.*
1 – aérien (voir *lettre de transport*)
2 – à ordre
3 – à personne dénommée, – nominatif
4 – au porteur
5 – avec réserves
6 – chef, – direct

7 – de transbordement
8 – dit custody B/L

9 – dit port B/L

10 – fluvial

11 – maritime
12 – mentionnant le chargement sur le pont
13 – net, – sans réserves
14 – reçu à bord, – ,,embarqué''
15 – (libellé) reçu pour embarquement, reçu à quai

16 – en trois exemplaires
17 jeu complet de –s
18 l'un (des –s) étant accompli, les autres restent sans valeur

19 suivant –
20 émettre, rédiger un –
connaître
bien connu
consciencieux

12 slowing down of economic activity
13 improvement in the economic conditions, cyclical recovery
14 business cycle downturn

15 cyclical sensitive

16 cyclical overheating
cyclical
1 – unemployment
2 – fluctuations
3 economic prospects
4 – recovery
knowledge
1 profound – of
2 it came to our –
3 to bring to one's –
4 to note contents of...
bill of lading (B/L)
1 Air Transportation Waybill
2 B/L to order
3 B/L to a named person, (*Amer.*) straight B/L
4 B/L to bearer
5 foul (dirty) B/L
6 through B/L, transit B/L

7 transhipment B/L
8 custody B/L

9 port B/L

10 Inland Waterway B/L

11 ocean B/L
12 B/L mentioning the stowage on deck
13 clean B/L
14 shipped B/L, on board B/L
15 received for shipment B/L, alongside B/L

16 B/L drawn in 3 copies
17 full set of bills of lading
18 one (of the bills of lading) being accomplished the others to stand void

19 as per B/L
20 to issue (make out) a B/L
to know
well-known
scrupulous

conseil m.
 1 – d'administration
 2 – de famille
 3 – d'entreprise
 4 – des gouverneurs
 5 – des prises
 6 – des prud'hommes
 7 – économique
 8 – en publicité
 9 –s en matière d'investissements
 10 (avocat) –

 11 demander des –s, prendre – de qqn
 12 donner des –s
 13 suivre un –
 14 sur le – de
conseiller m.
 1 – économique
 2 – fiscal
 3 – juridique
consensuel
consentement m.
 1 – exprès
 2 – tacite
 3 par – mutuel
consentir à
 – un prêt
conservateur m. **des hypothèques**
conservatoire
 1 actes, mesures f. pl. –s

 2 saisie f. –
considération f.
 1 en – de
 2 mériter –
 3 ne pas entrer en –
 4 prendre en –
 5 jouir de la – générale [haute]
 6 veuillez agréer (l'assurance de) ma
considéré, tout bien –

considérer comme
consignataire m.
 – (*dépositaire*)
consignateur m.
consignation f.
 1 caisse f. de – (voir *caisse*)
 2 facture f. de –
 3 marchandises f. pl. en –
 4 donner en –
 5 envoyer en –
consigne f.
 déposer à la –

advice
 1 board of directors
 2 family council
 3 (works)council
 4 Board of Governors
 5 prize court
 6 conciliation board
 7 economic council
 8 advertising consultant
 9 expert advice on investments
 10 counsel, consulting barrister

 11 to ask one's –
 12 to give –
 13 to follow an –
 14 at the suggestion (advice) of
adviser, counsel(l)or
 1 economic adviser
 2 tax consultant
 3 legal adviser
consensual
consent
 1 formal –
 2 tacit –
 3 by mutual –
to agree to
 to grant a loan
registrar of mortgages

 1 measures of conservation, conservancy measures
 2 seizure for security
consideration
 1 on account of
 2 to be worthy of –
 3 to be out of question
 4 to take into –
 5 to be highly respected
 6 yours respectfully, yours faithfully
all things considered, on further consideration
to consider as
consignee
 depositary
consignor, consigner
consignment

 2 – invoice
 3 goods on –
 4 to give in –
 5 to send on –
cloak room, left-luggage office
 to deposit in the –

consigner / 76

consigner — to deposit
consolidation *f.* (*dette*) — consolidation
  – (*d'un marché à prime*) — exercise of an option
consolider — to consolidate
  1 – une dette flottante — 1 a floating debt
  2 – un marché à prime — 2 to exercise an option
  3 dette consolidée — 3 consolidated debt
consolidés *pl.* — consols
consommateur *m.* — consumer
  1 demande *f.* des –s — 1 consumers' demand
  2 groupe *m.* de –s — 2 group of –s
consommation *f.* (voir aussi *tête*) — consumption
  1 – de courant — 1 – of current
  2 – intérieure — 2 home (domestic) –
  3 – journalière — 3 daily –
  4 – mondiale — 4 world –
  5 accroissement *m.* de la – — 5 rise in consumption

  6 biens *m. pl.* de – — 6 consumer(s') (consumption) goods

  7 biens de – durables — 7 consumer durables, consumer durable goods

  8 crédit *m.* à la – — 8 consumer's credit

  9 dépenses *f. pl.* de – — 9 consumer spending, – consumers' expenditure

  10 fins *f. pl.* de – — 10 purposes of –
  11 fonction *f.* de – — 11 – function
  12 habitudes *f. pl.* de – — 12 consuming (consumption) habits
  13 impôt *m.* sur la – — 13 – tax

  14 marchandises (mises) *f. pl.* en – — 14 goods for home (domestic) –

  15 prêt *m.* de – — 15 simple loan
  16 propension *f.* de – — 16 propensity to consume
  17 restriction *f.* de – — 17 curtailment of –
  18 société coopérative de – — 18 cooperative society

consortium *m.* — consortium, syndicate
  – de banques — syndicate of bankers
constituer — to form, to constitute
  1 – une hypothèque — 1 to create a mortgage
  2 – une rente à... — 2 to settle an annuity on...

  3 – une société — 3 to form a company
constitution *f.* — constitution
  1 – (*loi fondamentale*) — 1 –
  2 – d'hypothèques — 2 creation of mortgage
  3 – de rente — 3 settlement of an annuity
  4 – de réserves — 4 building up of reserves
  5 – d'une société — 5 formation of a company
  6 frais *m. pl.* de – — 6 formation expenses, promotion expenses

77 / construction

construction *f.*
1 – de logements
2 – mécanique
3 – navale
4 en cours de –
5 activité *f.* de la –
6 autorisation *f.* (permis *m.*) de –
7 frais *m. pl.* de –
8 marché *m.* de la –
9 société *f.* de –

consul *m.*
1 – de carrière
2 – général
3 – honoraire, – marchand

consulaire
1 agent *m.* –
2 certificat *m.* –
3 facture *f.* –
4 frais *m. pl.* –s
5 rapports *m. pl.* –s
6 visa *m.* –

consulat *m.*
– général

consultatif
1 commission consultative
2 voix consultative

consulter
container *m.*
contact *m.*
1 entrer en – avec

2 prendre – avec...
contacter

contenance *f.*
1 – (*bouteille*)
2 – (*champ*)
contenir
– 5 litres
contentieux
1 affaires contentieuses, le –
2 service *m.* du – (*d'une banque etc.*)

contenu *m.*
dont le – a eu notre meilleure attention
contestation *f.*
contester
une créance contestée
contigu à
contingent *m.*
– d'importation

building
1 home building, housing
2 engineering
3 ship –
4 in progress of (under) construction
5 construction activity
6 – licence
7 – expenses
8 construction market
9 – company

consul
1 career –
2 – general
3 honorary –

consular
1 – agent
2 – certificate
3 – invoice
4 consulage, – fee
5 – reports
6 – visa

consulate
– general

consultative, advisory
1 advisory committee
2 consultative voice

to consult
container
contact
1 to come into – with, to get into touch with, to approach
2 to contact...
to contact

1 content
2 content, area
to contain
– 5 liters

1 contentious matters
2 legal department

contents
we duly noted –, – of which had our careful attention
dispute
to contest
a contested claim
contiguous to
quota
import –

contingentement / 78

contingentement *m.*	**fixing of quotas**
contingenter	**to fix (establish) quotas**
contractant	**contracting**
les –s, les parties –es	– parties
contracter	**to contract**
1 – une assurance	1 to conclude an insurance, to take out an insurance policy
2 – un bail	2 to enter into a lease
3 – des dettes	3 – debts
4 – un emprunt	4 – a loan
5 – des obligations	5 to enter into engagements
contractuel	**contractual**
obligations –les	contractual obligations
contraire	**contrary**
1 – à	1 – to
2 – au contrat	2 – to contract
3 – aux statuts	3 – to (against) the articles
4 au –	4 on the –
5 dans le cas –	5 in the – case
6 jusqu'à preuve (du) –	6 until the – is proved, in the absence of evidence to the –
7 sauf avis –	7 unless you advise us the –, unless we hear from you to the –
8 sauf convention –	8 unless otherwise agreed
9 intérêts *m. pl.* –s	9 conflicting (opposing) interests
contrat *m.*	**contract**
1 contraire au –	1 contrary to –
2 suivant –	2 by –, as per –
3 – aléatoire	3 aleatory –
4 – à la grosse	4 bottomry bond
5 – à titre onéreux	5 onerous –
6 – bilatéral	6 bilateral –
7 – collectif de travail	7 collective labo(u)r –
8 – d'affrètement	8 – of affreightment
9 – d'apprentissage	9 articles of apprenticeship
10 – d'assurance	10 – of insurance
11 – d'échange	11 exchange –, barter agreement
12 – de livraison	12 – of delivery
13 – de location	13 hire –
14 – de louage de service	14 – for hire of service
15 – de mariage	15 marriage settlement
16 – de représentation	16 agency –
17 – de société	17 deed (articles) of partnership
18 – de transport	18 – of carriage

19 – de travail
20 – de vente
21 – synallagmatique
22 – translatif de la propriété
23 – type

24 – unilatéral
25 durée *f.* d'un –
26 exécution *f.* d'un –
27 objet *m.* d'un –
28 projet *m.* d'un –
29 renouvellement *m.* d'un –
30 rupture *f.* de –
31 stipulations *f. pl.* (termes) d'un –
32 dresser un –
33 exécuter un –

34 passer un –
35 renouveler un –
36 résilier un –
37 rompre un –
38 se conformer au –
39 s'engager par –

40 stipuler par –

contrebande *f.*
1 – de guerre
2 commerce *m.* de –
3 –, marchandises de –

4 faire la –
contrebandier *m.*
contre-caution *f.*
contre-expertise *f.*
contrefaçon *f.*
1 méfiez-vous des –s
2 protéger contre la –
contrefaire
1 – un article, un objet
2 – une signature
contremaître
contremander
contremarque *f.*
contre-ordre *m.* (voir *contrordre*)
contre-partie *f.* (*comptabilité*)
1 compte *m.* (de) –
2 fonds *m.* de –

contre-partie *f.*
contre-passation *f.* **contre-passement** *m.*
– (*lettre de change*)

---

19 labour –
20 sale –, – of sale
21 synallagmatic –
22 conveyance
23 skeleton –

24 unilateral –
25 life (term) of a –
26 fulfilment of a –
27 subject (subject matter) of a –
28 draft –
29 renewal of a –
30 breach of –
31 terms of a –
32 to draw up a –
33 to execute (fulfil) a –

34 to enter into a –
35 to renew a –
36 to cancel a –
37 to break a –
38 to comply with the –
39 to –

40 to stipulate by –

contraband
1 – of war
2 – trade (traffic)
3 – goods

4 to –, to smuggle
contrabandist, smuggler
countersecurity
countervaluation, resurvey
imitation
1 beware of –s
2 to protect from –
to counterfeit, to imitate
1 to imitate an article
2 to forge a signature
foreman
to countermand
countermark

contra
1 – account
2 counterpart funds

other party, other side
writing back, reversal, contraing

re-endorsement

contre-passer
  1 – un article

  2 – (*lettre de change*)
contre-poser
contre-position *f.*
contresignataire *m.*

contresignature *f.*

contresigner

  – (*lettre, adresse*)
contre-valeur *f.*
  1 – en or
  2 compte *m.* –
contribuable *m.*
  – retardataire
contribuant *m.*
contribuer (à)
  1 – aux frais
  2 – proportionnellement

contribution *f.* (*part*)
  1 – aux frais
  2 apporter une – valable à ...
contribution *f.* (*créanciers*)
contribution *f.* (voir aussi *impôt, taxe*)
  1 – foncière
  2 – (in)directe
  3 bureau *m.* des –s
  4 feuille *f.* de –
  5 inspecteur *m.* des –s
  6 receveur *m.* des –s
  7 rôle *m.* des –s
contrôle *m.*
  1 – bancaire
  2 – des changes
  3 – des prix
  4 – du bilan
  5 – physique
  6 appareil *m.* de –
  7 marque *f.* de –
  8 numéro *m.* de –
  9 talon *m.* de –
  10 être soumis au –
  11 effectuer (exercer) le – sur
  12 soumettre au –
contrôler
contrôleur *m.*
  – des contributions
contrôleur *adj.* horloge contrôleuse
contrordre *m.*

  1 to write back (reverse, contra) an entry, an item
  2 to endorse back
to misenter
misentry
... who countersigns

countersignature

to countersign

  to frank
countervalue
  1 equivalent in gold
  2 counterpart account
taxpayer, ratepayer
  ratepayer in arrears
contributor
to contribute to, towards
  1 to contribute towards the expenses
  2 to contribute proportionally, in proportion to
contribution
  1 – towards the expenses
  2 to make a valuable – to
distribution
tax, rate
  1 land tax
  2 (in)direct tax
  3 collector's office
  4 tax form
  5 surveyor of taxes
  6 tax (rate) collector
  7 register of taxes
control
  1 supervision of banking
  2 exchange –
  3 price –, – over prices
  4 balance sheet audit
  5 physical –s
  6 –(ling) (checking) apparatus
  7 – stamp
  8 check number
  9 counterfoil, (*Amer.*) stub
  10 to be subject to –
  11 to exercise – over
  12 to submit to –
to control
controller
  inspector of taxes
control watch, check clock
counterorder

convaincre
  convaincu que
convenance *f.* (voir aussi *raison*)
  à votre (meilleure) –

convenir
  1 – d'un (du) prix
  2 comme convenu
  3 dès que cela vous conviendra
  4 entre... il est convenu ce qui suit... ;
    ... ont convenu (sont convenus de) ce qui suit
  5 il est expressément convenu que...

  6 prix convenu
convention *f.* (*traité*)
  1 – monétaire
  2 – (*accord*)
  3 – écrite, par écrit
  4 – expresse
  5 – matrimoniale

  6 – tacite
  7 – verbale
  8 contraire à la –
  9 sauf – contraire

  10 passer une –
  11 signer une –
conventionnel
conversion *f.*
  1 – (*de monnaies*)
  2 – de crédits à court terme

  3 – d'entreprise

  4 – (*d'une société*) en...
  5 – d'un emprunt
  6 – en titres nominatifs
  7 cours *m.* de –
  8 emprunt *m.* de –
  9 tableau *m.* de –
convertibilité *f.*

  1 – externe
  2 rétablissement *m.* de la libre –
  3 suspension *f.* de –
convertible
convertir
  1 – en francs belges
  2 – un billet de banque en espèces

to convince
  convinced that

  at your convenience

  1 to agree upon a price
  2 as agreed upon
  3 at your earliest convenience
  4 it is mutually agreed between ... that, ... have agreed as follows

  5 it is expressly agreed and understood that...
  6 price agreed upon
convention
  1 monetary –
  2 agreement
  3 written agreement
  4 express agreement
  5 marriage settlement

  6 tacit agreement
  7 verbal agreement
  8 contrary to agreement
  9 unless otherwise agreed

  10 to make an agreement
  11 to sign an agreement
by agreement, contractual
conversion
  1 –
  2 funding of the short term credits

  3 conversion of enterprises

  4 conversion into...
  5 – of a loan
  6 – into registered securities
  7 rate of –
  8 – loan
  9 – table
convertibility

  1 external (non resident) –
  2 restoration of free –
  3 suspension of –
convertible
to convert
  1 – (turn) into Belgian francs
  2 – a banknote into cash

convocation / 82

3 – un emprunt
4 – des valeurs
convocation *f.*
1 – des actionnaires

2 – d'une assemblée

3 avis *m.* de –

4 recevoir une –
convoquer
1 – les actionnaires

2 – une assemblée générale

coopération *f.*
coopératif *adj.*
coopérative *f.*

1 – d'achats

2 – de consommation

3 – de crédit
4 – de crédit agricole

5 – de production
coordonnée *f.*
copartageant *m.*
copie *f.*
1 – au net
2 – au papier carbone
3 – authentique
4 – certifiée conforme
5 – de lettre de change
6 – du capitaine
7 pour – conforme

8 suivant – ci-jointe
9 faire une –
10 garder –
11 prendre (tirer) –
copie *m.* de lettres
copier
1 encre *f.* à –
2 machine (presse) *f.* à –
copossesseur *m.*
copossession *f.*
copropriétaire *m.*
copropriété *f.*
coque *f.*
corbeille *f.* (*bourse*)
– à papier

3 – a loan
4 – securities
calling, convening
1 calling the shareholders together

2 convening a meeting

3 convening notice for a meeting, notice convening the meeting
4 to receive a notice for a meeting
to call, to convene
1 to call shareholders together, to convene the shareholders

2 to call (convene) a general meeting

co-operation
co-operative
co-operative society

1 purchasers' association

2 consumers' –, co-operative store

3 credit co-operative
4 agricultural co-operative credit society
5 producers' co-operative
co-ordinates
joint sharer
copy
1 clean (fair) –
2 carbon –
3 certified –, true –
4 certified –
5 – of (a bill of) exchange
6 captain's –
7 certified true –, I certify this a true –
8 as per enclosed –
9 to make out a –
10 to keep a –
11 to take a –
(copy) letter book
to copy, to make a copy of
1 copying ink
2 copying machine, copying press
joint owner
joint ownership
co-proprietor, joint proprietor
joint ownership, co-property
hull
corbeille
 waste–paper basket

83 / corporation de droit public

corporation *f.* de droit public	public (municipal) corporation, body
corps *m.*	
1 – (*d'un effet*)	1 body
2 – (*d'un navire*)	2 hull, body
3 périr – et biens	3 to perish crew and cargo
correspondance *f.* (voir aussi *courrier, vente*)	correspondence
1 – active	1 active –
2 – commerciale	2 commercial –
3 – volumineuse	3 considerable –
4 par –	4 by –
5 dépouiller sa –	5 to open the mail, to go (look) through one's –
6 entrer en – avec	6 to enter into – with
7 être en – avec	7 to stand (to be) in – with
8 faire (tenir) la –	8 to conduct (attend) the –
correspondance *f.* (*train*)	connection
manquer la –	to miss – (correspondence) with
correspondancier *m.*	correspondence clerk
correspondant *m.*	correspondent
1 –s dans le monde entier	1 –s in all parts of the world, all over the world
2 – étranger (*banque*)	2 – abroad
correspondre	to correspond (with)
– avec	– with
corriger	to correct
1 – des épreuves	1 to read (printer's) proofs
2 corrigé des prix	2 adjusted for prices
3 corrigé des variations saisonnières	3 seasonally adjusted
cosignataire *m.*	co-signatory
cotation *f.*	quotation
1 – à terme	1 forward –
2 – à vue	2 sight –
3 – certaine (voir *certain*)	
4 – des cours	4 – of prices
5 – en pourcents	5 – in percentages
6 – incertaine (voir *incertain*)	
7 – par titre, par unité	7 – per unit
8 – successive	8 consecutive quotation
9 – télégraphique	9 tape –
cote *f.*	quotation
1 – comparative	1 comparative –
2 – d'appréciation	2 marks awarded
3 – de clôture	3 closing –

cote / 84

4 – des changes
5 – des cours
6 – en banque
7 – faible
8 – la plus élevée
9 – officielle, – de la bourse
10 – provisoire
11 – variable
12 admission *f.* à la –
13 demande *f.* d'admission à la –

14 admettre à la –
15 demander l'admission à la –

16 être admis à la – officielle

cote *f.* (*impôts*)
– personnelle
côté *m.*
1 – le plus fort (*compte*)
2 – de l'adresse
3 – du débit
coté
1 – à...
2 être – à la bourse
3 valeurs –es (à la bourse)
4 valeurs non –es
coter
1 – en pourcents
2 – le change, le cours
3 – des pièces
4 – le prix
5 – par titre
coteur *m.*
cotisation *f.*

1 – aux assurances sociales
2 – obligatoire
3 – ouvrière
4 – patronale

5 payer (verser) sa –
coulage *m.*
coulant (*accommodant*)

coulisse *f.*

coulissier *m.*
coupe-papier *m.*
coupon *m.*
1 – accepté à l'escompte
2 – arriéré
3 – attaché

4 exchange –
5 – of prices
6 unquoted list
7 weak –
8 the highest –
9 quoted list, official –
10 provisional –
11 consecutive –
12 admission to –
13 application for admission to –

14 to admit to –
15 to apply for admission to –

16 to enjoy an official –

assessment
capitation
side
1 the stronger –
2 address –
3 debit –
quoted
1 quoted at...
2 to be – on the Stock Exchange
3 listed securities
4 unlisted securities
to quote
1 – in percentages
2 – the exchange
3 to mark documents
4 – the prices
5 – per unit
marking clerk
share, contribution, (*association*)
subscription
1 social insurance contribution
2 compulsory contribution
3 employee's contribution
4 employer's contribution, payments under Social Security
5 to pay one's subscription
leakage
accommodating

coulisse, (*Amer.*) **curb market**

coulissier, outside broker
paper knife
coupon
1 – accepted for discount
2 – in arrear
3 cum (with) –

85 / coupon-réponse

4 – de dividende

5 – détaché (ex –)
6 – d'intérêts
7 – domicilié
8 – échu
9 – périmé
10 – pris à l'encaissement
11 – remis à l'encaissement
12 les –s sont épuisés
13 détenteur m. de –s
14 feuille f. de –s

15 impôts m. pl. sur les –s
16 remise f. des –s, contre...
17 détacher des –s
18 encaisser des –s
19 payer des –s
coupon-réponse m.
couponnier m.
coupure f.

1 en –s de... (titres)
2 en –s de vingt francs
3 en petites –s (billets de banque)
4 en unités et en –s de (voir unité)
coupure f. (coupon) d'action
coupure f. de journal
courant
1 affaires –es
2 année –e
3 dépenses –es
4 intérêts –s
5 monnaie –e
6 être de pratique –e
7 être de vente –e

courant m.
1 –s commerciaux
2 consommation f. de –
3 coupure f. de –
4 économie f. de –
5 pénurie f. de –
courant m. (mois)
1 dans le – du mois
2 du 15 –

3 fin –
4 – d'affaires
5 – du marché
6 au – de la branche
7 être au – de (informé)

4 dividend –

5 ex –, ex dividend
6 interest –
7 domiciled –
8 due –
9 lapsed –
10 – accepted for collection
11 – sent for collection
12 the coupon sheet is exhausted
13 – holder
14 – sheet

15 – tax
16 against delivery of –s
17 to cut off (to detach) –s
18 to cash –s
19 to pay –s
reply coupon
coupon clerk
denomination

1 in –s of, in the – of
2 in twenty-franc notes
3 in small –s

subshare
press cutting
current
1 – (pending) affairs
2 – year
3 – expenditure
4 running interest
5 – money
6 to be the usual practice
7 to have a ready sale

current
1 trade –s
2 consumption of –
3 power cut
4 saving of –
5 shortage of electric –
current (present) month
1 in the course (during) the month
2 of the 15th inst.

3 at the end of the present month
4 turnover
5 market price
6 well up in the trade
7 to be fully informed

courbe / 86

8 être au – (*sans arriéré*)
9 se remettre au – (*arriéré*)
10 tenir au – de
courbe *f.*
1 – de(s) coût(s)
2 – de demande
3 – d'offre
4 – du chômage
5 – de recette
6 – de recette moyenne
7 – de recette totale
courir
1 – le risque de
2 les intérêts courent à partir de...

3 cette lettre de change a encore... jours à –
courrier *m.* (v. *poste, correspondance*)
1 – du matin
2 – du soir
3 – envoyé, – au départ

4 – reçu, – à l'arrivée

5 le premier –
6 par le même –
7 par prochain –
8 par retour du –
9 par – avion
10 par – bateau
11 par – séparé
12 ouverture *f.* du –
13 transfert *m.* –
14 dépouiller le –

15 distribuer le –
16 faire son –
17 lire son –
cours *m.* (voir aussi *change*)
1 – acheteur (*change*)
2 – acheteurs, – Argent
3 – acheteurs réduits
4 – argent (voir – *acheteurs*)
5 – à terme (*change*)
6 – à terme (*valeurs*)
7 – trois mois
8 – au comptant
9 – à vue (*change*)
10 – d'achat
11 – d'après-bourse
12 – de clôture
13 – de compensation

8 to be up to date
9 to make up arrears
10 to keep in touch with, informed on
curve
1 cost –
2 demand –
3 supply –
4 unemployment –
5 revenue –
6 average revenue –
7 total revenue –
to run
1 – a risk
2 interest runs (accrues) from

3 this bill has still... days to –

post, correspondence
1 early mail, morning mail
2 evening mail
3 letters sent out, outgoing letters, post, mail
4 letters received, incoming letters, post, mail
5 the first post
6 by the same post
7 by next mail
8 by return of post
9 by air mail
10 by sea mail
11 by separate post
12 opening of the letters, of the mail
13 mail transfer
14 to open the mail, to go (look) through one's correspondence
15 to distribute the post
16 to do one's correspondence
17 to read one's correspondence
rate, price
1 buying rate
2 prices bid, buyers
3 buyers over

5 forward rate
6 settlement price
7 three months' rate   [spot rate
8 price for cash, cash price, (*change*)
9 demand rate
10 cost
11 street price, price after hours
12 closing price, closing rate
13 making up price

14 – de conversion (*monnaie*)
15 – d'émission

16 – de déport
17 – de l'intérêt
18 – de l'option, – du stellage

19 – de l'ou
20 – de prime
21 – de rachat
22 – de report
23 – de souscription
24 – demandés (voir –*acheteurs*, –*argent*)
25 – de(s) change(s), – du change
26 – des changes (des devises) à terme
27 – des changes (de devises traitées) au comptant
28 – d'introduction
29 – d'ouverture
30 – du chèque
31 – du comptant (*change*)
32 – du disponible (*marchandises*)
33 – du dont
34 – du jour
35 – du livrable
36 – du marché
37 – du marché libre
38 – du stellage
39 – faits
40 – favorable
41 – fictif
42 – fixe
43 – forcé
44 – hors banque, hors bourse
45 – le plus bas
46 – le plus haut
47 – limité
48 – maximum
49 – minimum
50 – modifié
51 – moyen
52 – offerts (voir – *vendeurs*)
53 – officiel
54 – papier
55 – pratiqués
56 – précédent
57 – surfaits
58 – télégraphique
59 – tel quel
60 – vendeur (*change*)
61 – vendeurs, – papier (P)

14 rate of conversion
15 issue price, price of issue

16 backwardation rate
17 rate of interest
18 put and call price, price of double option
19 put price
20 option price
21 buying in price
22 contango rate, carry-over rate
23 subscription price

25 rate of exchange, foreign exchange
26 forward exchange rate
27 spot exchange rate

28 opening price
29 opening price
30 cheque (check) rate
31 spot price, spot rate
32 spot price, price ex store
33 call price
34 price of the day
35 forward price, terminal price
36 market price
37 free market price
38 put and call price
39 business done, bargains done
40 favo(u)rable rate
41 nominal rate
42 fixed rate
43 forced exchange
44 unofficial price
45 lowest price, bottom price
46 highest price, top price
47 limited price
48 maximum price, rate
49 minimum price, rate
50 modified exchange
51 average (middle) price

53 official rate
54 price offered, sellers
55 business done, bargains done
56 previous price
57 unduly high prices
58 tape price
59 tale quale rate
60 selling rate
61 price offered, sellers

cours / 88

62 – vendeurs réduits

63 au – de
64 au-dessous du –
65 au-dessus du –
66 dernier –
67 premier –
68 les – baissent
69 les – montent
70 les – s'effondrent

71 les – s'effritent
72 les – fléchissent

73 le – se maintient
74 les – se raffermissent
75 les – sont bas
76 les – sont élevés
77 les – sont fermes
78 amélioration *f.* des –
79 baisse *f.* des –
80 bénéfice *m.* de –
81 calcul *m.* des –
82 chute *f.* des –
83 cote *f.* des –
84 écart *m.* des –
85 dégringolade *f.* (effondrement *m.*) des –
86 effritement *m.* des –
87 fixation *f.* des –
88 fléchissement *m.* des –
89 fluctuations *f. pl.* des –
90 hausse *f.* des –
91 mouvement *m.* des –
92 niveau *m.* des –
93 recul *m.* des –
94 relèvement *m.* des –
95 stabilisation *f.* des –
96 stabilité *f.* des –
97 valeur *f.* du –
98 faire baisser les –
99 faire monter les –
100 fixer le –
cours, en – (voir *en cours*)
cours *m.* (*circulation*)
1 – forcé
2 avoir –

3 avoir – légal
4 n'avoir plus –
court
1 être – de
2 être (à) – d'argent

62 sellers over

63 at the rate of
64 below the rate
65 above the rate
66 closing price
67 opening price
68 the exchange falls, declines
69 the exchange rises, advances
70 the exchange slumps

71 prices crumble, ease off
72 prices sag, droop, are on the decline

73 the exchange remains (keeps) firm
74 the exchange hardens
75 prices are low
76 prices are high
77 prices are firm
78 improvement in prices, price [improvement
79 fall in prices
80 market profit
81 calculation of exchange
82 (rapid) fall of prices
83 price quotation
84 difference in price
85 slump of prices

86 crumbling of prices
87 fixing of prices
88 decline in prices
89 fluctuations in the rate of exchange
90 rise in exchange
91 movement in prices
92 price level
93 decline in prices
94 recovery in prices
95 price stabilization
96 firmness of prices
97 rate of exchange
98 to force down prices
99 to force up prices
100 to fix the exchange
currency

1 forced exchange
2 to be current, to be tender, to have currency
3 to be legal tender, to have lawful –
4 to be no longer current
short
1 to run (to be) – of
2 to be (to run) – of money

3 à – terme
4 crédit à – terme
5 dépôts *m. pl.* à – terme
6 effet –, papier –
7 emprunt *m.* à – terme
courtage *m.*

1 – de change
2 – officiel
3 maison *f.* de –
4 taux *m.* de –
5 tarif *m.* des –s

courter (*march.*)
courtier *m.*
1 – assermenté
2 – de change
3 – d'assurances
4 – de marchandises
5 – d'escompte
6 – maritime
7 – marron
8 – officiel
coût *m.*
1 – assurance, fret
2 – constant
3 – de production
4 – de la vie

5 – des facteurs
6 – fixe
7 – fixe moyen
8 – marginal
9 – moyen
10 – prévisionnel
11 – réel
12 – total
13 – total moyen
14 – variable
15 – variable moyen
coûtant, au prix –
coûter
1 – cher
2 coûte que coûte
coûteux
coutume *f.*
–s de la place
couvert (voir *couvrir*)
couverture *f.*
1 – métallique
2 – or
3 – suffisante
4 en – de

89 / courtage

3 –dated
4 short (–term) credit
5 deposits at – notice
6 – bill
7 –dated loan
brokerage, commission

1 exchange brokerage
2 official brokerage
3 broker's firm, brokerage house
4 commission rate
5 scale of commissions, brokerage tariff
to offer for sale
broker
1 sworn –
2 bill –, exchange –
3 insurance –
4 produce –
5 bill –
6 ship –
7 outside –
8 inside –
cost
1 –, insurance, freight
2 constant –s
3 – of production
4 – of living

5 factor –s
6 fixed –
7 average fixed –
8 marginal –s
9 average –s
10 – estimate
11 costing
12 total –s
13 average total –s
14 variable –s
15 average variable –s
at cost, at cost price
to cost
1 to be dear, expensive
2 at all costs
dear, expensive
custom
local –s, usages of the place

cover, margin
1 metallic cover, cover in metal
2 gold reserve
3 ample security, ample cover
4 as cover

5 sans –
6 achat *m.* de –
7 coefficient *m.* de –
8 moyens *m. pl.* de –
9 remise *f.* en – (règlement) de
10 vente *f.* de – (*march.*)
11 demander une – de 30 %
12 fournir la –

couvrir
1 – l'assurance
2 – un découvert
3 – un déficit
4 – les frais
5 – une perte
6 – le risque
7 – qqn (*rembourser*)
8 – qqn des frais
9 – qqn du montant
10 l'emprunt est couvert
11 largement couvert (*emprunt*)
couvrir, se –
– en... (*bourse*)
craint l'humidité !
crayon *m.*
1 au –
2 – de couleur
3 gomme *f.* à –
4 taille- – *m.*

créance *f.*
1 – active, – à recouvrer
2 – chirographaire
3 – douteuse
4 – exigible
5 – garantie
6 – gelée
7 – hypothécaire
8 – irrécouvrable
9 – litigieuse
10 – ordinaire
11 – passive
12 – principale
13 – privilégiée
14 – recouvrable
15 titre *m.* de –
16 mauvaise –
17 admettre une – (au passif)
18 amortir une – douteuse
19 contester une –
20 reconnaître une –
21 recouvrer des –s
22 vérifier des –s

5 without cover, uncovered
6 covering purchase
7 cover ratio
8 resources, cover funds
9 remittance in cover of
10 hedging selling
11 to require a cover (margin) of 30 %
12 to provide (send) cover

to cover
1 – the insurance
2 – a short (a bear) account
3 to meet (make good) a deficit
4 – the expenses
5 to make good a loss
6 – the risk
7 – a person for
8 to reimburse a person
9 – someone for the amount
10 the loan is fully subscribed
11 largely oversubscribed
to cover oneself, to hedge
to cover, to hedge
to be kept dry !
pencil
1 in –, pencilled
2 coloured –
3 – eraser
4 – sharpener

debt, claim
1 outstanding debt
2 unsecured debt
3 doubtful debt
4 debt due
5 secured debt
6 frozen debt
7 mortgage debt
8 irrecoverable (unrecoverable) debt
9 contested claim
10 ordinary debt
11 debt
12 principal debt
13 privileged (preferential) debt
14 recoverable (collectable) –
15 acknowledgment of debt
16 bad debt
17 to admit a claim
18 to write off a bad debt
19 to contest a claim
20 to acknowledge a claim
21 to recover (collect) debts
22 to verify claims

créancier *m.*
1 – chirographaire
2 – de la faillite
3 – d'une lettre de change
4 – gagiste
5 – hypothécaire
6 – nanti
7 – obligataire
8 – opposant
9 – ordinaire
10 – privilégié

11 – saisissant
12 assemblée *f.* des –s
13 commission *f.* des –s
14 réunion *f.* des –s (*pour la vérification des créances*)
15 admettre comme –
16 convoquer les –s
17 désintéresser, satisfaire les –s

création *f.*
1 – d'argent
2 – de crédit
3 – d'un chèque
4 – d'une maison de commerce

crédit *m.* (*compt.*)
1 par le – de votre compte
2 avis *m.* de –

3 côté *m.* du –

4 note *f.* de –
5 extourner au –
6 passer (porter) au –

7 passer (porter) au – de qqn

crédit *m.*
1 – à court terme
2 – à découvert

3 – à la consommation

4 – à la production

5 – à long terme
6 – à moyen terme

7 – au consommateur
8 – aux classes moyennes
9 – bloqué
10 – confirmé
11 – consenti par le fournisseur

creditor
1 unsecured –
2 – of bankrupt's estate
3 holder of a bill
4 lienor, pledgee
5 – on mortgage
6 secured –
7 bond –
8 opposing –
9 ordinary –
10 preferential –

11 attaching –
12 meeting of –s
13 board of –s
14 creditors' meeting (for proof of debts)
15 to admit as –
16 to call the –s
17 to satisfy (pay off) the –s

creation
1 – of money
2 – of credit
3 writing out of a cheque (check)
4 foundation of a house of business

credit, credit side, creditor side
1 to the credit of your account
2 credit advice

3 credit side, creditor side

4 credit note
5 to recredit
6 to pass (enter, place) to the credit

7 to pass (enter, place) to one's credit, to the credit of one's account

credit
1 short (-term) –
2 blank –

3 consumer('s) –

4 productive –, for productive purposes
5 long (-term) –
6 medium-term –

7 consumer –
8 middle-class –
9 frozen –
10 confirmed –
11 – granted by supplier

crédit / 92

12 – (de) courrier
13 – de banque, – bancaire
14 – de caisse
15 – de compte courant, – comptable
16 –s d'engagement
17 – d'escompte
18 – de transition
19 – d'exportation
20 – d'importation
21 – divisible
22 – documentaire (voir ce mot)
23 – en banque
24 – en blanc
25 – en clearing
26 – en compte courant
27 – épuisé
28 – foncier
29 –s gelés
30 – (il)limité
31 – immobilier
32 – intérimaire
33 – irrévocable
34 – mobilier
35 – non confirmé
36 – ouvert par câble
37 – par acceptation
38 – personnel
39 – pour le financement d'autos
40 – réalisable par acceptation, remboursement de banque
41 – réalisable par négociation
42 – réalisable par payement
43 – réel
44 – révocable
45 – revolving, – rotatif
46 – revolving cumulatif
47 – saisonnier
48 – supplémentaire
49 – sur notoriété
50 – transférable
51 – transitoire
52 – utilisable à vue
53 – utilisable contre remise des documents suivants
54 – utilisable par tirages

55 à –
56 à valoir sur mon –
57 fixed credits
58 banque *f.* de –
59 bénéficiaire *m.* d'un –

12 mail –
13 bank –
14 cash –, cash advance
15 – in current account, book –
16 budgetary commitments
17 discount –
18 standby –, interim –
19 export –
20 import –
21 divisible –

23 – at (with) the bank
24 blank –
25 clearing assets
26 in current account –
27 – abated
28 loan on landed property
29 frozen –s
30 (un)limited –
31 – on real property
32 interim loan
33 irrevocable –
34 – on personal property
35 unconfirmed –
36 – opened by cable
37 acceptance –
38 personal –
39 motor car –, auto loan
40 (documentary) acceptance –

41 – available by (requiring) negotiation
42 – requiring payments
43 – on real estate
44 revocable –
45 revolving –

46 revolving cumulative –
47 seasonal –
48 supplementary –
49 unsecured –
50 transferable –
51 interim loan
52 – available at sight
53 – available against delivery of the following documents
54 – utilizable (available) by drafts on

55 on –
56 against my –
57 fixed –s
58 – bank
59 beneficiary of –

93 / crédit documentaire

60 conditions *pl.* du –
61 contrôle *m.* du –
62 création *f.* de –
63 demande *f.* de –

64 dépassement *m.* de –
65 établissement *m.* de –
66 expansion *f.* de –

67 facilité *f.* de –
68 forme *f.* de –
69 gonflement *m.* du volume du –
70 instrument *m.* de –
71 lettre de – (voir *lettre*)
72 limite *f.* de –
73 octroi *m.* de –s

74 ouverture *f.* d'un –
75 pénurie *f.* de –s
76 plafond *m.* du –
77 politique *f.* de –
78 prorogation *f.* (de la durée) d'un –
79 resserrement, restriction *f.* du –

80 retrait *m.* d'un –
81 risque *m.* de – (voir aussi *assurance*)
82 structure *f.* du –
83 union *f.* du –
84 utilisation *f.* de –s
85 volume *m.* de –
86 acheter à –
87 accorder un –
88 amputer un –
89 annuler un –
90 avoir du –
91 confirmer un –
92 dépasser un –
93 ébranler le –
94 nuire au –
95 octroyer un –
96 jouir de –
97 ouvrir un – en faveur de... jusqu'à concurrence de...
98 proroger (la durée d')un –
99 restreindre le –
100 retirer un –
101 utiliser un – entièrement ou partiellement
102 vendre à –
crédit documentaire *m.*
 1 ordre *m.* d'ouvrir un –
 2 ouverture *f.* d'un –

60 – terms
61 – control
62 creation of –
63 application for –

64 excess of –
65 – institution
66 – expansion

67 line of –
68 type of –

69 inflation of the volume of –
70 instrument of –

72 limit of –
73 granting of –s

74 opening of a –
75 – stringency
76 – ceiling, – limit
77 – policy
78 extension of –
79 credit restriction, curtailment of –, – squeeze

80 withdrawal of a –
81 – risk
82 – structure
83 – union
84 use of –s
85 volume of –
86 to buy on –
87 to grant (allow) a –
88 to curtail (reduce) a –
89 to cancel a –
90 to have good –
91 to confirm a –
92 to exceed (surpass) a –
93 to shake the –
94 to prejudice the –
95 to grant a –
96 to enjoy –
97 to open a – to the extent of... in favo(u)r of...
98 to extend a –
99 to restrict the –
100 to withdraw a –
101 to take up a – in whole or in part

102 to sell on –
documentary credit
 1 order to open a –
 2 opening of a –

crédité / 94

3 modifier un –
4 notifier au bénéficiaire l'ouverture d'un –

crédité m.

créditer
1 – en compte courant
2 – quelqu'un de...

3 – un compte de...

4 dont veuillez nous – sous avis

créditeur m.
1 –s divers
2 – en compte courant
3 –s pour effets à l'encaissement

créditeur adj.
1 colonne créditrice
2 compte –
3 intérêts –s
4 nombre –
5 pays –
6 position créditrice

7 solde – en compte
8 vos soldes –s chez nous
9 garder un solde – dans son compte
10 votre compte est –

créer
1 – un chèque
2 – un effet de commerce
3 – une hypothèque
4 – une maison de commerce

creux m.
– saisonnier

criée f.
vente f. à la –

crieur m. (vente publique)

crise f.
1 – économique
2 – financière
3 – monétaire
4 une – éclate
5 années f. pl. de –
6 symptômes m. pl. de –
7 déclencher une –
8 lutter contre la –
9 traverser une –

3 to modify (amend) a –
4 to notify the opening of a – to the beneficiary

credited party, person

to credit
1 to pass to current account
2 – someone with...

3 – an account with, to carry... into an account
4 with which please credit us, under advice

creditor
1 sundry –s
2 – on current account
3 –s for bills received for collection

1 credit column
2 creditor account
3 credit interest
4 credit product
5 creditor nation
6 creditor position

7 credit balance on account
8 your credit balances with us
9 to keep a balance on one's account
10 your account is in credit

to create
1 to write out a cheque (check)
2 to issue (draw up) a bill
3 – a mortgage
4 to found a house of business

low point, trough
seasonal –

auction room
sale by auction, auction sale

crier

crisis
1 economic –
2 financial –
3 monetary –
4 a – breaks out
5 years of –
6 – symptoms
7 to bring about a –
8 to struggle against a –
9 to pass (go) through a –

croiser
  nos lettres se sont croisées
croissance *f.*
  1 – économique
  2 taux *m.* de –
croix *f.* (v. *marquer*)
cueillette (voir *affrètement, charge*)
cuir *m.*
  1 articles *m. pl.* en –, –s
  2 commerce *m.* des –s
culture *f.* (intensive, extensive)

cuprifères *pl.*
curatelle *f.*
  1 être en –
  2 mettre sous –
curateur *m.*
cyclique

to cross
  our letters have crossed
growth
  1 economic –
  2 – rate

leather
  1 – goods
  2 – trade
cultivation (intensive, extensive)

copper shares, coppers
guardianship
  1 to be under –
  2 to place under –
trustee, guardian
cyclical

D

dactylo, dactylographe *f.*

  1 bureau *m.* pour –
  2 salle *f.* des –s

dactylographie *f.*
  central *m.* de –

dactylographier

dame-jeanne *f.* (*pl.* –s–s)
dans
  1 – huit jours
  2 – les quinze jours
  3 – les trois jours après la réception

darse *f.*
date *f.*
  1 – de la poste
  2 – de l'avis (d'ouverture de crédit)
  3 – de l'échéance
  4 – de l'envoi
  5 – de valeur, d'entrée en valeur
  6 – d'expiration
  7 – extrême
  8 à – fixe
  9 à trois mois de –

  10 de même –
  11 en – de ce jour

typist

  1 typewriter table
  2 typewriter room

typewriting, typing
  typewriter room

to type, to typewrite

demijohn
in
  1 – eight days
  2 within a fortnight
  3 within three days of receipt

darsena, open basin
date
  1 – as postmark
  2 – of the notification
  3 due –, date of maturity
  4 – of despatch
  5 value –
  6 expiry –
  7 latest –
  8 at fixed –
  9 at three months' –, three months after –
  10 of the same –
  11 under this day's –, dated this day

dater / 96

12 votre lettre en – du 24 décembre

13 porter une –
dater
1 à – d'aujourd'hui

2 lettre datée du 1er avril
dateur *m.*
débâcle financière

débarcadère *m.*
débardeur *m.*
débarquement *m.*
 1 en –
 2 lieu *m.* de –
débarquer
débaucher (ouvriers)
débattre du prix
débit *m.* (*vente*)
 1 avoir un bon –, être de bon –
 2 d'un – facile
débit *m.* (*magasin*)
 1 – de tabac
 2 – de vin
débit *m.* (*compt.*)
 1 – et crédit
 2 à votre –
 3 par le – de notre compte, chez vous, sous avis
 4 avis *m.* de –

 5 côté *m.* du –
 6 note *f.* de –
 7 inscrire (porter) au – de
débiter
 1 – de
 2 – un compte de

 3 – qqn de

 4 dont veuillez nous – sous avis

débiteur (*adj.*)
 1 colonne débitrice
 2 intérêts –s
 3 nombres –s
 4 pays –
 5 solde –
 6 le solde de votre compte est –
débiteur *m.* (voir aussi *céder*)
 1 – délégué
 2 – en compte courant

12 your letter –d 24th December

13 to bear a –
to date
1 from to-day

2 letter under date (dated) 1st April
date stamp
slump, crash

landing stage
docker
unloading, unshipment
 1 under discharge
 2 – berth
to unload, to discharge, to unship
to attract (entice) away
to bargain down the price
sale
 1 to go off (sell) readily, quickly
 2 saleable, of ready sale
shop
 1 tobacconist's –
 2 wine –
debit
 1 – and credit
 2 to your –
 3 to the – of our account with you, under advice
 4 – advice

 5 – side
 6 – note
 7 to pass (carry, put, enter) to the – of
to debit
 1 – with
 2 – an account with, to place (enter, put, carry) to the debit of an account
 3 – with, to charge to the account of

 4 with which please debit us, under advice
debit...
 1 – column
 2 – interest
 3 – products
 4 debtor nation
 5 – balance
 6 your account is in –
debtor
 1 delegated –
 2 credit account –

97 / débitrice

2 –s douteux
3 – gagiste
4 – hypothécaire
5 – insolvable
6 –s par acceptations (*bilan*)
7 – principal
8 – saisi
9 – solidaire
10 (compte) –s
11 grand livre des –s
débitrice *f.*
déblocage *m.*
débloquer
 fonds débloqués
débordé
 – de travail
débouché *m.*
 1 ouverture *f.* de nouveaux –s
 2 assurer un – à
 3 chercher de nouveaux –s
 4 ouvrir un –
 5 trouver un –
débours, déboursés *pl.*

 1 note *f.* de –
 2 recouvrer (rentrer dans) ses –

déboursement *m.*
débourser
debout, tenir – (*caisse*)
débrayer
début *m.*
 1 au – de l'année
 2 au – de mai
 3 dès le –
 4 du – à la fin
débutant *m.*

décacheter (*lettre*)
décaissement *m.*
décaisser
décartellisation *f.*
décès *m.*
(voir aussi *acte, cause, déclaration*)
décharge *f.*
 1 – (quitus) aux administrateurs

 2 – finale
 3 à notre –
 4 constituer la –
 5 donner –
 6 donner – (*quittance*)

2 doubtful (dubious) – s
3 pledger
4 – in mortgage, mortgagor
5 insolvent –   [tances
6 liabilities of customers for accep-
7 principal –
8 distrainee, person distrained
9 joint –
10 – account
11 –s' ledger
debtor
unblocking, release
to unblock
 released funds
overwhelmed
 – with work
outlet, market, opening
 1 opening up of new markets
 2 to assure an outlet to
 3 to look for new outlets
 4 to create new openings
 5 to find an outlet, a market
disbursement, outlay, (*ch. de fer*)
paid-on charges
 1 disbursement account
 2 to recover one's disbursements

disbursement
to disburse, to lay out, to spend
keep upright
to stop work
beginning
 1 at (by) the – of the year
 2 in the – of May
 3 from the –
 4 from – to end
beginner

to open, to unseal
paying out (of cash)
to pay out of cash
deconcentration, decartelization
decease, death

discharge
 1 ratification of the actions of the
   board of directors

 2 full –
 3 to our –
 4 to be the –
 5 to grant –
 6 to give –, to –

déchargement / 98

7 dont veuillez nous donner – | 7 from which please – us

8 obtenir – | 8 to obtain discharge
déchargement *m.* | **unloading, discharge**
1 en – | 1 under discharge
2 port *m.* de – | 2 port of discharge
décharger | **to unload, to discharge**
1 – un compte | 1 to discharge an account
2 – d'une obligation | 2 to release (to discharge) from an obligation

déchéance *f.* (*jur.*) | **loss, forfeiture**
déchiffrer | **to decode, to decipher, to translate**

déchu, être – d'un droit | to lose (forfeit) a right

décider | **to decide, to resolve**
1 – d'une chose | 1 to decide on...
2 se – | 2 to decide
décimal | **decimal**
1 fraction –e | 1 – fraction
2 système – | 2 – system
décimale *f.* | **decimal**
calculé jusqu'à la 5ᵉ – | calculated to 5 places (points) of –s
décisif | **decisive**
voix décisive | casting vote
décision *f.* | **decision**
1 – arbitrale | 1 arbitrator's award
2 arriver à une – | 2 to come to a –
3 prendre une – | 3 to take a –
4 réserver une – | 4 to delay a –
5 se réserver la – | 5 to reserve one's –
déclarant *m.* | **declarant**
déclaration *f.* | **declaration, statement**
1 – de décès | 1 notification of death
2 – de faillite | 2 declaration of bankruptcy
3 – de mariage | 3 notification of marriage
4 – fausse, fausse – | 4 false declaration
5 – sous serment | 5 sworn statement
6 faire une – par écrit | 6 to issue a statement
déclaration *f.* (de valeur) | **declaration of value**
1 – au-dessous de la valeur | 1 declaration under the value
2 – au-dessus de la valeur | 2 declaration above the value
3 – d'impôts (de revenu) | 3 return of income
4 faire la – de son revenu | 4 to make a return of one's income
déclaration (en douane) *f.* | **customs declaration**

1 – d'acquittement de droits | 1 duty-paid entry
2 – de libre entrée | 2 declaration for free importation
3 – de libre sortie | 3 declaration for free exportation
4 – de libre transit | 4 declaration for free transit
5 – d'entrée | 5 entry (declaration) inwards
                        [entrepôt |
6 – d'entrée en entrepôt, de mise en | 6 warehousing entry

99 / déclaré

7 – de (mise en) consommation | 7 entry for home use
8 – de sortie | 8 entry (declaration) outwards
9 – de transit | 9 transit entry
10 – pour produits exempts de droits, libres | 10 free entry, entry for duty-free goods

déclaré
1 lettre *f.* avec valeur –e
2 marchandises –es
3 valeur –e

déclarer
1 – à la douane
2 – au-dessus de la valeur
3 – un dividende
4 je soussigné,... déclare par la présente
5 rien (quelque chose) à –

déclarer (se –)
1 – acheteur (*aff. à prime*)
2 – vendeur

décliner
1 – une offre
2 – la responsabilité

décommander

décompte *m.* (*déduction*)
1 – (*calcul*)
2 – (*compte détaillé*)
3 – des intérêts dus
4 – d'une somme
5 – après encaissement
6 – final
7 faire le – (*déduire*)
8 faire le – (*calculer*)

décompter une somme

déconfiture *f.* (*non-commerçant*)

découvert *m.* (*déficit*)
1 – (*d'un compte*)
2 – (*bourse*)
3 à –
4 le compte est à –, de...

5 acceptation *f.* à –
6 achat *m.* à –
7 acheteur *m.* à –
8 avances *f. pl.* à –
9 baissier *m.* à –
10 compte *m.* à –
11 crédit *m.* à –

12 dépôt *m.* à –

declared
1 letter with value insured
2 entered goods
3 – value

to declare, to state
1 to declare at the custom house
2 to overvalue
3 to declare a dividend
4 I, the undersigned declare hereby
5 anything to declare?

1 to call the shares
2 to put the shares

to decline
1 – an offer
2 – responsibility

to countermand

deduction
1 calculation, working out the charges
2 detailed account
3 calculation of the interest due
4 – of a sum
5 settlement on receipt of...
6 final settlement
7 to deduct
8 to calculate, (charges) to work out

to deduct a sum

insolvency

shortage
1 overdraft
2 bear account, bears
3 without cover, uncovered
4 the account is overdrawn to the extent of...

5 uncovered acceptance
6 bull purchase
7 bull purchaser
8 unsecured advances
9 uncovered bear
10 overdrawn account
11 blank credit

12 unsealed deposit

décrocher / 100

13 opérations *f. pl.* à -
14 rachat *m.* de -
15 vendeur *m.* à -
16 vente *f.* à -
17 acheter à -
18 combler un -
19 mettre un compte à -

20 tirer à -
21 vendre à -
décrocher (le récepteur) (*tél.*)
de cujus *m.*
dédit *m.*
  payer un -
dédommagement *m.*
dédommager de
  se -
dédouanement *m.*

dédouaner
  marchandises dédouanées

déductible (*frais*)
déduction *f.*
1 - faite des frais
2 faire - des intérêts
3 après - des frais
4 sans - de frais
5 sans - pour différence du vieux au neuf

6 sous - de
7 sous - d'escompte
déduire
  à - de...
défaire
1 - un marché
2 se - de (*actions*)
défalcation *f.*
  - faite des frais
défalquer
défaut *m.* (voir aussi *vice*)
1 -s apparents
2 -s cachés
3 - de fabrication
4 - de forme
5 - de nouvelles (*assur. mar.*)
6 -s inhérents, propres à

7 à - de
8 à - d'accord
9 à - de payement
10 (Mr X) et à son -,...

13 bear transactions
14 bear covering
15 bear seller, short seller
16 bear sale, short sale
17 to buy a bull, to bull
18 to make up a deficit
19 to overdraw an account

20 to draw in blank
21 to sell a bear, to short, to sell short
to take up(remove) the receiver
testator
forfeit, penalty
  to pay the forfeit
indemnification
to indemnify for...
  to compensate oneself for
clearance through the customs

to clear (through the customs)
  cleared goods

deductible
deduction
1 after deducting the expenses
2 to make - of interests
3 after deducting the expenses
4 without - of charges
5 without - new for old

6 less
7 less discount
to deduct
  to be deducted from...

1 to cancel (undo) a bargain
2 to unload, to part with
deduction
  after deducting the expenses
to deduct
defect, fault
1 patent defects
2 latent defects
3 defect of manufacturing
4 defect of form, faulty drafting
5 absence of news
6 inherent defects

7 in default of
8 in default of agreement
9 in default of payment
10 and failing him,...

défavorable

1 change *m.* −
2 circonstances *f. pl.* −s

défectueux
emballage −

défendeur *m.*

défendre
se − (*cours*)

défense *f.* (voir aussi *interdiction*)
1 − d'afficher
2 − de fumer
3 − d'entrer

4 − de parquer

déficit *m.*
1 − de caisse
2 −s et excédents de caisse

3 combler un −
4 accuser, présenter un −
5 il résulte un −
6 se solder par un −
7 se trouver devant un −

déficitaire
1 balance *f.* commerciale −
2 solde *m.* −

déflation *f.*
1 politique *f.* de −
2 de −

déflationniste
mesure *f.* −

dégât *m.* (voir aussi *dommage*)
1 les −s occasionnés

2 −s causés par l'eau
3 −s causés par le gel
4 −s causés par l'incendie
5 −s matériels
6 causer des −s
7 évaluer les −s

dégeler (*crédit*)

dégonflement *m.*

dégressif

degré *m.*
1 − de liquidité
2 − de parenté
3 − d'emploi
4 − d'utilisation de la capacité

dégrèvement *m.* d'impôts

dégrever
1 − (*impôts*)

unfavo(u)rable
1 − exchange
2 − circumstances

defective
deficient (insufficient) packing

defendant

to defend
to be maintained

(voir aussi *interdiction*)
1 post (stick) no bills
2 no smoking (allowed here)
3 no admittance

4 no parking here

deficit
1 shortage in the cash
2 cash shorts and overs

3 to meet a −
4 to show a −
5 a − arises
6 to close with a −
7 to be faced with a −

1 adverse balance of trade
2 debit (adverse) balance

deflation
1 deflationary policy
2 deflationary

deflationary
− measure

damage
1 the − done (occasioned)

2 − by water
3 − by frost
4 − by fire
5 material −, − to property
6 to cause −
7 to estimate the −

to unfreeze, to thaw

reduction

degressive

degree
1 liquidity ratio
2 − of relationship
3 level of employment
4 − of capacity utilization

reduction (abatement) of taxes

1 to diminish taxes

dégringolade / 102

2 – une propriété | 2 to disencumber a property
dégringolade *f.* des prix | **slump in prices**
dégringoler (*prix*) | **to slump down**
délai *m.* (*remise*) | **delay**
  1 – (*temps*) | 1 time
  2 – d'acceptation | 2 term of acceptance
  3 – de chargement | 3 time of loading
  4 – de déchargement | 4 time of discharging
  5 – de grâce | 5 days of grace
  6 – de livraison | 6 time (term) of delivery
  7 courts –s de livraison | 7 short deliveries
  8 – d'embarquement | 8 time for shipment
  9 – de payement | 9 time of payment
  10 – de planche, – de starie | 10 laytime
  11 – de préavis | 11 (period of) notice
  12 – de prescription | 12 term of limitation
  13 – de rigueur | 13 latest time, date
  14 – de surestarie | 14 days of demurrage
  15 – de validité | 15 term of validity
  16 – de vue | 16 time after sight
  17 dans le – de 8 jours | 17 within 8 days
  18 dans le – de 1 mois | 18 within a month
  19 dans le plus bref – | 19 in the shortest possible time
  20 dans un – de... | 20 within a period of
  21 sans – | 21 without delay
  22 demande *f.* d'un – | 22 request for a respite
  23 expiration *f.* du – | 23 end of the time (allowed)
  24 prolongation *f.* du – | 24 extension of time
  25 accorder un – de payement | 25 to grant a –, an extension of payment
  26 demander un – | 26 to ask for a –
  27 dépasser un – | 27 to exceed a term
  28 observer un – | 28 to keep to a term
  29 prolonger (proroger) un – | 29 to extend a term
  30 cela ne peut subir aucun – | 30 it cannot be delayed
délai-congé *m.* | **(period of) notice**
délaissé (*valeurs*) | **neglected**
délaissement *m.* | **abandonment**
  – du navire et des facultés assurées (*à l'assureur*) | – of the ship and the insured goods
délaisser à l'assureur | **to abandon to the underwriter**
délégation *f.* | **delegation**
  1 – de pouvoir | 1 – of powers
  2 – d'une dette | 2 – of a debt
  3 par – | 3 on the authority of
délégué *m.* | **delegate**
déléguer | **to delegate**
  – ses pouvoirs à... | – one's powers to
délibération | **deliberation, consideration**
  1 les –s (résolutions) prises par... | 1 the resolutions passed by...
  2 après – | 2 after consideration
  3 mettre en – | 3 to submit for discussion

103 / délibérer

délibérer sur	to deliberate on, to consider
delivery-order *m.* (*bon de livraison à valoir sur connaissement*)	delivery order
délivrance *f.*	handing over, delivery
– des titres	delivery of the certificates
délivrer	to deliver, to hand over
1 – des billets	1 to deliver tickets
2 – des coupons	2 to deliver coupons
3 – les documents contre payement	3 to deliver the documents against payment
4 – des valeurs	4 to deliver securities
déloyal	dishonest, unfair
demain	to-morrow
de – en huit	– week
demande *f.*	demand
1 – accumulée	1 backlog (stored-up) –
2 – croissante	2 increasing –
3 – de (*marchandises*)	3 – for
4 – de biens de consommation	4 – for consumers' goods
5 – des consommateurs	5 consumers' –
6 – de crédit	6 application for credit
7 – d'emploi	7 application for a situation
8 bulletin *m.* de – d'emploi	8 application form
9 lettre *f.* de – d'emploi	9 letter of application
10 „–s d'emploi" (*annonces*)	10 situation wanted
11 – de pension	11 pension claim
12 – de prix	12 inquiry of price
13 – de renseignements	13 inquiry, request for information
14 – de tonnage	14 inquiry for tonnage
15 – dérivée	15 derived –
16 – effective	16 effective –
17 – élastique	17 elastic –
18 – excédentaire	18 excess –
19 – externe, extérieure	19 – from abroad
20 – fixe	20 inelastic –
21 – intérieure, – interne	21 domestic (home) –
22 – manuscrite (*emploi*)	22 self-written application
23 seules sont retenues les –s manuscrites	23 self-written applications only
24 – mondiale	24 world –
25 – reconventionnelle	25 counterclaim
26 – saisonnière	26 seasonal –
27 conformément à votre –	27 in compliance with your request
28 en faible –	28 in limited –
29 sur – (voir aussi *prospectus*)	29 on application
30 sur – (présentation)	30 on –, at sight
31 sur sa –	31 on his request
32 la – dépasse l'offre	32 the – exceeds the offer

demandé / 104

33 il y a une forte – de... | 33 there is a keen – for...
34 accroissement *m.* de la – | 34 increase in –
35 courbe *f.* de – | 35 – curve
36 élasticité *f.* de la – | 36 elasticity of –
37 fléchissement *m.* de la – | 37 decline (slackening) in –
38 formule *f.* de – | 38 application form
39 pression *f.* de la – | 39 pressure of –, – pressure
40 accéder à (accorder) une – | 40 to grand a request
41 débouter d'une – | 41 to reject a claim
42 faire face à la – | 42 to satisfy the –
43 refuser une – | 43 to decline a –
44 répondre à une – | 44 to comply with a –
45 être en faible – | 45 to be in limited –, request

demandé *m.* (*tél.*) — called (distant) subscriber
demandé — demanded
1 fort – | 1 in great request, much in request
2 peu – | 2 in limited request, demand
3 action, fr.... – et... offert | 3 share fr... bid and... offered
4 prix – | 4 price asked

demander — to demand, to request
1 – le payement | 1 to ask for payment
2 – des renseignements | 2 to apply for information
3 – quelque chose à quelqu'un | 3 to demand someone to do...
4 ,,on demande tout de suite'' | 4 wanted immediately
5 ,,on demande un correspondancier'' | 5 wanted a correspondence clerk
6 on vous demande au téléphone | 6 you are wanted on the telephone

demandeur *m.*
1 – (*jur.*) (demanderesse *f.*) | 1 plaintiff
2 – (*tél.*) | 2 caller, calling subscriber

démarche *f.* — step
faire les –s nécessaires pour... — to take the necessary –s towards

démarcheur *m.* (*banque, assur.*) — canvasser
– en publicité — advertising –

démarquer — to remove the marks
démarqué (*article*) — marked down

démarrage *m.* — start
période *f.* de – — starting period

déménagement *m.* — removal
1 avis *m.* de – | 1 notice of –
2 entreprise *f.* de – | 2 furniture removers, – contractor
3 frais *m. pl.* de – | 3 – expenses
4 voiture *f.* de – | 4 furniture van, pantechnicon van
5 pour cause de – | 5 on account of –

déménager — to remove
demi — half
1 une fois et –e | 1 one and a – times
2 une heure et –e | 2 one and a – hours

105 / demi-douzaine

3 un mètre et –	3 one metre (meter) and a –
4 trois mètres et –	4 three and a – metres (meters)
demi-douzaine f.	half dozen
demi-gros m.	wholesale dealing in small quantities
demi-ouvré (*produit*), demi-pro- [duit]	semimanufactured product
démission f.	resignation
1 accepter la –	1 to accept the –
2 donner (offrir) sa –	2 to tender one's –
démissionner	to resign
démographique	demographic
1 politique f. –	1 population policy
2 statistique f. –	2 population statistics
démonétisation f.	demonetization, withdrawal from circulation
démonétiser	to demonetize, to withdraw from circulation
démonstrateur m.	demonstrator
„démonstration f. sans engagement"	ask for free demonstration
dénationalisation f. (*industries*)	denationalization
dénationaliser	to denationalize
deniers publics	public money
dénomination f.	denomination, name
sous la – de...	under the name (style) of...
dénommé, ci-après – (*contrat*)	hereinafter referred to as...
dénoncer	to give notice
– un contrat	–, to terminate a contract
denrée f.	commodities, produce
1 -s alimentaires	1 foodstuffs
2 -s alimentaires, boissons et tabac	2 food, beverages and tobacco
3 -s coloniales	3 colonial produce
dépanneuse f.	breakdown lorry
départ m.	departure
1 courrier m. au –	1 outgoing mail
2 date f. de – (*navire*)	2 sailing date
3 dépêche f. de –	3 sailing telegram
4 liste f. des -s	4 sailing list, sailing schedule
5 port m. de –	5 port of –, of sailing
département m. (voir aussi *service*)	service, department
dépassement m.	excess
dépasser	to exceed
1 – les attentes	1 – expectations
2 – un crédit	2 – a credit
3 montants ne dépassant pas...	3 amounts not exceeding...
4 montants dépassant...	4 amounts exceeding..., in excess of...
dépendance f. (*hôtel*)	annex to...
avec -s	with outbuildings
dépens pl. (d'un procès)	costs of a law suit
être condamné aux –	to be ordered to pay costs

dépense *f.* (voir aussi *frais*) — expense, expenditure

1. –s accessoires — incidental expenses
2. –s courantes — running expenses
3. –s de fonctionnement — operational expenditure
4. –s d'exploitation — working expenses
5. –s diverses — sundry expenses
6. –s effectives — actual expenses
7. –s extraordinaires — extraordinary expenditure
8. –s fixes — fixed expenditure
9. –s prévues — contemplated expenditure
10. –s publiques — public (authority) expenditure, government spending
11. –s supplémentaires — additional expenses
12. –s et recettes — receipts and expenditure
13. augmentation *f.* des –s — increase of expenses
14. diminution *f.* des –s — diminution of expenses
15. réduction *f.* des –s — spending cuts, cuts in expenditure
16. entraîner des –s considérables — to involve considerable expenses
17. faire face (pourvoir) aux –s — to defray the expenses
18. réduire les –s — to cut down (to curtail, prune) expenses
19. rembourser qqn de ses –s — to reimburse someone for his expenses
20. se mettre en –s — to incur expenditure

dépenser — to expend, to spend
déplacé (v. *effet*)
déplacement *m.* (*navire*) — displacement
dépliant *m.* — folder

déport *m.* — backwardation
1. – (*bonification*) —
2. opérations *f. pl.* de – — – business
3. taux *m.* du – — – rate

déposant *m.* — depositor
– (*caisse d'épargne*) —

déposé — deposited
1. marque –e — registered trade mark
2. montant – — amount –

déposer — to deposit
1. – à — with
2. – à la caisse d'épargne — to put in the savings bank
3. – à la poste — to post
4. – au greffe — in the registry
5. – de l'argent en banque — money at a bank
6. – son bilan — to file one's petition in bankruptcy
7. – dans la boîte aux lettres — to put into the letter box
8. – la garantie chez... — the security with...
9. – en nantissement — to pledge

107 / dépositaire

10 – des titres dans une banque | 10 to lodge securities at a bank

11 – des titres en garde | 11 – securities in safe custody

12 – des titres au siège social (*assemblée*) | 12 – securities at the company's office

13 les titres que vous avez déposés chez nous | 13 your shares deposited with us

dépositaire *m.* | **depositary**

dépôt *m.* | **deposit**
  1 –s | 1 –s
  2 – à la caisse d'épargne | 2 savings bank –
  3 – à court terme | 3 – at short notice
  4 – à découvert | 4 unsealed –
  5 – à échéance fixe | 5 fixed –, – at fixed date
  6 – à long terme | 6 – at long notice
  7 – à préavis | 7 – at notice
  8 – à un mois de préavis | 8 – at one month's notice
  9 – à terme | 9 time –
 10 – à vue | 10 demand –, sight –, – at (on) call
 11 – à vue et à un mois au plus (*bilan*) | 11 –s at call and at up to one month's notice
 12 – cacheté | 12 sealed –
 13 – de garantie | 13 –
 14 –s d'épargne | 14 savings –s
 15 – de virement | 15 – on giro account
 16 – en banque | 16 bank –
 17 – en compte courant | 17 – on current account
 18 – en numéraire | 18 cash –
 19 – libre, – en garde | 19 safe custody
 20 – (de) titres | 20 stock –
 21 – de titres en nantissement | 21 securities lodged as collateral
 22 – de titres pour (en vue de) l'assemblée | 22 –ing of securities with a view to attending the meeting
 23 – contre – de titres | 23 against – of securities
 24 argent *m.* mis en – | 24 –s
 25 augmentation *f.* des –s | 25 growth of (increase in) –s
 26 avoir *m.* en – | 26 bank –
 27 banque *f.* de – | 27 – bank
 28 compte *m.* de – (voir aussi *compte*) | 28 – account

dépôt / 108

28 intérêt *m.* de –	28 – interest
29 livret *m.* de –	29 depositor's book
30 mise *f.* en –	30 –
31 récépissé *m.* de –	31 – receipt
32 sommes mises en – chez	32 sums placed on – with...
33 taux *m.* des –s	33 – (rate of interest)
34 tirages couverts par un – de titres	34 drafts covered by the – of securities
35 avoir en –	35 to have in custody
36 mettre de l'argent en – chez...	36 to place money on – with...
37 retirer un –	37 to withdraw a –
38 recevoir des –s, recevoir en –	38 to receive –s, money on –
39 tenir des valeurs en – (en gage)	39 to keep securities as a –
dépôt *m.* (*magasin*)	depot, warehouse
dépôt *m.* de bilan	filing one's petition in bankruptcy
dépouiller son courrier	to go through one's correspondence, post
dépréciation *f.*	depreciation
déprécier	to depreciate
se –	to fall in value, –
dépression *f.*	depression, low point
déprimer	to depress
1 – les prix	1 – prices
2 marché déprimé	2 depressed market
dernier	last
1 ces dernières années	1 in the – few years
2 – cours	2 closing quotation
3 dernière répartition	3 final dividend, distribution
dérogation *f.*	derogation
1 – à...	1 – from (to, of), departure from
2 en – à cette règle	2 this rule notwithstanding
3 par (en) – à la loi	3 in – of the law
dérogatoire, clause *f.* –	derogatory clause
déroger à	to depart from, to derogate from
déroutement *m.*	change of route, deviation from the normal route
désabonnement *m.*	discontinuance of subscription
désabonner, se –	to withdraw (discontinue) one's subscription
désaccord *m.*	disagreement
désachalander	to take away the custom, the business
se –	to lose one's custom
désapprovisionné (*compte*)	overdrawn
désarmer (*navire*)	to lay up
désarrimer (*cargaison*)	to shift
se – (*cargaison*)	–
désavantage *m.*	disadvantage
à notre –	to our –

désavantageux	**disadvantageous**
désendettement m.	**reduction of indebtedness**
désépargne f.	**dissaving**
déséquilibre m.	**disequilibrium, lack of balance**
éliminer un –	to cure a disequilibrium
déshypothéquer	**to free from mortgage, to disencumber**
désignation f.	**designation**
1 – du contenu	1 description of contents
2 – des marchandises	2 description of goods
3 – du navire	3 naming of the ship
désigner	**to designate**
désinflation f.	**disinflation**
désinflationniste	**disinflationary**
1 mesure f. –	1 – measure
2 politique f. –	2 – policy
désintéresser (*créanciers*)	**to satisfy, to pay off**
désirer	**to wish**
laisser à –	to leave much to be desired
desservir	**to serve (a town, a port)**
dessus (*emballage*)	**top, topside up**
destinataire m. (*lettre*)	**addressee**
– (*marchandises*)	consignee
destinateur m.	**sender, consignor**
destination f.	**destination**
1 immeuble par –	1 immovable by –
2 lieu m. de –	2 place of –
3 navire m. à – de...	3 ship bound for...
4 pays m. de –	4 country of –
5 port m. de –	5 port of –
6 train m. à – de...	6 train for...
7 arriver à –	7 to arrive at –
destiné à...	**destined for...**
détacher	
1 – un chèque du carnet	1 to tear out a cheque (check) from the book
2 – les coupons	2 to detach coupons from
3 – suivant le pointillé	3 to detach along the dotted line
détail m.	**detail**
1 –s d'un compte	1 –s of an account
2 pour plus amples –s	2 for further particulars
3 donner tous les –s	3 to enter into all –s, to give full particulars
4 entrer dans le(s) –(s)	4 to go into the –s
détail m. (*commerce*)	**retail trade**
1 prix m. – de	1 retail price

détaillant / 110

2 vente *f.* en – | 2 retail sale

3 faire le – | 3 to do a –
détaillant *m.* | **retailer, retail dealer**

détailler | **to detail**
1 – *(vendre)* | 1 to retail
2 description détaillée | 2 detailed description
3 facture détaillée | 3 specified invoice
4 liste détaillée | 4 detailed list
détaxe *f.* | **remission (reduction) of charges, duties**

détaxer | **to remit (to reduce) duties**

détenir | **to detain, to hold**

1 – un gage | 1 to hold a security
2 – en garantie | 2 to hold as security
détente *f.* | **easing**
détenteur *m.* | **holder**
1 – de bonne foi | 1 bona fide –
2 – de mauvaise foi | 2 mala fide –
3 – de titres | 3 stockholder
4 – d'obligations | 4 debenture –
5 – du gage | 5 – of a security
6 tiers – | 6 third –
déterminer le poids | **to ascertain the weight**
déthésaurisation *f.* | **dishoarding**
détourné (voir *déplacé*) |
détournement *m.* | **embezzlement, misappropriation**
  commettre des –s | to embezzle
détourner | **to misappropriate, to embezzle**
détresse, navire *m.* en – | **ship in distress**
détriment *m.* | **detriment**
1 à votre – | 1 to your disadvantage, –
2 au – de | 2 to the – (prejudice) of
dette *f.* | **debt**
1 – active | 1 book –, active –

2 –s arriérées | 2 arrears
3 – chirographaire | 3 unsecured –
4 – consolidée | 4 consolidated –
5 – convertible | 5 convertible –
6 – d'argent | 6 money –
7 –s de clearing | 7 clearing –s
8 – de jeu | 8 gambling (gaming) –
9 – d'honneur | 9 – of hono(u)r
10 – exigible | 10 due –
11 – extérieure | 11 external –
12 – flottante | 12 floating –
13 – foncière | 13 land charge
14 – fondée | 14 funded –
15 – hypothécaire | 15 mortgage –

16 – inexigible	16 – not due
17 – obligataire	17 bonded –
18 – passive	18 (passive) –
19 – portable	19 – payable at the payee's address
20 – prescrite	20 prescribed –
21 – privilégiée	21 preferential –
22 – publique	22 public – [debtor
23 – quérable	23 – payable at the address of the
24 – solidaire	24 joint and several –
25 – unifiée	25 unified (consolidated) –
26 – véreuse	26 bad –
27 accablé (criblé) de –s	27 charged (burdened) with –s
28 amortissement *m.* de –s	28 discharge of debts
29 extinction *f.* d'une –	29 extinction (discharge) of a –
30 montant *m.* de la –	30 amount of indebtedness
31 non-reconnaissance *f.* (répudiation *f.*) d'une –	31 repudiation of a –
32 réduction *f.* de –s	32 reduction of –s
33 règlement *m.* de –s	33 payment of –s
34 remise *f.* de –	34 remission of a –
35 reprise *f.* de –s	35 assignment of –s
36 titre *m.* de – foncière	36 land charge deed
37 acquitter une –	37 to pay a –
38 amortir une –	38 to amortize a –
39 avoir des –s	39 to have –s
40 contracter (faire) des –s	40 to contract (make) –s
41 se décharger (se libérer) d'une –	41 to redeem (liquidate) a –
42 purger de –s	42 to free from –s
43 reconnaître une –	43 to acknowledge a –
44 recouvrer une –	44 to recover (collect) a –
45 rembourser une –	45 to reimburse (redeem) a –
46 remettre une –	46 to cancel a –
deuxième	**second**
– de change (voir aussi *première*)	– of exchange
dévaluation *f.*	**devaluation**
bruits *m. pl.* de –	– rumo(u)rs
dévaluer	**to devalue**
devanture *f.*	**shop window**
développer	**to develop**
1 – nos relations d'affaires	1 – our business relations
2 se –	2 –, to extend
déviation *f.* (*navire*)	**change of route, deviation**
dévier	**to deviate (from one's course)**
devis *m.*	**estimate**
1 – estimatif	1 preliminary –
2 établir un –	2 to draw up an –
devises *f. pl.* (étrangères) (voir aussi *change*)	**foreign exchange**
1 – à terme	1 forward exchanges
2 – (traitées) au comptant	2 spot exchange

devoir / 112

3 – dures
4 – molles
5 avoir *m.* en –
6 compte *m.* en –
7 cours *m.* des –
8 effet *m.* en –
9 marché *m.* des –
10 octroi *m.* de –
11 office *m.* des –
12 pénurie *f.* de –
13 réglementation *f.* des –

14 rentrées *f. pl.* de –
15 réserve *f.* de (en) –

16 restrictions *f. pl.* en matière de –

17 sorties *f. pl.* de –
18 transfert *m.* de –
19 se procurer des –

devoir
1 montant dû
2 sommes qui sont ou pourraient nous être dues

3 en due forme
4 nous devons votre adresse à
5 cela est dû à une négligence

6 cela est dû à son expérience

diagramme *m.*
dictaphone *m.*
dictée *f.* (*d'une lettre*)
 prendre sous –
dicter
dictionnaire *m.*
 consulter le –
différé
1 action –e
2 annuité –e
3 télégramme –
différence *f.*
1 – de 10 % en plus ou en moins

2 – de cours
3 – de prix
4 – du vieux au neuf (voir aussi *déduction*)
5 – en moins

3 hard currency
4 soft currency
5 currency assets
6 account in foreign currency
7 – rate
8 bill in foreign currency
9 – market
10 allocation (allotment) of currency, [of –
11 foreign currency control office
12 scarcity of –
13 currency regulations

14 inflow of –
15 currency reserves, cushion of foreign exchange
16 exchange restrictions

17 outflow of –
18 transfer of currency
19 to provide oneself with foreign currency

to owe
1 sum due
2 sums that are or may become due to us

3 in due form
4 we owe your address to
5 it is due (to be imputed) to negligence

6 it is owing to his experience

diagram
dictaphone
dictation
 to write under –
to dictate
dictionary
 to refer to (consult) the –
deferred
1 – share
2 – annuity
3 – telegram
difference
1 – of 10 % more or 10 % less

2 – of exchange
3 – in price
4 new for old

5 deficit

113 / différenciation

6 – en plus
7 cela fait une grande –
différenciation *f.* **du produit**
différend *m.*
  1 partager le –
  2 régler un –
différent
  1 – de
  2 à –es reprises
  3 tout à fait –
différentiation *f.* *(math.)*
différentiel
  1 calcul –
  2 droits –s
  3 fret *m.* de transport –
  4 tarif –
différer *(être différent)*
  1 – beaucoup de...
  2 – de prix
différer le payement
difficile
  il est – de
difficulté *f.*
  1 –s grandissantes
  2 –s insurmontables
  3 aplanir des –s
  4 entraîner des –s
  5 éprouver des –, rencontrer des –s
  6 être (se trouver) en –s
  7 faire (soulever) des –s
  8 faire face aux –s
  9 présenter des –s
  10 surmonter des –s
diligence *f.* *(soin)*
  1 – *(promptitude)*
  2 – *(zèle)*
  3 à la – de... *(jur.)*
  4 en toute –
  5 faire –
  6 faire ses –s contre... *(jur.)*
diligent (voir *partie*)
dimanche *m.*
  1 –s et jours de fête
  2 le –
dimension *f.*
diminuer
  1 – le personnel
  2 – les prix
  3 la demande diminue
  4 les prix diminuent
diminution *f.*
  1 – de prix

6 surplus
7 that makes all the –
product differentiation
difference, dispute
  1 to split the difference
  2 to settle (adjust) a difference
different
  1 – from
  2 at – times
  3 totally –
differentiation
differential
  1 – calculus
  2 – duties
  3 – freight rate
  4 – tariff
to differ
  1 – largely from
  2 – in price
to defer (postpone) the payment
difficult
  it is – to
difficulty
  1 growing difficulties
  2 insuperable difficulties
  3 to remove difficulties
  4 to involve (give rise to) difficulties
  5 to encounter difficulties
  6 to be involved in difficulties
  7 to raise difficulties
  8 to face difficulties
  9 to present difficulties
  10 to surmount difficulties
care
  1 dispatch, haste
  2 diligence, application
  3 at the suit of...
  4 with all possible dispatch
  5 to make haste
  6 to take proceedings against...

Sunday
  1 –s and public holidays
  2 on –s
size
to diminish, to lessen, to reduce
  1 to reduce (cut down) the staff
  2 to reduce prices
  3 the demand is slackening
  4 prices fall, decline, go down
diminution, reduction
  1 price reduction, reduction in price

2 – des recettes
3 – des salaires
4 – de la valeur

5 accuser une –
6 subir une –
dire
1 disons...
2 à vrai –
3 cela ne veut pas – que
4 c'est à – (c. à d.)
5 il va sans –

6 pour ainsi –
directeur m.
1 – adjoint
2 – commercial
3 – de banque
4 – de succursale
5 – des achats
6 – de vente
7 – général
8 – gérant
9 – régional
10 – technique
direction f.
1 – de créanciers
2 – générale
3 changement m. de la –
4 comité m. de –
5 sous la – de
directorat m.
directrice f.
diriger
dirigisme m.
disagio m.
accuser un – de...
discrédit m.
1 jeter le – sur
2 tomber en –
discret (v. aussi *renseignement*)
discrétion f.
1 – assurée, sous assurance de –
2 demander la –
discrimination f.
– de prix
discussion f.

1 sans –
2 bénéfice m. de –

3 mettre en –
4 ouvrir une –

2 falling off in the receipts
3 reduction of wages
4 decrease in value

5 to show a diminution
6 to experience a diminution
to say
1 say...
2 to tell the truth
3 this is not – that
4 that is – (i.e.)
5 it goes without saying

6 so to speak, as it were
manager
1 assistant –
2 commercial –
3 bank –
4 branch –
5 buying –
6 sales – (director)
7 general –
8 managing director
9 district –
10 technical –
management
1 committee of creditors
2 general –
3 alteration in the –
4 managing committee
5 under the direction of
managership
manageress
to manage, to direct, to run
dirigisme

to stand at a discount of
discredit
1 to bring – on, to –
2 to fall into –
discreet
discretion
1 absolute privacy guaranteed
2 to ask for –
discrimination
price –
discussion

1 without –
2 benefit of –

3 to bring up for –
4 to open the –

115 / discuter

discuter une question	to discuss a question
dispache *f.*	average statement, average adjustment
établir la –	to adjust the average
dispacheur *m.*	average adjuster
dispatch *m.*	dispatch, despatch
– money (*prime de rapidité*)	dispatch (despatch) money
disponibilité *f.*	availability
disponibilités *f. pl.*	available funds, liquid assets
1 – en caisse et en banque	1 cash in hand and at bankers
2 – en quête d'emploi	2 available funds in quest of employment
disponible	available
1 – et réalisable	1 – and liquid assets
2 le – (*marchandises*)	2 spot market
3 avoir *m.* –	3 liquid assets
4 capital *m.* –	4 – funds
5 cours (prix) *m.* du –	5 spot rate, spot price
6 marchandise *f.* –	6 spot goods, disposable goods
7 fonds *m. pl.* –s	7 liquid assets
8 solde *m.* –	8 – balance
9 stock *m.* –	9 stock in warehouse, supply on spot
10 transactions *f. pl.* en –	10 spot transactions
11 vente *f.* en –	11 spot sale
12 vendre en –	12 to sell for spot (immediate) delivery
disposé	
1 bien –	1 cheerful
2 nous sommes tout –s à...	2 we are fully prepared to; we shall be glad to...
3 mieux – (*bourse*)	3 better in tone, more cheerful
disposer	to dispose
– de grands capitaux	to command a large capital, an ample supply of capital
disposer (*tirer*)	to draw
1 – un chèque sur...	1 – a cheque (check) on
2 – un effet sur une banque	2 – a bill on a bank
3 – (d'un montant) par quittance postale	3 to collect an amount through the post office
4 – (d'un montant) par remboursement	4 to take an amount forward, to cash on delivery
5 – sur qqn d'une somme de...	5 – on... for a sum
6 – sur un compte par chèque	6 – on an account by cheque
7 – sur qqn en une traite	7 – a bill on...
disposition *f.* (*marché*)	tone

disposition / 116

disposition *f.*
1 −s (de l'article...)
2 −s testamentaires
3 nous sommes à votre entière −
4 mettre à votre −
5 prendre des −s
6 tenir à votre −
disposition *f.* (*traite*)
1 − à vue
2 vos −s sur (qqn)
3 vos −s sur (un compte)
4 avis *m.* de −
5 versements et −s sur un compte
dissolution *f.* (*société*)
dissoudre (*société*)
distinction *f.*
la plus haute − à l'exposition de...
distraction *f.* (*détournement*)
− (*prélèvement*)
distraire (*détourner*)
− (*prélever*)
distribuer
1 − un dividende
2 − des lettres
distributeur *m.*
distribution *f.*
1 − (*commerce*)
2 − d'un bénéfice
3 − du dividende
4 − de lettres
5 − de porte en porte (*poste*)
divers *pl.*
divers
à −es reprises
dividend-warrant *m.*

dividende *m.* de... % (*liquidation;* voir aussi *répartition*)
dividende *m.*
1 −s accrus, − accumulés
2 − arriéré
3 − brut
4 − cumulatif
5 − de l'année 1964
6 − fictif
7 − final
8 − intérimaire
9 − net
10 − non réclamé

disposal
1 provisions
2 testamentary dispositions
3 we are entirely at your −
4 to place at your −
5 to make arrangements
6 to hold at your −
draft
1 sight −
2 your −s on...
3 your drawings
4 advice of −
5 payments (deposits) and drawings (withdrawals) on an account
dissolution
to dissolve
distinction
highest reward at the... exhibition
embezzlement
setting aside, appropriation
to embezzle
to set aside, to appropriate
to distribute
1 − a dividend
2 − letters
distributor, dealer
distribution
1 −
2 − of profits
3 − of the dividend
4 delivery of letters
5 house-to-house distribution
sundries
sundry
at − times
dividend warrant

dividend of... %

dividend
1 accumulated (accrued) −s
2 overdue −
3 gross −
4 cumulative −
5 − over the year 1964
6 sham −, fictitious −
7 final −
8 interim −
9 net −
10 unclaimed −

117 / diviser

11 – privilégié
12 – proposé
13 – provisoire
14 – récupérable
15 – semestriel
16 – statutaire
17 – supplémentaire
18 avec –
19 ex –
20 blocage *m.* des –s
21 coupon *m.* de –
22 déclaration *f.* de –

23 distribution *f.* de –

24 fixation *f.* du –
25 fonds *m.* de –
26 impôt *m.* sur le –
27 limitation *f.* du –
28 passation *f.* de –
29 répartition *f.* de –
30 réserve *f.* de –

31 solde *m.* de –
32 avoir droit à un –
33 déclarer un –
34 distribuer un –
35 donner un –
36 fixer un –
37 passer un –
38 proposer un – de...

39 payer un –
40 toucher un –

diviser
1 – en
2 – 16 par 2
3 capital divisé en... actions de... chacune

diviseur *m.*
1 – fixe
2 le plus grand commun –

division *f.*
1 – du travail
2 bénéfice *m.* de –

divisionnaire (voir *monnaie*)
dock *m.* (voir aussi *bassin*)
docker *m.*
doctrine *f.* (*jur.*)
– et jurisprudence *f.*

11 preferential –, preference –
12 proposed –
13 interim –
14 cumulative –
15 halfyearly –
16 statutory –
17 extra –
18 cum –
19 ex –
20 – limitation
21 – coupon
22 – announcement

23 distribution of the –

24 fixation of the –
25 undistributed profits
26 – tax
27 – limitation
28 passing of the –
29 distribution of the –
30 – reserve

31 final –
32 to be entitled for a –, to rank for a –
33 to declare a –
34 to distribute a –
35 to pay a –
36 to fix a –
37 to pass a –
38 to recommend (propose) a – of...

39 to pay a –
40 to collect a –

to divide
1 – into
2 – 16 by 2
3 capital divided into... shares of... each

divisor
1 steady –
2 the highest common factor

division
1 – of labo(u)r
2 benefit of –, beneficium divisionis

dock
docker
doctrine
– and case-law

document / 118

document *m.*
1. –s d'embarquement, –s d'expédition
2. –s contre acceptation
3. –s contre payement
4. comptant contre –s
5. contre remise des –s
6. levée *f.* de –s
7. lever des –s
8. présenter des –s
9. refuser des –s
10. nous déclinons toute responsabilité quant à l'authenticité et la validité des –s
11. nous vous libérons des –s

documentaire
1. crédit – (voir *crédit doc.*)
2. encaissements *m. pl.* –s
3. traite *f.* –

documentation *f.*
doit *m.* (voir *débit*)
dollar *m.*
1. – financier, – titre
2. cours *m.* du –

domaine *f.*
1. – financier
2. – public
3. tomber dans le – public
4. dans le – de l'économie
5. Administration *f.* des –s

domicile *m.*
1. – d'origine
2. – élu
3. – fiscal
4. – légal
5. – réel
6. sans – fixe
7. changement *m.* de –
8. élection *f.* de –
9. élection de – est faite à... (*acte*)
10. livraison *f.* franco à –
11. prise *f.* à –
12. remise *f.* à –
13. changer de –
14. élire – à
15. établir son –

document
1. shipping –s
2. –s against acceptance
3. –s against payment
4. cash against –s
5. against delivery of the –s
6. taking up (retiral, lifting) of –s
7. to take up (retire, lift) –s
8. to present –s
9. to refuse –s
10. we decline all responsibility as to the authenticity and validity of the –s
11. we discharge you from the –s

documentary
2. – collections
3. – draft (bill), draft with documents attached

documents

dollar
1. security –
2. – exchange, rate for –s

domain, field
1. financial field, matters
2. common (public) property
3. to become common property
4. in the economic field, in the field of economy
5. Crown Land Commissioners

domicile
1. original –, – of origin
2. elected –, – of election, of choice
3. residence for tax purposes
4. legal –
5. place of residence
6. of no fixed abode
7. change of residence
8. election of –
9. ... is elected as –
10. delivery free –, carriage paid
11. collection (at residence)
12. delivery (at home)
13. to change residence
14. to elect – in
15. to take up one's –, residence

16 prendre à –
17 remettre à –
domiciliataire m.
domiciliation f.

1 commission f. de –
2 payement m. d'une –
domicilié
1 coupon –
2 traite –e
domicilier

1 – des acceptations
2 – un effet à une banque

3 – dans une place autre que...

dommage m. (voir aussi *dégât*)
  1 – corporel
  2 – matériel
  3 calcul m. du –
  4 causer du –
  5 être responsable du –
  6 évaluer le –
  7 régler les –s
  8 subir du –
  9 supporter le –
  10 il est – que
dommageable
dommages-intérêts m. pl.

1 demande f. en –

2 intenter une action en –
3 obtenir des –
4 payer des –
5 réclamer des –
donation f.
1 – entre vifs
2 acte m. de –
donneur m.
1 – à la grosse
2 – d'aval
3 – de faculté (voir *faculté*)
4 – d'ordre
5 – d'option, – de stellage

dont m. (*bourse*)
1 acheter un –

2 vendre un –

doré sur tranche

---

16 to collect from home
17 to deliver at home
paying agent
domiciliation

1 domicile commission
2 payment of a –, of a domicile
domiciled
1 – coupon
2 – bill, domicile
to domicile

1 – acceptances
2 – a bill at (with) a bank

3 – at a place other than...

damage
  1 – to persons
  2 material –, – to property
  3 calculation of –
  4 to cause –
  5 to be liable (responsible) for the –
  6 to estimate the –
  7 to settle the –
  8 to suffer –
  9 to bear the –
  10 it is a pity that
damageable
damages

1 claim for –

2 to enter an action for –
3 to receive (recover) –
4 to pay –
5 to claim –
grant, donation
1 donation (gifts) inter vivos
2 deed of donation

1 lender on bottomry
2 guarantor

4 principal
5 taker for (seller of) a put and call

call, call option, buyer's option
1 to give for the call, to buy a call option
2 to take for the call, to sell a call option
gilt-edged

dos *m.* (*effet*)
au - de l'effet
dossier *m.*
1 titres qui reposent sous votre -

2 placer sous votre -

3 retirer des titres du -

douane *f.* (voir aussi *droits*)
 1 la -
 2 assujetti aux (passible de) droits de -
 3 exempt de -
 4 administration *f.* de la -
 5 agent *m.* de -
 6 agent *m.* en -

 7 bureau *m.* de la -
 8 déclaration *f.* en -
 9 dépôt *m.* de -
 10 droits *m. pl.* de -
 11 entrée *f.* en - (*navire*)
 12 faire l'entrée en -
 13 expédition *f.* en - (*navire*)
 14 faire l'expédition en -
 15 inspecteur *m.* des -s
 16 franchise *f.* de -

 17 réglementation *f.* de -
 18 remboursement *m.* des droits de -

 19 timbre *m.* de -
 20 visite *f.* de la -
 21 affranchir des droits de -

 22 payer la -
douanier *m.*
douanier (*adj.*)
 1 barrières douanières
 2 abaisser les barrières douanières
 3 fermeture douanière
 4 formalités douanières
 5 accomplir les formalités douanières
 6 recettes douanières
 7 tarifs -s
 8 union douanière
double *m.*
fait en -

double
 1 - emploi (*compt.*)

back
on the - of the bill
dossier, file
1 securities in your deposit

2 to place into your deposit

3 to withdraw securities from the deposit
customs
 1 - authorities
 2 dutiable

 3 duty-free, exempt from -
 4 - (custom house) authorities
 5 - officer
 6 - agent, custom house broker

 7 - office
 8 - declaration
 9 - warehouse
 10 -, - duties
 11 clearance inwards
 12 to clear inwards
 13 clearance outwards
 14 to clear outwards
 15 - inspector
 16 exemption from - duty

 17 - regulations
 18 drawback

 19 - seal
 20 - inspection
 21 to exempt from - duty

 22 to pay -, - duties
customs officer
customs...
 1 - barriers, tariff walls, - walls
 2 to lower - barriers
 3 - seal
 4 - formalities
 5 to observe - formalities
 6 - collections
 7 - tariffs
 8 - union
duplicate
done in -

double
 1 duplication

121 / doublé, doublure

2 – emploi (*fig.*)
3 – étalon
4 – prime

5 – valable pour simple

doublé *m.*, **doublure** *f.* (voir aussi *faculté*)
1 – à la baisse

2 – à la hausse

douteux
douzaine *f.*
1 à la –
2 la –
drawback *m.*
droit *m.* (*loi*)
1 – aérien
2 – bancaire
3 – civil
4 – commercial
5 – commun
6 – coutumier
7 – de change, – cambial
8 – des gens
9 – des obligations
10 – des sociétés
11 – fiscal
12 – formel
13 – international
14 – international privé
15 – international public

16 – interne
17 – jurisprudentiel
18 – légal
19 – maritime
20 – matériel
21 – naturel
22 – positif
23 – public
24 de – public

25 société *f.* de – anglais
droit *m.*
1 –s civils
2 – corporel   [aussi *faculté*]
3 – d'acheter encore autant (voir

2 duplication
3 – standard
4 – option, put and call option

5 (receipt) in duplicate valid for one option to double

1 put of more, seller's –

2 call of more, buyer's –

doubtful
dozen
1 by the –
2 per –
drawback
law
1 air (aerial) –
2 bank –
3 civil –
4 commercial –
5 common –
6 customary –
7 exchange –
8 – of nations
9 – of contracts
10 company –
11 fiscal –
12 formal –
13 international –
14 private international –
15 public international –

16 municipal –
17 case-law
18 statutory –
19 maritime –
20 material –
21 natural –
22 substantive –
23 public –
24 of public –

25 company under the English –
right
1 civil –s
2 corporeal –
3 call of more

droits / 122

4 – d'auteur	4 copyright, (*somme*) royalties
5 – de gage	5 lien
6 – de préavis	6 – of notice
7 – de préemption	7 – of pre-emption
8 – de préférence	8 preferential –
9 – de rachat	9 power of redemption
10 – de recours	10 – of recourse
11 – de rétention	11 lien
12 – de souscription	12 (application) –s
13 – de suite (par hypothèque)	13 – on a property even after it has passed into the hands of third parties
14 – de superficie	14 leaseholder's building –
15 –s de tirage	15 drawing –s
16 – de vendre encore autant (voir aussi *faculté*)	16 put of more
17 – de vote	17 – of vote
18 – d'opposition	18 – of appeal
19 – d'option	19 – of option
20 – incorporel	20 incorporeal –
21 – personnel	21 personal –
22 – réel	22 real –
23 avec –, – attaché	23 with –s, cum new
24 ex –, – détaché	24 ex –s, ex new
25 de plein –	25 with good –
26 de quel –	26 on what authority
27 avoir le – de	27 to be entitled to
28 conférer le – à	28 to entitle to..., to grant the –
29 dénier le –	29 to deny a –
30 être dans son –	30 to be within one's –s
31 exercer un –	31 to exercise a –
32 faire valoir son –	32 to assert one's –s
33 jouir d'un –	33 to enjoy a –
34 renoncer à un –	34 to renounce (relinquish) a –
35 se réserver le –	35 to reserve to oneself the –
36 user d'un –	36 to use a –
droits *m. pl.* (*taxes*)	**duties, dues**
1 – acquittés	1 duty-paid
2 – ad valorem	2 ad valorem duties
3 – de bassin	3 dock dues, dockage
4 – de douane	4 customs (duties)
5 – de garde (*banque*)	5 charge for safe custody
6 – de magasinage (garde)	6 rent, storage
7 – d'emplacement	7 market dues
8 – d'enregistrement	8 registration fees
9 – d'entrée	9 import duties
10 – de phare	10 light dues

123 / dû

11 – de pilotage	11 pilotage (dues)
12 – de port	12 harbo(u)r dues
13 – de quai	13 wharfage, quayage
14 – de réciprocité	14 reciprocal duties
15 – de sortie	15 export duties
16 – de stationnement (*ch. de fer*)	16 demurrage charge
17 – de statistique	17 statistical dues
18 – de succession	18 legacy (estate) duties
19 – de timbre	19 stamp duty
20 – de transit	20 transit duties
21 – différentiels	21 differential duties
22 – non acquittés	22 in bond
23 – prohibitifs	23 prohibitive duties
24 – protecteurs	24 protective duties
25 – spécifiques	25 specific duties
26 assujetti aux –, passible de –, soumis aux –	26 dutiable, liable to duty
27 exempt de –	27 duty-free
28 remboursement *m.* des – perçus à l'entrée	28 drawback
29 affranchir (libérer) de –	29 to exempt from duty
30 imposer, établir des –	30 to lay on (impose) duties
31 percevoir des – [trée	31 to levy duties
32 rembourser des – perçus à l'en-	32 to pay the drawback

dû (*adj.*) (voir aussi *devoir*) — **due**
1 en – temps — 1 in due course
2 en due forme — 2 in due form

dû *m.* — **due**
réclamer son – — to claim one's –

ducroire *m.* — **del credere**
1 – (*commission*) — 1 – commission
2 commissionnaire – *m.* — 2 – agent
3 être – — 3 to undertake the –

dûment — **duly**
dumping *m.* — **dumping**
duopole *m.* — **duopoly**
duplicata *m.* — **duplicate**
1 – de lettre de voiture — 1 Counterfoil Waybill
2 émettre un – — 2 to issue a –

duplicateur *m.* — **duplicator, duplicating machine**
durée *f.* — **duration**
1 – de travail — 1 hours of labo(u)r
2 – de validité — 2 – of validity
3 – d'un contrat — 3 term of a contract
4 – d'une société — 4 – of a company
5 de courte – — 5 of short –
6 proroger la – — 6 to extend the term

E

écart *m.*
 1 – de 5 % en plus ou en moins
 2 – des cours
 3 – de prime (différence entre le cours à prime et le ferme)

échange *m.* (voir aussi *circulation, mouvement*)
 1 –s commerciaux
 2 –s de biens
 3 –s de correspondance
 4 –s de lettres
 5 –s de marchandises et de services
 6 – de notes
 7 – de titres
 8 – d'idées
 9 –s triangulaires
 10 en – de
 11 commerce *m.* d'–
 12 instrument *m.* (moyen *m.*) d'–
 13 termes *m. pl.* de l'–
 14 valeur *f.* d'–
échangeable

échanger
 1 – les anciennes actions contre des actions nouvelles
 2 – des billets de banque contre de l'or
 3 – des coupons
 4 – des certificats (titres) provisoires contre les titres définitifs
 5 – des vues
 6 on n'échange pas les objets achetés
 7 correspondance échangée
échantillon *m.*
 1 – à référence
 2 – gratuit
 3 – moyen
 4 – sans valeur
 5 – type
 6 sur –
 7 carte *f.* d'–

difference
 1 tolerance of 5 % more or 5 % less
 2 – of exchange
 3 ecart (margin between prices for firm stock and option stock)

exchange

 1 commercial intercourse, commercial traffic
 2 goods- and capital movements
 3 – of correspondence
 4 – of letters
 5 – of goods and services
 6 – of notes
 7 – of securities
 8 – of views, of ideas
 9 three-cornered (triangular) trade
 10 in – for
 11 (trade by) barter
 12 medium of –
 13 terms of trade
 14 value in –
exchangeable

to exchange
 1 to exchange old shares for new ones
 2 to exchange banknotes for gold
 3 to collect coupons
 4 to exchange the scrips for the definite shares or bonds
 5 to exchange views (ideas)
 6 no goods exchanged
 7 correspondance exchanged
sample
 1 reference –
 2 free –
 3 average –, bulk –
 4 – of no value
 5 type –
 6 by –
 7 – card

125 / échantillonnage

8 collection *f.* d'–s — 8 – assortment, range of –s
9 envoi *m.* d'–s — 9 – packet, pattern parcel
10 foire *f.* d'–s — 10 – fair
11 livre *m.* d'–s — 11 – book, pattern book
12 prise *f.* d'–s — 12 sampling, – taking
13 salle *f.* d'–s — 13 – room
14 envoyer comme – — 14 to send by – post
15 être conforme à l'– — 15 to be up to –
16 prélever des –s — 16 to draw –s
17 soumettre des –s — 17 to submit –s
18 vendre sur – — 18 to sell on (by) –

échantillonnage *m.* — **sampling**
échantillonner — **to sample**
échantillonneur *m.* — **sampler**
échapper (voir aussi *nom*) — **to escape** [memory
cela m'a échappé — it has escaped my attention, my

échéance *f.*
1 – (*effet*) — 1 bill
2 – (*terme*) — 2 tenor, currency, term
3 – (*valeur*) — 3 value
4 – (*date*) — 4 due date, maturity date
5 – à 3 mois de date — 5 (maturity) 3 months after date; at three months' date
6 – à 3 jours de vue — 6 (maturity) at 3 days' sight
7 – (à date) fixe — 7 fixed date
8 –s de fin de mois — 8 end of month maturity
9 – moyenne — 9 average due date
10 – d'un coupon — 10 coupon date
11 – d'une police — 11 expiry of a policy
12 à l'– — 12 at maturity, when due

13 avant l'– — 13 before (prior to) maturity
14 besoins *m. pl.* de l'– — 14 end of month requirements
15 dépôt *m.* à – fixe — 15 fixed deposit
16 effet *m.* à courte – — 16 short bill, short-dated bill

17 effet *m.* à longue – — 17 long bill, long-dated bill
18 jour *m.* de l'– — 18 date of maturity
19 lendemain *m.* de l'– — 19 day after maturity [currency
20 terme *m.* d'– — 20 term (time) of payment, tenor,
21 valeur *f.* à l'– — 21 value day of maturity
22 veille *f.* de l'– — 22 one day before maturity

23 faire face à une – — 23 to meet a bill
24 faire face aux besoins de l'– mensuelle — 24 to meet end of month requirements

25 payer à l'– — 25 to pay at maturity
26 arriver, venir à – — 26 to fall due, to mature
échéancier *m.* — **bill diary**

échelle *f.* — **scale**
1 – (*intérêts*) — 1 ladder

échelon / 126

2 – des salaires
3 – mobile
4 – sociale
5 sur une large –
6 méthode f. à –s
échelon m.
  1 à l'– le plus élevé
  2 expédition f. par –s
échelonner
  1 – les payements sur...

  2 les versements s'échelonnent
  3 intérêts échelonnés
échoir
  1 le coupon échoit le...
  2 l'effet échoit le...
échouement m.
  – avec bris
échouer
  1 – à l'examen
  2 – un navire (sur le rivage)
éclairage m.
économat m. (*banque*)
économe m. (*banque*)
économe (*adj.*)
économétrie f.
économétrique
économie f.
  1 –s
  2 – contrôlée
  3 – de frais
  4 – de guerre
  5 – de marché
  6 – d'entreprise
  7 – de temps
  8 – dirigée

  9 – libre
  10 – libre des marchés
  11 – mondiale
  12 – nationale
  13 – planifiée
  14 – politique
  15 – rurale
  16 – sociale
  17 branche f. de l'–
  18 commission f. des –s
  19 mesure f. d'–

  20 politique f. d'–s
  21 pour des raisons f. pl. d'–
  22 faire une – de...

2 wage –
3 sliding wage –
4 social –, social ladder
5 on an extensive (large) –
6 steps method, "ladder" system
step
  1 at the highest level
  2 shipment by instalments

  1 to spread payments over...

  2 instalments are spread over...
  3 graduated interests, varied rates
to fall due
  1 the coupon becomes payable on...
  2 the bill falls due (matures) on...
stranding
  – with break
to fail
  1 – at an examination
  2 to beach a ship
lighting
stationery department
stationery clerk
economical, sparing
econometrics
econometric
economy
  1 savings
  2 controlled –
  3 – in expenses
  4 war –
  5 market –
  6 business economics
  7 saving of time
  8 planned –

  9 free –
  10 free-market –
  11 world –
  12 national –
  13 planned –
  14 political –
  15 husbandry
  16 social –
  17 sector of –
  18 —(retrenchment) committee
  19 economical measure, measure of –

  20 policy of retrenchment
  21 for reasons of economy
  22 to save...

127 / économique

23 faire des –s
24 faire des –s (*réduire les dépenses*)
économique
1 crise *f.* –
2 géographie *f.* –
3 ministère *m.* des Affaires –s
4 reprise *f.* –
5 situation *f.* –
6 vie *f.* –
économique (*d'un appareil e. a.*)
économiquement
les – faibles
économiser
pour –

économiste *m.*
écoulé
1 exercice –
2 le 15 du mois –
écoulement *m.*
écouler
1 s'– facilement

2 s'– lentement

écouteur *m.* (*tél.*)
1 décrocher l'–
2 raccrocher l'–
écrire
1 – à quelqu'un
2 – à la machine
3 – (sous le numéro) K 70 bureau du journal
4 machine *f.* à –
5 prière *f.* d'– lisiblement
écrit
1 – à la main
2 – à la machine
3 – en chiffres
4 convention –e
5 déclaration –e
6 preuve –e
7 confirmer par –
8 coucher (mettre) par –

écritoire *f.*
écriture *f.*
1 – à la machine
2 – lisible
écriture *f.* (*compt.*)

1 –s comptables
2 – d'ordre

---

23 to save money
24 to curtail (retrench) expenditure
economic
1 – crisis
2 – geography
3 Department of – Affairs
4 – recovery
5 – situation, conditions
6 – life
economical
economically
lower-income groups
to economize, to save
in order to economize, for reasons of economy
economist
ultimo
1 past trading year
2 on the 15th –
placing, sale
to place, to sell
1 to go off steadily, to find a ready sale
2 to sell slowly

receiver
1 to remove (take up) the –
2 to replace the –
to write
1 – to...
2 to typewrite, to type
3 write to K 70

4 typewriter
5 please write distinctly, very clearly
written
1 hand—
2 typewritten
3 expressed in figures
4 – agreement
5 – statement
6 – proof
7 to confirm in writing
8 to put down in writing

inkstand
writing
1 typewriting
2 legible –, hand
entry

1 accounts
2 suspense –

3 – de clôture, – d'inventaire
4 – de contrepassement
5 – de redressement
6 – d'inventaire, (voir – de clôture)
7 – inverse (voir –s de contrepassement)
8 –s passées au crédit
9 – rectificative (voir – de redressement)
10 – transitoire
11 faux *m.* en –s
12 arrêter les –s
13 contrepasser une –
14 passer –
15 passer – conforme
16 rectifier une –
17 tenir les –s

éditeur *m.*

édition *f.*
1 – de midi
2 – du dimanche
3 – du matin
4 – du soir
5 – spéciale
6 maison *f.* d'–s
7 société *f.* d'–s

effectif *adj.*

effectif *m.* du personnel

effectuer
1 – des démarches
2 – des payements
3 – un versement
4 le payement s'effectue comme suit

effet *m.* (*résultat*)
1 –s secondaires
2 – suspensif
3 – utile
4 à – rétroactif
5 à cet –
6 en –
7 prendre – (*loi*)

8 sortir ses pleins –s

effet (de commerce) *m.* (voir aussi *lettre de change, papier, traite*)
1 – à courte échéance

2 – à date (échéance) fixe
3 – à délai de date
4 – à délai de vue

3 closing –
4 reversing (transfer) –
5 correcting –

8 entries to the credit side

10 suspense –
11 forging of documents
12 to balance the books
13 to reverse (transfer, contra) an –
14 to make an –
15 to book in conformity
16 to adjust an –
17 to keep the books

publisher

edition
1 noon –
2 Sunday –
3 morning –
4 evening –
5 special –
6 publishing house, firm
7 publishing business

effective, real

strength of staff, number of employees

to effect, to execute
1 to take steps
2 to effect (make) payments
3 to make (effect) a payment
4 payment is effected (made) as follows

effect
1 incidental consequence
2 suspensive –
3 practical –
4 retrospective
5 for this purpose
6 indeed
7 to become operative, to take (come into) –
8 to have its full –

bill of exchange

1 short bill, short-dated bill

2 day bill
3 bill after date
4 bill after sight

129 / effet (de commerce)

5 – à l'encaissement	5 bill for collection
6 – à l'escompte	6 bill for discount
7 – à longue échéance	7 long bill, long-dated bill
8 –s à ordre	8 order paper, paper to order
9 –s à payer	9 bills payable
10 journal *m.* des –s à payer	10 bills payable book
11 –s à recevoir	11 bills receivable
12 journal *m.* des –s à recevoir	12 bills receivable book
13 – à renouvellement	13 windmill, kite
14 – à trois mois	14 three months' bill
15 – à usance	15 bill at usance
16 – à vue	16 sight bill
17 – au porteur	17 bearer paper, paper to bearer
18 – avec protêt	18 protested bill
19 – accepté	19 accepted bill
20 – avalisé	20 guaranteed bill
21 – bancable	21 bankable bill
22 –s brûlants	22 hot bills
23 –s creux	23 house bills, pig on pork
24 – de complaisance	24 accommodation bill
25 –s de finance	25 finance bills
26 – déplacé,	26 bill payable on another place than that of issue, out of town bill
27 –s documentaires, –s avec documents attachés	27 documentary bills, bills with attached documents
28 – domicilié	28 domiciled bill
29 – du Trésor	29 Treasury bill
30 – échu	30 due bill
31 – en devises	31 bill in foreign currency, currency bill
32 – endossé	32 endorsed bill
33 – en pension	33 bill on deposit
34 –s en portefeuille	34 bills in case
35 –s en souffrance	35 bills in suspense
36 – escomptable	36 discountable bill
37 – escompté	37 bill discounted
38 – fictif	38 fictitious bill
39 – impayé	39 unpaid bill
40 – innégociable	40 unnegotiable bill
41 – libellé en monnaie étrangère	41 bill in foreign currency
42 – libre	42 clean bill
43 – négociable	43 negotiable bill

effet (de commerce) / 130

44 – nominatif	44 unnegotiable bill
45 – non accepté	45 dishono(u)red bill
46 – protesté	46 protested bill
47 – réescompté	47 bill rediscounted
48 – rendu, retourné, renvoyé	48 bill returned, dishono(u)red bill
49 – ,,sans frais''	49 bill "without charges"
50 – sur l'étranger	50 foreign bill
51 – sur l'intérieur	51 inland bill, home bill
52 – sur place	52 local bill
53 délai *m.* d'un –	53 currency of a bill
54 envoi *m.* des –s aux correspondants	54 dispatch of bills to correspondents
55 montant *m.* d'un –	55 amount of a bill
56 parties intervenantes d'un –	56 parties to a bill
57 portefeuille *m.* d'–s	57 bill case
58 porteur *m.* (détenteur *m.*) d'un –	58 bearer (holder) of a bill
59 preneur *m.* (bénéficiaire *m.*) d'un –	59 payee
60 remise *f.* d'–s à l'encaissement	60 remittance of bills for collection
61 remise *f.* d'–s à l'escompte	61 remittance of bills for discount
62 accepter un –	62 to accept a bill
63 domicilier un –	63 to domicile a bill
64 encaisser un –	64 to collect a bill
65 endosser un –	65 to endorse a bill
66 envoyer des –s à l'encaissement	66 to send bills for collection
67 envoyer des –s à l'escompte	67 to send remittances for discount
68 escompter un –	68 to discount a bill
69 faire bon accueil à un –	69 to hono(u)r a bill
70 faire protester un –	70 to have a bill noted
71 négocier un –	71 to negotiate a bill
72 ne pas honorer un –	72 to dishono(u)r a bill
73 présenter un – à l'acceptation	73 to present a bill for acceptance
74 présenter un – de nouveau	74 to present a draft once more
75 recouvrer un – (voir *encaisser un–*)	
76 renouveler un –	76 to renew a bill
77 retirer un –	77 to withdraw a bill
78 retourner un –	78 to return a draft

effets *m. pl.* (voir aussi *titres*)
1 – publics
2 – publics mobilisables à la Banque Nationale
3 – publics réescomptables à la Banque Nationale

effondrement *m.* des cours

effondrer, s'–
effort *m.*
1 –s soutenus, suivis
2 de vains –s
3 faire tous ses –s
4 faire un dernier –
5 ne reculer devant aucun –

effritement *m.* des cours
effriter, s'–
égal
1 cela nous est –
2 sans –

égaler
1 (10 moins 5) égale...
2 rien n'égale

égalisation *f.* (voir aussi *fonds*)
égaliser
égalité *f.*
– fiscale

égard *m.*
1 à cet –
2 à l'– de

3 à tous –s
4 eu – à

5 par – pour
6 avoir – à

égaré
élaborer
élasticité *f.*
1 – croisée (de la demande)
2 – de la demande
3 – de l'offre
4 – de substitution
5 – -prix
6 – -revenu

élastique (*demande*)
élection *f.*
– du bureau
électricien *m.*
électricité *f.*
électrification *f.*
électrifier

---

securities, stocks and shares
1 government securities
2 treasury bills negotiable with the National Bank
3 treasury bills rediscountable with the National Bank

slump in prices, collapse of prices

to slump down to...
effort
1 continuous –s
2 useless –s
3 to make every –, to do one's utmost
4 to make a last –
5 to spare no –s

crumbling of prices
to crumble
equal
1 it is all the same to us
2 unequalled

to equal
1 equals...
2 nothing can compare with...

equalization
to equalize
equality
fiscal –

consideration
1 in this respect
2 with regard (respect) to

3 in every respect
4 having regard to, considering, in – of
5 out of – (respect) for
6 to take into –, into account

mislaid, lost
to work out
elasticity
1 cross-elasticity
2 – of demand
3 – of supply
4 – of substitution
5 price –
6 income –

elastic
election
– of the committee, of the board
electrician
electricity
electrification
to electrify

électrique

électrique — **electric**
1 centrale f. - — 1 electricity works, power station
2 courant m. - — 2 - current

électronique — **electronic**
industrie f. - — electronics industry

élevage m. — **stock breeding**

élévateur m. — **elevator**

élévation f. — **rise, raising**
- du taux d'escompte — the raising of the bank rate

élevé — **high**
à des prix –s — at - prices

élever (prix) — **to raise**
1 s'- à — 1 to amount to
2 s'élevant à... — 2 amounting to...

éleveur m. — **stock breeder**

éligibilité f. — **eligibility**

éligible — **eligible**

élire — **to elect**
1 - domicile — 1 - domicile, one's residence
2 - un président — 2 - a chairman, a president
3 - ... président — 3 - ... chairman

émancipation f. — **emancipation**

- restreinte — restricted -

émancipé — **emancipated**

émargement m. (l'action) — **signing, initialling, receipting (in the margin)**

1 - (annotation) — 1 marginal note
2 contre - au carnet — 2 against signature in the book

3 feuille f. d'- — 3 pay sheet

émarger — **to sign, to initial, to receipt (in the margin)**

1 - (salaire) — 1 to draw one's salary
2 - au budget — 2 to be in the civil service

emballage m. — **packing**

1 - à retourner — 1 - to be returned

2 - compris — 2 - included
3 - défectueux — 3 defective -
4 - d'origine — 4 original -
5 - en caisses — 5 - in cases
6 - factice — 6 dummy (pack)
7 - insuffisant — 7 insufficient -
8 - maritime, - pour transport par mer — 8 seaworthy -, - for shipment
9 - non compris, - en sus, - à part — 9 - extra

10 –s retournés vides — 10 returned empties
11 –s vides — 11 empties

133 / emballer

12 l'– n'est pas porté en compte

13 caisse *f.* d'–
14 carton *m.* d'–
15 frais *m. pl.* d'–
16 papier *m.* d'–
17 toile *f.* d'–
18 retourner l'– vide

emballer (v. aussi *mer*)
 – dans des (en) caisses
emballeur *m.*
embarcadère *m.*
 – (*chem. de fer*)
embargo *m.*
1 lever l'–

2 mettre l'– sur

embarquement *m.*
1 à l'–
2 billet *m.* (bon) d'– (*billet de bord*)

3 délai *m.* d'–
4 documents *m. pl.* d'–
5 frais *m. pl.* d'–
6 permis *m.* d'–
7 place *f.* (emplacement) d'–
8 port *m.* d'–
9 reçu pour –
embarquer
1 poids embarqué

2 poids net embarqué
3 s'– pour
embarras *m.*
1 – d'argent, – pécuniaire
2 être dans l'–
3 mettre dans l'–
4 tirer d'–
embauchage *m.*
embouteillage *m.* (*circulation*)
émetteur *m.*
émetteur *adj.*
1 banque émettrice

2 société émettrice
émettre
1 – des actions au cours de
2 – des actions au pair
3 – des billets de banque
4 – un chèque

12 no charges for –

13 – case
14 – cardboard
15 – charges
16 – paper
17 – cloth
18 to return empties

to pack
 – in cases
packer
landing stage
 departure platform
embargo
1 to raise the –

2 to lay an – on, to embargo

shipment
1 on –
2 mate's receipt

3 time for –
4 shipping documents
5 shipping charges, loading charges
6 shipping note
7 loading berth
8 loading port
9 received for –
to ship
1 shipping weight, loaded weight

2 loaded net weight
3 to embark for
difficulty
1 pecuniary (money) difficulties
2 to be embarrassed (for money)
3 to embarrass
4 to free from –
recruitment, engaging, taking on
congestion, traffic block
issuer
issuing
1 – bank

2 – company
to issue
1 – shares at...
2 – shares at par
3 – bank notes
4 – a cheque (check)

5 – un emprunt | 5 – (to float) a loan
6 – une traite sur | 6 – a bill
émigration *f.* | emigration
émigrer | to emigrate
émission *f.* | issue
  1 – au-dessous du pair | 1 – below par, – at a discount
  2 – au-dessus du pair | 2 – above par, – at a premium
  3 – au robinet | 3 – on tap
  4 – de billets de banque | 4 – of bank notes
  5 – d'un chèque | 5 – of a cheque (check)

  6 – d'un emprunt | 6 – (floatation) of a loan

  7 – d'obligations | 7 bond –
  8 – d'une traite | 8 – of a draft

  9 –s en cours | 9 current –s
  10 – (il)limitée | 10 (un)restricted issue
  11 nouvelles –s | 11 new –s, emissions
  12 banque *f.* d'– | 12 bank of issue, note issuing bank
  13 conditions *pl.* d'– | 13 – terms, terms of –
  14 cours *m.* d'–, prix d'– | 14 rate of –, price of –

  15 date *f.* d'– (*traite*) | 15 date of –
  16 frais *pl.* d'– | 16 – expenses
  17 impôt *m.* sur les –s | 17 tax on the – of securities
  18 lancement *m.* de nouvelles –s | 18 bringing out of new –s
  19 (maison *f.* d'–) | 19 issuing house

  20 marché *m.* des –s | 20 new – market
  21 prime *f.* d'– | 21 share premium
  22 service *m.* des –s (*banque*) | 22 issue department
  23 type *m.* d'– | 23 type of –
emmagasinage *m.* | storing, warehousing
emmagasiner | to store, to warehouse
émoluments *m. pl.* | emoluments
empêchement *m.* | impediment
  en cas d'– | in case of inability to...
empêcher | to impede, to prevent
  1 être empêché de... | 1 to be prevented from...
  2 nous ne pouvons nous – de | 2 we cannot refrain from..., we cannot but...

emphytéose *f.* | long lease
emphytéote *m.* | leaseholder
emphytéotique, bail – | long lease, ninety-nine year lease
emplacement *m.* | space
  – réservé aux mentions de service | – for service instructions

emplettes *f. pl.*, faire ses – | to go shopping
emploi *m.* | employment, place
  1 – vacant | 1 vacancy
  2 – d'une somme | 2 use (employment) of a sum

3 degré *m.* d'–
4 dégression *f.* de l'–

5 demande *f.* d'–
6 ,,demandes d'–''
7 mode *m.* d'–
8 ,,offres d'–''
9 ,,agiter avant –''
10 chercher un –
11 être en quête d'– (*capitaux*)
12 être sans –
13 solliciter un –
employé *m.*
1 – de banque
2 – de bureau
3 – du guichet
employée *f.*
employer
1 – 100 ouvriers

2 – une somme
employeur *m.*
1 association *f.* d'–s
2 risque *m.* de l'–
emporter, à – (*boissons, glace, etc.*)
emprunt *m.*
1 – (à) 3 %
2 – à court terme
3 – à la grosse
4 – à long terme
5 – à lots
6 – à primes
7 – à taux progressif, à intérêts croissants
8 – au jour le jour
9 – avec option de change
10 – colonial
11 – communal
12 – consolidé
13 – convertible
14 – d'amortissement
15 – de conversion

16 – de guerre
17 – de stabilisation, de valorisation
18 – d'État, du gouvernement
19 – de villes
20 – en unités de compte

21 – extérieur
22 – forcé
23 – gagé, garanti
24 – hypothécaire

3 level of employment
4 decline in employment

5 application for a situation
6 situations wanted
7 directions for use
8 situations vacant
9 shake before using
10 to look out for a situation
11 to be in quest of investment
12 to be out of employment
13 to apply for a situation
employee, clerk
1 bank clerk
2 (office) clerk
3 counter clerk
(lady)clerk
to use
1 to employ (give employment to) 100 hands
2 – a sum
employer [tion
1 employers' association, confedera-
2 employers' liability
for off-consumption
loan
1 3 % –, – (bearing interest) at 3 %
2 short (–dated) –, short-term –
3 bottomry –
4 long-dated –, long-term –
5 lottery –
6 premium –
7 loan bearing interest at varied (different) rates
8 day-to-day –
9 – with currency option
10 colonial –
11 municipal –
12 consolidated –
13 – in the form of convertible bonds
14 redemption –
15 conversion –

16 war –
17 stabilization –
18 government –
19 municipal –
20 unit of account –

21 foreign (external) –
22 forced (compulsory) –
23 secured –
24 mortgage –

emprunter / 136

25 – indexé	25 indexed –, – tied (linked) to an index
26 – intérieur	26 internal –
27 – non gagé	27 unsecured –
28 – obligataire, – (par) obligations	28 debenture –
29 emprunt-or	29 gold –
30 – perpétuel	30 perpetual –
31 – privé	31 privately placed –
32 – public	32 public –
33 – remboursable par tirage au sort	33 – redeemable by lot, by drawing
34 – révalorisé	34 revalorized –
35 – sur titres	35 – on stock
36 – volontaire	36 voluntary –
37 l'– a été couvert	37 the – was fully subscribed
38 l'– a été largement couvert, a été couvert plusieurs fois	38 the – was largely oversubscribed, was subscribed several times over
39 par voie d'–, par appel à l'–	39 by the issue of –s
40 amortissement *m.* d'un –	40 redemption of a –
41 émission *f.* d'un –	41 issue (floatation) of a –
42 intérêts *m. pl.* sur –	42 – interest
43 placement *m.* d'un –	43 placing of a –
44 produit *m.* de l'–	44 proceeds of –
45 service *m.* d'un –	45 service of –
46 accorder un –	46 to grant a –
47 amortir un –	47 to redeem a –
48 contracter (faire) un –	48 to contract a –
49 émettre un –	49 to issue a –
50 lancer un –	50 to float a –
51 négocier un –	51 to negotiate a –
52 placer un –	52 to place a –
53 rembourser un –	53 to repay a –
54 souscrire à un –	54 to subscribe to a –
emprunter (à)	**to borrow (from)**
1 – sur hypothèques	1 to borrow on mortgage
2 – sur police	2 to borrow on a policy
3 – sur titres	3 to borrow on securities
emprunteur *m.*	**borrower**
1 – à la grosse	1 – on bottomry
2 – sur gages	2 mortgagor
encadré, partie –e d'une ligne noire, d'un trait gras	**portion surrounded by heavy black lines, outlined in heavy rule**
encaissable	**collectible, collectable**
encaisse *f.*	**cash on hand, cash balance**
1 – métallique	1 cash and bullion in hand
2 encaisse-or	2 gold coin and bullion
encaissement *m.* (voir aussi *recouvrement*)	**collection**
1 –s documentaires sur l'étranger	1 documentary –s abroad

137 / encaisser

2 –s hors Bruxelles	2 –s outside Brussels
3 à l'–	3 for –
4 sauf –	4 under usual reserve
5 **affaires** *f. pl.* d'–	5 – business
6 **banque** *f.* d'–	6 – bank
7 **bordereau** *m.* d'–	7 list of bills for –
8 **conditions** *f. pl.* d'–	8 conditions of –
9 **courtage** *m.* pour l'–	9 – charge
10 **décompte** *m.* des –s	10 statement of –s
11 **effet** *m.* à l'–	11 bill for –
12 **frais** *m. pl.* d'–	12 – charges
13 **rayon** *m.* d'–	13 – area
14 **remise** *f.* à l'–	14 remittance for –
15 **service** *m.* d'–	15 – department
16 **tarifs** *m. pl.* d'–	16 – rates
17 „**valeur** à l'–"	17 value for –
18 **effectuer** (faire) l'–	18 to effect (undertake) the –
19 se **charger** de l'– d'effets	19 to attend to –s of drafts
20 **donner** à l'–	20 to hand in for –
22 **envoyer** à l'–	22 to send for –
23 **présenter** à l'–	23 to present for –
24 **recevoir** à l'–	24 to receive for –
25 **soigner** l'– de...	25 to attend to the – of

encaisser
 1 – de l'argent
 2 – un chèque
 3 – des coupons
 4 – des effets
encaisseur *m.*
 1 – (*guichet*)
 2 banquier –
encan, vente *f.* à l'–
encart *m.*

enchère *f.*
 1 – au rabais
 2 folle –
 3 vente *f.* aux –s
 4 mettre une – sur
 5 vendre aux –s
enchérir

 1 – (*augmenter en prix*)
 2 – (*des marchandises*)
 3 – sur qqn
enchérissement *m.*

to collect
 1 – (cash) money
 2 to cash a cheque (check)
 3 to cash coupons
 4 – bills
collector
 1 receiver, receiving cashier
 2 collecting banker
sale at auction
tip-in, inset

bid
 1 Dutch auction
 2 irresponsible –; forfeit
 3 auction
 4 to make a – for
 5 to sell by auction
to bid

 1 to rise in price, to get dearer
 2 to raise the price
 3 to outbid someone
rise in price, increase of price

enchérisseur m.
  au dernier et plus offrant –
encombrant
  marchandises –es
encombré
  le marché est – de
encombrement m. (*trafic*)
  1 – (*guichet*)
  2 – (*marché*)
  3 – (*espace*)
  4 fret m. suivant –
encore
  – que
encourir
  1 – des frais
  2 – un risque
  3 – une responsabilité
en cours
  1 – de construction

  2 – de fabrication
  3 – d'exécution
  4 affaires f. pl. –

  5 contrats m. pl. –
  6 émissions f. pl. –
  7 engagements m. pl. –
  8 exercice m. –
  9 intérêts m. pl. –
  10 mois m. –
  11 négociations f. pl. –
  12 ordres m. pl. –
  13 travaux m. pl. –

encours m. (voir aussi *risque*)

  1 – cédant

  2 – tiré
encre f.
  1 – à copier, – communicative
  2 – à tampon
  3 – de Chine
  4 – indélébile (à marquer)
  5 – pour stylos, stylographique
  6 – sympathique
  7 à l'– rouge
  8 corrigé à l'–
  9 tache f. d'–
encrier m.
endéans (mieux: *dans*)
endettement m.
endetter, s'–

bidder
  to the highest –
bulky
  – goods
           [with
the market is glutted (overstocked)
congestion
  1 crowding
  2 glut
  3 space occupied, measurement
  4 measurement freight
still
  although

  1 to incur expenses
  2 to run (incur) a risk
  3 to incur responsibilities
current
  1 in progress of construction, under construction
  2 in process of manufacture
  3 in progress
  4 pending affairs, outstanding business
  5 running contracts
  6 – issues
  7 running engagements
  8 – year
  9 running interest
  10 running month   [proceeding
  11 negotiations in progress, now
  12 orders in hand
  13 works in progress

liabilities on bills of exchange

  1 liability as transferor, (*tireur*) as maker
  2 liability as drawee
ink
  1 copying –
  2 stamping –
  3 Chinese (Indian) –
  4 indelible –, marking –
  5 fountain pen ink
  6 sympathetic (invisible) –
  7 in red –
  8 corrected in –
  9 – blot
inkpot, inkstand

indebtedness, running into debt
to run into debt

139 / endommagement

endommagement *m.*	damage
endommager	to damage
endossable	endorsable
endossataire (endossé) *m.*	endorsee
endossement *m.*, endos *m.*	endorsement, indorsement
1 – à forfait (sans garantie)	1 qualified endorsement (without recourse)
2 – conditionnel	2 conditional endorsement
3 – (à titre) pignoratif („valeur en garantie")	3 endorsement "value as security"
4 – (à titre) de procuration („valeur à l'encaissement")	4 endorsement "only for collection"
5 – en blanc	5 blank endorsement, endorsement in blank
6 – irrégulier	6 irregular (restrictive) endorsement
7 – partiel	7 partial –
8 – régulier	8 regular endorsement, endorsement in full
9 – restrictif	9 restrictive (restricted) endorsement
10 munir (revêtir) de son endos	10 to endorse
11 transférer (transmettre) par voie d'–	11 to transfer by endorsement, to endorse over
endosser	to endorse, to indorse
1 – en blanc	1 to endorse in blank
2 – la responsabilité	2 to assume the responsibility
3 dûment endossé	3 duly endorsed
endosseur *m.*	endorser, indorser
1 – précédent	1 preceding (previous) endorser
2 – subséquent	2 subsequent endorser
énergie *f.* (v. *atomique*)	energy
production *f.* d'–	power production
fourniture *f.* d'–	power supply
engagement *m.* (voir aussi *suite*)	engagement
1 – (*par le patron*)	1 –
2 – à court terme	2 short-term obligation
3 –s actuels et futurs	3 present and future –s
4 –s à la baisse	4 bear –s, commitments
5 –s à la bourse	5 stock exchange commitments
6 –s à la hausse	6 bull –s, commitments
7 – à l'essai	7 trial –
8 –s à l'étranger	8 foreign liabilities
9 – d'acceptation	9 acceptance liability
10 –s en cours	10 current (running) –s

engager / 140

11 – ferme	11 firm –, firm undertaking
12 –s nostro	12 liabilities on nostro account
13 –s par endossement	13 liabilities in respect of endorsements
14 sans –	14 without –
15 ,,démonstration *f.* sans –"	15 ask for free demonstration
16 offre *f.* sans –	16 offer without –
17 contracter (prendre) un –	17 to enter into an –
18 entraîner des –s	18 to involve liabilities
19 faire honneur (face) à ses –s, remplir ses –s	19 to fulfil (carry out) one's –s
20 manquer à un –	20 to break an –
engager	**to bind**
1 – (*mettre en gage*)	1 to pledge, to pawn
2 – de l'argent dans une affaire	2 to put money in a business
3 – un employé	3 to engage a clerk
4 – un équipage	4 to engage a crew
5 – sa parole	5 to pledge one's word
6 – la responsabilité	6 to involve the responsibility
7 cela ne vous engage à rien	7 it does not bind you to anything
engager, s'– (*équipage*)	**to sign on**
1 – chez...	1 to take service with
2 – à	2 to engage oneself to..., to undertake to
3 – dans (*spéculations*)	3 to engage in...
engrais *m. pl.*	**manure**
– chimiques	fertilizers
enlever	
1 – des marchandises (*à la gare*)	1 to remove (collect) goods
2 s'– (*s'écouler*)	2 to sell readily
enquête *f.*	**inquiry**
1 – pilote	1 pilot survey
2 faire une –	2 to make inquiries (into)
enquêter sur	**to inquire into**
enrayer (*hausse*)	**to check**
enregistrement *m.*	**registration**
1 bureau *m.* d'–, l'–	1 registry
2 frais *m. pl.* d'–	2 registration fee
enregistrer	**to register, to file**
1 – un acte	1 to register (file) a deed
2 faire – ses bagages	2 to register luggage
enregistreur	
caisse enregistreuse	cash register
enseigne *f.*	**sign (board)**
1 – au néon	1 neon sign
2 – lumineuse	2 illuminated (electric) sign
3 à bon vin point d'–	3 good wine needs no bush
entamer	
1 – son capital	1 to encroach upon (to dip into) one's capital

141 / entendre

2 – des négociations | 2 to open negotiations

3 – des poursuites contre | 3 to institute proceedings against

4 – un stock | 4 to draw on a stock

entendre | **to hear**
1 – par | 1 to understand by
2 donner à – à qqn | 2 to give a person to understand
3 s'– avec | 3 to come to an understanding with
4 s'– sur un prix | 4 to agree upon a price

5 les prix s'entendent comptant | 5 the prices are... cash
6 bien entendu si... | 6 of course if
7 c'est entendu | 7 that is all right (agreed)
8 il est bien entendu (convenu) que | 8 it is further clearly (expressly) understood that

entente *f.* | **understanding**
en-tête *m.* | **heading**
1 – de lettre | 1 letterhead
2 papier *m.* à – | 2 headed letter paper
entier | **whole**
1 en – | 1 in full
2 nombre – | 2 whole number
entièrement | **fully, entirely**
entrave *f.* | **hindrance (obstacle) to**
constituer une – à | to hinder, to hamper
entraver | **to hinder, to hamper**
entrée *f.* | **entrance**
1 – et sortie (*bâtiment*) | 1 way in and way out
2 – et sortie (d'un pays) | 2 entering and leaving (the country)
3 –s et sorties de caisse | 3 cash receipts and payments

4 – interdite | 4 no admittance
5 – libre | 5 admission free
6 – principale | 6 main –
7 – en douane (*navire*) | 7 clearance inwards
8 faire l'– en douane | 8 to clear inwards
9 – en fonction | 9 – into office
10 "– en jouissance immédiate" | 10 with immediate possession
11 – en possession | 11 taking possession of
12 – en vigueur | 12 coming into force
13 libre – sur le marché | 13 free access to market
14 carte *f.* d'– | 14 ticket
15 date *f.* d'– en valeur (*intérêts*) | 15 value date
16 prix *m.* d' – | 16 admission, admission charge

entremise *f.* par l' – de | **through the agency of**
entrepont *m.* | **steerage**
passager *m.* d'– | – passenger
entreposage *m.* | **storage, bonding**
entreposer | **to bond, to storage**

marchandises entreposées | bonded goods

entreposeur *m.* — bonded store keeper, warehouse keeper

entrepositaire *m.* — bonder
entrepôt *m.* — bonded warehouse
1 – fictif — 1 private –
2 – réel — 2 public –
3 en – — 3 bonded, in bond
4 certificat *m.* d'– — 4 warehouse warrant
5 frais *m. pl.* d'– — 5 warehousing charges, storage
6 marchandises *f. pl.* en – — 6 bonded goods, goods in bond
7 vente *f.* en – — 7 sale in bond, in –
8 mettre en – — 8 to store in bond
9 sortir de l'– — 9 to take (release) from bond
10 vendre en – — 10 to sell in bond

entreprendre — to undertake
entrepreneur *m.* — contractor
1 – (*de bâtiments*) — 1 builder and –
2 – de pompes funèbres — 2 undertaker
3 – de transports — 3 cartage –

4 profit *m.* de l'– — 4 entrepreneur's profit
5 rémunération *f.* de l'– — 5 entrepreneur's remuneration
6 revenu *m.* de l'– — 6 entrepeneur's income
entreprise *f.* — undertaking, enterprise
1 – à forfait — 1 work by contract
2 – à fort coefficient de capital — 2 capital-intensive enterprise
3 – à fort coefficient de travail — 3 labo(u)r-intensive enterprise
4 – agricole — 4 agricultural undertaking
5 – commerciale — 5 commercial (business) undertaking
6 – concessionnaire — 6 concessionary company
7 – de déménagement — 7 furniture removers, removal contractors
8 – de pompes funèbres — 8 undertaking business
9 – de roulage, – de transports — 9 cartage contractors, carrying company
10 – d'une personne — 10 one-man business
11 – d'utilité publique — 11 public utility concern
12 – familiale — 12 family business
13 – industrielle — 13 industrial undertaking
14 – viable — 14 concern that pays its way
15 grande – — 15 large concern
16 moyenne – — 16 medium-sized concern
17 petite – — 17 minor concern
18 chef *m.* d'– — 18 head of business
19 femmes chefs d'–s — 19 women executives
20 conseil *m.* d'– — 20 works council
21 économie *f.* d'– — 21 business economics

143 / entrer

22 journal *m.* d'– (*personnel*)
23 presse *f.* d'–
24 règlement *m.* d'–
25 travail *m.* à l'–
26 diriger une –
entrer
1 – (*compt.*)
2 – dans un port
3 – en considération
4 – en condition
5 – en fonction
6 – en vigueur
7 défense d'–

entresol *m.*

entretenir
1 qqn de

2 – en bon état

3 – un compte chez
4 – une correspondance avec

5 – une langue
6 – des relations avec
7 – un service
8 s'– avec... de...
9 bien entretenu
entretien *m.* (*conversation*)
1 – (*maison*)
2 – (*subsistance*)
3 frais *m. pl.* d'–

4 accorder un –
5 avoir un – avec
6 être de grand –
entrevue *f.* (voir aussi *rendez-vous*)
solliciter une – avec

enveloppe *f.*

1 – à fenêtre, fenestrée, à panneau
2 – affranchie (*pour la réponse*)
3 – deuil
4 sous –
5 patte *f.* d'une –
6 mettre sous –
environ
envoi *m.*
1 – (*chose envoyée*)
2 – à titre d'essai
3 – à vue

22 staff magazine, house journal
23 industrial press
24 works regulation
25 contract work
26 to direct an undertaking
to enter
1 to enter
2 – a port
3 to be taken into account
4 to go into service
5 – upon one's office, duties
6 to come into force
7 no admittance

entresol

to maintain
1 to talk to (converse with) someone about
2 to keep in repair
3 to keep an account with (at)
4 to carry on (keep up) a correspondence with
5 to keep up a language
6 – relations with
7 – a service
8 to converse with someone about, on
9 in good repair
conversation
1 maintenance, upkeep
2 living
3 maintenance charges

4 to grant an interview
5 to have an interview with
6 to require considerable upkeep
interview, appointment
to ask for an appointment (interview) with
envelope

1 panel –, window –
2 stamped addressed –
3 black-bordered –
4 under cover
5 flap of an –
6 to put in an –
about
sending, forwarding
1 packet, parcel, consignment
2 goods sent on trial
3 goods sent on approval

envoyer / 144

4 – chargé, – de valeur déclarée
5 – contre remboursement
6 – d'argent
7 – de fonds
8 – d'espèces
9 – en franchise de port, – franco
10 – exprès
11 – gratuit sur demande
12 – groupé
13 un – par chemin de fer
14 – postal

15 – recommandé
16 contre – de...
17 date *f.* d'–
18 prêt à l'–
envoyer
1 – à vue
2 – comme colis postal
3 – par chemin de fer

4 – par la poste
5 – un télégramme
envoyeur *m.*
épargne *f.*
1 – -construction
2 – dépôt
3 – en vue d'un but précis
4 – forcée
5 – mobilière, en valeurs

6 les –s
7 les –s individuelles
8 la petite –
9 capital *m.* d'–
10 compte *m.* à une caisse d'–
11 dépôts *m. pl.* d'–
12 encouragement *m.* de l'–
13 fonction *f.* d'–
14 formation *f.* de l'–
15 forme *f.* d'–
16 habitudes *f. pl.* d'–
17 institution *f.* d'–
18 livret *m.* (de caisse) d'–
19 protection *f.* de l'–
20 taux *m.* d'–
21 encourager l'–
22 vivre de ses –s
épargner (pour)
1 – du temps
2 n'– ni peine ni temps
3 s'– la peine
4 propension *f.* à –

4 insured packet
5 cash on delivery parcel [money
6 cash remittance, consignment of
7 remittance of funds, remittance
8 specie consignment [in cash
9 post free parcel
10 express packet
11 post free on application
12 joint consignment
13 railway consignment
14 postal packet

15 registered packet
16 on receipt of
17 date of dispatch
18 ready for dispatch
to send
1 – on approval
2 – by parcel post
3 – by rail

4 – by post
5 to despatch a telegram
sender
economy
1 saving for building purposes
2 saving through deposit accounts
3 saving for a specific purpose
4 forced (compulsory) savings
5 saving through investment in securities
6 savings
7 private (individual) savings
8 small savings, the small savers
9 savings capital
10 savings account
11 savings bank deposits
12 encouragement to (of) savings
13 savings function
14 formation of savings
15 form of savings
16 savings habits
17 savings institution
18 savings bank book
19 protection of savings
20 savings ratio
21 to encourage savings
22 to live on one's savings
to save (for)
1 – (spare) time
2 to spare neither time nor pains
3 – oneself the trouble
4 propensity –

épave f. (*navire*) — wreck
1 –s (*maritimes*) — 1 wreckage, jetsam, stranded goods
2 –s flottantes — 2 flotsam
3 droit m. d'– — 3 shore rights
épeler — to spell
épicerie f. — grocer's shop

– (*marchandises*) — groceries
épicier m. — grocer

épingler — to pin
épongement m. — skimming off, draining off
éponger (*pouvoir d'achat excédentaire*) — to skim off
épreuve f. (*imprimerie*) — (printer's) proof
1 – écrite et orale — 1 oral and written examination
2 à toute – — 2 foolproof
3 corriger des –s — 3 to read proofs
épuisement m. — exhaustion
– des réserves — – of the reserves
épuiser — to exhaust
1 – une lettre de crédit — 1 – a letter of credit
2 l'article est épuisé — 2 the article is out of stock
3 les coupons sont épuisés — 3 the coupon sheet is exhausted
4 le livre est épuisé — 4 the book is out of print
5 le stock est épuisé — 5 the stock is exhausted
équilibre m. — equilibrium, balance
1 garder l'– — 1 to keep the balance
2 perdre l'– — 2 to lose the balance
3 rétablir l'– — 3 to restore (redress) the balance, the equilibrium
4 rompre l'– — 4 to disturb the equilibrium
équilibrer — to balance

équipage m. — crew
équipe f. — shift
1 – de nuit — 1 night –
2 chef m. d'– — 2 foreman
3 travailler en 3 –s — 3 to work (in) 3 –s
équipement m. — equipment, outfit
– industriel — plant, industrial equipment
équiper — to equip, to outfit
équivalent adj. — equivalent
équivalent m. — equivalent
1 l'– en francs — 1 the – in francs
2 payer l'– — 2 to pay the –
équivaloir à — to be equivalent to
erreur f. — error, mistake
1 – de calcul — 1 mistake of (in) calculation, error in calculation
2 – typographique — 2 misprint, printer's error
3 par – — 3 by mistake, erroneously
4 sauf – — 4 if we are not mistaken
5 sauf – ou omission — 5 errors and omissions excepted

erroné / 146

6 une – s'est glissée dans

7 rectification *f.* d'une –
8 faire –
9 faire une –

10 induire en –
11 réparer une –

erroné
erronément
escale *f.*
  faire – dans un port (à)

escomptable
escompte *m.* (*remise*)
1 – au comptant, – de caisse
2 – sur marchandises, – remise, – d'usage
3 moins un – de 5 %

4 sans –
5 faire un – de 5 %
6 jouir d'un –
escompte *m.* (*banque*)
1 – en dedans, – rationnel

2 – en dehors, – commercial, – irrationnel
3 – hors banque
4 – officiel
5 – privé (voir – *hors banque*)
6 remis à l'–
7 banque *f.* d'–
8 bordereau *m.* d'–
9 conditions *f. pl.* –
10 courtier *m.* d'–
11 crédit *m.* d'–
12 frais *m. pl.* d'– (*agios*)
13 maison *f.* d'–
14 marché *m.* de l'–
15 politique *f.* d'–
16 promesse *f.* d'–
17 taux *m.* d'–
18 abaissement *m.* (réduction *f.*) du taux d'–
19 élévation *f.* (majoration *f.*) du taux d'–
20 abaisser (réduire) le taux d'–

21 élever (majorer) le taux d'–
22 prendre à l'–
23 remettre à l'–, présenter à l'–

6 an error has crept into

7 rectification of a mistake
8 to be wrong, to be mistaken
9 to make a mistake, to commit an error
10 to mislead
11 to rectify an error

erroneous, wrong
erroneously, by mistake
call, port of call
  to call at a port, to make a call at

discountable
discount
1 cash –, – for cash
2 trade –

3 less 5 % –

4 without –
5 to allow a – of 5 %
6 to enjoy a –
discount
1 true (arithmetical) –

2 bankers' –

3 private rate of –, market –
4 bank (rate of) –

6 sent for –
7 – bank
8 list of bills for –
9 – terms
10 – broker
11 – credit
12 – charges
13 – house
14 – market
15 – policy
16 – promise
17 – rate
18 lowering of the – rate

19 raising of the – rate

20 to lower the – rate

21 to raise the – rate
22 to take on –, to –
23 to tender for –

147 / escompter

escompter — to discount, to take on discount
1 – une hausse — 1 to discount (reckon upon, allow for) a rise
2 faire – — 2 to negotiate

escompteur *m.* — discounter
escroc *m.* — swindler
escroquerie *f.* — swindle
espacement *m.* — spacing
 barre *f.* d'– — space bar
espèces *f. pl.* — cash
1 – en caisse et en banque — 1 – in hand and at bankers
2 – monnayées — 2 coin, specie
3 en – sonnantes — 3 in hard –
4 avoir *m.* en – — 4 – assets
5 bordereau *m.* d'– — 5 specification
6 dividende *m.* en – — 6 – dividend
7 payement *m.* en – — 7 – payment
8 prestation *f.* en – — 8 payment in –
9 recettes *f. pl.* en – — 9 – receipts
10 titres *m. pl.* contre – — 10 shares for –
11 échanger des billets contre – — 11 to exchange notes for coin

espérer — to hope
1 nous osons – que — 1 we venture – that, we trust that
2 espérant que, — 2 hoping to
3 résultat espéré — 3 the result hoped for
espoir *m.* — hope
1 dans l'– que — 1 in the – that, hoping to
2 exprimer l'– — 2 to express the –
3 renoncer à tout – — 3 to abandon (relinquish) all –
essai *m.* — trial
1 à titre d'– — 1 on –, by way of –
2 balance *f.* d'– — 2 – balance
3 commande *f.* à titre d'– — 3 – order
4 envoi *m.* à titre d'– — 4 goods sent on –
5 vente *f.* à l'– — 5 sale on –
6 un mois à l'– (*emploi*) — 6 a month on –
7 faire un – — 7 to make a –
essayer — to try
essence *f.* — petrol, (*Amer.*) gasoline
1 pompe *f.* à – — 1 – pump
2 réservoir *m.* à – — 2 – (fuel) tank
3 faire le plein d'– — 3 to fill up with –
essences *f. pl.* — varieties of trees
essor *m.* — progress
1 – de l'industrie — 1 upward surge of industry
2 – économique — 2 economic –
3 prendre un grand – — 3 to make great strides

estampillage *m.* — stamping
par – des titres — by – the shares
estampille *f.* — stamp, mark
– de pesage — weight stamp
estampiller — to stamp
actions estampillées — stamped shares
estaries *f. pl.* — lay days
ester en justice — to go to law

capacité *f.* d'– — capacity to sue
estimation *f.* — estimate, valuation
1 – des frais — 1 estimate of charges
2 d'après une – approximative — 2 at a rough estimate
3 valeur *f.* d'– (estimative) — 3 appraised value
estimée *f.* **(lettre)** — esteemed letter
estimer — to estimate, to value
1 – à — 1 to estimate at
2 nous estimons que — 2 we think that
établir — to establish, to found
1 – un budget — 1 to draw up a budget
2 – un compte — 2 to make out (draw up) an account
3 – une maison de commerce — 3 to found a business
4 – une moyenne — 4 to average
5 – un prix — 5 to establish (fix) a price
6 – une quittance — 6 to make out a receipt
7 s'– dans une ville — 7 to settle in a town
8 s'– comme... — 8 to establish oneself as...
9 être établi à son compte — 9 to be in business for one's own account
10 établi à... (*entreprise*) — 10 established (situated) in...
établissement *m.* — establishment, foundation
1 – (*succursale*) — 1 branch
2 – (*de prix*) — 2 fixation
3 – de banque — 3 banking establishment
4 – d'un compte — 4 drawing up of an account
5 – du bilan — 5 drawing up of a balance sheet
6 – de crédit — 6 credit institution
7 – du prix de revient — 7 costing
8 – financier — 8 financial institution
9 – principal — 9 principal place of business, main establishment
10 droit *m.* d'– — 10 right of establishment
11 frais *m. pl.* de premier – — 11 initial expenses
12 liberté *f.* d'– — 12 freedom of establishment
étalage *m.* — window
1 à l'– — 1 in the –
2 avarié par l'– — 2 window-soiled, shopworn
3 concours *m.* d'– — 3 – dressing competition
4 éclairage *m.* d'– — 4 – illumination
5 être à l'– — 5 to be in the –
6 mettre à l'– — 6 to display
étalagiste *m.* — window dresser

étaler
1 marchandises étalées
2 – sur (*échelonner*)

étalon *m.* (*monnaie*)
1 étalon-argent
2 – boiteux
3 – de change-or
4 – de lingots-or
5 – de numéraire-or
6 – métallique
7 étalon-or
8 – -or de change (voir – *de change-or*)
9 – -or lingot (voir – *de lingots-or*)
10 étalon-papier
11 – unique
12 – de(s) valeur(s)
13 double –
14 abandon *m.* de l'– or

15 retour *m.* à l'– or

état *m.*
1 – Providence
2 banque *f.* d'–
3 contrôle *m.* de l'–
4 intervention *f.* de l'–

état *m.* (*situation*)
1 – de fortune
2 – des choses
3 – du marché
4 – d'innavigabilité (*navire*)
5 en – d'innavigabilité
6 – de navigabilité
7 en – de navigabilité
8 en bon –
9 en bon – et conditionnement apparents

10 en mauvais –
11 être en – de...
12 ne pas être en – de
13 mettre en –

état *m.* (*liste*)
1 – civil (*la condition*)
2 – civil (*bureau*)
3 officier *m.* de l'– civil
4 registre *m.* de l'– civil

5 – de caisse
6 – de compte

7 – des dettes actives et passives
8 – des frais, des dépenses

149 / étaler

to display
1 the goods displayed
2 to spread over

standard
1 silver –
2 limping (halting) –
3 gold exchange –
4 gold bullion –
5 gold specie –
6 metallic –
7 gold –

10 paper –
11 single –
12 – of value
13 double –
14 departure from the gold –

15 return to the gold –

state
1 welfare –
2 – bank, government bank
3 – supervision
4 – interference

state, condition
1 financial position
2 state of affairs
3 state of the market
4 unseaworthiness
5 unseaworthy
6 seaworthiness
7 seaworthy
8 in good condition
9 in apparent good order and condition

10 in bad condition
11 to be able (to be in the position) to
12 not to be able, to be unable
13 to enable

statement
1 civil status
2 registry office
3 mayor (**official**) acting as registrar
4 register of births, marriages and deaths

5 cash –
6 state (position) of the account

7 account of liabilities and assets
8 – of expenses

étatisation / 150

9 – des lieux	9 inventory of premises, of fixtures
10 – de mutation	10 list of staff transfers
11 – de payement	11 pay schedule
12 – de situation	12 position
13 – nominatif	13 list of names, nominal roll
14 – récapitulatif	14 recapitulative –
15 – trimestriel	15 quarterly –
étatisation *f.*	**nationalization**
étatiser	**to nationalize**
éteindre (*jur.*)	**to extinguish**
– une dette	– a debt
étendre	**to extend**
s'– sur (2 ans)	– over...
étendue *f.* (*dommage*)	**extent**
étiquetage *m.*	**labelling**
étiqueter	**to label**
étiquette *f.*	**label**
1 – annexe	1 enclosure –
2 – d'adresse	2 address –
3 – gommée	3 gummed –
étonnant	**surprising**
il n'est guère – que	it is not – that, no wonder that
étonnement *m.*	**astonishment**
à mon grand –	to my great –
étonner	**to astonish**
1 s'– de	1 to be astonished at
2 nous sommes étonnés que	2 we are astonished (surprised) that
étranger *m.*	**foreigner**
étranger *adj.*	**foreign**
1 à l'–	1 abroad
2 avoirs *m. pl.* à l'–	2 assets held abroad
3 capitaux –s	3 – capital
4 créances *f. pl.* à l'–	4 claims on foreign countries
5 dettes *f. pl.* envers l'–	5 external debts
6 emprunts contractés à l'–	6 external loan
7 langues étrangères	7 – languages
8 monnaie étrangère	8 – currency
9 représentant *m.* à l'–	9 representative abroad
10 transactions *f. pl.* avec l'–	10 foreign business
étroit (*marché*)	**limited, narrow**
être à l'–	to be in strained circumstances
étroitesse *f.* (*marché*)	**limitedness, narrowness**
étude *f.*	**study**
1 – d'avocat	1 solicitor's office
2 – de notaire	2 notary's office
3 mettre à l'–	3 to make a – of

151 / évaluation

évaluation (voir aussi *estimation*) f.	valuation
evaluer (voir aussi *estimer*)	to value
évasion f. de capitaux	flight (exodus) of capital
évasion fiscale	tax evasion
événement m.	event
attendre les –s	to assume an expectant attitude
éventuel	possible, contingent
réclamations –les	complaints, if any
éventuellement	on occasion, should the occasion arise, possibly, if necessary
éviction f.	eviction, dispossession
évolution f.	evolution
– des prix	trend (course) of prices
ex-coupon	ex coupon
ex-dividende	ex dividend
ex-droit	ex rights, ex claim, ex new
ex-magasin	ex works
ex-répartition	ex allotment
exact	exact, accurate
1 être – à payer	1 to be punctual in paying
2 c'est tout à fait –	2 that is quite correct
3 le montant –	3 the exact amount
exactitude f.	accuracy
– (*payer*)	punctuality
examen m. (*épreuve*)	examination
1 – concours	1 competitive –
2 – d'admission, – d'entrée	2 entrance –
3 – de passage	3 removing (end-of-year) –
4 – de sortie, – final	4 final –
5 sujet m. d'–	5 – paper
6 échouer à l'–	6 to fail in (at) an –
7 faire l'–	7 to examine
8 passer (subir) un –	8 to go in for an –
9 réussir à l'–	9 to pass an –
10 se présenter (soumettre) à un –	10 to go in for an –
examen m.	examination
1 – médical	1 medical –
2 – minutieux	2 close –
3 après – approfondi, après plus ample –	3 on closer (exhaustive) –
4 faire l'– de	4 to examine
5 soumettre à un –	5 to submit to an –
6 la question est à l'–	6 the matter is under –, consideration
examinateur m.	examiner
examiner	to examine
1 – une affaire	1 to investigate a matter
2 – des marchandises	2 – goods
3 – minutieusement	3 – closely, minutely
4 en examinant nos livres	4 on looking through (over) our books
excédent m.	surplus
1 – budgétaire	1 budget –

excéder / 152

2 – de bagages
3 – de caisse
4 – de charge
5 – de dépenses
6 – des exportations
7 – de mesure
8 – de poids
9 – de population
10 – de production
11 – de recettes

12 – monétaire
13 somme *f.* en –
excéder
1 – les espérances

2 les recettes excèdent les dépenses de...
excepté
exception *f.*
1 – à la règle
2 à l'– de
3 par –
4 sans –
5 les –s confirment la règle
6 faire –
exception *f.* (*jur.*)
 soulever une – contre
exceptionnel
1 cas –
2 mesure – le

exceptionnellement

exclure
exclusif
1 agent –
2 droit –
3 vente exclusive
exclusion *f.*
à l'– de

excuse *f.*
1 comme –
2 lettre *f.* d'–
3 faire (présenter) ses –s
4 veuillez agréer nos –s

excuser
1 – qqn de
2 s'– de
exécuter
1 s'– (*actionnaire*)

2 excess luggage (baggage)
3 cash –
4 excess freight
5 excess of expenditure
6 excess of exports, export –
7 overmeasure
8 excess weight
9 – population
10 – produce
11 – of receipts

12 glut of money
13 sum in excess
to exceed
1 – hopes, expectations

2 the receipts exceed the expenses by...

except, besides
exception
1 – to the rule
2 with the – of
3 by way of –
4 without –
5 the – proves the rule
6 to make an –
plea
 to take exception to, to put in a –
exceptional
1 – case
2 – measure

by way of exception, as an exception, exceptionally
to exclude
exclusive
1 sole agent
2 – right
3 – sale
exclusion
to the – of, exclusive of

excuse
1 in –
2 letter of apology
3 to apologize, to offer apologies
4 please accept (kindly accept) our apology
to excuse
1 – someone for
2 to apologize for
to execute
1 to pay up

153 / exécuteur testamentaire

2 – un acheteur

3 – un contrat
4 – des ordres de vente
5 – un testament
6 – un vendeur

exécuteur testamentaire *m.*
exécutrice testamentaire *f.*
exécution *f.*
 1 – (*bourse*)
 2 – d'un acheteur

 3 – d'un gage
 4 – d'un vendeur

 5 – forcée
 6 – parée

 7 en – des articles...
 8 mise *f.* à –
 9 prompte – d'un ordre
 10 travaux *m. pl.* en voie d'–
 11 commencer l'– de
 12 mettre à –
exécutoire
 1 titre *m.* –
 2 avoir force –
exemplaire *m.*
 1 – du capitaine
 2 – gratuit
 3 en double –
 4 en triple –
 5 connaissement *m.* rédigé en 3 –s

 6 lettre *f.* de change à plusieurs –s

exemple *m.*
 par –
exempt
 1 – d'accise
 2 – de tous droits
 3 – de tout impôt
 4 – de tous impôts et taxes présents et futurs
 5 – du timbre
exemption *f.*
 – d'impôts
exempter de
exercer
 1 – un contrôle
 2 – un droit
 3 – un droit d'option

2 to sell out against a buyer

3 – (perform) a contract
4 – selling orders
5 to carry out the provisions of a will
6 to buy in against a seller

executor
executrix
execution, carrying out
 1 buying in and selling out
 2 selling out against a buyer

 3 realization of a pledge
 4 buying in against a seller

 5 forced execution
 6 summary execution

 7 in pursuance of sections...
 8 execution
 9 prompt execution of an order
 10 work in progress
 11 to take in hand
 12 to carry into execution
executory
 1 writ of execution
 2 to be enforceable
copy
 1 captain's –
 2 free –
 3 in duplicate
 4 in triplicate
 5 bill of lading drawn in 3 copies

 6 bills of exchange in a set

example
 for instance
free of, exempt from
 1 exempt from excise duty
 2 duty-free, free of duty
 3 free of all tax, tax free
 4 free of (exempt from) duties present and future
 5 exempt from stamp duty
exemption, exoneration
 exemption from taxation
to exempt (exonerate) from
to exert
 1 to exercise control
 2 to exercise a right
 3 to exercise an option

4 – une influence sur
5 – une pression sur
6 – une profession
exercice *m.*
exercice *m.* (social)
 1 – 1964 attaché
 2 – budgétaire
 3 – clôturé le...
 4 – écoulé
 5 – en cours
 6 – fiscal
 7 – (passé) sous revue
 8 ex –
 9 dividende *m.* de l'– 1964
 10 rapport *m.* de l'– 1964

 11 solde reporté à nouveau sur l'– suivant
 12 solde reporté de l'– précédent

exiger
exigibilité *f.* (*dette*)
 faire face aux –s
exigible (*dette*)
 1 dépôt *m.* – sur demande, sans préavis
 2 passif *m.* –

existence *f.*
 1 minimum *m.* nécessaire à l'–
 2 moyens *m. pl.* d'–
existence *f.* (*stock*)
 1 –s en caisse
 2 – en effets de commerce
 3 – en magasin
exode *m.* de capitaux

exonération *f.* (voir aussi *exemption*)
exonérer (voir aussi *exempter*)
 1 – de responsabilité

 2 – un montant
 3 montant exonéré
exorbitant
expansion *f.*
 1 – coloniale
 2 – commerciale
 3 – de crédit
 4 – économique
 5 – monétaire
 6 taux *m.* de l'–
 7 freiner l'–
expédier un acte
expédier un navire (*douane*)

4 to exercise an influence on
5 – pressure upon
6 to carry on (exercise) a profession, exercise, practice
financial year, trading year
 1 cum dividend 1964
 2 budgetary year
 3 financial year ended...
 4 past year
 5 present business year
 6 fiscal year
 7 year under review
 8 ex dividend
 9 dividend for the year 1964
 10 report for the year ended Dec. 31, 1964
 11 balance carried forward to next account
 12 balance brought forward from last account
to claim, to demand
(re)payability
 to meet current liabilities
due
 1 deposit repayable on demand

 2 current liabilities
subsistence
 1 minimum of –, – level
 2 means of –, of support
stock
 1 –s in the till
 2 – of bills of exchange
 3 – in trade, – on hand
flight of capital

exoneration, exemption
to exempt, to exonerate
 1 to relieve of liability

 2 to exempt an amount
 3 exempted amount
exorbitant
expansion
 1 colonial –
 2 –of trade
 3 – of credit
 4 economic –
 5 monetary –
 6 – rate
 7 to check (restrain) the –
to make a copy of a deed
to clear a ship outwards

155 / expédier

expédier (*envoyer*)
 1 – le courrier
 2 – par bateau
 3 – par la poste
 4 – un télégramme
expéditeur *m.* (*lettre*)
 1 – (*marchandises*)
 2 – (*agent*)
expédition *f.* (*d'un acte*)

 1 en double –
 2 pour – conforme

 3 délivrer une –
expédition *f.* (*du navire douane*)
expédition *f.* (*envoi*)

 1 ,,– immédiate''
 2 ,,– le plus tôt possible''
 3 – par bateau
 4 – par chemin de fer
 5 – par la poste
 6 – de marchandises
 7 –s partielles sont autorisées

 8 –s partielles sont interdites
 9 ,,prompte –''
10 avis *m.* d'–
11 bordereau *m.* d'–
12 date *f.* de l'–
13 frais *m. pl.* d'–
14 instructions *f. pl.* d'–

15 maison *f.* d'–

16 mode *m.* d'–
17 service *m.* d'–

expéditionnaire *m.* (*commis*)
expérience *f.*
 1 – de longue date
 2 par –
 3 acquérir de l'–
expérimenté
expert *m.*
 1 – assermenté
 2 – comptable

 3 –s de Lloyd's (*nommés par le Lloyd*)
 4 – en écritures
 5 – financier
 6 – fiscal
 7 à dire d'–

to dispatch, to send
 1 to dispatch the post
 2 to ship
 3 to dispatch by post
 4 to send (dispatch) a telegram
sender
 1 consignor
 2 forwarding agent
copy

 1 in duplicate
 2 certified true –

 3 to deliver a –
clearance outwards
despatch

 1 immediately
 2 (shipment) as soon as possible
 3 shipment
 4 forwarding (–) by rail
 5 – by post
 6 – of goods
 7 part shipments permitted, allowed

 8 part shipments prohibited
 9 prompt shipment
10 forwarding advice
11 – note
12 date of –
13 forwarding charges
14 forwarding (shipping) instructions

15 forwarding agency

16 mode of forwarding, of shipment
17 delivery department

forwarding (shipping) clerk
experience
 1 many (long) year's –
 2 from –
 3 to gain –
experienced, skilled
expert
 1 sworn –
 2 chartered accountant

 3 Lloyd's surveyors
 4 handwriting expert
 5 financial –
 6 fiscal –
 7 according to – advice

expertise / 156

8 avis *m.* d'–
9 comité *m.* des –s

10 consulter un –

11 nommer un –
12 soumettre à un –

expertise *f.*

1 certificat *m.* d'–
2 frais *m. pl.* d'–
expertiser
expiration *f.*
1 à l'– du terme
2 après – de
3 date *f.* d'–
expirer
1 le contrat expire
2 le terme est expiré
exploit *m.* (*d'huissier*)
1 – de saisie
2 – de saisie-arrêt, d'opposition
3 – de saisie-exécution
4 signifier un – à qqn
exploitant *m.*
1 – (huissier –)

2 – de cinéma
3 – forestier
exploitation *f.* (voir aussi *entreprise*)

1 – (*péjoratif*)
2 – à ciel ouvert (*mine*)
3 – à outrance (*sol*)
4 – agricole
5 – commerciale
6 – d'un brevet

7 – des chemins de fer
8 – de cinémas
9 – des mines
10 – forestière
11 – industrielle
12 – souterraine (*mine*)
13 en pleine –
14 arrêt *m.* d'–
15 bénéfice *m.* d'–
16 capital *m.* d'–
17 chef *m.* d'–
18 coefficient *m.* d'–
19 compte *m.* d'–

8 – advice
9 – committee

10 to consult an –

11 to assign an –
12 to submit to an –

survey

1 surveyor's certificate
2 – expenses
to survey
expiration, expiry
1 on the expiration of the term
2 after the expiration of
3 expiry date
to expire
1 the contract expires, terminates
2 the term has expired
writ
1 – of arrest
2 garnishment
3 – of execution
4 to serve a – upon a person
operator, owner
1 process server

2 cinema proprietor, exhibitor
3 grower
working

1 exploitation, (*ouvriers*) sweating
2 open working
3 exhaustive cultivation
4 farming, agricultu al undertaking
5 commercial und rtaking, business
6 exploitation (utilization) of a patent
7 – of railways
8 operation of cinemas
9 – of mines, mining
10 exploitation of forests
11 industrial undertaking, concern
12 underground work
13 in – condition
14 closing down of works (plant)
15 trading profit
16 – capital
17 works (plant) manager
18 ratio of – expenditure
19 (trading) account

157 / exploiter

20 frais *m. pl.* d'– | 20 – expenses
21 lieu *m.* d'– | 21 place of business
22 matériel *m.* d'– | 22 – plant
23 mise *f.* en – | 23 putting into operation
24 pertes *f. pl.* d'– | 24 operating losses
25 résultats *m. pl.* d'– | 25 trading results
26 être en – | 26 to be in operation
27 mettre en – | 27 to put into operation

exploiter | **to work**
1 – les clients | 1 to exploit the customers
2 – un commerce | 2 to carry on a business
3 – une mine | 3 – a mine

exportateur *m.* | **exporter**
exportateur *adj.* | **exporting**
exportation *f.* | **export, exportation**
1 – de... en (vers)... | 1 export from... to...
2 – de capitaux | 2 export of capital
3 –s invisibles | 3 invisible –
4 articles *m. pl.* d'– | 4 export goods
5 autorisation *f.* d'– | 5 export permit
6 commerce *m.* d'– | 6 export trade
7 crédit *m.* d'– | 7 export credit
8 excédent *m.* d'– | 8 export surplus
9 licence *f.* d'– | 9 export licence
10 maison *f.* d'– | 10 export firm
11 port *m.* d'– | 11 port of exportation
12 possibilité *f.* d'– | 12 export possibility
13 prime *f.* d'– | 13 export bounty
14 restrictions *f. pl.* d'– | 14 export restrictions
15 taxe *f.* à l'– | 15 export duty

exporter | **to export**
– de... en (vers)... | – from... to...

exposant *m.* | **exhibitor**

exposé *m.* | **statement, account**
– des motifs | explanatory statement

exposer | **to exhibit**
1 – (*envoyer à une exposition*) | 1 –
2 articles exposés | 2 exhibits
3 les frais exposés | 3 expenses incurred

exposition *f.* (voir aussi *foire*) | **exhibition**
1 – ambulante | 1 travelling –
2 – universelle | 2 universal –
3 comité *m.* de l'– | 3 – committee
4 envoi *m.* (à une –) | 4 exhibit
5 salle *f.* d'– | 5 show room
6 stand *m.* d'– | 6 stand (at an –)
7 terrains *m. pl.* de l'– | 7 – grounds

exprès / 158

exprès
1 ,,–''
2 distribution *f.* par –
3 envoi *m.* par –
4 lettre *f.* par –
expressément
exprimer
1 – sa gratitude
2 – ses regrets
expropriation *f.*
– pour cause d'utilité publique
exproprier
expulsion *f.* d'un locataire
e_xtension *f.* (*tél.*)

extension *f.*
1 donner de l'– à (*affaires*)
2 prendre de l'–
extinction *f.*
1 – de bail
2 – d'une dette
3 – d'une hypothèque
extourne *f.*

extourner
– au crédit
extrait *m.*
1 – conforme
2 – de
3 – d'actes d'état civil
4 – de compte
5 – de compte-titres
6 – de votre compte arrêté au 31 décembre

7 – de mariage
8 – de naissance
9 – journalier

10 – mortuaire
extrajudiciaire
extraordinaire
assemblée *f.* –
extrinsèque

1 express
2 express delivery
3 express parcel
4 express letter
expressly
to express
1 – one's thanks
2 – one's regret
expropriation
– for public purposes
to expropriate
ejection (eviction) of a tenant
extension...

extension
1 to extend
2 to extend

1 termination of a lease
2 paying off of a debt
3 extinction of a mortgage
contraing, reversal

to contra, to write back
to recredit
extract
1 certified true –
2 abstract of
3 certificate   [account
4 abstract (extract, statement) of
5 statement of custodianship account
6 statement of your account made up to Dec. 31

7 (copy of) marriage certificate
8 (copy of) birth certificate
9 daily abstract, daily statement of account
10 certificate of death
extrajudicial
extraordinary
– meeting
extrinsic

F

fabricant *m.*
du – au consommateur
fabrication *f.*
1 – belge

manufacturer, maker
from producer to consumer
manufacture   [gian make
1 Belgian-made article, article of Bel-

2 – d'un faux document
3 – de la fausse monnaie
4 – en série
5 de – indigène
6 défaut *m.* de –
7 frais *m. pl.* de –
8 procédé *m.* de –
9 secret *m.* de –
fabrique *f.*
1 marque *f.* de –
2 prix *m.* de –
3 déposer une marque de –
fabriquer
face *f. (monnaie)*
face, faire –
1 – aux dépenses
2 – à ses engagements

facile
facilité *f.*
1 –s de crédit
2 –s de payement

3 demander des –s de payement
4 donner toutes les –s à...

5 pour plus de –
faciliter
façon *f. (prix)*
fac-similé *m.*
factage *m. (prix)*
1 – *(transport)*
2 entreprise *f.* de –
facteur *m.*
1 – des postes
2 – en douane
facteur *m. (élément)*
1 – coûts
2 –s de la production
3 au coût des –s
facture *f.*
1 – consulaire
2 – d'achat
3 – d'avoir, – de crédit
4 – de...
5 – de consignation
6 – de débit
7 – de vente
8 –s envoyées
9 – fictive
10 – finale
11 – originale
12 – provisoire

2 forging of a document
3 coining of counterfeit money
4 mass production
5 home-made
6 defect of manufacturing
7 manufacturing cost
8 manufacturing process
9 manufacturing secret
manufactory, factory
1 trade mark
2 makers' price, manufacturing cost
3 to register a trade mark
to manufacture
obverse, head side

1 to defray the expenses
2 to fulfil one's engagements

easy
easiness
1 line of credit
2 facilities for payment, easy terms

3 to ask for easy terms
4 to grant facilities to

5 for convenience sake
to facilitate
manufacturing cost
facsimile
carriage
1 parcels cartage
2 parcels delivery company

1 postman
2 customs agent, custom house broker
factor
1 cost –, – in costs
2 –s of production
3 at – costs
invoice, bill
1 consular invoice
2 purchase invoice
3 credit note
4 invoice of (for)
5 consignment invoice
6 debit note
7 sale invoice
8 outgoing invoices
9 pro forma invoice
10 final invoice
11 original invoice
12 provisional invoice

facturer / 160

13 —s reçues — 13 invoices inwards
14 — simulée — 14 pro forma invoice
15 selon — ci-jointe — 15 as per invoice inclosed
16 montant *m.* de la — — 16 invoice amount
17 prix *m.* de — — 17 invoice price
18 valeur *f.* de — — 18 invoice value
19 acquitter une — — 19 to receipt an invoice
20 envoyer une — — 20 to send an invoice
21 faire (dresser) une — — 21 to make out an invoice
22 présenter (remettre) une — — 22 to hand an invoice

facturer (à...) — **to invoice (to)**
1 machine *f.* à — — 1 invoicing (billing) machine
2 montant facturé — 2 amount invoiced

facturier *m.* (*employé*) — **invoice clerk**

facturier *m.* (*livre*) — **invoice book**
1 — d'entrée — 1 purchase book
2 — de sortie — 2 sales book

faculté *f.* — **right**
— de rachat, de réméré — option of repurchase

faculté *f.* (voir aussi *doublure*) — **option (to double, to treble** *etc.*)
1 — de lever double, — à la hausse — 1 call of more, buyer's option to double
2 — de lever quadruple — 2 call of three times more, buyer's option to quadruple
3 — de livrer double, — à la baisse — 3 put of more, seller's option to double
4 — de livrer triple — 4 put of twice more, seller's option to treble
5 donneur *m.* de — lever double — 5 taker for a call of more
6 donneur *m.* de — livrer double — 6 taker for a put of more
7 preneur *m.* de — de lever double — 7 giver for a call of more
8 preneur *m.* de — de livrer double — 8 giver for a put of more

facultés *f. pl.* (*assur.*) — **cargo**
1 — assurées — 1 insured goods
2 assurance *f.* sur — — 2 insurance of —
3 assurance *f.* sur corps et — — 3 insurance of hull and —
4 délaissement *m.* du navire et des — assurées — 4 abandonment of the ship and the insured goods

faible — **weak**
1 — quantité — 1 small quantity
2 tendance *f.* — — 2 — tendency

faiblir (*cours*) de... à... — **to weaken from... to...**

failli *m.* — **bankrupt**

1 – réhabilité
2 commerçant –
faillir
faillite f. (v. aussi *dividende*)

1 déclaration f. de –
2 intéressé dans une –
3 masse f. de la –
4 ouverture f. de la –
5 procédure f. de –
6 requête f. en déclaration de –
7 syndic m. de la –
8 déclarer en –
9 se déclarer en –
10 demander la déclaration en – de
11 être déclaré en –
12 être en –
13 faire –, tomber en –
faire (v. aussi *face*)
1 – des affaires avec
2 – des frais
3 – de son mieux
4 – le commerce de...
5 – un prix
6 cela fait ensemble combien ?
faire-part m.
1 – de décès

2 – de mariage

3 le présent avis tient lieu de –
fait en double

– à Bruxelles, le 30 août...

fait m.
1 – accompli
2 –s de guerre
3 au –
4 en – de...
5 il est un –
6 tout à –
falsification f.
1 – de chèque
2 – de traites
falsifier
– une signature
familial
1 allocation –e
2 salaire –
famille f.
1 – nombreuse
2 chef m. de –

1 discharged –
2 – trader
to fail, to become bankrupt
bankruptcy, failure

1 declaration of bankruptcy
2 involved in a bankruptcy
3 bankrupt's estate
4 opening of bankruptcy proceedings
5 bankruptcy proceedings
6 bankruptcy petition
7 assignee of a bankrupt's estate
8 to adjuge bankrupt
9 to file one's petition
10 to present a petition against
11 to be adjudicated bankrupt
12 to be bankrupt
13 to go bankrupt, to fail
to make
1 to do business with
2 to incur expenses
3 to do one's best
4 to deal in...
5 to realize a price
6 how much is that altogether ?
card, notice
1 notification of death

2 wedding card

3 no cards
done in duplicate

(given) – at Brussels on the 30th day of August

fact
1 accomplished –
2 acts of war
3 after all
4 in point of
5 it is a matter of –
6 quite, wholly
falsification
1 forgery of a cheque (check)
2 forging of bills
to falsify
to forge a signature
family...
1 – allowance
2 – wage
family
1 large –
2 householder, head of the –

farde / 162

```
3 conseil m. de –                          3 – council
4 membres m. pl. de la –                   4 members of the –
5 nom m. de –                              5 surname
```
farde *f.* (*Belg.*)   folder
fascicule *f.*   part, section
  par –   in parts
f.a.s.   free alongside ship

faussaire *m.*   forger
fausser   to falsify
faute *f.*   fault, mistake
  1 – de   1 for want of
  2 – de frappe, – dactylographique   2 typing error, typist's error
  3 – de payement   3 in default of (failing) payment
  4 – de preuves   4 for lack (in the absence) of evidence
  5 – d'impression   5 misprint, printer's error
  6 sans –   6 without fail
  7 corriger une –   7 to correct a mistake
  8 être en –   8 to be in fault
  9 faire une –   9 to make a mistake
faux   false, wrong
  1 fausse adresse   1 wrong address
  2 – chèque   2 forged cheque (check)
  3 – cours   3 nominal rate, made-up price
  4 fausse déclaration   4 false declaration
  5 – frais   5 incidental expenses
  6 – fret   6 forfeit freight
  7 fausse monnaie   7 base coin
  8 – monnayeur   8 false coiner
  9 – numéro   9 wrong number
  10 – poids   10 false weight
  11 fausse signature   11 false signature
faux *m.* **en écritures**   forgery
  faire un –   to commit a –, to forge
faveur *f.*   (*Amer.*) favor, (*Gr. Br.*) favour
  1 en – de   1 in – of
  2 en votre – (*avantage*)   2 to your advantage
  3 en votre – (*payement*)   3 in your –
  4 solde *m.* en votre –   4 balance in your –
  5 demander une – à...   5 to beg a – of...
  6 être en –   6 to be in –
  7 faire (accorder) une – à...   7 to do someone a –
favorable   (*Amer.*) favorable, (*Gr.Br.*) **favourable**
  1 cours *m.* –   1 – exchange
  2 perspectives *f. pl.* –s   2 – prospect, outlook
  3 dans le cas le plus –   3 at best
  4 à des conditions –s   4 on – terms
  5 profiter d'une occasion –   5 to make use of a – occasion
  6 trouver un accueil –   6 to meet with a – reception
favorablement   favourably, (*Amer.*) favorably
favoriser   to favour, (*Amer.*) to favor
  1 – le commerce   1 to encourage (promote) the trade

163 / félicitation

2 nous espérons que vous nous favoriserez de vos ordres [vorisée
3 clause *f.* de la nation la plus fa-
4 nation la plus favorisée
félicitation *f.*

1 lettre *f.* de –s

2 présenter des –s à l'occasion de

3 recevoir les –s
féliciter de...

femme *f.* **de journée**
fermage *m.*
ferme *f.*
1 bail *m.* à –
2 donner à –
3 prendre à –
ferme *adj.*
1 cours *m. pl.* –s
2 marché *m.* – (*pas à prime*)
3 offre *f.* –
4 prise *f.* – (*émission*)
5 prix *m. pl.* –s
6 tendance *f.* –
7 le marché est –
8 acheter – (*actions*)
9 être – en clôture (*actions*)
10 offrir –
11 prendre – (*emprunt*)
12 vendre – (*actions*)
fermer
1 – à (*actions*)
2 – à clef
3 – un compte
4 – une lettre
5 – une usine
6 nos bureaux seront fermés du... à...
7 les magasins ferment à 6 heures
fermeté *f.* (*marché, prix*)
fermeture *f.*
1 – des bureaux
2 – des guichets
3 – des magasins
4 – d'un compte
5 heure *f.* de –
ferraille *f.*
ferré
1 voie –e
2 par voie –e

2 we hope you will favour us (to be favo(u)red) with your orders

3 most-favo(u)red-nation clause
4 most favo(u)red nation
congratulation

1 congratulatory letter

2 to offer one's –s on...

3 to receive –s
to congratulate upon

charwoman
rent
lease
1 farming –
2 to –
3 to take on –
firm
1 – rates
2 – bargain, – deal
3 – offer
4 – underwriting
5 – prices
6 – tendency
7 the market is –, steady
8 to buy –
9 to close –
10 to offer –
11 to take –
12 to sell –
to close
1 – at
2 to lock
3 – an account
4 – a letter
5 – down a factory
6 our office will be closed from... to...

7 shops close (shut up) at 6 o'clock
firmness
closing
1 – of the office
2 – of the offices (to the public)
3 – of shops
4 – of an account
5 – time
scrap
rail... railway
1 railway
2 by rail

ferroviaire / 164

3 communication *f.* par voie –e ferroviaire
ferroviaires *pl.*
feu *m.*
 1 le – rouge (*circul.*)

 2 donner le – vert
feuille *f.* (v. aussi *coupons*)
 1 – (*imprimerie*)
 2 – de contribution, d'impôt
 3 – de coupons

 4 – de déclaration d'impôt
 5 – de liquidation (*bourse*)
 6 – d'émargement, – de paie
 7 – de présence (*réunion*)
 8 – de route
 9 – de transfert
 10 – de versement
 11 – volante
 12 à –s mobiles
feuillet *m.*
 à –s interchangeables
fiche *f.*
 classement *m.* par –s (répertoire sur –s)
fichier *m.*

fictif
 1 actif –
 2 dividende –
 3 facture fictive
 4 marché –
fidéicommis *m.*
 1 appelé *m.* au – (à la substitution)

 2 grevé *m.* de – (de substitution)
fidéicommissaire *m.*

fidéicommissaire *adj.*
 1 héritier *m.* –
 2 substitution *f.* –

fidéjusseur *m.*
fiduciaire *m.*
fiduciaire *adj.*
 1 administration *f.* –
 2 base *f.* –
 3 circulation *f.* –
 4 contrat *m.* –
 5 héritier *m.* –

 6 monnaie *f.* –
 7 opérations *f. pl.* –s

3 railway connection
rail..., railway...
railways, railway stocks
fire
 1 (to show) the red light

 2 to give the go ahead, (green light)
sheet
 1 –
 2 notice of assessment
 3 sheet of coupons

 4 (form of) return
 5 clearing –
 6 pay –, wages –
 7 attendance –, list of those present
 8 waybill
 9 transfer deed
 10 paying in slip
 11 loose –
 12 loose-leaf...
leaf
 loose–...
(index) card
 card index system
card index

sham, fictitious
 1 fictitious assets
 2 fictitious dividend, sham dividend
 3 pro forma invoice
 4 fictitious bargain
trust
 1 beneficiary of a –

 2 trustee, heir on –
beneficiary of a trust

fideicommissary
 1 – heir, feoffee in trust
 2 constitution of a trust

surety
fiduciary, trustee
fiduciary
 1 trusteeship
 2 trust basis
 3 – circulation
 4 trust indenture, trust deed
 5 – heir, trustee, heir on trust

 6 common money
 7 trust transactions

165 / figurer

8 société *f*. – | 8 accounting and auditing firm
figurer dans les livres | to figure (appear) in the books

filature *f*. | **spinning mill**
file, faire la – | to queue, (*Amer.*) to line up
filiale *f*. | **subsidiary company**
filière *f*. (*bourse*) | **connected contract**
1 – (*document*) | 1 string, (*valeurs*) trace

2 – tournante | 2 ring
3 arrêter une – | 3 to end a string
4 émettre une – | 4 to start a string
5 endosser une – | 5 to endorse a string
filigrane *m*. | **watermark**
fin *f*. | **end**
1 – courant, à la – du mois | 1 at the – of the present month
2 – janvier | 2 at the – of January
3 – prochain | 3 at the – of next month
4 à cette – | 4 to that –
5 aux –s de... | 5 for
6 en – de compte | 6 finally
7 vers la – de l'année | 7 towards the close (end) of the year
8 bonne – | 8 happy issue
9 sauf bonne – (*encaissement*) | 9 under reserve, under usual reserve

10 mener à bonne – | 10 to bring to an –
11 mettre – à | 11 to put an – to
12 prendre – | 12 to terminate
13 toucher à sa – | 13 to come (to draw) to an –
fin *adj*. | **fine**
or – | – gold
final | **end..., final**
1 règlement – | 1 final settlement
2 résultat – | 2 final result
3 solde – | 3 final balance
finalement | **finally, at last**
finance *f*. | **finance, world of finance**
1 les –s | 1 finances
2 ses –s (*moyens*) | 2 his resources, finances
3 les –s publiques | 3 public finance

4 la haute – | 4 high finance
5 administration *f*. des –s | 5 Finanz department
6 ministère *m*. des –s | 6 ministry of finance, (*Gr. Br.* Exchequer; *Amer.*, Treasury Department)
7 ministre *m*. des –s | 7 Minister of Finance (*Gr. Br.* Chancellor of the Exchequer; *Amer.* Secretary of the Treasury)
8 monde *m*. de la – | 8 finance, world of finance
9 moyennant – | 9 for a consideration
financement *m*. | **financing**
1 – au moyen de capitaux étrangers | 1 – with outside capital
2 – de l'exportation | 2 – of exports, export –

financer / 166

8 – par propres fonds
financer
financier *m.*
financier *adj.*
  1 aide financière
  2 crise financière
  3 difficultés financières, embarras –s
  4 entreprise financière
  5 gestion financière
  6 journal –
  7 mesures financières
  8 milieux –s
  9 monde –
  10 moyens –s
  11 opérations financières
  12 presse financière
  13 rubrique financière
  14 situation financière
finir
firme *f.*
  la – mentionnée sur le bulletin ci-joint
fisc *m.*
fiscal
  1 année –e
  2 autorités –es
  3 bague (bandelette) –e
  4 charges –es
  5 conseiller –
  6 dette –e
  7 droit –
  8 droits fiscaux
  9 loi –e
  10 privilèges fiscaux
  11 réforme –e
  12 timbre –
  13 serrer la vis –e
fiscalité *f.*
  1 – excessive
  2 poids *m.* de la –
fixation *f.*
fixe
  1 dépôt *m.* à terme –
  2 droit *m.* –
  3 prix *m. pl.* –s
  4 revenu *m.* –
  5 valeurs *f. pl.* à intérêt –
fixe *m.*
fixer
  1 – les conditions
  2 – une date

8 self –
to finance
financier
financial
  1 – assistance
  2 – crisis
  3 – difficulties, embarrassments
  4 – enterprise
  5 – conduct of finances, – management
  6 – paper
  7 – measures
  8 – circles
  9 – world
  10 – means
  11 – operations
  12 – press
  13 – part
  14 – position
to end
firm
  the – mentioned on the enclosed slip

fiscal (revenue) authorities
fiscal, revenue...
  1 fiscal year, tax year
  2 taxation authorities
  3 fiscal (revenue) band
  4 fiscal charges
  5 tax consultant
  6 tax liability
  7 fiscal law
  8 fiscal duties, fiscal taxes
  9 fiscal law
  10 tax privileges
  11 tax reform
  12 revenue stamp
  13 to turn the tax screw
fiscality
  1 excessive taxation
  2 burden of taxation, tax burden
fixing
fixed
  1 – deposit
  2 – duty
  3 – prices
  4 – income
  5 –interest securities
fixed salary
to fix
  1 – (stipulate) the terms
  2 – a date

167 / fléchir

3 – un prix
fléchir (*cours*)

fléchissement *m.*
flexibilité *f.* (*taux*)
flexible (*taux, cours*)
florin *m.*
– hollandais
100.000 –s
flot, à –
1 à terre ou –
2 remettre –
3 vendre –
flottant
1 dette –e
2 dock –
3 grue –e
4 marchandises –es, sous voile
5 police –e
flotte *f.*
– commerciale, marchande
fluctuation *f.*
1 –s de conjoncture
2 –s des prix
3 –s monétaires
4 –s saisonnières
5 éprouver (subir) des –s
6 sujet à des –s
fluctuer
– entre... et...   [*cépissé*]
fluvial (voir aussi *connaissement, ré-*
par la voie –e
flux *m.*
1 – monétaire
2 – réel
foi *f.*
1 de bonne –
2 de mauvaise –
3 en – de quoi

4 acheteur *m.* de bonne –
5 porteur *m.* de bonne –
6 de source digne de –
7 faire –
8 les 2 textes faisant également –

foire *f.* (voir aussi *exposition*)
1 – commerciale
2 – d'automne
3 – d'échantillons
4 – de printemps
5 – internationale de Bruxelles
6 administration de la –

3 – a price
to sag, to droop, to give away

sagging, drooping
flexibility
flexible
florin, guilder
Netherlands –
100.000 –s
afloat
1 ashore or –
2 to refloat
3 to sell –
floating
1 – debt
2 – dock
3 – derrick
4 goods afloat, on passage
5 – policy
fleet
merchant –
fluctuation
1 cyclical –s
2 price –s
3 –s of currency
4 seasonal –s
5 to undergo –s
6 liable (subject) to –s
to fluctuate
– between... and...
fluvial, river...
by inland waterways
flow
1 – of money
2 – of goods
faith
1 in good –, bona fide
2 in bad –, mala fide
3 in witness whereof

4 purchaser in good –, bona fide buyer
5 holder in good –
6 from a reliable source
7 to attest, to have probatory force
8 both texts being equally authentic

fair
1 commercial –
2 autumn –
3 sample –
4 spring –
5 Brussels International –
6 – management committee

fois / 168

  7 bâtiments *m. pl.* de la –
  8 stand *m.* de –
  9 visiteur *m.* de la –
fois
  1 une –
  2 deux –
  3 trois –
  4 une – pour toutes
  5 payement *m.* en une –
  6 payer en une –
  7 souscrit plusieurs –
folio *m.*
foliotage *m.*
folioter
folioteuse *f.*
foncier
  1 crédit –
  2 impôt –
  3 propriétaire –
  4 propriété foncière
  5 rente foncière
fonction *f.*
  1 les –s de président
  2 entrée *f.* en –
  3 entrer en –
  4 être en –
  5 rester en –
  6 – commerciale
fonctionnaire *m.*
fondateur *m.*
  part *f.* de –
fondation *f.*
fondé
fondé *m.* de pouvoir

fondement *m.*
  1 – juridique
  2 dénué de tout –
fonder
  1 – une dette
  2 – une maison de commerce
  3 – une société
  4 fondé en 1903
fonds *m.*
  1 – d'amortissement
  2 – d'assurance
  3 – de chômage
  4 – d'égalisation des changes
  5 – de garantie
  6 – de grève
  7 – de péréquation
  8 – (commun) de placement

  7 exhibition building
  8 exhibition stand
  9 visitor to the –
time
  1 once
  2 twice
  3 three –s
  4 once for all
  5 payment in full, in one amount
  6 to pay in a single sum
  7 subscribed several –s over
folio
foliation
to foliate, to folio
numbering machine
land..., landed
  1 land bank
  2 land tax
  3 landed proprietor
  4 landed property
  5 ground rent
function
  1 the duties (–s) of a chairman
  2 assumption of one's office, duties
  3 to enter upon one's office, duties
  4 to hold office
  5 to remain (continue) in office
  6 – of trade
official
founder
  founder's share
foundation
well-founded
attorney, proxy (holder), signing (managing, confidential) clerk
base
  1 jurisdictional basis
  2 groundless, without foundation
to found
  1 – a debt
  2 – a business
  3 to form (establish) a society
  4 established in 1903
fund
  1 sinking –
  2 insurance –
  3 unemployment –
  4 exchange equalization –
  5 guarantee –
  6 strike –
  7 equalization –
  8 mutual –, investment trust

169 / fonds

9 – de placement à capital fixe | 9 closed end investment trust
10 – de placement à capital variable | 10 open end investment trust
11 – de prévoyance | 11 contingency –
12 – de prévoyance (au profit) du personnel | 12 staff provident –
13 – de renouvellement | 13 renewal –
14 – de réserve | 14 reserve –
15 – de roulement | 15 working capital
16 – de secours | 16 relief –
17 – de stabilisation monétaire | 17 currency stabilization –
18 – en caisse | 18 cash in hand
19 – Monétaire International | 19 International Monetary Fund
20 – nécessaires | 20 – required, necessary –s
21 – secret | 21 secret –
22 – social | 22 partnership –s, company's –s
23 à – perdu | 23 à fonds perdu
24 appel *m*. de – (voir aussi *appel*) | 24 call (for –s) upon shareholders
25 bailleur *m*. de – | 25 money lender
26 mise *f*. de – | 26 capital invested, stake, outlay
27 placement *m*. à – perdu | 27 doubtful investment
28 être en – | 28 to be in –s
29 faire les – de... | 29 to supply the capital for
30 fournir les – | 30 to furnish –s
31 placer à – perdu | 31 to invest in a life annuity

fonds (*valeurs*) | **funds**
1 – consolidés | 1 consols
2 – d'état | 2 Government stocks
3 – publics | 3 public –
4 détenteur *m*. de – publics | 4 fundholder

fonds de commerce *m*. | **business, goodwill**
1 acheter un – | 1 to buy a business, a goodwill
2 vendre un – | 2 to sell a business (goodwill)

fonds (*de terre*) *m*. | **land, estate**
1 – assujetti (servant) | 1 servient tenement
2 – dominant | 2 dominant tenement

fongible | **fungible**

forcé (voir aussi *épargne*) | **forced**
1 cours – | 1 – rate of exchange
2 emprunt – | 2 compulsory loan
3 vente –e | 3 – sale
4 nous nous voyons –s de | 4 we are – (compelled) to...

force *f*. | **force**
1 majeure | 1 force majeure
2 – probante | 2 probatory –
3 par la – des choses | 3 by the – of circumstances

4 acquérir – de loi
5 passer en – de chose jugée

forclore
forclusion *f.*
forfait *m.*
1 endossement *m.* à –

2 prix *m.* à –
3 somme fixée à –
4 travail *m.* à –
5 acheter à –
6 travailler à –
forfaitaire
1 prix *m.* –
2 somme *f.* –
formalité *f.*
1 –s nécessaires, requises
2 exempt de –s
3 avec dispense de toutes les –s que la loi autorise à supprimer
4 accomplir (remplir) les –s

5 être sujet à une –
format *m.*
– de poche
formation *f.*
1 – du marché des capitaux
2 – des prix
3 – de réserves
4 – d'une société

5 – professionnelle
forme *f.*
1 en bonne et due –

2 pour la –
3 sous – de
4 vice *m.* de –
formel
1 ordre –
2 refus –
formellement
former
1 – des réserves
2 – une société
3 se – une opinion
formulaire *m.* (*carnet*)
– (*Belg.*) (*formule*)
formule *f.* (*Belg.* formulaire)
1 – de chèque
2 – de réponse
3 – de télégramme

4 to obtain – of law
5 to become final, to become res judicata
to estop
estoppage
contract
1 endorsement without recourse

2 – price, agreed price
3 agreed sum, lump sum
4 work by –
5 to buy by the lump
6 to work by the job (by the piece)
by contract, agreed
1 agreed price, contract price
2 lump sum
formality
1 necessary formalities
2 free from –
3 with exemption from all formalities that may legally be waived
4 to comply with the formalities, to observe (fulfil) the formalities
5 to be subject to a –
size
pocket –
formation
1 – of a capital market
2 determination of prices
3 building up of reserves
4 – of a company

5 vocational training
form
1 in due –

2 for form's sake
3 in the shape of, in... –
4 informality, faulty drafting
formal
1 strict order
2 – (absolute) refusal
formally
to form
1 to build up reserves
2 – (constitute) a company
3 – an opinion
formulary
form
form
1 cheque –
2 reply –
3 telegram –

4 – en blanc
5 – imprimée
6 remplir une –
formule *f.* (*phrase*)
1 – de début
2 – de politesse (*lettre*)
3 – finale
formuler
– des objections
fort
1 –e commande
2 –e hausse
3 –e somme
4 prix –

5 se faire – de
6 se porter – pour
fortune *f.*
1 – immobilière

2 – mobilière
3 – nationale
4 élément *m.* de –
5 état *m.* de –

6 perte *f.* de –
7 avoir de la –

8 faire –
fortunes *f. pl.* de mer (*assur.*)
fournir
1 – à la dépense, aux frais
2 – aux besoins de
3 – caution
4 – un chèque sur
5 – une couverture
6 – en nantissement
7 – des fonds
8 – la preuve
9 – des renseignements
10 – une traite sur
11 – sur
12 se – chez

fournissement *m.* (*apport*)
fournisseur *m.*
– de la Cour
fourniture *f.*
1 –s
2 –s de bureau
fraction *f.*
1 – décimale
2 – ordinaire

171 / formule

4 blank –
5 printed –
6 to fill up a –
form, formula
1 opening formula, sentence
2 complimentary close
3 formal ending
to formulate
to raise objections
strong
1 large (big) order
2 big rise
3 big sum, large amount
4 full price

5 to take it upon oneself to...
6 to answer for...
fortune
1 immovable property

2 personalty, personal property
3 national wealth
4 item of property
5 financial position, financial status

6 loss of wealth
7 to be well off, to be a person of means

8 to make a –
perils of the sea
to furnish
1 to contribute to the expense
2 to provide for the needs
3 to give security
4 to draw a cheque (check) upon
5 to provide cover
6 to lodge as collateral   [finance
7 to provide (supply) with funds, to
8 – evidence
9 to supply (furnish) information
10 to draw a bill on
11 to draw on
12 to be a customer of

contribution
supplier, dealer
purveyor to H. M. the Queen (King)
supplying
1 requisites
2 stationery, office requisites
fraction
1 decimal –
2 vulgar (common) –

fractionnaire / 172

3 – d'action
4 par 100 fr. ou – de 100 fr.

fractionnaire, nombre –
fractionnement *m.* (*actions*)
fractionner (*actions*)
fragile
„–"
frais *m. pl.*
 1 – accessoires
 2 – accidentels (faux –)
 3 – compris, – inclus

 4 – d'acquisition
 5 – d'administration
 6 – de banque
 7 – de bureau
 8 – de chauffage
 9 – d'éclairage
 10 – de confection (*titres*)
 11 – de constitution
 12 – de course
 13 – de déménagement
 14 – de déplacement

 15 – de douane
 16 – de fabrication
 17 – de manutention
 18 – d'emballage
 19 – d'emmagasinage
 20 – d'encaissement
 21 – **d'entrepôt**
 22 – d'entretien

 23 – **d'envoi**
 24 – de justice
 25 – de port
 26 – de premier établissement
 27 – de protêt
 28 – de publicité
 29 – de remboursement
 30 – de remise en état
 31 – de représentation

 32 – de sauvetage
 33 – d'escompte
 34 – de séjour (*d'hôtel*)
 35 – de stationnement (*wagon*)
 36 – de téléphone
 37 – de transbordement
 38 – de transport
 39 – de voyage
 40 – d'expédition

3 – of share
4 for each 100 fr. or fractional part thereof, or – of 100 fr.

fractional number
splitting
to split
fragile
 –, glass, with care
charges, expenses
 1 accessory (additional) –
 2 incidental expenses
 3 including all charges, charges included

 4 cost of acquisition
 5 administrative expenses, costs
 6 bank charges
 7 office expenses
 8 heating expenses
 9 lighting expenses
 10 cost of printing
 11 formation expenses
 12 porterage
 13 removal expenses
 14 travelling expenses, (*choses*) removal expenses

 15 customs charges
 16 manufacturing cost
 17 handling costs
 18 packing charges
 19 warehouse charges
 20 collecting charges
 21 warehousing –
 22 upkeep expenses

 23 forwarding –
 24 law costs
 25 postage
 26 initial expenses
 27 protest charges
 28 advertising costs
 29 cash-on-delivery charges
 30 reconditioning expenses
 31 expenses of (official) entertainment

 32 salvage charges
 33 discount charges
 34 hotel expenses
 35 demurrage (charge)
 36 telephone –
 37 transhipment –
 38 cost of carriage
 39 travelling expenses
 40 forwarding charges

173 / franc

41 – d'exploitation
42 – d'impression
43 – divers
44 – extraordinaires
45 – fixes
46 – généraux

47 – inclus

48 – non compris

49 à – communs
50 à grands –
51 à nos –
52 à peu de –

53 à propres –
54 aux – de
55 aux – du perdant

56 déduction faite de tous les –
57 faux –
58 menus –
59 plus les – (voir – *non compris*)
60 sans –
61 y compris les – (voir – *inclus*)
62 augmentation *f.* des –
63 centre *m.* de –
64 compte *m.* de –
65 évaluation *f.* de –
66 note *f.* de –
67 réduction *f.* des –
68 condamner aux –
69 contribuer aux –
70 entraîner des –
71 faire de grands –
72 faire face aux –
73 intervenir dans les –
74 mettre en –
75 occasionner des –
76 rembourser les –
77 rentrer dans ses –
78 répartir les –
79 se mettre en –
80 supporter les –
franc (voir aussi *franco*)
1 – d'avarie(s)
2 – d'avaries au-dessous de 3 %
3 – d'avaries communes
4 – de toute avarie
5 – de capture et de saisie

6 – de casse

41 working expenses
42 cost of printing
43 sundry expenses
44 extra charges
45 fixed (standing) charges
46 general expenses, overhead expenses, overheads
47 including all charges, charges included
48 exclusive expenses

49 at joint cost
50 at a great expense
51 at our expense
52 at a small expense, at a moderate charge
53 at one's expense
54 at the expense of
55 at the loser's risk

56 all charges deducted
57 incidental expenses
58 out-of-pocket expenses

60 free of charge

62 increase of cost
63 cost center
64 account of charges
65 estimate of the cost
66 note of charges
67 diminution of the expenses
68 to condemn to the costs
69 to contribute to the expenses
70 to involve expenses
71 to incur heavy expenses
72 to defray the expenses
73 to contribute to the expense
74 to put to expenses
75 to cause expenses
76 to reimburse (refund) the expense
77 to recover one's expenses
78 to apportion the expenses
79 to go to expense
80 to bear the expenses
free
1 – of (from) average
2 – from average under 3 %
3 – of general average
4 – of all average
5 – from capture, seizure and detention
6 – from breakage

franc / 174

7 – de commission
8 – de port
9 – de port (*poste*)
10 – de tous droits (frais)
11 – de tout droit de douane
12 – de tous impôts et taxes présents et futurs
13 – d'impôts
14 port –
15 trois jours –s
16 zone franche

franc *m.*
1 – belge
2 – français
3 – or
4 – papier
5 – suisse

franchise *f.*
1 – à déduire
2 – de bagages, – de poids
3 – douanière
4 – postale
5 la – est atteinte

6 en – (*douane*)
7 franc d'avaries au-dessous de la –

franco (voir aussi *franc*)
1 – Rotterdam
2 – à bord
3 – à bord du navire dans le port de départ
4 – à domicile
5 – bord-bord
6 – (de) commission
7 – de douane
8 – de fret et de droits
9 – d'emballage
10 – de port
11 – de port (*poste*)
12 – de tous frais
13 – gare...
14 – le long du navire

15 – quai...
16 – rendu
17 – (sur) wagon

frappe *f.*
1 – libre
2 – douce (*machine à écrire*)

frapper
1 – d'une amende

---

7 – of commission
8 carriage paid
9 post –
10 – of all charges
11 duty –
12 – from present and future taxes
13 tax –
14 – port
15 three clear days
16 – zone

franc
1 Belgian –
2 French –
3 gold –
4 paper –
5 Swiss –

exemption, freedom
1 deductible franchise
2 free luggage (baggage) allowance
3 exemption from (customs) duty
4 exemption from postal duty
5 the average touches the margin

6 free of duty
7 free of average under the franchise

free
1 – Rotterdam
2 – on board
3 – on board the ship in the port of departure
4 – domicile, carriage paid
5 free in and out
6 – of commission
7 – of customs duties
8 freight and duty paid
9 packing free
10 carriage paid
11 post –
12 – of all charges
13 – station...
14 – alongside ship

15 – on quay
16 – delivered
17 – on rail, free on truck

coinage, minting
1 free coinage
2 light touch

1 to fine

2 – d'un impôt
3 – de la monnaie
4 – de nullité
fraude *f.*
1 – fiscale
2 commettre une –
3 introduire en –
frauduleux
freiner
frère *m.*
..., –s
fret *m.* (*prix, cargaison*)
1 – à forfait
2 – à l'aller
3 – à payer d'avance
4 – au long cours
5 – au temps, – à terme
6 – au voyage
7 – de distance, – proportionnel
8 – de retour
9 – mort, – sur le vide
10 – payable d'avance
11 – payé
12 – payé d'avance
13 – suivant encombrement
14 – supplémentaire
15 assurance *f.* sur le –
16 contrat *m.* du –
17 marché *m.* des –s
18 note *f.* de –
19 taux *m.* du –
20 donner à – (*navire*)
21 prendre à –
22 prendre du –
fréter
fréteur *m.*
– et affréteur
frontière *f.*
fuite *f.* de capitaux
fusion *f.*, **fusionnement** *m.*

– bancaire
fusionner

1 – deux sociétés

2 se –
fût *m.*
1 –s vides
2 en –s

2 to tax
3 to coin
4 to render void
fraud
1 tax dodging
2 to commit a –
3 to smuggle in
fraudulent
to check, to restrain
brother
..., brothers
freight
1 through –
2 outward –
3 – to be prepaid
4 ocean –
5 time –
6 voyage –
7 distance –, pro rata –
8 homeward (return) –
9 dead –
10 – payable in advance, prepayable
11 – paid
12 – prepaid
13 measurement –
14 additional –, extra –
15 – insurance
16 – contract
17 – market
18 – note
19 – rate
20 to – out
21 to charter a ship
22 to take in –
to freight (out)
shipowner
 owner and charterer
frontier
flight of capital
fusion, merging, amalgamation

 bank merger, banking amalgamation
to fuse, to merge, to amalgamate

1 to amalgamate two companies

2 to amalgamate, to fuse, to merge
cask, barrel
1 empties
2 in casks, in barrels

G

gabarit *m.* de chargement	loading gauge
gâcher (*le marché*)	to spoil
gagé	pledged
gage *m.*	pledge, security
1 – immobilier	1 pledge of real property
2 – mobilier	2 pledge of movables
3 – non retiré	3 unredeemed pledge
4 affecté en –	4 set aside as pledge
5 complément *m.* de –	5 additional pledge
6 dépréciation *f.* du –	6 depreciation of the pledge
7 détenteur *m.* du –	7 pledgee
8 donneur *m.* du –	8 pledger
9 estimation *f.* du –	9 valuation of the pledge
10 emprunteur *m.* sur –	10 pledger, pledgor
11 exécution (*réalisation f.*) du –	11 realization of the pledge
12 mise *f.* en –	12 pledging, pawning
13 prêteur *m.* sur –	13 pledgee, pawnbroker
14 détenir en –	14 to hold in pledge
15 donner en –	15 to pledge, to put in pledge
16 emprunter sur –	16 to borrow on pledge
17 mettre en –	17 to give (put) in pledge
18 prêter sur –	18 to lend upon pledge
19 retirer un –	19 to redeem a pledge
20 suppléer au –	20 to supplement the pledge
gager (*mettre en gage*)	to pledge, to pawn
susceptible d'être gagé	acceptable as collateral
gager (*payer*)	to pay wages to
gages *m. pl.*	wages
être aux – de	to be in the pay of
gageur *m.*	pledger, pledgor, pawner
gagiste, créancier –	pawnee, pledgee, secured creditor
gagnant *m.*	winner
numéro –	winning number, –
gagner	to win
1 – de l'argent	1 to earn money
2 – un lot	2 to draw a prize
3 – 5 points	3 to gain 5 points
4 – un procès	4 – a case
5 – du temps	5 – time
6 – sa vie	6 to earn one's living
7 – qqn pour	7 – over someone to
8 – beaucoup sur...	8 to have (make) large profit on
9 – gros	9 to earn (make) big money
10 il gagne 7.000 francs par mois	10 he earns 7000 francs a month
gagneur *m.*	gainer, winner

gain *m.* (voir aussi *salaire*)
1 – de quelques points, (*actions*)
2 – de temps
3 réalisation *f.* d'un –
4 réaliser de gros –s

garage *m.*
garagiste *m.*
garant *m.*
1 – solidaire
2 je me porte – de…
3 se porter (rendre) – pour qqn

garantie *f.*
1 – (*émission*)
2 – de banque
3 – de bonne fin (*d'un effet*)

4 – de crédit à l'exportation

5 – de l'État
6 – de solvabilité
7 –s données
8 – personnelle
9 –s reçues de tiers (*bilan*)
10 avec 1 an de –

11 sans – de notre part
12 sous la – de l'État

13 avance *f.* contre –
14 commission *f.* de – (*émission*)
15 contrat *m.* de –
16 fonds *m.* de –
17 lettre *f.* de – (*connaissement*)
18 syndicat *m.* de – (*émission*)

19 titres déposés en –
20 ,,valeur –''
21 fournir une –

garantir
1 – une émission
2 – par hypothèque

3 garanti pur
4 garanti sur facture
garçon *m.* de bureau
garçon *m.* de course(s)
garçon *m.* de recette(s)
garde *f.* (en dépôt)
1 – (en dépôt) de titres
2 droit *m.* de –
3 déposer des titres en –
4 mettre en – contre

profit
1 a gain of a few points
2 saving of time
3 realization of –s
4 to make large –s

garage
garageholder
guarantor, surety
1 joint surety
2 I can vouch for
3 to become a surety for

[surety
guarantee, guaranty, security,
1 underwriting
2 bank guaranty
3 guarantee of the protection (meeting) of a bill

4 export credits guarantee

5 state (government) guarantee
6 guarantee of solvency
7 guarantees given, granted
8 personal security
9 guarantees received
10 guaranteed (with guarantee) for 1 year, under one year's guarantee
11 without guarantee on our part
12 under government guarantee, state-guaranteed
13 advance against security
14 underwriting commission
15 contract of guarantee
16 guarantee fund
17 letter of indemnity
18 underwriting syndicate, underwriters

19 stocks lodged as security
20 value as security
21 to give a guarantee
to guarantee
1 to underwrite an issue
2 to secure by mortgage

3 warranted pure
4 guarantee on invoice
office messenger
errand boy, messenger boy
collecting clerk, bank messenger
safe custody
1 – of securities
2 charge for –
3 to place securities in –
4 to warn against

garde-meuble / 178

5 prendre des titres en –
garde-meuble *m.*

garder
gare *f.*
 1 – d'arrivée
 2 – de chemin de fer
 3 – de départ, – d'expédition
 4 – de destination
 5 – de réception
 6 – de tête de ligne
 7 – de triage
 8 – des (aux) marchandises
 9 – frontière
 10 – intermédiaire
 11 – maritime
 12 – restante, en –
 13 – terminus
 14 chef *m.* de –
gaspillage *m.*
 – de temps et d'argent
gaspiller
gâter
 – le marché
Gatt *m.* (Accord général sur les tarifs douaniers et le commerce)
gaz *m.*
 consommation *f.* de –
gelé (*crédit*)
gêne pécuniaire *f.*
général
 1 d'une façon –e
 2 en –
genre *m.*
 1 ce – d'affaires
 2 de ce –
 3 de tout –
 4 du dernier –
gens d'affaires *m. pl.*
gens de maison *m. pl.*
gens de mer *m. pl.*
géographie économique *f.*
gérance *f.*
gérant *m.*

 1 – d'affaires
 2 directeur – *m.*
gérante *f.*
gérer
 – en bon père de famille

gestion *f.*
 1 – d'affaires

5 to accept securities in custody
furniture repository

to keep
station
 1 – of arrival
 2 railway –
 3 – of departure, forwarding –
 4 – of destination
 5 receiving –
 6 terminal –
 7 marshalling yard
 8 goods –
 9 frontier –
 10 intermediate –
 11 harbo(u)r –
 12 to be called for
 13 terminal –
 14 stationmaster
waste
 – of time and money
to waste
to spoil
 – the market
Gatt (General Agreement on Tariffs and Trade)
gas
 – consumption
frozen
pecuniary (financial) difficulties
general
 1 in a – way
 2 in –
kind
 1 this line (–) of business
 2 of this nature
 3 of all –, of every description
 4 of the latest fashion
business men
domestic staff, servants
seamen
economic geography
management
manager

 1 business –
 2 managing director
manageress
to manage, to run
 to act as a prudent administrator

management
 1 – (conduct) of affairs

179 / global

2 – de biens, de fortune
3 – d'entreprise
4 séminaire *m.* pour la – d'entreprise
5 – de portefeuille

6 – directe

7 – financière
8 mauvaise –
9 frais *m. pl.* de –
10 rapport *m.* de –

global
1 estimation –e
2 montant –
gold-point *m.*
1 – d'entrée
2 – de sortie
3 atteindre le –
gomme (à effacer) *f.*
1 – à crayon
2 – à encre
3 – pour machine à écrire
4 affaires *f. pl.* à la –
gommé
1 à bord –
2 enveloppe –e
3 étiquette –e
gonflement *m.*
– du volume du crédit
gonfler
se –
goulot *m.* **d'étranglement**
goût *m.*
1 dans ce –
2 avoir un – de...
3 c'est une affaire de –
gouverne, pour votre –

gouvernement *m.*
gouverneur *m.*
– de la banque
grâce *f.*
1 – à
2 délai *m.* (jours) de –
gracieux, à titre –
grand
1 –e banque
2 –e ville
3 – en – nombre
grand livre *m.*
1 – à feuilles mobiles

2 – of property
3 business management
4 business management seminar
5 – of securities

6 direct –

7 financial management
8 mismanagement
9 administrative expenses
10 report, annual report

total
1 rough estimate
2 – amount
gold point
1 import –, incoming –
2 export –, outgoing –
3 to reach the –
india-rubber, eraser
1 pencil eraser
2 ink eraser
3 typewriter eraser
4 bogus transactions
gummed
1 with – edge
2 – envelope
3 – label
inflation, swelling
inflation of the volume of credit
to inflate, to increase, to swell
to swell
bottleneck
taste
1 of that sort
2 to – like
3 it is a matter of –
for your guidance

government
governor
– of the bank

1 thanks to
2 days of grace
gratuitously
big, large
1 big bank
2 large (big) town
3 in large numbers
ledger
1 loose-leaf –

grand magasin / 180

2 – de la dette publique
3 – des valeurs
4 – général
5 compte *m.* du –
grand magasin *m.*
graphique *m.*
graphique, industrie –
gratification *f.*
 – de Noël
gratis
grattage *m.*
gratter
grattoir *m.*
gratuit (à titre –)
 1 entrée –e
 2 prêt –
 3 remise –e
 4 ... est –
gré (v. aussi *savoir*)
 1 à –
 2 à votre –
 3 au – de
 4 au – de l'acheteur, du vendeur
 5 de plein –
 6 arrangement *m.* de – à –
 7 vente *f.* de – à –
 8 nous vous saurions infiniment – de, nous vous en saurions beaucoup de –
 9 vendre de – à –

gréement *m.*
greffe *m.* (*tribunal*)

 déposer au –

greffier *m.* (*tribunal*)
grève *f.*
 1 – d'avertissement
 2 – de la faim
 3 – des cheminots
 4 – des dockers, – du port
 5 – des mineurs
 6 – des transports
 7 – de protestation
 8 – de surprise
 9 – de sympathie, – de solidarité
 10 – du bâtiment
 11 – du zèle

 12 –s, émeute et mouvements populaires (*assur.*)

2 register of national debt
3 securities –
4 general –
5 – account
department store
graph, chart
printing and allied industries
gratuity, bonus
 Christmas bonus
gratis
erasure, scratching out
to erase, to scratch out
penknife, eraser
gratuitous
 1 admission free
 2 – loan
 3 free delivery
 4 no charge is made for

 1 at discretion
 2 at your discretion
 3 in the discretion of
 4 at buyer's, (seller's) option
 5 freely
 6 amicable settlement
 7 sale by private treaty
 8 we shall be much obliged if you will, you would greatly oblige us by.

 9 to sell by private contract

rigging
clerk's office, clerk of the court's office
 to lodge at the –, to lodge with the clerk of the court
clerk of the court
strike
 1 warning –
 2 hunger –
 3 railway –
 4 dock –, dockers' –

 5 coal –
 6 transport –
 7 protest –
 8 lightning –
 9 sympathetic –
 10 – of building workers
 11 working to rule, work-to-rule

 12 –, riot and civil commotion

181 / grevé

13 – générale
14 – non organisée, – sauvage
15 – partielle
16 – perlée
17 – sur le tas
18 – symbolique
19 une – a éclaté
20 la – est terminée
21 allocation *f.* de –
22 briseur *m.* de –
23 comité *m.* de –
24 droit *m.* de –
25 fonds *m.* de –
26 piquet *m.* de –
27 décréter une –
28 décommander une –
29 se mettre en –
grevé *m.* (*jur.*) (voir *fidéicommis*)
grever
 1 – le budget de...
 2 – d'hypothèque

 3 – (*un envoi*) de remboursement

 4 grevé de dettes
gréviste *m.*
griffe *f.*
 1 – de pesage
 2 – de réception
gros
 1 – bénéfices
 2 – se commande
 3 – ses coupures
 4 – se somme
 5 à – intérêt
 6 gagner –
gros *m.* (commerce de (en) –)
 1 maison *f.* de –

 2 marchand *m.* en –

 3 prix *m.* de –

 4 indice *m.* des prix de –
 5 acheter en –
 6 faire le –

 7 vendre en –
grosse *f.* (*copie*)
grosse *f.* (12 × 12)
 vendre à la –
grosse *f.* (aventure)
 1 – sur corps

13 general –
14 wild-cat –
15 partial –
16 go slow –, ca'canny –
17 sit-down –, stay-in –, sit-in –
18 token –
19 a – has broken out
20 the – has been settled, has come [to an end
21 – pay
22 – breaker
23 – committee
24 right to –
25 – fund
26 – picket
27 to call a –
28 to call off a –
29 to go on –

to encumber, to weight
 1 to burden the budget with
 2 to mortgage, to encumber with mortgage
 3 to put a trade charge on, to charge with reimbursement
 4 encumbered (burdened) with debts
striker
stamped signature
 1 weight stamp
 2 reception stamp
large, big
 1 large profits
 2 large order
 3 big denominations
 4 large sum, big amount
 5 at high interest
 6 to earn (make) big money
wholesale trade
 1 wholesale house

 2 wholesale dealer

 3 wholesale price

 4 wholesale price index
 5 to buy in bulk
 6 to deal wholesale

 7 to sell wholesale
copy, engrossment
gross
 to sell by the –
bottomry
 1 –

grossiste / 182

2 – sur facultés (marchandises)
3 contrat *m.* à la –
4 emprunteur *m.* (preneur) à la –
5 prêteur *m.* (donneur) à la –
6 emprunter à la –
7 prêter (donner) à la –
grossiste *m.*

groupage *m.*
service *m.* de –

groupe *m.*
groupement *m.*
– professionnel
grouper
grue *f.*
droit *m.* de –
guerre *f.*
  1 – de tarifs
  2 années *f. pl.* d'après –
  3 années *f. pl.* d'avant –
  4 assurance *f.* contre risque de –
  5 bénéfice *m.* de –
  6 clause *f.* de –
  7 emprunt *m.* de –
  8 faits *m. pl.* de –
  9 impôts *m. pl.* sur les bénéfices de –
 10 risques *m. pl.* de –
guichet *m.*
  1 à – ouvert
  2 au –
  3 commission de – (*émission*)
  4 fermeture *f.* des –s
  5 heures *f. pl.* d'ouverture des –s
    (voir *heure*)
  6 ruée *f.* sur les –s d'une banque

  7 salle *f.* des –s

  8 payable à nos –s
  9 s'adresser au – n°...
 10 payer au –
 11 présenter au –
 12 prêter ses –s (*émission*)

 13 vendre au – (*valeurs*)

guichetier *m.*
guichetière *f.*
guide, carte *f.* –
guide-papier *m.* (*de machine à écrire*)

2 respondentia
3 – bond
4 borrower (taker) on bottomry
5 lender on –
6 to borrow (take, raise) money on –
7 to lend (advance) money on –
wholesaler

joint cargo, grouping
  joint cargo service

group, batch
group
  professional –
to group, to batch
crane
  cranage
war
  1 tariff (rate) –
  2 postwar years
  3 prewar years
  4 – risk insurance
  5 – profits
  6 – clause
  7 – loan
  8 acts of –
  9 – profits tax
 10 – risks
counter, window
  1 on demand, presentation
  2 at (over) the counter
  3 selling agent's commission
  4 closing of the offices

  6 run on a bank, bank run

  7 counters, main hall

  8 payable at our counters
  9 apply at counter (window) n°
 10 to pay over the counter
 11 to hand in over the counter
 12 to receive subscription, application

 13 to sell over the counter

counter clerk
counter clerk
tab card, guide card
paper guide

H

habitude *f.* — custom
  comme d'– — as usual
habituel — usual
haler — to tow
halle *f.* — covered market
hallier *m.* — stall keeper
hangar *m.* — shed
hasardeux (*spéculation*) — risky
hausse *f.* — rise
  1 – de prix — 1 – in price(s)   [boom]
  2 – subite (*cours, prix*) — 2 sudden – (sudden and sharp =
  3 forte – — 3 sharp –
  4 la – (*les spéculants*) — 4 the bulls
  5 mouvement *m.* de – — 5 upward movement
  6 opération *f.* à la – — 6 bull transaction
  7 position *f.* à la – (*acheteur*) — 7 bull position
  8 liquider une position à la hausse — 8 to liquidate a bull position
  9 prime *f.* à la – — 9 call option

  10 spéculateur *m.* à la – — 10 bull (operator)
  11 accuser une – — 11 to show a –
  12 avoir une tendance à la – — 12 to show a rising tendency, a tendency to –, an upward trend
  13 enrayer la – — 13 to arrest the upward movement
  14 être à la –, être en – — 14 to be rising, to be up
  15 être (jouer, spéculer) à la – — 15 to speculate (go) for a –

  16 subir une – — 16 to experience a –
hausser — to raise
  1 – le prix — 1 to advance (raise) the price
  2 les cours haussent — 2 rates rise, advance, go up, are rising

haussier *m.* — bull, bull operator

haut — high
  1 la –e Autorité (*charbon, acier*) — 1 the High Authority
  2 –e mer — 2 – sea
  3 la –e finance — 3 – finance
  4 aux plus –s prix — 4 at the –est prices
  5 en – de la page — 5 at the top of the page
hauteur *f.* — height
  1 à la – du temps — 1 up-to-date, abreast of the times
  2 rester à la – du progrès — 2 to keep abreast with the progress
hebdomadaire — weekly
  bulletin *m.* – — – report
hectogramme *m.* — hectogram
hectolitre *m.* — hectolitre
hectomètre *m.* — hectometer
hedging, opération – — hedging transaction

héritage / 184

héritage *m.*
 répudier un –
hériter de...
héritier *m.*
 1 – légal
 2 – réservataire

 3 les –s Peters
héritière *f.*
hésiter
heure *f.*
 1 – d'arrivée
 2 –s de bourse
 3 –s de bureau, aux –

 4 – de départ
 5 –s de grande affluence

 6 –s de pointe
 7 – d'été
 8 –s de travail
 9 –s d'ouverture (des guichets)

 10 –s supplémentaires [à part
 11 les –s supplémentaires sont payées
 12 faire des –s supplémentaires
 13 à trois –s
 14 trois –s
heure-homme *f.* (*pl.* –s-s)
heure-machine *f.*
heureuse arrivée
 vendre à l'–
hier
 votre lettre d'–
hinterland *m.*
hivernage *m.*
 port *m.* d'–
holding *m.* et *f.*

homme *m.* **d'affaires**
homme *m.* **de confiance**
 l'– de
homme *m.* **de paille**
homme-sandwich *m.*
honnête
honnêteté *f.*
honneur *m.*
 1 membre *m.* d'–
 2 parole *f.* d'–
 3 nous avons l'– de vous informer que

 4 faire – à sa signature

inheritance
 to renounce a legacy
to inherit from
heir
 1 heir-at-law
 2 person to whom the legal portion is due
 3 Peters –s
heiress
to hesitate
hour
 1 time of arrival
 2 stock exchange –s
 3 during business –s

 4 time of departure
 5 busy (rush) –s

 6 peak –s
 7 summer time
 8 working –s
 9 office (banking) –s, counter business –s
 10 overtime, overtime –s
 11 overtime is paid extra
 12 to work overtime
 13 at three o'clock
 14 three –s
man-hour, labo(u)r-hour
machine hour
safe arrival
 to sell to arrive, for arrival
yesterday
 your letter of –
hinterland
wintering
 – port
holding company

business man
reliable man
 the confidential agent of
man of straw
sandwich man
honest
honesty, probity
(*Amer.*) honor, (*Gr. Br.*) honour
 1 honorary member
 2 word of –
 3 we have (we have the pleasure) to inform you
 4 to – one's signature

185 / honorable

5 faire – à une signature | 5 to – a signature
6 faire – à une traite | 6 to – a bill, to pay due – to a bill
7 ne pas faire – à une traite | 7 to dishono(u)r a draft
8 intervenir pour l'– d'une signature | 8 to intervene for the – of a signature
9 se faire – de | 9 to consider (deem) it an –

honorable respectable, (*firme*) of high standing
honorabilité *f.* respectability, (*firme*) standing
honoraires *pl.* fees
honoré esteemed
1 votre –e du... | 1 your – letter of
2 vos –s ordres | 2 your valued orders
honorer (*Amer.*) to honor, (*Gr. Br.*) to honour
1 – une traite | 1 to – (meet) a bill
2 ne pas – une traite | 2 to dishono(u)r a bill

horaire *m.* (*trains, avion*) time table
hors banque
1 escompte *m.* – | 1 private (rate of) discount
2 papier *m.* – | 2 prime trade bills
horloge *f.* clock
1 – centrale | 1 master –
2 – contrôleuse | 2 check –
hôtel *m.* hotel
1 – de premier rang | 1 first-class –
2 à l'– ... | 2 at the ... –
hôtelier, industrie hôtelière hotel industry
hot money hot money
houillère *f.* coal mine
huile *f.* oil
huilerie *f.* oil mill
huissier *m.* (*bureaux*) usher [server
1 – (*justice*) | 1 bailiff, sheriff's officer, process-
2 signifier un exploit d'– à... | 2 to serve a writ of execution upon...

huit eight
1 dans les – jours | 1 within – days
2 d'aujourd'hui en – | 2 to-day (this day) week
3 de demain en – | 3 to-morrow week
4 d'hier en – | 4 a week from yesterday
5 tous les – jours | 5 every – days
huitaine, remettre à – to adjourn for a week
humidité *f.* humidity
craint l'– | keep dry

hypothécable mortgageable

hypothécaire mortgage...
1 affectation *f.* – | 1 – charge
2 caisse *f.* – | 2 – bank (company)
3 charge *f.* – | 3 – charge
4 contrat *m.* – | 4 – deed
5 créancier *m.* – | 5 mortgagee

hypothécairement / 186

6 débiteur *m.* –
7 dette *f.* –
8 inscription *f.* –
9 certificat *m.* d'–
10 marché *m.* –
11 obligation *f.* –
12 prêt *m.* –
13 radiation *f.* –
14 rente *f.* –
hypothécairement
hypothèque *f.*
 1 – conventionnelle
 2 – de premier rang
 3 – générale
 4 – judiciaire
 5 – maritime, sur navires
 6 – pour sûreté d'un crédit
 7 deuxième –
 8 grevé d'–s
 9 libre (franc) d'–
10 première –, – en (de) premier rang
11 en (sur) première –
12 susceptible d'–
13 bureau *m.* des –s
14 au bureau des –s
15 conservateur *m.* des –s
16 constitution *f.* d'une –

17 extinction *f.* de l'–
18 mainlevée *f.* d'–
19 purge *f.* d'–

20 rang *m.* d'une –
21 amortir une –
22 avoir une – sur...
23 constituer une –
24 emprunter sur –
25 grever d'–
26 prendre une –
27 prêter sur –
28 purger une –
hypothéquer

6 mortgagor
7 – debt
8 registration (recording) of –
9 – certificate
10 – market
11 – bond, – debenture
12 – loan
13 entry of satisfaction of –
14 – rate
by mortgage, on mortgage
mortgage
 1 – resulting from a contract
 2 first –
 3 general –
 4 – by order of the court
 5 – on ships
 6 equitable –
 7 second –
 8 burdened (encumbered) with –
 9 unencumbered
10 first (prior) –
11 on first –
12 mortgageable
13 – registry
14 at the recording office
15 recorder of –s
16 creation of a –

17 extinction of –
18 release of –
19 redemption of –

20 rank of a –
21 to redeem a –
22 to have a – on...
23 to create a –
24 to borrow on –
25 to –
26 to raise a –
27 to lend on –
28 to redeem (to pay off) a –
to mortgage

I

ici
1 – Dupont (*tél*)
2 d'– là

3 d'– peu

here
1 Dupont speaking
2 by that time, between now and then
3 before long, ere long

187 / identification

identification *f.*	**identification**
identifier	**to identify**
identique	**identical**
identité *f.*	**identity**
1 carte *f.* d'–	1 – card
2 prouver l'–	2 to prove the –
illégal	**unlawful, illegal**
actes illégaux	illegal (unlawful) acts
illégalité *f.*	**illegality**
illicite	**illicit**
illimité	**unlimited**
illisible (*signature*)	**illegible**
imitation *f.* (voir aussi *contrefaçon*)	**imitation**
– cuir	– leather
imiter (voir aussi *contrefaire*)	**to imitate**
– une signature	to forge a signature
immatriculation *f.*	**registration, registry**
immatriculer	**to register**
immédiatement	**immediately**
immeuble *m.* (voir aussi *locaux*)	**real property**
– à vendre	premises (property) for sale
immeuble *adj.*	**real, immovable, fixed**
1 – par destination	1 immovable by destination, fixture
2 – par nature	2 immovable by (in) nature
3 biens *m. pl.* –s	3 fixed property, real estate, immovable property
immigration *f.*	**immigration**
immigrer	**to immigrate**
immobilier	**real, immovable**
1 agent –	1 estate agent
2 fortune immobilière	2 immovable property
3 marché –	3 real estate (property) market
4 saisie immobilière	4 seizure of immovable property
5 société immobilière (voir *société*)	
6 vente immobilière	6 sale of real estate, of property
immobilisation *f.*	**immobilization, locking up**
1 – de capitaux	1 immobilization (lock-up) of capital, sterilization of money
2 les –s	2 capital expenditure
immobiliser	**to immobilize, to lock up, to tie up**
1 – des capitaux	1 to immobilize (lock up) capital
2 actif immobilisé	2 fixed assets
impair	**odd, uneven**
impartial	**impartial**
impasse *f.*	
1 arriver (entrer) dans (aboutir à) une –	1 to come to a deadlock
2 sortir de l'–	2 to break the deadlock

impatience / 188

impatience *f.*
impayé
 1 chèque –
 2 comptes –s
 3 la traite est revenue –e

 4 rester –
impayé *m.*, – retourné, – rendu

impeccable (*qualité*)
importance *f.*
 1 – du crédit
 2 – du dommage
 3 de grande –
 4 de la plus haute –

 5 de peu d'–
 6 d'après (selon) l'– de la commande

 7 attacher une – à

important
 1 firme –e
 2 somme –e
importateur *m.*
importateur *adj.*
 pays –
importation *f.*
 1 les –s
 2 – en provenance de.
 3 – invisible
 4 articles *m. pl.* d'–
 5 commerce *m.* d'–

 6 droits *m. pl.* d'–
 7 excédent *m.* d'–
 8 licence *f.* d'–

 9 liste *f.* des –s
 10 maison *f.* d'–
 11 pays *m.* d'–
 12 possibilités *f. pl.* d'–
 13 prime *f.* d'–

 14 restriction *f.* d'–
 15 taxe *f.* à l'–
 16 valeur *f.* d'–
importer
 1 – d'Italie
 2 – en Suisse
imposable
 1 marchandises *f. pl.* –s

impatience
unpaid
 1 – cheque, (check)
 2 unsettled accounts
 3 the bill was returned dishono(u)red, has suffered dishono(u)r
 4 to remain –
bill returned dishono(u)red, unpaid

unimpeachable, perfect
importance
 1 the amount (size) of the credit
 2 the extent of the damage
 3 of great –
 4 of paramount (the utmost) –

 5 of little –
 6 according to the – (extent) of the order
 7 to attach – to

important
 1 – firm
 2 large (substantial, considerable) sum
importer
importing, import
 importing country
import, importation
 1 the imports
 2 imports from
 3 invisible import, invisibles
 4 imports, import articles
 5 import trade

 6 import duties
 7 excess (surplus) of imports
 8 import licence

 9 import list
 10 import firm
 11 importing country
 12 possibilities of importations
 13 bounty on importation, import bounty
 14 restriction of import
 15 tax on imports
 16 import value
to import
 1 – from Italy
 2 – into Switzerland
taxable
 1 dutiable goods

2 matière *f.* –
3 revenu *m.* –
imposer
  1 – quelqu'un pour...
  2 marchandises imposées
  3 prix imposé
imposition *f.*
  1 – multiple
  2 double –
  3 année *f.* d'–
impossibilité *f.*
  se trouver dans l'–
impossible
impôt *m.* (voir aussi *contribution, exempt, fiscal, taxe*)
  1 –s cédulaires
  2 – de capitation
  3 – de consommation
  4 – de luxe, – somptuaire
  5 –s directs
  6 – du timbre
  7 – foncier
  8 –s indirects
  9 – progressif
  10 – retenu à la source
  11 – successoral
  12 – sur les bénéfices
  13 – sur les bénéfices de guerre
  14 – sur les bénéfices exceptionnels
  15 – sur les bénéfices industriels et commerciaux
  16 – sur les boissons
  17 – sur les super-bénéfices
  18 – sur le capital

  19 – sur le chiffre d'affaires
  20 – sur les coupons
  21 – sur les exportations
  22 – sur les opérations de bourse
  23 – sur les plus-values
  24 – sur le revenu
  25 – sur le revenu des valeurs mobilières
  26 – sur les sociétés
  27 – sur les tantièmes
  28 – sur les traitements et salaires
  29 assujetti à l'–
  30 passible d'–
  31 assiette *f.* de l'–

  32 augmentation *f.* des –s
  33 crédit *m.* d'–
  34 déclaration *f.* d'–

2 – article
3 assessable income
to tax, to charge with duty
  1 to assess someone at...
  2 taxed goods
  3 price laid down by...
imposition
  1 multiple taxation
  2 double taxation
  3 year of assessment
impossibility
  to find oneself in the –
impossible
tax

  1 schedule –
  2 capitation –, head –, poll –
  3 consumption –
  4 luxury –
  5 direct –es
  6 stamp duty
  7 land –
  8 indirect –es
  9 progressive (graduated) –
  10 – deducted at source
  11 death duty, estate duty
  12 – on profits
  13 excess profits duty
  14 excess profits –
  15 tax on incomes derived from trade and manufacture
  16 beverage –
  17 excess profits –
  18 – on capital, capital levy

  19 turnover –
  20 coupon –
  21 – on exports
  22 – on exchange dealings
  23 increment value –
  24 income –
  25 stockholder's –

  26 corporation –, corporate –
  27 – on allocated portion of profits
  28 salary –, – on wages
  29 liable to (for) –
  30 taxable
  31 basis of assessment

  32 increases in taxation
  33 – credit
  34 return of income

imprimé / 190

35 détournement *m.* d'–	35 defraudation of –es
36 exonération *f.* de l'–	36 exemption from taxation
37 moins-perçu *m.* d'–s	37 shortfall in – revenue
38 objet *m.* de l'–	38 taxable article
39 payement anticipé d'–s	39 prepayment of –es
40 payement *m.* d'arriérés d'–	40 payment of – arrears
41 perception *f.* des –s	41 collection of –es
42 peréquation *f.* des –s	42 equalization of –es
43 poids *m.* des –s	43 burden of taxation, – burden
44 receveur *m.* (percepteur *m.*) des –s	44 – collector
45 réduction *f.* des –s	45 – reduction, – cut, – rebate
46 rendement *m.* (produit *m.*) des –s	46 – proceeds, – yield
47 répartition *f.* des –s	47 distribution of taxation
48 réserve *f.* pour les –s	48 reserve for taxation
49 restitution *f.* d'–s	49 reimbursement (refund) of –es
50 exempter d'–s	50 to exempt from –es
51 frapper (grever) d'–s	51 to burden with taxation
52 lever des –s	52 to levy –es
53 payer l'– sur…	53 to pay – on…
54 retenir des –s à la source	54 to deduct –es at the source
imprimé *m.*	**printed paper, printed book**
1 ,,–s'' (*poste*)	1 printed matter
2 –s (*formules*)	2 printed forms
3 – à taxe réduite	3 – at a special reduced rate
imprimer	**to print**
imprimerie *f.*	**printing house**
imprimeur *m.*	**printer**
improductif (*capitaux*)	**unproductive, dead, lying idle**
imputable à	**due (attributable) to**
frais *m. pl.* –s sur (à) un compte	expenses chargeable to an account
imputation *f.*	**charging**
1 – des frais à (sur) un compte	1 – of the expenses to an account
2 – des payements à une dette	2 appropriation of a payment to a debt
imputer	**to attribute**
1 – sur le crédit consenti	1 to deduct from the granted credit
2 – une dépense sur le (au) compte…	2 to charge an expense to the… account
3 – un payement à (sur) une dette	3 to apply a payment to a debt
4 être imputé au budget	4 to come within the budget
inaliénable	**unalienable**
droits *m. pl.* –s	– rights
inanimé (*bourse*)	**dull, lifeless**
incalculable	**incalculable**
incapable	**unable**

191 / incapacité

1 – (*jur.*)   1 under a disability, incapable
2 – de travailler   2 unfit for work

incapacité *f.*   **incapacity**
 1 – (*jur.*)   1 disability, –
 2 – de travail   2 disablement
 3 – légale   3 absence of legal capacity
 4 – partielle de travail   4 partial disablement
 5 – permanente de travail   5 permanent disablement
 6 – temporaire de travail   6 temporary disablement

 7 – totale de travail   7 total disablement
incertain   **uncertain**
 1 cotation –e   1 movable (–, indirect, variable) exchange, quotation in foreign currency

 2 donner l'–   2 to quote in foreign currency, to quote variable exchange
incessibilité *f.*   **untransferability**

incessible   **untransferable**
incidence *f.*   **incidence**
 1 – de... sur...   1 – of... upon..., effect of... on...

 2 – des droits de douane sur   2 – of customs duties upon
 3 – d'un impôt   3 – of a tax

inclure (voir aussi *ci-inclus*)   **to enclose in**
 – (*clause*)   to insert... in
inclusivement   **inclusive of**
 jusqu'au... –   till the... inclusive
incomplet   **incomplete**
inconnu   **unknown**
 si – à l'adresse, prière de retourner à...   if undelivered, please return to...

incontestable   **incontestable**
inconvertible   **inconvertible, unconvertible**
 papier monnaie – en...   paper money inconvertible into
incorporation *f.*   **incorporation**

incorporer à   **to incorporate into**

incoté   **unquoted**
indéchiffrable   **undecipherable**
indemnisation *f.*   **indemnification**
indemniser de...   **to indemnify (compensate) for...**
indemnité *f.* (voir *allocation*)   **indemnity**
 1 – d'accouchement   1 maternity benefit
 2 – de caisse   2 cash indemnity
 3 – de chômage   3 dole, unemployment benefit
 4 – de déplacement   4 travelling allowance
 5 – de logement   5 lodging (housing) allowance

6 – de maladie	6 sickness benefit
7 – de représentation	7 entertainment allowance
8 – de sauvetage	8 (remuneration for) salvage
9 – de séjour	9 hotel allowance
10 – de séparation	10 separation allowance
11 – de vie chère	11 cost-of-living bonus
12 – d'expropriation	12 compensation for expropriation
13 – en argent, en espèces	13 pecuniary compensation
14 – en nature	14 allowance in kind
15 – forfaitaire	15 agreed consideration
16 allouer une –	16 to award an indemnity
17 avoir droit à une –	17 to be entitled to indemnity
18 être tenu à une –	18 to be liable for indemnity
19 payer une –	19 to pay damages
20 réclamer une –	20 to claim damages, compensation
index *m.* (v. aussi *indice*)	**index**
1 l'– est de (s'établit, s'inscrit, se situe) à ...	1 the – stands at ...
2 l'– est passé de ... à ...	2 the – rose from... to...
3 l'– est tombé de 2 points	3 the – fell by 2 points
4 l'– est en hausse de 2 points	4 the – rose by 2 points
5 clause *f.* –	5 index clause
6 rattaché à (au mouvement de) l'–	6 tied to the –, index-tied
7 salaire lié à l'–	7 wages linked to the –
8 – (*d'un livre*)	8 index
indexé	**indexed, index-linked**
1 emprunt –	1 – loan, loan linked (tied) to an index
2 obligation –e	2 index-bond, index-linked bond
indicateur *m.*	
1 – des chemins de fer	1 railway guide
2 – téléphonique	2 telephone directory
indication *f.* (v. *carnet, sauf*)	**indication**
1 – du mode d'emploi	1 directions for use
2 –s de service (voir aussi *emplacement*)	2 service instructions
3 à titre d'–	3 for your guidance –
indice *m.*, **nombre** –(voir aussi *index*)	**index number**
1 – de la production	1 production index
2 – de la production industrielle	2 index of industrial production
3 – des (cours d')actions	3 share price indices
4 – des prix à la consommation	4 consumer price –
5 – des prix au détail	5 retail price –
6 – des prix de gros	6 wholesale price index
7 – des prix du commerce extérieur	7 price index of the external trade

193 / indiquer

8 – des prix et des salaires	8 prices and wages index
9 – des quantités	9 quantity index
10 – des quantités ponderées par les valeurs	10 quantity index weighted by prices
11 – des valeurs mobilières	11 – of securities
12 – du coût de la vie	12 cost-of-living index, figure
13 – du volume des exportations	13 volume index of exports
14 – de la valeur des exportations	14 value-index of exports
15 – (non) pondéré	15 (un)weighted index
indiquer	**to indicate**
1 – la route	1 to specify the route
2 ainsi qu'il est indiqué	2 as indicated
indivis	**undivided, (property) held indivisum**
par –	jointly
indivision *f.*	**joint possession, property held in common, indivisum**
pour sortir d'–	to determine the joint possession
indû	**undue, not due**
l'–	what is not due
indûment	**unduly**
industrialisation *f.*	**industrialization**
industrialiser	**to industrialize**
industrie *f.*	**industry**
1 – à domicile	1 home –
2 – alimentaire	2 food(stuff)–
3 – ayant des perspectives de croissance	3 growth industry
4 – chimique	4 chemical –
5 – cotonnière	5 cotton –
6 – d'articles de consommation	6 – producing consumer goods, consumer goods –
7 – de base	7 basic –
8 – de la chaussure	8 shoe –
9 – de l'emballage	9 packaging –
10 – de produits d'investissement	10 investment goods –
11 – de transformation des métaux	11 metal-using –
12 – diamantaire	12 diamond –
13 – du charbon, du fer et de l'acier	13 coal, iron and steel –
14 – du papier	14 paper –
15 – du verre	15 glass –
16 – du vêtement	16 clothing –
17 – électrotechnique	17 electric equipment producing –
18 – hôtelière	18 hotel –
19 – lainière	19 woollen –
20 – lourde	20 heavy –
21 – métallurgique	21 metallurgy
22 – minière	22 mining –
23 – saisonnière	23 seasonal –
24 – transformatrice, – de transfor- [mation	24 processing –
25 branche *f.* d'–	25 branch of –

industriel / 194

26 fédération *f.* des –s
27 petite –
industriel
  1 action –le
  2 banque –le
  3 centre –
  4 concentration –le
  5 entreprise –le
  6 esthétique –le
  7 exposition –le
  8 obligation –le
  9 parc –
10 pays –
11 propriété –le
12 valeurs –les
industriel *m.*
inébranlé
inéchangeable
inescomptable
inestimable
inexécution *f.*
inexigible
inflation *f.*
  1 – de crédit
  2 – des coûts de revient
  3 – des prix
  4 – des salaires
  5 – galopante
  6 – importée
  7 – latente
  8 – ouverte
  9 – par la demande

10 – par les coûts
11 – rampante
12 – refoulée, – contenue
13 lutte *f.* contre l'–
14 combattre l'–
inflationniste, inflatoire

  1 pression (poussée) –
  2 spirale *f.* –
  3 tendances *f. pl.* -s
inflexion *f.*, **point d'** –
influence *f.*
  1 sous l'– de
  2 sphère *f.* d'–
  3 avoir (exercer) de l'– sur
  4 subir l'– de
information *f.* (v. *renseignement*)
  1 à titre d'–
  2 pour votre –
  3 demande *f.* d'–

26 federation of industries
27 small (-scale) –
industrial
  1 – share, –
  2 – bank
  3 – centre
  4 – concentration
  5 – undertaking, enterprise
  6 – design
  7 – exhibition
  8 – bond
  9 – park, trade estate
10 – country
11 patent rights
12 –s
manufacturer
unshaken
unexchangeable
undiscountable
unestimable
non-performance
not demandable, undue
inflation
  1 credit –
  2 cost-induced –
  3 price –
  4 wage –
  5 galloping –
  6 imported –
  7 concealed –
  8 open –
  9 demand-induced –, demand-pull –

10 cost-induced –, cost-push –
11 creeping –
12 pent-up –
13 fight (struggle) against –
14 to combat (to fight against) –
inflationary, inflatory

  1 – pressure
  2 inflation (–) spiral
  3 – tendencies
flex (inflexion) point
influence
  1 under the – of
  2 sphere of –
  3 to have (exercise, exert) – on
  4 to feel the – of
information
  1 by way of –
  2 for your –
  3 inquiry

4 source f. d'–
5 aller aux –s, prendre des –s sur

6 donner (fournir) des –s
informé m.
1 plus ample –
2 jusqu'à plus ample –
[tage]
informer (voir aussi *honneur, avan-*
1 bien (mal) informé
2 je vous informe que

3 s'– de... auprès de...
infrastructure f.
ingénieur m.
1 – civil
2 – conseil
3 – des mines
ingérence f.
– de l'état
ininflammable
initial
capital –
initiale f.
initiative f.
1 – privée
2 de notre propre –
3 de sa propre –
4 syndicat m. d'–

5 manquer d'–
6 prendre l'–
injection f. (*de monnaie*) **dans**
injuste
innavigabilité f. (*navire*)
innavigable (*navire*)
innovation f.
introduire des –s
inopportun
inscription f.
1 – comptable
2 – hypothécaire (voir *hypothécaire*)
3 –s nominatives
4 –s sur le grand livre de la dette publique
5 – sur le registre du commerce
6 date f. d'–
inscrire
1 – un article
2 – une hypothèque sur
3 – un nom
4 – dans (sur) un livre
5 – sur une liste

4 source of –
5 to make inquiries about

6 to furnish (supply) –
inquiry
1 closer (further) –
2 until further –, until further information is available
to inform
1 well (ill)-informed
2 I inform you that

3 to inquire of... about...
infrastructure
engineer
1 civil –
2 consulting –
3 mining –
interference
government –
non-inflammable
initial
initial capital
initial
initiative
1 private –
2 on our own –
3 on his own –
4 association for the encouragement of touring
5 to be lacking –
6 to take the –
injection into...
unjust
unseaworthiness
unseaworthy
innovation
to introduce –s
inconvenient
inscription, entry
1 entry

3 inscribed stock
4 inscribed Government stock

5 – in the trade register
6 date of –
to enter
1 to – (to post) an item
2 to register a mortgage on
3 to – a name
4 to – in a book
5 to – on a list

inscrire / 196

6 être inscrit au bilan pour... fr.

7 être inscrit à la cote officielle

inscrire, s −
1 − à
2 − en baisse (*actions, cours*)
3 − en hausse (*actions, cours*)
insérer
1 − une annonce dans un journal

2 − une clause dans...
3 prière d'−

insertion *f.* (*annonce*)

1 − gratuite
2 frais *m. pl.* d'−

insister
1 − sur (un fait)
2 − sur le payement immédiat
3 − vivement pour que...
insolvabilité *f.*

insolvable
inspecter
inspecteur *m.*
1 − des contributions
2 − d'une société d'assurances
3 − du travail
inspection *f.*
1 − de livres
2 − d'un navire
instabilité *f.*
instable
installation *f.*
instamment (*prier*)
instance *f.*
1 en première (dernière) −
2 prier avec −
institution *f.*
− de crédit
instructions *f. pl.*
1 − relatives à l'expédition
2 conformément à vos −
3 dans l'attente de vos −
4 sauf − (voir *sauf*)
5 selon les −
6 agir contrairement aux −
7 se conformer (s'en tenir) aux −

8 donner des −

6 to appear (stand) in the balance sheet at... fr.
7 to be quoted in the official list

1 to be quoted at
2 − to be marked down
3 − to be marked up
to insert
1 to − an advertisement in a newspaper
2 to − a clause in
3 for the favo(u)r of publication in your columns
insertion

1 free −
2 advertising charges

to insist
1 − on
2 − on immediate payment
3 to urge strongly that
insolvency

insolvent
to inspect, to examine
inspector
1 surveyor of taxes
2 − of an insurance company
3 factory −
inspectation, examination
1 examination of books
2 survey of a ship
instability, unsteadiness
unsteady
equipment, fittings and fixtures
urgently
instance
1 in the first (the last) −
2 to request urgently
institution
credit −
instructions
1 shipping −
2 in accordance with your −
3 awaiting your −

5 according to (as per) −
6 to act contrary to the −
7 to comply with the −

8 to give −

197 / instrument

  9 exécuter des –
  10 suivre les –
instrument *m.* **de crédit**

instrument *m.* **de payement**
instruments *m. pl.* **de ratification**
  1 dépôt *m.* des –
  2 échange *m.* des –
insu, à notre –
insuffisant
  emballage –
insuffisamment
  – affranchi
insurmontable
intangible
  valeurs *f. pl.* –s
intégral
  1 calcul –
  2 payement –
intégralement
  – libéré, versé
intégration *f.*
  – économique
intention *f.*
  nous n'avons pas l'– de
interdiction *f.* (*défense*)
  1 – de commerce
  2 – d'exportation
  3 – d'importation
interdiction *f.* (*jur.*)

  1 – judiciaire
  2 frapper d'–
interdit *m.* (*jur.*)

interdit (voir aussi *défense*)
  1 entrée –e
  2 passage –
intéressé *m.*

  1 –s d'une lettre de change

  2 – dans une faillite
  3 les –s sont priés de…

intéresser qqn à…
  – aux bénéfices
intéresser, s –
  1 – à…
  2 – dans une entreprise

intérêt *m.*
  1 – assurable

  9 to carry out –
  10 to follow the –
credit instrument, instrument of credit

instrument of payment
instruments of ratification
  1 deposit of –
  2 exchange of –
without our knowledge
insufficient
  – packing
insufficiently
  – prepaid
unsurmountable
intangible
  – assets
integral
  1 – calculus
  2 payment in full
in full
  fully paid
integration
  economic –
intention
  we have no – to…
prohibition
  1 interdiction of commerce
  2 – of export
  3 – of import
deprival of the exercise of certain rights
  1 judicial interdiction
  2 to impose judicial interdiction on
person under judicial disability

prohibited
  1 no admittance
  2 no thoroughfare
interested party

  1 parties to a bill

  2 involved in a bankruptcy
  3 those interested are invited

to interest someone in…
  to give a share in the profits

  1 to take an interest in
  2 to interest oneself in an enterprise

interest
  1 insurable –

intérêt / 198

2 -s réciproques
3 contraire aux -s
4 dans l'- de
5 dans votre propre -
6 communauté *f.* d'-
7 sphère *f.* d'-
8 agir aux mieux de vos -s
9 agir contre ses propres -s
10 avoir des -s dans une entreprise

11 il a tout - à...
12 concilier les -s
13 éveiller l'-
14 favoriser les -s de...
15 nuire aux -s
16 servir les -s de qqn
17 veiller aux -s de..., sauvegarder les -s de...

intérêt *m.*
1 à 5 % d'-
2 -s accumulés, accrus
3 - à échoir
4 - à recevoir
5 -s arriérés
6 - composé
7 - courant
8 - couru
9 - créditeur
10 - créditeurs supérieurs au taux officiel
11 - débiteur
12 - de capital
13 - de retard, - moratoire
14 - différé
15 -s dus, - exigibles
16 -s échus
17 - élevé
18 - fixe
  à -
19 -s intercalaires, intérimaires
20 -s noirs
21 -s rouges
22 - simple
23 - usuraire
24 - variable
25 avec -
26 ex -
27 l'- court à partir de

28 portant un - de...
29 productif d'-
30 non productif d'-s
31 calcul *m.* des -s

2 mutual -s
3 contrary to the -s
4 in the - of
5 in your own -
6 community of -s
7 sphere of -   [advantage
8 to act in your -, to your best
9 to act against one's own -
10 to have an - (to be interested) in an undertaking
11 it is in his - to
12 to reconcile the -s
13 to awake -
14 to promote the -s of...
15 to prejudice the -s
16 to serve the -s of
17 to promote (to attend to, to look after) the -s of

interest
1 at the rate of 5%, at 5 % -
2 accrued -
3 accruing -
4 - receivable
5 arrears of -
6 compound -
7 running -
8 accrued -
9 credit -
10 creditor-interest above the official rates
11 debit -
12 - on capital
13 - of deferred payment, - of default
14 deferred -
15 - due, payable
16 outstanding -
17 high -
18 fixed -
  fixed - bearing...
19 interim -
20 black -
21 red -
22 simple -
23 usurious -
24 variable -
25 cum -
26 ex -, excluding -
27 - is due (accrues) from

28 bearing - at...
29 interest-bearing
30 no interest bearing
31 computation of -

199 / intérimaire

32 capital *m.* et –s	32 principal and –
33 compte *m.* d'–s	33 – account
34 coupon *m.* d'–s	34 – coupon
35 jouissance *f.* d'–s	35 enjoyment of –
36 jours *m. pl.* d'–s	36 days of –
37 perte *f.* d'–s	37 loss of –
38 prêt *m.* à –	38 loan on –
39 prêt *m.* sans –	39 advance free of –
40 service *m.* des –s	40 service of a loan
41 table *f.* d'–s	41 – table
42 taux *m.* d'–	42 rate of –
43 conversion *f.* du –	43 conversion of the rate of –
44 réduction *f.* du –	44 reduction of the rate of –
45 bonifier des –s	45 to pay –
46 calculer les –s	46 to calculate (compute) the –
47 capitaliser les –s	47 to capitalize the –
48 compter des –s	48 to charge –
49 emprunter à –	49 to borrow (take) at –
50 joindre l'– au principal	50 to add the – to the capital
51 placer à –	51 to put out at –
52 prêter à –	52 to lend out at –
53 (rap)porter des –s	53 to yield –

intérimaire — **interim**
dividende *m.* –   – dividend

interligne *m. (espace entre 2 lignes)* — space between two lines
interligne *m. (écriture entre 2 lignes)* — interlineation
intermédiaire *m.* — intermediary, middleman
  1 –s s'abstenir   1 no agents need apply, no agents wanted
  2 par l'– de   2 through the intermediary (agency, medium) of
  3 par votre –   3 through your agency
  4 commerce *m.* –   4 intermediate trade
  5 port *m.* –   5 intermediate port
  6 servir d'–   6 to act as intermediary
international — **international**
  1 commerce –   1 – trade
  2 droit –   2 – law
interpénétration *f.* — **interpenetration**
interprétation *f.* — **interpretation**
  susceptible d'–s diverses   open to several –s

interprète *m.* — **interpreter**
interpréter — **to interpret**
interrompre — **to interrupt, to break**
interruption *f.* — **interruption, break**
  1 – de voyage   1 break of a journey
  2 sans –   2 without interruption
intervenant *m.* — **acceptor for hono(u)r, supra protest**

intervenir / 200

intervenir
— (*pour l'honneur d'une signature*)
intervention *f.*
1 — de l'état
2 acceptation *f.* par —, sous protêt

3 point *m.* d'—
4 payer par —
intervertir (*chiffres*)
intra-communautaire (CEE)
intrinsèque
valeur *f.* —
introduction *f.*
1 — de la semaine de 5 jours
2 lettre *f.* d'—
introduire
1 — ... auprès de...
2 — à la (en) bourse
3 — des innovations
4 — sur le marché
5 — une action en dommages-intérêts
6 bien introduit (*dans une branche*)
inutile
— de dire
invalider

invendable
invendu
inventaire *m.*
1 — annuel (*action*)

2 — avec prisée
3 — comptable
4 — des marchandises
5 — effectif
6 — théorique
7 sous bénéfice d'—

8 établissement *m.* d'un —

9 livre *m.* des —s
10 valeur *f.* d'—
11 vente *f.* pour cause d'—
12 dresser (établir, faire) l'—

inventeur *m.*
invention *f.*
brevet *m.* d'—
inventorier

— (*titres*)
investir
1 — à court terme

to intervene	
to accept for hono(u)r	
intermediary	
1 state interference	
2 acceptance for hono(u)r, supra protest	
3 intervention point	
4 to pay by intervention	
to transpose	
intra-Common Market	
intrinsic	
— value	
introduction	
1 — of the five-day week	
2 letter of —	
to introduce	
1 — ... to...	
2 — (*Amer.* to list) on the Exchange	
3 — novelties	
4 — on the market	
5 to bring an action for damages	
6 with a wide connection	
useless	
needless to say	
to invalidate	
unsal(e)able	
unsold	
inventory	
1 annual stocktaking	
2 — with valuation	
3 detailed account	
4 stocktaking	
5 actual balance	
6 balance as shown by books	
7 under beneficium of —	
8 stocktaking	
9 stock book	
10 stocktaking value	
11 stocktaking sale	
12 to draw up an —, to take stock	
inventor	
invention	
patent	
to inventory, to take stock	
to value	
to invest	
1 — at short term	

201 / investissement

2 – des capitaux dans
3 – d'un pouvoir
4 capital investi
investissement *m.* (voir aussi *placement*)
  1 – à court terme
  2 –s à l'étranger
  3 – de capitaux
  4 – d'équipement
  5 –s étrangers

  6 –s improductifs
  7 –s industriels
  8 – **mal orienté**
  9 –s privés
  10 –s productifs
  11 – des propres ressources
  12 –s publics
  13 nouveaux –s
  14 banque *f.* d'–
  15 compte *m.* d'–
  16 crédit *m.* d'–

  17 dépenses *f. pl.* d'–

  18 excédent *m.* d'–
  19 financement *m.* d'–s
  20 fins *m. pl.* d'–
  21 plan *m.* d'–
  22 politique *f.* d'–
  23 préfinancement *m.* des –s
  24 programme *m.* d'–s
  25 projet *m.* d'–s
  26 valeurs *f. pl.* d'–
  27 volume *m.* des –s

  28 faire des –s
  29 financer les –s par leurs propres ressources
investisseur *m.*
  1 –s institutionnels

  2 – privé
invisible (*importations*)
invitation *f.*
  sur l'– de
inviter à
irrachetable (*obligations*)
irrécouvrable
  créances –s
irréductible (voir *souscription*)
irrégularité *f.*
irrégulier

2 – capital in
3 – with a power
4 invested capital
investment

  1 short-term –
  2 –s in foreign countries, –s abroad
  3 – of capital, capital –
  4 – in equipment
  5 foreign –s

  6 unproductive (non-productive) –s
  7 industrial, –s
  8 misdirected –, misinvestment
  9 private –s
  10 productive –s
  11 – from one's own resources
  12 publics –
  13 new –s
  14 – bank
  15 – account
  16 – credit

  17 – expenditure, – spending, capital outlays

  18 excess of –s
  19 – financing
  20 – purposes
  21 – plan
  22 – policy
  23 prefinancing of –s
  24 – program(me)
  25 – projects
  26 – securities
  27 volume of –s

  28 to effect –s
  29 to invest out of one's own resources

investor
  1 institutional –s

  2 private –
invisible, invisibles
invitation
  at the – of
to invite to
irredeemable
irrecoverable
  – debts

irregularity
irregular

irremboursable / 202

irremboursable (*obligations*)
irresponsable
irrévocable
italique *m.*
  1 (caractère) –
  2 en –
  3 imprimer en –s
item *m.*

irredeemable
irresponsible
irrevocable
  1 italic
  2 in italics
  3 to print in italics, to italicize
item

J

jauge *f.*
  1 – brute
  2 – nette
jaugeage *m.*
  certificat *m.* de –
jauger
  1 – un navire
  2 le navire jauge 4.000 tonnes
jet *m.* à la mer
  – et enlèvement par la mer (les lames)
jeter
  1 – une cargaison à la mer
  2 – par dessus bord
  3 – sur le marché
  4 marchandises jetées à la mer
jeton *m.* (*guichet*)
  – de présence
jeu *m.*
  1 – complet de connaissements
  2 – de bourse
  3 – de lettres de change
joindre à
  1 joindre au capital
  2 ci-joint
  3 les documents ci-joints
  4 nous vous remettons ci-joint, veuillez trouver ci-joint
jouer
  1 – à la bourse
  2 – à la baisse
  3 – à la hausse
joueur *m.*
  1 – à la baisse

tonnage
  1 gross register –
  2 net register –
measurement
  certificate of –

  1 to measure a ship
  2 the ship is of 4.000 tons
jettison
  – and washing overboard
to cast, to throw
  1 to jettison cargo
  2 to throw over board
  3 to throw on the market
  4 goods jettisoned
token
  attendance fee
game
  1 full set of bills of lading
  2 stock gambling
  3 set of bills of exchange
to add to
  1 to add to the capital
  2 enclosed, herewith, annexed
  3 the enclosed documents
  4 we enclose herewith, we are enclosing herewith, enclosed please find
to play, to gamble
  1 to gamble on the stock exchange
  2 to speculate for a fall, to go a bear
  3 to speculate for a rise, to go a bull
gambler
  1 bear operator, bear

2 – à la hausse

jouir
1 – d'une bonne réputation
2 – d'un droit (privilège)
3 – de l'estime

4 – d'une réduction
5 – de l'usufruit
6 – de la préférence

jouissance *f.*
1 – coupon 10
2 – d'intérêts
3 – 15 janvier, 15 juillet

4 – du 1ᵉʳ mars prochain

5 – 1 décembre (*maison*)
6 avec – immédiate

7 droit *m.* de –
8 (époque *f.* de) –

jour *m.*
1 – calendrier
2 – de bourse
3 ... –s de date   [*pas*]
4 – de fête (*où les banques n'ouvrent*
5 – de grâce
6 – de la déclaration des noms
7 – de (la) réponse des primes
8 – de la liquidation

9 – de payement
10 – de planche
11 – de repos
12 – de(s) reports
13 – de starie
14 – de surestarie
15 ... –s de vue
16 – d'exposition, – de visite (*avant la vente*)
17 –s d'intérêt
18 – férié
19 – férié bancaire
20 – férié légal
21 – franc
22 – non férié, – ouvrable, – ouvrier
23 – ouvrable (*pendant lequel le temps permet de travailler*)
24 – ouvré

25 le deuxième – ouvrable après le – de réception
26 – plein

---

203 / jouir

2 bull operator, bull

to enjoy
1 – an excellent reputation
2 – a right
3 – esteem, to stand in esteem

4 to receive a discount
5 to hold in usufruct
6 – the preference

enjoyment
1 cum (with) coupon 10
2 right of interest
3 interest due 15th January, 15th July

4 bearing interest from 1st March next
5 possession on December 1st
6 with immediate possession, entry of possession
7 usufruct
8 due date of coupon

day
1 calendar –
2 exchange –
3 ... –s after (from) date
4 bank holiday
5 – of grace
6 name –, ticket –
7 option declaration –
8 settling –, pay –

9 pay –
10 lay –
11 – of rest
12 contango –
13 lay –
14 – of demurrage
15 ... –s after sight
16 show –

17 –s of interest
18 holiday
19 bank holiday
20 public (statutory) holiday
21 clear –
22 working –
23 weather working –

24 worked –, – of work
25 the second working – after (following) the – of receipt
26 clear –

journal / 204

27 à 8 –s de date
28 à 8 –s de vue
29 à partir de ce –
30 au – le – (v. *argent, prêt*)
31 dans huit –s
32 de ce –
33 notre télégramme de ce –

34 par –
35 tous les –s
36 jusqu'à ce –
37 les livres sont à –

38 compter les mois à 30 –s

39 mettre les livres à –
40 tenir les livres à –

journal *m.*
 1 – de la bourse
 2 – d'entreprise (*pour le personnel*)
 3 – du dimanche
 4 – financier
 5 – hebdomadaire
 6 – local
 7 – officiel
journal *m.* (*compt.*)
 1 – auxiliaire, – analytique
 2 – de bord
 3 – des achats
 4 – des effets à payer
 5 – des effets à recevoir

 6 – des rendus, – des retours
 7 – des ventes
 8 – grand livre
 9 article *m.* de –
 10 entrer (inscrire, passer) au –
journalier *m.*
journaliser
journée *f.*
 1 – de 8 heures
 2 – de travail
 3 – de travail (*ouvrage*)
 4 – chômée
 5 – perdue
 6 femme *f.* de –
 7 homme *m.* de –
 8 travailler à la –
judiciaire
 1 enquête *f.* –
 2 hypothèque *f.* –

27 at 8 –s' date
28 at 8 –s' sight
29 from to –
30 from – to –
31 in eight –s
32 to-day's
33 our to-day's telegram, telegram of to-day's date

34 a –
35 every –
36 up to this –
37 books are kept up to date

38 to reckon (take) a month at 30 –s

39 to post up the books
40 to keep books up to date

newspaper
 1 financial –
 2 staff magazine, house journal
 3 Sunday paper
 4 financial –
 5 weekly paper
 6 local paper
 7 the Gazette
journal
 1 subsidiary –
 2 log book
 3 purchase book
 4 bills payable book
 5 bills receivable book

 6 returns book
 7 sales book
 8 combined journal and ledger
 9 – item
 10 to journalize, to enter in the –
day labo(u)rer
to journalize
day
 1 8-hour working –
 2 working –
 3 –'s work
 4 – not worked
 5 lost –
 6 charwoman
 7 – labo(u)rer
 8 to work by the –
judicial
 1 – inquiry
 2 mortgage by order of the Court

3 pouvoir m. –
4 vente f. –
5 par les voies –s
judiciairement
judicieux
juge m.
– au tribunal de commerce
jugement m. (*tribunal*)
1 – (*opinion*)
2 – déclaratif de faillite
3 – par défaut
juger
1 – nécessaire de
2 chose jugée (voir aussi *force*)
juré
juridiction f.
jurisprudence f.

jusque
1 jusqu'à nouvel avis
2 jusqu'à preuve du contraire
3 jusqu'au 15 janvier
justificatif
1 numéro – (*de journal*)
2 pièce justificative
justification f.
justifier
1 – de (*donner la preuve*)
2 – (*rendre compte*)
3 se –
4 se – (*être justifié*)
5 s'il est justifié que
juxtaposition f.

3 – power
4 sale by order of the Court
5 legally
judicially
judicious, discerning
judge
judge in commercial court
judgment
1 opinion, judgment
2 adjudication in bankruptcy
3 – by default
to judge
1 to think it necessary to
2 res judicata
sworn
jurisdiction
jurisprudence, precedents, holding of the courts
until, till
1 till further advice
2 until the contrary is proved
3 until the 15th January
voucher
1 – copy, checking copy
2 –, documentary evidence
justification
to justify
1 to prove
2 to account for, to vindicate
3 to justify (vindicate) oneself
4 to be justified
5 if it is proved that
juxtaposition

K

kiosque m.

krach m.
– bancaire

kiosk, newsstand

crash
banking failure

L

lacune f.
combler une –
laissé pour compte m.

laissez-passer m. (*douane*)

laminoir m.

gap
to fill (bridge) a –, to meet a want
goods left on hand, refused

transire

rolling mill

lancer
1 – un article
2 – un emprunt
3 – une mode
4 – une nouvelle entreprise
5 – un prospectus
6 – des titres sur le marché

langage *m.*
1 – boursier
2 – chiffré
3 – clair
4 – convenu

langue *f.*
1 –s étrangères
2 posséder une –

languir
le marché languit

languissant
1 commerce –
2 état – du marché

large (*marché*)

légal
monnaie –e

légalisation *f.*

légaliser
1 – une signature
2 copie légalisée

légataire *m.*
1 – particulier
2 – universel

légende *f.* (*monnaie*)

législation *f.*
1 – commerciale
2 – du travail
3 – en matière fiscale
4 – en vigueur
5 – sur la lettre de change

legs *m.*

léser les intérêts

lest *m.*
1 en (sur) –
2 prendre du –

lester

letter of hypothecation *f.*

lettre *f.* (*caractère*)
1 – de référence
2 en toutes –s
3 somme *f.* en –s
4 s'en tenir à la –

lettre *f.*
1 – en date du... courant

---

to launch
1 to put an article on the market
2 to float a loan
3 to initiate (set) a fashion
4 – a new enterprise
5 to send out (issue) a prospectus
6 to throw shares on the market

language
1 stock exchange parlance
2 cipher –
3 plain –
4 code –

language
1 foreign –s
2 to be proficient in a –

to languish
the market is dull, languid

languishing
1 – trade
2 – state of the market

free, broad

legal
– tender

legalization

to legalize
1 – (authenticate) a signature
2 legalized copy

legatee
1 specific –
2 sole –

legend

laws, legislation
1 commercial laws
2 labo(u)r legislation
3 fiscal (tax) legislation
4 laws in force
5 bills of exchange laws

legacy

to injure the interests...

ballast
1 in –
2 to take in –

to ballast

letter of hypothecation

letter
1 reference
2 in words at length
3 amount in words
4 to stick to the –

letter
1 – dated ... inst., of ... inst.

207 / lettre

2 votre – d'hier
3 par –
4 – suit (*télégr.*)
5 – assurée, – chargée
6 – avion
7 – circulaire (*poste*)
8 – d'affaires, – commerciale
9 – d'avis
10 – (d'avis) de non-attribution, de retour de souscription
11 – (d'avis) de répartition, (*actions*)
12 – de change (voir ce mot p. 404)
13 – de condoléance
14 – de confirmation
15 – de convocation

16 – de crédit (voir ce mot p. 404)
17 – de félicitations

18 – de gage
19 – de garantie, – d'indemnité
20 – de licenciement
21 – de marque
22 – de mer
23 – d'envoi
24 – de poursuite, – de rappel, – de relance
25 – de rappel (*pour payement*)
26 – de recommandation

27 – de remercîment
28 – de transport aérien

29 – de voiture
30 duplicata *m.* de – de voiture

31 – de voiture ferroviaire
32 – de voiture émise par transporteurs routiers
33 – d'excuse
34 – d'introduction
35 délivrer à Mr... une – d'introduction
36 – insuffisamment affranchie
37 – non datée
38 – par exprès
39 – recommandée
40 – retournée
41 en-tête *m.* de –
42 suite *f.* de –
43 adresser une – à
44 affranchir une –
45 fermer une –

2 your yesterday's –
3 by –, in writing
4 writing
5 insured –
6 air mail –
7 circular letter
8 business –, commercial –
9 (letter of) advice, advice note
10 – of regret

11 – of allotment

13 condolatory –, – of condolence
14 letter of confirmation
15 notice convening the meeting

17 congratulatory –

18 letter of hypothecation
19 – of indemnity
20 notice of dismissal
21 –s of marque, of mart
22 sea –
23 accompanying –
24 follow-up –

25 – of reminder
26 – of recommendation, of introduction
27 – of thanks
28 Air Consignment Note, (*Amer.*) Air Bill of Lading
29 waybill
30 Counterfoil Waybill

31 Railway Bill of Lading
32 Trucking (companies) Bill of Lading
33 – of apology
34 – of introduction
35 to hand Mr... a – of introduction
36 insufficiently stamped –
37 undated –
38 express –
39 registered –
40 returned –
41 letterhead
42 follower, continuation sheet
43 to address a – to
44 to stamp a –
45 to close a –

lettre de change / 208

46 mettre une – à la poste
47 plier une –
lettre *f.* **de change** (voir aussi *change, copie, effet, traite*)
1 – à l'extérieur
2 – à 3 mois
3 – à date fixe
4 – à délai de date
5 – à délai de vue
6 – à plusieurs exemplaires

7 législation *f.* sur la –
lettre *f.* **de crédit** (v. *transmission*)
1 – circulaire, – pour voyageurs
2 – commerciale
3 – confirmée
4 – épuisée
5 – simple
6 émettre une – sur...
7 émis en vertu de la –
8 épuiser une –
9 inscrire les payements au dos de la –

levée *f.* (*poste*)
1 dernière –
2 – des documents

3 – d'impôts
4 – de la prime
5 – des scellés
6 – des titres (*bourse*)
7 – personnelles, – de compte

lever (*boîte aux lettres*)
1 – un dépôt (*titres*)
2 – les documents

3 – des impôts
4 – une option
5 – une prime

6 – les scellés
7 – une séance
8 – les titres

levier *m.*
1 – de dégagement du chariot
2 – de dégagement du papier
3 – d'interligne
4 – porte-caractères
lez (lès) (Anvers)
liasse *f.*

46 to post a –, to take a – to the post
47 to fold a –
bill of exchange

1 foreign bill
2 three months' bill
3 day bill
4 bill after date
5 bill (payable) after sight
6 bills of exchange in a set

7 bills of exchange law
letter of credit
1 circular –, travel(l)er's –
2 commercial –
3 confirmed –
4 exhausted –
5 special –
6 to issue a – on...
7 drawn under –...
8 to exhaust a –
9 to endorse the payments on the back of the –

clearing, collection
1 last collection
2 taking up (retiral, lifting) of the documents
3 levy of taxes
4 call for the premium
5 taking off the seals
6 taking up (taking delivery) of stock
7 personal drawings

to clear
1 to withdraw deposited securities
2 to take up (retire, lift) the documents
3 to collect (levy) taxes
4 to take up an option
5 to take up an option

6 to take off the seals
7 to close a meeting
8 to take up (take delivery of) stock

lever
1 carriage release –
2 paper release –
3 line spacer
4 type bar
near (Antwerp)
bundle

libellé *m.*
1 – d'un article de journal
2 colonne *f.* du –

libeller
1 libellé comme suit
2 libellé en dollars
3 être libellé au porteur

libéralisation *f.*
1 – du commerce
2 – du cours du dollar

libéraliser

libération *f.*
1 – des échanges commerciaux
2 – (intégrale) d'une action
3 en – de
4 jusqu'à leur complète –

libératoire
avoir force –

libérer
1 – une action de 20%
2 – une action entièrement
3 – un débiteur
4 – d'une obligation
5 – d'une responsabilité
6 – le trafic des payements internationaux
7 action entièrement (intégralement) libérée
8 action non entièrement libérée
9 cette action est libérée de 10%
10 montants *m. pl.* à – sur titres et participations (*bilan*)

libérer, se – (*actions*)
1 – de dettes
2 – d'un engagement
3 – par anticipation

liberté *f.*
1 – d'action
2 prendre la – de

libre
1 – à l'entrée
2 – des droits de douane
3 – d'hypothèques
4 – frappe
5 – service
6 dépôt *m.* –
7 entrée *f.* –

wording
1 narration of a journal entry
2 description column

to word
1 reading (running) as follows
2 expressed (denominated) in dollars
3 to be made out to bearer

liberalization
1 – of commerce
2 freeing of the dollar

to liberalize

relief
1 liberalization of commerce
2 payment in full of a share
3 in full payment of
4 until (their) payment in full, until (they are) fully paid up

to be legal tender

to relieve
1 to pay (a call of) 20%
2 to pay up a share in full
3 to release a debtor
4 to – of (discharge from) an obligation
5 to – of (discharge from) a liability
6 to liberalize international payments
7 fully paid up share
8 partly paid up share
9 this share is 10% paid
10 amounts callable on subscribed shares and participations

to pay up in full
1 to free (clear) oneself from debts
2 to free oneself from an obligation
3 to pay up in advance

liberty
1 freedom of action
2 to take the – of (to)

free
1 duty-free, uncustomed
2 duty-paid
3 unmortgaged, unencumbered
4 – coinage
5 self-service
6 safe custody
7 admission –

libre-échange / 210

8 marchandises *f. pl.* –s
9 marché *m.* –
10 papier *m.* –
11 quitte et – (voir *quitte*)
12 traite *f.* –
13 avoir la main –
14 vous êtes – de..
libre-échange *m.*
zone *f.* de –
libre-échangiste *m.*
librement
licence *f.*

1 – de fabrication
2 – de vente
3 – d'exportation
4 – d'importation
5 porteur *m.* de –
6 sous –
licenciement *m.*
1 – de personnel
2 – sans préavis
3 lettre *f.* de –
licencier
licitation *f.*

lier
1 opération liée
2 ordre lié
3 se – par contrat
4 se considérer lié
lieu *m.* (voir aussi *état*)
1 – de départ
2 – de destination
3 – de livraison
4 – d'émission (*traite*)
5 – de payement

6 avoir –
7 donner – à...
8 ...n'aura pas –
ligne *f.*
1 la – sur l'Amérique
2 – de charge
3 – de chemin de fer
4 – de conduite
5 – de navigation
6 – de tramway
7 – principale (*tél.*)
8 – privée (*tél.*)
9 – supplémentaire (*tél.*)
10 en – ascendante

8 – goods
9 – market
10 unstamped paper

12 clean bill
13 to have – hand
14 you are allowed to
free trade
– area
free trader, free tradist
freely
licence, license

1 manufacturing –
2 selling –
3 export –
4 import –
5 licensee
6 under a licence
dismissal
1 laying off
2 – without notice
3 notice of –
to dismiss, to lay off
sale by auction of property held indivisum

to bind
1 combined deal, swap transaction
2 contingent order
3 to bind oneself by contract
4 to consider oneself bound
place
1 – of departure
2 – of destination
3 – of delivery
4 – of issue
5 – of payment

6 to take –
7 to give rise to...
8 ... will not take place
line
1 – to America
2 load –
3 railway –
4 – of conduct
5 shipping –
6 tram(way) –
7 exchange –
8 private –
9 extension –
10 in ascending –

11 en – collatérale
12 en – descendante
13 en – directe
limitation *f.*
1 – du dividende

2 – de production
limite *f.*
1 – d'âge
2 – de crédit
3 – de poids
4 dépasser une –
5 étendre la –
6 fixer une –
7 lié à une –

8 s'en tenir à une –, observer une –

limiter
lingot *m.*
1 – d'or
2 or *m.* en –s
liquidateur *m.* (*de société*)
nommer un –
liquidation *f.*
1 – (*mise en vente*)
2 – d'une affaire

3 – forcée
4 – judiciaire
5 – totale
6 – volontaire
7 société *f.* en –
8 entrer en –
9 être en –
10 procéder à la –
liquidation *f.* (*bourse*)
1 – de fin de mois

2 – de quinzaine

3 opération *f.* de – de quinzaine
4 – prochaine
5 achat *m.* en –
6 caisse *f.* de –
7 compte *m.* de –
8 feuille *f.* de –
9 jour *m.* de – (voir *jour*)
10 vente *f.* en –
liquide
1 argent *m.* –
2 dette *f.* –
3 marchandises *f. pl.* –s

---

211 / limitation

11 in collateral –
12 in – of descent
13 in direct –
limitation
1 – of dividend

2 – of production
limit
1 age –
2 – of credit
3 – of weight
4 to exceed a –
5 to raise the –
6 to fix a –
7 bound to a –

8 to keep within the –s, to adhere to a –

to limit
ingot
1 ingot, gold bar
2 ingot (bar) gold
liquidator
to appoint a –
liquidation, winding up
1 selling off
2 settlement of a transaction

3 compulsory liquidation
4 winding up by the Court
5 clearance sale
6 voluntary liquidation, winding up
7 company in –
8 to go into liquidation
9 to be in liquidation
10 to proceed to liquidation
settlement, account
1 end month settlement, account

2 mid month settlement, fortnightly settlement, account
3 η dealing for the –
4 next account
5 buying for the account
6 clearing house
7 liquidating account
8 clearing sheet

10 sale for the account
liquid
1 ready money, available cash
2 – debt
3 wet goods

liquider / 212

liquider
 1 – une affaire
 2 – une dette
 3 – (*des marchandises*)
 4 – une position à la hausse
 5 – une société

liquidité *f.*
 1 –s
 2 – de banques
 3 –s de premier rang
 4 –s monétaires
 5 –s quasi-monétaires (quasi-monnaie)
 6 coefficient *m.* (degré *m.*) de –

 7 préférence *f.* pour la –

liste *f.*
 1 – des abonnés
 2 – des actionnaires
 3 – de correspondants
 4 – des départs
 5 – des passagers
 6 – de présence
 7 – des signatures autorisées
 8 – de souscripteurs
 9 – des tirages
 10 – noire
 11 – nominative
 12 cette – annule et remplace toutes nos –s antérieures
 13 dresser une –
 14 mettre sur la –
 15 rayer de la –
litige *m.*
 1 en –
 2 en cas de –
 3 objet *m.* du –
 4 point *m.* en –
 5 régler un –
litigieux
 valeur litigieuse
livrable *m.*
 cours *m.* du –
livrable *adj.*
 vendre – à terme
livraison *f.*
 1 – à domicile
 2 – à terme
 3 – franco domicile
 4 – partielle
 5 – des titres
 6 à (contre) –

 1 to settle a transaction
 2 to pay off (liquidate) a debt
 3 to sell off, to clear
 4 to close (liquidate) a bull position
 5 to wind up a company

liquidity
 1 liquid assets
 2 bank –
 3 first grade –
 4 primary –
 5 secondary –, near-money
 6 – ratio

 7 – preference

list
 1 – of subscribers
 2 – of shareholders
 3 – of correspondents
 4 sailing –, sailing schedule
 5 passenger –
 6 – of those present
 7 – of authorized signatures
 8 – of subscribers, applicants
 9 – of drawings
 10 black –
 11 nominal –
 12 this – cancels and replaces all our previous lists
 13 to make out a –
 14 to enter on a –
 15 to strike off the –
litigation
 1 in –
 2 in case of contest
 3 matter at issue
 4 point at issue
 5 to settle a dispute
litigious
 value of the matter at issue
forward, terminal, (*grains*) **futures**
 forward price
deliverable
 to sell for future delivery
delivery
 1 – at residence
 2 forward –
 3 – free domicile
 4 partial –
 5 – of stock
 6 on –

213 / livre

7 après –
8 par (en) –s (*ouvrage*)
9 prompte –
10 conditions *f. pl.* de –
11 **délai** *m.* de –
12 jour *m.* de –
13 lieu *m.* de –
14 prix *m.* à –
15 retard *m.* dans la –
16 terme *m.* de –
17 demander – (*titres*)
18 être de bonne – (*titres*)
19 être de mauvaise – (*titres*)
20 faire – (*titres*)
21 prendre – (*titres*)
22 prendre – (*marchandises*)
23 vendre à –
livre *f.* (*mesure, monnaie*)
1 – sterling
2 en –s sterling
3 – turque
4 – à terme
5 – transférable
livre *m.* (voir aussi *registre*)
1 – à feuilles mobiles
2 – à souche(s)
3 – auxiliaire
4 – d'achats
5 – d'actionnaires
6 – d'adresses
7 – de balance
8 – de bord
9 – de caisse
10 – d'échéances
11 – de commandes
12 –s de commerce
13 – **de commission**
14 – **de comptabilité**, – de compte(s)
15 – de copies de lettres
16 – de dépenses
17 – d'effets
18 – de magasin
19 – de ménage
20 – de paye
21 – des acceptations
22 – des comptes courants
23 – **des créanciers**
24 – **des débiteurs**
25 – des effets à payer
26 – des effets à recevoir
27 – des entrées
28 – des inventaires
29 – des réclamations

7 after –
8 in parts
9 prompt –
10 terms of –
11 time (term) of –
12 day of –
13 place of –
14 forward price
15 delay in –
16 term of delivery
17 to demand –
18 to be good –
19 to be bad –
20 to deliver stock
21 to take up stock
22 to receive, to take – of
23 to sell for future –
pound
1 – sterling
2 in –s sterling
3 Turkish –
4 forward pound
5 transferable sterling
book
1 loose-leaf –
2 counterfoil –, stub –
3 subsidiary –
4 purchase –, bought –
5 share register, register of members
6 address –
7 balance –
8 log –
9 cash –
10 bill diary
11 order –
12 account –s
13 commission –
14 account –
15 letter –
16 – of charges
17 bill –
18 warehouse –
19 housekeeping –
20 wages –
21 acceptance –
22 account current –
23 creditors' ledger
24 debtors' ledger
25 bills payable –
26 bills receivable –
27 purchase –
28 stock –
29 claims –

livrer / 214

30 – des rendus
31 – des sorties
32 – de(s) ventes
33 clôture *f.* des –s
34 teneur *m.* de –s
35 tenue *f.* des –s
36 tenue *f.* des –s en partie double
37 tenue *f.* des –s en partie simple
38 arrêter (balancer, clôturer) les –s
39 en examinant nos –s
40 inscrire dans (porter sur) les –s
41 produire les –s
42 tenir les –s
livrer
1 – à domicile
2 – à terme fixe
3 – des marchandises
4 – des titres (*bourse*)
5 à – (plus tard)
6 livré en entrepôt
7 livré franco domicile
8 livrez à l'ordre de...
9 livré sur warrant
10 marché *m.* à –
11 prime à – (voir *prime*)
livret *m.* (voir aussi *carnet*)
1 – de caisse d'épargne
2 – de compte
3 – de dépôts
4 – de famille, de mariage (voir *carnet*)
5 – d'ouvrier
6 – horaire
livreur *m.*
livreuse *f.*
locataire *m.*
 – d'un coffre-fort
locatif
1 réparations locatives

2 risque –
3 valeur locative
location *f.*
1 – (*prise à louage*)
2 – de coffres-forts
3 – de places (*théâtre*)
4 – **de voitures**
5 en –
6 bureau *m.* de – (*places*)

7 conditions *f. pl.* de –
8 contrat *m.* de –
9 indemnité *f.* de –
10 prix *m.* de –

30 returns –
31 sales –
32 sales –
33 balancing of the –s
34 bookkeeper
35 bookkeeping
36 bookkeeping by double entry
37 bookkeeping by single entry
38 to balance the –s
39 on examining our –s
40 to enter in the –s
41 to produce the –s
42 to keep the –s
to deliver
1 – at residence
2 to furnish at a fixed term
3 – goods
4 – stock
5 for future delivery
6 bonded terms
7 delivery free domicile
8 deliver to the order of
9 stored terms
10 transaction for forward delivery

book(let)
1 savings bank book
2 pass book
3 depositor's book, deposit book

5 workman's record
6 time table
deliverer
delivery van
tenant, lessee
hirer of a safe
tenant's
1 tenant's repairs, repairs incumbent upon the tenant
2 tenant's risks
3 rental value
letting
1 renting, hiring
2 renting of safes
3 booking of seats
4 **car hiring**
5 on hire
6 box office

7 terms of tenancy
8 hire contract
9 allowance for rent
10 rent

215 / location-vente

location-vente *f.*
locaux *pl.*
 1 – commerciaux, pour le commerce
 2 – pour exposition
 3 – pour magasins
lock-out *m.*
logement *m.*
 1 allocation *f.* de –
 2 crise *f.* du –
 3 pénurie *f.* de –
 4 problème *m.* du –
loi *f.*
 1 – cadre
 2 – des finances
 3 – de Gresham
 4 – de l'offre et de la demande
 5 – en vigueur
 6 – fondamentale (*Allem.*)
 7 – sur...
 8 – sur les établissements incommodes ou insalubres
 9 – sur les sociétés anonymes
 10 – sur le timbre
 11 contraire à la –
 12 d'après la –
 13 par la –
 14 infraction *f.* à la –

 15 interprétation *f.* de la –
 16 projet *m.* de –
 17 contrevenir à la –
 18 éluder la –

 19 être régi par une –, fonctionner sous le régime d'une –
 20 observer la –

loisir *m.*
 utilisation *f.* (organisation) des –s
long
 1 – cours
 2 crédit *m.* à – terme
 3 emprunt *m.* à – terme
 4 papier –
 5 traite *f.* à longue échéance
lot *m.* (*de marchandises*)
 1 en –s
 2 diviser en –s
lot *m.* (*de loterie*)
 1 le gros –
 2 emprunt *m.* à –s
 3 obligation *f.* à –s
 4 gagner un –

---

hire purchase
premises
 1 business –
 2 exhibition –
 3 shop –
lock-out
housing
 1 rent subsidy
 2 housing shortage
 3 housing shortage
 4 housing problem
law
 1 outline –, skeleton –
 2 Finance Act
 3 Gresham's –
 4 – of supply and demand
 5 – in force
 6 basic constitutional –
 7 – on...
 8 Public Nuisance Act

 9 Companies Act
 10 stamp act
 11 contrary to the –
 12 according to the –
 13 by –
 14 transgression of a –

 15 interpretation of the –
 16 bill
 17 to contravene the –
 18 to evade the –

 19 to be governed by a –

 20 to observe the –, to comply with the –

leisure
 use (spending) of leisure
long
 1 – navigation
 2 long-term credit
 3 long-term loan
 4 long-dated bill, long bill
 5 long-dated bill
lot, parcel
 1 in lots
 2 to lot, to parcel out
lottery ticket
 1 first prize
 2 lottery loan
 3 prize bond
 4 to draw a prize

loterie / 216

loterie *f.* | lottery
  billet *m.* de – | lottery ticket
lotir | to parcel out, to lot

lotissement *m.* | parcelling out
louage *m.* | hiring
  1 – | 1 letting
  2 – de service | 2 hire of services
  3 donner à – | 3 to let
  4 prendre à – | 4 to rent, to take on hire
louer (*donner à louage*) | to let
  1 – (*prendre à louage*) | 1 to rent, to hire
  2 – au mois | 2 to hire (let) by the month
  3 – pour 3 ans | 3 to rent (let) for 3 years
  4 à – | 4 to be let
loup *m.* (*bourse*) | stag (premium hunter)
lourd (*marché*) | heavy
lourdeur *f.* (*marché*) | heaviness
loyal | loyal
  1 marchandises –es | 1 genuine goods
  2 qualité –e et marchande | 2 fair average quality
loyer *m.* | hire, rent
  1 – arriéré | 1 arrears of rent
  2 – de l'argent | 2 price of money
  3 – d'un coffre-fort | 3 hire of safe
  4 – élevé | 4 high rent
  5 blocage *m.* des –s | 5 rent restriction
  6 contrôle *m.* des –s | 6 control of rents
  7 impôt *m.* sur les – | 7 rent tax
  8 loi *f.* sur les –s | 8 rent restriction act
  9 donner à – | 9 to let
  10 prendre à – | 10 to take on hire, to rent
lu et approuvé | read and confirmed
lubrifiants *m. pl.* | lubricants
lucratif | lucrative, profitable
  association *f.* sans but – | non-profit association, institution
lucre *m.* | lucre
  amour *m.* (esprit) du – | profit motive
luxe *m.* | luxury
  1 articles *m. pl.* de – | 1 articles of –, fancy goods
  2 édition *f.* de – | 2 de luxe edition
  3 industrie *f.* de – | 3 fancy goods industry
  4 taxe *f.* de – | 4 – tax

M

machine *f.* | machine
  1 – à additionner | 1 adding –, adder
  2 – à additionner et à soustraire | 2 adding-substracting –
  3 – à adresser | 3 addressing –
  4 – à affranchir | 4 franking –

217 / *madame*

5 – à calcul(er)	5 calculating –
6 – à copier	6 copying –
7 – à dicter	7 dictating –
8 – à écrire	8 typewriter
9 – à écrire comptable	9 typewriter accounting –
10 – à écrire et à calculer	10 typewriter calculating –
11 – à écrire portative	11 portable typewriter
12 – à écrire silencieuse	12 noiseless typewriter
13 – à facturer	13 invoicing –
14 – à polycopier	14 duplicating –
15 – à statistiques (*par cartes perforées*)	15 statistical –
16 – à sténographier	16 shorthand –, stenograph
17 – agrafeuse	17 stapling –, stapler
18 – agricole	18 agricultural –
19 – comptable	19 bookkeeping –, accounting –
20 – de bureau	20 office –
21 – interprète (*cartes perforées*)	21 interpreter
22 – outil	22 machine tool
23 – ouvre-lettres	23 letter opener
24 – poinçonneuse (*cartes perforées*)	24 punch, punching –
25 – tabulatrice	25 tabulator, tabulating –
26 – textile	26 textile –
27 – trieuse (*cartes perforées*)	27 sorter
28 écrit (tapé) à la –	28 typewritten
29 fait à la –	29 machine-made

madame *f.* (*adresse*) — Mrs X
1 – (*lettre*) — 1 Madam
2 mesdames et messieurs — 2 ladies and gentlemen
mademoiselle (*adresse*) — Miss X
– (*lettre*) — Madam ; Miss + the name
magasin *m.* (*de réserve*) — warehouse, store
1 – (*boutique*) — 1 shop
2 – à prix uniques — 2 one-price store
3 – à rayons multiples — 3 department(al) store
4 – à succursales multiples (v. *maison*)
5 – bien assorti — 5 well furnished shop
6 –s généraux — 6 bonded warehouses
7 – libre service — 7 self-service shop
8 grand – — 8 department(al) store
9 demoiselle *f.* de – (*vendeuse*) — 9 shop assistant, shop girl
10 garçon *m.* de – — 10 errand boy
11 livre *m.* de – — 11 stock book
12 marchandises *f. pl.* en – — 12 goods on hand, goods in stock
13 stock *m.* en – — 13 stock in trade, on hand
14 avoir en – — 14 to have in stock

magasinage / 218

15 être en –
16 mettre en –
17 ouvrir un –
18 pris en –
19 tenir un –
magasinage *m.*
(frais de) –
magasiner
magasinier
main *f.*
1 de première –
2 entre les –s de
3 fait à la –
4 changer de –s
5 remettre en –(s) propre(s)
main courante *f.*
main-d'œuvre *f.*
1 – agricole
2 – féminine
3 – qualifiée, spécialisée

4 pénurie *f.* de –
5 prix *m.* de –
6 recours *m.* à la – étrangère

mainlevée *f.*
1 – de la saisie
2 – de l'interdiction
3 – d'une hypothèque
4 donner – (de saisie)
maintenir
1 se – à (*cours*)
2 la hausse se maintient
maison *f.*
1 – affiliée
2 – à appartements (multiples)
3 – à succursales multiples

4 – bourgeoise
5 – d'armement
6 – de banque
7 – de commerce
8 – de commission
9 – de confiance

10 – de détail
11 – d'éditions
12 – de gros
13 – de maître
14 – de premier ordre
15 – de rapport
16 – de vente par correspondance
17 – d'exportation

15 to be in stock
16 to take (lay) in stock
17 to open a shop
18 ex store
19 to keep a shop
storage, warehousing [house rent
warehouse (storage) charges, ware-
to store, to warehouse
storekeeper, warehouseman
hand
1 at first –
2 in the –s of
3 hand-made
4 to change –s
5 to deliver to... personally
waste book
labo(u)r, manpower, labor force
1 agricultural workers
2 womanpower, female labo(u)r
3 skilled labo(u)r
                    [manpower
4 scarcity (shortage) of labo(u)r, of
5 cost of labo(u)r, making
6 resort to foreign –

withdrawal
1 replevin
2 withdrawal of interdiction
3 release of mortgage
4 to grant replevin
to maintain
1 to be maintained
2 the rise is sustained, maintained
house
1 subsidiary company
2 block of flats
3 multiple shops (*one type of goods*),
chain stores

4 private –
5 shipping –, shipowner's firm
6 banking –
7 business –, firm
8 commission –
9 trustworthy –

10 retail business
11 publishing –
12 wholesale firm
13 residence mansion
14 high-class firm
15 revenue-earning house
16 mail-order house
17 export firm

18 – d'habitation
19 – d'importation
20 – mère
21 – succursale
22 – sérieuse
23 ancienne – X
maître m. de l'ouvrage
majoration f.
  subir une –
majorer
  1 majoré des frais
  2 – (*pour souscription*)

majoritaire, participation –
majorité f.
  1 – absolue
  2 – des deux tiers
  3 – des trois quarts
  4 – écrasante
  5 – qualifiée
  6 – relative
  7 à la – des suffrages (des voix)
  8 à la grande –
  9 faible –
  10 la grande – de...

  11 décision f. de la –
  12 atteindre sa –
maladie f.
  – professionnelle
malaise m.
malhonnête(té)
mali m.
malversation f.
mandant m.
mandat m. (*fonction*)
  1 – général
  2 – impératif
  3 – spécial
  4 le – de Mr X expire (*conseil d'administration*)
  5 son – est expiré
  6 leur – est renouvelable

  7 durée f. du –
  8 se démettre de son –
mandat m. (*de payement*)
  1 – d'encaissement (recouvrement) postal
  2 – de remboursement
  3 – de virement postal

  4 – international, – sur l'étranger

---

18 dwelling –
19 import firm
20 parent –, head office
21 branch –
22 – of good standing
23 late X
building owner
increase
  to experience a rise
to increase
  1 plus charges
  2 to subscribe for more than actually desired
majority interest
majority
  1 absolute –
  2 two-thirds –
  3 three-quarters –
  4 overwhelming –
  5 qualified –
  6 relative –
  7 by a – of votes
  8 by a large –
  9 narrow –
  10 the great (vast) – of...

  11 – decision
  12 to attain one's –
illness
  occupational (industrial) disease
depression of trade
dishonest(y)
shortage, short
embezzlement
principal, mandator
mandate
  1 general power
  2 binding (mandatory) instructions
  3 special (particular) power
  4 Mr X retires by rotation

  5 his – has expired
  6 they may be re-appointed, their term of office is renewable
  7 term of office
  8 to resign
order to pay
  1 (postal) collecting order

  2 trade charge money order
  3 postal transfer form

  4 international money order

mandataire / 220

5 – postal, – poste
6 envoyer par – postal
7 – télégraphique
8 établir un –
mandataire *m.*

mandater

– des frais de voyage
maniement *m.* (*affaires*)
– d'argent
manier (*affaires*)
1 – de l'argent
2 – des machines
manifeste *m.*
– de douane

manipulation *f.*

–s (*financières*)
manœuvre *f.* de bourse

manquant *m.*
manque *m.*
1 – à gagner

2 – d'argent
3 – de confiance
4 – de fonds
5 – de place
6 – de poids
7 – en caisse
8 3 sacs de –
manquer
1 – (*faire faillite*)
2 – à ses engagements

3 – à la livraison
4 – de
5 – un train
6 l'article manque
7 les marchandises qui manquent
8 il manque 6 balles

9 il nous manque les capitaux nécessaires
10 nous ne manquerons pas de...

manteau *m.* (*de titre*)
manufacture *f.*
1 la – de (*fabrication*)
2 – de soie
3 – de tabacs

5 post office order
6 to send by post office order
7 telegraphic money order
8 to issue an order to pay
mandatary, agent, proxy, attorney

to issue an order for (to authorize) the payment of
– travelling expenses
management, conduct
handling of money
to conduct, to manage
1 to handle money
2 to handle machines
manifest, ship's manifest
customs manifest

handling

manipulations
manipulation on the stock exchange
short, shortage, deficiency
short, shortage, deficiency
1 loss of profit

2 lack (want) of money
3 lack of confidence
4 want of capital
5 lack of accommodation
6 short weight
7 shortage (deficiency) in the cash
8 there are 3 bags short, missing
to be missing
1 to fail, to default
2 to fail one's engagements

3 – on delivery
4 to be in need of
5 to miss a train
6 we are short of this article
7 the missing goods
8 there are 6 bags short, 6 bags are missing
9 we need (are short of) the necessary capital
10 we shall not fail to

certificate
manufactory, factory, works
1 the manufacture of
2 silk mill
3 tobacco manufactory

manufacturer
articles manufacturés
manufacturier m.
manufacturier adj.
industrie manufacturière
manuscrit
demandes –es à... sous le numéro...

manutention f. (*gestion*)
1 – (*marchandises*)
2 frais m. pl. de –

manutentionner
maquiller (*bilan*)
marasme m.

marc m.
1 au – le franc, au – la livre
2 au – le franc de la valeur
marchand m.
1 – ambulant
2 – de journaux
3 – de poisson
4 – en...
5 – en (au) détail

6 – en gros
7 – forain
8 il y a –!
9 trouver –
marchand adj.
1 marine –e
2 navire –
3 prix –
4 qualité loyale et –e

5 valeur –e
marchandage m.
marchander
marchandises f. pl.
1 – acquittées
2 – avariées
3 – de contrebande
4 – de cubage
5 – de grande vitesse
6 – d'encombrement
7 – d'entrepôt, ent~
8 – de petite vitmation
9 – de ret~

10

to manufacture
manufactured articles
manufacturer
manufacturing
– industry
hand-written, in writing
application in own handwriting to...

management
1 handling
2 loading charges ; handling costs

to handle
to fake, to cook
stagnation

1 pro rata, proportionally
2 pro rata (in proportion) to the value
dealer, trader
1 pedlar, hawker
2 newsagent
3 fishmonger
4 dealer in...
5 retailer

6 wholesaler, wholesale dealer
7 booth (stall) keeper
8 I bid
9 to find a buyer
merchant
1 mercantile marine
2 merchant man, trading vessel
3 trade price
4 fair average qua~

5 sale value, market v~lue
bargaining, haggle
to bargain.
goods
1 ~ggled (contraband) –
~easurement –
5 fast train –, speed –
6 bulky –
7 bonded –
8 – sent by – train, slow –
9 returns, – returned

10 bulky goods
11 – for home use, home consumption

marché / 222

12 – en cueillette
13 – en transit
14 – en vrac
15 – flottantes
16 – franches de douane
17 – inflammables
18 – libres
19 – liquides
20 – non acquittées
21 – passibles de droits
22 – périssables

23 – retournées
24 – sèches
25 désignation *f.* des –
26 échange *m.* des –
27 libérer les –

marché *m.* (*transaction*)
1 – à facultés
2 – à prime
3 – à prime pour lever
4 – à prime pour livrer
5 – à terme (*crédit*)
6 – à terme, – à livrer

7 – à terme ferme

8 – au comptant

9 – ferme
10 annuler un –
11 conclure (passer) un –

marché *m.*
1 après bourse
2 – à terme

3 – à terme de devises
4 – au comptant
5 – Commun
6 dans le – Commun
7 association *f.* au – Co…
8 entrée *f.* dans le – Com…
9 adhérer au – Commun
10 – d'outre-mer
11 – de l'argent
12 – de l'escompte
13 – de marchandises
14 – des acheteurs
15 – des capitaux
16 – des changes
17 – des changes à terme
18 – des émissions

12 general –
13 transit –
14 – in bulk, loose –, bulk –
15 afloat
16 duty-free –
17 inflammable –
18 free –
19 wet –
20 uncustomed –
21 dutiable –
22 perishable –

23 returns, – returned
24 dry –
25 description of –
26 exchange of –
27 to release –

bargain, transaction
1 option to double (treble, quadruple)
2 option bargain
3 call option, buyer's option
4 put option, seller's option
5 transactions on credit
6 (*commod*) forward transactions (*securities*) settlement bargain
7 transaction for future delivery during specified periods
8 cash bargain, dealings for cash, cash business
9 firm bargain
10 to cancel a purchase
11 to strike a bargain

market
1 street –
2 (*securities*) settlement –; (*grains*) futures –; (*prod.*) terminal –
3 forward exchange –
4 cash –, spot –
5 **Common** –
6 in the Common –
7 association with the Common –
8 entry into the Common –
9 to join the Common –
10 overseas –
11 money –
15 …nt –
16 fo…y –
17 forw…
18 new is…

223 / marché

19 – des frets	19 freight –
20 – des matières premières	20 commodity –
21 – des titres, des valeurs	21 stock – (share –)
22 – des vendeurs	22 sellers' –
23 – du crédit	23 credit –
24 – du travail	24 labo(u)r –
25 – en banque (coulisse)	25 outside –, (*Amer.*) curb –
26 – en bourse (parquet)	26 official –
27 – extérieur	27 foreign –
28 – hors cote	28 – in unlisted securities
29 – intérieur	29 home –, domestic –
30 – libre	30 free –
31 cours *m.* du –	31 free – price
32 – libre des devises	32 free exchange –
33 – libre de l'or	33 free gold –
34 – mondial	34 world –
35 – des matières premières	35 – of raw materials
36 – monétaire	36 money –
37 titres négociables sur le – monétaire	37 money – paper
38 – noir	38 black –
39 – officiel	39 official –
40 – ouvert	40 open –
41 – over the counter (N. York)	41 over the counter –
42 sur le –	42 in (on) the –
43 le – est :	43 the – is :
44 agité	44 excited
45 animé	45 brisk, animated, lively
46 bien disposé	46 in good tone, cheerful
47 calme	47 calm, quiet
48 déprimé	48 depressed
49 étroit	49 limited, narrow
50 faible	50 weak
51 ferme	51 firm
52 hésitant, indécis	52 unsteady
53 inactif	53 dull
54 languissant	54 dull
55 large	55 broad, free
56 lourd	56 depressed, heavy
57 mou	57 flat
58 résistant	58 strong
59 soutenu	59 steady
60 aisance (facilité) *f.* du –	60 easiness of the –
61 analyse *f.* du –	61 – analysis
62 bulletin *m.* du –	62 – report
63 droits *m. pl.* du –	63 – dues
64 étroitesse *f.* du –	64 limitedness of the –
65 étude *f.* du –	65 – research
66 faiblesse *f.* du –	66 weakness of the –
67 fermeté *f.* du –	67 firmness of the –
68 fluctuations *f. pl.* du –	68 – fluctuations
69 hésitation *f.* du –	69 hesitancy of the –
70 instabilité *f.* du –	70 unsteadiness of the –
71 jour *m.* du –	71 – day

72 lourdeur *f.* du –
73 orientation *f.* du –
74 place *f.* du –
75 prix *m.* du –
76 raffermissement *m.* du –
77 rapport *m.* du –
78 relèvement *m.* du –
79 résistance *f.* du –
80 secteur *m.* du –
81 situation *f.* du –
82 technique *f.* du –
83 tendance *f.* (tenue *f.*) du –

84 agir sur le –
85 conquérir le –
86 dominer le –
87 encombrer le –
88 être sur le –
89 fournir le –
90 gâcher le –
91 jeter sur le –
92 mettre sur le –
93 ouvrir le – à…
94 refouler du –
marge *f.* (*bord*)
1 comme en –

2 en –
3 note *f.* en –

4 noter en –
marge *f.* (*surplus*)
 1 – (*couverture*)
 2 – bénéficiaire, – de bénéfice

 3 – commerciale
 4 – de sécurité, de sûreté

 5 – de crédit
 6 – en espèces
 7 – supplémentaire
 8 obligation *f.* de fournir une – supplémentaire
 9 appel *m.* de –

 10 faire un appel de –

 11 déposer une – en espèces
 12 laisser une – suffisante

 13 maintenir une – de…
 14 porter la – à…
margeur *m.*

72 heaviness of the –
73 trend of the –
74 – place
75 – price
76 hardening of the – tendency
77 – report
78 revival of the –
79 strength of the –
80 section of the –
81 state of the –
82 – technique
83 tendency of the –

84 to act on the –
85 to conquer (capture) the –
86 to dominate the –
87 to overload (encumber) the –
88 to be in the –
89 to supply the –
90 to spoil the –
91 to throw on the –
92 to put (to bring) on the –
93 to open the – to…
94 to oust from the –
margin
1 as per –, as in the – hereof

2 in the –
3 marginal note

4 to write in the –
margin
 1 –, cover
 2 profit –, – of profit

 3 trading (profit) –, trade –
 4 safety –

 5 credit –, (*acc. bilatéral*) swing
 6 – in cash
 7 further (additional) cover
 8 liability to put up additional cover

 9 call for additional cover, – call

 10 to make a call for additional cover

 11 to deposit a – in cash
 12 to leave a sufficient –

 13 to maintain a – of…
 14 to bring the – up to…
marginal stop

marginal (v. *courbe, coût, utilité*)
1 charbonnages marginaux
2 entreprise –e
3 notes –es

4 productivité –e
5 recette –
6 unité –

marginer
marié, femme –e
marine *f.* (v. aussi *marchand*)
marital
  autorisation –e

maritime
1 agence *f.* –
2 assurance *f.* –
3 assureur *m.* des risques –s
4 commerce *m.* –
5 droit *m.* –
6 gare *f.* –
7 mouvement *m.* –
8 navigation *f.* –
9 nouvelles *f. pl.* –s

10 risque *m.* –
11 trafic *m.* –
12 transport *m.* –
13 valeurs *f. pl.* –s
marquage *m.*
marque *f.*
1 – (*sorte*)

2 – de choix
3 – de commerce, de fabrique
4 – déposée

5 – d'origine
6 –s principales
7 – sur les caisses
8 bonne – de cigares
9 toutes les –s d'autos
10 liste *f.* des –s
11 loi *f.* sur les –s
12 vin *m.* de –

marquer
1 – (*les prix*)
2 – d'une croix
3 marqué et numéroté

4 encre *f.* à –
5 fil *m.* à –

marginal
1 – mines
2 – enterprise
3 – notes

4 – productivity
5 – revenue
6 – product

to margin, to write in the margin
married woman
marine
marital
  husband's authorization

marine
1 shipping agency
2 – (maritime) insurance
3 – underwriter
4 sea-borne trade
5 maritime law
6 harbo(u)r station
7 shipping movement
8 maritime navigation
9 shipping intelligence

10 – (maritime) risk
11 sea traffic
12 – transport
13 shipping shares
marking
mark
1 (*cigars, liqueurs etc.*) brand, (*machines*) make

2 choice brand
3 trade –
4 registered trade –

5 – of origin
6 leading –s
7 –s on the cases
8 a good brand of cigars
9 all makes of cars
10 list of –s
11 Merchandise Marks Act
12 wine of a well-known brand

to mark
1 to price, –
2 – with a cross
3 marked and numbered

4 marking ink
5 marking thread

225 / marginal

masse / 226

masse *f.*
 1 – active
 2 – des créanciers
 3 – de la faillite
 4 – passive
 5 créancier *m.* de la –
 6 dette *f.* de la –
 7 production *f.* en –
matériaux *m. pl.*
 – de construction
matériel *m.*
 1 – d'emballage
 2 – roulant
mate's receipt *m.*

matière *f.*
 1 –s adjuvantes
 2 –s d'alimentation
 3 – de remplacement
 4 –s d'or et d'argent
 5 – explosible
 6 –s fissiles
 7 – imposable
 8 –s premières
 [mières
 9 approvisionnement *m.* en –s pre-
 10 besoins *m. pl.* de –s premières
 11 pénurie *f.* de –s premières
 12 prix des –s premières
 13 en – de...

mauvais (v. aussi *récolte*)
 –e administration
maximisation *f.*
maximiser
maximum *m.*
 au – (tout au plus)
maximum *adj.*
 1 cours *m.* –
 2 montant *m.* –
 3 prix *m.* –
mécanique
mécanisation *f.*
mécaniser
mécanographie *f.* comptable
mécompte *m.*

mécompter, se –

meilleur
 à – marché, à – compte
méfiance *f.*
méfiant

mass
 1 assets
 2 – (body) of creditors
 3 bankrupt('s) estate
 4 liabilities
 5 creditor of a bankrupt
 6 debt of the estate
 7 – production
materials
 building –
stock
 1 packing material
 2 rolling –
mate's receipt

material
 1 adjuvants, auxiliaries
 2 foodstuffs
 3 substitute, surrogate
 4 gold and silver bullion
 5 explosive
 6 fissile material
 7 taxable article
 8 raw materials, (*exchange*) commodities
 9 supplying with raw materials
 10 raw materials requirements
 11 scarcity of raw materials
 12 prices of raw materials
 13 in the matter of

bad
 mismanagement
maximation, maximization
to maximize
maximum
 at most, not exceeding
maximum
 1 – price
 2 – amount
 3 – price
mechanical
mechanization
to mechanize
machine posting
miscalculation, mistake

to miscalculate

better
 cheaper
distrust
distrustful

227 / méfier (se)

méfier, se –
membre m.
  1 – actif
  2 – ordinaire
  3 – du comité
  4 – du comité de direction
  5 – du conseil d'administration

  6 carte f. de –

mémoire m. (voir aussi *poste*)
  1 pour –

  2 note f. pour –

mémorandum m.
mémorial m. (*brouillard, main courante*)
mensualité f.
  par –s
mensuel
  1 payement –
  2 rapport –
mensuellement
mention f.
  1 –s de service
  2 – écrite
  3 –s imprimées sur...
  4 faire – de
mentionner
  1 mentionné ci-dessous
  2 mentionné ci-dessus
  3 comme mentionné ci-contre
  4 comme mentionné ci-dessous
  [haut
  5 comme mentionné ci-dessus, plus
  6 en mentionnant
menu
  1 –s frais
  2 –e monnaie
mer f.
  1 haute –
  2 par –
  3 sur –
  4 emballé pour transport par –
  5 jet m. à la –
  6 marchandises jetées à la –
  7 port m. de –
  8 risques m. pl. de –
  9 transport m. par –
  10 jeter à la –
mercantile
  système m. –

to distrust
member
  1 active –
  2 ordinary –
  3 – of the committee
  4 – of the managing committee
  5 – of the board

  6 membership card

bill, account
  1 as a memorandum, on record, not valued
  2 pro memoria item

memorandum
waste book, (*Amer.*) **scratch pad**

monthly allowance, pay
  in monthly instalments
monthly
  1 – payment
  2 – report
monthly
mention
  1 service instructions
  2 written –
  3 notices printed on
  4 to make – of
to mention
  1 below-mentioned
  2 above-mentioned, referred to above
  3 as mentioned opposite
  4 as mentioned (stated) at foot, below

  5 as mentioned above
  6 stating
small
  1 petties, petty expenses
  2 small change
sea
  1 open (high) –
  2 by –
  3 at –
  4 packed for transport by –
  5 jettison
  6 goods jettisoned
  7 seaport
  8 – risks
  9 transport by –
  10 to throw into the – (overboard)
mercantile
  – system

mercantilisme / 228

mercantilisme *m.*
merci
  non –
mercuriale *f.*
mérite *m.*
  en reconnaissance de ses –s
merit-rating *m.*

message *m.*
  – téléphonique
messageries *f. pl.*
mesure *f.*
  1 –s conservatoires

  2 –s de précaution, de sûreté

  3 –s de rétorsion
  4 – discriminatoire
  5 –s sévères, – de rigueur
  6 par – de prudence
  7 être en – de
  8 mettre en – de
  9 prendre les –s nécessaires
mesure *f.*
  1 – de capacité
  2 à – que
  3 au fur et à – du besoin
  4 dans une large –
  5 dans la – du possible

  6 fait sur –
  7 vendre à la –
mesureur *m.*
  peseurs et –s jurés
métal *m.*
  1 – précieux
  2 métaux non ferreux
métallique
  1 monnaie *f.* –
  2 réserve *f.* –
métallurgie *f.*
métallurgique
  industrie *f.* –
méthode *f.*
  1 – de financement
  2 – des nombres
  3 – des parties aliquotes
  4 – de travail
  5 – directe, – progressive [soldes
  6 – hambourgeoise, – à échelles, – par
  7 – indirecte, rétrograde
métier *m.*
  chambre *f.* des –s

mercantilism
thank you
  no, thank you
official list
merit
  in recognition of his services
merit rating

message
  telephonic – [company
parcels service, parcels delivery
measure
  1 –s of conservation

  2 –s of precaution, precautionary measures
  3 retaliatory –s
  4 discriminatory –
  5 stringent –s
  6 as a precautionary –
  7 to be able to
  8 to enable to
  9 to take the necessary –s, steps
measure, size
  1 cubic measure
  2 as, in proportion as
  3 according to requirements
  4 to a large extent
  5 as far as possible, within possibility

  6 made to measure
  7 to sell by measure
measurer
  sworn weighers and –s
metal
  1 precious –
  2 non-ferrous –s
metallic
  1 – money
  2 – reserve
metallurgy
metallurgic(al)
  – (metal) industry
method
  1 – of financing
  2 product –
  3 – of the aliquot parts
  4 – of working
  5 forward –
  6 balance –, steps –
  7 backward –
trade
  chamber of trade

mètre *m.*
1 – carré
2 – courant
3 – cubique
4 trois –s

métropole *f.*
1 – (*par rapport aux colonies*)
2 – commerciale

metteur *m.* **en page**

meuble (voir aussi *titre*)
biens *m. pl.* –s

meuble *m.*

1 – classeur
2 –s meublants

mévendre
mévente *f.*
microfilm *m.*
mieux *m.*
mieux
1 au –
2 au – de vos intérêts

3 sauf – (*bourse*)
4 ordre *m.* au –

5 acheter au –
6 faire de son –
7 vendre au –

milieu *m.*
1 –x boursiers
2 –x commerciaux
3 –x économiques
4 –x financiers

mille
par –

milliard *m.*
millier *m.*
en –s de francs (*tableau*)

million *m.*
en –s de francs (*tableau*)

mine *f.*
1 – de houille
2 – d'or

mineur *m.* (*ouvrier*)
mineur *m.* (*jur.*)
minier
concession minière

minimum *m.*
1 au –
2 – vital (voir *existence*)
3 montant *m.* –

metre, (*Amer.***) meter**
1 square –
2 running –
3 cubic –
4 three –s

metropolis
1 mother country, home country
2 commercial –

make-up man

personal, movable
personal estate, movable property, mov(e)ables

piece of furniture, (*meubles*) **furniture**

1 filing cabinet
2 household furniture

to sell at a sacrifice
selling at a loss
microfilm
improvement
better
1 at best
2 to your best advantage, in your best interests

3 or –
4 order at best

5 to buy at best
6 to do one's utmost
7 to sell at best

middle
1 exchange circles
2 business circles
3 business circles
4 financial circles

thousand
per –

one thousand millions, milliard;
(*Amer. aussi*) **billion**
in thousands of francs

million
in –s of francs

mine
1 coal –
2 gold –

miner
infant
mining
– concession

minimum
1 at the least

3 – amount

ministère / 230

4 poids *m.* –
5 réduire au –
ministère *m.*
 1 – de l'Agriculture
 2 – de l'Intérieur
 3 – des Affaires économiques
 4 – des Affaires étrangères

 5 – des Finances

 6 – du Commerce et de l'Industrie

 7 le – Public
ministre *m.*
 1 – des Affaires économiques
 2 – des Affaires étrangères

 3 – des Affaires sociales
 4 – de l'Agriculture
 5 – du Commerce
 6 – du Commerce et de l'Industrie
 7 – des Finances

 8 – de l'Intérieur
 9 – du Travail
 10 – des Travaux publics
 11 – des Transports
 12 – d'État
 13 Premier –
minorité *f.*
 1 – (*jur.*)
 2 rapport *m.* de la –
 3 être en –
minque *f.*
 – au beurre

minuscule *f.*
minute *f.* (*d'un acte*)
 1 – (*d'une lettre*)
 2 faire une –
minuter
mise *f.* (*jeu*)
 1 – (aux enchères)
 2 – à bord
 3 – à la retraite
 4 – à l'eau
 5 – à pied
 6 – à prix
 7 – au nominatif (*actions*)
 8 – au point

4 – weight
5 to reduce to the –
ministry
 1 Department (Board) of Agriculture
 2 – of Home Affairs, Home Office
 3 – for Economic Affairs
 4 – of Foreign Affairs, (*Gr.Br.*) Foreign Office, (*Amer.*) State Department
 5 Finance Department, (–*Gr. Br.*) the Exchequer, (*Amer.*) Treasury Department
 6 Department of Commerce and Industry, Board of Trade
 7 the Public Prosecutor
minister
 1 – of (for) Economic Affairs
 2 – for Foreign Affairs, (*Gr. Br.*) Foreign Secretary, (*Amer.*) Secretary of State
 3 – of Social Affairs
 4 – of Agriculture
 5 – of Trade, of Commerce
 6 – of Commerce and Industry
 7 – of Finance, (*Gr. Br.*) Chancellor of the Exchequer, (*Amer.*) Secretary of the Treasury [Secretary
 8 – of the Interior, (*Gr. Br.*) Home
 9 – of Labo(u)r
 10 – of Public Works
 11 – of Transport
 12 – of State
 13 Prime –
minority
 1 infancy
 2 – report
 3 to be in the (a) –
mart
 butter – (auction)

small letter, minuscule
original
 1 draft
 2 to make a draft
to draw, to draft
stake
 1 bid
 2 loading on board
 3 pensioning off
 4 launching
 5 dismissal
 6 upset price
 7 conversion into registered shares
 8 rectification

231 / miser

9 – de fonds
10 – en bouteilles
11 – en chantier
12 – en circulation
13 – en demeure

14 – en exécution
15 – en exploitation
16 – en gage
17 – en marche
18 – en pages
19 – en payement (*dividende*)
20 – en possession

21 – en valeur (*portefeuille*)
22 – en vente
23 – en vigueur
24 – hors
25 – sociale
miser
mission *f.*
1 – commerciale
2 – spéciale
3 sans –
4 avoir – de (pour)
mitoyen, mur –

mitraille *f.*
mobilier (*adj.*)
1 biens –s
2 fortune mobilière
3 impôt –

4 saisie mobilière
5 valeurs mobilières
6 vente mobilière
mobilier *m.*
– de bureau
mobilisable
mobilisation *f.* (*capital*)
– de fonds

mobiliser
1 – de l'argent
2 – des fonds
mobilité *f.*
1 – de la main-d'œuvre
2 – professionnelle
mode *m.*
1 – d'emploi
2 – de payement
3 – de transport
4 – d'expédition

9 capital invested, stake
10 bottling
11 laying down
12 circulation, issue
13 summons, injunction

14 carrying out, putting into effect
15 putting into operation
16 pledging, pawning
17 putting into operation, starting
18 layout, making up, make-up
19 payment, making payable
20 putting into possession

21 turning to account
22 putting up for sale
23 putting into force
24 disbursement
25 stake
to bid
mission
1 trade –
2 special –
3 without authority
4 to be commissioned to
party wall

scrap metal
personal, movable
1 personal estate, mov(e)ables
2 personalty, personal property
3 tax on movables

4 seizure of movables
5 transferable securities
6 sale of personal property
furniture
office –
mobilizable
mobilization, setting free
raising of money

to mobilize
1 to set money free, to mobilize
2 to raise funds
mobility
1 labo(u)r –, – of man power
2 occupational –
mode
1 directions for use
2 – of payment
3 – of transport
4 – of conveyance

mode / 232

mode *f.*
1 articles *m. pl.* de –
2 couleur *f.* à la –
3 journal *m.* des –s
4 ne plus à la –
5 devenir la –
6 être à la –
7 lancer une –
8 passer de –
modèle *m.*
moderne
moderniser

modicité *f.* (*prix*)
modification *f.*
1 – aux statuts

2 – d'un crédit documentaire
3 – d'un contrat
4 apporter des –s à...
5 subir des –s
modifier
modique
moindre
de – qualité
moins *m.*
moins
1 – les frais
2 15 – 5 égale...
3 10 francs de –   [(voir *écart*)
4 écart *m.* de... en plus ou en –
5 plus ou –
moins-perçu *m.*
moins-value *f.*

mois *m.*
1 – courant
2 le 10 du – courant
3 – écoulé
4 le 10 du – écoulé
5 – précédent
6 – prochain
7 à trois mois de date
8 dans le délai d'un –
9 – par –
10 commencement *m.* du –
11 dernier jour du –
12 fin *f.* du –
13 milieu *m.* du –
14 première moitié du –
15 papier *m.* à 3 –
moitié *f.*
à – prix

fashion
1 millinery
2 fashionable colour
3 fashion journal
4 out of –
5 to come into –
6 to be in –
7 to bring into –
8 to go out of –
specimen
modern
to modernize

lowness
modification, alteration
1 alteration in the articles of association
2 amendment of a credit
3 alteration of a contract
4 to effect alterations in...
5 to undergo alterations
to modify
moderate
smaller
of inferior quality
minus sign
less
1 – charges
2 15 – (minus) 5 equals...
3 10 francs short

5 more or –
deficiency in receipts
decrease of value, depreciation, deficit
month
1 current (present) –
2 the 10th instant
3 last –
4 the 10th of last –
5 previous –
6 next –
7 three –s after date
8 within a –
9 monthly
10 beginning of the –
11 last day of the –
12 end of the –
13 middle of the –
14 first half of the –
15 three months' paper
half
at – (the) price

mollir (*bourse*) — to flag, to slacken, to ease
monde *m.* — world
  1 – financier — 1 – of finance
  2 correspondants dans le – entier — 2 correspondants in all parts of (throughout) the –, all over the –

mondial — world...
  1 besoins mondiaux de... — 1 world's needs of
  2 commerce – — 2 – trade
  3 consommation –e — 3 – consumption
  4 crise –e — 4 – crisis
  5 économie –e — 5 – economy
  6 firme –e — 6 firm of world-wide reputation
  7 guerre –e — 7 – war
  8 marché – — 8 – market
  9 prix mondiaux — 9 – market prices
  10 production –e — 10 – production, output
  11 de réputation –e — 11 world-known, world-famous
  12 stock – — 12 – stock, supply

monétaire — monetary, money...
  1 assainissement *m.* – — 1 monetary rehabilitation
  2 circulation *f.* – — 2 circulation of currency, monetary circulation
  3 convention *f.* – — 3 monetary convention
  4 crise *f.* – — 4 monetary crisis
  5 dépréciation *f.* – — 5 depreciation of currency, of money
  6 fluctuations *f. pl.* –s — 6 fluctuations of currency
  7 fonds – international — 7 international monetary fund
  8 marché *m.* – — 8 money market
  9 politique *f.* – — 9 monetary policy
  10 question *f.* – — 10 currency problem
  11 réforme *f.* – — 11 currency reform
  12 réserve *f.* – — 12 supply of currency
  13 situation *f.* – — 13 monetary situation
  14 stabilité *f.* – — 14 stability of currency
  15 stabilisation *f.* – — 15 currency stabilization
  16 système *m.* – — 16 monetary system
  17 union *f.* – — 17 monetary union
  18 unité *f.* – — 18 monetary unit
  19 valeur *f.* – — 19 money value
  20 voile *m.* – — 20 veil of money

monétisation *f.* — monetization
monétiser — to monetize
monnaie *f.* — money
  1 – ayant cours, – courante, – en cours — 1 current coin
  2 – belge — 2 Belgian –
  3 – d'appoint — 3 odd –, small change
  4 – d'argent — 4 silver –, silver currency
  5 – d'échange, de change — 5 – of exchange
  6 – d'or — 6 gold –, gold currency

monnayable / 234

7 – de compte
8 – de papier
9 – dépréciée
10 – divisionnaire, – d'appoint
11 – droite
12 – étalon
13 – étrangère
14 – fictive
15 – fiduciaire
16 – flottante
17 – intrinsèque
18 – légale
19 – métallique
20 – nationale
21 – neutre
22 – réelle
23 – saine
24 – scripturale, – de banque
25 fausse –
26 menue (petite) –
27 conversion *f.* d'une – en une autre

28 convertibilité *f.* des –s

29 complète et libre –

30 papier *m.* –
31 pièce *f.* de –
32 titre *m.* de –
33 battre (frapper) de la –
34 rappeler (retirer) de la –
monnayable
monnayage *m.*
(droit de) –
monnayer
1 – un lingot
2 or *m.* à –
monnayeur *m.*
faux –
monométallisme *m.*
monopole *m.*
1 – de l'état
2 – du tabac
3 – de la vente

4 – de fait
5 position *f.* de –
6 accorder le –
7 avoir le – de...
8 obtenir le –
monopoleur, monopolisateur *m.*
monopolisation *f.*
monopoliser

7 – of account
8 (convertible) paper –
9 depreciated currency
10 divisional coin
11 standard –
12 standard –
13 foreign currency
14 token –
15 common –
16 floating currency
17 standard –
18 lawful –, tender
19 metallic –
20 home currency
21 neutral money
22 effective (real) –
23 sound currency
24 deposit –, bank –
25 counterfeit (bad) –
26 change
27 conversion of a currency into another one

28 convertibility of currencies

29 free and complete convertibility

30 (inconvertible) paper –
31 coin
32 fineness
33 to coin –
34 to withdraw coins
coinable
coinage, minting
mintage
to coin, to mint
1 to coin (mint) an ingot
2 standard gold
coiner, minter
counterfeiter, false coiner
monometal(l)ism
monopoly
1 Government –
2 tobacco –
3 exclusive sale, –

4 actual –
5 – position
6 to grant the –
7 to hold a – of
8 to obtain the –
monopolist
monopolization
to monopolize

235 / monsieur

monsieur *m.*	**gentleman**
1 – (*lettre*)	1 (Dear) Sir
2 cher – (X)	2 Dear Sir, Dear Mr. X
3 Messieurs	3 Gentlemen, Dear Sirs
4 – E. Ladrieux (*adresse*)	4 Mr. E. Ladrieux ; E. Ladrieux, Esq.
5 Messieurs Wouters & Legrand	5 Messrs. W. & L.
6 – et Madame... (*adresse*)	6 Mr. and Mrs...
montant *m.* (voir aussi *somme*)	**amount**
1 – brut	1 gross –
2 – de moins de...	2 sum of less than
3 – dépassant...	3 sum exceeding...
4 – exonéré	4 exempted –
5 – maximum	5 maximum –
6 – minimum	6 minimum –
7 – net	7 net –
8 – total	8 total –
9 d'un – de	9 to the – of, amounting to
10 jusqu'au – de	10 up to..., to the extent (amount) of
11 chèque *m.* d'un – de	11 cheque (check) for...
montée *f.*	**rise**
1 – des prix	1 – in (of) prices
2 – des salaires	2 – in (of) wages
monter	**to rise**
1 – une affaire	1 to start a business
2 – en flèche	2 to shoot up, to soar, to rocket
3 faire – les cours	3 to raise (force up) prices
4 se – à	4 to amount to
5 les prix montent	5 prices are rising
morale *f.* des affaires	**business ethics**
moratoire *m.* (v. *intérêt*)	**moratorium**
décréter un –	to announce a –
mortalité *f.*	**mortality**
table *f.* de –	life (mortality) table
morte-saison *f.*	**dead season**
mot *m.*	**word**
1 – de code	1 code –
2 – de repère	2 key – [key
3 –s guides (*tel.*)	3 identification –s, telephone spelling
4 – mutilé (*télégr.*)	4 mutilated –
5 au bas –	5 at the lowest figure
6 en d'autres –s	6 in other –s
7 en un –	7 in one –, briefly
motivation *f.*, recherche de –	**motivation research**
motiver	**to give reasons for**
décision motivée	reasoned decision
mou (*bourse*)	**flat, easy**
mouillage *m.*	**anchorage**
(lieu de) –	anchorage
mouiller	**to anchor**
mouilleur *m.*	**damper**
mouvement *m.* (voir aussi *circulation*, *échange*)	**movement**
1 – ascensionnel	1 upward –

moyen / 236

2 – boursier	2 turnover, sales on the Exchange
3 – commercial	3 commercial traffic
4 – conjoncturel	4 cyclical –
5 – d'affaires important	5 considerable volume of business
6 – dans le personnel	6 staff transfers, staff changes
7 – de baisse	7 downward –, retrograde –
8 – de caisse	8 cash transactions
9 – de hausse	9 upward –
10 – de l'épargne	10 savings –
11 – de l'or	11 gold –
12 – des acceptations bancaires	12 circulation of bank acceptances
13 – des capitaux	13 capital –s
14 – d'escompte	14 discount transactions
15 – des cours	15 – of prices
16 – des devises	16 currency dealings, exchange operations
17 – des grèves, – gréviste	17 strike –
18 – des marchandises et des capitaux	18 – of goods and capital
19 – des navires (*journal*)	19 shipping news, shipping intelligence
20 – des payements internationaux	20 international payments
21 – des personnes	21 – of workers, transfer of manpower, (free) – of labo(u)r
22 – des prix	22 – of prices
23 – des salaires	23 wage –s
24 – des valeurs	24 circulation of securities
25 – de transit	25 transit traffic
26 – d'un compte	26 turnover (of an account)
27 – du port	27 – of the port, traffic of the port
28 – international du commerce et des payements	28 international commerce and payments
29 – maritime	29 shipping traffic, shipping –
30 –s monétaires	30 –s of money
31 compte *m.* à grand –	31 active account
32 compte *m.* sans –	32 account without turnover
33 entrave *f.* au – des marchandises	33 trade restrictions
34 libération *f.* du – des marchandises	34 liberalization of the –s of goods
moyen	**middle, average**
1 cours –	1 average price
2 échéance –ne	2 average due date
3 qualité –ne	3 average quality

moyen *m.*
1 au – de
2 –s de communication
3 –s de payement
4 –s de production
5 –s de transport
6 –s d'existence
7 –s disponibles
8 –s étrangers
9 –s financiers
10 –s flottants, liquides
11 –s limités, faibles
12 –s propres

13 disposer d'amples –s

14 voies et –s
moyennant
– payement
moyenne *f.*
1 – annuelle
2 – arithmétique
3 – géométrique, proportionnelle

4 – mensuelle
5 – pondérée
6 en –

7 prendre la –
multiple *m.*
50 francs et –s
multiplicateur *m.* (*écon.*)
multiplication *f.*

table *f.* de –
multiplier
3 multiplié par 4 égale...

mutation *f.*
1 –s (*personnel*)
2 – de propriété
3 état *m.* de –
mutuel
1 accord –
2 assurance –le

3 société –le, une –le
4 société *f.* d'assurance –le contre l'incendie

means
1 by – of
2 – of communication
3 – of payment
4 capital goods
5 – of transport
6 – of subsistence
7 available –
8 borrowed capital
9 pecuniary –
10 liquid resources
11 limited –
12 own –, resources

13 to have ample – (funds) at one's disposal
14 ways and –
for, by means of, in return for
on payment
average
1 yearly –
2 arithmetic(al) mean
3 geometrical mean, mean proportional

4 monthly –
5 weighted –
6 on an –

7 to take the –
multiple
50 francs and –s
multiplier
multiplication

– table
to multiply
3 multiplied by 4 equals...

transfer
1 (staff)transfers
2 – (conveyance) of property
3 list of staff –s
mutual
1 – agreement
2 – insurance

3 – society
4 – fire insurance company

N

nantir
  1 – quelqu'un

  2 – des valeurs
  3 créancier nanti

nantir, se –

  – de...
nantissement *m. (action)*

  1 – *(acte)*
  2 – *(objet)*
  3 sur – de...
  4 avances *f. pl.* sur –
  5 prêt *m.* sur –
  6 titres *m. pl.* remis (déposés) en –

  7 donner (remettre) en –
  8 emprunter sur –
  9 prêter sur –
  10 tenir (détenir) en –
nation la plus favorisée
  clause *f.* de la –
nationalisation *f.*

nationaliser
nationalité *f.*
nature *f.*, en – (v. *prestation, règlement*)
naufrage *m.*
  faire –
naufragé *m.*
navigabilité *f.*
  1 (bon état de) –
  2 en mauvais état de –
navigable
  – (*en état de naviguer*)
navigation *f.*
  1 – au long cours
  2 – au tramping, – irrégulière
  3 – de cabotage
  4 – intérieure, fluviale
  5 – maritime
  6 compagnie *f.* de –
  7 compagnie *f.* de – aérienne

  8 entraver la –
navire *m.* (voir aussi *bateau*)
  1 – abandonné
  2 – abordé

to pledge, to secure
  1 to secure someone by...

  2 to pledge securities
  3 secured creditor

to secure oneself by

to provide oneself with
pledging, hypothecation

  1 contract of pledge
  2 collateral security, pledge
  3 on security of
  4 advances against security
  5 loan on security
  6 securities lodged as collateral

  7 to pledge
  8 to borrow on security
  9 to lend on collateral (security)
  10 to hold in pledge
most favoured nation
  – clause
nationalization

to nationalize
nationality
in kind
(ship)wreck
  to suffer –
shipwrecked (person)
navigability
  1 seaworthiness
  2 unseaworthy
navigable
  seaworthy
navigation
  1 long (foreign) –, ocean –
  2 tramp –
  3 coasting –
  4 inland –
  5 maritime –
  6 shipping company
  7 air line company

  8 to impede –
ship
  1 derelict
  2 – collided with

239 / né

3 – abordeur
4 – à passagers
5 – citerne
6 – de mer
7 – de tramping, – irrégulier
8 – marchand, – de commerce
9 – pétrolier
10 – régulier
11 le long du –

12 par le premier –
13 affréter un –
14 armer un –
15 fréter un –

né
Madame X, –e Y

nécessaire
1 estimer –
2 faire le –
3 rendre –

nécessité *f.* (voir aussi *produit*)
1 –s du service
2 se trouver dans la –

négatif
négligence *f.*
négligent
négliger
1 négligé (*valeur*)
2 les fractions de... sont négligées

négoce *m.*
faire le –
négociabilité *f.*

négociable

1 – en bourse
2 papier –

3 valeurs *pl.* –s

négociant *m.*
négociation (voir aussi *affaires, marché, opérations*)
1 –s à prime
2 –s à terme
3 –s au comptant
4 – d'un effet

5 – d'un emprunt

6 des –s sont en cours

---

3 colliding –
4 passenger –
5 tank vessel, tanker
6 seagoing –, ocean –
7 tramp
8 merchant man, trading vessel
9 oiler, oil ship
10 liner
11 alongside vessel

12 by first available steamer
13 to charter (take in freight) a vessel
14 to fit out a –
15 to freight (out) a –

born
Mrs X, née Y ; Mrs X, maiden name (born) Y

necessary
1 to judge –
2 to do the needful, –
3 to necessitate

necessity
1 requirements of the service
2 to be under the –

negative
negligence
negligent
to neglect
1 neglected
2 fractions of... are ignored

trade, trading
to trade
negotiability

marketable

1 negotiable on the stock exchange
2 negotiable paper

3 – securities

trader, merchant
negotiation

1 option bargains
2 dealings for the settlement
3 cash transactions
4 – of a bill

5 – of a loan

6 –s are in progress

négocier / 240

7 entamer des –s

8 reprendre les –s

9 rompre les –s
négocier
1 – un effet
2 – un emprunt

3 – un emprunt (*placer*)
négocier, se – (*effet*)
– (en bourse)

net
1 – d'impôts
2 bénéfice –
3 montant –
4 perte –te
5 prix –
6 produit –
7 mettre au –
neuf
flambant –
niveau *m.* (v. aussi *échelon*)
1 – des prix
2 – des salaires
3 – de vie élevé

4 – le plus bas
5 – le plus élevé
6 atteindre un –
7 maintenir les prix à un même –
nivellement *m.*
niveler
noir
1 – sur blanc
2 liste –e
3 marché –
nolis *m.* (*fret*)
nolissement *m.* (*affrètement*)
nom *m.*
1 – de baptême, petit –
2 – de famille
3 – de jeune fille
4 – d'emprunt
5 – social
6 dont le – m'a échappé

7 (inscrit, libellé) au – de
8 compte *m.* ouvert en votre –
9 changement *m.* de –
10 agir au – de
11 apposer son – sous...

7 to enter into (open) –s

8 to take up –s

9 to break off –s
to negotiate
1 – a bill
2 – a loan

3 to place a loan
to be negotiated
to be dealt in on the exchange

net
1 free of tax
2 – profit
3 – amount
4 – loss
5 – price
6 – proceeds
7 to make a fair (clean) copy
new
brand-new
level
1 – of prices
2 wage –
3 high standard of living

4 the lowest –, low, trough
5 the highest –, peak –
6 to reach a –
7 to maintain prices at the same –
levelling
to level
black
1 in – and white
2 – list
3 – market
freight
chartering
name
1 Christian –
2 surname
3 maiden –
4 assumed –
5 – of firm, style
6 whose – has slipped my memory

7 in the – of
8 account opened in your –
9 change of –
10 to act on behalf of
11 to put one's – to

nombre m.
1 – élevé
2 – entier
3 – fractionnaire
4 – impair
5 – pair
6 au – de 1.000
7 en grand –
8 en –s ronds
9 ne pas être en – (*assemblée*)
nombres m. pl. (*calcul des intérêts*)
1 – créditeurs
2 – débiteurs
3 – noirs
4 – rouges
5 balance f. des –
6 méthode f. des –
nombre index, indice (voir aussi *index*)
nomenclature f.

nominal
1 appel –
2 par appel –
3 valeur –e
4 sans valeur –e
nominatif
1 action nominative
2 liste nominative
3 mise f. au –

4 valeurs nominatives
nomination f.
– de...
nommé
1 – ci-après (*contrat*)

2 un – X
3 le susnommé
nommément
nommer
1 – (*à un poste*)
2 – à vie
3 – des experts
4 – ...son héritier
5 – président

6 être nommé à la présidence

non acceptable
non-acceptation f.
non accepté
non-accomplissement m.

number
1 high –
2 whole –
3 fractional –
4 odd (uneven) –
5 even –
6 to the – of 1000, 1000 in –
7 in large –s
8 in round –s
9 the quorum is not complete
products
1 credit –
2 debit –
3 black –
4 red –
5 balance of –
6 product method
index number

nomenclature, list

nominal
1 call-over, roll call
2 by call-over
3 – value, face value
4 without – value
nominal
1 registered share
2 list of names
3 conversion into registered shares

4 registered securities
nomination, appointment
appointment as
named
1 hereinafter – (called)...

2 a certain Mr. X
3 the above-named
by name
to call
1 to appoint
2 to appoint for life
3 to appoint experts
4 to appoint... one's heir
5 to appoint (as) chairman

6 to be elected chairman, to the presidency
unacceptable
non-acceptance
unaccepted
non-fulfilment

non acquitté	unsettled
non affranchi	unpaid
non appelé (*capital*)	uncalled
non-arrivée *f.*	non-arrival
non assuré	uninsured
non avenu	void
non bancable	unbankable
non-commerçant *m.*	non-trader
non confirmé	unconfirmed
non-conformité *f.*	non-conformity
non coté	unquoted, non-quoted
non cumulatif	non-cumulative
non daté	undated
non emballé	unpacked
non-embarquement *m.*	non-shipment
non endommagé	undamaged
non entièrement libéré	partly paid
non-exécution *f.*	non-execution
non-livraison *f.*	non-delivery
non monnayé	uncoined
non payé	unpaid
non-payement *m.*	non-payment
en cas de –	in case of –
non périmé	unexpired
non réclamé	unclaimed
non remboursable (*emprunt*)	irredeemable
non-résident *m.* (*change*)	non-resident
non-responsabilité *f.*	non-liability
non rétribué	honorary
non signé	unsigned, "signature missing"
non-valeur *f.* (*créance*)	bad debts
1 – (*marchandises*)	1 unsal(e)able goods
2 – (*titres*)	2 worthless securities
non-vente *f.*	non-sale
normalisation *f.*	standardization
commission *f.* de –	– committee
normaliser	to standardize
nostro	nostro...
1 compte *m.* –	1 – account
2 engagements *m. pl.* –	2 – liabilities
notaire *m.*	notary
1 étude *f.* de –	1 notary's office
2 frais *m. pl.* de –	2 notary's fees
3 résidence *f.* du –	3 notary's residence
4 dressé par devant –	4 drawn up before a –
notarié, acte –	notary's (notarial) deed
note *f.*	note
1 – (*facture*)	1 bill, invoice, account

2 – de commission
3 – de couverture (*assur.*)
4 – de crédit
5 – de débit
6 – de frais
7 – de poids
8 – marginale
9 suivant la – ci-jointe
10 prendre – d'une commande
11 prendre – du contenu
12 nous avons pris bonne – de

noter
1 – une adresse
2 – une commande
3 notez bien !
4 notez bien que
notice *f.*
la – légale prescrite par ... a paru dans ... (*émission*)

notification *f.*
1 – du protêt
2 donner – de
3 jusqu'à – expresse de son retrait

4 – (*créd. doc.*)
5 commission *f.* de –
notifier

1 – au bénéficiaire (*crédit doc.*)

2 veuillez – par courrier, par câble, par telex
notoriété *f.*
1 acte *m.* de –

2 crédit *m.* sur –
3 il est de – publique

4 sur –
nourrir (voir *action*)
nouveau
1 nouvelle édition
2 nouvelle émission
3 nouvelle feuille de coupons
4 1 action nouvelle contre 2 anciennes
5 de –
6 jusqu'à nouvel avis
7 pour une nouvelle période de 3 mois

2 commission account
3 cover –
4 credit –
5 debit –
6 – of expenses
7 weight –
8 marginal –
9 as per account enclosed
10 to note (take down) an order
11 to take – of the contents
12 we have taken due – of

to note
1 – an address
2 to book an order
3 mind you ! mark !
4 please note that

the advertisement in compliance with... was issued in...

notification, notice
1 notification of protest
2 to give notice of
3 until (its) withdrawal is expressly notified to
4 notification, advising
5 advising commission
to notify

1 to notify the beneficiary, to advise... to the beneficiary
2 please advise by mail, by cable, by telex
notoriety
1 identity certificate, statutory declaration
2 unsecured credit
3 it is a matter of common knowledge, it is notorious that
4 unsecured, without security

new
1 – edition
2 – issue
3 – sheet of coupons
4 1 – share for two old ones

5 again
6 till (until) further advice
7 for a further period of 3 months

nouveauté / 244

8 report *m.* à - de l'exercice précédent
9 solde *m.* à - (*compt.*)

10 (re)porter à - (*compt.*)
nouveauté *f.*
1 haute -
2 magasin *m.* de -
nouvel an *m.*
vœux *m. pl.* de -

nouvelle *f.*
1 assurance *f.* sur bonnes ou mauvaises -s
2 défaut *m.* de -s (*navire*)
3 bonnes -s
4 mauvaises -s
5 perdu sans -s
novation *f.*
nu (*sans emballage*)
1 - propriétaire

2 -e propriété
nucléaire
1 fission *f.* -
2 industrie *f.* -
3 réacteur *m.* -
4 recherche *f.* -
nuitée *f.* (*hôtel*)
nul
1 - et non avenu
2 affaires presque -les
3 son crédit est presque -
4 considérer comme - et non avenu
5 déclarer -
nullité *f.*
1 - d'un contrat
2 déclaration *f.* de -
3 demande *f.* en -
numéraire *m.*
en -
numérique
bordereau *m.* -
numéro *m.*
1 - d'appel (*télescripteur*)
2 - d'appel, - de téléphone

3 faux - d'appel
4 - de commande
5 - de référence, - de renvoi

6 - d'habitation [tion (*auto*)
7 - minéralogique, - d'immatricula-

8 balance brought forward from previous account
9 balance (carried forward) to next account

10 to carry forward to - account
novelty
1 great -
2 millinery
New Year
New Year's wishes, compliments of the season

news
1 insurance "schip lost or not lost"

2 want of -
3 good -
4 bad -
5 missing
novation
naked, unprotected
1 bare owner

2 bare ownership
nuclear
1 - fission
2 - industry
3 - reactor
4 - research
one night's lodging
null
1 - and void
2 business almost nil
3 his credit is nil
4 to consider as - and void
5 to declare - and void
nullity
1 - of a contract
2 declaration of -
3 plea of -
specie, (hard) cash
in cash, for cash
numerical
- list
number
1 call -
2 call -

3 wrong call -
4 order -
5 reference -

6 house -
7 car -

245 / numérotage

8 – d'ordre
9 – du district postal
10 – justificatif
11 composer le – (tel.)
numérotage m.
numéroter

numéroteur m.

8 running –, rotation –
9 postal zone –
10 voucher copy
11 to dial the –
numbering
to number (consecutively)

numerator

O

obérer de dettes

objecter

objection f.
1 écarter des –s
2 faire (soulever) des –s

objet m.
1 – : (lettre)
2 l'– de la présente est
3 –s d'art
4 – d'un contrat

5 – de l'impôt
6 –s de valeur (coffre)
7 la société a pour –
obligataire adj.
1 créancier m. –
2 dette f. –
3 emprunt m. –
obligataire m.
registre m. des –s
obligation f.

1 – à 4 %
2 – portant un intérêt de 4 %
3 – à intérêt variable
4 – à la souche, – non souscrite
5 – à lots
6 – amortie
7 – amortissable
8 – à option de change
9 – à primes
10 – à revenu fixe
11 – à revenu variable
12 – à taux progressif, à intérêts croissants
13 – au porteur

to burden with debts

to object against

objection
1 to remove –s
2 to raise (make) –s against

object
1 re : ; subject :
2 this letter (the – of the present) is to
3 –s of art
4 subject (subject matter) of a contract
5 taxable article
6 valuables
7 the – of the company is
debenture...
1 bond creditor
2 – debt
3 – loan
debenture holder
debenture register
debenture, bond

1 4 % bond
2 bond bearing interest at 4 %
3 variable-interest bearing debenture
4 unissued debenture
5 lottery (prize) bond
6 redeemed debenture
7 redeemable debenture
8 – with currency option
9 premium bond
10 fixed-interest bearing debenture
11 variable-yield debenture
12 graduated-interest debenture

13 bearer debenture

obligation / 246

14 – chirographaire
15 – communale

16 – convertible
17 – définitive
18 –s en portefeuille
19 – étrangère
20 – hypothécaire
21 – indexée
22 – industrielle
23 – nominative

24 – non remboursable
25 – or, – à garantie de change
26 – participante
27 – privilégiée

28 – rachetable, remboursable
29 – remboursée
30 – sortie (au tirage)
31 capital *m.* –s
32 dette *f.* d'–s
33 émission *f.* d'–s
34 emprunt *m.* –s (obligataire)
35 perte *f.* sur émission d'–s
36 porteur *m.* d'–s

37 prime *f.* sur émission d'–s
38 remboursement *m.* d'–s
39 émettre des –s
40 racheter, rembourser des –s
obligation *f. (engagement)*
1 – de faire un versement supplémentaire
2 avoir des –s envers...
3 contracter des –s

4 délier (libérer) d'une
5 faire honneur à ses –s
6 imposer l'– de
7 il lui incombe l'– de
8 se soustraire à une –
obligatoire
obligeance *f.*
avoir l'– de
obligé *m.*
– *(lettre de change)*
obliger
1 il est obligé de
2 nous vous sommes très obligés

3 vous nous obligeriez beaucoup en...

14 simple (naked) debenture
15 municipal bond

16 convertible debenture
17 definitive bond
18 unissued bonds
19 foreign bond
20 mortgage bond (debenture)
21 index-bond
22 industrial bond
23 registered bond

24 irredeemable (perpetual) bond
25 gold bond
26 profit sharing (participating) bond
27 priority bond, preference bond

28 redeemable bond
29 redeemed bond
30 drawn bond
31 debenture capital
32 bonded debt
33 issue of debentures, debenture issue
34 debenture loan
35 discount on bonds
36 bondholder, debenture holder

37 bond agio, premium on bonds
38 redemption of bonds
39 to issue bonds
40 to redeem bonds
obligation
1 liability to put up additional cover

2 to be under an –
3 to enter into engagements, to undertake –s

4 to release from an –
5 to fulfill one's –s
6 to impose the – to
7 he is under the – to...
8 to withdraw from one's –
compulsory
kindness
to have the – to, to be so kind as to...
obligor
party liable on a bill of exchange
to oblige
1 he is obliged (bound) to
2 we are much obliged to you

3 we shall be much obliged if you will, you will (would) greatly oblige us by

247 / oblitérateur

4 nous nous voyons obligés

5 s'— à…
oblitérateur *m.*
oblitérer (*timbre*)
observation *f.*
  colonne *f.* pour les —s
observer (*contrat*)
 — (*délai*)
obstacle *m.*
  1 écarter des —s
  2 mettre des —s à qqn

occasion *f.*
  1 — (*achat*)
  2 à la première —
  3 à cette —, en cette —
  4 à l'—
  5 à l'— de
  6 d'—
  7 dès que l'— se présente

  8 si l'— se présente
  9 livres *m. pl.* d'—
  10 voiture *f.* d'—
  11 manquer l'—, laisser passer l'—
  12 profiter d'une —

  13 saisir l'—
occupation *f.*
  1 — accessoire
  2 — principale
occuper
  1 — 200 ouvriers
  2 — le rez-de-chaussée

  3 être occupé à…
  4 être très occupé

  5 occupé (*tel.*)

occurence, en l' —
octroi *m.*
octroyer
offert (*bourse*)
  1 demandé… et —…
  2 cours —s (vendeurs)

  3 être — à…
office *m.*
  1 — de brevets d'invention
  2 — de compensation
  3 — de placement

4 we feel obliged to

5 to undertake to
cancel(ling) stamp
to cancel, to obliterate
remark, observation
  remarks column
to observe, fulfil, live up to
  to keep to
obstacle
  1 to remove —s
  2 to put —s in one's way

occasion
  1 (chance) bargain
  2 at the first opportunity
  3 at this juncture, on this occasion
  4 on —, when an opportunity occurs
  5 on the — of
  6 second-hand
  7 should an — (opportunity) present itself
  8 when the opportunity offers
  9 second-hand books
  10 second-hand (used) car
  11 to miss (neglect) the opportunity
  12 to avail oneself of (take advantage of) an opportunity
  13 to take the opportunity
business, work
  1 additional occupation
  2 chief business

  1 to give employment to 200 hands
  2 to occupy (live on) the ground floor

  3 to be occupied in…
  4 to be very busy, to be very much pressed with business
  5 (line) engaged, the number is engaged, (*Amer.*) the line is busy
in the present case
granting
to grant

  1 … bid, … offered
  2 prices offered, sellers

  3 to be on offer at…
office
  1 Patent —
  2 clearing —
  3 labo(u)r exchange

4 – de publicité | 4 advertising agency
5 – de tourisme | 5 travel agency
6 – du commerce extérieur | 6 foreign trade agency
7 d'– | 7 officially
8 d'– (*sans plus*) | 8 automatically
9 il l'a fait d'– | 9 he did it of his own accord

10 grâce aux bons –s de | 10 by the good – of
officiel | **official**
officieux | **semiofficial**
offrant, au plus – | **to the highest bidder**
offre *f.* | **offer**
  1 – acceptable | 1 acceptable bidding
  2 – avec échantillons | 2 sampled –
  3 ,,–s d'emploi'' | 3 ,,situation vacant''
  4 – de service | 4 tender (offer) of service
  5 – de souscription (*émission*) | 5 tender, – for subscription

  6 – de vente | 6 – for sale
  7 – excédentaire | 7 excess –
  8 – ferme | 8 firm –
  9 – par écrit | 9 written –
  10 – sans engagement | 10 – without engagement
  11 – spéciale | 11 special –
  12 – et demande | 12 supply and demand
  13 courbe *f.* d'– | 13 supply curve
  14 loi *f.* de l'– et de la demande | 14 law of supply and demand

  15 cette – est valable jusque... | 15 this – is still firm till...

  16 l'– excède la demande | 16 the – exceeds the demand

  17 accepter une – | 17 to accept an –
  18 décliner (refuser) une – | 18 to decline an –
  19 demander une – | 19 to ask an –
  20 faire une – | 20 to make an –
  21 profiter d'une – | 21 to take advantage of an –
  22 recevoir une – | 22 to receive an –
  23 retirer une – | 23 to withdraw an –
offrir (voir aussi *offert*) | **to offer**
  1 – à la (en) vente | 1 – for sale
  2 – des avantages | 2 – advantages
  3 – des perspectives | 3 – prospects
  4 – un prix | 4 to bid a price
  5 – ferme | 5 – firm
  6 – sans engagement | 6 – without engagement
  7 – sauf vente | 7 – if unsold
oisif (*capital*) | **idle, dead**
oligopole *m.* | **oligopoly**
oligopolique | **oligopolistic**
once *f.* | **ounce**
onéreux, à titre – | **by onerous title, for a valuable consideration**

onglet *m.*
opération *f.* (voir aussi *affaire, marché, négociation*)
1 – à découvert, – à la baisse

2 – à la hausse
3 –s à prime
4 –s à terme (*crédit*)
5 –s à terme, – à livrer

6 –s à terme ferme

7 –s au comptant

8 –s de banque
9 toutes –s de banque

10 –s de bourse
11 –s de change

12 –s de change à terme

13 –s de change au comptant

14 –s de crédit
15 –s de déport
16 –s de report

17 –s fermes
18 –s financières
19 –s liées

opéré, avis *m.* d –
opérer un payement
opposition *f.*
1 bulletin *m.* (liste) des –s

2 valeurs frappées d'–

3 mettre – sur
optant *m.*
option *f.*
1 – (*double prime*)

2 – du change
3 – du double

4 coût *m.* d'–
5 droit *m.* d'–

tab, thumb index
dealing, transaction

1 bear transaction, dealing for a fall

2 bull transaction, dealing for a rise
3 option dealings, option bargains
4 credit operations
5 (*commod.*) forward transactions; (*securities*) bargains for the account, settlement (time) bargains
6 transactions for future delivery during specified periods
7 cash transactions, dealings for cash [tions
8 banking business, banking opera-
9 every description (kind) of banking business, banking business of every description transacted
10 stock exchange transactions
11 exchange transactions, exchange business
12 forward exchange transactions, business
13 spot exchange transactions, business
14 credit operations, business
15 backwardation business
16 contango business

17 firm dealings
18 financial transactions
19 swaps, swap transactions

advice of purchase (or sale)
to effect a payment
opposition
1 list of stopped bonds

2 stopped bonds

3 to stop
taker of an option
option
1 double –, put and call

2 – of the exchange
3 call of more, buyer's – to double

4 – money
5 right of –

optionnaire / 250

6 avoir l'– de

7 exercer son droit d'–, lever une –
8 prendre à –
optionnaire *m.*
or *m.*
 1 – au titre
 2 – en barres, en lingots
 3 – fin
 4 – monnayé
 5 – sans titre
 6 d'–, en –
 7 afflux *m.* d'–
 8 agio *m.* sur l'–
 9 barre *f.* d'–
 10 bloc *m.* d'–
 11 pays *m. pl.* du bloc-or
 12 clause *f.* –or
 13 commerce *m.* de l'–
 14 cours *m.* de l'–
 15 couverture *f.* –or
 16 emprunt *m.* –or
 17 étalon *m.* –or
 18 abandon *m.* de l'étalon-or
 19 retour *m.* à l'étalon-or

 20 exportation *f.* de l'–
 21 franc *m.* –or
 22 importation *f.* d'–
 23 lingot *m.* d'–
 24 marché *m.* libre de l'–
 25 monnaie *f.* (d')–
 26 mouvement *m.* de l'–
 27 obligation *f.* –or
 28 parité *f.* –or
 29 pièce *f.* d'–
 30 point *m.* d'– (voir *point*)
 31 prime *f.* sur l'–
 32 prix *m.* de l'–
 33 réserve *f.* –or
 34 sortie *f.* de l'–
 35 thésaurisation *f.* d'–
 36 titre *m.* de l'–
 37 valeur *f.* –or
 38 versement *m.* en –
ordinaire
 1 comme d'–
 2 d'–
ordonnée *f.*
ordre *m.* (*rang*)
 1 – de grandeur
 2 du même – de grandeur
 3 – du jour (voir ce mot)

6 to have the refusal of, to have an – on
7 to exercise one's right of –
8 to take in –
giver of an option
gold
 1 essayed –
 2 bar –, ingot –
 3 fine –
 4 coined –
 5 unessayed –
 6 –
 7 influx of –
 8 premium on –
 9 bar of –
 10 – block
 11 – block countries
 12 – clause
 13 – trade
 14 rate of –
 15 – cover
 16 – loan
 17 – standard
 18 departure from the – standard
 19 return to the – standard

 20 – export
 21 – franc
 22 importation of –
 23 ingot of –
 24 free – market
 25 – coin
 26 movement of –
 27 – bond
 28 – parity
 29 – coin

 31 – premium
 32 price of –
 33 – reserve
 34 efflux (outflow, drain) of –
 35 – hoarding
 36 fineness of –
 37 value in –
 38 payment in –
ordinary
 1 as usual
 2 usually
ordinate
order
 1 – of magnitude
 2 of the same – of magnitude

251 / ordre

4 – public (*jur.*)	4 public policy
5 contraire à l'– public	5 contrary to public policy
6 pour des raisons d'– public	6 for reasons of public policy
7 de premier – (v. *titres*)	7 first-classe, first-rate
8 en bon – (*lettre*)	8 in good –, duly
9 par – alphabétique	9 in alphabetical –
10 par – chronologique	10 in chronological –
11 par – numérique	11 in numerical –
12 pour le bon –	12 for the sake of good –, for regularity's sake
13 numéro *m.* d'–	13 running number
ordre *m.* (*commande*)	**order** [account
1 – à terme	1 – for the settlement, for the cash –
2 – au comptant	2
3 – au cours	3 – to sell or to buy at the current price
4 – au dernier cours	4 – at the closing price
5 – au mieux	5 – at best
6 – au premier cours	6 – at the opening price
7 – d'achat	7 buying –
8 – de bourse	8 stock exchange –
9 – de payement	9 – to payment
10 – de payement par lettre, par courrier	10 mail transfer –
11 – de payement télégraphique	11 telegraphic transfer –
12 – d'essai (à titre d'essai)	12 trial –
13 – de vente	13 selling –
14 – de virement	14 – to transfer
15 – d'ouvrir (*un crédit*)	15 – to open
16 –s en carnet, en portefeuille	16 –s in hand, unfilled –s
17 –s en titres	17 stock –
18 – ferme	18 firm –
19 – illimité	19 unlimited –
20 – lié	20 contingent –
21 – limité	21 limited –
22 – permanent	22 standing –
23 – permanent (*paiements périodiques*)	23 standing –
24 – stop loss	24 stop-loss –
25 – télégraphique	25 cable –
26 – valable jusqu'à... inclus	26 – valid up to and including...
27 – valable jusqu'à révocation	27 – available till revoked
28 Anvers à l'– de	28 Antwerp for –s
29 à l'– de	29 to the – of
30 à l'– de moi-même	30 to our own –
31 à Monsieur X ou à son –	31 to Mr. X or –

ordre/du jour / 252

32 d'– et pour compte de
33 dans l'attente de vos honorés –s

34 jusqu'à nouvel –
35 payable à l'– de
36 pour moi à l'– de
37 suivant votre –
38 billet *m.* à –
39 chèque *m.* à –
40 clause *f.* à –
41 compte *m.* d'–

42 connaissement *m.* à –
43 donneur *m.* d'–
44 papiers *m. pl.* (effets) à –
45 port *m.* d'–
46 annuler un –
47 considérer un – comme annulé
48 exécuter un –
49 favoriser de vos –s
50 noter un –
51 passer un –
52 payez à l'– de Monsieur...

53 placer un –
54 recueillir des –s
55 transmettre un –
ordre du jour *m.*
  1 l'– étant épuisé

  2 points *m. pl.* à l'–
  3 être à l'–
  4 inscrire (mettre) à l'–

  5 passer à l'–

  6 rayer de l'–
organisation *f.*
  1 – bancaire
  2 – centrale
  3 – des entreprises
  4 – de Coopération et Développement Économiques

  5 – Européenne de Coopération Économique

organiser
orientation *f. (bourse)*

  – professionnelle
orienté
  la tendance est –e à la hausse

32 by – (on behalf) and for account of
33 trusting (we hope) to receive (to be favo(u)red with) your –s

34 till further notice
35 payable to the – of..., to... or –
36 for me to the – of
37 as per your –
38 promissory note, note of hand
39 cheque to –
40 – clause
41 contingent (suspense) account

42 B/L to –
43 principal
44 bills (paper) to –, – paper
45 port of call
46 to cancel an –
47 to consider an – as cancelled
48 to execute (fulfil) an –
49 to favo(u)r with your –s
50 to book an –
51 to pass an –
52 pay to the – of Mr...

53 to place an – with...
54 to collect –s
55 to transmit an –
order of the day, agenda
  1 there being no further (this being all the) business
  2 items of the agenda [agenda
  3 to be on the order of the day, on the
  4 to put down on the agenda

  5 to proceed (pass to) the business of the day
  6 to remove from the agenda
organization
  1 bank –
  2 central –
  3 business (industrial) –
  4 – for Economic Cooperation and Development

  5 – for European Economic Cooperation

to organize
trend, tendency

  vocational guidance
oriented
  to show an upward trend

original
facture –e
original m. l'–
origine f.
 1 d'– anglaise
 2 certificat m. d'–

 3 emballage m. d'–
 4 marque f. d'–
 5 pays m. d'–
 6 port m. d'–
oscillation f.
osciller
outillage m.
outiller
outre-mer
 1 commerce m. d'–
 2 possessions f. pl. d'–
ouverture f.
 1 – d'un compte
 2 – d'un crédit
 3 – de la faillite
 4 – de nouveaux débouchés
 5 bilan m. d'–
 6 cours m. d'–
 7 demande f. d'– d'un compte
 8 heures f. pl. d'– des guichets

ouvrable, jour – (non férié)
 jour m. – (quand le temps permet de travailler)
ouvré, par heure –e
ouvre-lettres m.
ouvrier m. (voir aussi travailleur)
 1 – agricole
 2 – à la journée
 3 – à la tâche, – aux pièces
 4 – du fond (mine)
 5 – du jour, de surface (mine)
 6 – d'usine
 7 – manuel
 8 – (non) qualifié
 9 – saisonnier
 10 – spécialisé
 11 classe ouvrière
 12 maisons ouvrières
 13 mouvement –
 14 parti –
 15 question ouvrière
 16 train –
ouvrière f.
ouvrir
 1 – un compte à la banque

original
– invoice
the original
origin
 1 of English –
 2 certificate of –

 3 original packing
 4 mark of –
 5 country of –
 6 port of departure
fluctuation
to fluctuate
plant, equipment
to equip with plant
oversea
 1 oversea(s) trade
 2 oversea(s) possessions
opening
 1 – of an account
 2 – of a credit
 3 – of bankruptcy proceedings
 4 – of new markets
 5 – balance
 6 – rate
 7 request to open an account
 8 office (banking) hours, counter business hours

working day
weather working day

per hour worked
letter opener
workman, worker
 1 agricultural (farm) labo(u)rer
 2 day lab(ou)rer
 3 piece worker
 4 underground worker
 5 surface worker
 6 factory hand
 7 manual worker
 8 (un)skilled worker
 9 seasonal worker
 10 skilled worker
 11 working class
 12 workmen's dwellings
 13 labo(u)r movement
 14 labo(u)r party
 15 labo(u)r question
 16 workmen's train
woman worker
to open
 1 an account at the bank

2 – le courrier
3 – un crédit à...
4 – un débouché
5 – la faillite
6 – une séance
7 – une souscription
8 – une succursale
9 la souscription (*d'un emprunt*) est ouverte le...

10 ,,côté *m.* à –''
11 ouvert toute l'année

2 – the letters
3 – a credit in favour of...
4 to create new openings
5 – bankruptcy proceedings
6 – a meeting
7 – a subscription
8 – (start) a branch
9 applications will be received on...

10 open here
11 open all the year round

P

page *f.*
1 – d'annonces
2 – de couverture
3 – de droite
4 – de gauche
5 – spécimen
6 dernière – (verso)
7 première –
pagination *f.*
paginer

1 – à livre fermé
2 – à livre ouvert
paiement (voir *payement*)
pair *m.*
1 – commercial
2 – du change, – intrinsèque
3 au –
4 être au –
5 être au-dessous du –
6 être au-dessus du –
7 change *m.* au –
8 cours *m.* du –
9 émission *f.* au –
10 remboursable au –
11 valeur *f.* du –
palan *m.* (*navire*)
sous –
palette *f.* (*transport*)
panier *m.* à papier
panique *f.*
1 – sur la (en) bourse
2 causer (produire) une –
3 une – se produisit
panne *f.*
avoir une –

page
1 advertising –
2 cover
3 right-hand –
4 left-hand –
5 specimen –
6 back –
7 front –
pagination, paging
to page, to paginate

1 to page
2 to folio

par
1 commercial –
2 (mint) – of exchange
3 at –
4 to be at –
5 to be below –, to be at a discount
6 to be above –, to be at a premium
7 exchange at –
8 – (of exchange)
9 issue at –
10 repayable at –
11 – value
tackle
at ship's rail. under ship's –
pallet, pallet board
waste-paper basket
panic
1 – on the stock exchange
2 to raise a –
3 a – set in
breakdown
to have a –

255 / panneau

panneau *m.*
  1 – d'affichage
  2 – réclame

papeterie *f.*

  – (*usine*)

papier *m.*
  1 – à calquer
  2 – à écrire
  3 – à en-tête
  4 – à lettre(s)
  5 – brouillon
  6 – buvard
  7 – carbone
  8 – carboné
  9 – d'affaires

  10 – d'emballage
  11 – deuil
  12 – gommé
  13 – libre
  14 – machine
  15 – ministre
  16 – pelure
  17 – réglé
  18 – sans fin
  19 – timbré

papier (*cotation*)
  1 coter... –
  2 cours *m.* –

papier (voir aussi *effet, lettre de change, traite*)
  1 – à 3 mois
  2 – à ordre
  3 – au porteur
  4 – à vue
  5 – bancable
  6 – brûlant
  7 – commerçable
  8 – commercial, – de commerce
  9 – court, à courte échéance
  10 – creux

  11 – de complaisance

  12 – de haut commerce, – hors banque
  13 – déplacé, – sur le dehors

  14 – doré sur tranche
  15 – fait
  16 – long, – à longue échéance

board, hoarding
  1 poster hoarding, (*Amer.*) billboard
  2 advertisement hoarding

stationer's shop

  paper mill, paper factory

paper
  1 tracing –
  2 writing –
  3 headed note paper
  4 letter –
  5 scribbling –, (*Amer.*) scratch –
  6 blotting –
  7 carbon –
  8 carbac, carbonized –
  9 business papers, (*poste*) commercial papers
  10 packing –
  11 black-edged (bordered) –
  12 gummed –
  13 unstamped –
  14 typewriting –
  15 official foolscap
  16 tissue –
  17 lined –
  18 endless –
  19 stamped –

price offered (sellers)
  1 to be on offer at...
  2 prices offered

paper, bill

  1 three months' bill
  2 bills to order, order paper
  3 bearer paper, paper to bearer
  4 sight bills
  5 bankable bills
  6 hot bills
  7 negotiable paper
  8 trade paper, trade bills
  9 short paper (bills)
  10 house bill, pig on pork

  11 accommodation paper

  12 prime (fine) trade bills

  13 bill payable on another place than that of issue
  14 gilt-edged paper
  15 guaranteed paper
  16 long paper, bills

papillon / 256

17 – monnaie
18 – négociable
19 – non bancable
20 – sur le dehors (voir – *déplacé*)
21 – sur place
22 beau –
23 –s valeurs
papillon *m.*
paquebot *m.*
Pâques *m.* (*à* –)
paquet *m.*
  – d'actions
parafe, paraphe *m.*
  apposer son –
parafer, parapher
parafeur *m.* (*livre*)
paragraphe *m.*
  article 2, – 3
paraître, vient de –
parastatal (semi-public)
  les (établissements) parastataux (*Belg.*)
pari passu
parité *f.*
  1 –s du change
  2 – des monnaies
  3 – du pouvoir d'achat
  4 – de voix
  5 – or
  6 calcul *m.* des –s
  7 point *m.* de –
  8 prix *m.* de – (*agric. Amér.*)
  9 table *f.* des –s
parquage *m.*
parquer
  défense de –
parquet *m.* (*bourse*)
part *f.*
  1 – aux bénéfices
  2 – d'apport
  3 – de fondateur, – bénéficiaire
  4 – de syndicat, – syndicataire
  5 – sociale
  6 à –s égales
  7 d'une –
  8 de votre –
  9 entre... d'une (de première) –, et ... d'autre (de deuxième) –
  10 emballage *m.* à –
  11 faire – de qch. à qqn
  12 prendre en mauvaise –

17 (inconvertible) paper money
18 negotiable paper
19 unbankable paper

21 local bill
22 first-rate bill
23 paper securities
slip
liner
Easter (*at* –)
parcel
  block of shares
initials
  to put one's –
to initial
signature folder
section
  article 2, – 3
just out, just published
quasi public
  semi-official (semipublic) institutions

pari passu
parity
  1 exchange parities
  2 mint par (of exchange)
  3 purchasing power –
  4 equality of votes
  5 gold –
  6 calculation of parities
  7 – point
  8 – price
  9 table of parities
parking
to park
  no parking here, parking prohibited
official market
share
  1 – in the profits
  2 vendor's –
  3 founder's –
  4 – of underwriting
  5 ,,part sociale''
  6 in equal parts
  7 on the one hand
  8 on your part
  9 between... of the one part and... of the other part
  10 packing extra
  11 to inform someone of...
  12 to take it ill, in bad part

257 / partage

partage *m.* — division, distribution
1 – de succession, – successoral / division in a succession
2 – de voix / equality of votes

partager — to divide
1 – le bénéfice / – the profit
2 – la différence, le différend / to split the difference
3 – une opinion / to share an opinion

partance *f.* — sailing
1 par premier bateau en – / by first available steamer
2 être en – / about to sail, outward bound

partenaire, pays –s (CEE) — partners

participant *m.* — participant, sharer

participation *f.* — participation
1 – à une entreprise / 1 – in an undertaking
2 – aux bénéfices / 2 profit sharing, share in profits
3 – dans une société / 3 – in a company
4 – majoritaire / 4 majority holding, stake, interest
5 – minoritaire / 5 minority holding, stake, interest
6 –s syndicales / 6 syndicate –s
7 en – / 7 on joint account
8 association *f.* en – / 8 particular partnership
9 compte *m.* de – / 9 joint account
10 entreprise *f.* à – / 10 joint undertaking
11 opérations *f. pl.* en – / 11 transactions on joint account

participer (à) — to participate (in)
1 – aux bénéfices / 1 to share in the profit
2 – à un congrès / 2 to attend a congress
3 – à une entreprise / 3 to participate (to be interested) in an undertaking

particulier (voir aussi *privé*) — private
1 compte – / 1 – account
2 intérêts –s / 2 – interests

particulier *m.* — private person

partie *f.* — part
1 – aliquote / 1 aliquot –
2 – de marchandises / 2 parcel (lot) of goods
3 en – / 3 partly
4 en –s égales / 4 in equal –s
5 en grande – / 5 to a large extent
6 en majeure – / 6 for the greater –
7 comptabilité en – double (voir *comptabilité*)
8 livraison *f.* par –s / 8 delivery in instalments
9 vente *f.* en –s / 9 sale in lots

partie f. (*personne*)
1 – adverse
2 – comparante
3 –s contractantes

4 les –s en cause
5 –s intéressées
6 – intervenante
7 – la plus diligente
8 – prenante

partiel
1 acceptation –le
2 expéditions –les sont autorisées
3 expéditions –les sont interdites
4 payement –

partir
1 – pour
2 à – de
3 à – d'aujourd'hui

4 à – du 1 février
5 parti en voyage
6 „parti sans laisser d'adresse"

parvenir
1 – à destination
2 faire –
3 votre lettre nous est parvenue

4 il est parvenu à...

passage m. (*mer*)
1 – (*magasins*)
2 – souterrain
3 billet m. de –
4 prix m. de –

passager m.

passation f.
1 – d'un acte

2 – d'un dividende
3 – d'écritures en compte
4 – d'ordres

passavant m.

passé
le 15 du mois –

passeport m.
1 – (*d'un navire*)
2 bureau m. des –s
3 photo f. de –
4 se faire délivrer un –
5 viser un –

party
1 opposing –, the other side
2 appearer
3 contracting parties

4 the parties concerned
5 parties interested
6 intervening –
7 the willing –, the first mover
8 payee, receiver

partial
1 – acceptance
2 part shipments allowed, permitted
3 part shipments prohibited
4 – payment, part payment

to leave, to start
1 to leave for...
2 from
3 from to-day onwards

4 as from February 1st
5 away on journey, voyage
6 gone away, no address

1 to reach (arrive at) destination
2 to send
3 your letter reached us, has come to hand

4 he succeeded in...

passage
1 arcade
2 subway
3 passenger ticket
4 passage money, fare, (*plane*) air fare

passenger

1 drawing up a deed

2 passing of a dividend
3 making entries, entering
4 giving orders, placing orders

transire

past, last
the 15th of last month

passport
1 –, clearance
2 – office
3 – photo
4 to have a – issued
5 to put a visa to (to visa, to visé) a –

259 / passer

passer (*mettre en circulation*)
ne plus – (*monnaie*)
passer
1 – aux profits et pertes
2 – en compte (voir aussi *valeur*)
3 – un acte
4 – un article au journal
5 – un contrat
6 – un dividende

7 – écriture

8 – écriture conforme
9 – une lettre de change à l'ordre de...

10 – un marché

11 – un montant
12 – un montant au débit

passible
1 – de droits
2 – d'impôts

passif
1 balance commerciale passive
2 bilan – des payements
3 solde –

passif *m.*
1 – envers tiers
2 – éventuel
3 – exigible
4 – non exigible
5 actif et –
6 côté *m.* du –
7 prise *f.* en charge du –
8 porter au –

patente *f.* de santé

1 – brute, – suspecte
2 – nette

patience *f.*
prendre –

patron *m.*

patronage *m.*
sous le – de

patronal
1 association –e
2 cotisation –e

patronat *m.*

patte *f.* (*d'enveloppe*)

pavillon *m.*
1 baisser le –

to utter, to pass
to be out of circulation

1 to post to profit and loss account
2 to place to account
3 to draw up a deed
4 to post an entry to the journal
5 to enter into a contract
6 to pass a dividend

7 to enter up, to enter

8 to enter (book) accordingly
9 to endorse over a bill of exchange to the order of...

10 to make a bargain, to enter into a bargain

11 to enter an amount
12 to pass an amount to the debit

liable to, subject to
1 liable to duty
2 liable for tax

passive
1 adverse balance of trade
2 – balance of payment
3 debit balance

liabilities
1 – toward third parties
2 contingent –
3 current –
4 non-current –
5 assets and –
6 liability side
7 taking over of the –
8 to enter on the liabilities side

bill of health

1 suspected –
2 clean –

patience
to have –

employer, principal

patronage
under the – of

employer's, of employers
1 employers' association
2 employer's contribution

the employers

flap

flag
1 to lower the –

payable / 260

2 battre – français
3 hisser le –
4 naviguer sous – étranger

payable
1 – à la banque
2 – à l'arrivée
3 – à l'échéance
4 – à nos caisses, à nos guichets
5 – à 3 mois de date

6 – à 3 jours de vue

7 – à terme échu
8 – au (le) 15 mars
9 – au comptant sans escompte
10 – au comptant avec 2 % d'escompte
11 – au porteur
12 – à vue, à présentation
13 – d'avance

14 – dans 3 mois
15 – en
16 – par acomptes

paye *f.*
1 feuille *f.* de –
2 jour *m.* de –
3 sachet *m.* à –

payement (paiement) *m.*
1 – anticipatif (v. par anticipation)
2 – anticipé
3 – arriéré
4 – au comptant
5 – contre documents
6 – différé
7 – du solde
8 – échelonné
9 – en espèces, en numéraire
10 –s internationaux
11 – mensuel
12 – par acomptes
13 – par anticipation
14 – par chèque
15 –s par chèques et virements
16 – par intervention
17 – partiel
18 –s périodiques
19 – postérieur
20 – supplémentaire
21 – télégraphique

22 – trimestriel
23 au lieu de (comme) –
24 contre –, moyennant – de

---

2 to fly the French colo(u)rs
3 to hoist the –
4 to sail under foreign –

payable
1 – at the bank
2 – on arrival
3 – when due, at maturity
4 – at our counters, offices
5 – at 3 months' date, at 3 months after date
6 – at 3 days' sight, 3 days after sight
7 – at maturity
8 due (payable) 15th of March
9 – net cash
10 – 2 % discount for cash
11 – to bearer
12 – at sight, on presentation
13 – in advance

14 – in 3 months
15 – in
16 – by instalments

wage; wage payment
1 pay sheet, wages sheet
2 pay-day
3 wage packet, pay packet

payment

2 anticipated –, – before due date
3 – in arrear
4 cash –
5 – against documents
6 deferred –
7 – of balance
8 – by instalments
9 – in cash
10 international –s
11 monthly –
12 – by instalments
13 – in advance
14 – by cheque (check)
15 cashless – s
16 – for hono(u)r
17 part –
18 periodical –s
19 subsequent –
20 additional –
21 telegraphic transfer

22 quarterly –
23 instead (by way) of –
24 on – of

261 / payer

25 en – de
26 accord *m.* de –
27 balance *f.* des –s, (voir aussi *balance*)
28 cessation *f.* des –s
29 conditions *f. pl.* de –
30 délai *m.* –
31 difficultés *f. pl.* de –
32 documents *m. pl.* contre –
33 facilités *f. pl.* de –
34 instrument *m.* de –
35 jour *m.* de –
36 lieu *m.* de –
37 mandat *m.* de –
38 mode *m.* de –
39 mouvement *m.* des –s internationaux
40 libération *f.* du mouvement des –s internationaux
41 moyens *m. pl.* de –
42 ordre *m.* de suspendre les –s
43 promesse *f.* de –
44 refus *m.* de –
45 retard *m.* de –
46 sommation *f.* de –
47 sursis *m.* de –
48 suspension *f.* des –s
49 terme *m.* de –
50 accepter en –
51 accorder un sursis de –

52 avancer le –
53 cesser les –s
54 différer le –
55 échelonner les –s
56 être en retard avec le –
57 exiger le –
58 faciliter le –
59 faire un –, effectuer un –
60 obtenir un –
61 refuser le –
62 remettre le –
63 reprendre les –s
64 solliciter un sursis de –
payer
 1 – à livraison
 2 – au comptant
 3 – au comptant compté
 4 – d'avance

 5 – en compte
 6 – en espèces
 7 – en nature

25 in – of
26 –s agreement
27 **balance of –s**

28 suspension of –
29 terms of –
30 delay, respite
31 financial difficulties
32 documents against –
33 easy terms, easy –
34 tender
35 pay day, day of –
36 place of –
37 money order
38 mode of –
39 international –s

40 liberalization of international –s

41 means of –
42 stop – order
43 promise to pay
44 refusal to pay
45 delay of –
46 application (demand) for –
47 delay of –
48 stoppage of –
49 term of –
50 to accept in –
51 to grant a delay of –, an extension of the term of –
52 to advance the –
53 to stop –s
54 to postpone the –
55 to spread –s over...
56 to be in arrears with the –
57 to demand (to ask for) –
58 to facilitate the –
59 to make (effect) a –
60 to obtain –
61 to refuse –
62 to postpone (defer) the –
63 to resume –s
64 to ask for a delay of –
to pay
 1 – on delivery
 2 – cash
 3 – cash down, spot cash
 4 to prepay

 5 – on account
 6 – in cash
 7 – in kind

8 – en partie
9 – en supplément
10 – en trop
11 – intégralement
12 – par acomptes
13 – par anticipation
14 – par chèque
15 – par intervention
16 – ponctuellement
17 – rubis sur l'ongle
18 avoir à –

payez
1 – à l'ordre de M...
2 – au porteur
3 – par cette première de change, la seconde ne l'étant (voir *première*)

payeur *m.*
1 – ponctuel
2 mauvais –

pays *m.*
1 – à change élevé
2 – à change faible
3 – créditeur
4 – débiteur
5 – de destination
6 – de provenance
7 – d'origine
8 – en voie de développement
9 – exportateur
10 – importateur
11 – industriel
12 le – membre (*communauté*)
13 – producteur
14 – signataire
15 – sous-développés
16 des – tiers
17 – transitaire
18 monnaie *f.* du –

pécuniaire
1 avantages *m. pl.* –s
2 embarras *m. pl.* –s
3 perte *f.* –

péniche *f.*

pension *f.* (voir *retraite*)
1 – alimentaire
2 – de retraite
3 – de survie
4 – de veuve
5 – de vieillesse
6 – d'invalidité
7 – viagère
8 âge *m.* de la –
9 caisse *f.* de –

8 – in part
9 to make an additional payment, [– extra
10 to overpay
11 – in full
12 – by instalments
13 – in anticipation, to prepay
14 – by cheque (check)
15 – by intervention, for hono(u)r
16 – promptly
17 – to the last farthing, cent
18 to have –

1 pay to the order of Mr...
2 pay to bearer

payer
1 punctual –
2 bad –

country
1 – with a high rate of exchange
2 – with a low rate of exchange
3 creditor nation
4 debtor nation
5 – of destination
6 last – of exportation
7 – of origin
8 developing
9 exporting –
10 importing –
11 industrial –
12 the member –
13 producing –
14 signatory –
15 underdeveloped countries
16 third countries
17 transit –
18 currency of the –

pecuniary
1 – advantages
2 – difficulties
3 – loss

lighter, barge

pension
1 alimony
2 (retiring) –
3 survivors' –
4 widow's –
5 old-age –
6 invalidity –
7 – for life
8 pensionable age
9 – fund

263 / pensionné

10 effet *m.* en –
11 versements *m. pl.* pour la –
12 verser pour sa –
pensionné *m.*
pensionner

pénurie *f.*
1 – aiguë
2 – d'argent
3 – de capitaux
4 – de devises
5 – de dollars
6 – de fret
7 – de main-d'œuvre
8 – des matières premières
9 il y a – de...
percepteur *m.* (*impôts*)
– des postes
perception *f.* (*impôts*)
perception *f.* (*bureau*)
percevoir
perdre
1 – un procès
2 – sur les marchandises
3 considérer comme perdu
4 se –

5 emballage perdu
père *m.* **de famille**
1 en bon – (*gérer*)
2 placement *m.* de –
péréquation *f.*
1 – des impôts
2 – des salaires

3 caisse *f.* de – (*charbonnages*)
4 faire la –
perforateur *m.*
perforer
 carte perforée (voir *machine*)
perforeuse *f.* **de chèques**
péricliter
périmé
période *f.*
1 – comptable
2 – correspondante
3 – de comparaison
4 – d'essai
5 – entre les deux guerres
6 – sous revue, – considérée

7 – suspecte

10 bill in pawn
11 superannuation contribution
12 to contribute towards one's –
pensioner
to pension, to pension off

scarcity
1 pressing shortage
2 lack (want) of money
3 – (shortage) of capital
4 shortage of foreign currency
5 dollar shortage
6 – of freight
7 labo(u)r shortage
8 – of raw materials
9 there is a – of
tax collector
postmaster
collection
collector's office
to collect
to lose
1 – a lawsuit
2 – on the goods
3 to give up for lost
4 to get lost

5 packing included
head of the family
1 as a prudent administrator
2 gilt-edged investment
equalization
1 – of taxes
2 – of wages

3 – fund
4 to equalize
perforator
to perforate
 punch(ed) card
cheque perforator, protector
to decline, to be on the decline
expired, out of date
period
1 accounting –
2 corresponding –
3 comparable –
4 trial –
5 inter-war –
6 – under review

7 – before the declaration of bankruptcy

8 – transitoire
9 courte –

10 la longue –

11 pour la – allant jusqu'au...
périodique
périodique m.
périssable (*marchandises*)

permanent
permettre
 1 nous nous permettons de...

 2 si le temps le permet
 3 nos moyens ne le permettent pas
permis m.
 1 – de bâtir, construire
 2 – de conduire
 3 – de débarquement
 4 – de douane
 5 – d'embarquement
 6 – de séjour
 7 – de transbordement
 8 – d'exportation, – de sortie
 9 – d'importation, – d'entrée
personnalité civile, morale

 1 acquérir la –

 2 demander la –

personne *f.*
 1 – civile, morale

 2 – physique
 3 „parlant à sa –'' (*huissier*)

 4 se présenter en –
personnel *adj.*
 1 „-le'' (*lettre*)
 2 fortune –le
 3 garantie –le
 4 levées –les, prélèvements –s

 5 strictement – (*billet*)
personnel m.

 1 – administratif
 2 – de bureau
 3 – qualifié
 4 chef m. du –
 5 diminution f. de –

8 – of transition
9 short-run –, short-run

10 the long-run –, the long-run

11 for the – up to...
periodical
periodical
perishable

permanent, standing
to permit
 1 we beg to..., we are taking the liberty to
 2 weather permitting
 3 we cannot afford it
permit, licence, license
 1 building licence, permit
 2 driver's licence
 3 landing permit
 4 customs permit
 5 shipping note
 6 permission to reside
 7 transhipment permit
 8 export permit
 9 import licence
incorporation, legal status

 1 to acquire legal status, to be incorporated
 2 to apply for a charter of incorporation
person
 1 body corporate, corporate body, legal entity, legal –
 2 natural –
 3 speaking to him in –, writ served to the party concerned
 4 to apply in –
personal
 1 –
 2 private means
 3 – security
 4 – drawings

 5 not transferable
staff, personnel

 1 clerical staff
 2 office staff
 3 skilled staff
 4 – (personnel) manager
 5 staff reduction

265 / personnellement

6 effectif *m.* du –	6 strength of the staff
7 fonds *m.* de pension (de prévoyance) pour le –	7 staff pension fund
8 licenciement *m.* de –	8 dismissal, laying off
9 manque *m.* de –	9 shortage of –
10 membre *m.* du –	10 member of the staff
11 recrutement *m.* du –	11 staff recruitment, engaging of staff
12 rendement *m.* du –	12 output of the staff
13 service *m.* du –	13 staff (personnel) department
14 faire partie du – de...	14 to be on the staff of...
15 manquer de –	15 to be understaffed
personnellement	**personally**
perspective *f.*	**prospect**
perte *f.* (*titres*)	**discount**
1 être en –, faire –	1 to be (stand) at a –
2 se négocier à... de –	2 to be dealt in at... –
perte *f.*	**loss**
1 à –	1 at a –
2 en cas de –	2 in case of –
3 – au (sur le) change	3 – on exchange
4 – brute	4 gross –
5 – d'argent	5 – of money
6 – de bénéfice	6 – (of profit)
7 – de place	7 cost of collection, collecting charges
8 – de poids	8 – in weight
9 – de temps	9 waste (–) of time
10 – d'intérêts	10 – of interest
11 – en capitaux	11 – of capital
12 – nette	12 net –
13 – partielle (*assur.*)	13 partial –
14 – sèche	14 dead –
15 – totale (*assur.*)	15 total –
16 – totale constructive	16 constructive total –
17 grosse –	17 heavy –
18 opération *f.* à –	18 business at a –
19 compenser une –	19 to make good a –
20 couvrir (combler) une –	20 to cover a –
21 entraîner (causer) une –	21 to cause a –
22 réparer une –	22 to make good (repair) a –
23 subir (essuyer) de grosses –s	23 to suffer heavy –es
24 vendre à –	24 to sell at a –
pesage *m.*, **pesée** *f.*	**weighing**
estampille *f.* de –	weight stamp
pèse-lettre *m.* (*pl.* –s)	**letter scale**
peser	**to weight**
peseur *m.*	**weigher**
– et mesureur	measurer and –
petit	**small**
1 –e exploitation	1 – undertaking
2 –e industrie	2 – (–scale) industry

pétrolier / 266

3 -e monnaie
4 - rentier
pétrolier
1 industrie pétrolière
2 (valeurs) pétrolières
pétrolier *m.*
peu
  sous -
photo *f.*
1 - de 6 sur 9
2 - de face
3 - de passeport
photocopie *f.*
photocopier
pièce *f.*
1 - de 5 francs
2 - de monnaie
3 -s de rechange
4 - d'or
5 par -
6 à la - (*étoffe*)
7 dix -s
8 10 frs. -
9 salaire *m.* à la -
10 travail *m.* à la -
11 travailler à la -
12 vendre à la -
pièce (*document*) *m.*
1 - comptable
2 -s de bord
3 - de caisse
4 -s jointes (annexes)
5 vignettes -s jointes
6 - justificative, - à l'appui
pied *m.* (v. aussi *prime*)
1 -s humides (*bourse*)
2 10 -s
3 sur - (*avant la récolte*)
4 sur - (*bétail*)
pignoratif (v. aussi *endossement*)
acte -
pilotage *m.*
  - (*droits*)
pilote *m.*
1 - (*avion*)
2 bateau *m.* -
pince-notes *m.*
pique-notes *m.*
place *f.* (voir aussi *emploi, vacant*)
1 - bancable
2 - boursière

3 - cambiste, - de change

3 - change
4 - investor

1 oil industry
2 oils, oil shares
oiler, oil ship
few
  shortly
photo(graph)
1 6 by 9 -
2 full-face -
3 passport -
photocopy, photostat
to photostat
piece
1 five-franc -
2 coin
3 spare parts
4 gold coin
5 by the -
6 in the -
7 ten
8 10 francs each, apiece
9 - work wages
10 - work
11 to work by the -, to do - work
12 to sell singly, by the -
document
1 bookkeeping voucher
2 ship's papers
3 cash voucher
4 enclosure
5 enclosure stamps
6 voucher (in support)
foot
1 pushers selling valueless scrip
2 10 feet
3 standing
4 on the hoof, livestock

contract of pledge
pilot service
  pilotage (dues)
pilot
1 -
2 - boat
letter clip
bill file
place
1 banking -
2 - in which a (stock) Exchange is
   located [market
3 - of exchange, foreign exchange

267 / placement

3 – de commerce, marchande
4 – non bancable
5 payable dans une autre –
6 sur –
7 sur cette –
8 sur notre –
9 sur votre –
10 connaissance *f.* de la –
11 faute de –

12 frais *m. pl.* de –
13 jour *m.* de –
14 papier *m.* (effet) sur –
15 prix *m.* de –
16 transactions *f. pl.* de la –
17 voyageur *m.* de –
18 être sur la – (*marché*)
19 faire la –

20 retenir des –s
21 retenir une – à bord   [*ment*]
placement *m.* (voir aussi *investisse-*
1 – à court terme
2 – à report

3 – à revenus fixes
4 – à revenus variables
5 – avantageux

6 – d'actions dans le public

7 – d'argent, – de capitaux
8 – de commandes chez...

9 – de père de famille
10 – de tout repos, – sûr
11 – en valeurs
12 – intéressant
13 bureau *m.* de – (*emplois*)
14 valeurs *f. pl.* de –
15 faire un –
placer (*argent*)
1 – à court terme
2 – à intérêts

3 – des actions
4 – des actions dans le public

5 – de l'argent
6 – un emprunt
7 – des marchandises

8 – un ordre

3 commercial –
4 non-bank –
5 payable at another –
6 on the spot
7 at this –
8 in our city, at (in) our –
9 in your city, at (in) your –
10 local knowledge
11 owing to pressure on our space, for want of space

12 local charges
13 market day
14 local bill
15 spot price
16 local business
17 town traveller
18 to be in the market
19 to do the –, to canvass the town

20 to book –s
21 to book one's passage
investment
1 short-term –
2 – on contango

3 fixed-yield –
4 variable-yield –
5 profitable –

6 placing shares with the public

7 capital –
8 placing orders with...

9 gilt-edged –
10 safe –
11 – in securities
12 attractive –
13 employment agency
14 – securities
15 to make an –
to invest
1 – on short terms
2 to put out at interest

3 to issue shares
4 to place shares with the public

5 – money
6 to place a loan
7 to place goods

8 to place an order

placier / 268

9 – des titres en garde
10 – des titres en report
11 – en viager
placier *m.*
plafond *m.*
– du crédit
plaindre, se – (de)
1 avoir à –
2 on se plaint généralement que

plainte *f.*
1 – bien fondée
2 – mal fondée
3 donner lieu à –
4 examiner une –
5 formuler des –s
6 porter – *(jur.)*
7 porter – contre
8 retirer sa –

plaisir *m.*
1 avec –
2 nous avons le – de vous faire savoir

plan *m.*
1 – cadastral
2 – d'alignement
3 – d'amortissement
4 – d'arrimage
5 – de campagne
6 – d'ensemble
7 – de tirage
8 – quinquennal
9 exécuter un –
10 faire (dresser, établir) un –
11 soumettre un –
planche *f.*
1 – à billets
2 jours *m. pl.* de –
planification *f.*, économique
plastique
(matières –s)
plate-forme *f. (tram)*
plein
1 – emploi
2 – pouvoir
3 – tarif
4 de – gré
5 en – hiver
6 en –e mer
7 en –e saison
8 en –e ville

9 to deposit securities in safe custody
10 to lend stock on contango
11 to invest in life annuities
town traveller
limit
credit –, credit ceiling
to complain (about)
1 to have cause for complaint
2 there is a general complaint that

complaint
1 well-founded (justified) –
2 unfounded (groundless) –
3 to give cause for –
4 to inquire into a –
5 to formulate –s
6 to bring an action against
7 to lodge a – against
8 to withdraw one's charge

pleasure
1 with –
2 we have – in informing you, we have the – to inform (of informing) you
plan
1 cadastral survey
2 building line
3 redemption table
4 stowage –
5 – of action
6 general –
7 – of drawing
8 five-year –
9 to execute a –
10 to draw up a –
11 to submit a –
board
1 note printing press
2 lay days
economic planning

plastics, plastics materials
platform
full
1 – employment
2 – power
3 – rates
4 of one's own free will
5 in the middle of winter
6 on the high (open) sea
7 at the height of the season
8 right in the town

269 / plein

plein *m.*
1 – (*assur.*)
2 tableau *m.* des –s
3 battre son –

4 faire le – (d'essence)
5 fixer les –s (*assur.*)
plénier, séance plénière

pléthore *f.* de...
pli *m.*
1 – (*lettre*)
2 – avec valeur déclarée, – chargé
3 – cacheté
4 sous – cacheté
5 sous – fermé
6 sous – recommandé
7 sous – séparé

plier
(prière de) ne pas –
plus *m.* (*signe*)
plus
1 – ou moins
2 – les frais
3 différence en – (voir *différence*)
4 d'autant – que
5 de – en –
6 10 mois et –
7 pour – de sécurité
8 5 – 3 égale...
plus-value *f.*
exonération *f.* des –s
poids *m.*
1 – abattu (*bétail*)
2 – à vide   [– rendu
3 – au débarquement, – délivré,
4 – brut
5 – des impôts, de la fiscalité
6 – embarqué
7 – et mesures
8 – maximum
9 – minimum
10 – mort
11 – moyen
12 – net
13 – net débarqué
14 – net embarqué
15 – rendu (voir – *au débarquement*)
16 – spécifique
17 – total
18 – utile
19 – vif, vivant (*bétail*)

1 maximum limit, line
2 table of limits
3 to be at the full, to be at its height

4 to fill up with (petrol, gasoline)
5 to fix a limit
plenary assembly meeting

plethora of, glut of...
envelope, cover
1 letter
2 insured letter
3 sealed letter
4 in a sealed envelope
5 in a closed envelope
6 under registered cover
7 under separate cover

to fold
keep flat, please don't fold, bend
plus
more
1 – or less
2 and costs

4 the – as
5 – and –
6 10 months and –
7 for better security
8 5 plus 3 equals
appreciation, increase in value
exemption of capital gains
weight
1 carcass –, dressed –
2 – when empty
3 delivered –
4 gross –
5 burden of taxation
6 shipping (loaded) –
7 –s and measures
8 maximum –
9 minimum –
10 dead –
11 average –
12 net –
13 unloaded. net –
14 loaded net –

16 specific gravity, specific –
17 total –
18 useful load
19 live –, – on the hoof

poinçonner / 270

20 au – (*vendre*)
21 bon –
22 certificat *m.* de –
23 certification *f.* de –
24 déclaration *f.* de –
25 différence *f.* de –
26 excédent *m.* de –
27 manque *m.* de –
28 note *f.* de –
29 perte *f.* de –
30 unité *f.* de –
31 dépasser le –
32 perdre de –
poinçonner
poinçonneuse *f.*
point *m.* (*signe*)
  1 – d'exclamation
  2 – d'interrogation
  3 – virgule
  4 deux –s
point *m.*
  1 – bas
  2 – d'entrée de l'or
  3 – de saturation
  4 – de sortie de l'or
  5 – d'inflexion (*courbe*)
  6 à son – maximum
  7 de ce – de vue
  8 atteindre le – de l'or
  9 baisser de 2 –s
10 être sur le – de
11 gagner 2 –s
12 hausser de 2 –s
pointage *m.*
pointer avec
pointillé *m.*
  à détacher suivant le –

police *f.*
  1 – à forfait
  2 – à ordre
  3 – à terme
  4 – au porteur
  5 – au voyage
  6 – avec participation au bénéfice
  7 – d'abonnement
  8 – d'assurance contre incendie
  9 – (d'assurance) dotale

10 – (d'assurance) maritime
11 – (d'assurance) sur la vie
12 – de chargement (*ports médit.*)
13 – dotale (voir – *d'assurance dotale*)

20 by –
21 draft
22 certificate of –
23 certification of –
24 declaration of –
25 difference of –
26 excess of –
27 short –
28 – note
29 loss of –
30 unit of –
31 to exceed the –
32 to lose –
to punch
punching machine, punch
stop
  1 note of exclamation
  2 question mark
  3 semicolon
  4 colon
point
  1 low, low –
  2 import gold –
  3 saturation –
  4 export gold –
  5 flex –, inflexion –
  6 at its peak
  7 from this – of view
  8 to reach the gold –
  9 to decline 2 –s
10 to be on the – of, to be about to
11 to gain 2 –s
12 to rise 2 –s
ticking off, checking
to tick off, to check
perforation, dotted line
  tear off along the dotted line

policy
  1 open – for a specific amount
  2 – to order
  3 time –
  4 – to bearer
  5 voyage –
  6 participating –
  7 floating (open) –
  8 fire insurance –
  9 portion (insurance) –, dowry insurance –
10 marine (insurance) –
11 life (insurance) –
12 bill of lading

14 – évaluée
15 – flottante
16 – générale
17 – libérée
18 – maritime (voir – *d'assurance maritime*)
19 – mixte
20 – nominative
21 – non évaluée

22 – omnium (voir – *tous risques*)
23 – ouverte
24 – provisoire
25 – sans part aux bénéfices
26 – **tous risques d'auto** (omnium)

27 – universelle
28 avenant *m.* de –
29 détenteur *m.* de –
30 timbre *m.* de –
31 valeur *f.* de rachat d'une –
32 établir une –
33 prendre une – [*médit.*]
police *f.* **de chargement** (*ports*
politique *f.*
 1 – agricole

 2 – commerciale
 3 – de conjoncture
 4 – de crédit
 5 – de dividende
 6 – déflationniste
 7 – de la porte ouverte
 8 – de l'argent à bon marché

 9 – de l'argent cher
10 – d' (de l')open market
11 – de plein emploi
12 – des prix
13 – de restriction des crédits
14 – des salaires, – salariale
15 – d'escompte
16 – du commerce extérieur
17 – économique
18 – en matière de change
19 – extérieure
20 – financière
21 – inflationniste
polycopier
polypole *m.*
ponctualité *f.*
ponctuel(lement)

14 valued –
15 floating (open) –
16 general –
17 paid up –

19 mixed –
20 named –
21 open (unvalued) –

23 open –
24 covering note
25 – without profits
26 all risks –, automobile all-in –, comprehensive –

27 world-wide –
28 endorsement
29 – holder
30 – stamp
31 surrender value of a –
32 to make out a –
33 to take out a –
bill of lading
policy
 1 agricultural –

 2 trade –
 3 cyclical –
 4 credit –
 5 dividend –
 6 – of deflation
 7 – of the open door
 8 cheap-money –

 9 dear-money –
10 open-market –
11 full-employment –
12 price –
13 **restrictive credit –**
14 wage –
15 discount –
16 external trade –
17 economic –
18 exchange –
19 foreign –
20 financial –
21 – of inflation
to manifold, to stencil
polypoly
punctuality
punctual(ly)

pondération f.
  coefficient m. de –
pondéré
  1 moyenne –e
  2 vote –
pont m. (*navire*)
  – supérieur
pont m.
  – à bascule, – à peser
pontée f.
  chargé en –
pool m.
  – de l'acier
population f.
  1 – active
  2 accroissement m. de –
  3 densité f. de la –
  4 diminution f. de la –
  5 excédent m. de –
port m. (*taxe*)
  1 – de lettres
  2 – compris
  3 – dû (à recevoir)
  4 – payé, perçu (franc de –)
  5 – payé par le destinataire
  6 – supplémentaire
  7 frais m. pl. de port
  8 envoi – payé
  9 envoyer franc de –
port m. (*d'un navire*)
  – en lourd
port m.
  1 le – d'Anvers
  2 – aérien
  3 – à (de) marée
  4 – à (de) transit
  5 – d'arrivée
  6 – d'attache
  7 – de chargement
  8 – de déchargement
  9 – de départ
  10 – de destination
  11 – de détresse
  12 – d'embarquement
  13 – de mer
  14 – d'enregistrement
  15 – de relâche
  16 – d'escale
  17 – de transbordement
  18 – d'expédition
  19 – d'ordres
  20 – fluvial
  21 – franc

weighting
  – coefficient
weighted
  1 – average
  2 – vote
deck
  upper –
bridge
  weighbridge
deck cargo, deck load
  shipped on deck
pool
  steel –
population
  1 working –, labo(u)r force
  2 increase in –
  3 density of –
  4 decrease (fall) in –
  5 surplus –
postage
  1 –
  2 – included
  3 carriage forward, carriage to pay
  4 carriage paid, – (post) paid
  5 – will be paid by addressee
  6 additional –
  7 –
  8 carriage-paid consignment
  9 to send post paid
burden, burthen
  dead-weight capacity
port
  1 the – of Antwerp
  2 airport
  3 tidal harbo(u)r
  4 – of transit
  5 – of arrival
  6 home –
  7 – of loading
  8 – of discharge
  9 – of departure
  10 – of destination
  11 – of distress
  12 shipping –, l(o)ading –
  13 seaport
  14 – of registry
  15 – of refuge, of necessity
  16 – of call
  17 – of transhipment
  18 shipping –
  19 – of call for orders
  20 river –, inland –
  21 free –

273 / porte

22 autorités *f. pl.* du –	22 harbo(u)r authorities
23 capitaine *m.* de –	23 harbo(u)r master
24 droits *m. pl.* de –	24 harbo(u)r dues, – dues
25 police *f.* de –	25 harbo(u)r police
26 règlements *m. pl.* du –	26 – regulations
27 arriver à bon –	27 to come safe into –
28 entrer dans un –	28 to enter an harbo(u)r
29 faire escale dans un –	29 to call at a –
30 quitter le –	30 to leave the –
porte *f.*	**door**
– ouverte	open –
portée *f.* (*navire*) (voir *port*)	**burden, burthen**
portefeuille *m.*	**portfolio**
1 d'assurances	1 insurance book
2 – (d')effets	2 bills, bills in case
3 – (de) titres (valeurs)	3 stocks and shares, investments; security holdings
4 – documentaire	4 documentary collections (in hand)
5 actions *f. pl.* en –	5 shares in –, unissued shares
6 composition *f.* d'un –	6 composition of a –
7 gestion *f.* de –	7 management of securities
8 ordres *m. pl.* en –	8 orders in hand, unfilled orders
9 service *m.* du – (effets)	9 bills department
10 traites *f. pl.* en —	10 bills in the bill case
11 avoir... titres en –	11 to have... securities in –
12 composer un –	12 to compose a –
portefeuilliste *m.*	**investor**
porte-mine(s) *m.*	**propelling pencil**
porte-monnaie *m.*	**purse**
porte-plume *m.*	**penholder**
– (à) réservoir	fountain pen
porter	**to bear**
1 – à compte à nouveau	1 to carry forward for new account
2 – à domicile	2 to deliver at home
3 – au crédit	3 to pass to the credit
4 – au crédit du compte de...	4 to pass to the credit of, to credit... for
5 – au débit	5 to enter to the debit
6 – au journal	6 to journalize
7 – aux livres	7 to book
8 – de... à...	8 to bring (raise) from... to...
9 – en compte à	9 to charge at
10 portez en compte suivant avis	10 place to account as per advice
11 – les frais en compte à M...	11 to charge someone for the expenses
12 – en décharge	12 to deduct
13 – intérêt	13 – interest

porteur / 274

14 – des intérêts à partir de
15 – la mention
16 – un nom
17 – une signature

18 être porté dans les livres pour
porteur *m.* (*gare*)
porteur *m.* (*détenteur*)
  1 – d'actions
  2 – de bonne foi
  3 – d'un chèque
  4 – d'une lettre de crédit
  5 – d'une lettre de gage
  6 – de licence
  7 – d'obligations
  8 – de la présente
  9 – d'une procuration
  10 – de télégrammes
  11 – d'une traite
  12 par –
  13 payable au –
  14 tiers *m.* –
  15 être au –
portion *f.* (*d'un héritage*)
  1 – disponible
  2 – légitime
portuaire
  1 installations *f. pl.* –s

  2 tarifs *m. pl.* –s
position *f.*
  1 – à cheval (– mixte)
  2 – acheteur, à la hausse, haussière
  3 – débitrice
  4 – créditrice
  5 – de place
  6 – d'un compte

  7 – financière
  8 – sociale
  9 – vendeur, à la baisse, baissière
  10 liquider une –
  11 réaliser une –

  12 reporter une –
  13 transmettre une –
posséder
  – une langue
possesseur *m.*
  – (*de valeurs*)
possession *f.*
  1 – de fait
  2 – trentenaire

14 – interest from
15 – the mention, to be marked
16 – a name
17 – a signature

18 to stand in the books at
porter
bearer
  1 shareholder
  2 bona fide holder
  3 – of a cheque (check)
  4 holder of a letter of credit
  5 holder of a mortgage bond
  6 licensee
  7 bondholder
  8 – (of this letter)
  9 holder of a proxy
  10 telegraph messenger
  11 holder of a bill of exchange
  12 by messenger
  13 payable to –
  14 second endorser
  15 **to be (payable) to –**
portion
  1 freely disposable –
  2 legal (legitimate) –
port...
  1 – equipment, harbo(u)r installations

  2 – rates, harbour tariffs
position
  1 straddle
  2 bull –, bull account
  3 debtor –
  4 creditor –
  5 market –
  6 – of an account

  7 financial –
  8 social standing
  9 bear –, short –, bear account
  10 to liquidate (close) a –
  11 to realize a –

  12 to carry over (continue) a –
  13 to carry over a –
to possess, to own
to be well up (versed) in a language
owner, possessor
holder
possession
  1 actual –
  2 thirty years' –

275 / possessions

3 – vaut titre (voir *meuble*)

4 nous sommes en – de votre lettre
5 prise *f.* de –
6 entrer en –
7 mettre en – de
8 prendre en –
possessions *f. pl.* (*biens*)
 1 – de la société
 2 – d'outre-mer
possibilité *f.* (v. *exportation*)
possible
 1 aussitôt que –

 2 autant que –
 3 dans la mesure du –

 4 si –
 5 faire tout son –
postal
 1 boîte –e
 2 colis –
 3 numéro *m.* du district –
 4 quittance –e
 5 récépissé –
 6 services postaux
 7 tarif –
 8 trafic –
postdater
poste *m.*
 1 – créditeur
 2 – de bilan
 3 – débiteur
 4 – de mémoire
 5 présenté avec un – de... pour mémoire
 6 – (*tel.*) 144
poste *f.* (v. aussi *courrier*)
 1 par la –
 2 – aérienne, – avion
 3 – pneumatique
 4 – restante
 5 administration *f.* des –s

 6 bon *m.* de –
 7 bureau *m.* de –
 8 date *f.* de la –
 9 par – ordinaire
 10 mettre à la –, poster
post-scriptum *m.*
 mettre (faire) un –
pot-de-vin *m.*
potentiel *m.* **de production**

3 – is title

4 we are in receipt of your letter
5 taking –
6 to enter into –
7 to put in – of
8 to get into (to take) –
possessions, properties
 1 properties of the company
 2 oversea(s) possessions
possibility
possible
 1 as soon as –

 2 as much as –
 3 as far as –

 4 if –
 5 to do one's utmost, all one can
postal
 1 post (office) box
 2 – parcel
 3 – zone number
 4 – collection order
 5 – receipt
 6 – services
 7 rates of postage, – rates
 8 – traffic
to postdate, to date forward
item, heading
 1 credit item, credit entry
 2 – of the balance sheet
 3 debit item, debit entry
 4 entry for memory, reminder entry
 5 shown pro memoria at the value of...
 6 extension 144
post
 1 by –
 2 air mail
 3 pneumatic –
 4 to be (left till) called for
 5 postal authorities

 6 postal order
 7 – office
 8 date as – mark
 9 by regular mail
 10 to post
postscript
 to make (add) a –
hush money
output potential

« pour acquit » / 276

"pour acquit" — received (with thanks)
pour-cent *m.* — percentage
 1 – en dedans — 1 (– on the smaller number)
 2 – en dehors — 2 (– on the larger number)
 3 – simple — 3 –
 4 à quel – ? — 4 at what rate per cent?
 5 en – — 5 in –s

pour cent — per cent
 1 un demi – — 1 one half –
 2 à 4 – — 2 at 4 –
 3 emprunt *m.* à 4 – — 3 loan of 4 –, 4 – loan
 4 diminuer de 10 – — 4 to reduce by 10 –
 5 rapporter 4 – d'intérêt — 5 to bear 4 – interest

pourcentage *m.* — percentage
 1 – élevé — 1 high –
 2 calcul *m.* du – — 2 calculation of –
pour copie conforme — certified true copy
pour mémoire (voir aussi *poste*) — pro memoria, as a memorandum
 montant mentionné – — pro memoria figure
pour mille — per thousand

„poussez" (*porte*) — push
pouvoir *m.* — power
 1 –s publics — 1 public authorities
 2 – pour assemblée générale — 2 proxy for general meeting

 3 plein – (voir aussi *procuration*) — 3 full –
 4 avoir plein – — 4 to have full –
 5 donner plein – — 5 to give full –
 6 munir de plein – — 6 to furnish (invest) with full –
pouvoir *m.* d'achat — purchasing (buying) power
 1 excédentaire, en excès — 1 excess (excessive) –
 2 augmentation *f.* du – — 2 increase of –
 3 maintien *m.* du – — 3 maintenance of –
 4 parité *f.* du – — 4 – parity
pratique *f.* — practice
 1 – bancaire — 1 banking –
 2 – de nombre d'années — 2 a many years experience
 3 dans la – — 3 in –
 4 c'est de – courante — 4 it is usual
 5 acquérir la – — 5 to acquire a –
 6 avoir de la – — 6 to have a –
pratique (*adj.*) — practical
 1 connaissance – — 1 workable knowledge
 2 examen – — 2 – examination
pratiqué
 1 cours –s (*bourse*) — 1 bargains done
 2 prix –s — 2 ruling prices
préachat *m.* — prepayment
préalable — previous
 1 au – — 1 previously, before hand

277 / préalablement

2 sans avis –
3 accord *m.* –
préalablement
préavis *m.*
1 délai *m.* de –
2 à trois mois de –
3 à 7 jours de –
4 sans –
5 donner un – de 3 jours
précédent *m.*
1 créer un –
2 sans –
précompte *m.*
précompter
préemption *f.*
droit *m.* de –
préfabriqué

préférence *f.* (*priorité*)
1 de –
2 droit *m.* de –
3 accorder (donner) la – à
4 avoir la – sur

préférentiel (voir aussi *privilégié*)
tarif –
préférer à
préfinancement *m.*
préjudice *m.* (*dommage*)
1 sans – de
2 causer (porter) – à

préjudiciable
préjudiciel
préjudicier
préjuger, sans – de
prélèvement *m.*
1 –s d'avances de caisse
2 – d'échantillons
3 – d'intérêts sur le capital
4 –s exceptionnels
5 –s personnels

6 – sur le capital
7 –s sur compte courant
8 – sur la fortune
9 – sur la fortune immobilière
10 – sur la réserve de dividende

11 – sur le salaire
prélever
1 – une commission sur...

2 without – advice
3 – agreement
previously
notice
1 term of –
2 at three months' –
3 at 7 days' –
4 without –; at call
5 to give a three days' –
precedent
1 to set (create) a –
2 unprecedented
previous deduction
to deduct beforehand
pre-emption
right of –
prefabricated (prefab)

preference
1 by –
2 right of claim
3 to give the – to
4 to rank before, to have the – over

preferential
– tariff
to prefer to
prefinancing
prejudice, damage
1 without – to
2 to be prejudicial to, to cause (inflict) damage (loss) to
prejudicial to
pre-judicial
to be prejudicial to   [to...
without prejudicing..., prejudice
withdrawal
1 drawing of cash advances
2 taking samples, sampling
3 payment of interest out of capital
4 extraordinary levy
5 personal drawings

6 capital levy
7 drawings on current account
8 property levy
9 levy on real estate
10 – from the dividend reserve

11 deduction from the wages

1 to draw (charge) a commission on...

premier / 278

2 – des échantillons
3 – une somme de... pour ses besoins personnels
4 – des titres sur le dossier „nantissement"
5 réserves *f. pl.* à – sur les bénéfices

6 somme prélevée sur... pour...

premier (v. *frais*, *main*)
première *f.* de change
  payez par cette – la seconde ne l'étant

prendre
1 – un billet pour...
2 – un brevet
3 – une commande
4 – cours à partir de...
5 – en considération

6 – en mauvaise part
7 – ferme (*emprunt*)
8 – intérêt à

9 – la liberté
10 – des marchandises de qqn
11 – le nom et l'adresse
12 – note
13 – part à
14 – possession

15 – rang après
16 – réception
17 être très pris
18 mon temps est pris

preneur *m.*
1 – (*acheteur*)
2 – à la grosse
3 – d'assurance
4 – d'un effet
5 – de faculté de lever double

6 – de faculté de livrer double

7 – de stellage, – d'option
8 bailleur *m.* et –

9 trouver –s
prénom *m.*
préposé *m.*
  – de la douane

2 to take samples
3 to draw a sum for one's personal requirements
4 to withdraw securities from deposit

5 reserves to be appropriated out of profits
6 sum taken (appropriated) from... to...
first
first of exchange
  pay this our –, second of the same tenor and date being unpaid

to take
1 – a ticket for
2 – out a patent
3 – an order
4 to run from...
5 – into consideration

6 – ill, in bad part
7 – firm
8 – an interest in

9 – the liberty (– leave) to
10 to buy (draw) goods from
11 – name and address
12 – note
13 – part in
14 – possession of

15 to rank after
16 – delivery
17 to be pressed with business
18 my time is taken up

taker
1 buyer
2 borrower on bottomry
3 insurance –
4 payee of a bill
5 giver for a call of more

6 giver for (buyer of) a put of more

7 giver for a put and call
8 the lessor and the lessee

9 to find buyers
Christian name
servant, official
  customs official

près Paris
prescription *f.*
  1 – acquisitive
  2 – extinctive
  3 – trentenaire
  4 délai *m.* de –
  5 loi *f.* de –
  6 frappé de –
prescription *f.* (*instructions*)
  1 suivant les –s
  2 se conformer aux –s
prescrire (*jur.*)

  1 dette prescrite
  2 être prescrit
prescrire (*ordonner*)
  1 à la date prescrite
  2 dans le délai prescrit
  3 dans la forme prescrite
présence *f.* (v. aussi *liste*)
  1 en – de...
  2 jetons *m. pl.* de –

présent (voir aussi *présente*)
  1 la –e (voir *présente*)
  2 – et à venir, – et futur
  3 le – accord
  4 dans le cas –
  5 dans la situation –e
  6 à –
  7 à – que
  8 jusqu'à –
  9 étaient –s
  10 être – en personne
présentateur *m.* (*effet*)
présentation *f.*
  1 – à l'acceptation
  2 – au payement
  3 – de candidats
  4 à –
  5 payable à (sur) –
  6 sur – des factures
  7 sur – du coupon

présente, la –

  1 au reçu de la –

  2 par la –, les –s
  3 le porteur de la –
présenter
  1 – à l'acceptation

---

near Paris
prescription, limitation
  1 acquisitive (positive) prescription
  2 extinctive (negative) prescription
  3 thirty years' prescription
  4 term of limitation
  5 statute of limitation
  6 barred by (the statute of) limitation
instruction
  1 according to –s
  2 to conform to –s
to become barred by statute, to become void by prescription
  1 statute barred debt
  2 to be barred by limitation
to prescribe
  1 on the date fixed
  2 within the prescribed time
  3 in the prescribed form
presence
  1 in – of
  2 attendance fees

present

  2 – and future
  3 the – agreement
  4 in the – case
  5 in the – situation
  6 at –, at the – time
  7 now that
  8 so far, up to the –, as yet
  9 –..., those – were...
  10 to be – personally
presenter
presentation
  1 – for acceptance
  2 – for payment
  3 nomination
  4 on –
  5 payable on demand, on –
  6 on production of the invoices
  7 on – of the coupon

the present (letter), this letter

  1 on receipt of the present

  2 hereby, by these presents, herewith
  3 bearer of this letter
to present
  1 – for acceptance

présidence / 280

2 – à l'encaissement
3 – à l'escompte
4 – au payement
5 – les billets (*ch. de fer*)
6 – des excuses

7 – les factures
8 – un rapport à l'assemblée générale

9 – un solde de...   [tera
10 la première occasion qui se présen-
11 permettez-moi de vous –
12 se – en personne
présidence *f.* (*société*)
1 pendant sa –
2 sous la – (*réunion*)

3 être nommé à la –

président *m.* (*d'un pays*)
1 – (*de société*)
2 Monsieur le –
3 discours *m.* du – (*ass. génér.*)
présider
1 – une assemblée

2 présidé par...

presse *f.*
1 campagne *f.* de –
2 moments *m. pl.* de –
3 nouvelles *f. pl.* de –
4 avoir une bonne –

5 être sous –
6 sortir de –

presse-papiers *m.*
presser
l'affaire presse
pression *f.*
1 – de la demande
2 – inflationniste
3 groupe *m.* de –
prestation *f.*
1 – de capitaux
2 –s de services
3 – d'un serment
4 – en nature

5 – en argent
prêt *m.*
1 – à (de) consommation

2 – for collection
3 – for discount
4 – for payment
5 to produce tickets
6 to tender apologies, to offer an apology to
7 to produce invoices
8 – a report to the general meeting

9 to show a balance of   [arise
10 the first opportunity which may
11 may I introduce... to you?
12 to apply in person
chairmanship
1 during his –
2 ... in the chair, presided over by... under the – of,... presiding
3 to be elected chairman

president
1 chairman
2 Mister (Mr.) chairman
3 chairman's address
to preside, to be in the chair
1 to preside at (over) a meeting, to be chairman of a meeting
2 to be presided over by... ; ... (was) in the chair
press
1 – campaign
2 rush hours
3 – news
4 to have a good –

5 to be in the –
6 to come out

paper weight
to expedite
the matter is urgent
pressure
1 demand pull, – of demand
2 inflationary –
3 – group
achievement
1 furnishing, provision of capital
2 (performance of) services
3 taking of an oath
4 allowance (benefit) in kind

5 allowance in money
loan
1 simple –, – for consumption

281 / prêt

2 – à court terme | 2 short –
3 – à intérêts | 3 – on interest
4 – à la grosse (aventure) | 4 bottomry –
5 – à la grosse sur corps | 5 bottomry –
6 – à la grosse sur facultés | 6 respondentia –
7 – à long terme | 7 long-term (period) –
8 – au jour le jour | 8 day-to-day –
9 – à usage (*commodat*) | 9 free –
10 – gagé, – garanti | 10 secured –
11 – gratuit | 11 advance free of interest
12 – hypothécaire | 12 – on mortgage
13 – lombard | 13 lombard –, – on collateral
14 – maritime (voir – à la grosse) |
15 –s personnels | 15 personal –s
16 – sur gage, – sur nantissement | 16 – on collateral, lombard –
17 – sur signature | 17 signature –
18 – sur titres | 18 – on stock, on securities
19 – usuraire | 19 usurious –
20 à titre de – | 20 as a –
21 banque *f.* de –s sur navires | 21 ship-mortgage bank
22 caisse *f.* de –s | 22 – bank
23 contrat *m.* de – | 23 contract of –
24 demande *f.* de – | 24 application for a –
25 société *f.* de –s | 25 – society
26 taux *m.* du – sur gage | 26 rate for advances on collateral
27 titre *m.* de – | 27 – certificate
28 conclure un – | 28 to contract a –
29 consentir un – | 29 to allow a –
30 donner à titre de – | 30 to give as a –
31 recevoir à titre de – | 31 to receive as a –

prêt (*adj.*) | **ready**
– à l'envoi | – for dispatch

prête-nom *m.* | **dummy, man of straw**

prêter | **to lend**
1 – à | 1 – to
2 – à intérêt | 2 – at interest
3 – à la grosse | 3 – on bottomry
4 – sur hypothèque | 4 – on mortgage
5 – sur gage, nantissement | 5 – on security
6 – sur titres | 6 – on stock
7 se – à | 7 – oneself to

prêteur *m.* | **lender**
1 – à la grosse | 1 – on bottomry
2 – sur gage, sur nantissement | 2 – on security, pledgee
3 – sur hypothèque | 3 mortgagee

preuve *f.* | **proof**
1 comme – de | 1 as – of
2 jusqu'à – du contraire | 2 until the contrary is proved
3 faire – de | 3 to give – of
4 fournir la – | 4 to furnish –, to prove

prévaloir / 282

prévaloir, se – de

prévision *f.*
 1 –s budgétaires
 2 –s de récolte
 3 d'après les –s
prévision (*bilan*) (v. *provision*)
prévoyance *f.*
 1 – sociale
 2 fonds *m.* de – (voir *fonds*)
prévu, être –
prier
 1 nous vous prions de...
 2 en vous priant de...
prière *f.*
 1 – d'adresser la réponse à...

 2 – d'écrire lisiblement

 3 – de fermer la porte
 4 – de nous faire savoir
 5 – d'insérer (voir *insérer*)
 6 – de rappeler dans votre réponse nos références...
prime *f.*
 1 – à la baisse, (voir – *pour livrer*)
 2 – à la hausse, (voir – *pour lever*)
 3 – annuelle
 4 – d'assurance
 5 – d'émission
 6 – de remboursement
 7 – de rendement
 8 – de renouvellement (*assur.*)
 9 – d'(à l') exportation
 10 – d'importation

 11 – directe (voir – *pour lever*)
 12 dont (voir – *pour lever*)
 13 – du change   [*livrer*]
 14 – indirecte, – inverse (voir – *pour*
 15 – ou (voir – *pour livrer*)
 16 – pour lever, – pour l'acheteur, – simple à la hausse

 17 – pour livrer, – pour le vendeur, – simple à la baisse, – renversée

 18 – sur les actions
 19 – sur obligations
 20 – sur l'or
 21 double – (option)

to pride oneself of, to avail oneself of
prospect
 1 estimates
 2 crop prospect
 3 according to the estimates

precaution
 1 state insurance

to be provided for
to request, to ask
 1 we would request you; please...
 2 with the request
request
 1 all communications to be addressed to...
 2 please write distinctly, clearly

 3 please close the door
 4 please inform us

 6 in your reply (in replying) please quote...
premium

 3 annual –
 4 insurance –
 5 share –
 6 redemption –
 7 merit bonus
 8 renewal –
 9 export bounty
 10 bounty on importation, import bounty

 13 exchange –, – on exchange

 16 call, call option, buyer's option

 17 put, put option, seller's option

 18 – on shares
 19 – on bonds
 20 – on gold
 21 double option, put and call, put and call option

283 / principal

22 abandon *m.* de la –	22 abandonment of the option money
23 cours *m.* de la –	23 option price
24 écart *m.* de – (différence entre le cours ferme et le cours à prime)	24 ecart (difference between the prices of firm stock and option stock)
25 jour *m.* de la réponse des –s	25 option (declaration) day
26 levée *f.* de la –	26 call for the –
27 marché *m.* à –	27 option bargain
28 opérations *f. pl.* à –	28 option business
29 payeur *m.* de la –	29 giver of the rate
30 pied *m.* de la – (limite de la –)	30 limit price at which the option is abandoned
31 receveur *m.* de la –	31 taker of the (option) rate
32 réponse *f.* des –s	32 option declaration
33 (taux *m.* de la) –	33 (option) rate
34 ristourne *f.* de – (*assur.*)	34 return of –
35 abandonner la –	35 to abandon an option
36 être en –, faire –	36 to be at a –
37 lever la –	37 to call for the –
principal (*adj.*)	**principal**
1 créancier –	1 – creditor
2 débiteur –	2 – debtor
3 siège –	3 head office
principal *m.*	**main point**
– et intérêts	principal and interest
priorité *f.*	**priority, preference**
1 – d'hypothèque	1 priority of mortgage
2 droit *m.* de –	2 priority right
3 avoir un droit de – sur	3 to rank in priority to
prise *f.*	
1 – à bord	1 taking on board
2 – à commission (*émission*)	2 taking on a commission basis
3 – de bénéfices	3 profit taking
4 – en charge (v. aussi *passif*)	4 taking over
5 – en dépôt	5 acceptance for deposit
6 – ferme (*émission*)	6 taking firm
7 commission *f.* de – ferme	7 underwriting commission
8 contrat *m.* de – ferme	8 underwriting agreement
9 prix d'achat de – ferme	9 price to underwriters
10 syndicat *m.* de – ferme	10 underwriting syndicate
prise *f.* (*mar.*)	**prize**
tribunal *m.* des –s	– Court
prise *f.* à domicile	**collection (at residence)**
1 frais *m. pl.* de –	1 collecting charges
2 service *m.* de remise et –	2 collection and delivery service
prisée *f.*	**valuation, estimate**
priser	**to value**
priseur *m.*	**appraiser, valuer**
privé	**private**
1 banque –e	1 – bank

privilège / 284

2 bureau –
3 compte –
4 entreprise –e
5 escompte –
6 personne –e
7 prélèvements –s, personnels

8 propriété –e
9 signature –e
privilège *m.*
1 – (*droit de préférence*) sur...
2 – de souscription

3 jouir d'un –
privilégié
prix *m.*
1 – acceptable
2 – à forfait
3 – actuels
4 – approximatif
5 – au comptant
6 – avantageux
7 – contractuel
8 – convenu

9 – coûtant
10 calcul *m.* du – coûtant
11 – d'achat
12 – d'après-guerre
13 – d'avant-guerre
14 – de base
15 – de catalogue
16 – de clôture
17 – de détail
18 – de direction
19 – de fabrique
20 – de facture
21 – de faveur
22 – défiant la concurrence, compétitifs
23 – de gros
24 – de la prime
25 – de main-d'œuvre
26 – demandé
27 – de mise en vente
28 – d'émission

29 – de rachat (*police*)
30 – de revient
31 – dérisoire
32 – désavantageux
33 – de soutien
34 – de transport

2 – office
3 – account
4 – enterprise
5 – discount
6 – person
7 personal drawings

8 – property
9 – signature
privilege
1 lien upon...
2 application right

3 to enjoy a –
preferential, preferred
price
1 acceptable –
2 contract –
3 ruling –es
4 approximate –
5 cash –
6 favo(u)rable –
7 contract –
8 – agreed

9 cost –
10 costing, cost accounting
11 purchase –
12 postwar –s
13 prewar –s
14 basis (basic) –
15 list –
16 closing –
17 retail –
18 basic (guiding) –
19 manufacturer's –, maker's –
20 invoice –
21 preferential –
22 competitive –s

23 wholesale –
24 option –, – of option
25 cost of labour
26 demand –, – asked
27 selling off –
28 issue –

29 surrender value
30 cost
31 ridiculously low –
32 unfavo(u)rable –
33 supported (pegged) –
34 carriage charge

285 / prix

35 − de vente
36 − de vente au détail
37 − de vente imposé
38 − d'inventaire
39 − d'occasion
40 − d'ouverture
41 − du fret
42 − du jour
43 − du marché noir
44 − du report
45 − élevé
46 − en vigueur
47 − exorbitant
48 − fermes
49 − fixe
50 − forfaitaire
51 − fort
52 − imposé
53 système des − imposés (par le fabricant aux revendeurs)
54 − inabordables
55 − libellés en monnaie étrangère
56 − marqué
57 − maximum
58 − minimum
59 − modique
60 − moyen
61 − net
62 − obtenu
63 − offert
64 − prohibitifs
65 − raisonnable
66 − réduit
67 − réel
68 − rémunérateur
69 − sacrifiés
70 − standard
71 − tous frais compris
72 − unique
73 magasin *m.* à − unique
74 − unitaire
75 − usuraire
76 − variable
77 à moitié −
78 à tous les −
79 à tout −
80 à vil −

81 au-dessous du −
82 au-dessus du −
83 au − de
84 bas −
85 le plus haut −

35 selling −
36 retail −
37 fixed selling −
38 stocktaking −
39 bargain −
40 opening −
41 rate of freight
42 current −
43 black market −
44 contango rate, carry over rate
45 high −
46 ruling −s
47 exorbitant −
48 firm (steady) −s
49 fixed −
50 contract −, agreed −
51 selling −, full −
52 fixed (selling) −
53 system of fixed −s for resale

54 prohibitive −s
55 −s expressed in foreign currency
56 marked −
57 maximum −
58 minimum −
59 moderate −
60 average −
61 net −
62 − obtained
63 offered −
64 prohibitive −s
65 reasonable −
66 reduced −
67 actual −
68 remunerative −
69 ruinous (slaughter) −s
70 standard −
71 inclusive −
72 one −
73 one-price store
74 unit −
75 usurious −
76 variable −
77 at half −
78 in all − ranges
79 at any −
80 dirt cheap, knock-out −

81 below the −
82 above the −
83 at the − of
84 low −
85 the highest −

prix / 286

86 tout dernier −
87 les − baissent

88 les − montent
89 les − se maintiennent
90 les − sont 5 % plus bas que
91 les − tendent à la hausse

92 affichage *m.* des −
93 amélioration *f.* des −
94 augmentation *f.* des −
95 baisse *f.* des −

96 blocage *m.* des −
97 calcul *m.* des −
98 chute *f.* des −
99 consolidation *f.* des −
100 contrôle *m.* des −
101 demande *f.* de −
102 différence *f.* de −
103 diminution *f.* de −

104 disparité *f.* des −
105 écart *m.* de −
106 évolution *f.* des −
107 fixation *f.* du −
108 fixation *f.* du − (par les autorités)
109 fluctuation *f.* de −
110 formation *f.* des −
111 hausse *f.* des −

112 indication *f.* des −
113 indice *m.* des −
114 indice *m.* des − de gros
115 liste *f.* des −
116 mise *f.* à −
117 montée *f.* des −
118 mouvement *m.* des −
119 niveau *m.* des −
120 office *m.* de contrôle des −

121 rabaissement *m.* des −

122 rajustement *m.* des −
123 réduction *f.* de −
124 réglementation *f.* des −
125 repli *m.* des −
126 stabilisation *f.* des −
127 stabilité *f.* des −
128 structure *f.* des −
129 afficher les −
130 atteindre un −
131 augmenter de −

86 lowest −
87 −s decline, go down, fall

88 −s advance
89 −s remain firm, are maintained
90 −s are 5 % lower
91 −s show an upward tendency, tend upwards

92 placarding of − lists
93 improvement in −s
94 rise (increase of) in −s
95 fall in −s

96 − stop
97 calculation of −s
98 collapse (drop) of −s
99 consolidation of −s
100 − control, control over −s
101 − inquiry
102 − difference
103 diminution of −s

104 difference in −
105 difference in −
106 trend (course) of −s
107 fixation of the −
108 price fixing (by the authorities)
109 fluctuation of −s
110 − determination
111 rise of −s

112 quotation of −s
113 −s index
114 wholesale − index
115 − list
116 upset −
117 rise of (in) −s
118 − movement
119 level of −s
120 office of − administration, − control office

121 lowering of −s, cut in −

122 adjustment of −s
123 reduction in −
124 − regulation
125 fall in −s
126 strengthening of −s
127 − stability
128 − structure
129 to bill (post up) − lists
130 to reach a −
131 to rise (advance) in −

132 augmenter les – de...
133 calculer le –
134 convenir d'un –
135 demander un –
136 demander (le) –
137 diminuer de –
138 diminuer les – de...
139 établir (fixer) un –
140 faire baisser les –
141 faire hausser les –

142 marquer les –
143 noter un –
144 obtenir un –
145 offrir un –
146 rabattre du –

prix-courant m.
– sur demande

probabilité f.
1 calcul m. des –s
2 selon toute –
probable
probant, force –e
procédé m. (industrie)
procédure f.
1 – (jur.)
2 – d'annulation de titres adirés

3 – de faillite
procès m.
1 frais m. pl. de –
2 gagner son –
3 intenter un – à...
procès-verbal m. (séance)
1 le – est lu et adopté

2 approuver le –
3 rédiger le –
4 inscrire au –
procès-verbal m. (police)
dresser – contre...

prochain
1 le 15 du mois –
2 fin – (bourse)
3 par le – courrier
procuration f.
1 – collective
2 – en blanc
3 – générale

132 to raise (increase) –s by...
133 to calculate the –
134 to agree on a –
135 to ask a –
136 to inquire the –
137 to fall in –
138 to reduce (lower) –s by...
139 to set (fix) a –
140 to depress (force down) –s
141 to push up (force up) –s

142 to mark, to –
143 to note a –
144 to obtain a –
145 to offer a –
146 to make a reduction on the –, to take off the –
price list
– on application

probability
1 calculus (theory) of –
2 in all likelihood, –
probable
probatory force
process
proceedings
1 procedure
2 public advertisement of securities which have been lost
3 bankruptcy proceedings
action
1 cost of proceedings
2 to win one's case
3 to bring an – against..., to sue
minutes
1 the – were read and confirmed

2 to approve (adopt) the –
3 to draw up the –
4 to enter on the –
policeman's report
to make a report, to take down one's name and address
next
1 the 15th prox, the 15th of – month
2 end – (account)
3 by – mail
procuration
1 joint (power of) –
2 blank power of attorney
3 general power

producteur / 288

4 – individuelle
5 – réciproque
6 – spéciale
7 par – (p. pon)

8 cette – est valable (voir *valable*)
9 la – est expirée
10 avoir la –
11 conférer (donner) la –
12 investir d'une –
13 signer par –
producteur *m.*

1 centre –
2 pays –
productif
– d'intérêts
production *f.*

1 – agricole
2 – à la chaîne
3 – annuelle
4 – d'automobiles
5 – en masse

6 – en série

7 – industrielle
8 – journalière
9 – mondiale
10 la – surpasse les besoins

11 appareil *m.* de –
12 augmentation *f.* de –

13 baisse *f.* de la –
14 capacité *f.* de –

15 centre *m.* de –

16 diminution *f.* de la –
17 excédent *m.* de –
18 frais *m. pl.* de –
19 indice *m.* de la –
20 moyens *m. pl.* de –
21 perte *f.* de –
22 potentiel *m.* de –
23 processus *m.* de –
24 ralentissement *m.* de la –
25 restriction *f.* de –

26 surplus *m.* de –
27 unité *f.* de –

4 individual proxy
5 reciprocal proxy
6 special power
7 per – (p. p.), by proxy

9 the – has lapsed
10 to have power of –, to hold the –
11 to grant power of –
12 to confer powers of attorney on
13 to sign by –
producer

1 producing center, region
2 producing country
productive
interest-bearing
production, output

1 agricultural –
2 moving-band (flow) production
3 annual –, output
4 car output, automobile output
5 mass production

6 serial manufacture

7 industrial –
8 daily production
9 world production
10 the production exceeds the demand

11 production machinery
12 increase in production

13 decline in production
14 producing capacity, capacity of output

15 producing centre
[output
16 diminution of production, fall in
17 surplus produce
18 cost of production
19 production index
20 capital goods
21 loss of production, loss in output
22 – potential
23 process of –
24 falling off in –
25 restricted production

26 surplus of production
27 unit of –

289 / production

production *f.* (*de pièces*)
  sur – de
productivité *f.*
  1 accroissement *m.* de la –
  2 mesure *f,* de la –
produire
  – de l'intérêt
produire (*exhiber*) **des documents**
produit *m.* (*compt.*)
produit *m.* (voir aussi *article*)
  1 – agricole

  2 –s définitifs
  3 – de marque
  4 –s de première nécessité
  5 – demi-ouvré
  6 – du pays, – indigène
  7 –s finis
  8 –s industriels
  9 – manufacturé
  10 –s mi-finis
  11 –s préliminaires
  12 les –s principaux de... (*pays*)
  13 – semi-ouvré
produit *m.* (*rapport*)
  1 – brut
  2 – national brut
  3 – national net
  4 – national au coût des facteurs

  5 – national au prix du marché

  6 – net
  7 – d'une vente
profession *f.*
  1 – d'architecte
  2 – libérale
  3 sans –
  4 adresse et –

professionnel *m.* (*bourse*)
  les –s

professionnel
  activité –le
profit *m.* (v. *maximisation*)
  1 – espéré
  2 –s et pertes
  3 au – de
  4 compte *m.* des pertes et –s
  5 faire son – de, mettre à –
  6 vendre à –
profitable

production
  on – of
productivity, productiveness [vity
  1 stepping up (raising) of producti-
  2 – measurement
to produce
  to bear (yield) interest
to produce documents
product in process
product
  1 agricultural product

  2 finally finished goods
  3 branded good
  4 essential (indispensable) products
  5 semimanufactured article
  6 home –, domestic –
  7 finished goods
  8 manufactures, products of industry
  9 manufactured article, manufacture
  10 semifinished goods
  11 goods for further processing
  12 staple commodity
  13 semifinished product
proceeds, yield
  1 gross proceeds
  2 gross national product
  3 net national product
  4 national product at factor cost

  5 national product at market prices

  6 net proceeds
  7 proceeds of a sale
profession
  1 – of an architect
  2 liberal –   [tion
  3 on independant means, no occupa-
  4 address and –, occupation, description

professional
  the –s

professional
  – activity
profit
  1 imaginary (anticipated) –
  2 – and loss
  3 in favo(u)r of
  4 – and loss account
  5 to profit by, to take advantage of
  6 to sell at a –
profitable

profiter / 290

profiter
 1 – à
 2 – de
 3 – de *(tirer un bénéfice)*
 4 – d'une occasion

progrès *m.*
 faire des –
progressif (v. *emprunt, impôt*)
 à taux –
progression *f.*
 1 – arithmétique, – par différence
 2 – géométrique, – par quotient
 3 être en –
prohiber
prohibitif (v. *droits, prix*)
 1 système –
 2 lois prohibitives
prohibition *f.*
 1 – d'entrée, – d'importation
 2 – d'exportation
projet *m.* *(plan)*
 1 abandonner un –
 2 former un –
projet *m.* (1ʳᵉ *rédaction*)
 1 en –
 2 – de budget
 3 – de contrat
 4 – de loi
 5 – de réponse
 6 – de statuts
prolongation *f.*
 – du délai
prolonger
promesse *f.*
 1 – *(document)*
 2 – d'actions
 3 – de paiement
 4 tenir une –
promotion *f.*
 – des ventes
prompt
 1 –e expédition
 2 –e réponse
promptitude *f.*
propagande *f.*
 1 brochure *f.* de –
 2 département *m.* de – *(banque)*

propension *f.*
 1 – à la consommation
 2 – à l'épargne, à épargner
 3 – marginale

 1 to be profitable to
 2 to profit by
 3 to benefit, to profit by
 4 to take advantage of an opportunity
progress
 to make –
progressive
 at a – rate
progression
 1 arithmetic progression
 2 geometric progression
 3 to be growing
to **prohibit**
prohibitive
 1 – system
 2 prohibitory laws
prohibition
 1 – of import
 2 – of export
plan
 1 to give up a –
 2 to draw up a –
draft
 1 in –
 2 – budget
 3 – contract
 4 – bill
 5 – reply
 6 – articles
prolongation
 extension of the time
to **prolong**, to **extend**
promise
 1 promissory note
 2 – of share
 3 – to pay
 4 to keep a –
promotion
 sales –
prompt
 1 – shipment
 2 early reply
promptitude
propaganda
 1 advertising brochure
 2 publicity department, new-business department
propensity
 1 – to consume
 2 – to save
 3 marginal –

291 / proportion

proportion f.
1 à –
2 à (en) – de
3 hors de toute –
proportionnel
1 – à
2 directement – à
3 inversement – à
proportionnellement
propos, à ce –
proposer
1 – un concordat de...
2 – un dividende
3 – pour un emploi
proposition f.
1 – d'assurance
2 – de dividende
3 accepter une –
4 prendre une – en considération
5 repousser une –
6 soumettre une –
propre
1 de sa – main
2 en – personne
3 en main – (voir *remettre*)
4 pour son – compte
5 le – (biens –s)
6 avoir en –
propriétaire m.
1 – f.
2 – (*d'une maison louée*)
3 – de la marchandise
4 – foncier
5 changement m. de –
6 changer de –
propriété f.
1 – bâtie
2 – foncière
3 – grevée
4 – immobilière
5 – industrielle
6 – intellectuelle
7 – mobilière
8 – privée
9 nue –
10 pleine –
11 acte m. translatif de –
12 droit m. de –
13 mutation f. de –
14 protection f. de la – industrielle
15 titre m. de –
16 tranfert m. de –
17 acquérir la –

proportion
1 in –
2 in – to
3 out of all –
proportional
1 – to
2 directly – to
3 inversely – to, in inverse ratio to
proportionally to, pro rata
in this connection
to propose
1 – a composition of...
2 to recommend a dividend
3 to put forward for a post
proposal, proposition
1 proposal of insurance
2 recommendation of dividend
3 to accept (agree to) a proposition
4 to take a proposition into consideration
5 to reject a proposition
6 to submit a proposition
own
1 (written) in one's – hand
2 in person, personally
3 personally, into (his) – hands
4 for one's – account
5 separate property
6 to possess in one's – right
owner, proprietor
1 proprietress
2 landlord
3 owner of the goods
4 landed proprietor
5 change of ownership
6 to change the proprietor
property
1 built on –
2 landed –, landed estate
3 encumbered –
4 real –, real estate
5 industrial –, patent rights
6 intellectual –
7 personal estate
8 private –
9 bare ownership
10 freehold, unrestricted ownership
11 deed of conveyance
12 ownership
13 transfer (conveyance) of –
14 protection of industrial – rights
15 title deed
16 conveyance, transfer of –
17 to acquire the –

prorata *m.*	**proportion, share**
1 au –	1 pro rata, in proportion
2 au – de	2 pro rata to, in proportion to, proportionately
prorogation *f.*	**prolongation, extension**
proroger	**to prolong, to extend**
1 – (*séance*)	1 to adjourn
2 – un terme	2 to extend a term
prospecter (*mine*)	**to prospect**
– (*clients*)	to canvass (*par prospectus*) to circularize
prospecteur *m.* (*clientèle*)	**canvasser**
prospection *f.* (*terrain*)	**prospecting**
1 droit *m.* de –	1 prospecting concession
2 – (*clientèle*)	2 canvassing
prospectus *m.*	**prospectus**
1 – d'émission	1 issue –
2 – sur demande	2 – on application, – may be obtained at
3 distribuer (lancer) un –	3 to issue (give out, send out) a –
prospère	**prosperous**
prospérité *f.*	**prosperity**
protecteur	**protective**
1 droits *pl.* –s	1 – duties
2 système *m.* –	2 – system
3 tarif *m.* –	3 – tariff
protection *f.*	**protection**
association *f.* pour la – des détenteurs de titres	association for the – of security holders
protectionnisme *m.*	**protectionism**
protectionniste *adj.*	**protectionist**
protectionniste *m.*	**protectionist**
protestable	**protestable**
protester (contre)	**to protest (against)**
1 faire – une traite	1 to have a bill protested
2 ce que vu, j'ai protesté ledit effet	2 wherefore I now do protest the said bill
3 traite protestée	3 protested (noted) bill
4 revenir protesté	4 to be returned protested
protêt *m.*	**protest**
1 – authentique	1 certified –
2 – du capitaine du navire	2 – of the ship's master
3 – en matière de lettres de change	3 – of a bill
4 – faute d'acceptation	4 – for non-acceptance
5 – faute de payement	5 – for non-payment
6 – simplifié	6 single –

293 / provenance

7 acte *m.* de –
8 délai *m.* de –
9 frais *m. pl.* de –
10 levée *f.* de –

11 faire (lever) –
12 faire dresser –
13 notifier un –
provenance *f.* (voir aussi *origine, pays*)
provision *f.* (*bilan*)
1 –s pour créances douteuses
2 –s pour impôts
provision *f.* (*stock*)
1 – en magasin
2 faire des –s
3 faire – de
provision *f.* (*couverture*)
1 – (*de lettre de change*)
2 – insuffisante
3 sans –
4 chèque *m.* sans –

5 défaut *m.* de – (*lettre de change*)
6 fourniture *f.* de –
7 fournir –
8 verser une (somme par) –
provisionnel
provisoire
public *m.* (voir aussi *placer*)
public *adj.*
  vente publique
publication *f.* (*action*)

1 – (*ce qui est publié*)
2 – obligatoire
publicitaire *adj.*
1 cadeau *m.* –
2 concours *m.* –
3 dessin *m.* –
4 film *m.* –
5 valeur *f.* –
publicitaire *m.*
publicité *f.*
1 – dans les cinémas, – cinéma, sur l'écran
2 – lumineuse
3 – métro
4 – murale
5 – par radio
6 – télévision
7 – agence *f.* de –
8 – agent *m.* de –
9 – budget *m.* de –

7 deed of –
8 time for protesting
9 – charges
10 making of the –

11 to draw up a –
12 to have a bill noted
13 to give notice of a –
origin
reserve
1 bad debts –
2 – for taxation
stock
1 – of stores
2 to lay in –
3 to lay in a – of
provision, funds
1 consideration, funds
2 insufficient funds
3 no funds, no effects
4 cheque (check) without sufficient funds to meet it, dud cheque

5 absence of consideration
6 providing of funds
7 to provide funds [security
8 to pay a deposit, to pay a sum as
provisional
provisional
public
public
– sale
publication

1 –, published book
2 compulsory –
advertising
1 – gift
2 – competition
3 – design
4 – film
5 – value
publicity (advertising) man
publicity, advertising
1 cinema (screen) advertising

2 electric sign advertising
3 underground railway –
4 mural (wall) advertising
5 radio advertising
6 television advertising
7 advertising (publicity) agency
8 advertising agent
9 advertising budget

publier / 294

10 campagne *f.* de –
11 chef *m.* de (la) –
12 démarcheur *m.* en –

13 département *m.* de la –
14 dessinateur *m.* en –
15 frais *m. pl.* de –

16 page *f.* de –
17 faire de la –
publier
pupillaire
1 deniers *m. pl.* –s
2 placement *m.* –
3 valeurs *f. pl.* –s
pupille *m.*
patrimoine *m.* de –
pur
–e soie
purge *f.* (*hypothèques*)
purger
1 – un bien de dettes
2 – une hypothèque

10 publicity campaign
11 advertising (publicity) manager
12 advertising canvasser, (*Amer.*) space salesman
13 publicity department
14 commercial designer
15 advertising charges, cost of advertising
16 advertising page
17 to advertise
to publish
pupi(l)lary, concerning a ward
1 ward's patrimony
2 safe investment
3 gilt-edged stock
ward
ward's patrimony
pure
– silk
paying off, redemption
to free, to clear
1 to free (clear) a property from debt
2 to pay off (redeem) a mortgage

Q

quai *m.*
1 à –
2 connaissement libellé ,,reçu à –''
3 droit *m.* de –
4 décharger au –
5 rendu (livré) à –
quai *m.* (*chem. de fer*)
1 – d'arrivée
2 – de chargement
3 – de déchargement
4 – de départ
quaiage *m.* (voir *quayage*)
qualifié
1 – (*ouvrier*)
2 majorité –e
qualité *f.*
1 nom, adresse et –
2 – courante
3 – demandée, désirée
4 – de membre
5 – inférieure
6 – loyale et marchande

quay
1 ex –
2 alongside B/L
3 wharfage
4 to discharge at the –
5 free on –
platform
1 arrival –
2 goods –
3 unloading –
4 departure –

qualified, competent
1 skilled
2 qualified majority
quality
1 name, address and description
2 fair average –
3 required –
4 membership
5 poor (inferior) –
6 fair average –

7 – moyenne
8 – supérieure
9 bonne –
10 mauvaise –
11 meilleure –
12 première –
13 en sa – de
14 selon la –
15 vendre sur – vue
quantième m.
quantitatif
quantité f.
1 en – suffisante
2 en grande –
3 par –s de...
4 (pris) par –s de

5 par petites –s
quantum m.
– des bénéfices
quarantaine f.
1 pavillon m. de –
2 port m. de –
3 faire –
4 lever la –
5 mettre en –
quayage m.
question f.
1 une – d'argent
2 une – de temps
3 – pendante
4 – sociale
5 la personne en –

6 résoudre une –
7 soulever une –
8 traiter une –
questionnaire m.
quittance f.
1 – à valoir

2 – comptable

3 – en double
4 – en double valant pour simple
5 – finale
6 – pour solde de compte

7 – valable
8 contre –
9 dont –

7 medium –
8 superior –
9 good –
10 poor (inferior) –
11 better –
12 first –
13 in the capacity of
14 according to the –
15 to sell on approval
day
quantitative
quantity
1 in sufficient –
2 in large quantities
3 for a – of
4 for quantities of..., when ordering...

5 in small quantities
amount
 proportion of profits
quarantine
1 – flag
2 – harbo(u)r, station
3 to perform –
4 to raise the –
5 to –, to put in –
wharfage, quayage
question
1 a matter of money
2 a matter of time
3 outstanding (open) question
4 social –
5 the person in –

6 to solve a –
7 to raise a –
8 to treat a –
list of questions
receipt
1 – on account

2 accountable –

3 – in duplicate
4 – in duplicate valid for one
5 – in full discharge
6 – for the balance

7 valid –
8 against –
9 – whereof is hereby acknowledged

quittance / 296

10 suivant –
11 carnet m. de –s
12 formulaire m. de –
13 timbre m. de –
14 donner – de
15 établir une –
quittancer
quitte et libre
quitter
 ne quittez pas (*tél.*)
quitus m., donner – à...
quorum m.

 le – n'est pas atteint

quota m.
 1 les –s sont épuisés
 2 système m. des –s
quote-part f.
 recevoir sa –
quotient m.
quotité f.
 – disponible

10 as per –
11 – book
12 – form
13 – stamp
14 to give a –
15 to issue a –
to receipt [clear
free and unencumbered, free and
to leave
 hold the line (wire) please
to give quittance to
quorum

 a – is not present

quota
 1 –s are exhausted
 2 – system
quota, share, proportion
 to receive one's share
quotient
amount, proportion
 freely disposable portion

R

rabais m.
 1 – pour revendeurs
 2 – spécial
 3 avec un – de 5 %
 4 grand – (*réduction de prix*)
 5 vente f. au –
 6 accorder un –

 7 nous accordons un-aux revendeurs
 8 réclamer un –
 9 vendre au –
 10 vendre au – (*à prix réduits*)

rabaissement m.
rabaisser
 – un prix
rabat m. de prix
rabattre
 – du prix

raccordement m. (voir *voie*)
raccrocher l'écouteur
rachat m.
 1 – (*exécution*) [découvert
 2 – des baissiers, – des vendeurs à

discount
 1 trade –
 2 extra rebate
 3 with a reduction of 5 %
 4 great reduction
 5 sale by Dutch auction
 6 to grant a rebate

 7 we grant a – to trade
 8 to claim a rebate, reduction
 9 to sell by Dutch auction
 10 to sell at a –, at reduced prices

lowering
to lower
 – a price
reduction in price
to deduct
 to take off the price

to replace the receiver
repurchase, buying back
 1 buying in against
 2 buying back of bear sellers

3 – d'une obligation
4 – d'une police
5 – d'un vendeur
6 droit *m.* de –
7 valeur *f.* de – (*police*)
8 vente *f.* avec faculté de –

rachetable
racheter
  1 – (*exécution*)

  2 – une créance
  3 – une hypothèque
  4 – une obligation
  5 – une police
  6 – des titres
  7 – un vendeur

racheteur *m.*
radiation *f.*
  1 – d'un article de compte

  2 – d'une liste
  3 – d'une inscription hypothécaire

radier (voir aussi *biffer, rayer*)
  1 – une liste
  2 – une inscription hypothécaire

radio (télé)gramme *m.*
raffermir, se – (*cours*)
raffermissement *m.* (*cours*)
raison *f.*
  1 à – de
  2 à – de 1 nouvelle action pour... (voir *action*)
  3 à plus forte –
  4 en – de...

  5 en – directe
  6 en – inverse de
  7 pour – de santé

  8 pour des –s personnelles, de convenance personnelle
  9 pour cette –
  10 pour n'importe quelle –
  11 sans aucune –
raison *f.* (*sociale*)
  1 sous la – sociale...
  2 changer de –
  3 signer sa –

---

3 redemption of a debenture
4 surrender of a policy
5 buying in against a seller
6 option of repurchase
7 surrender value
8 sale with option of repurchase

redeemable
to buy back
  1 to buy in against

  2 to buy off a claim
  3 to redeem a mortgage
  4 to redeem a debenture
  5 to surrender a policy
  6 – stock
  7 to buy in against a seller

repurchaser
striking out
  1 crossing out an item in an account

  2 striking off the list
  3 entry of satisfaction of mortgage

to strike out
  1 to strike off a list
  2 to cancel the registration of a mortgage

radiotelegram
to harden, to stiffen
hardening, stiffening
reason
  1 at the price of

  3 all the more
  4 in consideration of, owing to, on account of
  5 in direct ratio
  6 in inverse ratio to
  7 for health –s, on account of ill health, owing to ill-health
  8 on personal grounds

  9 for that –
  10 for any –
  11 without any –
firm, name, style
  1 under the style of
  2 to change the firm
  3 to sign one's firm name

raisonnable / 298

raisonnable (*prix*) | **reasonable**
rajustement *m.* | **adjustment**
  1 – d'un différend | 1 settling of a difference
  2 – des salaires | 2 – of wages

ralentissement *m.* | **slackening**
rajuster | **to adjust**
rang *m.* | **rank**
  1 – d'une créance | 1 – of a debt
  2 – d'une hypothèque | 2 – of a mortgage

  3 de premier – | 3 first-class, first-rate
  4 par – d'ancienneté | 4 by seniority, according the seniority
  5 hypothèque *f.* en premier – | 5 first mortgage
  6 prendre – après | 6 to – after
  7 prendre – avant... | 7 to – before...
  8 prendre le même – (*créanciers*) | 8 to – equally with
  9 prendre le même – que (*actions*) | 9 to – pari passu with
ranimer, se – | **to recover**
rapatriement *m.* | **repatriation**
rapatrier (*capitaux*) | **to repatriate**
rappel *m.* | **reminder**
  1 – de compte, un –   [lance] | 1 –
  2 lettre *f.* de – (de poursuite, de re-rappeler | 2 follow-up letter

  1 – à... | 1 to remind... of...
  2 je ne me rappelle pas que | 2 I do not remember that
  3 à – dans la réponse s. v. p. (voir *réponse, référence*)
  4 se – | 4 to remember
rapport *m.* (*proportion*) | **ratio**
rapport *m.* (*compte rendu*) | **report**
  1 – (*d'une conférence*) | 1 report
  2 – annuel | 2 annual –
  3 – des affaires sociales | 3 social –
  4 – des commissaires | 4 auditors' –
  5 – de gestion | 5 directors' –, annual –

  6 – d'expertise | 6 survey –

  7 – de mer, – du capitaine | 7 captain's –
  8 – intérimaire | 8 interim –
  9 – mensuel | 9 monthly –
  10 année *f.* du – | 10 year under review
  11 entendre un – | 11 to hear a –
  12 faire un – sur | 12 to report about, to make a – on
rapport *m.* (*revenu*) | **yield, return**
  1 de bon – | 1 profitable

  2 maison *f.* de – | 2 revenue-earning (tenement) house
  3 donner un loyer d'un grand – | 3 to command a high rent
rapport *m.* (*relation*) | **relation**
  1 –s de commerce | 1 business –s

299 / rapporter

2 mettre en – avec	2 to bring into contact (touch) with
3 se mettre en – avec	3 to communicate with, to get into touch with, to approach
4 sous ce – (voir *propos*)	4 in this respect
rapporter (*faire un rapport*)	to report
rapporter (*produire*)	to yield, to produce
1 – ...par an	1 to bring in ... a year
2 – de l'argent	2 to bring in (to yield) money
3 – des bénéfices	3 to yield profit
4 – des intérêts	4 to bear (yield) interest
5 – un intérêt de 4 %	5 to yield 4 %
6 – peu	6 to bring in little, to yield a bad return
rapporteur *m.* (*conférence*)	reporter
rare	rare
l'argent est –	money is scarce, tight
rareté *f.*	tightness, scarcity
ratification *f.*	ratification, confirmation
ratifier	to ratify, to confirm
rationalisation *f.*	rationalization
rationaliser	to rationalize
rationnement *m.*	rationing
suppression *f.* du –	abolition of –
rature *f.*	erasure
1 sans –s ni surcharges	1 without –s or corrections
2 approuver les –s	2 to consent to deletions
ravitaillement *m.*	supply of foodstuffs
rayer	to strike out, to cross, to delete
rayez les mentions qui ne conviennent pas	delete as required, strike out words not applicable (inappropriate words)
rayon *m.* (*magasin*)	department
chef *m.* de –	departmental chief
réaction *f.*	reaction
réagir	to react
réalisable	realizable
1 le –	1 liquid resources
2 actif *m.* –	2 – assets
réalisation *f.*	realization
1 – d'un bénéfice	1 making of profit
2 – d'un stock	2 – of a stock of goods
3 – d'un gage	3 – of a pledge
réaliser	to realize
1 – un bénéfice	1 – a profit
2 – des économies	2 to effect (–) savings
3 – sa fortune	3 – one's assets
4 – un gage	4 – a pledge
5 – des marchandises	5 – goods

6 – sa position | 6 – one's position, account

7 – de titres | 7 to sell out securities

réapprovisionner | to restock with
réassurance *f.* | reinsurance

réassurer | to reinsure
réassureur *m.* | reinsurer
rebut *m.* | rubbishy goods, trash
  1 –s | 1 dead letter, dead postal packets
  2 bureau *m.* des –s (*poste*) | 2 dead-letter office
  3 marchandises *f. pl.* de – | 3 rubbishy goods, trash
  4 mettre au – (*marchandises*) | 4 to reject
récapitulatif | recapitulative
  état – | – statement
récapituler | to recapitulate, to summarize
recensement *m.* | census
  – des entreprises | industrial –
récépissé *m.* (voir aussi *acquit, reçu,* [*quittance*] | receipt
  1 – aérien | 1 air –
  2 – de dépôt | 2 deposit –
  3 – de poste aérienne | 3 air mail –
  4 – de souscription | 4 application –
  5 – de versement (de fonds) | 5 call –
  6 – des chemins de fer | 6 Railway (railroad) Consignment Note
  7 – d'entrepôt | 7 warehouse – [Note
  8 – fluvial | 8 Inland Waterway Consignment
  9 – postal | 9 postal –
  10 – warrant | 10 warrant
réception *f.* | receipt
  1 – (*marchandises*) | 1 taking delivery
  2 – (*travaux*) | 2 taking over, acceptance
  3 – (*hôtel*) | 3 reception desk
  4 à la – de… | 4 on – of
  5 dans les 3 jours après la – | 5 within 3 days of –
  6 accusé *m.* de – | 6 acknowledg(e)ment of –

  7 cachet *m.* (timbre) de – | 7 reception stamp
  8 valeur *f.* jour de – | 8 value day of reception
  9 accuser – de | 9 to acknowledge – of

  10 donner une – | 10 to hold a reception
  11 prendre – de | 11 to take – (delivery) of
  12 souhaiter la bonne – | 12 to wish safe –
réceptionnaire *m.* | consignee, receiver
réceptionner | to check and take delivery

  – (*travaux*) | to inspect and take over
récession *f.* | recession
recette *f.* (v. aussi *courbe*) | receipt
  1 – annuelle | 1 yearly –

301 / recette

2 – brute
3 –s de caisse
4 –s des douanes
5 – effective
6 –s et dépenses
7 –s fiscales
8 – journalière
9 – nette
10 –s ordinaires
11 – prévue
12 garçon m. de –
13 faire la – d'une banque
recette f. (*bureau*)
– des douanes
receveur m.
1 – des contributions
2 – des douanes et accises
3 – de l'enregistrement
4 – de la prime
5 – du timbre
recevoir
1 nous avons reçu votre honorée du...
2 nous avons dûment reçu

3 recevez nos salutations (très, bien, les plus) distinguées
4 ... ne reçoit personne
5 reçu... frs
6 reçu à valoir
rechange m.
frais m. pl. de –

recherche f.
1 – (*travaux*)
2 – conjoncturelle
3 – économique
4 – opérationnelle
5 – scientifique
6 institut m. de –s
recherché
1 être peu –

2 être très –

réciprocité f.
1 convention f. de –
2 à titre de –
3 par –
4 appliquer la –
réciproque
nos intérêts –s
réciproques pl. (*arithm.*)
réciproquement

2 gross –
3 cash –s
4 customs –s
5 actual –
6 –s and expenditure, payments
7 inland revenue
8 daily –
9 net –
10 regular –s
11 calculated –
12 collecting clerk
13 to do the receiving
tax collector's office
receiver's office for the customs
collector, receiver
1 tax collector
2 collector of customs
3 registrar (of deeds)
4 taker of the rate
5 stamp collector
to receive
1 we are in receipt of your letter of
2 we have duly received

3 yours faithfully, yours truly, very truly yours
4 at home to nobody
5 received from
6 received on account
redraft, re-exchange
redraft charges

research
1 – work
2 cyclical –
3 economic –
4 operational (operations) –
5 scientific –
6 – institute
in demand, in request
1 to be in little demand

2 to be in great demand

reciprocity
1 – agreement
2 reciprocally
3 by –
4 to grant –
reciprocal
our mutual (–) interests
reciprocals
reciprocally

réclamant *m.* | claimant

réclamation *f.* | claim

1 – fondée
2 en cas de –
3 toute – pour être valable doit être faite dans les 8 jours

1 founded –
2 in the event of a –
3 any – must be made, if at all, within 8 days of receipt of the goods

4 lettre *f.* de –
5 registre *m.* des –s
6 admettre une –
7 faire droit à une –
8 refuser une –
9 retirer une –

4 letter of complaint
5 complaint (request) book
6 to admit a –
7 to entertain a –
8 to reject (refuse) a –
9 to drop withdraw) a –

réclame *f.* (voir aussi *publicité*) | advertising

1 – lumineuse
2 – murale
3 article *m.* de –
4 panneau *m.* –
5 semaine *f.* de –
6 vente *f.* –
7 faire de la –
8 aux fins de –

1 illuminated sign
2 mural –
3 leading line, leading article
4 advertising billboard
5 shopping week
6 bargain sale
7 to advertise
8 for advertisement purposes, with a view to advertisement

réclamer | to claim

1 – (*exiger de retour*)
2 – auprès de
3 – contre
4 – des dommages-intérêts
5 – son dû
6 – le montant
7 – le payement
8 – le remboursement
9 dividende non réclamé
10 marchandises non réclamées

1 – back
2 – on
3 to protest (to appeal) against
4 – damages
5 – one's due
6 – the amount
7 to demand (ask) for payment
8 – the reimbursement
9 unclaimed dividend
10 unclaimed goods

récognitif, acte – | act of acknowledgment

récognition *f.* | recognition

récoler | to check

récolte *f.* | crop, harvest

1 – abondante
2 – sur pied
3 maigre –
4 mauvaise –
5 nouvelle –
6 évaluation *f.* de la –
7 financement *m.* de la –
8 prévisions *f. pl.* de –
9 rentrer la –

1 large (plentiful) –
2 standing –
3 poor (scanty) –
4 poor –, failure of the –
5 new –
6 – estimate
7 financing of harvest and crops
8 – outlook, prospect
9 to gather –

303 / recommandable

recommandable	recommendable
recommandataire *m.*	referee in case of need
recommandation *f.*	recommendation
1 – d'une lettre	1 registration of a letter
2 sur la – de	2 on the – of, at the suggestion of
3 frais *m. pl.* de – (*lettre*)	3 registration fee
4 lettre *f.* de –	4 letter of –
recommander (*lettre*)	to register
1 „recommandé"	1 registered
2 lettre recommandée	2 registered letter
3 sous pli recommandé	3 under registered cover
4 faire – une lettre	4 to have a letter registered
recommander	to recommend
1 – ... à quelqu'un	1 – ... to
2 – à l'attention de...	2 – to one's attention
3 nous nous recommandons à vos ordres ultérieurs	3 we solicit the favour of your further orders
re(ré)conduction *f.*	renewal
– tacite	tacit reconduction, – by tacit agreement
reconnaissance *f.* de dette	acknowledgment of debt
reconstituer	to build up again, rebuild
– le cheptel	to build up the livestock again
reconstruction *f.*	reconstruction
Banque Internationale pour la – et le Développement	International Bank for – and Development
reconvention *f.*	counterclaim
recopier	to recopy, to copy again
record *m.*	record
1 chiffre *m.* –	1 – figure
2 battre le –	2 to beat the –
recouponnement *m.*	renewal of coupons
recouponner	to renew the coupons
recours *m.*	recourse
1 – contre l'endosseur	1 – to the endorser
2 – contre des tiers	2 – against a third party
3 – irrégulier	3 – to a prior party
4 – régulier	4 regular –
5 bénéficiaire *m.* du –	5 beneficiary of a –
6 droit *m.* de –	6 right of –
7 sans –	7 without –
8 soumis au –	8 liable to –
9 il n'y a pas de – contre	9 there is no – for it
10 s'assurer contre le – des tiers	10 to insure against a third party claim
11 avoir – à	11 to resort to
12 exercer (avoir) – contre	12 to have – against
recouvrable	recoverable, collectible

recouvrement / 304

recouvrement m. (voir aussi *encaissement*) — recovery, collection
1. —s — outstanding debts
2. — de créances — collection of debts
3. — d'impôts — collection of taxes
4. en — de... — for the collection of
5. affaires f. pl. (opérations) de — — collecting business
6. agence f. de —s — debt collecting agency
7. effet m. au — — draft for collection
8. frais m. pl. de — — collecting charges
9. remise f. en — — remittance for collection
10. service m. de — — collecting department
11. tarif m. de —s — collection tariff, collection rates
12. „valeur en —" (voir aussi *valeur*) — value for collection
13. envoyer au — — to hand in (remit) for collection
14. faire (effectuer) le — — to undertake the collection

recouvrer — to collect
1. — (*acquérir de nouveau*) — to get back
2. — une créance — to recover (collect) a debt
3. — une traite — — a bill
4. créances f. pl. à — — outstanding debts
5. faire — par la poste — — money through the post office

recta, payer — — to pay exactly on time
rectificatif — correcting
écriture rectificative — — entry
rectification f. — correction
1. — de bilan — balance sheet adjustment
2. — d'un compte — adjustment of an account

rectifier — to rectify
— une erreur — to correct an error

recto m. — right-hand page
1. au — d'un effet — on the face of a bill
2. — d'une carte postale — address side of a postcard

reçu m. (voir aussi *quittances, récépissé*) — receipt
1. — à valoir — — on account
2. — de bord — mate's —
3. — de souscription — application —
4. — de versement — deposit —
5. au — de... — on — of

recul m. — decline
marquer un — — to fall off
reculer (*cours*) — to fall back, to recede, to relapse
récupérable — recoverable
récupérer ses déboursés — to recoup one's disbursements
se récupérer de ses pertes — to recoup oneself for one's losses
rédaction f. (*journal*) — staff
— (*action*) — drawing up
reddition f. **de comptes** — rendering of accounts

redevable
 1 – de l'impôt
 2 être – de...

redevable *m.*

redevance *f.*
 1 – annuelle
 2 – foncière

rédhibition *f.*

rédhibitoire
 vice *m.* –

rédiger
 1 – un contrat
 2 – une lettre
 3 rédigé en français
 4 connaissement rédigé à l'ordre de

redressement *m.*
 1 – d'un compte

 2 – économique

 3 – financier

 4 écriture *f.* de –

redresser
 1 – un compte
 2 – une erreur
 3 se – (*cours*)

redû *m.*

réductible (voir *souscription*)

réduction *f.*
 1 – considérable, sensible
 2 – de capital
 3 – des dépenses

 4 – de l'escompte (du taux de l'escompte)
 5 – de personnel
 6 – des prix
 7 – des salaires
 8 – pour différence du vieux au neuf (voir *déduction*)
 9 – pour perte de poids au déballage, au déchargement
 10 tableau *m.* de –

réduire
 1 – les dépenses
 2 – le personnel
 3 – le taux de l'escompte
 4 à prix réduits
 5 tarif réduit

indebted, liable
 1 liable for tax
 2 to owe...

debtor

fee, (*concessions*) **royalties**
 1 yearly rental
 2 ground rent

redhibition

redhibitory
 – defect, defect that makes a sale void

to draw up, to write out
 1 to draft a contract
 2 to draw up a letter
 3 drawn up in French
 4 bill of lading made out to the order of

rectification
 1 – (adjustment) of an account

 2 economic recovery

 3 financial recovery

 4 correcting entry

to rectify
 1 – (adjust) an account
 2 – (correct) an error
 3 to firm up, to harden

balance due

reduction
 1 substantial –
 2 – of capital
 3 curtailment of expenses

 4 lowering of the rate of discount

 5 staff –
 6 price –
 7 cut in wages

 9 deduction for waste of goods in unpacking
 10 – table

to reduce [expenses
 1 – (curtail, cut down, prune) the
 2 to reduce the staff
 3 – the rate of discount
 4 at reduced prices
 5 reduced tariff

rééducation professionnelle

frais *m. pl.* de –
réel
1 crédit –
2 droit –
3 valeur –le
réélection *f.*
1 se présenter à la –

2 ne pas se présenter à la –

rééligibilité *f.*
rééligible
réélire
réemploi *m.*, de –
rééquipement *m.*
réescompte *m.*
réescompter
réévaluation *f.*
1 – (*monnaie*)

2 –s (*bilan*)
réévaluer
réexpédier
– une lettre (*à une nouvelle adresse*)
réexpédition *f.*
réexportation *f.*
réexporter
réfaction *f.*
référence *f.*
1 –s commerciales
2 –s de banque
3 –s de premier ordre, d'excellentes –s
4 sans bonnes –s inutile de se présenter

5 avoir de bonnes –s
6 demander les –s d'usage
7 donner des –s
8 indiquer des –s
9 veuillez trouver nos –s en bas de la présente
référence *f.* (*renvoi*)
1 –s à rappeler s. v. p. ; prière de rappeler dans votre réponse nos –s

2 ,,votre –'' (*lettre*)
3 échantillon *m.* de –

4 numéro *m.* de –

référer
(en) nous référant à

occupational resettlement, retraining

cost of –
real
1 credit on – estate
2 – right
3 – value
re-election
1 to offer oneself for – (re-appointment) [–
2 to decline to stand (*Amer.* : run) for
re-eligibility
re-eligible
to re-elect
second-hand, used
re-equipment
rediscount
to rediscount
revaluation
1 upward –, up-valuation

2 adjustment of values
to revalue
to reforward
to redirect a letter
reforwarding
re-export, re-exportation
to re-export
rebate, allowance
reference
1 trade –s
2 bank –s
3 high –s
4 applications without testimonials will not be considered
5 to have good –s
6 to ask for the usual –s
7 to furnish –s
8 to state –s
9 please find our –s below

reference
1 in your reply (in replying) please quote... ; for – please quote

2 your –
3 – sample

4 – number

to refer
with reference to, referring to

refinancement *m.*
  crédits *m. pl.* de –
réflation *f.*
reflux *m.* (*or*)
réforme *f.*
  1 – bancaire
  2 – fiscale
  3 – monétaire
refus *m.*
  1 – d'acceptation
  2 – de payement
  3 en cas de –
refuser
  1 – d'accepter un effet
  2 – de payer
  3 – de payer un effet
  4 – de prendre livraison des marchandises
régie *f.*

  1 – de l'État
  2 – des impôts indirects
  3 en –

régime *m.*
  1 – de la communauté des biens
  2 – de la communauté réduite aux acquêts

  3 – de la séparation des biens

  4 – dotal
régional
régir
  1 conditions régissant votre compte

  2 être régi par une loi (fonctionnant sous le régime de la loi...)
registre *m.* (voir aussi *livre*)
  1 – à feuillets mobiles
  2 – à souche(s)
  3 – des actionnaires

  4 – du cadastre
  5 – du commerce
  6 – de l'état civil
  7 – des hypothèques
  8 extrait *m.* du –
  9 inscrire sur le (au) –
règle *f.*
  1 – conjointe, – de chaîne
  2 – de trois
  3 –s de La Haye

refinancing
  – credits
reflation
reflux
reform
  1 banking reform
  2 tax(ation) –
  3 reorganization of currency
refusal
  1 non-acceptance, – to accept
  2 non-payment, – to pay
  3 in case of –
to refuse   [bill
  1 – to accept a bill, to dishono(u)r a
  2 – payment
  3 – to pay a bill
  4 – to take delivery of the goods

management

  1 state –
  2 excise administration
  3 under direct – of the State

system
  1 joint estate
  2 community of goods acquired during marriage

  3 separation of goods and property, separate maintenance
  4 dotal -
regional
to rule, to manage
  1 terms for the conduct of your account
  2 to be governed by (to be subject to) a law
register
  1 loose-leaf book
  2 counterfoil book
  3 share –, – of members

  4 land (cadastral) –
  5 trade –
  6 – of births, marriages, and deaths
  7 – of mortgages
  8 extract from a –
  9 to enter in the –
rule
  1 chain –
  2 – of three
  3 Hague –s

règle / 308

4 –s de Vienne
5 –s d'York et d'Anvers
6 –s et usances uniformes relatives aux crédits documentaires

7 en – générale
8 il est de – que
9 pour la bonne –

10 exception *f.* à la –
11 être en –
12 trouver en –
règle *f.* (*objet*)
1 – à calculer
2 – plate
règlement *m.*
1 – amiable
2 – d'avaries

3 – de compte
4 – des créances
5 – d'une dette

6 – d'une facture
7 – de l'indemnité (*assur.*)
8 – en espèces
9 – en nature
10 – mensuel
11 – trimestriel
12 en – de votre compte
13 en – de (*facture*)

14 en – de cette affaire
15 en – final, intégral
règlement (*ordonnance*)
1 – d'atelier
2 – de bourse
3 – d'entreprise
4 – de service
5 – de port
6 – d'ordre
7 – d'ordre intérieur
8 –s douaniers
réglementation *f.* (règlementation)
1 – du change

2 – du marché
3 – du travail
réglementer (règlementer)
régler
1 – à l'amiable
2 – au comptant
3 – une affaire

4 Vienna –s
5 York-Antwerp –s
6 uniform customs and practice for commercial documentary credits

7 as a general –
8 it is the – that, it is customary that
9 for the sake of regularity, for order's sake
10 exception to the –
11 to be in order
12 to find in order
ruler, rule
1 slide rule
2 flat rule
adjustment
1 amicable settlement
2 – of average

3 settlement of an account
4 – of claims
5 settlement of a debt

6 settlement of an invoice
7 payment (settlement) of the claims
8 payment in specie, in cash
9 payment in kind
10 monthly settlement
11 quarterly accounts
12 in settlement of your account
13 in settlement of

14 in settlement of this business
15 in full settlement
regulations
1 shop (working) rules
2 stock exchange –
3 works –
4 service –
5 port –
6 standing orders
7 rules, internal –
8 customs –
regulation
1 control of exchanges, exchange –

2 – of the market
3 – of labo(u)r
to regulate
to regulate
1 to settle amicably
2 to settle in cash
3 to settle a business

309 / régression

4 – une affaire de commun accord	4 – a matter by mutual agreement
5 – un compte	5 to pay an account
6 – les comptes (*arrêter*)	6 to close the accounts
7 – une dette	7 to settle a debt
8 – les dommages	8 to settle the damage
9 – une facture	9 to settle (pay off) a bill
10 – un montant	10 to settle an amount
11 – le solde	11 to pay the balance
12 affaires *f. pl.* à –	12 matters in suspense, to be settled
13 non réglé (*compte*)	13 outstanding, unsettled
14 tenir une affaire pour réglée	14 to regard an affair as done with

régression *f.* — drop
1 – du chômage — 1 decrease in unemployement
2 être en – — 2 to be falling

regret *m.* — regret
1 à notre grand – — 1 much to our –, with great –
2 nous avons le –, nous sommes au – de — 2 we much regret that, we deeply regret to have to
3 exprimer son – — 3 to express one's –

regrettable — regrettable
1 il est – que — 1 it is – (it is a matter of regret) that
2 c'est d'autant plus – que — 2 it is the more to be regretted as

regretter — to regret [that
1 nous regrettons vivement que... (de) — 1 we are very sorry (we much regret)
2 notre regretté collègue — 2 our lamented colleague

régularisation *f.* — regularization
fonds *m.* de – des changes — currency equalization fund

régulariser — to regularize
régularité *f.* — regularity
régulier — regular
régulièrement — duly, properly
acheter – — to take regularly
réhabilitation *f.* (*banqueroute*) — discharge
réhabiliter — to discharge
réimportation *f.* — reimport, reimportation
réimporter — to reimport
réimpression *f.* — reprint
réinscrire — to re-enter
réinstallation *f.* indemnité de – — resettlement allowance
réintégrer — to reinstate
être réintégré dans la vie économique — to be reabsorbed into economic life

réinvestir — to reinvest
réinvestissement *m.* — reinvestment
réitéré — repeated
remercîments –s — – thanks
réitérer — to repeat
rejeter(*décliner*) — to decline

relâche f.
 1 – forcée

 2 port m. de –
relâcher dans un port
relation f. (*rapport*)
relation f.
 1 –s d'affaires, commerciales

 2 –s avec l'étranger, –s extérieures
 3 –s de longue (vieille) date, anciennes –s
 4 –s humaines (*entreprises*)

 5 –s suivies
 6 –s tendues
 7 (service m. des) –s étrangères
 8 avoir de nombreuses –s
 9 développer nos –s
 10 entrer en –s d'affaires avec

 11 entretenir des –s

 12 étendre les –s
 13 être en – avec
 14 mettre en – avec

 15 se mettre en – avec

 16 nouer des –s avec

 17 rester en – avec

 18 rompre les –s
relevé m.
 1 – de caisse
 2 – de compte
 3 – des dettes actives et passives
 4 – de fin de mois
 5 faire un – de compte

relèvement m.
 1 – (*reprise, redressement*)

 2 – du commerce
 3 – des salaires
 4 – des tarifs
 5 – du taux d'escompte
 6 – économique

relever
 1 – un compte

call, putting in
 1 compulsory call

 2 port of refuge
to call at a port
relation, connection
relation
 1 business connection, –s

 2 foreign –s
 3 long-standing –s

 4 human –s

 5 continuing (lasting) –s
 6 strained –s
 7 foreign department
 8 to have numerous (extensive) –s
 9 to develop our –s
 10 to enter into business – (to open up a business connection) with...
 11 to keep up –s, to have business relations with
 12 to extend the –s
 13 to be in touch with
 14 to bring into connection (to place in touch) with
 15 to get into –s (to get into touch) with
 16 to enter into –s with, to establish –s with
 17 to continue the –s with, to keep in touch with
 18 to break off –s
statement, return
 1 cash statement
 2 statement (abstract) of account
 3 statement of assets and liabilities
 4 monthly statement, return
 5 to draw up (make out) a statement of account

raising, rise
 1 recovery, revival

 2 revival of business
 3 increase of wages
 4 raising of tariffs
 5 raising of (the rate of) discount
 6 economic recovery

to raise
 1 to make out a statement of account, to abstract an account

311 / relever de

2 – une erreur, une faute
3 – un fait
4 – une industrie
5 – un navire
6 – quelqu'un de ses engagements

7 – quelqu'un de ses fonctions
8 – les salaires
9 se – (*marché, cours, affaires*)
relever de (*dépendre de*)
relié (*livre*)
non – (voir aussi *broché*)
reliquat *m.*
  1 – d'un compte
  2 payement *m.* d'un –
reliquataire *m.*

remarque *f.*
  faire des –s
remarquer
  nous vous faisons –

remballer
rembarquer

remboursable
1 – au pair
2 – en espèces
3 – par... francs
4 emprunt *m.* – en 10 ans
5 emprunt *m.* non –
6 obligations *f. pl.* –s
remboursement *m.*

  1 – anticipé
  2 – au pair
  3 – de dette
  4 – des droits de douane
  5 – des frais

  6 – d'une obligation
  7 – d'une somme

  8 – partiel
  9 contre –
10 en – de ce tirage

11 délai *m.* de – (*emprunt*)
12 envoi *m.* contre –
13 grevé d'un – (*colis*)

14 prime *f.* de –
15 appeler au – les obligations

---

2 to discover (point out) an error
3 to note a fact
4 to revive an industry
5 – a ship
6 to relieve someone of his engagements

7 to relieve someone of his office
8 – wages
9 to recover
to be dependent on
bound
unbound
remainder, balance
  1 balance of an account
  2 payment of the balance
debtor for the balance

observation
  to make –s
to observe
  we draw your attention to, attention must be drawn to the fact that

to repack
to reship

repayable
1 – at par
2 – in cash
3 – at... francs
4 loan – in 10 years
5 irredeemable loan
6 redeemable bonds
repayment, reimbursement, refund

  1 accelerated redemption
  2 repayment at par
  3 repayment of a debt
  4 drawback
  5 reimbursement of the expenses

  6 redemption of a bond
  7 repayment (reimbursement) of a sum

  8 partial reimbursement
  9 charges forward, cash on delivery
10 in reimbursement of this drawing

11 term of redemption
12 cash-on-delivery parcel
13 on which a trade charge is to be collected
14 redemption premium   [bonds
15 to give notice of withdrawal of

16 se couvrir par – | 16 to reimburse oneself

17 demander le – d'un emprunt | 17 to call in a loan
18 disposer d'un montant par – | 18 to take an amount forward

19 envoyer contre – | 19 to send ,,cash on delivery''
20 réclamer le – | 20 to demand (require) repayment

rembourser | **to repay, to reimburse, to refund**
1 – au pair | 1 to pay off at par
2 – une dette | 2 to pay a debt
3 – des droits de douane | 3 to pay the drawback

4 – un effet | 4 to pay (retire) a bill
5 – un emprunt | 5 to pay off (return) a loan
6 – les frais à quelqu'un | 6 to reimburse someone for his expenses

7 – une obligation | 7 to redeem a bond
8 – une somme | 8 to repay a sum
9 – quelqu'un | 9 to reimburse someone

10 se – | 10 to reimburse oneself, to repay oneself

11 se – du montant | 11 to reimburse oneself for

12 veuillez vous – de... sur... | 12 please reimburse yourselves for... upon...

remembrement *m.* **des biens ruraux** | **reparcelling out of land, consolidation of strip holdings**
remerciement *m.* | **thanks**
1 avec mes –s (*objet retourné*) | 1 returned with –
2 avec mes –s anticipés | 2 thanking you beforehand, in anticipation
3 lettre *f.* de – | 3 letter of –
4 recevoir avec ses –s | 4 to receive with –
5 réitérer des –s | 5 to repeat –
6 rendre des –s | 6 to reciprocate –
remercier | **to thank**
1 nous vous remercions beaucoup de... | 1 we thank you very much for

2 – quelqu'un de... | 2 – a person for...

3 – d'avance | 3 – in advance
4 ce dont nous vous remercions d'a- [vance | 4 for which we thank you in advance
5 en vous remerciant d'avance, nous vous prions | 5 thanking you in anticipation (beforehand) we remain
remercier (*congédier*) | **to dismiss**
réméré, vente *f.* **à –** | **sale with option of repurchase**
remettant, remetteur *m.* | **remitter**
remetteur, banquier *m.* **–** | **remitting banker**
remettre (*différer*) | **to postpone, to adjourn**
remettre (*faire grâce de*)
1 – ... % sur... | 1 to allow... % on
2 – une dette | 2 to remit a debt

313 / remettre

remettre (*livrer*)	**to deliver, to hand over**
1 – à l'encaissement, en recouvrement	1 to remit for collection
2 – à l'escompte	2 to remit for discount
3 – de l'argent	3 to remit (send) money
4 – des documents à	4 to hand over documents to
5 – en main(s) propre(s)	5 to deliver (to...) personally
6 – une lettre à...	6 to deliver a letter to...
7 – des pièces	7 to hand in, to hand over documents
8 nous avons l'avantage de vous – ci-joint...	8 we have pleasure in handing you herein, enclosed we are handing you
remise *f.* (*retardement*)	**postponement, adjournment**
remise *f.* (*commission*)	**commission**
remise *f.* (*réduction*)	**allowance, discount**
1 – d'une dette	1 remission of a debt
2 accorder une forte –	2 to grant a substantial reduction
3 faire une – de...	3 to make an allowance of..., to allow a discount of...
remise *f.* (*effet de commerce*)	**remittance**
1 –s et tirages	1 –s and drawings
2 – à vue	2 sight –
3 – documentaire	3 documentary draft
4 – simple	4 clean draft
5 encaisser des –s	5 to collect –s
6 envoyer une –	6 to send a –
remise *f.* (*livraison*)	**delivery, handing over**
1 – (*envoi de valeurs*)	1 remittance
2 – à domicile	2 delivery (at residence)
3 – d'argent, – en espèces	3 remittance in cash
4 – d'un effet à l'encaissement	4 remittance of a bill for collection
5 – de télégrammes	5 delivery of telegrams
6 contre – des coupons	6 against delivery (on presentation) of coupons
7 contre – des documents	7 against delivery of the documents
8 faire une – de fonds	8 to make a remittance of funds
remise *f.* **en état**	**overhauling, reconditioning**
frais *m. pl.* de –	reconditioning expenses
remisier *m.* (*bourse*)	**remisier**
remorquage *m.*	**towage**
frais *m. pl.* de –	–, – charges
remorque *f.*	**trailer**
prendre à la –	to take in tow
remorquer	to tow [stance
se faire –	to be towed, to take towage assi-
remorqueur *m.*	**tug (boat)**

remplacement *m.*
1 en – de

2 frais *m. pl.* de –

3 valeur *f.* de –

remplacer
1 – un article par...
2 – quelqu'un
remplir
1 – les conditions

2 – les formalités
3 – une formule
4 – un montant
5 – ses obligations

rémunérateur

1 affaire rémunératrice
2 placement –
rémunération *f.*

1 – d'un capital
2 en – des apports

3 égalité *f.* des –s entre les travailleurs masculins et les travailleurs féminins
rémunérer
rencaisser
renchérir
1 – (*hausser le prix*)
2 – sur
renchérissement *m.*
renchérisseur *m.*
rendement *m.*
1 – d'un capital
2 – des actions
3 – des impôts

4 – du personnel
5 – individuel
6 – intéressant

7 – moyen (*d'une action*)
8 à gros –

9 à plein –
10 le – de ce placement est de 5 %

11 augmentation *f.* de –

replacement
1 in the place of

2 cost of –

3 value of –

to replace
1 to substitute (–) an article by
2 – someone
to perform
1 to comply with (fulfil, perform) the conditions
2 to comply with the formalities
3 to fill up a form
4 to fill in an amount
5 to fulfil one's obligations

remunerative
[ness
1 profitable (lucrative, paying) busi-
2 – investment
remuneration, consideration

1 return on a capital
2 as consideration (payment) for the transfer
3 equal remuneration for men and women

to remunerate
to recash
to rise in price
1 to raise the price
2 to outbid
rise (increase, advance) in price
runner-up
yield, return
1 yield of capital, return on capital
2 return (yield) of shares
3 yield of taxes, tax proceeds

4 output of the staff
5 individual output, output per man
6 fair return, attractive rate of interest
7 average –
8 high yield...

9 at a full capacity
10 this investment yields 5 %

11 increase in output

rendez-vous *m.*	**appointment**
prendre – avec... pour...	to accept (arrange, make) an appointment with... for...
rendre	**to return**
1 – 4 %	1 to yield 4 %
2 – bien	2 to pay well
3 – de l'argent	3 to return money
4 – compte de	4 to give (render) account of
5 – service à	5 to render a service to
6 – visite à	6 to pay a visit to
7 – la monnaie d'un billet de 100 francs	7 to give change for a hundred-franc note
8 se – caution	8 to stand (become) surety
rendu	
1 – à domicile	1 delivered at residence
2 – à quai	2 free on quay
3 – à l'usine	3 free factory
4 – en gare	4 free at station
5 – en wagon	5 free on truck
6 – franco bord	6 delivered free on board
7 poids –	7 delivered weight
rendus *m. pl.*	**returns**
renflouer	**to (re)float**
rengager (*en service*)	**to re-engage**
– (*gage*)	to repledge, to repawn
renoncer à	**to renounce, to waive**
renouvelable	**renewable**
renouveler	**to renew**
1 – un bail	1 a lease
2 – un contrat	2 a contract
3 ne pas – un contrat	3 to determine a contract
4 – un crédit	4 to extend a credit
5 – un effet	5 – a bill
6 – une feuille de coupons	6 – a sheet of coupons
7 – le stock	7 to restock
renouvellement *m.*	**renewal**
1 – de l'année	1 turn of the year
2 – de bail	2 – of lease
3 – de feuilles de coupons	3 – of sheet of coupons
4 – de stock	4 restocking
5 – d'une traite	5 – of a bill
6 fonds *m.* de –	6 – fund
renseignement *m.* (voir aussi *information*)	**information**
1 –s sur...	1 – about
2 –s complémentaires	2 supplementary –, further particulars
3 –s complets	3 full –
4 –s contradictoires	4 conflicting –

5 –s de crédit | 5 credit report
6 –s demandés | 6 – required
7 –s exacts | 7 accurate –
8 –s fournis | 8 the – supplied
9 –s satisfaisants | 9 satisfactory –
10 – strictement confidentiels | 10 strictly confidential –
11 –s sûrs | 11 reliable –
12 ... et autres –s | 12 ... and further particulars
13 à titre de – | 13 by way of –
14 pour –s s'adresser ici | 14 inquire within
15 pour de plus amples –s s'adresser à | 15 for further particulars apply to...

16 bulletin *m.* (*fiche*) de –s | 16 – slip
17 bureau *m.* de –s | 17 inquiry office, – bureau
18 demande *f.* de –s | 18 inquiry, request for –
19 fiche *f.* de –s | 19 – slip
20 communiquer des –s à des tiers | 20 to communicate – to third parties

21 demander des –s | 21 to apply for –
22 donner des –s sur... | 22 to give – (particulars) on, about...
23 faire un usage discret de –s | 23 to use – with the greatest discretion, to make a confidential use of...

24 prendre des –s sur | 24 to make inquiries about

renseigner quelqu'un sur... | **to inform someone about**
se renseigner sur | to inquire (to make inquiries) about, as to

rentabilité *f.* | **profitableness, productiveness, productivity, earning capacity**

1 calcul *m.* de – | 1 calculation of the net return

2 limite *f.* de – | 2 limit of profitability
rente *f.* | **rent, annuity, income**
1 – annuelle | 1 yearly income
2 – consolidée | 2 consolidated annuities, consols
3 – de survie, – réversible | 3 survivorship annuity
4 – différée | 4 deferred annuity
5 – foncière | 5 ground rent
6 –s françaises | 6 French rentes
7 – perpétuelle | 7 perpetual annuity
8 – rachetable, remboursable | 8 redeemable annuity
9 – sur l'état | 9 government annuity
10 – viagère | 10 life annuity
11 – viagère immédiate | 11 immediate annuity
12 assurance *f.* de –s | 12 annuity insurance
13 racheter une – | 13 to redeem an annuity
14 vivre de ses –s | 14 to live on one's income
rentier *m.* (*détenteur de fonds publics*) | **fundholder**
1 – (*qui vit de ses rentes*) | 1 person of independent means
2 – viager | 2 life annuitant
3 petit – | 3 small investor

317 / rentrée

rentrée *f.* — collection, receipt
1. les –s — receipts, payments received
2. –s (*en magasin*) — returns inwards
3. –s (*effets*) — paid bills
4. – d'argent — receipt of money
5. – des classes — reopening of schools
6. – des impôts — collection (getting in) of taxes
7. –s fiscales — revenue receipts
8. –s journalières — daily receipts
9. –s et sorties de caisse — cash receipts and payments
10. d'une – difficile — difficult to collect
11. sauf – — under usual reserve
12. veuillez nous remettre le montant après la – — please remit the amount when cashed, received

rentrer — to come in
1. – dans ses fonds — to get back his money
2. – dans ses frais — to recover one's expenses
3. – difficilement (mal) — – badly
4. faire – des créances — to collect debts
5. il rentre de l'argent — money is coming in

renverser, „ne pas –" — (keep) this side up, keep upright

renvoi *m.* — return, sending back
1. – (*ajournement*) — postponement
2. – (*employé*) — dismissal
3. – (*référence*) — reference
4. un folio, sans – — one sheet, no marginal alteration
5. numéro *m.* de – — reference number

renvoyer — to return
1. – (*ajourner*) — to postpone
2. – (*personnel*) — to dismiss
3. – à — to refer to
4. veuillez nous – la formule incluse, revêtue de votre signature — please return the enclosed form duly signed

réorganisation *f.* — reorganization

– financière — financial reconstruction

réorganiser — to reorganize
réouverture *f.* — reopening
réparation *f.* — repair
1. –s d'entretien — keeping in –
2. –s des maladies professionnelles — compensation for industrial diseases
3. –s locatives — tenant's –s
4. –s usufruitières — usufructuary's –s

réparer / 318

5 atelier *m.* de –
6 frais *m. pl.* de –
réparer
– un navire
répartir
1 – au prorata, proportionnellement
2 – par (suivant) ...
3 – des actions
4 – les avaries d'après
5 – les bénéfices entre...
6 – un dividende
7 – les frais entre...
8 – un risque
9 – sur 2 années
répartition *f.*
1 – d'après (par)...
2 – de l'avarie
3 – du bénéfice
4 – des contributions
5 – du dividende

6 – des frais

7 – géographique
répartition *f.* (*titres*)
1 avis *m.* de –

2 libération *f.* à la –
3 ... à verser à la –
répartition *f.* (*liquidation*)
1 – de 10 %
2 dernière –
3 première et unique –
4 état *m.* (liste *f.*) de –
repasser (*un compte*)
répercussion *f.* sur

répertoire *m.*

– sur fiches
répertorier
répéter
– (*jur.*)
répit *m.*
jours *m. pl.* de –
repli *m.* des prix
répondant *m.*

répondre
1 – (*se porter garant*)
2 – de (*être responsable*)
3 ne répond pas (*tél.*)
4 – à l'attente

5 repairing shop
6 cost of –s
to repair
– a ship
to divide, to apportion [rata
1 to distribute proportionally, pro
2 to classify according to
3 to allot shares
4 to apportion the average according
5 to distribute the profits among
6 to distribute a dividend
7 to apportion the expenses among
8 to spread a risk
9 to spread over 2 years
division, distribution
1 classification according to...
2 adjustment of averages
3 appropriation of the profit
4 assessment of taxes
5 distribution of the dividend

6 apportionment of the expenses

7 geographical distribution
allotment
1 – letter

2 payment in full on –
3 ... to pay on –
dividend
1 – (distribution) of 10 %
2 final –, distribution
3 first and final distribution, –
4 notice of –
to re-examine
repercussion (impact) on

index, list

card index
to index
to repeat
to claim back
respite
days of grace
fall in prices
surety

to reply, to answer
1 to be security
2 to be liable for
3 sorry, there is no reply
4 to come up to (answer) expectations

319 / réponse

5 ne pas – à l'attente

6 – à une lettre

7 – à une prime
8 – négativement
9 veuillez nous – par retour du courrier
réponse *f.*
1 – affirmative
2 – au porteur

3 – définitive
4 – des primes (*bourse*)
5 jour *m.* de la – des primes
6 – négative
7 – par fil
8 – payée
9 carte postale avec – payée
10 télégramme *m.* avec – payée
11 – tardive
12 – s'il vous plaît

13 il n'y a pas de –

14 dans l'attente de votre –
15 en – à votre lettre

16 prière d'adresser la – à

17 prière de rappeler dans votre –

18 laisser sans –
19 rester sans –
report (*prorogation du marché*) *m.*

1 – (*écart entre comptant et terme*)

2 –s et avances sur titres

3 – et déport
4 opération *f.* de –

5 placement *m.* de fonds en –
6 taux *m.* de –
7 donner en – (*se faire reporter*)

8 placer de l'argent en –

9 prendre en – (reporter)

5 to fall (be) short of expectation

6 to answer (reply) to a letter

7 to declare an option
8 to answer in the negative
9 we shall be glad to have a reply by return (of post)
reply, answer
1 favo(u)rable answer
2 please answer by bearer

3 conclusive answer
4 option declaration
5 option declaration day
6 refusal
7 reply by wire
8 reply paid
9 reply post card
10 prepaid telegram
11 delayed reply
12 an answer will oblige, the favo(u)r of an answer is requested
13 there is no answer

14 awaiting your reply
15 in reply to your letter

16 all communications to be addressed to...

17 in your reply (in replying) please quote

18 to leave unanswered
19 to receive no reply
contango, continuation, carrying over

1 difference between cash and settlement prices

2 advances and loans on negotiable securities

3 contango and backwardation
4 contango business, carrying over (continuation) of a bargain

5 investment on contango
6 contango rate, rate of continuation
7 to give on stock

8 to employ money on contango

9 to take in stock, to continue

report / 320

report *m.* (*du journal au grand livre*)	posting
report *m.* (*transport d'une somme*)	carrying forward
report *m.* (*somme transportée*)	amount carried forward
1 „–" (*haut de la colonne*)	1 brought forward
2 – à nouveau	2 balance carried forward to next account
3 – à l'exercice suivant	3 balance to next account
4 – antérieur, – de l'exercice précédent	4 balance (brought forward) from last account
reporté *m.*	giver (on stock)
reporter (*prendre en report*)	to take in, to carry (borrow) stock, to take the rate
1 se faire – (*donner en report*)	1 to give on, to give the rate, to lend stock
2 – une position à la prochaine liquidation	2 to carry over (continue, contango) a position to the next account
3 faire – des titres	3 to give on (to give the rate on, to lend) stock
4 faire – une position à la prochaine liquidation	4 to give on (to give the rate on) a position for the next account
5 titres reportés	5 stock taken in, stock borrowed, stock carried
reporter (*compt.*)	to carry (to bring) forward
1 „à –", „reporté" (*bas de la colonne*)	1 carried forward, forward
2 – à nouveau	2 to carry forward to new account
reporteur *m.*	taker
reprendre	
1 – le commerce de...	1 to take over a business from...
2 – le travail	2 to resume work
3 les affaires reprennent	3 business is improving, recovers
4 les cours (se) reprennent	4 prices recover, rally
5 le marché se reprenait	5 the market recovered, rallied
représentant *m.*	representative
1 – de commerce	1 commercial agent
2 – exclusif, seul –	2 general –
représentation *f.*	representation, agency
1 – exclusive	1 sole agency
2 frais *m. pl.* de –	2 expenses of (official) entertainment
3 contrat *m.* de –	3 agency contract
4 confier la – à	4 to entrust the agency to...
représenter	to represent
1 – à l'acceptation	1 – for acceptance
2 représenté judiciairement et extrajudiciairement	2 represented at law and otherwise
3 capital représenté par... actions	3 capital divided into... shares
4 emprunt représenté par... obligations de – chacune	4 loan divided into... bonds

5 certificat m. représentant... actions | 5 certificate representing... shares

reprise f.
1 – des affaires
2 – des payements
3 – économique
4 – des travaux

5 – vigoureuse des cours
6 une – s'est produite
7 être en – (*cours*)
reproche m.
reprocher
reproduction f.
1 – interdite
2 droit m. de –
répudiation f.
1 – d'une dette
2 – d'un héritage
répudier (*dette*)
– (*héritage*)
réputation f.
1 – mondiale
2 bonne, excellente –
3 avoir la – d'être...
4 avoir la – d'(être) un mauvais payeur
5 jouir d'une bonne –

6 maintenir sa –
7 nuire à la –
8 perdre sa –
requis
réquisitionner
réseau m.
1 – de succursales
2 – local
3 – téléphonique
réservataire, héritier m. –

réservation f. (voir aussi *location*)
bureau m. de – (des passages)
réserve f.
1 sans –
2 sous – d'approbation

3 sous (avec) cette –
4 sous – de nos droits
5 sous – des dispositions du paragraphe 3
6 sous les –s d'usage
7 sous toutes –s
8 accepter sous –
9 faire des –s

[ness
1 recovery (revival, pickup) of busi-
2 resumption of payment
3 economic recovery
4 resumption of business

5 a brisk (sharp) rally of prices
6 a rally occurred
7 to recover, to rally
reproach
to reproach
reproduction
1 ,,copyright (reserved)''
2 copyright
repudiation
1 – of a debt
2 renunciation of a succession
to repudiate
to renounce, to relinquish
reputation
1 world-wide –
2 good (established) –
3 to be reputed to be...
4 to be known as a bad payer
5 to enjoy a good –

6 to keep up one's –
7 to damage (to injure) the –
8 to fall into discredit, to lose one's –
requisite, required
to requisition
network
1 branch networks, – of branches
2 local line
3 telephonic system
heir entitled to the legal portion

reservation, booking
booking office
reserve
1 without –, unreservedly
2 with the – of (subject to) approval

3 with the – that
4 without prejudice to our rights
5 subject to the provisions of paragraph 3
6 under usual –
7 with all –
8 to accept with –
9 to make –s

réserve / 322

10 observer une –, se tenir sur la – | 10 to adopt a reserved attitude, to maintain an attitude of reserve

réserve *f.*
1 – cachée
2 – de capital
3 –s de (en) devises

4 – de prévoyance
5 – disponible
6 – d'or
7 – extraordinaire
8 – fiscale

9 – latente (voir – *cachée*)
10 – légale
11 – légale (*succession*)

12 –s mathématiques
13 – métallique
14 – obligatoire
15 – occulte
16 – par réévaluation du portefeuille-titres
17 – pour créances douteuses

18 – pour différence de cours
19 – pour éventualités diverses
[actions
20 – prime d'émission, – prime sur
21 – statutaire
22 – visible
23 accumulation *f.* de –s
24 capital *m.* de –
25 compte *m.* de –
26 création *f.* de –s
27 fonds *m.* de –
28 accumuler des –s
29 affecter à la –

30 constituer (créer) des –s
31 fixer la –
32 mettre à contribution la –

33 verser une somme au fonds de –

réserver
1 – bon accueil (voir *accueil*)
2 – une décision
3 – la partie jusqu'à...
4 – une partie des bénéfices pour...

reserve
1 hidden (secret) –
2 capital –
3 (foreign) currency –s

4 contingency –
5 available –
6 gold –
7 extraordinary –
8 – for taxation

9
10 legal –
11 legal portion, portion that must devolve on the heirs
12 fund to cover liabilities
13 bullion (metallic) –
14 required –s
15 secret –
16 – derived from re-evaluation of securities portfolio
17 – for doubtful (bad) debts

18 – for loss on investments
19 contingency –

20 premium –
21 – provided by the articles
22 visible –
23 accumulation of –s
24 – capital
25 – account
26 building up of –s
27 – fund
28 to accumulate –s
29 to put to the –, to transfer to – funds
30 to build up –s
31 to fix the –
32 to draw on the –s

33 to place a sum to the –

to reserve

2 to delay a decision
3 to give the refusal of the parcel till
4 – a part of the profit for...

5 – une place	5 – a place ; (*boat, plane*) to book a passage for...
6 tous droits réservés	6 all rights reserved
7 se – le droit de...	7 – the right to...
résident *m.* (*change*)	**resident** (person inside the Territory)
résidentiel, quartier –	**residential quarter**
résidu *m.* (voir *rompu*)	
résiliation *f.*	cancellation, termination
résilier	to cancel, to terminate
– un contrat	to terminate a contract
résistant (voir *marché*)	
résolution *f.*	resolution
1 –s d'une assemblée	1 –s of a meeting
2 projet *m.* de –	2 draft –
résolutoire, clause *f.* **–**	avoidance clause
résoudre	to cancel, to terminate, to avoid
– (*un problème*)	to solve
respecter (*contrat*)	to comply with, to live up to
– (*délai*)	to keep to
responsabilité *f.*	responsibility, liability
1 – civile	1 civil liability
2 – contractuelle	2 contractual –, – out of contract
3 – de l'employeur, patronale	3 employers' liability
4 – (il)limitée	4 (un)limited liability
5 – non contractuelle	5 non-contractual –
6 – solidaire	6 joint and several liability
7 sans aucune – de notre part	7 without any responsibility on our part
8 sous sa propre –	8 on one's own responsibility
9 la – incombe à...	9 the responsibility lies (rests) with...
10 sentiment *m.* de –	10 sense (feeling) of –
11 assumer la –	11 to undertake (assume) the responsibility
12 décharger d'une –	12 to relieve of (free, release from) the responsibility
13 décliner toute –	13 to decline all responsibility
14 déterminer la –	14 to establish the responsibility
15 engager la – de...	15 to involve the liability of...
16 engager sa –	16 to assume responsibility
17 entraîner de la –	17 to involve a responsibility
18 exonérer (libérer) d'une – (voir *décharger*)	
19 s'affranchir (se libérer) d'une –	19 to free oneself from a responsibility
20 se soustraire à une –	20 to withdraw from a responsibility
responsable	**responsible, liable**
1 solidairement –	1 jointly and severally liable
2 tenir (rendre) – de	2 to hold responsible for

resserrement m. (argent)	tightness, tightning, scarceness
politique f. de – monétaire	tight money policy
ressort m. (compétence)	province, competence
1 de votre –	1 within your province
2 pas de notre –	2 outside our province, not in our line
ressortir (paraître)	appear
1 comme il ressort de...	1 as appears from...
2 de... il ressort que	2 from... it emerges that
ressortir à	to belong to
ressortissants pl. (d'un pays)	nationals
ressource f.	resource
1 –s financières	1 means, sources of revenue
2 –s personnelles, propres	2 private means, own –s
3 sans –s	3 without means of support
restant m.	remainder, surplus
1 – de compte	1 balance of an account
2 – en caisse	2 cash in hand
restant (adj.)	remaining
somme –e	remainder, balance, – amount
reste m.	rest, remainder
rester	to remain
1 il me reste (100 francs)	1 I have... left
2 il ne me reste qu'à vous remercier	2 it only remains for me to thank you
3 10 moins 3, il reste 7	3 3 from 10 leaves 7
restituer	to return
restitution f.	return, restitution
– des droits d'entrée	drawback
restreindre	to restrict
1 – le crédit	1 – the credit
2 – les dépenses	2 – the expenses
3 se – à	3 – oneself to
restreint	restricted
1 avec des moyens –s	1 with limited means
2 responsabilité –e	2 limited liability
3 transactions –es	3 – dealings
restrictif (clause, mesure)	restrictive
restriction f.	restriction f.
1 – de crédit	1 credit –
2 – de la production	2 – of output
3 –s aux exportations	3 – on exportations
4 –s quantitatives	4 quantitative –s
5 suppression f. des –s	5 abolition of –s
6 affranchir des –s	6 to remove –s, to free from –s
7 être soumis à des –s	7 to be subject to –s
8 imposer des –s	8 to impose –s
résultat m. (voir aussi clause)	result
1 –s d'une affaire	1 trading –s

2 – d'exploitation, de l'exercice

3 – favorable
4 compte *m.* de –s
5 sans –
6 aboutir à un –
7 donner un – avantageux
résulter
1 il résulte de...
2 il en résulte une difficulté
3 il en résulte un solde de...
4 il en résulte que...
retard *m.*
1 – à la livraison
2 en – de versements (*actions*)

3 sans –
4 contribuable *m.* en –
5 intérêts *m. pl.* de –
6 payement *m.* en –
7 arriver avec –
8 éprouver du –
9 être en – (*payement*)
10 être en – pour son loyer
11 être trois jours en – (*navire*)
12 être en – de 20 minutes (*train*)
13 cela ne peut souffrir un –
retardataire, contribuable *m.* –
retarder
1 – le payement
2 expédition retardée
3 l'horloge retarde
4 ma montre retarde (je retarde) de 5 minutes
retenir, je retiens 5 (*arithm.*)
retenir
1 – une chambre

2 – un montant
3 – ... sur le salaire
retention, droit *m.* de –

retenue *f.*
1 – à la source
2 – d'un montant
3 – sur les salaires
retirer
1 – de l'argent de...

2 – des actions
3 – de la circulation

4 – un crédit

2 trading –s

3 satisfactory –
4 profit and loss account
5 without any –
6 to come to a –
7 to give a favo(u)rable –

1 from... it appears
2 thence arises a difficulty
3 it shows a balance of
4 hence it follows that...
delay
1 – in delivery
2 in arrear with calls

3 without –
4 ratepayer in arrears
5 interest on arrears
6 payement in arrear
7 to arrive with –
8 to be delayed
9 to be in arrear with
10 to be behind with the rent
11 to be three days overdue
12 to be 20 minutes overdue
13 it brooks (admits of) no –
taxpayer in arrears
to delay
1 to defer (–) payment
2 delayed (late) despatch
3 the clock is slow
4 my watch is 5 minutes slow

I carry 5
to bear in mind
1 to reserve (engage) a room, to book accommodation
2 to deduct an amount
3 to deduct... from the wages
lien

deduction
1 – at source
2 retention of an amount
3 – from wages
to retire, to withdraw
1 to withdraw money from

2 to pay off shares
3 to withdraw from circulation

4 to withdraw a credit

retour / 326

5 – un dépôt	5 to withdraw a deposit
6 – un gage	6 to redeem a pledge
7 – des marchandises (*gare, magasin*)	7 to collect (remove) goods
8 – une offre	8 to withdraw an offer
9 – des titres d'un dépôt	9 to withdraw securities from a deposit
10 – une traite	10 to retire a bill
11 se – des affaires	11 to retire from business

retour *m.*   **return**

1 –s (voir aussi *effet de –, marchandises de –*)	
2 – à l'envoyeur	2 to be returned to sender
3 – sans frais	3 protest waived in case of dishon(o)ur, incur no expenses
4 à mon – de voyage (voir aussi *voyage*)	4 on my – home (from abroad)
5 par – du courrier (voir aussi *répondre*)	5 by – (of post)
6 billet *m.* d'aller et –	6 – ticket
7 chargement *m.* de –	7 – cargo
8 compte *m.* de –	8 statement of –
9 effet *m.* de –	9 bill returned, dishono(u)red
10 frais *m. pl.* de –	10 redraft charges
11 fret *m.* de –	11 – freight
12 marchandises *f. pl.* de –	12 returns, goods returned
13 prime *f.* de –	13 – premium
14 registre *m.* des –s	14 –s book

retourner   **to return**

1 – à l'expéditeur	1 – to the sender
2 – un effet	2 – a draft
3 – une remise	3 – a remittance
4 si inconnu à l'adresse prière de – à...	4 in case of non-delivery (if undeliverable as addressed) please return to
5 prière de nous – l'accusé de réception ci-joint, revêtu de votre signature	5 please sign and return the enclosed acknowledgement
6 marchandises retournées	6 returns, goods returned
7 wagons retournés vides	7 wagons returned empty

retrait *m.*   **withdrawal**

1 – d'argent	1 – of money
2 – d'un dépôt	2 – of a deposit
3 – d'un gage	3 redemption of a pledge
4 – de marchandises	4 removal of goods

retraite *f.* (*effet*)   **redraft, re-exchange**
retraite *f.* (*pension*)   **pension**

1 âge *m.* de la –	1 pensionable age

327 / retraité

  2 caisse *f.* de –
  3 droit *m.* à la –

  4 ayant –
  5 mise *f* à la –
  6 demande *f.* de –
  7 pension *f.* de –
  8 demander sa mise à la –
  9 mettre à la –
 10 prendre sa –

retraité *m.*

rétribution *f.*
rétroactif, effet –
rétrocession *f.*
rétrograder (*actions*)
réunion *f.* (voir *assemblée, séance*)
  1 – d'actionnaires
  2 – de créanciers
  3 – du bureau
  4 – privée
  5 – urgente
  6 salle *f.* de –
  7 tenir une –
réunir (*une assemblée*)
  se –
réussir
  1 – à un examen
  2 nous avons réussi à...
révalorisation *f.*
  – de la livre sterling
révaloriser (*emprunt*)
revendable
revendeur *m.*
  escompte *m.* pour –s
revendication *f.*
  –s de salaires
revendiquer
revendre
  1 – (*exécution*)
  2 – un acheteur

  3 – des titres
revenir
  1 – sur une décision
  2 revenant sur notre lettre
  3 cela nous revient à
  4 il nous revient que
  5 il vous revient encore 100 francs
  6 la somme nous revenant
  7 sommes vous revenant ou à vous revenir

  2 superannuation fund
  3 pensionable (–) rights

  4 pensionable, entitled to a –
  5 pensioning
  6 application for a –
  7 retiring –
  8 to apply for one's –
  9 to pension off, to pension
 10 to retire on a –

pensioner

remuneration
retrospective effect
retrocession
to fall back, to relapse
meeting
  1 – of shareholders
  2 – of creditors
  3 – of the board
  4 private –
  5 emergency –
  6 assembly room
  7 to hold a –
to convene, to call together
  to meet
to succeed (in)
  1 to pass an examination
  2 we succeeded in...
revalorization
  revaluation of the pound
to revalorize
resaleable
reseller, retailer
  trade discount
claim
  wage(s) –s
to claim
to resell
  1 to sell out against
  2 to sell out against a buyer

  3 to sell out stock
to come back
  1 to reconsider a decision
  2 reverting to our letter
  3 it costs us
  4 we learn that
  5 you have still 100 francs to get
  6 the amount due to us
  7 sums due or to become due to you

revente f.
1 – (*exécution*)
2 – d'un acheteur
3 – de titres

revenu m.
1 –s accessoires
2 – annuel de...
3 – cadastral

4 – (provenant) de ...
5 – de capitaux
6 – du travail
7 – de valeurs mobilières
8 – de l'entreprise
9 – dérivé
10 – disponible
11 – fixe
12 – foncier
13 – imposable
14 – minimum
15 – national
16 – national au coût des facteurs
17 – national au prix du marché
18 – national brut
19 – national net
20 – national réel
21 – net
22 –s professionnels
23 –s publics
24 – réel
25 déclaration f. de –s
26 distribution f. des –s
27 échelon m. (tranche f.) de –s
28 effet m. de –
29 formation f. du –
30 groupes m. pl. à grands –s
31 groupes m. pl. à bas (faibles) –s

32 groupes m. pl. à –s moyens
33 impôt m. sur le –
34 niveau m. de –
35 nivellement m. des –s
36 nouvelle répartition des –s
37 source f. de –s
38 utilisation f. du –
révérend, au –..
revers m. (*monnaie*)
revêtir d'une signature

revient, prix m. de – (v. *prix*)
revirement m. (*changement*)
– (*dette*)
reviser, réviser

resale
1 selling out against
2 selling out against a buyer
3 selling out stock

income
1 additional –
2 annual – of...
3 rent of land and buildings

4 – from...
5 funded –
6 earned –
7 – from securities
8 entrepeneur's –
9 derived –
10 disposable –
11 fixed –
12 – from real estate
13 taxable –
14 minimum –
15 national –
16 national – at factor cost
17 national – at market prices
18 gross national –
19 net national –
20 real national –
21 net –
22 receipts from earnings
23 public (government) revenue
24 real –
25 return of one's –
26 income distribution
27 – bracket
28 – effect
29 formation of –s
30 higher – groups, higher – brackets
31 lower income groups, brackets

32 middle income groups, classes
33 – tax
34 level of –
35 levelling of –s
36 redistribution of –
37 source of –
38 spending of –
Reverend...
reverse(side)
to appose a signature, to sign

(sudden) turn, change
 making over
to revise

329 / reviseur

reviseur *m.*
révocable (voir aussi *crédit*)
révocation *f.*
  valable jusqu'à –
révoquer
revue, année passée sous –
revue *f.* (*publication*)
riche
richesse *f.*
risque *m.* (voir aussi *encours*)

  1 – cédant
  2 – tiré
risque *m.* (*danger*)
  1 –s additionnels
  2 – assuré
  3 – choisi
  4 – de change
  5 – de conversion et de transfert
  6 – du crédit
  7 – de guerre
  8 – de mer
  9 – d'entrepreneur
10 – de transfert
11 – de transport
12 – d'incendie
13 –s habituels
14 – locatif
15 –s politiques et sociaux
16 –s spéciaux
17 à vos –s et périls
18 à ses –s et périls
19 au – de
20 aux –s et périls de
21 aux –s de l'expéditeur
22 tous autres –s
23 premier –
24 assurance *f.* au premier –
25 assurance *f.* contre tous –s (voir aussi *police*)
26 assurance *f.* contre les –s de crédit
27 assurance *f.* contre le – du remboursement au pair
28 capital à –s (*voir* capital)
29 dossier *m.* (livre *m.*) des –s (*traites*)

30 répartition *f.* des –s
31 surveillance *f.* des –s (*traites*)
32 assumer le –
33 comporter des –s

34 courir le – de
35 couvrir le –

auditor
revocable
revocation
  available until –
to revoke
year under review
review
rich
richess
liabilities on bills of exchange

  1 liability as transferor, as maker
  2 liability as drawee
risk
  1 additional –s
  2 – subscribed
  3 eligible –
  4 exchange (rate) –
  5 conversion and transfer –
  6 credit –
  7 war –
  8 sea –s
  9 contractor's –
10 transfer –
11 transport –
12 fire –
13 usual –s
14 tenant's third party –
15 political and social –s
16 special –s
17 at your –
18 at one's own –
19 at the – of
20 for account and – of
21 at sender's –
22 all other perils
23 premier risque, first –, first loss
24 first loss insurance
25 insurance against all –s

26 credit insurance
27 insurance against risks of redemption at par

29 liability ledger, liability book, liability cards
30 spreading (distribution) of –s
31 control of liabilities
32 to undertake the –
33 to be attended with –s

34 to run the – of...
35 to cover the –

risquer / 330

36 présenter un –
37 souscrire un –
38 les marchandises voyagent, sauf convention contraire, aux –s et périls de l'acheteur
risquer
ristourne *f.*
1 – (*compt.*)
2 – (*excédent*)
3 – (*réduction*)
4 – de droits de douane
5 – de prime

6 faire – de
7 faire une – sur
ristourner (*excédent*)
1 – (*compt.*)
2 – une police

robinet ouvert, (*émission*)
rodage, en –
rôle *m.*
1 – des contributions
2 – d'équipage
3 sortir à tour de –

rompre
1 – les négociations
2 – une charge
3 – un marché

4 – les relations
rompu à
– aux affaires
rompu *m.* (*action*)

rond
1 – en affaires
2 en chiffres –s
3 une somme –e
rossignol *m.*
rotation *f.*
1 – des stocks
2 fréquence *f.* de –
3 période *f.* de –
4 vitesse *f.* de – (*stocks*)
5 vitesse *f.* de – (*capitaux*)
rouille et oxydation (*assur.*)
roulant
1 capital –
2 matériel –
roulement *m.*
1– de capitaux

36 to present –s
37 to underwrite a –
37 the goods travel, unless otherwise agreed, at buyer's –

to risk, to venture
return
1 transfer, writing back
2 refund, –
3 rebate, allowance
4 drawback
5 – of premium

6 to make – (refund) of
7 to make an allowance on
to return, to refund
1 to write back, to transfer
2 to cancel (to annul) a policy

on tap
running in
list
1 assessment book
2 crew –
3 to retire by (in) rotation

to break
1 – off negotiations
2 – bulk
3 to call off a deal

4 – off relations
experienced in
– business
fraction, share fraction, residual fraction
round
1 businesslike
2 in – figures
3 a – sum of
drug
circulation
1 turnover of stocks, stock turnover
2 frequency of turnover
3 period of turnover
4 speed (rate) of turnover
5 velocity of –
rust and oxidation
rolling
1 floating capital
2 – stock
rotation
1 turnover of capital

2 fonds *m.* de – | 2 working capital

3 tableau *m.* de – | 3 – roll
„rouler, ne pas culbuter" | to be rolled not tipped
route *f.* | road
 1 en – | 1 on the way
 2 transport *m.* par – | 2 – transport
 3 indiquer la – | 3 to specify the route
routier, carte routière | road map, route map
routine *f.* | routine
ruban *m.* | ribbon
 – pour machine à écrire | typewriting –
rubis sur l'ongle | to the last farthing, cent
rubrique *f.* | heading
 1 – collective | 1 collective –
 2 – de la cote | 2 section of the list
 3 mentionné en – | 3 above-(mentioned)

 4 sous cette – | 4 under this –
 5 réuni sous la – | 5 lumped under the –
ruée *f.* sur"' (v. *guichet*) | rush (run) on...
ruiner | to ruin
rupture *f.* | breaking
 1 – d'un contrat | 1 breach of contract
 2 – d'un engagement | 2 breach of an engagement
 3 – d'un marché | 3 calling off of a deal
 4 – des relations | 4 – off of relations
rythme *m.* | rhythm

S

sabotage *m.* | sabotage, rattening
saboter | to ratten, to sabotage
sac *m.* | sack
 1 10 –s de pommes de terre | 1 10 –s of potatoes
 2 en –s | 2 bagged, in bags
sacrifice *m.* | sacrifice
 faire un – | to make a –
sacrifier | to sacrifice
 1 articles sacrifiés | 1 sacrified goods, goods sold at a sacrifice
 2 prix sacrifiés | 2 slaughter prices, ruinous prices

sain | sound
 1 – et sauf | 1 safe and –
 2 chargement – | 2 – cargo
 3 monnaie –e | 3 – currency
 4 valeur –e | 4 – value
saisie *f.* | seizure
 1 – arrêt | 1 attachment, garnishment
 2 – conservatoire | 2 – for security
 3 – exécution | 3 execution

saisir / 332

4 – gagerie | 4 writ of execution on furniture
5 – immobilière, – réelle | 5 – of real property
6 – mobilière | 6 – of movable property
7 – revendication | 7 – under a prior claim
saisir | **to seize**
– une occasion | to take an opportunity
saisissable | (*goods*) **distrainable**, (*income*) **attachable**
saison *f.* | **season**
1 – précédente | 1 previous –
2 à l'approche de la – | 2 on the approach of the –
3 la – bat son plein | 3 the – is at its height
4 en pleine (haute) – | 4 at the height of the –
5 par suite de la – avancée | 5 on account of the advanced –
6 morte | 6 dull (dead) –
7 vente *f.* de fin de – | 7 end- of – sale, clearance sale

saisonnier | **seasonal**
1 articles –s | 1 – articles
2 baisse saisonnière | 2 – drop
3 besoins –s | 3 – requirements
4 chômage – | 4 – unemployment
5 chutes saisonnières | 5 – declines
6 crédit – | 6 – credit
7 demande saisonnière | 7 – demand
8 facteurs –s | 8 – factors
9 fléchissement *m.* – des ventes | 9 – decline in sales
10 fluctuations saisonnières | 10 – fluctuations
11 hausse saisonnière | 11 – rise
12 influences saisonnières | 12 – influences
13 ouvrier – | 13 – worker
14 reprise saisonnière | 14 – revival
15 travail – | 15 – work
salaire *m.* (voir aussi *appointements*) | **wage(s), pay**
1 – à forfait, – à la tâche | 1 contractual wages, job wage
2 – à la pièce, – aux pièces | 2 piece (work) wages
3 – à l'heure, – horaire | 3 hourly wages
4 – au temps | 4 time wages
5 – annuel garanti | 5 guaranteed annual wage
6 – de base | 6 base rate
7 – de début | 7 initial –
8 – de rendement | 8 payment by results
9 – direct | 9 direct –
10 – familial | 10 family wage
11 – féminin | 11 women's –
12 – fixe | 12 fixed wages
13 – hebdomadaire | 13 weekly wages, earnings per week

333 / salarial

14 – indirect
15 – journalier
16 – lié à l'index
17 – masculin
18 – maximum
19 – mensuel
20 – minimum garanti
21 – nominal
22 – payé en nature

23 – réel
24 à travail égal – égal
25 augmentation *f.* de –
26 augmentation *f.* de – conventionnelle
27 augmentation *f.* de – extra-conventionnelle
28 blocage *m.* des –s
29 convention *f.* des –s
30 demande *f.* de –
31 disparité *f.* des –s
32 échelle *f.* des –s
33 échelle *f.* mobile des –s
34 formation *f.* des –s
35 impôt *m.* sur les –s
36 livret *m.* de –
37 montée *f.* des –s
38 mouvement *m.* des –s
39 niveau *m.* des –s
40 payement *m.* des –s
41 perte *f.* de –
42 politique *f.* des –s
43 prétentions *f. pl.* de –
44 rajustement *m.* des –s
45 réduction *f.* des –s
46 retenue *f.* sur les –s
47 round *m.* de relèvements de –s
48 taux *m.* des –s
49 zone *f.* de –s
50 bloquer les –s
51 toucher son –
salarial
1 dépenses –es

2 revenus salariaux
3 revendications –es
4 pause *f.* de revendications –es
salarié *m.*
salarié
1 travail –
2 travailleur –
salle *f.*
1 – d'attente
2 – des coffres(–forts)

14 indirect –
15 day's wages
16 wages linked to an index
17 men's –
18 maximum wages
19 monthly wages
20 minimum guaranteed wage
21 nominal (monetary) wages
22 remuneration in kind

23 real (actual) wages
24 equal pay for equal work
25 rise in wages, wage increase
26 contractual rise in –s
27 extra contractual rise in –s

28 wage stop, wage freeze
29 wages agreement
30 wage(s) claim
31 disparity in wage rates
32 wage(s) scale
33 sliding wage scale
34 formation of –
35 wages tax
36 wages book
37 rise of (in) –s
38 wage movements
39 wage level
40 payment of wages
41 loss of wages
42 wage policy
43 salary asked for
44 wage adjustment
45 reduction of (cuts in) wages
46 retention on (deduction from) –s
47 round of wage increases
48 rate of wages
49 wage zone
50 to freeze all wages
51 to receive (draw) one's salary
expenditure...
1 expenditure for wages

2 earned income
3 wage(s) claims
4 – pause, pause in – increases
wage earner
wage-earning, (*travail*) paid
1 paid labour
2 wage worker
room
1 waiting –
2 strong –

salon / 334

  3 – des dactylographes — 3 typewriter –
  4 – des guichets — 4 counters
  5 – des séances — 5 meeting (conference) –
  6 – de ventes — 6 sale –
  7 – d'exposition — 7 show –

salon *m.* — **saloon**
  1 – de coiffure — 1 hairdressing –
  2 – de l'automobile — 2 motor show
  3 – de thé — 3 tea-room

salutation *f.* — **greeting**
  avec mes meilleures –s, mes –s bien (très) distinguées — yours faithfully, very truly yours

sans — **without**
  1 – affaires (*bourse*) — 1 idle
  2 – (autre) avis (*lettre de change*) — 2 – (other) advice
  3 – avis contraire, – autre avis — 3 – further notice
  4 – cotation — 4 no quotation
  5 – date — 5 undated
  6 – engagement (*offre*) — 6 – engagement
  7 – engagement de notre part — 7 – any liability on our part
  8 – frais, retour – frais, – protêt — 8 no protesting, protest waived, – charges
  9 – nouvelles (*navire*) — 9 missing
  10 – préjudice de... — 10 – prejudice to
  11 – profession — 11 (of) no occupation
  12 – protêt (voir – *frais*)
  13 – recours (*effets*) — 13 – recourse
  14 – signature — 14 signature missing
  15 – valeur (*titres*) — 15 valueless, worthless

satisfaction *f.* — **satisfaction**
  donner entière – — to give full –

satisfaire — **to satisfy**
  1 – à la demande — 1 to meet the demand
  2 – ses créanciers — 2 – one's creditors
  3 – aux besoins — 3 – the needs

satisfait de — **satisfied with**

saturation *f.* — **saturation**
  point *m.* de – — – point

saturé — **satiated, saturated**
  le marché est – — the market is –, has reached the saturation point

sauf — **except**
  1 – avis contraire — 1 unless advised to the contrary, unless I hear to the contrary
  2 – bonne arrivée — 2 under reserve of good arrival
  3 – bonne fin (*effets*) — 3 under (usual) reserve
  4 – contrordre — 4 unless countermanded

335 / sauvegarde

5 – convention contraire	5 unless otherwise agreed
6 – dispositions contraires	6 save as provided otherwise
7 – encaissement	7 if cashed
8 – erreur ou omissions	8 errors and omissions excepted
9 – imprévu	9 circumstances permitting
10 – indications contraires dans les présentes	10 unless expressly otherwise stated herein
11 – instructions spéciales	11 unless special instructions (to the contrary)
12 – instructions différentes	12 unless otherwise instructed
13 – interdiction expresse	13 unless expressly prohibited
14 – l'approbation de...	14 subject to the approval of
15 – mieux (*bourse*)	15 or better
16 – rentrée	16 if cashed, under usual reserve
17 – stipulation expresse	17 unless expressly stipulated
18 – vendu, – vente	18 if unsold, subject to prior (intermediate) sale

sauvegarde *f.*, **clause** *f.* **de –**   saving clause
sauvetage *m.* (*marit.*)   salvage
  frais *m. pl.* de –   – charges
sauvegarder les intérêts   to protect (watch over) the interests
savoir   to know

1 prière de (veuillez) nous faire –   1 please let us know

2 nous avons l'honneur de vous faire –   2 we inform you that, we have (we have the pleasure) to inform you that

3 nous vous saurions infiniment gré (beaucoup de gré) de ...   3 we shall (should) be very much obliged if you will (would)...

4 pas que nous sachions   4 not that we know of
5 pour autant que je sache   5 as far as I know
6 reste à –   6 it remains to be seen whether

sceau *m.*   seal
scellé *m.*   seal

1 apposition *f.* des –s   1 sealing, fixing of the –s
2 bris *m.* des –s   2 breaking of the –s
3 levée *f.* des –s   3 unsealing, removing of –s

4 apposer (mettre) les –s   4 to affix the –s, to put under –
5 briser les –s   5 to break the –s
6 lever les –s   6 to take off (remove) the –s

sceller   to seal
script *m.*   scrip certificate
scriptural (voir *monnaie*)

séance *f.*   meeting
1 – de bourse   1 stock exchange session

seconde de change / 336

2 – de clôture
3 – tenante
4 en – publique
5 assister à une –
6 lever la –
7 ouvrir la –
8 tenir une –   [première]
seconde *f.* **de change** (voir aussi
secret *adj.*
secret *m.*
1 – bancaire
2 – de fabrication
3 – professionnel
4 tenu au –
secrétaire *m.*

1 – *f.* de ...
2 – adjoint
3 – communal
4 – général
5 – particulier
6 – trésorier
secrétariat *m.* (*office*)
– (*fonction*)
secteur *m.*
1 – économique
2 – industriel
3 – privé
4 – public
section *f.*
sécurité *f.*
1 – sociale
2 marge *f.* de –
selon
semaine *f.*
1 – de cinq jours
2 – de travail
3 – en cours
4 la – passée
5 – précédente
6 la – prochaine
semestre *m.*
semestriel(lement)
séminaire *m.*
1 organiser un –
2 participer à un –

sens *m.*
1 au – de la loi
2 au – figuré
3 au – propre
sentir
se faire –

2 closing session
3 pending (during) the –
4 in public session
5 to attend a –
6 to close the –
7 to open the –
8 to hold a –
second of exchange
secret
secret
1 banking secrecy
2 – of manufacture
3 professional secrecy
4 bound to secrecy
secretary

1 – to...
2 assistant –
3 town clerk
4 – general
5 private –
6 – and treasurer
secretariat, secretarial office
secretaryship
sector
1 economic –
2 industrial –, – of industry
3 private –
4 public –
branch
safety
1 social security
2 – margin
according to, in accordance with
week
1 five-day work(ing) –
2 working –
3 current –
4 last –
5 previous –
6 next –
half year
half yearly, semiannual(ly)
seminar
1 to hold a –
2 to attend a –

sense
1 within the meaning of the Act
2 in a figurative –
3 in a literal –
to feel
to be felt, to make itself felt

337 / séquestration

séquestration f.	sequestration
séquestre m. (personne)	sequestrator
séquestre m. (action)	sequestration
être sous –	to be in –
séquestrer	to sequester
biens séquestrés	property sequestered, sequestrated
série f.	series
1 – complète de connaissances	1 full set of bills of lading
2 en –	2 in –
3 articles m. pl. hors –	3 specially manufactured articles
4 fabrication f. en –	4 mass production, serial manufacture, standardized production
5 vente f. de fins de –	5 remnant sale
6 voiture f. de –	6 car of standard model
serment m.	oath
1 déclarer sous –	1 to declare on –
2 prêter –	2 to take an –
3 prêter – entre les mains de...	3 to take an – (to be sworn) before...
service m. (assistance)	service
1 – (département)	1 –, department
2 –s à la disposition de nos clients	2 –s at the disposal of our customers
3 –s administratifs	3 administrative department
4 – commercial	4 commercial department
5 – de dépôts de titres	5 safe custody department
6 – de factage	6 parcels cartage –
7 – de groupage	7 joint cargo –
8 – de jour	8 day –
9 – de la caisse	9 cash department
10 – de la comptabilité	10 accounts department
11 – de la correspondance	11 correspondence department
12 – de la prospection (clientèle)	12 canvassing
13 – de la publicité	13 advertising (publicity) department
14 – de l'économat (banque)	14 stationery department
15 – de l'escompte	15 discount department
16 – de l'expédition	16 dispatch department
17 – de l'expédition (courrier)	17 outward (outgoing) mail department
18 – de nuit	18 night –
19 – de recouvrement	19 collecting department
20 – de renseignements (tel.)	20 directory enquiry
21 – des achats	21 buying (purchasing) department
22 – des chèques et virements postaux	22 postal cheque (check) and clearing service
23 – des coffres-forts	23 safe deposit, safekeeping department
24 – des colis postaux	24 parcel post
25 – des coupons	25 coupon department

26 – des crédits | 26 credit department
27 – des crédits documentaires | 27 documentary credits department
28 – des émissions | 28 issue department
29 – des études financières et économiques (*banque*) | 29 financial research department
30 – des marchandises (*banque*) | 30 goods department
31 – des monnaies étrangères | 31 foreign currency department
32 – des ordres de bourse | 32 stock exchange orders
33 – des relations étrangères | 33 foreign department
34 – des renseignements commerciaux (*banque*) | 34 commercial information department
35 – des souscriptions | 35 loan subscription department
36 – des titres | 36 securities department
37 – des transferts, des virements | 37 department for transfer of funds
38 –s domestiques | 38 domestic –s
39 – du change | 39 exchange department
40 – du dépouillement (*courrier*) | 40 inward mail (mail sorting) department
41 – du personnel | 41 personnel (staff) department
42 – du portefeuille (*effets*) | 42 bills department
43 – extérieur | 43 outside –, (*personnel*) outdoor staff
44 – réciproque | 44 – in return, reciprocal –
45 au – de | 45 in the – of
46 à votre – | 46 at your –
47 en – (*bateau*) | 47 running
48 un – en vaut un autre | 48 one good turn deserves another
49 toujours disposé à vous rendre – | 49 always ready (glad) to reciprocate –
50 années *f. pl.* de – | 50 years of –
51 échanges *m. pl.* de –s | 51 exchange (movements) of –s

52 entrée *f.* en – | 52 entering the –
53 heures *f. pl.* de – | 53 office hours
54 indications *f. pl.* de – (voir aussi *case, emplacement*) | 54 – instructions
55 libre – | 55 self-service
56 nécessités *f. pl.* du – | 56 requirements of the –
57 offre *f.* de –s | 57 offer of –s
58 pli *m.* de – | 58 official letter (O.H.M.S.)
59 prestations *f. pl.* de – | 59 –s
60 règlement *m.* de – | 60 – regulation
61 tableau *m.* de – | 61 time table
62 vêtements *m. pl.* de – | 62 uniform
63 demander un – | 63 to ask a favour
64 entrer en – | 64 to enter upon one's duties
65 être au – de... | 65 to be employed by, to be on the staff of
66 mettre en – (*navire*) | 66 to place on the run
67 offrir ses –s à... | 67 to offer one's –s
68 nous vous offrons nos –s pour | 68 we offer you our –s for...
69 prendre en –, à son – | 69 to engage

339 / service

70 retirer du – (*navire*)
71 utiliser les –s de...
service *m.* (*paiement*)
 1 – de la dette
 2 – d'intérêt
 3 – d'un emprunt
 4 – financier
 5 établissement *m.* chargé du – financier
servir
servitude *f.*
seule *f.* de change
siège *m.*
 1 – administratif
 2 – d'exploitation
 3 – principal
 4 – social
 5 – statutaire
 6 au – de la société
 7 la société a son – à...

sieur *m.*, notre – X
signataire *m.*
signataire *m.* (*Belg.*)
signature *f.* (v. aussi *non signé*)
 1 – (*l'action*)
 2 – autorisée (voir *autorisé, liste*)
 3 – collective
 4 – en blanc
 5 – (il)lisible
 6 – légalisée
 7 – sociale
 8 – valable
 9 carte *f.* de spécimen de –

10 légalisation *f.* d'une –
11 liste *f.* des –s autorisées
12 spécimen *m.* de –
13 2 jeux de spécimen de –
14 déposer un spécimen de –
15 la – ne correspond pas avec le spécimen
16 pour être valable (...) doit porter 2 –s autorisées

17 apposer sa – au bas d'un accord

18 avoir la –

19 contrefaire (fausser) une –
20 honorer (faire honneur à) une –

21 légaliser une –
22 mettre sa –

70 to put out of commission
71 to utilize the –s of...
service
 1 debt –
 2 payment of interest   [on a loan
 3 – of a loan, payment of the interest
 4 – of a loan
 5 paying agent
to serve
easement, charge
sole of exchange
registered office
 1 administrative office   [workings
 2 principal place of business, (*mines*)
 3 head office
 4 –
 5 registered office
 6 at the head office
 7 the company's –s are at...,
   the business is established at...
Mr. X, our Mr. X.
signer, signatory
signature folder
signature
 1 the signing

 3 joint –
 4 blank –
 5 (il)legible
 6 legalized –
 7 joint –
 8 valid –
 9 – card

10 authentication (attestation) of a –
11 list of authorized –s
12 specimen (of) –
13 2 sets of the specimens of –
14 to enter a specimen of –
15 the – does not correspond to (agree with) the specimen
16 to be valid (...) must bear 2 authorized –s, (...) is only valid when signed by 2 authorized persons
17 to append a – to an agreement
18 to have the –, to hold the procuration, to have signatory power
19 to forge a –
20 to hono(u)r (protect) a –

21 to legalize a –
22 to put one's –

signer / 340

23 porter la – de
24 présenter à la –
25 revêtir de sa –
26 vérifier une –, l'authenticité d'une –

signer
 1 – en blanc
 2 – une lettre
 3 – par procuration
 4 – valablement
 5 signé X
 6 signé de propre main
 7 ... est déposé à –
 8 notre sieur X signera...

 9 personnes autorisées à –

 10 veuillez nous retourner l'accusé de réception ci-joint dûment signé

silo *m.*
simulé
 1 facture –e
 2 vente –e
sinistre *m.*
 1 – (*assur.*)
 2 – (*dommage*)
 3 avis *m.* de (déclaration *f.* du) –
 4 évaluer le –

sinistré *m.*

situation *f.*
 1 – critique
 2 – de la banque
 3 – de la caisse
 4 – d'un compte
 5 – du marché
 6 – économique
 7 – financière

 8 – hebdomadaire (*banque*)
 9 – mensuelle
 10 – monétaire
 11 – stable
situé
 maison bien –e
situer, se – (*index*)
slogan *m.*
social

23 to bear the – of...
24 to submit (present) for –
25 to appose one's – to
26 to verify a –

to sign
 1 – in blank
 2 – a letter
 3 – by proxy
 4 to be authorized –
 5 signed (sgd) X.
 6 signed personally (in own hand)
 7 it may be signed
 8 Mr. X. will sign...

 9 gentlemen authorized – on behalf of...

 10 please sign and return the present acknowledgment

silo
pro forma, sham
 1 pro forma invoice
 2 sham sale
accident, casualty
 1 claim
 2 damage, loss
 3 notice of loss
 4 to assess (estimate) the damage, the loss

victim of a disaster, sufferer, (*insur.*) **claimant**
situation
 1 critical –
 2 bank return, bank statement
 3 cash position
 4 state of an account
 5 state of the market
 6 economic –
 7 financial –, (*firm*) financial status, standing
 8 weekly statement, week's return
 9 monthly statement
 10 exchange position
 11 steady –
situated
 well-situated business
to be
slogan
social

341 / *sociétaire*

1 créanciers sociaux

2 malaise –
3 organisation –e de l'entreprise
4 question –e
5 sécurité –e
6 sous la raison –e

sociétaire *m.*
société *f.*
1 – absorbante (*fusion*)
2 – absorbée (*fusion*)
3 – affiliée
4 – anonyme
5 – à personne unique
6 – à portefeuille
7 – à responsabilité limitée

8 – civile

9 – commerciale
10 – coopérative (voir *coopérative*)
11 – d'assurance(s)
12 – de banque
13 – de capitaux
14 – d'économie mixte
15 – de construction
16 – de contrôle
17 – de famille
18 – de financement
19 – de personnes
20 – de personnes à responsabilité limitée
21 – de placement, d'investissement

22 – d'utilité publique
23 – en commandite par actions
24 – en commandite simple

25 – en liquidation
26 – en nom collectif
27 – en participation
28 – fiduciaire
29 – filiale
30 – financière
31 – Financière Internationale
32 – holding

33 – immobilière

34 – mère
35 – par actions

1 creditors of the company, company's creditors

2 – unrest
3 – planning in industry
4 – question
5 – security
6 under the style of X

member of the company
company
1 absorbing –
2 absorbed –
3 affiliated –
4 limited –
5 one-man –
6 holding –
7 limited liability –

8 – which performs habitually no acts of commerce, civil –

9 trading (commercial) –

11 insurance –
12 banking –
13 association of capital
14 partly private partly public –
15 building company
16 holding –
17 family business (concern)
18 financing –
19 association of persons
20 (association of persons enjoying limited liability)
21 investment trust, investment –

22 public utility –
23 – limited by shares
24 limited partnership

25 – in liquidation
26 partnership firm
27 special (particular) partnership
28 accounting and auditing firm
29 subsidiary –
30 finance –
31 International Finance Corporation
32 holding –

33 real estate –

34 parent –
35 joint stock –

sœur / 342

36 – privée

37 ouvrir une – privée au grand public

38 – sœur

39 acte *m.* de la –
40 but *m.* (objet *m.*) de la –
41 statuts *m. pl.* de la –

42 constituer une –
43 dissoudre une –
44 liquider une –
45 se retirer d'une –
46 transformer en –

sœur *f.*, X –s
soigné
1 exécution –e
2 service –
soigner
1 – l'acceptation
2 – l'assurance
3 – les intérêts

4 – le recouvrement
soin *m.*
1 apporter le plus grand – à
2 avoir – que
3 aux bons –s de
soit... *fr.*
„soldes" *m. pl.*
solde *m.*
1 – actif
2 – à nouveau, – à reporter

3 – ancien
4 – bénéficiaire
5 – créancier, créditeur
6 – créditeur en compte
7 – débiteur
8 – de caisse
9 – de dividende
10 – déficitaire
11 – disponible
12 – en banque
13 – en caisse
14 – en notre faveur
15 – en votre faveur
16 – excédentaire
17 – nouveau
18 – passif
19 – reporté de l'exercice précédent

36 private –, private (limited) –

37 to convert a private limited – into a public limited –

38 sister –

39 deed of partnership
40 objects of the –
41 articles of association, of partnership, company's articles

42 to constitute a –
43 to dissolve a –
44 to liquidate (wind up) a –
45 to withdraw from a partnership
46 to convert into a –

the sisters X
careful
1 – execution
2 – attention
to take care of
1 to procure acceptance
2 to attend to (effect) the insurance
3 to attend to (look after) the interests
4 to undertake the collection of
care
1 to bestow the utmost – on
2 to see that, to take – to
3 – of
say
remnant sale
balance
1 credit –
2 – (carried forward) to next account

3 old –
4 – in one's favo(u)r
5 credit –
6 – in account
7 debit –
8 cash –
9 final dividend
10 debit –
11 available –
12 bank –
13 – in hand
14 – in our favo(u)r, to your debit
15 – in your favo(u)r
16 surplus
17 new –
18 debit –
19 – brought forward from last account

343 / solder

20 en –
21 en – de
22 pour – de mon compte
23 pour – de tout compte

24 quittance *f.* pour – de compte

25 le – est de...

26 il résulte un – de...
27 établir le –
28 garder dans un compte un – créditeur minimum de...
29 présenter (accuser) un – de...
30 régler le –
31 reporter un – à nouveau

solder
1 – un compte
2 se – par

3 se – par un bénéfice de
4 se – par un déficit

5 le compte se solde par... en ma faveur

solidaire
1 codébiteur *m.* –
2 garant *m.* –
3 responsabilité *f.* –

solidairement
1 – responsable de
2 s'engager –

solliciter un emploi
solvabilité *f.*

fournir des renseignements sur la – de...

solvable

sommaire
relevé (état) *m.* –
sommairement
sommation *f.*
somme *f.* (voir aussi *montant*)
1 la – de... fr.
2 – d'argent
3 – disponible
4 – due
5 – en toutes lettres

20 on –
21 in settlement of
22 in settlement of my account
23 in full settlement

24 receipt for the –

25 the – amounts to, the account closes with...

26 it shows a –
27 to establish the –
28 to keep a minimum – on an account

29 to show a –
30 to pay the –
31 to carry the – forward to new account

to balance
1 to settle an account
2 to close with a balance of

3 to show (close with) a profit of
4 to show a deficit, to close with a deficit

5 the account closes with... in my favo(u)r

joint and several
1 – codebtor
2 guarantor in a – obligation
3 – liability

jointly and severally
1 – liable for
2 to engage jointly

to apply for a situation
solvability, solvency, financial status

to provide with information concerning the solvency, the financial standing, creditworthiness

solvent

summary
– statement
summarily
summons
sum, amount
1 the sum of
2 sum of money
3 available amount
4 amount due
5 sum in words, at length

6 – forfaitaire
7 – restante
8 – totale
9 –s vous revenant ou à vous revenir
10 –s qu'il doit ou pourrait nous devoir (voir *devoir*)
11 en – ronde
12 une grosse –
13 colonne *f.* des –s
14 arrondir une –
15 disposer d'une –

16 faire la –
17 parfaire une –
sommer
– de payer

sommet *m.*
1 conférence *f.* au –
2 atteindre un nouveau –

6 agreed sum
7 balance
8 sum total, total amount
9 sums due or to become due to you

11 in round sum, figures
12 a large (considerable) sum
13 amount column
14 to round off a sum
15 to have an amount at one's disposal
16 to add up
17 to make up a sum
to summon
to call on... to pay, to call for payment

top
1 summit conference
2 to reach a new peak, a new high

sortant
1 administrateur –
2 associé –
sortie *f.*
1 ,,–'' (*inscription*)
2 – (*des administrateurs*)
3 –s de caisse

4 – d'or
5 droits *m. pl.* de –

6 entrées *f. pl.* et –s

7 entrée *f.* et – (*d'un pays*)
8 point *m.* de – de l'or
sortir
1 – (*publication*)
2 – à tour de rôle

3 – du port
4 – du service
5 – ses effets
6 les administrateurs qui doivent – cette année sont messieurs...

souche *f.*
1 action *f.* à la –
2 carnet *m.* à –
3 livre *m.* (registre *m.*) à –

retiring
1 – director
2 – partner
going out
1 way out, exit
2 retirement
3 cash payments

4 outflow (efflux, drain) of gold
5 export duties

6 receipts and payments

7 entering and leaving the country
8 export gold point
to go out
1 to come out
2 to retire in rotation

3 to leave port
4 to leave (retire from) the service
5 to take effect
6 the directors who have to retire this year are Messrs...

counterfoil, stub
1 unissued share
2 counterfoil book
3 counterfoil book

souffrance
1 colis *m. pl.* en –
2 effets *m. pl.* en –
3 fonds *m. pl.* en –
4 lettre *f.* restée en –
5 marchandises *f. pl.* en – (*ch. d. fer*)
6 laisser un effet en –
7 laisser des marchandises en –

souhait *m.*
1 à –
2 les meilleurs –s de bonne année
3 réciproquer des –s

souhaiter
soulever
1 „– avec des chaînes, manier sans crampons"
2 – ici! (*transport*)
3 – une question

souligner
soulte *f.*
1 – (*actions*)
2 – (*succession*)
3 échange *m.* à raison de... actions nouvelles plus une – de... francs

soumettre
1 – à l'approbation de...
2 – des échantillons
3 – à un examen minutieux
4 – à la signature
5 soumis au droit de timbre
6 soumis à des fluctuations
7 soumis à l'impôt...

soumission *f.*
1 – cachetée
2 par (voie de) –
3 la – est ouverte jusqu'au...
4 les –s doivent être adressées à
5 (bulletin *m.* de) –
6 vente *f.* par –
7 faire une – pour
8 ouvrir la –
9 participer à une –

soumissionnaire *m.*
1 – au plus bas prix
2 le – au plus haut prix

soumissionner

---

1 undeliverable parcels
2 bills in suspense, dishono(u)red bills
3 suspended debenture bonds
4 dead letter, returned letter
5 goods on demurrage
6 to dishono(u)r a bill
7 to leave goods on demurrage

wish
1 as desired
2 kind (best) –es for the coming year
3 to reciprocate –es

to wish
to raise, to lift up
1 „hold with chains not with hooks"
2 heave here!
3 to raise (to bring up) a question

to underline
balance
1 – in cash, cash distribution
2 –
3 exchange at a rate of... new shares plus a cash distribution of...

to submit
1 – for approval to...
2 – samples
3 – to a careful examination
4 – (present) for signature
5 liable to stamp duty
6 subject to fluctuations
7 liable to tax, dutiable

tender
1 sealed –
2 by –
3 –s are invited for...
4 –s to be lodged with...
5 –
6 sale by –
7 to –, to send in a – for...
8 to put out for public –
9 to tender for a contract

tenderer
1 ... submitting the lowest tender
2 the highest bidder

to tender for, to submit (send in) for tender

source / 346

source *f.*
1 – de revenus
2 – d'informations
3 lever des impôts à la –
4 retenir à la – (impôts)
5 tenir de bonne –, de – sûre

sous-assurance *f.*
sous-bail *m.*

sous-bailleur *m.*
sous-chef *m.*
sous-consommation *f.*

souscripteur *m.*
1 – (*d'une lettre de change*)
2 – à des actions
3 – à un emprunt
4 – en espèces, en numéraire

souscription *f.* (*adjudication*)
les –s doivent être présentées avant...

souscription *f.* (*émissions*)
1 – à des actions
2 – à un emprunt
3 – (à titre) irréductible

4 – (à titre) réductible

5 – surpassée
6 par –
7 la – est ouverte du.. au ... à ...

8 à verser lors de la –
9 avis *m.* de retour de –
10 billet *m.* (bulletin *m.*) de –

11 banque (établissement) qui reçoit les –s
12 cours *m.* de la –
13 droit *m.* de –
14 cum –

15 ex –
16 exercer un –
17 liste *f.* de –
18 offre *f.* de –

19 titres *m. pl.* mis en –
20 clôturer la –
21 mettre en –, offrir à la –
22 ouvrir la –

souscrire
1 – (à)... actions

source
1 – of revenue, of income
2 – of information
3 to collect taxes at the –
4 to deduct at the –
5 to know (to have) from a reliable –

underinsurance
sublease, underlease

underlessor, sublessor
deputy chief clerk
underconsumption

subscriber, applicant
1 drawer, maker
2 applicant for shares
3 subscriber to a loan
4 cash subscriber

tender
–s must be delivered before...

application
1 – for shares
2 subscription for (to) a loan
3 – as of right for new shares, for letter of rights
4 – for excess shares, excess application
5 oversubscription
6 on –
7 applications will be received at... on.. and will close on...
8 to pay on –
9 letter of regret
10 form of –, – form

11 bank authorized to receive –s (subscriptions), selling agent
12 price of issue
13 – right
14 cum new (claim, rights)

15 ex claim; ex new
16 to exercise – rights
17 subscription list, list of –s
18 offer(ing) for subscription

19 securities offered for subscription
20 to close the – of –s
21 to offer for subscription
22 to invite –s (subscriptions) for...

to apply
1 – (subscribe) for... shares

347 / sous-directeur

2 – un abonnement

3 – un effet de commerce
4 – à un emprunt
5 – une liste
6 – pour un montant de...
7 actions souscrites
8 capital souscrit
9 souscrit entièrement
10 souscrit plusieurs fois
11 il a été souscrit pour un montant de
sous-directeur *m.*
sous-emploi *m.*
sous-estimation, sous-évaluation *f.*

sous-estimer, sous-évaluer
sous-locataire *m.*
sous-location *f.*

sous-louer
sous-main *m.*
sous-participation *f.*
sous-production *f.*
sous-produit *m.*
sous-secrétaire *m.*
soussigné *m.*

1 je –... déclare par la présente
2 le – déclare
3 les –s
4 le – de droite

soussigner
soustraction *f. (arith.)*
 – *(fraude)*
soustraire (de)
1 – *(fraude)*
2 se – à ses obligations

sous-traitant *m.*

soutenir
– des prix
soutenu *(bourse)*
soutien *m.*
1 – des prix
2 achats *m. pl.* de –
3 prix *m.* de –
spécial
spécialisé en (dans)
spécification *f.*
spécifier
 les conditions specifiées dans...

2 to subscribe (take out a subscription) to
3 to draw a bill of exchange
4 to subscribe to (for) a loan
5 to enter on a list
6 to subscribe for an amount of...
7 shares applied for, subscribed
8 subscribed capital
9 fully subscribed
10 applied for several times over
11 the subscriptions amount to...
submanager, assistant manager
under-employment
underestimation, undervaluation

to underestimate, to undervalue
sublessee, underlessee
subletting, underletting

to underlet, to sublet
writing pad, blotting pad
sub-participation
under-production
by-product [tary
under-secretary, assistant secre-
the undersigned

1 I –... hereby declare
2 – declares
3 the undersigned
4 writer whose signature appears on the right
to undersign
substraction
 abstraction
to substract (from)
1 to abstract
2 to evade (to back out of) one's obligations
subcontractor

to support
 to support prices
supported, steady
support
1 price support
2 supporting purchases
3 supported (pegged) price
special
specialized (in)
specification
to specify
 the conditions specified in...

spécifique
poids *m.* –
spécimen *m.*
– de signature (voir *signature*)
spéculateur *m.*
1 – à la baisse

2 – à la hausse
3 – en bourse
spéculatif
valeurs spéculatives
spéculation *f.*
1 – à la baisse

2 – à la hausse

3 – à cheval, – mixte
4 – avantageuse
5 – effrénée
6 – en bourse
7 – hasardeuse
8 – manquée, mauvaise –
9 – mixte (voir *à cheval*)
10 – sur les changes
11 – sur les valeurs
12 par –
13 achats *m. pl.* en –
14 esprit *m.* de –

15 opérations *f. pl.* de –

16 valeurs *f. pl.* de –

17 ventes *f. pl.* en –
18 se lancer dans (se livrer à) des –s

spéculer
1 – à la baisse

2 – à la hausse

3 – sur
sphère *f.*
1 – d'activité
2 – d'intérêts
spirale *f.*
– des prix et salaires

stabilisation *f.*
1 – des cours, des changes
2 – des monnaies
3 emprunt *m.* de –
stabiliser

---

specific
– weight
specimen

speculator
1 bear

2 bull
3 – on change, (*Amer.*) market –
speculative
– stocks
speculation
1 bear operation, – for (on) a fall

2 bull operation, – for (on) a rise

3 straddle, spread
4 favo(u)rable –
5 unbridled –
6 (stock) exchange –
7 hazardous –
8 bad (unsuccessful) –

10 – in exchanges
11 – on stock and shares
12 – on –
13 speculative buying
14 speculative spirit

15 speculative operations, transactions

16 speculative stocks

17 speculative selling
18 to engage in (embark on) speculations
to speculate
1 – for (on) a fall, to go a bear

2 – for a rise, to go a bull

3 – in
sphere
1 – (field) of activity
2 – of interests
spiral
wage-price spiral

stabilization
1 consolidation of exchange
2 – of currency
3 – loan
to stabilize

349 / stabilité

stabilité *f.*	**stability**
1 – des changes	1 – of currency rates
2 – des prix	2 price-, – of prices
stable	**stable**
1 – (*action*)	1 steady
2 monnaie – *f.*	2 – currency
stage *m.*	**period of probation, training period**
faire un –	to be on probation
stagiaire *m.*	**probationer,** (*industry*) **trainee**
stagnant	**stagnant**
être –	to be stationary
stagnation *f.*	**stagnation**
– des affaires	dullness in – (stagnation of) business
stand *m.* (*d'exposition*)	**stand**
standard *m.* de vie	**standard of living**
élévation (relèvement) *f.* du –	raising of (rise in) the –
standardisation *f.*	**standardization**
standardiser	**to standardize**
starie *f.*	**lay day**
stationnaire	**stationary**
stationnement *m.* (voir *défense, droits, frais*)	
statistique *f.*	**statistics**
1 Bureau *m.* (Institut) des –s	1 Statistical Office
2 machine à – (voir *machine*)	
3 taxe *f.* de –	3 statistical dues
4 établir une –	4 to compile –
statistique *adj.*	**statistical, statistic**
données *f. pl.* –s	statistical records
statutaire	**statutory**
1 amortissement *m.* –	1 – writing off
2 dividende *m.* –	2 – dividend
3 prescriptions *f. pl.* –s	3 provisions of the articles
4 réserve *f.* –	4 – reserve, reserve provided by the articles
statutairement	**in accordance with the articles**
statuts *m. pl.*	**articles of association, company's articles**
1 conformément aux –, selon les –	1 according to the –
2 modification *f. pl.* des –	2 change in the articles of association
3 publier les –	3 to publish the articles
4 rédiger des –	4 to draw up the articles
stellage *m.*	**put and call,** (*Amer.*) **spread**
1 donneur *m.* de –	1 taker for a –, seller of a –
2 preneur *m.* de –	2 giver for a –, buyer of a –

stencil / 350

stencil *m.* — stencil
stenciler — to stencil
sténodactylo(graphe) *f.* — shorthand typist
sténodactylographie *f.* — shorthand and typewriting
sténogramme *m.* — shorthand note
sténo(graphe) *m.* — shorthand writer, stenographer
sténographie *f.* — shorthand writing, stenography
sténographier — to take down (in shorthand)

sténographique — shorthand
sténotype *f.* — shorthand machine, stenograph
sténotypie *f.* — stenotypy
stérilisation *f.* (*de fonds*) — sterilization
 – d'argent — – of money
sterling *m.* — sterling
 1 bloc *m.* - — 1 – bloc
 2 zone *f.* - — 2 – area
stimulant *m.* — strong incentive (fillip) to...
stimuler (*affaires*) — to stimulate, to give a stimulus to
stipulation *f.* (v. aussi *sauf*) — stipulation
stipuler — to stipulate
 1 – des conditions — 1 – terms
 2 – par contrat — 2 – by contract
 3 le contrat stipule que... — 3 the contract stipulates that
stock *m.* — stock, (*Amer.* aussi) inventory
 1 –s charbonniers, des charbonnages — 1 coal –s
 2 –s considérables — 2 large (heavy) –s
 3 – disponible, - en magasin — 3 – in trade, – on hand

 4 –s excessifs — 4 inflated –s
 5 – mondial — 5 world –s
 6 – stratégique — 6 strategic stockpile
 7 – sur le carreau des mines — 7 pit-head –s

 8 –s visibles — 8 visible –, supply
 9 de – — 9 from –
 10 en – — 10 in –
 11 jusqu'à épuisement du – — 11 as long as the – lasts
 12 livrable de – — 12 deliverable from –
 13 pas en – — 13 out of –
 14 accumulation *f.* de –s — 14 – (inventory) accumulation
 15 constitution *f.* de –s — 15 stockbuilding, inventory building
 16 épuisement *m.* des –s — 16 exhaustion of –s
 17 reconstitution *f.*, renouvellement *m.* de – — 17 restocking, rebuilding (replenishment of –s)
 18 rotation *f.* des –s — 18 – turnover
 19 avoir en – — 19 to have (keep) in –
 20 compléter le – — 20 to complete a –
 21 constituer un – — 21 to build up –s
 22 entamer le – — 22 to draw on the –
 23 refaire ses –s — 23 to rebuild (replenish) –s
 24 travailler pour le – — 24 to work for –

stockage *m.* excessif — excessive building up of stocks
stock dividend — stock dividend

stocker — to stock, to place in stock
structure *f.* — structure, pattern
  1 – des prix — 1 price –
  2 – salariale — 2 wage –
style *m.* épistolaire — epistolary style
stylo(graphe) *m.* — fountain pen

  – à bille — ball(-point) pen
subdiviser — to subdivide
subdivision *f.* — subdivision
subir — to suffer
  1 – une majoration — 1 to experience a rise
  2 – des modifications — 2 to undergo alterations
  3 – une perte — 3 – a loss
subordination *f.* — subordination
subrogation *f.* — subrogation

subroger — to subrogate
  1 être subrogé aux droits de l'assuré — 1 to be subrogated in the rights of the assured
  2 demeurer subrogé aux droits d'un créancier — 2 to enter into the rights of the creditor
  3 subrogé tuteur — 3 deputy (surrogate) guardian
subside *m.* (v. aussi *subvention*) — subsidy
subsidiaire — subsidiary
substitution *f.* — substitution
  1 biens (produits) de – — 1 substitutional goods
  2 effet *m.* de – — 2 – effect
substituer — to substitute
subvenir aux besoins — to provide for the needs
subvention *f.* — subsidy, subvention

  1 – à l'exportation — 1 export –
  2 – de l'état — 2 state –
subventionner — to subsidize
succédané *m.* — substitute for
succès *m.* — success
  1 chance *f.* de – — 1 change of –
  2 couronné de – — 2 to be crowned with –
  3 sans – — 3 without –
successeur *m.* — successor
... –s — ...heirs
successif — successive
succession *f.* (*héritage*) — succession

  1 désistement *m.* de la – — 1 renunciation of an inheritance
  2 droits *m. pl.* de – — 2 legacy (estate) duties
successivement — successively
succursale *f.* — branch, branch office
  ouvrir une – — to open a branch

sucrier / 352

sucrier
 1 campagne sucrière
 2 culture sucrière
suffisamment
suffisant
suite *f.* (voir aussi *droit*)
 1 –s de la guerre
 2 comme – (faisant –) à notre lettre d'hier

 3 dans la –
 4 en – de quoi
 5 par – de, à la – de

 6 par – d'engagements antérieurs

 7 donner – à une demande

suite *f.* (*de lettre*)
suivant (*adj.*)
suivant
 1 – avis
 2 – connaissement
 3 – votre désir
 4 – vos instructions

 5 – la liste ci-jointe
suivre
 1 – une affaire
 2 – les instructions
 3 à –
 4 (avec prière de) faire –
 5 comme suit
 6 lettre suit
 7 relations suivies
sujet à
 1 – des droits
 2 – la casse
superbénéfice *m.*
superdividende *m.*
supérette *f.*
supermarché *m.*
suppléer
 1 – au gage
 2 avoir à –
supplément *m.*
 1 – (*billet*)
 2 – à (*journal*)
 3 – à (*texte*)
 4 –s d'un ouvrage
 5 payer un –
supplémentaire
 1 crédit *m.* –

sugar...
 1 sugar campaign
 2 sugar cultivation
sufficiently
sufficient, adequate
continuation
 1 after-effects of the war
 2 further to (referring to, in further reference to) our letter of yesterday

 3 for the future
 4 as a consequence of which
 5 in consequence of, owing to, on account of
 6 owing to previous engagements, commitments
 7 to comply with a request

follower, continuation sheet
following
according to
 1 as per advice
 2 as per bill of lading
 3 – (in pursuance of) your wish
 4 as per (–, in accordance with) your instructions
 5 as per list enclosed
to follow
 1 – up a matter (closely)
 2 – the instructions
 3 to be continued
 4 please forward
 5 as follows
 6 letter to follow
 7 lasting relations
liable to
 1 subject (liable) to duty
 2 subject to breakage
surplus profit
surplus dividend
superette
supermarket
to make up
 1 to supplement the pledge
 2 to have to pay the deficiency
supplement
 1 extra fare
 2 – (to)
 3 – to
 4 –s to a work
 5 to pay extra
supplementary, additional
 1 additional (further) credit

353 / supporter

2 frais *m. pl.* –	2 extra charges
3 payement *m.* –	3 additional payment
supporter	to bear
– les frais	– the expenses
supposer	to suppose
il est permis de –	it may be assumed
supputer	to calculate, to reckon
– les frais	to reckon the expenses
sûr	safe
sur	on, upon
3 m – 6 m	3 m by 6 m
surabondance *f.*	redundancy
sur-arbitre *m.*	umpire
surassurance *f.*	overinsurance
surcapacité *f.*	over-capacity
surcapitalisation *f.*	overcapitalization
surcapitaliser	to overcapitalize
surcharge *f.* (*texte*)	alteration, correction
– (*charge*)	overloading
surcharger (*texte*)	to correct, to alter
1 – (*charger trop*)	1 to overload
2 – (*des employés*)	2 to overwork
3 – un timbre-poste	3 to surcharge a postage stamp
4 marché surchargé de...	4 market overloaded with
surchauffe (v. *conjoncture*)	
surcroît *m.*	increase
1 – de dépenses	1 additional expenditure
2 – de travail	2 extra work, excess of work
surélever (*prix*)	to force up
sur-emploi *m.*	over-full employment, over-employment
surenchère *f.*	higher bid; outbidding
faire une – sur qqn	to outbid
surenchérir	to bid higher than, to outbid
– (*prix*)	to rise in price
surenchérissement *m.*	higher bidding
– (*prix*)	further rise in price
surenchérisseur *m.*	outbidder
surestaries *f. pl.*	days of demurrage
–, frais *m. pl.* de –	demurrage
surestimation *f.*	overestimate
surestimer	to overestimate
sûreté *f.*	safety, surety
1 pour – d'une dette	1 as surety (security) for a debt
2 pour – du payement de...	2 for better security for the payment of...
3 pour plus de –	3 for the sake of safety
surévaluation *f.*	overvaluation

surévalué / 354

surévalué	overvalued
surfaire	
1 – qqn	1 to overcharge someone
2 – (*marchandise*)	2 to ask too much for
3 il surfait souvent	3 he often overcharges
4 cours surfaits	4 unduly high prices
surhausser (*prix*)	to raise, to force up
surmenage *m.*	overworking
surmener	to overwork
se –	to overstrain oneself, –
suroffre *f.*	higher bid
surpassé (*émission*)	oversubscribed
surpayer (*personne*)	to overpay
– (*chose*)	– for, to pay too much for
surplus *m.*	surplus
payer le –	to pay the balance
surpoids *m.*	excess weight
– (*réduction*)	draft
surprime *f.*	additional premium, extra premium
surpris, agréablement –	agreeably surprised
surprix *m.*	excess price
surproduction *f.*	overproduction
surprospérité *f.*	super-boom
sursaturer	to supersaturate
sursis *m.* de payement	respite of payment
sur-souscrit	oversubscribed
surtare *f.*	supertare
surtaxe *f.*	extra-charge
1 – (*taxe supplémentaire*)	1 fee, surtax
2 – aérienne	2 air mail fee
surveiller	to supervise
survendre	to overcharge for
survente *f.*	overcharge
survie *f.*	survival
1 assurance *f.* de –	1 contingent (survivorship) insurance
2 pension *f.* de –	2 survivors' pension
survivant *m.*	survivor
sus(dé)nommé, susdit, susmentionné	above-named, aforesaid, aforementioned
suspendre ses payements	to suspend (stop) one's payments
suspens, en –	in suspense, in abeyance
1 écritures *f. pl.* en –	1 items in suspense
2 l'affaire est encore en –	2 this matter is still held over, still in abeyance
3 tenir en –	3 to hold over, to hold in abeyance

355 / suspension

suspension *f.* | suspension (stoppage) of payment
swap, opération – | swap operation
swing *m.* (*accord bilatéral*) | swing, credit margin
switch (opération) | switched transaction
sympathie *f.* | sympathy
  en – avec (*bourse*) | in – with
syndic *m.* | syndic
  – de faillite | trustee (receiver) in bankruptcy
syndical | syndicate...
  1 – (*mouv. ouvrier*) | 1 trade union...
  2 mouvement – | 2 trade union movement –
  3 opérations –es | 3 syndicate transactions
  4 participations –es | 4 syndicate participations
syndicat *m.* | syndicate
  1 – de banquiers | 1 – of bankers, banking syndicate
  2 – de faillite | 2 trusteeship
  3 – de garantie (*émission*) | 3 underwriting –, underwriters
  4 – d'émission | 4 issue –
  5 – de placement (*émission*) | 5 selling group
  6 – de prise ferme (*émission*) | 6 underwriting – (group)
  7 – d'initiative | 7 association for the encouragement of touring
  8 – financier | 8 financial –
  9 – houiller | 9 coal –
  10 – ouvrier | 10 trade union
  11 – patronal | 11 employers' federation
  12 – professionnel | 12 trade association
syndicataire *m.* | underwriter
syndiqué *m.* | trade unionist
syndiquer, se – (*émission*) | to syndicate, to form a syndicate
  se – (*ouvriers*) | to form a trade union
système *m.* | system
  1 – comptable | 1 accounting –
  2 – de clearing | 2 clearing –
  3 – douanier | 3 customs –
  4 – économique | 4 economic –
  5 – fiscal | 5 fiscal
  6 – monétaire | 6 monetary –
  7 suivant le –... | 7 on the... –
  8 employer un – | 8 to follow a –

T

table *f.* (*tableau*) | table
  1 – alphabétique (*livre*) | 1 index
  2 – de logarithmes | 2 logarithmic –s
  3 – de mortalité | 3 mortality –
  4 – de multiplication | 4 multiplication –
  5 – de parités | 5 parity –, – of par values
  6 – des matières | 6 – of contents
  7 – d'intérêts | 7 interest –

tableau / 356

tableau *m.*
  1 – comparatif
  2 – d'amortissement
  3 – d'avancement
  4 – de conversion
  5 – de distribution
  6 – de roulement
  7 – des tirages
  8 – récapitulatif
  9 – synoptique
  10 sous forme de –
  11 ainsi qu'il ressort (apparait) du – ci-après
tabulaire
  livres *m. pl.* –s
tabulateur *m.* (*mach. à écrire*)
tabulatrice *f.*
tacite
  1 consentement *m.* –
  2 convention *f.* –
talon *m.* (*chèque*)
  1 – (*titre*)
  2 contre (sur) remise du –
tampon *m.*
tangible
  valeurs *f. pl.* –s
tant *m.* **pour cent**
tantième *m.*
  1 – des administrateurs
  2 payement *m.* du –
  3 allouer un –
taper (à la machine)

tard
  au plus – le...
tardif
  fruits –s
tare *f.*
  1 – conventionnelle, – d'usage
  2 – estimée
  3 – extra
  4 – légale
  5 – moyenne
  6 – réduite
  7 – réelle
tare *f.* **de caisse**

tarer

tarif *m.*
  1 – à échelons, à paliers

table
  1 comparative –
  2 redemption –
  3 promotion list
  4 conversion –
  5 switch board
  6 roster
  7 plan of drawing
  8 recapitulative –, summary
  9 synoptic –
  10 in tabular form
  11 as the following – shows, as may be seen on the following –
tabular
  – books
tabulator
tabulator
tacit
  1 – consent
  2 – agreement
counterfoil, (*Amer.*) **stub**
  1 talon
  2 against delivery of the talon
pad, inking pad
tangible
  – assets
percentage
percentage, share, quote
  1 director's percentages of profit
  2 percentage distribution
  3 to allow a percentage of profits
to type, to typewrite

late
  not –r than, at the –st
late
  – fruit
tare
  1 customary –
  2 estimated –
  3 super –
  4 – assumed by the customs
  5 average –
  6 reduced –
  7 real –, actual –
shortage in the cash

to tare

tariff, rate
  1 graduated tariff

357 / tarifaire

2 – à forfait
3 – d'annonces
4 – de faveur
5 – dégressif
6 – de nuit
7 – de recouvrement (d'encaisse- [ments])
8 – des chemins de fer
9 – des imprimés
10 – des marchandises
11 – différentiel
12 – douanier ; – des douanes
13 – d'urgence (*télégr.*)
14 – en vigueur
15 – extérieur commun
16 – intérieur
17 – maximum
18 – minimum
19 – ordinaire (*télégr.*)
20 – postal
21 – préférentiel
22 – progressif
23 – réduit
24 – spécial
25 – uniforme
26 selon –
27 guerre *f.* des –s
28 majoration *f.* (relèvement *m.*) des –s
29 réduction *f.* du –
tarifaire
accord *m.* –
tarifer
tarification *f.*
tassement *m.* (*actions*)
tasser, se – de... à... (*actions*)
taudis *m.*
1 lutte *f.* contre les –
2 suppression *f.* des –
taux *m.*
1 – à vue
2 – d'assurance
3 – d'attribution
4 – de capitalisation
5 – de (du) change
6 – de conversion
7 – de fret
8 – de la natalité
9 – de la prime (*assur.*)
10 – de l'argent
11 – d'émission
12 – de réescompte
13 – d'escompte
14 – d'escompte hors banque, – privé

2 tariff as by contract
3 advertisement rates
4 preferential tariff
5 decreasing tariff
6 night charge
7 collection tariff
8 railway rates
9 printed-paper rate
10 goods rates
11 differential tariff
12 customs tariff
13 urgent rate
14 tariff in force
15 common external –
16 inland rate
17 maximum tariff
18 minimum tariff
19 ordinary rate
20 postal rates
21 preferential tariff
22 tariff based on a sliding scale
23 reduced rate
24 special rate
25 standard rate
26 according to tariff, as per tariff
27 tariff war
28 raising of tariffs
29 reduction of the tariff
tariff...
– agreement
to tariff
tariffing
setback
to have a setback from... to...
slum, hovel
1 slum-clearance campaign
2 elimination of slums
rate
1 demand –, sight –
2 –s of insurance
3 price of allotment
4 – of capitalization, yield
5 (rate of) exchange
6 – of conversion
7 freight –
8 birth –
9 – of premium
10 money –s
11 issue price, – of price
12 rediscount –
13 discount –, – of discount
14 market – of discount, private – of discount

taxateur / 358

15 – d'escompte officiel	15 bank – of discount
16 – d'intérêt	16 – of interest
17 – du déport	17 backwardation –
18 – du report	18 contango –, carry-over –, – of continuation
19 – d'usure (*dépréciation*)	19 – of wear and tear
20 – ferme	20 firm –
21 – forfaitaire	21 through –
22 – légal	22 legal –
23 – maximum	23 maximum –
24 – minimum	24 minimum –
25 – officiel (voir – *d'escompte*)	
26 – privé (voir – *d'escompte*)	
27 – uniforme	27 flat rate
28 à – différentiels constants	28 at fixed differential –
29 à – différentiels variables	29 at variable differential –
30 à – progressif, à intérêts croissants	30 with graduated interest
31 au – de...	31 at the – of...
32 à – réciproques	32 at reciprocal –
taxateur *m.*	appraiser, valuer
taxation *f.*	assessment
taxation *f.* des frais d'un procès	taxation of the costs of an action
taxe *f.* (voir aussi *impôt, contributions*)	duty, tax
1 – (*prix officiellement fixé*)	1 charge
2 – à l'exportation	2 tax on exports
3 – consulaire	3 consular fee
4 – de compensation (*France*)	4 compensation duties
5 – de consommation	5 consumption tax
6 – de séjour	6 visitors' tax
7 – de transmission (*titres*)	7 transfer duty
8 – de transmission	8 sales tax
9 – de luxe	9 luxury tax
10 – professionnelle	10 trade income tax
11 – supplémentaire	11 supplementary charge
12 – sur le chiffre d'affaires	12 turnover tax
13 – sur le revenu	13 income tax
14 – sur les spectacles	14 entertainment tax
15 – sur la valeur ajoutée	15 value-added tax, tax on value [added
taxer (*mettre un impôt*)	to assess, to tax
taxer (*des denrées*)	to fix the prices
– les dépens d'un procès	to tax the costs of an action
taxi *m.*	taxi, cab
technique *f.* de vente	selling technique
tel quel	tel quel, tale quale
télégramme *m.*	telegram
1 – conçu en ces termes, – ainsi conçu	1 – running as follows
2 – adressé poste restante (GP.)	2 – addressed poste restante

359 / télégraphe

3 – adressé télégraphe restant (TR.)

4 – à faire suivre (FS.)
5 – avec accusé de réception postal (PCP.)
6 – avec accusé de réception télégraphique (PC.)
7 – avec collationnement (TC.)
8 – avec réponse payée (RP.)
9 – chiffré
10 – codé
11 – de luxe (de félicitations) (Lx.)

12 – de presse
13 – de service
14 – différé
15 – en langage clair
16 – en langage convenu
17 – intérieur
18 – international
19 – lettre (LT.)
20 – multiple, – à adresses multiples (TM.)
21 – mutilé, tronqué
22 – ordinaire
23 – privé
24 – urgent (D.)

25 – téléphoné
26 échange *m.* de –s
27 échanger des –s
28 envoyer (expédier) un –
29 transmettre un – par téléphone

télégraphe *m.*
– restant
télégraphie *f.*
– sans fil
télégraphier
télégraphique
1 adresse *f.* –

2 bureau *m.* –
3 clé *f.* –
4 utiliser une –
5 communication *f.*
6 cotation *f.* –
7 cours *m.* –
8 mandat poste *m.* –
9 offre *f.* –
10 ordre *m.* –
11 remise *f.* –

3 – addressed telegraphe restant

4 – to follow the addressee
5 – with notice of delivery by post

6 – with notice of delivery by telegraph
7 with repetition, repetition-paid –
8 reply-paid –, prepaid-reply –
9 cipher –
10 code –
11 greetings –

12 press –
13 service –
14 deferred –
15 – in plain language
16 – in code
17 inland –
18 foreign –
19 letter –
20 multiple –, multiple-address –

21 mutilated –
22 ordinary –
23 private –
24 urgent –

25 telephoned –, – by telephone
26 exchange of –s
27 to exchange –s
28 to send a –
29 to telephone a wire, to tender a – by telephone

telegraph
– restant, to be called for
telegraphy
wireless –
to telegraph, to wire
telegraphic
1 – address

2 telegraph office
3 – key
4 to make use of a –
5 – message
6 tape quotation
7 tape price
8 – money order
9 – offer
10 cable order
11 – tranfer, cable transfer

télégraphiquement / 360

12 réponse *f.* –
13 tarif *m.* –

14 voie –, par voie –
télégraphiquement
télégraphiste *m.*
téléphone *m.*
 1 abonné *m.* au –
 2 bureau *m.* du –
 3 (bureau) central *m.* du –
 4 coup *m.* de –
 5 indicateur *m.* du –
 6 numéro *m.* de –, d'appel

 7 appeler au –
 8 on vous appelle au –
 9 toucher par – (voir *toucher*)
téléphoner
 – à
téléphonique

 1 appel *m.* –
 2 appareil *m.* –

 3 communication *f.* –
 4 entretien –
 5 ligne *f.* –
 6 réseau *m.* –
téléphoniquement
téléphoniste *m.* et *f.*

téléscripteur *m.*, **télex** *m.*
 1 abonné *m.* au réseau télex
 2 relié au réseau (service) télex (voir aussi *numéro d'appel*)
 3 par –
tempérament
 1 achat *m.* à –
 2 affaire *f.* à –

 3 crédit *m.* à –

 4 financement *m.* des achats à –
 5 marché *m.* à –

 6 vente *f.* à –

 7 contrat *m.* de vente à –

 8 contrôle *m.* sur les ventes à –
 9 restrictions *f. pl.* des ventes à –

12 reply by wire
13 – rate

14 by wire, telegraphically
telegraphically, by wire
telegraphist, (*Amer.***) telegrapher**
telephone
 1 – subscriber
 2 – office
 3 – exchange
 4 (telephone) call
 5 – directory
 6 – number

 7 to ring up, to call to the –
 8 you are wanted on the –

to telephone
 to ring up, to phone to
telephonic

 1 telephone call
 2 telephone

 3 call, telephone message
 4 – talk, conversation
 5 telephone line
 6 telephone network, system
telephonically, by phone
telephonist, (telephone) operator

telex, teleprinter
 1 telex subscriber
 2 on the teleprinter (network)

 3 by –, telexed

 1 instalment buying, hire purchase
 2 instalment transaction

 3 instalment credit, hire purchase credit
 4 hire purchase financing
 5 instalment transaction

 6 instalment sale, sale on the instalment (hire purchase) plan
 7 hire purchase (instalment) agreement
 8 hire purchase control
 9 hire purchase restrictions

361 / tempérer

10 système *m.* des ventes à –	10 instalment system, instalment plan
11 acheter à –	11 to buy on the instalment plan
tempérer (*economie*)	**to dampen**
temps *m.*	**time**
1 – (*cond. atmosphér.*)	1 weather conditions
2 à –	2 in –
3 ces derniers –	3 latterly
4 depuis quelque –	4 for some –
5 en (à) tout –	5 at any –
6 en – utile, voulu	6 in due course
7 épargne *f.* de –	7 saving of –
8 perte *f.* de –	8 loss of –
9 prendre beaucoup de –	9 it takes up (occupies) much –
10 si le – le permet	10 weather permitting
tenants et aboutissants *pl.*	**adjacent parts**
tendance *f.*	**tendency**
1 – du marché (voir aussi *marché*)	1 trend (–) of the market
2 – à la baisse	2 downward –, bearish –, (trend)
3 – à la hausse, ascensionnelle, ascendante	3 upward –, bullish –, (trend)
4 – faible	4 dull –
5 – ferme	5 firm –
6 avoir une – à la baisse	6 to show a falling (downward) –
teneur *f.*	**contents, terms**
1 – (*d'un corps*) en...	1 degree, content of...
2 – d'un contrat	2 wording (terms) of a contract
teneur *m.* de livres	**bookkeeper**
teneur *m.* de marché	**stockjobber**
tenir (v. aussi *tenu*)	**to keep**
1 – à (+ *infinitif*)	1 to desire, to make a point of...
2 – à ce que...	2 to be anxious (insistent) that...
3 – à (*une maison*)	3 to be contiguous (adjacent) to
4 – à bail	4 to hold on lease
5 – à jour	5 – up to date
6 – à la disposition de...	6 to hold at the disposal of...
7 – un article	7 – an article, to deal in an article
8 – une assemblée	8 to hold a meeting
9 – la caisse	9 – the cash
10 – un commerce de...	10 to deal (trade) in...
11 – un compte chez...	11 – an account with...
12 – compte de...	12 to take into account
13 – les livres à jour	13 – books up to date
14 – debout ! (*caisse*)	14 keep upright !
15 savoir à quoi s'en –	15 to know where one stands
16 se – ferme	16 – firm
17 se – aux instructions	17 to comply with instructions

tension / 362

tension *f.*
  1 −s sur le marché du travail
  2 − sociale
tenu
  1 être très −
  2 être − à (de)...
  3 être bien − (*action*)
  4 valeurs −es
tenue *f.*
  1 − des livres (v. *livre*)
  2 − (*disposition* : *marché*)
  3 − (*fermeté*)
  4 la bonne − (*bourse*)
  5 garder une − ferme
tenue *f.* (*toilette*)
  1 − de soirée
  2 − de ville (sombre)

terme *m.* (*mot*)
  1 −s d'un contrat
  2 − technique
  3 aux −s de
terme *m.* (*loyer de 3 mois*)
  payer son −
terme *m.* (*durée*) (voir aussi *achat, crédit, dépôt, devises, marché, vente*)
  1 − de bail
  2 − d'échéance (*effet*)
  3 − de grâce
  4 − de liquidation
  5 − de livraison
  6 − de payement
  7 − de préavis
  8 − de rigueur, − fatal
  9 à − échu
  10 à − fixe
  11 à court −
  12 à long −
  13 à moyen −

  14 le − échoit
  15 dollars *m. pl.* à −
  16 payements *m.* à (par) −s
  17 prolongation *f.* de −

  18 acheter à − (*crédit*)
  19 acheter à − (*bourse*)

  20 fixer un −
  21 payer en −s

  22 vendre à − (*crédit*)

pressure, tension
  1 pressures on the labo(u)r market
  2 social strains, social tension

  1 to be much pressed with business
  2 to be bound to...
  3 to be firm, hard
  4 firm stocks
bearing

  2 − tone
  3 firmness
  4 the good tone
  5 to maintain a firm tone
dress
  1 evening −
  2 morning −, − informal, (*Amer.*) street −
term
  1 the −s (wording) of a contract
  2 technical −
  3 by (under) the −s of
quarter's rent
  to pay the −
term

  1 − of a lease
  2 time of payment, currency, −
  3 time to pay
  4 date of settlement
  5 − of delivery
  6 − of payment
  7 − of notice
  8 final date, latest date
  9 on expiration of the −
  10 at a fixed time
  11 short-term..., short-dated, short
  12 long-term..., long-dated, long
  13 medium-term...

  14 the − expires
  15 forward dollars
  16 payment by instalments
  17 extension of time

  18 to buy on credit
  19 to buy for the settlement, for the **account**
  20 to fix a time
  21 to pay by instalments

  22 to sell on credit

23 vendre à – (*bourse*)

termes *m. pl.* de l'(d')échange

terminus *m.*
terrain *m.*
  1 – à bâtir
  2 – bâti
testament *m.*
  1 par –
  2 faire son –
testamentaire
  exécuteur *m.* –
testateur *m.*
testatrice *f.*
tête *f.*
  1 à la – de
  2 en – de (*page*)
  3 – de ligne (*ch. de fer*)
  4 20 –s de bétail
  5 par – d'habitant
  6 consommation *f.* de... calculée par – d'habitant
texte *m.* (voir *contenu*)
textile, industrie *f.* –, le –
textuel(lement)
thésaurisation *f.*
thésauriser
thésauriseur *m.*
ticker *m.*
ticket *m.*
  1 – d'entrée
  2 – de quai
tiers
  1 un –, une tierce personne
  2 – détenteur
  3 – porteur (*effet*)
  4 – possesseur
  5 pour compte d'un –

  6 fonds *m. pl.* de –
  7 risque *m.* du recours de –
timbrage *m.*
timbre *m.*
  1 – à dater, – dateur
  2 – adhésif, – mobile
  3 – de dimension

  4 – d'épargne
  5 – (de) quittance
  6 – de réception
  7 – de rabais

---

23 (*commod.*) to sell forward (*securities*) to sell for the settlement for the account

terms of trade

terminus, terminal point
land, ground
  1 building site, plot
  2 built on site, land
will
  1 by –
  2 to make one's –
testamentary
  executor of a will
testator
testatrix
head
  1 at the – of
  2 at the – (top) of
  3 terminus, terminal station
  4 20 – of cattle
  5 per – of population, per capita
  6 per capita consumption of...

text, wording
textile industry
textual, word for word
hoarding (of money)
to hoard (money)
hoarder
ticker
ticket
  1 –
  2 platform –
third
  1 – party, – person
  2 – holder
  3 second endorser
  4 – owner
  5 for account of a – party, of – parties

  6 – party funds
  7 – party risk
stamping
stamp
  1 date –, dater
  2 affixed, adhesive –
  3 – (according to size)

  4 savings bank –
  5 receipt –
  6 reception –
  7 trading (discount) –

timbré / 364

8 – fiscal
9 – non utilisé
10 – poste
11 – sec
12 – taxe
13 – vignette
14 exempt du –
15 soumis au droit de –
16 bureau *m.* du –
17 droit *m.* de –
18 „emplacement *m.* du – poste"
19 frais *m. pl.* de –
20 loi *f.* sur le –
21 apposer un – poste

22 oblitérer un –

timbré
1 document –
2 papier –
timbrer
– une lettre
tirage *m.* (*au sort*)
1 –s annuels
2 – au sort
3 amortissable par –
4 sorti au –
5 jour *m.* de –
6 liste *f.* des –s
7 tableau *m.* des –s
tirage *m.* (*effet*)
1 votre – sur nous
2 avis *m.* d'un – sur...
3 avis *m.* de – par chèque sur...

4 droits *m. pl.* de –s
5 utilisable au moyen de –s
tiré *m.*
tiré à part *m.*
tirer
1 – à courte échéance

2 – à vue

3 – au sort
4 – en l'air
5 – un chèque
6 – une traite sur

7 – sur

tireur *m.*
„**tirez**" (*porte*)

8 revenue –
9 unused –
10 postage –
11 impressed (embossed) –
12 postage due –
13 poster –
14 exempt from – duty
15 liable to – duty
16 – office
17 – duty
18 affix – here
19 – charges
20 – act
21 to affix a –

22 to obliterate (cancel) a –

stamped
1 – document
2 – paper
to stamp
– a letter
drawing
1 annual –s
2 prize –
3 redeemable by –
4 drawn
5 – day
6 list of –s
7 plan of –
drawing, draft, making out
1 your drawing on us
2 advice of a drawing upon...
3 advice of cheque (check) drawn on...

4 drawing rights
5 available by drawings
drawee
off-print
to draw
1 – at short sight

2 – at sight

3 – lots
4 to kite
5 – a cheque (check)
6 – a bill on

7 – on

drawer, (*Amer.*) **maker**
pull

titre m. (*monnaie*) | **fineness**
titre

1 à – de payement
2 à – de prêt
3 à – de réciprocité
4 à – d'essai
5 à – d'information
6 à – gracieux, gratuit
7 à – onéreux
8 à – provisoire
9 à quelque – que ce soit
10 nommer directeur à – personnel

1 in payment
2 as loan
3 reciprocally
4 on approval
5 by way of information
6 gratis, free of charge
7 for a consideration, for value
8 provisionally
9 on any ground whatsoever
10 to grant the honorary rank of...

titre m. (*certificat, droit*) | **certificate**

1 – au porteur
2 – authentique
3 – d'action
4 – de créance
5 – définitif (v. *échanger*)
6 – de possession
7 – de propriété
8 – de rente
9 – d'obligation
10 – multiple
11 – nominatif
12 – paré
13 – provisoire (v. *échanger*)

14 – unitaire
15 en fait de meubles possession vaut –

1 bearer –
2 valid title
3 share –
4 proof of debt
5 definite (definitive) –
6 possession title
7 deed of property, title
8 government bond
9 debenture bond
10 multiple –
11 registered –
12 executory deed
13 scrip

14 – for a single share
15 in respect of movables possession is title

titres (voir aussi *traiter, valeurs*) | **stocks, shares, securities**

1 – activement travaillés
2 – adirés
3 – à lots
4 – à revenu fixe (voir *valeurs*)
5 – à revenu variable (voir *valeurs*)
6 – à terme
7 – au comptant
8 – au porteur
9 – contre espèces
10 – de bonne livraison
11 – de père de famille, – de tout repos
12 – de placement
13 – de premier ordre
14 – de spéculation
15 – déposés en cautionnement pour compte propre
16 – frappés d'opposition
17 – libérés

1 active securities, stocks actively dealt in (traded)
2 lost certificates
3 prize bonds

6 forward securities [market
7 securities quoted on the spot
8 bearer securities
9 shares for cash
10 good delivery stock
11 safe investments
12 investment securities
13 first rate securities, blue chips
14 speculative securities
15 securities pledged as guarantee for own account
16 stopped bonds
17 fully paid stock

titres / 366

18 – nominatifs	18 registered stock
19 – remis en nantissement	19 securities lodged as collateral
20 achat et vente de –	20 purchase and sale of stock
21 avances *f. pl.* sur –	21 advances on securities
22 compte *m.* –	22 stock account
23 confection *f.* de –	23 printing of certificates
24 délivrance *f.* des –	24 delivery of the certificates
25 dépôt *m.* de –	25 deposit of securities
26 dépôt *m.* de – en nantissement	26 securities lodged as collateral
27 dépôt *m.* de – pour (en vue de) l'assemblée	27 depositing of securities, with a view to attending the meeting
28 détenteur *m.* (possesseur *m.*) de –	28 stockholder
29 échange *m.* de –	29 exchange of securities
30 échange *m.* titre pour titre	30 exchange share for share, one for one
31 estampillage *m.* de –	31 stamping of –
32 garde *f.* de –	32 safe custody of securities
33 levée *f.* des – (*terme*)	33 taking up of stock
34 livraison *f.* des – (*terme*)	34 delivery of stock
35 nantissement *m.* de –	35 pledging of securities
36 portefeuille *m.* de –	36 security holding
37 prêt *m.* sur –	37 loan on stock
38 réfection *f.* de –	38 reprinting of certificates
39 répartition *f.* de –	39 allotment of securities
40 service *m.* des –	40 securities department
41 transfert *m.* de –	41 transfer of securities
42 coter par titre	42 to quote per unit
43 délivrer les –	43 to deliver the certificates
44 demander livraison des – (*terme*)	44 to require delivery of stock
45 déposer des – chez...	45 to deposit securities with
46 déposer des – au siège de la société	46 to deposit securities with (at) the head office of the company
47 échanger les certificats provisoires contre les – définitifs	47 to exchange the scrips for the definitive shares or bonds
48 lever des –, prendre livraison des –	48 to take up stock
49 livrer des –, faire livraison des –	49 to deliver (make delivery of) stock
50 placer des – sous un dossier (dépôt)	50 to lodge securities into a deposit

367 / titulaire

51 prendre livraison des – (voir *lever des* –)
52 prêter sur –
53 retirer des – d'un dossier (dépôt)
54 vendre des – à découvert
titulaire *m.*
1 – d'une action
2 – d'un compte
3 – d'une fonction
4 – d'un passeport
tolérance *f.*

1 – (monnayage)
2 – de 10 % en plus ou en moins

tomber
1 – d'accord
2 – un samedi
3 – dans le domaine public

4 „ne pas laisser –''
tombola *f.*
tonnage *m.*

1 certificat *m.* de –
2 droit *m.* de –
tonne *f.*
1 – de jauge
2 – métrique
tonneau *m.*
1 – (*poids*)
2 – d'affrètement (– de portée en lourd)
3 – de registre, – registre, – de jauge
tontine *f.*
total *adj.*
1 montant –
2 perte –e (voir *perte*)
3 recette –e
4 vente –e
total *m.*
1 – des recettes
2 – général, global
3 au (en) –
4 se monter en – à...
totalement
totalisateur *m.*
totaliser
totalité *f.*
touche *f.*
toucher
1 – ses appointements
2 – un chèque

52 to lend on stock
53 to withdraw – from a deposit
54 to sell a bear, to sell short
holder
1 – of a share
2 – of an account
3 occupant of an office
4 bearer of a passport
tolerance

1 remedy, –
2 – of 10 % more or 10 % less

to fall
1 to come to an agreement
2 – on a Saturday
3 to become public property, (*book*) to be out of its copyright
4 don't drop, not to be dropped
lottery (tombola)
tonnage

1 – certificate, bill of –
2 – duty
ton
1 measurement –
2 metric –
barrel
1 ton
2 freight ton, shipping ton

3 register ton
tontine
total
1 – (aggregate) amount

3 gross receipts
4 complete sale
the whole
1 – of the receipts
2 grand total
3 in all, in the aggregate
4 to total..., to total up to...
totally
totalizator
to totalize, to sum up
totality, whole
key
to receive, to draw
1 to draw one's salary
2 to cash a cheque (check)

tourisme / 368

  3 – un intérêt de...
  4 – un traitement fixe
  5 – à un port
  6 – qqn par téléphone
  7 le plus durement touché
  8 profondément touché
  9 ne pas –
tourisme *m.*
touriste *m.*
touristique
  1 franc *m.* – (touriste)
  2 trafic *m.* –
tourner s'il vous plaît

tout
  1 en – ou en partie
  2 en –es coupures
  3 (pendant) –e l'année

tradition *f.* (*actions*)
traduction *f.*
  1 – de l'allemand en français

  2 – exacte
traducteur *m.*
  – assermenté
traduire
  1 – de... en...
  2 se – par
trafic *m.* (*négoce*)
trafic *m.* (voir aussi *circulation, mouvement*)
  1 – aérien (postal)
  2 – commercial
  3 – (des) marchandises
  4 – (des) paiements
  5 – (des) voyageurs
  6 – de transit
  7 – frontalier
  8 – postal
  9 – routier
  10 – touristique
trafiquant *m.*
  1 – (*pej.*), trafiqueur
  2 – du marché noir
trafiquer
  – (*péjor.*)
train *m.*
  1 – de 8 heures
  2 – de marchandises
  3 – de voyageurs
  4 – direct
  5 – (d')ouvrier(s)

  3 to receive an interest of...
  4 to draw a fixed salary
  5 to touch at a port
  6 to contact (reach) someone by te-[lephone
  7 the most affected
  8 deeply touched
  9 do not touch
touring
tourist
tourist
  1 – franc
  2 – traffic
please turn over

whole
  1 in – or in part
  2 in any denomination
  3 throughout the year, all the year round
tradition, delivery
translation
  1 – from German into French

  2 faithful –
translator
  sworn –
to translate
  1 – from... into...
  2 to show...
trade
traffic

  1 air (mail) –
  2 commercial –
  3 goods –, (*Amer.*) freight –
  4 payments
  5 passenger –
  6 transit –
  7 frontier –
  8 postal –
  9 road –
  10 tourist –
trader
  1 trafficker
  2 black marketeer
to trade
  to traffic (in)
train
  1 the eight o'clock –
  2 goods –, (*Amer.*) freight –
  3 passenger –
  4 through –, non-stop –
  5 workmen's –

369 / traite

6 – express
7 – omnibus
8 dans le –
9 par le –
10 ce – ne circule pas le...
11 changer de –
12 manquer le –
13 prendre le – pour

traite *f.* (voir aussi *effet, lettre de change, papier*)
1 – à courte échéance
2 – à date fixe
3 – à délai de date
4 – à délai de vue
5 – à longue échéance
6 – à trente jours
7 – à trois mois
8 – à vue
9 – avisée
10 – documentaire

11 – domiciliée

12 – en foire
13 – en l'air
14 – en plusieurs exemplaires

15 – en souffrance
16 – libre

17 – sur l'extérieur
18 – sur l'intérieur
19 la – échoit le 15 janvier

20 avis *m.* de –

21 exemplaire *m.* de –

22 terme *m.* (d'échéance) d'une –
23 accepter une –
24 donner avis d'une –
25 encaisser une –
26 endosser une –
27 envoyer une – à l'encaissement
28 escompter une –

29 faire bon accueil à (honorer) une –

30 faire protester une –
31 négocier une –

6 express –
7 stopping –, omnibus –
8 on the –
9 by –
10 this – doesn't run on...
11 to change –s
12 to miss one's –
13 to take the – for

draft

1 short bill
2 day bill
3 bill after date, time –
4 bill after sight
5 long bill
6 bill at 30 days
7 three month's bill
8 sight –, – at sight
9 advised –
10 documentary –, bill with documents attached

11 domiciled –

12 fair bill
13 kite, windmill
14 bills in a set

15 bill in suspense
16 clean bill

17 foreign –
18 inland –
19 the – falls due on January 15th

20 advice of –

21 via

22 term, tenor, currency
23 to accept a –
24 to advise a –
25 to collect a bill
26 to endorse a bill
27 to send a bill for collection
28 to discount a –

29 to hono(u)r a –

30 to have a bill protested
31 to negotiate a –

traité / 370

32 présenter une – à l'acceptation

33 présenter une – à l'encaissement
34 présenter une – au payement
35 recouvrer une – (voir *encaisser*)
36 retourner une –
37 tirer une (faire) – sur...

traité *m.*
1 – de commerce
2 – de compensation
3 – de réciprocité

4 – de Rome
traitement *m.*
traitement *m.* (*salaire*)
1 – de base
2 – fixe
3 – initial
4 retenue *f.* sur le –
5 toucher un – fixe
traiter
1 – avec
2 – des affaires
3 – un marché
4 – des opérations de banque
5 se – à...
6 il s'est traité peu d'affaires en...

7 titres traités
tramp *m.*

tramping *m.*
navire *m.* de –
tranche *f.*
1 – (*emprunt*)
2 par – de 1000 francs

transaction *f.* (*compromis*)
accepter (conclure) une –

transaction *f.* (voir aussi *opération*)
1 –s annuelles
2 –s commerciales

3 –s de banque, bancaires

4 –s de bourse

5 –s en bourse
6 –s de compensation
7 –s de réciprocité
8 peu de –s sur...

32 to present a – for acceptance

33 to present a – for collection
34 to present a – for payment
35
36 to return a –
37 to draw a bill on...

treaty
1 commercial –
2 compensation agreement
3 reciprocity agreement

4 Rome –
treatment
salary
1 basic –
2 fixed –
3 initial –
4 retention on (reduction from) wages
5 to draw a fixed –

1 to deal (transact) with
2 to transact business
3 to transact a business, a bargain
4 to transact banking business
5 to be dealt in (sold) at...
6 transactions in... are few

7 securities dealt in
tramp (steamer)

tramping
tramp
portion
1 portion, instalment
2 per – of 1000 francs, for each 1000 francs

compromise, arrangement
to agree to a compromise

transaction, business, dealing
1 annual turnover
2 commercial (business) transactions

3 banking business, banking transactions

4 exchange business, dealings in stocks and shares

5 transactions on Change
6 compensation transactions
7 reciprocity transactions
8 few dealings (transactions) in...

9 il y avait de nombreuses –s en...

10 sans –s
transbordement *m.*
1 – non autorisé
2 frais *m. pl.* de –
transborder (v. aussi *allège*)
transcrire
– (*compt.*)
transférable
transférer
1 – des actions
2 – un article de... à...
3 – un commerce à...
4 – son domicile
5 – la propriété
6 – le siège à ...
transfert *m.*
1 –s (câble et courrier)

2 – d'actions
3 – de capitaux

4 – de créances
5 – de devises
6 – de domicile
7 – de propriété
8 – dans les livres, comptes
9 – du siège social à ...

10 – télégraphique

11 accord *m.* sur les –s
12 autorisation *f.* de – (*créd. docum.*)
13 droit *m.* de – (*titres*)
14 opérations *f. pl.* de –
15 registre *m.* des –s (*actions*)
transformation *f.*
1 fermé pour cause de –
2 entreprise *f.* de –
transformer
– en société anonyme

transit *m.*
1 acquit *m.* de –
2 commerce *m.* de –
3 droits *m. pl.* de –
4 interdiction *f.* de –
5 liste *f.* de –
6 marchandises *f. pl.* de –
7 port *m.* de –
8 trafic *m.* de –
9 envoyer en –

9 much business was done in..., in... dealings were frequent
10 without dealings, transactions
trans(s)hipment
1 – not permitted
2 – charges
to trans(s)hip
to copy, to transcribe
to post
transferable
to transfer
1 shares
2 – an item from... to...
3 to remove a business to...
4 to change one's residence
5 – property
6 – the seat (registered office) to...
transfer
1 – (telegraphic and mail)

2 – of shares
3 – of capital

4 – of debts
5 currency –
6 change of one's residence
7 – of property
8 – in the books, in the accounts
9 – of the registered office to...

10 telegraphic (cable) –

11 – agreement
12 authority to –
13 – duty
14 – business
15 – register
transformation
1 closed for alterations
2 processing enterprise
to transform, to change
to convert (turn) into a limited company
transit
1 – bond
2 – trade
3 – dues, – duties
4 prohibition of –
5 – list
6 – goods
7 – port
8 – traffic
9 to forward in through freight

transitaire / 372

transitaire
transitaire *m.*
transiter
– des marchandises
transitoire
période *f.* –
translation *f.*
– de propriété
transmettre
1 – (*faire parvenir*)
2 – un ordre
3 – une propriété
4 – par (voie d') endossement
transmissible
transmission *f.*
1 – (*Com. L/C*)
2 – de câbles ou telex
3 – de propriété
4 – par endossement
5 taxe *f.* de – (*titres*)
transport *m.*
1 – aérien

2 – de marchandises
3 – fluvial
4 – par eau

5 – par route, – routier

6 – par terre, – terrestre
7 – par voie ferrée, par chemin de fer
8 – par voiture
9 – effectué par l'entreprise pour son propre compte
10 assurance *f.* contre les risques du –
11 contrat *m.* de –
12 entrepreneur *m.* de –
13 entreprise *f.* de –

14 frais *m. pl.* de –

15 mode *m.* de –
16 moyens *m. pl.* de –
17 risques *m. pl.* de –
18 société *f.* de –
19 tarifs *m. pl.* de –
transport *m.* (*cession*)
transport *m.* (*contrepassement*)
transporter
1 – (*céder*)
2 – (*contrepasser*)
transporteur *m.*

transit
forwarding agent
to pass in transit
to pass goods in transit
transitory
– (transition) period
transfer, conveyance
transfer (conveyance) of property
to transmit
1 –, to pass
2 – (send) an order
3 to transfer a property
4 to transfer by endorsement
transferable
transmission
1 –
2 – of cables or telex
3 conveyance (transfer) of property
4 transfer by endorsement
5 transfer duty
transport, conveyance
1 carriage by air

2 goods traffic, freight traffic
3 river transport
4 carriage by water, water carriage

5 road transport

6 land carriage
7 railway carriage, transport by rail

8 cartage
9 – effected by the enterprise for its own account
10 transport insurance
11 contract of carriage
12 cartage contractor
13 cartage contractors

14 transport charges

15 mode of conveyance
16 means of conveyance
17 transport risks
18 transport company
19 fares
transfer
transfer
to transport, to convey
1 to transfer, to make over
2 to transfer
carrier

transposition f. (chiffres)
transposer des chiffres
travail m.
1 – administratif
2 – à domicile
3 – à forfait
4 – à la chaîne

5 – à la machine
6 – à la main
7 – à la pièce, – aux pièces, – à la tâche
8 – à l'entreprise
9 – à temps partiel
10 – à temps plein, plein temps
11 – à temps réduit
12 – de bureau
13 – de nuit
14 – de plein air
15 – des enfants

16 – des femmes

17 – en cours (d'exécution)

18 – intellectuel
19 – manuel
20 – payé à la tâche
21 – payé au temps
22 – productif
23 – qualifié
24 – saisonnier
25 – supplémentaire
26 faire du – supplémentaire
27 accident m. du –
28 bourse f. du –
29 cessation f. du –
30 conditions f. pl. de –
31 conférence f. du –
32 conflits m. pl. du –
33 contrat m. de –
34 contrat collectif du –
35 division f. du –
36 durée f. du –
37 groupe m. de –
38 incapacité f. de –
39 législation f. du –
40 livret m. du –
41 marché m. du –
42 méthode f. de –
43 programme m. de mise au –
44 protection f. du –
45 réduction f. du temps de –
46 semaine f. de –

---

373 / *transposition*

transposition
to transpose figures
work, labour, (Amer.) labor
1 administrative work
2 home work
3 contract work
4 moving-band production, flow production
5 machine work
6 manual labour
7 piece work, job work
8 contract work
9 part-time work
10 full-time work
11 short-time work
12 office work, clerical work
13 night work
14 outdoor –
15 child labo(u)r, employment of children
16 women's labo(u)r, employment of women
17 work in progress

18 brain work
19 manual labo(u)r
20 work at piece-rates
21 work at time-rates
22 productive labo(u)r
23 skilled labo(u)r
24 seasonal work
25 overwork, overtime
26 to work overtime
27 industrial accident, [workmen injuries to
28 labo(u)r exchange
29 stoppage of labo(u)r
30 conditions of labo(u)r
31 labo(u)r conference
32 labo(u)r conflicts, disputes
33 labo(u)r contract
34 collective labo(u)r contract
35 division of labo(u)r
36 working hours
37 working group
38 disablement
39 labo(u)r legislation
40 workman's record
41 labo(u)r market
42 method of work, of labo(u)r
43 labo(u)r creation program(me)
44 protection of labo(u)r
45 cut in working time
46 working week, work week

travailler / 374

47 surcroît *m.* de –

48 avoir beaucoup de –
49 cesser le –
50 réduire la durée du –
travailler
1 – à perte
2 – dans...
3 – la clientèle

4 titres activement travaillés
travailleur *m.* (voir aussi *ouvrier*)
1 – à la pièce
2 – à temps reduit
3 – frontalier

4 – intellectuel
5 – manuel
6 –s migrants
7 – part-time
8 – saisonnier
9 – salarié
„travaux !"
traveller-chèque
trentenaire (voir *possession, prescription*)
trésor *m.* (*public*)
1 – *m.* (*banque*)
2 bon *m.* du –

trésorerie *f.* (*de l' État*)
1 – *f.* (*les finances*)
2 besoins *m. pl.* de –
3 faire face aux –
4 certificat *m.* de –
5 difficultés *f. pl.* de –

trésorier *m.*

triangulaire
échanges *m. pl.* –s
tribunal *m.*
1 – arbitral
2 – de commerce
3 – des prises
4 – des prud'hommes
5 toutes contestations relatives au présent contrat seront soumises aux tribunaux de...
6 comparaître devant le –
triennal (*durée*)
1 – (= *trisannuel*)
2 assolement –

47 pressure of work, extra work

48 to be fully supplied with work
49 to stop work
50 to reduce the hours of labo(u)r
to work
1 – at a loss
2 to be engaged at...
3 to visit customers

4 stock actively dealt in
worker
1 piece –
2 short-time –
3 frontier (border) –

4 brain –
5 manual –
6 migrant –s
7 part-time –
8 seasonal –
9 wage earner
road works
traveller's cheque, (*Amer.*) traveler's check

Treasury
1 treasury
2 – bond

Treasury
1 finances
2 cash requirements
3 to meet –
4 – certificate, (*Gr.Br.*) – bond
5 liquidity (cash) difficulties

treasurer

triangular
three-cornered trade, – transactions
court
1 – of arbitration
2 commercial –
3 prize – [disputes]
4 conciliation board (in industrial
5 all actions under the present contract shall be brought before the –s at...
6 to appear in –
triennial
1 recurring every third year [tation
2 three-field system, three-course ro-

trier | to sort
trieuse f. | sorter
trillion m. (*milliard de milliards*) | (*Gr.Br.*) trillion, (*Amer.*) one million trillion(s)
trimestre m. | quarter
  par – | quarterly
trimestriel(lement) | quarterly
triple | triple, treble
  en – (exemplaire) | in triplicate
triplicata m. | triplicate
triptyque m. | triptyque, tryptique
troc m. | barter, exchange
troisième f. de change | third of exchange
trucage, truquage m. (de bilan) | window dressing
trust m. | trust
  1 – de l'acier | 1 steel –
  2 formation f. d'un – | 2 trustification, formation of a –
trust (*commerce internat.*) |
  1 en – | 1 on a trust basis
  2 – letter, lettre de – | 2 trust letter, (*Amer.*) trust receipt

trustee m. | trustee
  convention de – (*titres*) | trust agreement, trust indenture
trust company (*Amer.*) | trust company
tutelle f. | guardianship
tuteur m. | guardian
  subrogé – | deputy –
tuyau m. (*renseignement*) | tip
  1 – de bourse | 1 stock exchange –
  2 donner des –x à (tuyauter) qqn | 2 to give –s to, to tip

U

unifié (v. aussi *dette*) | unified
unilatéral (*contrat*) | unilateral
union f. | union
  1 – de crédit | 1 credit society
  2 – douanière | 2 customs –
  3 – économique belgo-luxembourgeoise | 3 Belgo-Luxemburg Economic –
  4 – Européenne des Paiements | 4 European Payment –
  5 – monétaire latine | 5 Latin Monetary –
  6 – postale universelle | 6 Universal Postal –
unique | sole, unique
  prix – (voir aussi *magasin*) | one price
unité f. (v. aussi *marginal*) | unit
  1 – additionnelle | 1 additional –
  2 – de compte (v. *emprunt*) | 2 – of account
  3 – de mesure | 3 – of measure
  4 – de production | 4 – of output, of production
  5 –s et dizaines | 5 –s and tens
  6 – monétaire | 6 monetary –

urgence / 376

7 – produite
8 en –s et en coupures de...
urgence *f.*
 1 d'–
 2 il y a –

urgent
 1 – (*sur lettre*)
 2 besoin –
 3 cas –
 4 télégramme –
usage *m.*
 1 –s bancaires
 2 – domestique
 3 – du commerce
 4 –s du port de...
 5 – externe
 6 –s locaux
 7 à l'– de
 8 comme d'–
 9 contraire à l'– (commercial)
 10 d'après les –s
 11 – courant (*article*)
 12 pour – personnel
 13 prêt pour l'–
 14 sous les réserves d'–
 15 suivant les –s bancaires
 16 être d'–
 17 c'est d'– dans notre banque de...
 18 valeur *f.* d'–
usager *m.*
usance *f.*
 1 à –
 2 à deux –s, à double –
 3 lettre *f.* de change à –
 4 règles et –s... (voir *règle*)
usine *f.*
 à l'–
usuel
usufructuaire
usufruit *m.*
 avoir l'– de
usufruitier *m.*
usufruitier *adj.* (voir *réparation*)
usuraire
 intérêt – *m.*
usure *f.*
 prêter à –
usure *f.* (*dépréciation*)
usurier *m.*
utile
 1 en temps –
 2 juger –

7 – of product
8 in ones and in denominations of...
urgency
 1 urgently
 2 the case is pressing

urgent
 1 –
 2 – need
 3 emergency, – case
 4 – telegram
use
 1 bank custom
 2 domestic –
 3 usage of trade, trade custom
 4 usage (custom) of the port of
 5 for external – (application)
 6 local custom
 7 for the – (convenience) of
 8 as usual
 9 contrary to custom
 10 according to custom
 11 of everyday (daily) –
 12 for one's own –
 13 ready for –
 14 with the usual reserve
 15 according to bank custom
 16 to be usual, to be the custom
 17 it is a rule in our bank
 18 – value
user
usance
 1 at –
 2 at double –
 3 bill at –

works, factory
 ex works
usual
usufructuary
usufruct
 to hold in –
usufructuary

usurious
 – interest
usury
 to lend upon –
wear-and-tear
usurer
useful
 1 in due time, in due course
 2 to consider expedient

377 / utilisable

utilisable (v. aussi *crédit*)	**utilizable, available**
utilisation *f.* (v. aussi *capacité*)	**utilization**
utiliser	**to utilize**
1 – un crédit (par), au moyen de...	1 to avail a credit in...
2 – (*dans la fabrication*)	2 to work up, to manufacture
utilité *f.*	**use, utility**
1 (*expropriation*) pour cause d'– publique	1 for public use
2 – marginale	2 marginal utility

V

vacance *f.*	**vacancy**
pourvoir à (suppléer à) une –	to fill a –
vacances *pl.*	**holidays**
1 – de Pâques	1 Easter –
2 à mon retour (rentrant) de –	2 on my return from –, back from my vacation
3 en –	3 on holiday, on vacation
4 les grandes –	4 the summer –, the long vacation
5 pécule *m.* de –	5 holiday allowance
6 période *f.* (saison *f.*) des –	6 holiday (vacation) period
7 être en –	7 to be on holiday, on vacation
8 prendre des –	8 to take a (to go on) holiday
vacant	**vacant**
devenir –	to become –
vacations *f. pl.*	**attendance fee**
vague *f.*	**wave**
1 – d'achats	1 spending –
2 – de baisse	2 – of depression, slump
3 – de grèves	3 – (round) of strikes
4 – de hausses de salaire	4 – of wage increases
valable	**valid**
1 – jusqu'à révocation	1 available until revocation
2 – pour 3 jours (*billet*)	2 available (–) for 3 days
3 (*procuration*) rester – jusqu'à notification expresse de son retrait soit faite à...	3 remain – until such time as express notification of its withdrawal is received by
4 lettre *f.* de crédit – jusque	4 letter of credit available until
5 raisons *f. pl.* –s	5 sound reasons
valeur *f.*	**value**
1 – à l'encaissement	1 – for collection
2 – à l'état avarié	2 – in damaged condition, damaged
3 – à l'état sain	3 sound –
4 – ajoutée (v. *taxe*)	4 – added
5 – assurable	5 insurable –
6 – assurée	6 insured –
7 – au pair	7 par –
8 – cadastrale	8 cadastral –
9 – comptable	9 book –

10 – d'achat, d'acquisition	10 cost
11 – de bilan	11 balance sheet –
12 – d'échange	12 – in exchange
13 – déclarée	13 declared –
14 – de facture	14 invoice –
15 – d'émission	15 issue –
16 – de rachat (*police*)	16 surrender –
17 – de remboursement	17 redemption –
18 – de remplacement	18 – of replacement
19 – d'inventaire	19 – of stock, stocktaking –
20 – d'inventaire (*fonds de placement*)	20 break-up –
21 – du jour	21 current –
22 – d'usage	22 use –, – in use
23 – effective	23 real –
24 – en bourse	24 market –
25 – en compte	25 – in account
26 – en douane	26 customs –, – for customs purposes
27 – en garantie	27 – as security
28 – en marchandises	28 – received in goods
29 – en moi-même	29 – in myself
30 – en recouvrement	30 – for collection
31 – estimative	31 appraised –
32 – externe (*monnaie*)	32 external –
33 – faciale	33 face –
34 – de facture	34 invoice –
35 – fictive	35 fictitious –
36 – fiscale	36 rat(e)able –
37 – fournie (voir *clause de – fournie*)	
38 – imposable	38 taxable –
39 – interne (*monnaie*)	39 domestic (internal) –
40 – locative	40 rental –
41 – marchande	41 sale –, market –
42 – maximum	42 maximum –
43 – minimum	43 minimum –
44 – moyenne	44 average –
45 – nominale	45 nominal –, face –
46 d'une – nominale de	46 of a nominal – of...
47 sans désignation de – nominale	47 without par –
48 – non perçue	48 – uncollected
49 –or	49 – in gold
50 – reçue	50 – received
51 – reçue que passerez en compte, suivant avis de...	51 – received which place to account as advised
52 – réelle	52 real (actual) –
53 – totale	53 aggregate –
54 – vénale	54 sale (market) –
55 au-dessous de la –	55 below (under) –
56 au dessus de la –	56 above the –
57 de –	57 valuable
58 d'une – de	58 of the – of
59 sans –	59 worthless, valueless

379 / *valeur*

60 augmentation *f.* de –	60 increase in –
61 clause *f.* de – fournie	61 – given clause
62 déclaration *f.* de –	62 declaration of –
63 diminution *f.* de –	63 diminution of –
64 étalon *m.* (mesure *f.*) de –	64 standard of –
65 objets *m.* de –	65 valuables, objects of –
66 rectification *f.* de –	66 – adjustment
67 attacher une grande – à	67 to attach great – to
68 augmenter de –	68 to rise (increase) in –
69 augmenter la –	69 to raise the –
70 diminuer de –	70 to decline (fall) in –
71 diminuer la –	71 to reduce the –
72 estimer à sa juste –	72 to rate at its true –
valeur *f.* (*date*)	**value, value date**
1 – à l'échéance	1 value date of maturity
2 – (au) 1ᵉʳ juillet	2 value 1st July
3 – ce jour	3 value to-day
4 – le jour même	4 – same day
5 – du jour de réception	5 – day of receipt
6 – compensée	6 value compensated, value here and there the same day
7 date *f.* de –, d'entrée en –	7 value, value date
8 application *f.* de la –	8 valuation
9 appliquer une –	9 to apply a valuation
10 débiter – à l'échéance	10 to debit value day of maturity
valeurs *f. pl.* (voir aussi *titres*)	**securities**
1 – à lots	1 lottery bonds
2 – à revenu fixe	2 fixed-yield (fixed-interest bea-[ring] –
3 – à revenu variable	3 variable-yield –
4 – au porteur	4 bearer –
5 – bancaires, – de banque	5 bank shares
6 – coloniales	6 colonial shares
7 – cotées	7 quoted –
8 – de banque (voir – *bancaires*)	8 de banque (voir – *bancaires*)
9 – de bourse	9 stock exchange –
10 – de chemins de fer	10 railway shares
11 – d'électricité	11 electricity shares
12 – de mine, – minières	12 mining shares, mines
13 – de navigation	13 shipping shares
14 – d'entreprises en expansion, – dites croissantes	14 growth shares
15 – de père de famille	15 gilt-edged –
16 – de pétrole, – pétrolières	16 oil shares, oils
17 – de placement, de portefeuille	17 investment securities
18 – de spéculation, spéculatives	18 speculative shares
19 – de tout repos	19 safe investment
20 – dirigeantes, marquantes	20 leaders, leading shares

valider / 380

21 – en banque
22 – étrangères

23 – fiduciaires
24 – frappées d'opposition

25 – immobilières
26 – industrielles

27 – intangibles, – immatérielles
28 – minières,
29 – mobilières
30 – négociables
31 – nominatives
32 – non cotées
33 – pétrolières
34 – réalisables
35 – métallurgiques
36 – tangibles
valider
validité *f.*
1 délai *m.* (période *f.*) de –
2 proroger la –
valoir
1 – (*être de valeur*)
2 à – sur...

3 faire – ses droits
4 faire – son influence
valorisation *f.*
valoriser
varier de... à ...

vedettes *f. pl.* (*bourse*)
veille *f.*
1 à la – d'un jour de fête

2 la – de la réception
3 la – de l'échéance
4 la – ouvrable de la date fixée

veiller à
1 – l'exécution de
2 – vos intérêts

3 nous veillerons à ce que
veilleur *m.* de nuit
vénal, valeur –e

vendable
vendeur *m.*
1 – à découvert

21 unquoted (unlisted) –
22 foreign –

23 paper –
24 stopped bonds

25 property shares
26 industrial shares

27 intangible assets
28 mining shares, mines
29 stocks and shares
30 marketable –
31 registered –
32 unquoted –
33 oil shares, oils
34 realizable –
35 iron and steel shares
36 tangible assets
to make valid
validity (*ticket*) **availability**
1 term of validity
2 to extend the validity
to be in force
1 to be worth, to cost
2 on account of

3 to assert one's rights
4 to use one's influence
valorization
to valorize
to range between... and...

leaders, leading shares
day before
1 on the eve of an holiday

2 – receipt
3 – maturity
4 working – the day fixed

to look after
1 – the carrying out of
2 – (to promote) your interests

3 we shall see to it (take care) that
night watchman
sale value, saleable (marketable) value
saleable
seller; (*acte*) **vendor**
1 bear seller, short seller

381 / vendre

2 – (*stellage*)
3 – d'un dont, d'une prime directe
4 – d'un ou, d'une prime indirecte

5 cours – (*change*)
6 cours – (*titres*)
7 la place est –

vendre
1 – à crédit
2 – à découvert
3 – à l'amiable
4 – à l'essai
5 – (avec) perte
6 – à terme (*crédit*)
7 – à terme (*bourse*)

8 – au comptant
9 – au (en) détail
10 – au-dessous du prix
11 – au-dessus du prix
12 – au guichet
13 – au poids
14 – au rabais
15 – aux enchères
16 – avec profit
17 – de gré à gré
18 – dont
19 – en bloc
20 – en cargaison flottante
21 – ferme
22 – livrable à terme
23 – sous réserve d'arrivée
24 – sous voiles
25 – sur échantillon
26 – sur qualité vue
27 à –
28 être à –
29 ne pas se –
30 l'article ne se vend pas
31 se – difficilement

32 se – facilement

vente *f*
1 – à crédit
2 – à découvert
3 – à l'acquitté (à la consommation)
4 – à l'amiable, – de gré à gré
5 – à la criée, à l'encan
6 – à l'essai

2 taker for a put and call
3 taker for a call, seller of a call option
4 giver for a put, buyer of a put option
5 selling rate
6 prices offered, sellers
7 the market is a seller, seller's market

to sell
1 – on credit
2 – a bear
3 – privately
4 – on trial
5 – at (with) a loss
6 – on credit
7 (*commod.*) – forward; (*securities*) – for the settlement, for the account
8 – for cash
9 – by retail
10 – under the price
11 – above the price
12 – over the counter
13 – by weight
14 – by Dutch auction
15 – by auction
16 – with profit
17 – privately
18 to take for the call, – a call option
19 – in bulk
20 – afloat, on steaming terms
21 – firm
22 – forward, – for future delivery
23 – to arrive
24 – afloat, on steaming terms
25 – on (by) sample
26 – on approval
27 to be sold
28 to be for sale
29 to find no sale, no purchasers
30 the article doesn't catch
31 to go off (to sell) slowly, to be a slow sale
32 to go off well, to sell quickly

sale
1 – on credit
2 bear –, short –
3 duty-paid –, – ex bond
4 amicable –, private –
5 – by auction
6 – on trial

vente / 382

7 – à l'heureuse arrivée
8 – à livrer (*valeurs*)
9 – à réméré
10 – à tempérament
11 – à terme (*crédit*)
12 – à terme (*bourse*)

13 – à terme ferme
14 – au comptant
15 – au détail
16 – au rabais
17 – aux enchères
18 – comptant compté
19 – contre remboursement
20 – de fin de saison (voir *saison*)
21 – de la main à la main
22 –s de printemps
23 –s du fabricant au consommateur

24 – en cargaison flottante
25 – en (au) détail
26 – en disponible
27 – en entrepôt
28 – en gros
29 – exclusive
30 – facile
31 – ferme
32 – forcée
33 – judiciaire
34 – par correspondance
35 maison *f.* de – par correspondance
36 – par soumission
37 – pour cessation de commerce

38 – publique
39 – réclame
40 – sous voiles
41 – sur description
42 – sur échantillon
43 – sur qualité vue
44 – sur type
45 – volontaire
46 en – chez...
47 en – ici
48 en – partout
49 sauf –
50 bureau *m.* de –
51 campagne *f.* de –
52 chef *m.* de –
53 chiffres *m. pl.* de –
54 compte *m.* de –
55 comptoir *m.* de –
56 conditions *f. pl.* de –

7 – subject to safe arrival, – to arrive
8 – for delivery
9 – with option of repurchase
10 – on instalments, hire purchase (–)
11 – on credit
12 (*commod.*) forward –; (*securities*) for the settlement, for the account
13 – for future delivery during specified periods
14 cash –
15 retail –
16 Dutch auction
17 – by auction
18 cash down –
19 cash-on-delivery –

21 amicable –, private –
22 spring –s
23 direct – from producer to consumer
24 – of goods afloat
25 retail –
26 spot –
27 – in bonded warehouse
28 wholesale –
29 exclusive –
30 ready (brisk) –
31 firm –
32 compulsory (forced) –
33 judicial –, – by order of the Court
34 mail-order selling
35 mail-order house
36 – by tender
37 winding up –

38 public –
39 bargain – [terms
40 – of goods afloat, on steaming
41 – by description
42 – on (by) sample
43 – on approval
44 – on type
45 voluntary –
46 to be had from..., on sale at...
47 to be sold (had) here
48 on – everywhere
49 if unsold
50 selling agency, selling office
51 selling campaign
52 –s manager
53 –s figures
54 account –s
55 selling office, sales office
56 terms of –

57 contrat *m.* de –
58 jour *m.* de –
59 limite *f.* de –
60 monopole *m.* de –
61 ordre *m.* de –
62 organisation *f.* de –
63 possibilités *f. pl.* de –
64 prix *m.* de –
65 salle *f.* de –
66 service *m.* de –
67 valeur *f.* de –
68 effectuer la –
69 être de – difficile

70 être de – facile, de bonne –

71 mettre en –, offrir en –

72 se charger de la –
ventilation *f. (jur.)*
– *(compt.)*
ventiler *(jur.)*
– *(compt.)*

verbal
vérificateur *m. (douanes)*
 1 – comptable

 2 – des contributions
 3 – des poids et mesures
vérification *f.*
 1 – de la caisse
 2 – des comptes

 3 – des créances [créances
 4 réunion *f.* des créanciers pour – des
 5 – des livres
 6 – faite, après – de
 7 après – minutieuse de...
 8 avis *m.* de –
vérifier
 1 – un calcul
 2 – des comptes
 3 – les créances
 4 – les encaisses
 5 – l'exactitude de...
 6 – une facture

 7 – des marchandises
 8 – le poids
 9 en vérifiant nos livres
véritable *(produit)*

57 contract of –, deed of –
58 day of –
59 selling limit
60 selling monopoly
61 selling order
62 selling organization
63 possibilities of –
64 selling price
65 auction room
66 –s department
67 – (market, saleable) value
68 to effect the –
69 to go off slowly, to be a slow –

70 to be quick of –, to sell off readily, to find a ready –

71 to offer for –

72 to undertake the –
separate valuation
apportionment, analysis, breakdown
to value separately
to apportion, to analyse, (*Amer.*) to breakdown
verbal
examiner
 1 auditor

 2 surveyor of taxes
 3 inspector of weights and measures
examination
 1 cash revision, revision of the cash
 2 auditing of accounts

 3 – of claims
 4 creditor's meeting for proof of debts
 5 audit (of books)
 6 after verification
 7 on close verification of
 8 reconciliation, reconcilement
to verify, to examine
 1 to check an account
 2 to audit accounts
 3 to verify the claims
 4 to audit (check) the cash in hand
 5 to verify the correctness of...
 6 to check (examine) an invoice

 7 to examine goods
 8 to reweigh
 9 on examining our books
genuine, real

vérité *f.*
versé en
  – affaires
versement *m.*
  1 – à la banque
  2 – à la caisse d'épargne
  3 – anticipatif, par anticipation
  4 – d'appel de fonds de...
  5 – de libération, dernier –
  6 – de répartition

  7 – de souscription
  8 – s échelonnés
  9 – en une fois
  10 – s et dispositions sur un compte

  11 „–s et payements" (*guichet*)
  12 – initial (*vente à tempérament*)
  13 – supplémentaire
  14 – sur actions
  15 – télégraphique
  16 – contre – de...
  17 avis *m.* de –
  18 bordereau *m.* de –

  19 bulletin *m.* de –
  20 reçu *m.* de –

  21 appeler (exiger) un – de... % par action
  22 effectuer un –
  23 faire un – de... %
  24 régler par – ou virement

verser
  1 – entièrement (*actions*)
  2 – un acompte
  3 – un appel de fonds de... %
  4 – de l'argent à la banque
  5 – de l'argent à la caisse d'épargne

  6 – au crédit de...
  7 capital entièrement versé
verso *m.*
  1 au – d'un chèque
  2 le – et le recto

  3 comme indiqué au –
  4 inscrire les montants au – de la lettre de crédit
  5 voir au – (t.s.v.pl.)

truth
well up in
  – business matters
payment
  1 – into the bank
  2 deposit in the savings bank
  3 – in advance
  4 – of calls
  5 – of final call, final instalment
  6 allotment money

  7 application money
  8 – in (by) instalments
  9 – in full
  10 deposits and drawings on an account

  11 paying and receiving cashier
  12 initial down-payment
  13 additional –
  14 additional – of calls
  15 telegraphic remittance
  16 against – of...
  17 notice (advice) of paying in
  18 paying in slip, deposit slip

  19 paying in slip, deposit slip
  20 deposit receipt

  21 to make a call of... % per share

  22 to effect (make) a –
  23 to pay a call of... %
  24 to settle by paying in or transfer

to pay in
  1 – full
  2 to pay... on account
  3 – a call of... %
  4 to pay... into the bank
  5 to deposit money in the savings bank
  6 to pay (in)to the credit of...
  7 fully paid up capital
back
  1 on the – of a cheque (check)
  2 the left-hand page and the right-hand page
  3 as stated on the –, overleaf
  4 to endorse the amounts on the – of the letter of credit
  5 please turn over (P.T.O.)

vertu, en – de...
1 – l'article 18
2 – la loi
3 émis – la lettre de crédit

vétusté f. (*bâtiment*)

viable (*entreprise*)
viager, rente viagère
placer son argent en –
vice m. (voir aussi *défaut*)
1 – apparent
2 –s cachés
3 – de construction
4 – de forme
5 –s inhérents, propres
6 – rédhibitoire

vice-consul m.
vice-président m.
vidanges (voir *vides*)
vide
1 – en retour
2 des (bouteilles, caisses, etc.) –s
3 les caisses –s sont reprises à... pièce
4 on ne reprend pas les bouteilles (caisses) –s

vieillissement m. (*industrie*)
vieux (voir aussi *déduction*)
vignette f.
1 – pièces jointes
2 timbre m. –
vigueur f.
1 encore en –
2 mise f. en –
3 tarifs m. pl. en –
4 entrer en –
vil, à – prix
ville f. (v. aussi *tenue*)
1 – de commerce
2 – de province
3 „en – " (E.V.)
4 en cette –
5 en notre –
6 de votre –
7 emprunt m. de la –
virement m.
1 – au compte de...
2 – bancaire

on the strength of, in pursuance of
1 in pursuance (by virtue) of section 18
2 according to law
3 drawn under letter of credit

wear and tear

paying its way, viable
life annuity
to invest one's money in life annuities
defect
1 apparent (noticeable) –
2 hidden (latent) –s
3 constructional –
4 informality, faulty drafting
5 inherent –s
6 redhibitory –, – which cancels or voids the bargain

vice consul
vice president, vice chairman

empty
1 returned –
2 empties
3 – cases (empties) are returnable (taken back) at...
4 empties are not taken back

wearing-out
old
label
1 enclosure –
2 poster stamp
force
1 still in –
2 putting into –
3 rates in –
4 to take effect
dirt cheap, at a knock-out price
town
1 trading (commercial) –
2 provincial (country) –
3 local
4 in this –, place
5 in our city
6 in your –
7 municipal loan
transfer
1 – to the account of...
2 bank –

virer / 386

  3 – postal
  4 –s postaux (*système*)
  5 – télégraphique
  6 avis *m.* de – (*au bénéficiaire*)

  7 avis *m.* de débit du –

  8 banque *f.* de –
  9 compte *m.* de –
10 bulletin *m.* de –s collectifs
11 carnet *m.* de –s
12 mandat *m.* de – (postal)
13 ordre *m.* de – (banque)

14 paiements par chèques et –s
15 service *f.* des –s
16 (service des) chèques et –s postaux
17 effectuer (opérer) un –
18 payer (régler) par –

virer
– au compte de...

visa *m.*
  1 – consulaire, – du consul
  2 – sur un passeport
  3 apposer le – sur...

viser
  1 – (*des livres de commerce*)
  2 – un passeport

  3 – un effet

  4 être visé par une mesure
  5 visé à l'article...

visible
  1 exportations *f. pl.* –s
  2 réserve *f.* –
  3 stock *m.* –
  4 Monsieur... est-il –

visite *f.*
  1 – d'adieu
  2 – de la foire
  3 carte *f.* de –
  4 heures *f. pl.* de –
  5 rendre – à...

visite *f.* (*douane*)
  1 – des bagages
  2 – de la douane, douanière

  3 postal –
  4 clearing system
  5 telegraphic –
  6 notification of crediting, credit advice
  7 notification of debiting

  8 clearing bank
  9 – account
10 collective list of postal transfers
11 – order book
12 postal – form
13 order to –

14 cashless payments
15 –s   [ing service
16 postal cheques (checks) and clear-
17 to make a –
18 to pay by –

to transfer
– to the account of...

visa, visé
  1 consular visa
  2 visa on a passport
  3 to put the visa at..., to affix a visa, to visé

to visa, to visé
  1 to initial, to countersign
  2 to visé (visa) a passport

  3 to sight a bill

  4 to be affected by a measure
  5 referred to in (contemplated by) article...

visible
  1 – exports, –s
  2 – reserve
  3 – supply, stock
  4 can I see Mr... ?

visit, call
  1 parting visit
  2 attendance at the fair
  3 visiting card
  4 visiting hours
  5 to pay a visit to, to call on...

view, inspection
  1 examination of the luggage
  2 customs examinations

387 / visiter

visiter — to call, to visit
visiter (*douane*) — to view
– les bagages — to examine the luggage
visiteur *m.* — visitor, caller
– (*inspecteur*) — examiner, inspector
vite — rapid
 au plus –, aussi – que possible — as soon as possible
vitesse *f.* — speed
 1 – de rotation (voir *rotation*)
 2 par grande – — 2 by fast goods train, (*Amer.*) by fast freight
 3 par petite – — 3 by goods (freight) train
vitrine *f.* (*de magasin*) — show window, shop window
 – (*armoire*) — show case
vogue *f.*
 1 en – — 1 in use
 2 être très en – — 2 to be in great favour, vogue
voie *f.* — way
 1 –s et moyens — 1 –s and means
 2 – d'eau — 2 leak
 3 faire une – d'eau — 3 to spring a leak
 4 – de raccordement (*usine*) — 4 railway sidings, side line leading to factory
 5 – double — 5 double track
 6 – navigable — 6 waterway
 7 – simple — 7 single track
 8 en – de formation — 8 in process of formation
 9 par – d'affiche — 9 by poster
 10 par – d'emprunt — 10 by the issue of loan
 11 par – de mer — 11 by sea
 12 par – de terre — 12 by land
 13 par – ferrée — 13 by rail
 14 par la – des airs — 14 by air
 15 par la – hiérarchique — 15 through the official (usual) channels
 16 par la – la plus directe — 16 by the nearest –
 17 clause *f.* de – parée — 17 immediate execution clause
voile monétaire *m.* — veil of money
voiture (voir *lettre*, *occasion*)
voiturier *m.* — carrier, carter
voix — voice
 1 – additionnelle — 1 additional –
 2 – consultative — 2 advisory –
 3 – prépondérante — 3 casting vote
 4 à l'unanimité des – — 4 unanimously, with unanimity
 5 à la majorité des – — 5 by a majority of votes
  6 décider – exprimées — 6 to decide by a majority of the votes cast
 7 en cas de partage égal des – — 7 in case of an equal division (equality) of votes
 8 avoir – délibérative — 8 to have a right (to be entitled) to vote, to have a deliberative –
 9 mettre aux – — 9 to put to the vote

vol m.
1 –, pillage et disparition (*assur.*)
2 assurance *f.* contre le –

volant m. (*réserve*)
1 – (*document*)
2 la souche et le –
volet m. (*de document*)
1 – d'entrée (*triptyque*)
2 – de sortie (*triptyque*)
volume m.
1 – des affaires
2 – du commerce extérieur
3 expansion *f.* du – des exportations
volumineux
– (*encombrant*)
votation *f.*
mode m. de –
vote m.
1 – à mains levées
2 – par appel nominal
3 – par assis et levé

4 – par procuration
5 – plural

6 bulletin m. de –
7 droit m. de –
8 s'abstenir du –
9 procéder au –
voter
1 – une proposition
2 – sur...
vouloir
1 veuillez faire suivre
2 veuillez me faire savoir

3 veuillez nous envoyer
voyage m.
1 – à l'étranger
2 – d'affaires
3 – d'inspection
4 en –
5 à mon retour de – j'ai trouvé votre lettre
6 dès mon retour de –
7 agence *f.* de –
8 articles *pl.* de –
9 chèque m. de –

10 frais m. pl. de –
11 nécessaire m. de –
12 aller (partir) en –

theft
–, pilferage and non-delivery
2 theft (burglary) insurance

reserves
1 leaf
2 the counterfoil and the leaf
volet, part
1 volet of entry, importation voucher
2 volet of exit, exportation voucher
volume
1 – of business
2 external trade –
3 expansion in the – of exports
voluminous
bulky
voting
method of –
vote
1 – by show of hands
2 – by call-over, (*Amer.*) by roll call
3 – by rising or remaining seated

4 – by proxy
5 plural –

6 voting paper
7 right of voting
8 to abstain from voting
9 to proceed to the –
to vote
1 – (to approve) a proposal
2 – on...
to will
1 please forward
2 please (kindly) let me know, inform me
3 please send us
travel, journey, (*sea*) **voyage**
1 journey (trip) abroad
2 business tour, business travel
3 tour of inspection
4 on a journey, on a voyage
5 on my return home (from abroad) I found your letter
6 immediately on my return
7 tourist office
8 travelling requisites
9 traveller's cheque, (*Amer.*) traveler's check
10 travelling expenses
11 dressing case
12 to go on a journey

389 / *voyager*

13 être en –

14 être en – d'affaires
voyager
 1 – en affaires
 2 – pour une firme
 3 les marchandises voyagent, sauf convention contraire, aux risques et périls de l'acheteur
voyageur *m.*
 – de commerce
vrac
 1 en –
 2 cargaison *f.* en –
 3 chargé en –
 4 marchandises *f. pl.* en –
vu
 1 – à long terme
 2 – dans son ensemble

 3 – et approuvé
 4 – les circonstances
 5 – que
 6 au – de
vue *f.*
 1 à –
 2 à 3 jours de –
 3 à première –

 4 argent *m.* à –
 5 compte *m.* (de dépôts) à –

 6 (cours du) change *m.* à –
 7 dépôts *m. pl.* à –

 8 engagements *m. pl.* à –

 9 payable à –

 10 payable à 30 jours de –
 11 traite *f.* à –

 12 traite *f.* à délai de –

---

13 to be on a voyage, journey

14 to be away on business
to travel
 1 – on business
 2 – for a firm
 3 the goods travel, unless otherwise agreed, at buyer's risk

traveller
 commercial –

 1 in bulk
 2 bulk cargo
 3 laden in bulk
 4 goods in bulk
seen
 1 in the longer term
 2 taken as a whole

 3 – and approved   [stances
 4 in view of (considering) the circum-
 5 considering that
 6 on sight of
sight
 1 at –, on demand
 2 three days after –
 3 at first –, glance

 4 call money
 5 call deposit (demand deposit) account
 6 – rate, demand rate
 7 deposits at (on) call, sight deposits

 8 daily maturing obligations

 9 payable at –, on presentation

 10 payable at 30 days' –
 11 – bill

 12 bill payable after –

W

wagon *m.*
 1 – à bagages
 2 – à bestiaux
 3 – à marchandises
 4 – bâché

wag(g)on
 1 luggage van
 2 cattle –, cattle truck
 3 goods –, (*Amer.*) freight car
 4 sheeted –

warrant / 390

    5 – basculant
    6 – citerne
    7 – complet
    8 – couvert (fermé)
    9 – découvert (ouvert)
   10 – frigorifique
   11 – incomplet
   12 – non bâché
   13 wagon-lit
   14 wagon-restaurant
   15 franco sur –
warrant *m.*
    1 – cédule

    2 avances *f. pl.* sur –
    3 porteur *m.* du –
warranter
   marchandises warrantées

    5 tip –
    6 tank car
    7 full truck load
    8 covered –
    9 open truck
   10 refrigerated van (car)
   11 part truck load
   12 unsheeted –
   13 sleeping car
   14 dining car, restaurant car
   15 free on truck, on rail
warrant
    1 – issued in duplicate, one copy being the receipt and the other being the warrant
    2 advance on –
    3 bearer of the –
to secure by warrant
   goods covered by warrant

Z

zéro *m.*
zone *f.*
   1 – de libre-échange
   2 – dollar

   3 – franche
   4 – monétaire

   5 – sterling

nought, cipher
zone
   1 free trade area
   2 dollar area

   3 free –
   4 currency area

   5 sterling area

SUPPLÉMENT

abattement / 392

*abattement *m.,*
  – pour enfants à charge — tax abatement for children
*absorber (*une société*) — to take over
absorption *f.,* – (*société*) — take-over
  – du pouvoir d'achat — absorption of the purchasing power

accélérateur *m.* — accelerator
accélération, principe *m.* d'– — acceleration principle
*accès *m.* (*inf.*) — access
  – direct, sélectif — direct –, random –
  – parallèle — simultaneous (parallel) –
  – séquentiel — sequential –
  temps *m.* d'– — – time
accumulateur *m.* (*inf.*) — accumulator
*achat *m.,*
  – à l'essai (avec droit de retourner la marchandise) — purchase on approval
  – (ferme) à titre d'essai — (definite) purchase by way of trial
  –s d'accaparement — hoarding
  –s de panique — panic buying
  – de remplacement — replacement purchase
  – impulsif, par impulsion — impulsive buying
  comportement *m.* d'– — shopping behaviour
  intentions *f. pl.* d'– — buying intentions
  motif *m.* d'– — buying motive
  psychose *f.* d'–s — panic buying
*actif *m.,*
  – disponible et réalisable — current assets
  – immatériel — intangible assets
  incorporer dans l'– — to put on the assets side
*action *f.,*
  acquisition *f.* de ses propres –s — acquisition of own shares
  fractionnement *m.* d'–s — share split

actionnariat *m.* (*ouvrier*) — employee shareholding

*activité *f.,*
  – dans le bâtiment — building (construction) activity
  – économique — economic activity
  – relative (*stat.*) — potency ratio
actuariat *m.* — functions (profession) of an actuary

actuariel — actuarial
  calcul *m.* – — actuarial calculation
additionneur *m.* (*inf.*) — adder
adhésif *m.* — sticker, adhesive label
administration *f.*, des affaires — business administration
*adresse *f.* (*inf.*),
  – absolue — absolute address
  – de mémoire (*inf.*) — memory address
  – de retour (*inf.*) — return address
  – indexée (*inf.*) — indexed address
  – télex — telex address

393 / *affaires*

affacturage *m.*, — factoring
affaires
  en – — in business
  parti pour – — away on business
  rien que pour – — strictly for business
affectation *f.*,
  – aux réserves — allocation to reserves
  – du bénéfice net — appropriation of net profit
affichage *m.*,
  – des prix — price display

affichiste *m.* — **poster artist, designer**

âge *m.*,
  – limite — limiting age
  répartition *f.* par – — age distribution
agence *f.*,
  – de coupures de presse — clipping agency
  – immobilière — estate agency
agent *m.*,
  – immobilier — (real) estate agent
ajustement *m.* (*stat.*) — **fitting**
ajustement *m.*,
  – d'un compte — adjustment of an account
  – des prix — price adjustment
alerte *f.*,
  dispositif *m.* d''– — (burglar) alarm installation
algorithme *m.* (*inf.*) — **algorithm**
alléger,
  – les frais généraux — to cut down overhead expenses
  – les impôts, la charge fiscale — to reduce (lower) taxes
aménagement *m.* **du territoire** — **town and country planning**
amortissement *m.*,
  – dégressif — declining balance depreciation
  – linéaire — straight-line depreciation
  – pour dépréciation — amounts written off for depreciation

  dépenses *pl.* en – — depreciation expenses
  méthode *f.* d'– — depreciation method
  taux *m.* de l'– — depreciation rate
  pratiquer de larges –s — to write off liberally

amplitude *f.* (*stat.*) — **range**
analyse *f.*,
  – de fréquence — frequency analysis
  – de lecture — readership analysis
  – de régression — regression analysis
  – de tendance — trend analysis
  – de variance — analysis of variance
  – factorielle — factor analysis
  – par tris croisés — cross section analysis
  – séquentielle — sequential analysis
analyseur *m.* (*inf.*) — **analyser**

années / 394

– différentiel	differential –
*années,	
– de vaches grasses	years of plenty
– maigres	lean years
*annonce f.,	
– à clé, chiffrée	keyed advertisement
texte principal (d'une –)	body
*appel m.,	
– d'offres public	public invitation to tender
– d'offres restreint	limited invitation to tender
livraison f. sur –	delivery on request, on (at) call
marchandise f. (produit m.) d'–	loss leader
vente f. à livraison sur –	sale for delivery on call
vendre livraison sur –	to sell for delivery on call, on request
*apport m. **en numéraire, en espèces**	**contribution in cash**
approximation f. (*stat.*)	**approximation**
*archives,	
destruction f. d'–	records destruction
argument m. **de vente**	**selling argument**
*article m.,	
–s défraîchis	shop-soiled goods
–s de marque	branded article
assembler (*inf.*)	**to assemble**
*association f. (*stat.*)	**association**
coefficient m. d'–	coefficient of association
*assurance f.	**insurance**
– à terme fixe	fixed term –
– avec délai de carence	– with waiting period
– à temps	time policy
– aérienne	aviation –
– au profit d'un tiers	– for the benefit of another person
– collective	collective –
– contre les dégats des eaux	water damage –
– contre la tempête	storm and tempest –
– (de) groupe	group –
– défense en justice, frais de justice	legal expenses –
– de solde restant dû	life – of the outstanding-balance type
– du risque nucléaire	nuclear risks –
–études	educational –
– indexée	– with index clause
– libérée (de primes)	paid-up policy
– maternelle	maternity –
– pour son propre compte	– on own behalf
– pour compte de tiers	– for account of third parties
– sans examen médical	– without medical examination
– valeur à neuf	replacement value –
– valeur totale	full value –
assujetti aux –s sociales	**subject to social –**

395 / assuré

durée f. de l'–	period of –
marché m. des –s	– market
objet m. de l'–	object insured
obligation f. d'–	compulsory –
proposition f. d'–	– proposal
*assuré m.,	
– social	person covered by social insurance scheme
atomistique, concurrence – (parfaite)	atomistic competition
attitude f. (*mark.*)	**attitude**
étude f. d'–	attitude study
attribut m. (*stat.*)	attribute
audience f. (*mark.*)	**audience**
enquête f. d'–	audience research
habitude f. d'– TV	viewing habits
*augmenter de ... (*capital*)	**to raise, increase by...**
austérité f., politique f. d'–	**austerity policy**
programme m. d'–	austerity program(me)
autocode m. (*inf.*)	**autocode**
avancement m., possibilités pl. d'–	**prospects for promotion**
*avantage,	
–s accessoires	fringe benefits
–s en nature	allowance in kind
*avoir m.,	
– fiscal	tax credit
axiomatique (*stat.*)	**axiomatic**
balai m. (*inf.*)	**brush**
*balance f.,	
– du commerce extérieur	foreign trade balance
– des opérations courantes	balance of payments on current account
– des opérations en capital	balance of operations on capital account
– des prestations de services	balance of service transactions
*balance f. des paiements,	
déficit m. de la –	balance of payments deficit
détérioration f. de la –	deterioration of the balance of payments
déséquilibre m. de la –	disequilibrium of the balance of payments
bancable	**eligible for rediscount by the central bank**
*bancaire,	
place f. non –	non-bank place
secteur m. –	bank sector
secteur m. non –	non-bank sector
système m. –	banking system
*bande f.,	
– de fluctuation	margin of fluctuation

banque / 396

– magnétique (*inf.*)	magnetic tape
– perforée (*inf.*)	punched tape
– pilote	control tape
– transporteuse	conveyor, moving belt
*banque *f.*,	
– à succursales	bank with branches
– chargée de l'encaissement	collecting bank
– chef de file d'un syndicat	leading underwriter
– de dépôts et virements de titres	securities clearing bank
– membre d'un syndicat	bank member of a syndicate, underwriting bank
– remettante	remitting bank
*base *f.*,	
année *f.* de –	base year
période *f.* de –	base (reference) period
industrie *f.* de –	basic industry
produit *m.* de –	basic product
salaire *m.* de –	basic pay, basic wage
*bateau *m.*,	
– porte-barges	lash (lighter aboard ship)
bâtiment,	
ouvrier *m.* du –	building worker
*bénéfice *m.*,	
– après impôt	profit after tax
– avant amortissement	profit before depreciation
– avant impôt	pre-tax (before-tax) profit
se solder de nouveau par un –	to make profits again, to come out of the red
*bénéficiaire *m.*,	
premier – (*créd. doc.*)	first beneficiary
second –	second beneficiary
*bénéficiaire (*adj.*),	
dégagements –s	profit-taking
biais *m.* (*stat.*)	**bias**
biaisé (*stat.*)	**bias(s)ed**
non –	unbiassed
échantillon –	biassed sample
*biens *m.pl.*,	
– communs	joint property (of husband and wife)
– réservés	separate estate
*bilan *m.*,	
– de liquidation	statement of affairs
données *pl.* de –	balance sheet data
structure *f.* du –	balance sheet structure
*billet à ordre,	
souscripteur *m.* d'un –	maker of a promissory note
souscrire un –	to make out a promissory note
billing *m.* (*mark.*)	**billing**
binaire (*inf.*)	**binary**
digit –	– digit

nombres –s	– numbers
système *m.* –	– system
virgule *f.* –	– point
biquinaire (*inf.*)	**biquinary**
bit *m.* (*inf.*)	**bit**
– de contrôle	check –
– de parité	parity –
bloqué,	
crédits –s	frozen credits
fonds –s	frozen assets
**bloquer,	
– un chèque	to block a cheque
– les salaires	to freeze wages
boucle *f.* (*inf.*)	**loop**
boutique *f.*	**shop,** (*Amér.*) **store**
– (*mode*)	boutique
– bien assortie	well-stocked shop
étalage *m.* de –	shop-window
brader	**to sell at a knock-out price**
braderie *f.*	**jumble sale**
brocante *f.*	**dealing in second-hand goods, in curiosities**
**budget *m.*,	
– cyclique	cyclical budget
– d'exploitation	operating budget
– type (*stat.*)	average living expenditure
équilibrer le –	to balance the budget
réduire le – de...	to cut the budget by...
**budgétaire,	
contrôle *m.* –	budgetary control
gestion *f.* –	handling of budgetary expenditure
poste *m.* –	budget item
budgétisation *f.*	**budgeting**
budgétiser	**to budget**
buée *f.* **de cale**	**ship's sweat**
**but *m.*,	
à – lucratif	profit seeking
sans – lucratif	non-profit (seeking)
****cachet** *m.* **de la poste**	**(date of) postmark**
le – fait foi	date of postmark applies
cadeau *m.*	**present, gift**
– de Noël ; de Nouvel an	Christmas gift ; New Year's gift
–-réclame	advertising article, novelty
abonnement *m.* –	gift subscription
article *m.* –	gift ware
bon *m.* –	gift voucher
colis *m.* –	gift parcel

emballage *m.* –	gift packing
*cadre *m.*,	
–s moyens	middle (management) executives
les –s supérieurs	executive officers
formation *f.* des –s	management training
*caisse *f.*,	
– d'épargne à la construction	building and loan association, building society
– de sortie (*libre service*)	check-out
entrées *pl.* de –	cash receipts
*calculateur *m.* (*inf.*)	**computer**
– analogique	analog –
– numérique, digital	digital –
canal *m.* (*inf.*)	channel
cantine *f.* (**d'entreprise**)	**(industrial) canteen**
*capacité *f.*,	
– de stockage	storage capacity
– disponible	spare capacity
– exploitée à plein	full operating capacity
– inutilisée, non utilisée	unused (idle) capacity
utilisation *f.* de –	use of capacity
utiliser la – à plein	to work (run) to capacity
*capital *m.*,	
capitaux fébriles	hot money
– emprunté	borrowed capital
– en cas de décès (*assur.*)	sum payable at death
– et réserves	capital and reserves
augmentation *f.* de – par incorporation de réserves	capitalization of reserves
formation *f.* de capitaux	formation of capital
perte *f.* de –	capital loss
rendement *m.* du –	return on capital
caption *f.* (*publicité*)	**caption**
caractère *m.* (*inf.*)	**character**
caractère *m.* (*stat.*)	**characteristic**
– qualitatif	qualitative –
– quantitatif	quantitative –
carence *f.*	**lack ; insolvency**
délai *m.* de – (*assur.*)	waiting period
*cargaison *f.*,	
– complète	full cargo
– de retour	cargo homewards
*carnet *m.*,	
– de commandes bien garni, rempli	well-filled orderbooks

– de quittances	receipt book
caron m. **de bouteille**	**crowner**
carré m. (stat.)	**square**
– latin	latin –
moindres –s	least –s
somme f. des –s	sum of squares
*****carte** f.,	
––chèque, de chèques	cheque (guarantee) card
– de crédit	credit card
– de séjour (étranger)	residence permit
– verte d'assurance	insurance green card
*****cartel** m.,	
– de prix	price cartel
– de production	production combination
– régional	localized cartel
cartogramme m. (stat.)	**cartogram(me)**
cartonnage publicitaire m. (étalage)	**display carton**
casualisation f. (stat.)	**randomization**
*****céder à...** (commerce)	**to transfer (make over) to...**
cellule f. (inf.)	**cell**
central m. **téléphonique**	**telephone exchange**
centrale f. **nucléaire**	**nuclear power station**
*****centre** m.,	
– de calcul (inf.)	data processing centre
– de coûts	cost centre
– de recherches	research centre
– des affaires (quartier)	business centre
*****certificat** m.,	
– d'avarie	statement of loss
– de décès (assur.)	death certificate
– immobilier, foncier	property fund unit
– médical (assur.)	medical certificate
*****cession** f.,	
– de brevet	assignment of a patent
– de salaires	wage assignment
*****chaîne** f.,	
– de restaurants	chain of restaurants
– d'hôtels, hôtelière	hotel chain
production f. à la –	line production
chambre forte	**vault**
charge f. **de la preuve** (assur.)	**burden of proof**
chariot m. (libre service)	**trolley, shopping cart**
– de réapprovisionnement	trolley
*****chef** m.,	
– de file (émission)	syndicate leader, principal underwriter
– de produit	product (brand) manager
chemin m. **critique** (inf.)	**critical path**
*****chèque** m.,	
– garanti	guaranteed cheque

chi-carré / 400

révocation *f.* d'un –	stopping payment of a cheque
remplir un –	to write out a cheque
révoquer un –	to stop payment of a cheque
chi-carré (*stat.*)	**chi-square**
chiffres clés (*analyse d'entreprises*)	**key figures**
*chiffre *m.* **d'affaires**	
– (*agence de publicité*)	billing
– hors taxes	turnover all taxes deducted
– taxes comprises	turnover before tax
augmenter le –	to increase the sales
*choix *m.*	
– aléatoire (*stat.*)	random choice
– alternatif (*stat.*)	alternative choice
– intentionnel (*stat.*)	purposive choice
circuit *m.* (*inf.*)	**circuit**
– intégré	integrated –
*classe *f.* (*stat.*)	**class**
centre *m.* de la –	class mark
intervalle *m.* de –	class interval
limites de –	class limits
limite inférieure de la –	lower limit
limite supérieure de la –	upper limit
*classification *f.*,	
– décimale	Dewey decimal system
*clause *f.*,	
– "non à ordre"	clause not to order
–s surajoutées (*créd. docum.*)	superimposed clauses
*clé *f.*,	
–s en main, sur porte	turn-key
louer –s en main	to let with immediate possession
*clearing *m.*,	
avoir *m.* de –	clearing balance
*cliché *m.*	
– trait	line block
*climat *m.*,	
– de méfiance (*bourse*)	reserved tendency
– d'entreprise	social environment
– d'investissement	investment climate
coassureur *m.*	**co-insurer**
cocher	**to check, to tick off**
codage *m.*	**coding**
*code *m.*,	
– binaire (*inf.*)	binary code
– biquinaire	biquinary code
– mnémonique	mnemonic code
codeur *m.* (*inf.*)	**coder**

401 / coefficient

*coefficient m.,
−s bancaires | banking coefficients
− de corrélation | correlation coefficient
− de réserve obligatoire | minimum reserve ratio
− de variation | variation coefficient
collocation f. | **collocation in bankruptcy**

combinaison f. | **combination**
serrure f. à −s | combinationlock

*comité m.,
− de crédit | credit committee
command m. | **actual purchaser, principal**
*commande f.,
− d'essai | trial order
− ferme | definite order
−s intérieures | home-market orders
*commercial,
franc − | commercial franc
marché − (*devises*) | commercial market
*commission f.,
− d'engagement (*crédits*) | commitment commission
− de manipulation | handling charge
*communauté f.,
adhésion f. à la − | accession to the Community
pays pl. de la − | Community countries
commutation f. (*inf.*) | **switching**
compétivité f. | **competitiveness**

compilateur m. (*inf.*) | **compiler**
*comportement m.,
− de la clientèle | client behaviour
− du consommateur | consumer behaviour
composante f. (*stat.*) | **component**
− aléatoire | random −
− cyclique | cyclical −
− saisonnière | seasonal −
− de la variance | variance −
compris (y −) | **included, inclusive**

non − | not included, excluded
tout − (*hôtel*) | inclusive terms
*compromis m.
préférer un − à un procès (v. aussi *transiger*) | to prefer a compromise to a lawsuit
comptage m. | **count**
− de passants (*mark.*) | passenger −
*compte m.,
− annuel | annual account
− anonyme | anonymous account
− contre-partie | contra account
− d'épargne | savings account
− de régularisation | transitory items

comptoir-caisse / 402

– de répartition (*fonds de placement*)	distribution account
– détaillé	detailed (itemized) account
– numéroté, à numéro	numbered account
– salaires	salary account
– sans mouvement	dormant account
– séparé	segregated account
– spécial	special account
les bons – font les bons amis	short reckonings make long friends
suivant – remis	as per account rendered
intitulé (libellé) *m.* d'un –	name of an account
comptoir-caisse *m.* (*libre service*)	**cash-stand**
**concentration *f.*,	
courbe *f.* de – (*stat.*)	concentration curve
concepteur-rédacteur *m.*	**copy-writer**
**concurrence *f.*,	
– effective	workable competition
– illicite	illicit competition
– ruineuse	cut-throat competition
libre –	free competition
règles *pl.* de la –	rules of competition
conditionnement *m.*	**condition**
– (*emballage*)	packaging, package
grand –	economy size
confiance *f.* (*stat.*)	**confidence**
intervalle *m.* de –	– interval
limites de – (*stat.*)	– limits
seuil *m.* de – (*stat.*)	– level
configuration *f.* (*inf.*)	**configuration**
**conformité *f.*,	
présenter l'apparence de – avec les conditions	to appear on the face to be in accordance with the terms and conditions
**conjoncture *f.*,	
surchauffe *f.* de la –	overheating of the economy
**conjoncturel,	
recherche –le	cyclical research
reprise –le	economic recovery
tension –le	cyclical tension
politique –le	cyclical policy
**connaissement *m.*,	
– de groupage	collective Bill of Lading
couvert par le même –	covered by the same Bill of Lading
conservation *f.*, durée de – (*denrées*)	**shelf-life**
**consigne *f.* (*caution*)	**deposit**
consigné,	
emballage non –	no return
**consigner (*dans un rapport*)	**to register, to enter**
– l'emballage	to charge for packing

consolidé, bénéfice – | intercompany profit

bilan – | consolidated balance sheet

chiffre d'affaires – | consolidated sales, intercompany sales

compte – | intercompany account
*consommateur,
dernier –, – final | ultimate consumer
– potentiel | prospective consumer
association *f.* de –s | consumer association
choix *m.* du – | consumer's choice
éducation *f.* du – | consumer education

comportement *m.* du – | behaviour of the consumer

enquête *f.* auprès des –s | consumer survey
groupe-témoin *m.* de –s | consumer panel
habitudes *pl.* des –s | consumer habits

panel *m.* de –s | consumer panel
protection *f.* des –s | consumer protection
*consommation *f.,*
– par tête | consumption per capita
société *f.* de – | consumer society
taux *m.,* de –, quote-part réservée à la – | consumption ratio

unité *f.* de – | consumption unit
consortial, compte – | underwriting account
crédits consortiaux | syndicate credit
*consortium *m.,*
membre *m.* du – | syndicate member
*constituer (*mandataire*) | **to brief**
conteneur *m.* | **container**
– scellé | sealed –
navire –, navire porte-–s *m.* | container(-carrier)ship container vessel

port *m.* pour –s | container port
service *m.* de –s | container service
terminal *m.* à (pour) –s | container terminal
transport *m.* par –s | container transport

conteneurisation *f.* | **containerization**
contingence *f.* (*stat.*) | **contingency**
table *f.* de – | – table
contingent *m.* | **quota**
– annuel | annual –
– global | global –
– (à) d'exportation | export quota
fixation *f.* d'un – | fixation of a quota
réduction *f.* d'un – | reduction of a –
*contingenter (*limiter*) | **to curtail**
continu (*stat.*) | **continuous**

contractuel / 404

*contractuel,
  sur une base –le | on a contractual base
  rapports –s | contractual relationships
*contrat *m.*,
  – de trustee | trust agreement
  – de leasing | leasing agreement
  – de fret | freight contract
*contrôle *m.*,
  – budgétaire | budgetary control
  – de parité (*inf.*) | parity check
  – de la poubelle (*mark.*) | dustbin check
  – du crédit | credit control
  – interne | internal audit
  carte *f.* de – | control card
  interview *m.* de – (*mark.*) | check interview
*convention,
  – collective de travail | collective labour agreement

*conversion *f.* (*obligation*) | **conversion**
  cours *m.* de – | conversion price
  disagio *m.* de – | conversion discount
  prime *f.* de – | conversion premium
  termes *pl.* de – | conversion terms
*convertibilité *f.*,
  – intégrale | full convertibility
  – limitée, restreinte | limited convertibility
  restauration *f.* de la (retour *m.* à la) – | return to convertibility
*coopérative *f.*,
  – agricole | agricultural co-operative
  – de construction | building society
  – de vente | marketing co-operative
cooptation *f.* | **co-optation**
coopter | **to co-opt**
copy-platform (*mark.*) | **copy-platform**
copy-writer (voir *concepteur*)
correction *f.*, – de continuité (*stat.*) | **correction for continuity**
corrélation *f.* (*stat.*) | **correlation**
  – curvilinéaire | curvilinear –
  – de rang | rank –
  – illusoire | spurious –

  – linéaire | linear –
  – multiple | multiple –
  – négative | inverse (negative) –

  – positive | positive –
  coefficient *m.* de – | coefficient of –
  diagramme *m.* de – | – diagram

  fonction *f.* de – | – function
  surface *f.* de – | – surface
  table *f.* de – | – table
cotation *f.* (*de la barre d'or*) | **fixing**

405 / cote foncière

cote foncière	assessment on landed property
cote personelle	poll tax; head-money
*coupon m.,	
– semestriel	semi-annual coupon
coupon-réponse (mark.)	reply coupon, keyed coupon
*coupure de presse	
agence f. de –	clipping agency
service m. de –	clipping service
*courbe f. (stat.)	curve
– à main levée	free-hand –
– de concentration	concentration –
– de Gauss	normal –
– de la croissance	growth –
– de Lorenz	Lorenz –
– de mortalité	mortality –
– de production	production –
– d'indifférence	indifference –
– d'iso-coût	equal-cost –
– d'iso-produit	equal-product –
– en cloche	bell-shaped –
– en pointillé	dotted –
– en trait continu	continuous –
ajustement m. de la –	– fitting
rupture d'une ligne –	jump in a –
*cours m.	
– de change flottant	floating rate
– de change fixe	fixed exchange rate
– de change multiple	multiple exchange rate
– de change soutenu	pegged exchange rate
– plafond	ceiling rate, upper intervention limit
– plancher	floor rate, lower intervention limit
évolution f. des –	stock market trend
rapport m. –/bénéfice	price/earnings ratio
rapport –/cash flow	price/cash flow ratio
laisser flotter le – de change	to float the exchange rate
*coût m.,	
– de la main-d'œuvre, salarial	cost of labo(u)r
– de transport	cost of transport
évaluation f. du –	costing
unité f. de –	cost unit
covariance f. (stat.)	co-variance
*crédit m.,	
– à découvert	overdraft facilities
– à la construction	building credit
– à l'industrie	loan to industry, industrial loan
– s consortiaux	syndicate credit
– croisé	swap
– de démarrage	opening credit
– d'enlèvement (douane)	duty deferment
– de soudure	interim (bridging) loan

crédit-bail / 406

  – d'investissement | investment credit
  – non utilisé | unused credit
  en vertu (dans le cadre) du – | under the credit

encadrement *m.* de – | credit squeeze
montant *m.* du – | amount of a credit
avoir recours à un – | to make use of credit facilities
notifier un – | to advise a credit
crédit-bail *m.* | **leasing**
  – financier | financial lease
  – immobilier | real-estate –
***creux** *m.* | **cyclical low**
  – de la vague | trough of waves
creux *adj.*, heures creuses | off-peak hours
période (saison) creuse | slack season
***croissance** *f.*,
  accélération *f.* de la – | acceleration of growth
  courbe *f.* de – | growth curve
  perspectives *pl.* de – | growth prospects

ralentissement *m.* de la – | slowing down of the growth rate
rythme *m.* de – | growth pace
freiner la – | to curb growth
stimuler la – | to stimulate growth
curvilinéaire | **curvilinear**
cybernétique *f.* | **cybernetics**
***date** *f.*,
  – limite | deadline
***débiteur,**
  avoir un compte – | to be in the red
débrayage *m.* | **going to strike, stoppage of work**

décélération *f.* | **deceleration**
décile *m.* (*stat.*) | **decile**
***décision** *f.*,
  – prise par la direction | management decision

espace *m.* de – (*stat.*) | decision space
prise *f.* de – | decision making
table *f.* de – | decision table
théorie *f.* de la – | decision theory
décote *f.* | **tax rebate**
déductibilité *f.* | **deductibility**
défi *m.* | **challenge**
***déficit** *m.*,
  – budgétaire | budget deficit
  lourd – | heavy deficit
***déficitaire,**
  être – (*entreprise*) | to be in the red
  ne plus être – | to get out of the red
dégagement *m.* (*bourse*) | **sale**
***degré** *m.*,
  – d'invalidité | degree of disablement

407 / déjeuner

– de liberté	degree of freedom
déjeuner m.,	
– d'affaires	business lunch
– de travail	working lunch
*délai m.,	
– de carence (assur.)	waiting period
*demande f.,	
– fléchissante	slackening (lessening) demand
faible –	slack demand
forte –	keen (strong) demand
sur (simple) –	on demand
sur première –	upon first request
la – s'est affaiblie	demand is on the decrease
fonction f. de – (mark.)	demand function
modèle m. de – (mark.)	demand model
modification f. de la –	demand shifts
nouvelle flambée de la –	new sudden increase in demand
ralentissement m. de la –	slackening of demand
freiner la –	to curb the growth of demand
dénommé,	
un navire –	a named vessel
*dépassement m. (inf.)	**overflow**
*dépense f.,	
– déductible	allowable expense
–s d'équipement	equipment spending
–s d'investissement	investment expenditure
–s publicitaires	advertising expenditure
lourdes –s	heavy expenditure
menues –s	petties
plafond m. des –s	expenditure ceiling
ventilation f. des –s	expenditure breakdown
*dépositaire,	
banque –	custodian bank
dérouleur m. **de bande**	**tape unit**
désaisonnalisé	**seasonally adjusted**
désendetter	**to free of debts**
se –	to get out of debt
désinvestissement m.	**disinvestment**
desk research (voir étude sur documents)	
déstockage m.	**de-stocking**
*dette f.,	
–s à court terme	short-term liabilities
–s à long terme	long-term liabilities
–s comptables	accounts payable
*déviation f. (stat.)	**deviation**
– moyenne	average –
– quartile	quartile –
– standard	standard –

diagramme / 408

*diagramme *m.*,
 – à (en) bâtons, à colonnes — bar chart
 – à (en) secteurs — circle (pie) chart
 – de corrélation — correlation diagram
 – de dispersion — scatter diagram
 – de points — dot charter
 – logarithmique — logarithmic plot
 – temporel — time series chart
dichotomie *f.* (*stat.*) — **dichotomy**
digit *m.* (*inf.*) — **digit**
 – binaire — binary –
 – de contrôle — check –
digital (numérique) — **digital**
 calculateur – — – computer
*direction *f.*,
 fonction *f.* de – — executive post
 personnel *m.* de – — executive staff
 secrétaire *m.* de – — secretary to the director(s)
 secrétariat *m.* de la – — management secretariat
discontinu (*stat.*) — **discontinuous**
*discret (*stat.*) — **discrete**
dispersion *f.* (*stat.*) — **dispersion**
 coefficient *m.* de – — scatter coefficient
 diagramme *m.* de – — scatter diagram, chart
 mesures *pl.* de – — measures of –
display *m.* — **display carton**
disque magnétique *m.* (*inf.*) — **magnetic disk**
distorsion *f.* — **distortion**
 – de la concurrence — – of competition
distributeur *m.* **automatique** — **vending machine**
*distributeur *m.*,
 interview *m.* de –s — dealer interview
 panel *m.* de –s — dealer panel
*distribution *f.* — **distribution**
 – de porte en porte par la poste — house-to-house – through post-office

 – physique — physical distribution
 canaux *pl.* de – — trade channels

 entreprise *f.* de – — distributive trade
 étude *f.* de – — – research
 schéma *m.* de – — – pattern
distribution *f.* (*stat.*) — **distribution**
 – à 2 variables — bivariate –
 – à plusieurs variables — multivariate –
 – aléatoire — random –
 – binomiale — binomial –
 – de fréquence — frequency –
 – de fréquences cumulées — cumulative frequency –
 – de probabilité — probability –
 – discrète — discrete –
 – empirique — actual –
 – normale — normal –

409 / diversification

diversification f.
  – des produits
*dividende m.,
  – en actions

*document m.,
  – de groupage

  émetteur m. des –s (*créd. docum.*)
  présentation f. des –s

  émettre des –s
dol m.
*dollar m.,
  avoir m. en –s
  déficit m. en –s
  emprunt m. (libellé) en –s
  excédent m. de –s
  faiblesse f. du –
*dommage m. (*assur.*),
  – indirect
  évaluation f. du –
  montant m. du –
*dommages-intérêts,
  droit m. à des –
données pl. (*inf.*)
  – analogiques
  – de contrôle
  banque f. de –
  collecte f. de –
  entrée et sortie de –
  traitement m. des –

  transmission f. de –
*dossier m.,
  frais pl. de –
dotation f.
  – aux réserves

*douanier,
  facture douanière
  nomenclature douanière
  tarification douanière
  visite douanière
*droit m.,
  –s de tirage spéciaux
  cours m. du – de souscription
*durée f.,
  – de conservation (*denrées*)
  – moyenne de vie
*écart m. (*stat.*),
  – moyen
  – type

diversification
  product –

stock dividend

  groupage document

issuer of documents
presentation of documents

to issue documents
fraud

dollar holdings
dollar gap
dollar loan
dollar surplus
weakness of the dollar

indirect damage
appraisal of damage
amount of damage

right to claim for damages
data
  analog –
  control –
  – bank
  – collection, – gathering
  data input and output
  data processing

  – transmission

handling charge
endowment
  appropriation to the reserves

customs invoice
tariff nomenclature
customs tariffication
customs examination

special drawing rights
price of the (subscription) right

shelf-life
average life

mean deviation
standard deviation

*échantilllon / 410

*échantillon *m.*	
– de référence	reference sample
– gratuit	free sample
conforme à l' –	true to specimen (sample)
échantillon *m.* (*stat.*)	**sample**
– aléatoire, tiré au hasard	random –
– aréolaire	area –
– biaisé, – avec erreur systématique	bias(s)ed –
– choisi à dessein	purposive –
– en grappes	cluster –
– indirect	indirect –
– par quotas	quota –
– pondéré	weighted –
– probabiliste	probability –
– proportionnel	proportional –
– représentatif	representative –
– sans biais	unbias(s)ed –
– stratifié	stratified –
– systématique	systematic –
– universel	general purpose –
distribution *f.* d'–	sampling distribution
taille *f.* de l'–	– size
*échantillonnage *m.*, (*stat.*)	sampling
– à deux degrés	two-stage –
– à plusieurs degrés	multi-stage –
– simple	simple –
erreur *f.* d'–	– error
plan *m.* d'–	– plan, – design
point *m.* d'–	– point
taux *m.* (fraction *f.*) d'–	– rate
technique *f.* d'–	– technique
*échelle *f.*,	
à l'– européenne	at European level
à l'– nationale	on a national scale
*économie *f.*,	
– appliquée	applied economics
– de paix	paecetime economy
– mixte	mixed economy
relance *f.* de l'–	reactivation of the economy
relancer l'–	to reactivate (boost) the economy
*économique,	
biens –s	economic goods
croissance *f.* –	economic growth
isolement *m.* –	economic isolation
politique *f.* –	economic policy
écritures *pl.*, jeu *m.* d'–	book transfer
*éducation *f.*,	
– du consommateur	consumer education
– permanente	adult education

effectif m. (*stat.*) | size
effet m., |
– réescomptable | bill eligible for rediscount
– simple | clean draft

égal, |
à travail –, salaire – | equal pay for equal work
égalité f., |
– des salaires | equality of pay, in wages
emballage m., |
– à fenêtre | window pack
– à usage unique | throwaway packing, one-way package

– automatique | automatic packing
–-cadeau | gift packing
– de grande taille | economy size
– familial | family size
" – repris" | returnable packing
– sous vide | vacuum packing
– transparent | transparant package
date f. d'– | date of packing
matériel m. d'– | packaging material
emballement m., |
– des cours | boom in prices
émetteur m. (*connaissement*) | **issuer**
émettre (*connaissement*) | **to issue**
émeute f. | riot
assurance f. –s | riot and civil commotion insurance

émission f. (*connaissement*) | **issuance, issuing**
emploi m., |
changement m. d'– (dans l'entreprise) | job rotation

demandes d'– non satisfaites | the number of registered job seekers
offres d'– non satisfaites | unfilled (job) vacancies
politique f. de l'– | employment policy
demandeur m. d'– | job seeker

énergétique, politique f. – | energy policy
ressources –s | energy resources

énergie f., |
approvisionnement m. en – | power supply
besoins pl. en – | power needs
consommation f. d'– | power consumption
crise f. de l'– | energy crisis
ravitaillement m. en – | energy supply
secteur m. de l'– | energy sector
enquête f., |
– auprès des consommateurs | consumer survey
– auprès des détaillants | retailer survey
– auprès des distributeurs | dealer survey
– d'audience | audience research

ensemble / 412

- d'audience TV — viewer research
- de budgets — budget survey
- d'opinion — opinion survey
- permanente — continuous survey
- pilote — pilot survey
- par sondage — sample survey
- préliminaire — exploratory survey
- sur le terrain — field research

- omnibus — omnibus survey
bulletin *m.* d'– — questionnaire
ensemble *m.* (*stat.*) — **universe**
***entrée** *f.* (*inf.*) — **input**
—sortie — input-output
***entreprise** *f.*,
- artisanale — craftsman's establishment
- multinationale — multi-national (company)
libre – — free enterprise
environnement *m.* — **environment**
pollution *f.* de l'– — pollution of the –
protection *f.* (sauvegarde *f.*) de l'– — environmental protection
***envoi** *m.*,
- gare restante — parcel to be called for (at station office)

- poste restante — poste restante parcel
- sous bande — packet sent by bookpost
épargnant *m.* — **saver**
les petits –s — small –s
***épargne** *f.*,
- négative — negative savings, dissavings
–s oisives — idle savings
- positive — positive savings
goût *m.* de l'– — thriftiness
motivation *f.* de l'– — saving motives
plan *m.* d'– — savings scheme
propension *f.* à l'– — propensity to save

prime *f.* d'– — savings premium
***épargner**,
qui épargne gagne — waste not, want not

équidistant (*stat.*) — **equidistant**
érosion *f.* de la monnaie, monétaire — **erosion of the value of money**
***erreur** *f.* (*stat.*) — **error**
- aléatoire — random –
- d'échantillonnage — sampling –
- de deuxième espèce — – of second kind
- de jugement — – of judgment
- de mémoire — memory –
- de mesure — – of measurement
- de notation — – in notation
- de première espèce — – of first kind
- d'estimation — – in estimation

413 / escompte

– de transcription	transcription –
– probable	probable –
– systématique	systematic –
– type	standard –
courbe f. d'–	curve of –
marge f. d'–	margin of –, – band
théorie f. des –s	theory of –s
escompte m.,	
– d'effets	bill discount(ing)
– de factures	invoice discounting
plafond m. d'–	discount ceiling
espérance f., – mathématique (*stat.*)	mathematical expectation
– moyenne de vie (*assur.*)	average expectation of life
essence f.,	
bon m. d'–	petrol coupon
consommation f. d'–	petrol consumption
distribution f. d'–	petrol rationing
rationnement m. de l'–	petrol rationing
estimateur m. (*stat.*)	**statistic, estimator**
estimation f. (*stat.*)	**estimation**
– ponctuelle	point examination
erreur f. d'–	error in –
établissement m.,	
– payeur	paying agent
liberté f. d'–	freedom of settlement
étagère f. (*magasin*)	**shelf**
étalage m.,	
– de comptoir	counter display
– de masse	mass display
boîte f. d'–	display case
boîte f. d'– sur le comptoir	counter-display case
matériel m. d'–	window display material
étaler, s'– sur...	**to be spread over ...**
état m.,	
– défectueux	defective condition
étendue f. (*stat.*)	**range**
étiquette f.,	
– à bagages	luggage label
– de prix	price tag, price ticket
– de qualité	quality label
étude f.,	
– de distribution	distribution research
– de marketing	marketing research
– des supports publicitaires	media research
– d'opinion	opinion research
– sur documents	desk research
eurochèque m.	**eurocheque**
euro-dollar m.	**Eurodollar**
évaluation f.,	
– prudente	conservative esimate

événement *m.* (*stat.*) / event
- aléatoire / random –
- certain / certain –
- complémentaire / complementary –
- s s'excluant mutuellement / mutually exclusive –s
- fortuit / fortuitous –
- impossible / impossible –
- s indépendants / independent –s

éventail *m.* / **fan**
un large – de ... / a good range of ...

évolution *f.*
- conjoncturelle / cyclical trend
- des cours / trend of prices
- du marché / market development

exercice *m.*,
- incomplet / rump accounting year

expansion *f.*,
rythme *m.* d'– / rate of expansion
modération *f.* du rythme d'– / fall in the rate of expansion

expertise *f.*,
- du dommage / loss-assessment

exposition *f.*,
- en masse / mass display

extincteur *m.* / **fire extinguisher**
extinction *f.* (*assur.*) / **extinction**
système *m.* d'– automatique / sprinkler installation
(par eau diffusée)

extorquer / **to extort**
- de l'argent de ... / – money from ...

factor *m.* / **factor**

factoring *m.* (**affacturage** *m.*) / **factoring**
contrat *m.* de – / – contract
frais *pl.* de – / – fees
société *f.* de – / – company
système *m.* de – / – system

facturation *f.* / **billing**
facture *f.*,
suivant – remise / as per account rendered
fait *m.* **du prince** / **restraint of princes**

famille *f.*,
sans charges de – / without family encumbrance(s), dependants

entreprise *f.* de – / family partnership

soutien *m.* de – / bread winner
faute *f.*,
- inexcusable / inexcusable negligence
- lourde / gross negligence

415 / femme

– intentionnelle	deliberate negligence
*femme,	
– commerçante	tradeswoman, feme sole trader
– salariée	wage-earning woman
*fermé,	
– pendant les travaux de réparation	closed during restorations
*fermeture *f.*,	
– d'usine	factory shutdown (closure)
*fichier *m.* (*inf.*)	**file**
– d'entrée	input file
– principal	master file
*fiduciaire,	
à titre –	in a trust capacity, as trustee
field research (voir *enquête sur le terrain*)	
file *f.* **d'attente** (*inf.*)	**queue**
*fin *f.*,	
–s de série	oddments, remnants
*financier,	
franc –	financial franc
marché –	capital market
marché – (*devises*)	financial market
surface financière	financial standing
*firme *f.*,	
– de premier ordre	first-rate firm
– établie depuis longtemps	old-established firm
– solide	firm of good standing
image *f.* de –	corporate image
*fiscal,	
avoir –	tax credit
fraude –e	evasion of taxation
rentrées –es	tax yield
système –	tax system
flambée *f.*	
(nouvelle) – de la demande	sudden increase in demand
*fléchissement *m.*,	
– de la conjoncture	economic downturn
– des cours	decline in prices
flottaison *f.*	**float(ing)**
*flottant,	
cours –	floating rate
flottement *m.*	**float(ing)**
– commun	joint (concerted) –
– isolé	individual –
flotter (*monnaie*)	**to be floating**
laisser –	to float, to let free to float
*flux *m.*,	
– de biens	goods flow, flow of goods
– de revenus	earnings flow

*fonds *pl.,
 – disponibles | available funds
 – empruntés | borrowed funds
 – propres | own resources
fonds *m.* de placement immobilier | real-estate fund
*formation *f.*,
 – permanente, continue | adult education, lifelong education

fourchette *f.* (*écart*) | bracket
*fournisseur *m.*,
 – de navires | ship-chandler
fractile *m.* (*stat.*) | fractile
*frais *m. pl.*,
 – de chargement | loading charges shipping charges
 – de deblaiement (*assur.*) | cost of clearance of debris
 – de déchargement | landing charges
 – de dossier | handling charge
 – de tenue de compte | account keeping fee

 – de timbre | stamp duties
 – de traitement (*assur.*) | cost of treatment
 – d'expertise (*assur.*) | survey fees
 – judiciaires (*assur.*) | legal expenses
 – supplémentaires | extra charges, additional expenses
franchisage *m.* | franchising, franchise
*franchise *f.* (*mark.*) | franchise
 accord *m.* de – | franchise agreement
franchisé *m.* (*mark.*) | franchisee, franchised dealer
franchiseur *m.* (*mark.*) | franchisor
franchising *m.* (v. franchisage).
fréquence *f.* (*stat.*) | frequency
 – absolue | absolute –
 –s cumulées | cumulative frequencies
 – d'achat | buying –
 – observée | observed –
 – par cellule | cell –
 – relative | relative –
 courbe *f.* de – | – curve
 distribution *f.* de – | – distribution
 mesure *f.* de – | measure of –
 polygone *m.* de –s | – polygon
 table *f.* de –s | – table
frigo, mettre au – (*fig.*) | to put on ice
*frontière *f.*,
 contrôle *m.* à la – | border control
 gare *f.* – | frontier station
 passage *m.* de la – | border crossing
 point *m.* de passage de la – | border crossing point
 trafic *m.* passant les –s | cross-frontier traffic
 zone – *f.* | frontier area
*gage *m.*,
 acte *m.* d'affectation en – | mortgage deed
 droit *m.* de – | lien

réalisation f. d'un –	realization of a pledge
réaliser un –	to realize a pledge
galerie f. marchande	**shopping arcades, mall**
galette f.	**tin, brass, money**
gamme f.	**scale, range**
Gaussien .	**gaussian**
*****gestion** f.,	
rapport m. de –	management report
gondole f. (grand magasin)	**gondola**
étagère f. de –	– shelf
hauteur f. de –	height of –
tête f. de –	front end of –
*****graphique** m.,	
– à secteurs	pie chart
– de dispersion	scatter diagram
– de processus	process chart
– en barre	bar chart
– linéaire	line chart
*****graphique** adj.,	
représentation f. –	graphic presentation
grappe f.	**cluster**
échantillon m. en –s	– sample
*****grève** f.,	
– des acheteurs	buyers' strike
– spontanée	walk-out
– tournante	staggered strike
interdiction f. de la –	ban on a strike
préavis m. de –	strike notice
vague f. de –s	wave of strikes
briser une –	to break a strike
déclencher une –	to trigger off a strike
*****groupe** m.,	
– contrastant (mark.)	contrasting group
– d'âge	age group
– de contrôle (mark.)	control group
– de pression	lobby, pressure group
– de travail	working group
*****guichet** m.,	
– payeur	paying agent
– vendeur	selling agent
*****habitude** f.,	
–s d'audience T.V.	viewing habits
–s des acheteurs	buying habits
–s des consommateurs	consumer habits
–s d'écoute	listening habits
hachure f. (graphique)	**hatching**
hardware m. (matériel) (inf.)	**hardware**
hasard, au – (stat.)	**random**
choix m. au – (stat.)	random choice
nombres pl. au – (stat.)	random numbers

hearing *m.* | hearing
histogramme *m.* | histogram
***horaire** *m.* (*personnel*) | **working hours**
  – glissant | staggered –
  – variable | variable –
hôtesse *f.*,
  – d'accueil | hostess
  – de l'air | air hostess
hypermarché *m.* | **hypermarket**
hypothèse *f.* | **assumption**
  dans l'– où | on the – that, supposing that
  – nulle (*stat.*) | null hypothesis
îlot *m.* (*mark.*) | **island**
image *f.* (*mark.*) | **image**
  – de firme | corporate image
  – de marque | brand image
  – du produit | product image
***immigration** *f.*,
  – saisonnière | seasonal immigration
  contingent *m.* d'– | immigration quota
  politique *f.* d'– | immigration policy
  restrictions *pl.* à l'– | restrictions on immigration
***immobilier**,
  agence immobilière | estate agency
  agent – | estate agent
  fonds *m.* de placement – | real-estate fund
  placement *m.* – | investment in real estate
***immobilisations** *pl* | **fixed assets**
  – corporelles | tangible (fixed) assets
  –s incorporelles | intangible assets
implantation *f.* (d'une nouvelle industrie) | **establishment, setting up** (of a new industry)
***importation** *f.*,
  contingent *m.* d'– | import quota
  surtaxe *f.* sur les –s | import surcharge
***imposition** *f.*,
  – à la source | taxation at source
  accords *m. pl.* en matière de double – | antidouble tax treaty
***impôt** *m.*,
  – dégressif | degressive taxation
  paiement anticipé d'–s | prepayment of taxes
imprimante *f.* (*inf.*) | **printer**
  – à chaîne | chain –
  – par lignes | line –
  – par pages | page –
impulsif, achat – | impulsive buying
impulsion *f.* | **impulse**
  donner de l'– à | to give a stimulus (an –) to

*incorporation f.
- des réserves au capital — incorporation of reserves

incorporel — **intangible, incorporeal**
  actif – — intangible assets
  biens –s — incorporeal property
  droit – — incorporeal right
incrément m. (inf.) — **increment**
*indemnité f.,
- d'immobilisation (voiture) — compensation for loss of use
- kilométrique — mileage allowance
  montant m. de l'– (assur.) — indemnity
*index m., — index linking
  liaison f. à l'–
indexation f. — **indexation, index linking**

  clause f. d'– — escalator (index) clause
*indexé,
  salaire – — index-tied wage
indicatif m. (tél.) — **area code**
indicatif, prix – — **pilot price**
*indice m. — **index**
- composite — composite – number
- corrigé — corrected –
- corrigé des variations saisonnières — seasonally adjusted –
- des actions — share –
- en chaîne — chain –
- simple — simple – number
  calcul m. d'un – — calculation of an –
  élements pl. d'un – — – components
industrie f. — **industry**
- aéronautique — aircraft –
- automobile — (motor) car –
- clé — key –
- de la construction mécanique — engineering –
- de la construction navale — ship building –
- du bâtiment — building –
- du cuir — leather –
- extractive — extractive –
- graphique — printing and allied industries
- manufacturière — manufacturing –
- nationalisée — nationalized –
- pétrochimique — petrochemical –
- productrice de biens d'équipement — investment goods –
- textile — textile –
*inflation f.,
- potentielle — potential inflation
  danger m. d'– — inflation danger
  menace f. d'– — inflationary threat
  freiner l'– — to halt inflation

*information f. (inf.) — **information**
  entrée f. d'–s — data input

instruction / 420

sortie f. d'–s	data output
traitement m. électronique de l'–	electronic data processing
stocker des –s dans la mémoire	to stock (store) data
traiter l'–	to process data
*instruction f. (*inf.*)	**instruction**
– d'entrée-sortie	input-output –
– de branchement	branch –
insurrection f. (*assur.*)	**insurrection**
*intégration f.,	
– horizontale	horizontal integration
– verticale	vertical integration
interaction f. (*stat.*)	**interaction**
interbancaire	**interbank**
opérations –s	– dealings
intéressement m. du personnel	**employee profit sharing**
*intérimaire,	
bureau m. d'–s	interim agency
intervalle m. (*stat.*)	**interval**
– de classe	class –
– de confiance	confidence –
interview f. (*mark.*)	**interview**
– centrée	focused –
– de contrôle	check –
– dirigée	focused –
– de groupe	group –
– en profondeur	depth –
– par téléphone	telephone interview
intitulé m., – d'un compte	title of an account
*intracommunautaire	
commerce m. –	intra-community trade
invalidité f. (*assur.*)	**disablement**
– absolue, totale	total –
– partielle	partial –
– permanente	permanent –
– temporaire	temporary –
– totale	total –
assurance f. contre l'–	disability insurance
degré m. d'–	degree of disability
pension f. d'–	disability pension
*inventaire m.,	
stock m. à l'–, en fin d'exercice	closing stock
*investissement m.,	
– fixe	fixed investment
– net	net investment
mauvais –	mistaken (false) investment
climat m. d'–	investment climate
dépenses pl. d'–	capital expenditures
occasions (possibilités) pl. d'–	investment opportunities
propension f. à l'–	propensity to invest

*irrégularité f. (tendance)
*irrégulier (bourse)
*jeu m.,
 – d'entreprise
 libre – de la concurrence
 – d'écritures
*jouissance f.,
 – exercice 1975 (actions)

*jour m.,
 – des mères
 – des pères
 au premier – ouvrable qui suit
*journal m.
 – lumineux
 – parlé
*judiciairement,
 – et extrajudiciairement

kangourou m. (v. aussi *bateau porte-barges*) transport –
labo(ratoire) m.
 – de langues
laissé-pour-compte m.

 – (rossignol)
*langage m.
 – de programmation (inf.)
 – machine
lash (v. *bateau porte-barges*)
leasing m. (voir aussi *crédit-bail*)
 – à court terme
 – à long terme
 – brut
 – de biens d'équipement

 – de camions
 – d'entretien

 – de véhicules
 – financier
 – immobilier
 – net
 – opérationnel
contrat m. de –
demande f. de –
loueur m.
objet m. du –
opérations pl. de –
preneur m. (de –)
société f. de –
technique f. du –

irregularity
irregular

business (management) game
free play of competition
book transfer

entitled to dividend in the 1975 financial year

mother's day
father's day
on the first following business day

electric newspaper
broadcast news

judicially and extrajudicially

piggyback service

lab(oratory)
language –
returned (rejected) article

unsaleable article

programming language
machine language

leasing
short –
long –
gross lease, service lease
equipment –

truck –
maintenance –

vehicle –
finance –
real-estate leasing
net lease
operational –
 – agreement
application for –
lessor
 – object
 – operations
lessee
 – company
 – technique

léchage /de /vitrines / 422

léchage m. de vitrines	window-shopping
lecteur m. (inf.)	reader
– de bande magnétique	magnetic tape –
– de bande perforée	punched tape –
– de cartes	card –
– optique	optical –
*lettre f.,	
– d'accompagnement	accompanying letter
– d'avertissement	dunning letter, reminder
– de remise	remittance letter
*libéré,	
entièrement –	fully paid (up)
partiellement –	partially paid
*liberté f.,	
degré m. de – (stat.)	degree of freedom
libre-service m. (pl. libres-services)	self-service
– partiel	semi-self-service
commerce m. de gros à –	cash-and-carry (wholesale)
magasin m. (en) –	self-service store, shop
*lié,	
– à un délai	timed
– à l'index	index-tied
– par (un) contrat	bound by contract
lien m. (avec une monnaie)	link with (linked to)
*ligne,	
en dessous de la –	below the line
– en trait continu	continuous line
– pointillée	dotted line
ligne f. de crédit	line of credit
– non utilisée	unavailed –
demander une –	to ask for a –
dépasser la –	to run over the –
obtenir une –	to obtain a –
octroyer (accorder) une –	to grant a –
utiliser une –	to run a –
*limite f.,	
– des classes	limits of classes
– de tolérance (stat.)	tolerance limit
– d'indemnité (assur.)	limit of indemnity
linéaire	linear
linéarité f. (stat.)	linearity
*liquidité f.,	
acroissement m. des –s	increasing liquidity
besoins pl. en –s	liquidity requirements
création f. de –	liquidity creation
*liste f.,	
– aide-mémoire	check list
lister (inf.)	to list
*livraison f.,	
– sur appel	delivery on request

location f. financement	finance lease
logiciel m.	software
*****loisir** m.,	
industrie f. des –s	leisure industry
société f. de –s	leisure society
vêtements pl. –	leisure wear
machine f. distributrice automatique	vending machine
macro-économie f.	macroeconomics
macro-économique	macroeconomic
*****magasin** m.,	
– discount, minimarge	discount house, discount store, discounter
– libre service	self-service store
– spécialisé	specialty shop
emplacement m. du –	store location
entrée f. du –	shop entrance
équipement m. du –	shop equipment
sortie f. du –	shop exit
rester en – (non vendu)	to remain on the shelf
magnétique, bande f. –	magnetic tape
disque m. –	magnetic disc
tambour m. –	magnetic drum
*****main-d'œuvre** f.	
– bon marché	cheap labo(u)r
– étrangère	foreign labo(u)r
– familiale	family workers
– masculine	male labo(u)r force
– occasionnelle, temporaire	casual (occasional) workers
besoins m. pl. en –	manpower requirements
demande f. de –	labo(u)r demand
emploi m. de la –	employment of labo(u)r
*****mainmise** f.	seizure
– (fig.)	appropriation
– étrangère (sur les sociétés)	foreign control
*****maladie** f.,	
en cas de –	in the event of sickness
pour cause de –	because of sickness
allocation f. pour –	sickness allowance
assurance f. –	sickness insurance
caisse f. de –	sick-benefit fund
congé m. de –	sick-leave
*****mandataire** m.,	
constituer un –	to appoint a proxy
*****manipulation** f.,	
– monétaire	currency manipulation
manipuler (fin.)	**to manipulate**
maquillage m., – du bilan	window-dressing of the balance sheet
marathon m.	**marathon meeting**

marché *m.*,
- commercial (*change*) — commercial market
- financier (*change*) — financial market
- fractionné — market segment
- officiel — official market
- parallèle — parallel market
- partiel — sectional market
- potentiel — potential market
- -test — test market
- assainissement *m.* du – — market revitalization
- comportement *m.* du – — market behavio(u)r
- fraction *f.* du – — market segment
- mécanisme *m.* du – — market mechanism
- part *f.* du – — market share
- saturation *f.* du – — saturation of the market
- segmentation *f.* du – — market segmentation
- structure *f.* du – — market structure
- conquérir un nouveau – — to win a new market
- inonder le – (de) — to glut the market (with)
- sonder le – — to try the market
- regagner un – — to regain a market

*marché *m.* des changes** — **foreign exchange market**
- double – — two-tier –
- le – reste clos jusqu'à... — the – remains shut (closed) until...
- dédoublement *m.* du – — split of the – into two tiers
- dédoubler le – — to split the –
- fermer le – — to close the –
- instaurer le double – — to set up a two-tier market
- rouvrir le – — to reopen the –

marchéage *m.* (*aspect pratique du marketing*) — **marketing**

*marge *f.*
- pour les éventualités — margin for contingencies
- de fluctuations — fluctuation band, fluctuation margin
- élargie (*fluctuation*) — wider bands (margin)
- plus étroite (*fluctuation*) — narrower bands
- contraction *f.* des –s bénéficaires — shrinkage (narrowing) of profit margins
- élargissement *m.* des –s bénéficaires — increase of profit margins
- élargissement *m.* des –s de fluctuation — widening of the margin of fluctuation
- réduction *f.* des –s de fluctuation — reduction (narrowing) of the margins
- entamer les –s bénéficaires — to shrink the profit margins

*marginal,
- coût – — marginal cost
- produit – — marginal product
- propension –e à consommer — marginal propensity to consume
- propension –e à épargner — marginal propensity to save
- rendement – — marginal profit

425 / marketing

revenu –	marginal income
utilité –e	marginal utility
valeur –e	marginal value
marketing m. (côté théorique: *mercatique* f.; aspect pratique: *marchéage* m.)	**marketing**
– audit m.	– audit
chef m. du –	– manager
concept m. de –	concept of –
conseil m. en –	– consultant
département m. du –	– department
esprit m., –	– mindedness
étude f. de –	– research
fonction f. du –	– function
instruments m. pl. de –	– instruments
objectif m. –	– goal
politique f. de –	– policy
programme m. de –	– programme, – plan
spécialiste m. du –	marketer
stratégie f. de –	– strategy
technique f. du –	– technique
marketing mix m.	**marketing mix**
*marquage m. des prix	price labelling
*marque f.,	
– collective	collective mark
– de distributeur	private brand
fidélité f. à la –	brand loyalty
image f. de –	brand image
préférence f. de –	brand preference
test m. de notoriété de –	brand awareness test
*masse f.,	
– monétaire	volume of money
présentation f. de –	mass display
matériel m. (*inf.*)	**hardware**
matrice f. (*inf.*)	**matrix**
--mémoire	– memory
– de décodage	decoder –
maussade (*bourse*)	**dull, depressed**
maximisation f. **du profit**	**profit maximization**
*maximum m.,	
tableau m. des maxima (*assur.*)	table of maxima
fixer le – (*assur.*)	to fix the maximum
mécanisme m.	**mechanism**
– du marché	market –

média / 426

– des prix	price –
média *m.* (des –), (voir aussi *support*)	**medium** (media)
évaluation *f.* des –	media evaluation
recherche *f.* sur les –	media research
médiane *f.* (*stat.*)	**median**
***membre** *m.*,	
– à part entière	full member
– à vie	life member, member for life
– associé	associated member
–s fondateurs	foundation members
– payant	paying (subscribing) member
– permanent	permanent member
–s présents (*séance*)	members present
–s représentés (*séance*)	members represented
– suppléant	deputy member
état *m.* –	member state
état *m.* non –	non-member state
***mémoire** *f.* (*inf.*)	**store (storage, memory)**
– à accès sélectif	random-access –
– à accès immédiat	immediate (direct) access –
– à disques	disk –
– à ferrites	core –
– à tambour magnétique	magnetic drum –
– adressable	addressable store
– auxiliaire	auxiliary (backing, secondary) –
– centrale	main –
– de masse	mass(bulk) –, file –
– de travail	working –
– dynamique	dynamic store
– effaçable	erasable –
– externe	external –
– interne	internal –
– magnétique	magnetic –
– morte	read-only (fixed) –
– permanente	permanent –
– principale	main –
– tampon	buffer store
– temporaire	temporary –
capacité *f.* de –	– capacity
mot –	– word
programme *m.* en –	stored program
protection *f.* de –	– protection
nettoyer (vidanger) une –	to erase data
ménage *m.* (*famille*)	**household, family**
– (*entretien*)	household, housekeeping
– type (*calcul index*)	average family
argent *m.* de –	housekeeping money

427 / mensualisation

articles *pl.* de –	household articles
dépenses *pl.* du –	household expenses
femme de –	charwoman, daily (help)
mensualisation *f.* (*salaire*)	**paying by the month**
mercatique *f.* (*aspect théorique du marketing*)	**marketing**
mercuriale *f.*	**market price-list**
*message *m.*,	
– publicitaire	advertising message
*méthode *f.*,	
– d'évaluation	estimation method
– séquentielle (*mark.*)	sequential method
– simultanée	coincidental method
micro-économie *f.*	**microeconomics**
micro-économique	**microeconomic**
migration *f.*	**migration**
– alternante	commuting
– intérieure, interne	internal –
– internationale	international –
– saisonnière	seasonal –
*mine *f.*,	
– abandonnée, désaffectée	abandoned (shutdown) mine
– de renseignements	a mine of information
pris à la – (*prix*)	at the pit-head
carreau *m.* de –	pit-head
exploitation *f.* des –s	mining
ingénieur *m.* des –s	mining engineer
stocks *pl.* sur le carreau de la –	pit-head stocks
prix *m.* départ à la –	pit-head price, price at the pit-head
minimarge *m.*	**discount store, discounter**
*minimum *m.*,	
– d'existence	subsistence minimum
*mise *f.*,	
– à bord	loading on board
– à pied	temporary suspension
– en commun	pooling
mini-serpent *m.*	**worm, mini-snake**
mi-temps, à –	half-time
emploi *m.* à –	half-day job
travailleur *m.* à –	half-timer, half-time worker
travailler à –	to work half time
mobile *m.* (*mark.*)	**rotair(e)**
*modèle *m.*,	
– de demande (*mark.*)	demand model
– de croissance (*mark.*)	growth pattern
– de dépense (*mark.*)	spending pattern
*mois *m.*,	
le premier du –	the first of the month
au – (*payer, louer*)	by the month

moment / 428

par – (*gagner*)	per month, a month
moment *m.* (*stat.*)	**moment**
–s centrés	central –s
– empirique	frequency moment
monnaie *f.,*	
–clé	key (leading) currency
– de réserve	reserve currency
– forte	hard currency
– stable	stable currency
circulation *f.* de la –	money circulation
couverture *f.* de la –	currency cover
dépréciation *f.* de la –	depreciation of money
quantité *f.* de – (en circulation)	quantity of money
rareté *f.* de la –	scarcity of money
stabilisation *f.* de la –	currency stabilization
stabilité *f.* de la –	monetary stability
monoculture *f.*	**monoculture**
monopole *m.,*	
bénéfice *m.* de –	monopoly profits
situation *f.* (position *f.*) de –	monopoly position
monopsone *m.*	**monopsony**
motif *m.* d'achat	**buying motive**
motivation *f.*	**motivation**
étude *f.* de –	– research
moyen *m.,*	
– d'échange	medium of exchange
vivre au-dessus de ses –s	to live beyond one's means
moyenne *f.* (*stat.*)	**mean**
au-dessous de la –	below –
au-dessus de la –	above –
– harmonique	harmonic
– mobile	moving –
– quadratique	quadratic –
multinationale *f.*	**multi-national, multi-national company**
multiplicateur *m.*	**multiplier**
– d'exportation	export –
– d'investissement	investment –
effet *m.* de –	multiplier effect
multiprogrammation *f.* (*inf.*)	**multiprogramming**
multitraitement *m.* (*inf.*)	**multiprocessing**
nature *f.,*	
par –	by nature
navette *f.*	**commutation**
navetteur *m.*	**commuter**
navigation *f.,*	
– par poussage	pushing
– rhénane	navigation on the Rhine
droits *pl.* de –	navigation dues

*navire *m.*,
– porte-barges
– porte-conteneurs
fournisseur *m.* de –

propriétaire *m.* du –
nettoyage *m.*
– de bureaux
entreprise *f.* de –
entreprise *f.* de – (lavage) de vitres
personnel *m.* de –
*niveau *m.*,
au – le plus élevé
– des cours
– de signification, – critique
– record
élévation *f.* du – de vie

*Noël,
achats *pl.* de –
ventes *pl.* de –
noliser
*nombre *m.*,
le – rapport (*stat.*)
notarial
*note *f.*,
– d'hôtel
prendre des –s
présenter la – (*fig.*)
régler une –
porter sur la –
*notoriété *f.*,
– de la publicité
nuage *m.*, – de points (*stat.*)
*numéro
– de compte
– de contrôle
*objet *m.*,
– social, – d'une société

*obligation *f.*,
– subordonnée

*observation *f.* (*mark.*)
– aberrante, extrême
– (in)directe
obsolescence *f.*
*offre *f.*,
– de vente avec prime
– publique d'achat (*d'actions*)
– raisonnable
appel *m.* d'–s
opérateur *m.* (*inf.*)

lash (lighter aboard ship)
container vessel
ship-chandler

shipowner
cleaning
office –
– business
window-cleaning business
–staff

at the highest level
stock price level
level of significance
record level
raising of the standard of life

Christmas shopping, spending
Christmas sales
to charter

ratio
notarial

hotel-bill
to take notes
to present the bill
to settle an account
to charge... on the bill

advertising awareness
scatter of points

account number
check number

objects

subordinated bond

observation
outlier
(in)direct –
obsolescence

premium offer
take-over bid
reasonable offer
invitation of tenders
operator

opération f. (*inf.*) | operation
– arithmétique | arithmetic –
– logique | logic –
opérationnel, – (*usine*) | in working order
recherche – le | operational research
opinion f., enquête f. d'– | opinion survey
institut m. de sondage d'– publique | public opinion research centre
leader m. d'– | opinion leader
sondage m. de l'– publique | opinion research
opposition f., |
frapper d'– | to stop payment
mettre – à | to oppose

option f., |
– d'achat | purchase option
– de vente | seller's option
donneur m. d'– | taker for a put and call
opérations pl. à – | option dealings
or m., |
encaisse f. – | gold coin and bullion
ruée f. vers l'– | gold-rush
ordinateur m. (*inf.*) | computer
– de troisième génération | third generation –
– spécialisé | special purpose –
– universel | general purpose –
ordinogramme m. | **block diagram**
ordonnancement m. | **order to pay**

ordonnancer | **to pass for payment**
ordre m. du jour, |
– très chargé | heavy agenda
établir l'– | to fix (draw up) the agenda

organigramme m. | **organization chart**

outre-mer, |
banque f. d'– | oversea(s) bank
marchés pl. d'– | oversea markets
succursale f. d'– | oversea branch
ouverture, |
en dehors des heures d'– des guichets | outside the banking hours
palette f., |
marchandises pl. sur –s | palletized goods
transport m. sur –s | palletized transport
palettisation f. | **palletization**
palettiser | **to palletize**
panel m. | **panel**
– de consommateurs | consumer –
– de distributeurs | dealer –
membre m. d'un – | – member

panier m. (*libre-service*) | **basket**
– type (*stat.*) | food basket, shopping basket

mettre tous ses œufs dans un même –	to put all the eggs in one basket
*paquet *m.*,	
– de mesures	package of measures
para-étatique	**semi-public**
paramètre *m.* (*stat.*)	**parameter**
– nuisible	nuisance –
– statistique	statistic –
parc *m.*, **automobile**	**motor car fleet**
*parité *f.*,	
fixation *f.* de nouvelles –s	fixing new parities
modification *f.* des –s	parity alterations, parity change
réalignement *m.* (rajustement) *m.*) des –s	parities realignment
*part *f.*,	
– de fonds de placement	investment trust certificate
*partenaire *m.*,	
–s sociaux	management and labo(u)r
*participation *f.*,	
– syndicale	participation in a syndicate
prise *f.* de –	taking of holdings
acquérir une –	to secure an interest
partie civile *f.*	**plaintiff claiming damages**
se porter –	to bring a civil action against ...
*passif *m.*,	
incorporer dans le –, porter au –	to enter on the liabilities side
reprendre le –	to take over the liabilities
pause-café *f.*	**coffee break**
*pavillon *m.*,	
– de complaisance	flag of convenience
– de quarantaine, – jaune	flag of quarantine, yellow flag
– national	national flag
– neutre	neutral flag
le – couvre la marchandise	the flag covers the cargo
*payement *m.*,	
– des salaires par virement (de compte)	payment of wages by transfer
payer-prendre *m.*	**cash-and-carry**
*pays *m.*	
– de consommation	consuming country
– développés	developed countries
– non membres	non-member countries
– partenaires, – membres	member countries
– producteur de matières premières	raw material producing country
– voisin	neighbouring country
pécule *m.*, **– de vacances**	**leave (vacation) pay**

pension f., |
bénéficier d'une –, toucher une – | to draw (have) a pension
octroyer une – | to award (grant) a pension
percentile m. (*stat.*) | **percentile**
*perforateur m., |
– de bandes | tape punch
– de cartes | card punch
perforation f., – numérique | **numerical punching**
péril m. | peril
–s de la mer | – of the sea
– d'incendie | fire –
*période f., |
– budgétaire | budget period
– creuse | slack period
– de base | base period
– de démarrage | starting period
*personnel m., |
– féminin | female staff
– masculin | male staff
– temporaire | temporary personnel

avec un – trop nombreux | overstaffed
avec trop peu de – | understaffed
bureau m. du – | personnel office
charges pl. de – | staff expenditure
cotation f. (au mérite) du – | personnel (merit) rating
délégué m. du – | personnel representative
formation f. du – | staff training
local m. pour le – | staff room
politique f. en matière de – | staff policy
statut m. du – | staff regulations
manquer de – | to be understaffed
*perte f., |
– de (en) valeur | loss in value
– effective (*assur.*) | actual loss
– sensible | considerable loss
– totale effective (*assur.*) | actual total loss
accuser une – | to show a loss
supporter une – | to bear a loss
petro-dollar m. | **petro-dollar**
pétrole m. | petroleum, oil
approvisionnement m. en – | oil supplies
besoins pl. en – | oil needs
pays consommateur de – | oil consuming country
pays exportateur de – | oil exporting country
pays producteur de – | oil producing country
*pétrolier, crise pétrolière | oil crisis
politique pétrolière | oil policy
produits –s | oil products
situation pétrolière | oil situation
société pétrolière | oil company
*pilote , |
marché m. – | pilot (test) market

433 / piquet /de /grève

usine f. – | pilot factory
piquet m. **de grève** | **strike picket**
  constitution f. de –s | picketing
  installer des –s | to post (mount) –s
piste f. (inf.) | **track**
*placement m., |
  en quête de – | in quest of employment
*plafond m. | **upper limit, ceiling**
  cours m. – | ceiling rate, upper intervention limit
  relever le – | to raise the ceiling
plage f. (horaire) |
  – fixe | fixed working hours
  – mobile | staggered working hours
*plan m., |
  – comptable | chart of accounts
  – d'épargne | savings scheme
plancher m. | **lower limit**
  cours – | floor rate, lower intervention limit
planning m. | **planning**
*plein m., |
  – de conservation (assur.) | own retention
  contrôle m. des –s | control of the line limits
*plus-value f., |
  impôt m. sur les –s | betterment tax

*point, |
  un – chaud | a ticklish question, subject
  – d'achat | point of purchase
  – d'échantillonnage | sampling point
  – de rupture (inf.) | breakpoint
  – de seuil, – mort | break-even point
  – de vente | point of sale
  – d'intervention (voir aussi plafond, plancher) | intervention limit
  – faible | weak point
  être arrivé au – mort | to have reached a deadlock
  nuage m. de –s (stat.) | scatter of points
*police f., |
  – collective | group policy
  – combinée | comprehensive policy
  – individuelle | individual policy
  – mondiale | world-wide policy
  conditions pl. de – | policy conditions
  copie f. de – | copy of the policy
  frais pl. de – | policy fee, entrance fee
  numéro m. de – | policy number
  souscrire une – | to underwrite a policy
*politique f., |
  d'austérité | austerity policy
  – de l'emploi | employment policy
  – de libre-échange | free-trade policy
  – fiscale | fiscal policy
  – monétaire | monetary policy

population / 434

– de monnaie facile, de l'argent bon marché	easy-money policy
– des revenus	incomes policy
population *f.* (*stat.*)	**population, universe**
– finie	finite –
– hétérogène	heterogeneous –
– homogène	homogeneous –
– hypothétique	hypothetical population
– infinie	infinite –
*****portefeuille** *m.*,	
– -actions	shareholding, stockholding
– cédé (*assur.*)	portfolio ceded
– repris (*assur.*)	portfolio assumed
transfert *m.* de –	transfer of portfolio
poster	**to post**
post-test *m.*	**post test**
potentiel (*adj.*)	**potential**
client –	– customer
*****potentiel** *m.*	**potential, capacity**
– de croissance	growth –
– de main-d'œuvre	manpower (labo(u)r) potential
pour-compte, pourcompte *m.*	**undertaking to sell (sale of) goods on behalf of the sender**
poussage *m.*	**pushing**
navigation *f.* par –	pushing
poussée *f.*	**surge**
– de la consommation	upsurge of consumption
– de la demande	sudden increase in demand
– des salaires	wage push
– des prix	price upsurge
– inflationniste	inflationary tendency, pressure
poussette *f.* (**de marché**)	**shopping trolley**
pousseur *m.*	**push boat**
*****pouvoir** *m.*,	
– de signer	power to sign
– d'achat de la monnaie	purchasing power of money
absorption *f.* du – d'achat	absorption of the puchasing power
diminution *f.* du – d'achat	shrinkage in purchasing power
stabilité *f.* du – d'achat	stability of purchasing power
éponger le – d'achat	to mop up (absorb) purchasing power
*****pratique** *f.*,	
– d'affaires	business practice
libre – (*mar.*)	(free) pratique
donner libre – à	to admit to pratique
*****précompte** *m.*,	
– immobilier	withholding tax on income from real estate
– mobilier	withholding tax on income [come
– professionnel	withholding tax on professional in-

*préférence f.,
 – de goût (mark.)
 – de marque (mark.)
 – pour la liquidité

*prélèvement m.,
 – en espèces
*présentation f.
 – du produit
 – en vrac
*présenter,
 – la note (fig.)
présentoir m.
 – de comptoir
*presse f.,
 agence f. de coupures de –
 conférence f. de –
 représentant m. de la –
*pression f.,
 – fiscale
 –s salariales
 – spéculative
 forte – sur une monnaie
 subir une –
prêt-bail m.
pré-test m.

prétester
pretium doloris
prévention-incendie f. (assur.)
*prévision f.
 – à court terme
 – à long terme
 –s de ventes
price-earnings ratio m.

*prime f.
 – acquise (assur.)
 – à la construction
 – arriérée (assur.)
 – auto-payante

 – brute (assur.)
 – courante (assur.)
 – de base (assur.)
 – de conversion
 – de fidélité
 – de fin d'année
 – de risque (assur.)
 – de salissure
 – de vie chère
 – échue (assur.)

taste preference
brand preference
liquidity preference

withdrawal of cash
display
product design
bulk –

to present the bill
special promotion stand
counter display

press clipping bureau
press conference
representative of the press

pressure of taxation
wage pressure
speculative pressure
heavy pressure on a currency
to be under pressure
lend-lease
pretest

to pretest
smart money
fire prevention
forecast
 short term –
 long term –
 sales expectations
price/earnings ratio

premium
 earned –
 building subsidy
 – in arrear
 self-liquidating –, self-liquidator

 gross –
 current –
 basic –
 conversion –
 fidelity –
 Christmas bonus
 risk premium
 dirt money
 cost-of-living bonus
 – due

principal /d'un effet / 436

– faible (*assur.*) — low –
– fixe (*assur.*) — fixed –
– initiale (*assur.*) — initial –
– nette (*assur.*) — net –
– progressive (*assur.*) — increasing –
– ristournée (*assur.*) — returned –
– supplémentaire (*assur.*) — additional –
– unique (*assur.*) — single –
– variable (*assur.*) — variable –
calcul *m.* de – — calculation of –
fixation *f.* de la – (*assur.*) — fixing (assessment) of the –

majoration *f.* de – — increase of –
paiement *m.* des –s (*assur.*) — payment of –s
quittance *f.* de – (*assur.*) — – receipt
rabais *m.* sur la – (*assur.*) — – rebate
recettes de – (*assur.*) — – income

réduction *f.* de – — reduction in –

supplément *m.* de – — additional –
*principal *m.* d'un effet — **amount**
printemps *m.*, ventes *pl.* du – — **spring sales**
***prise** *f.*,
– de participation dans ... — participation in ...
– en charge — taking in charge
***prix** *m.* — **price**
– choc — knockdown –
– d'ami — special –
– d'émission (*fonds commun*) — issue –
– départ usine — – ex works (factory)
– de rachat, de remboursement (*fonds commun*) — resale –
– d'objectif — target –
– intéressant — attractive –
– pour le dernier consommateur — – to the ultimate consumer
– rendu — delivered –, free delivered

– rigide — rigid –
– stable — stabile –
– usine — – ex factory
équilibre *m.* des – — – equilibrium
marquage *m.* des – — – marking
mécanisme *m.* des – — – mechanism
poussée *f.* des – — – upsurge
soutien *m.* des – — – support
ajuster les – à — to adjust –s
pousser les – — to boost –s
***probabilité** *f.* (*stat.*) — **probability**
– à la taille — tail –
– de vie — average life expectancy, expectation of life

distribution *f.* de – — – distribution

calcul *m.* des –s	– calculus
théorie *f.* des –s	theory of probabilities
*procédure *f.*,	
– d'arbitrage	arbitration proceedings
processeur *m.* (*inf.*)	processor
*producteur *m.* (*assur.*)	**insurance agent**
*production *f.*	**production**
– (*assur.*)	new business
– de bière	beer output
– nationale	domestic –
– optimale	maximum output
– record	record output
– saisonnière	seasonal –
– par heure homme	output per man-hour
courbe *f.* de –	– curve
coût *m.* de –	– cost
facteur *m.* de –	factor of –
frais *pl.* de – (*assur.*)	new business expenses
niveau *m.* de la –	level of –
stade *m.* de –	stage of –
arrêter la – de ...	to discontinue the – of ...
augmenter la –	to step up –
freiner la –	to restrain –
ralentir la –	to slow (scale) down –
*productivité *f.*,	
– marginale	marginal productivity
prime *f.* de –	productivity bonus
accroître la –	to step up (lift) productivity
*produit *m.* (*article*)	**product**
–s alimentaires	foods, food products
–s complémentaires	complementary –s
– d'appel (*mark.*)	loss leader
– de substitution	substitute –
– factice	dummy
–s non alimentaires	non-foods
chef *m.* de –, spécialiste –	product manager, brand manager
diversification *f.* des –s	product diversification
lancement *m.* de –s nouveaux	launching of new products
*produit *m.* (*rapport*),	
– d'escompte	proceeds of a discounted bill
– intérieur brut	gross domestic product
– intérieur net	net domestic product
*professionnel,	
aptitude *f.* –le	professional qualification
cours *m.* de formation –le	training course
formation –le	vocational training
formation –le sur le tas	on-the-job training
programmation *f.*	**programming**
– automatique (*inf.*)	automatic –
– linéaire (*inf.*)	linear –

programme / 438

langage *m.* de – (*inf.*) — – language
programme *m.* (*inf.*) — **program**
– à longue échéance — long-range (forward) planning
– d'application (*inf.*) — application –
– de contrôle (*inf.*) — control –
– de fabrication — manufacturing –

– de service, utilitaire (*inf.*) — utility –, service –
– d'interprétation (*inf.*) — interpretive –
– d'investissement — investment –
– en mémoire (*inf.*) — stored –
– financier — financial –
– routier — road building –
bibliothèque *f.* de –s (*inf.*) — – library
établir un – — to work out a –
programmeur *m.* — **programmer**
***promesse** *f.*,
– d'achat — undertaking to buy
– de crédit — promise of a credit
– d'escompte — promise of discount
– de vente — undertaking to sell

promoteur *m.* — **promoter**
– (*constructions*) — property developer
***propriétaire** *m.*,
– actuel — present owner
– de navire — shipowner
– légitime — lawful owner
seul – — sole owner

prospect *m.* — **prospect**
***protection** *f.*,
– contre l'incendie — fire protection
– de l'épargne — protection of savings
– du consommateur — consumer protection
– des locataires — tenants protection
– du travail — labo(u)r protection
***provision** *f.*,
– pour amortissement — allowance for depreciation
– pour charges (obligations) imprévisibles — reserve for contingent liabilities
– pour dépréciation — provision for depreciation

–s pour pertes et charges — provision for losses and expenses

– pour retraites du personnel — pension reserve

–s pour risques — contingency reserve
***public** *m.*,
placer dans le – — to place with the public
***publicitaire**,
annonce *f.* – — advertisement
carte-réponse *f.* – — advertising reply card

cartonnage *m.* –	display
dépenses –s	publicity expenses
efficacité *f.* –	advertising effectiveness
émission *f.* –	commercial –
message *m.* –	advertising message
semaine *f.* –	publicity week
slogan *m.* –	advertising slogan
supports –s	advertising media
texte *m.* –	advertising copy
thème *m.* –	advertising theme
*****publicité** *f.*	
– à énigme	teaser advertisement
– au point de vente	point of sale advertising
– avec primes	gift scheme, free gift system
– d'appel	stopper
– d'association	tie-up advertising
– de masse	mass advertising
– de rappel	follow-up advertising
– directe	direct advertising
– directe par voie postale	direct mail
– institutionnelle	institutional advertising
– mensongère	misleading advertisement
– par affiches	billboard (poster) advertising
– par annonce	advertising
–presse	press advertising
– sélective, systématique	selective (systematic) advertising
conseil *m.* en –	advertising consultant
emplacement *m.* réservé à la –	advertising space
matériel *m.* de –	advertising material
voiture *f.* de –	advertising van
notoriété *f.* de la –	advertising awareness
puissance *f.* (*stat.*)	**power**
pupitre *m.* (**de commande**) (*inf.*)	**console, control desk**
pupitreur *m.* (*inf.*)	**console operator**
*****qualification** *f.*,	
– du travail	job evaluation
*****qualité** *f.*,	
contrôle *m.* de –	quality control
garantie *f.* de –	guarantee of quality
label *m.* (marque *f.*) de –	– label
normes *pl.* de –	quality standard
quantile *m.*	**quantile**
quartile *m.*	**quartile**
quasi-monnaie *f.*	**near-money**
*****question** *f.* (*mark.*)	**question**
– alternative	alternative –
– ambiguë	ambiguous –
– directe	direct –
– fermée	closed –

439 / *publicité*

– indirecte | indirect –
– filtre | filter –
– orientée | leading –
– ouverte | open-ended –
– piège | trick –
formulation f. de la – | – formulation
libellé m. de la – | wording of the –
*questionnaire m., |
établir un – | to make out a questionnaire
remplir un – | to fill in a questionnaire
*quittance f., |
– de prime | premium receipt
rack-jobber m. (*vendeur indépendant dans grand magasin*) | **rack-jobber**
rail m. | **rail**
par – | by –
route et – | road –
*raisonnable, |
délai m. – | reasonable time
prix m. – | reasonable price
avec un soin – | with reasonable care
*ralentissement m., |
– dans les affaires | slack times in business
*rappel m. (*visite*) (*mark.*) | **recall**
*rapport m., |
– cours/cash flow | price/cash flow ratio
– cours/bénéfices | price/earnings ratio
*rapport m. (*compte rendu*) |
– d'activité | progress report
– de gestion (*fonds commun*) | management report
raréfaction f. | **rarefaction**
rayonnage m. | **shelf**
réalignement m. | **realignment**
– des parités | parities –
– monétaire | – of currencies
réapprovisionnement m. | **replenishment, restocking**
*réassurance f., |
– en excédents | surplus reinsurance
– en excédent de sinistres | excess of loss reinsurance
– quote-part | quota-share reinsurance
– obligatoire | obligatory reinsurance
compagnie f. de – | reinsurance company
courtier m. de – | reinsurance broker
prime f. de – | reinsurance premium
traité m. (contrat) de – | reinsurance treaty, contract
traité m. de – en excédents | surplus reinsurance treaty
traité m. de – en excédent de sinistres | excess of loss reinsurance treaty
traité m. de – en quote-part | quota share (reinsurance) treaty
réassuré, le – | **reinsured**

recel m.	concealment
recherche f.,	
– auprès des consommateurs	consumer research
– de motivation	motivation research
– opérationnelle	operational research
– publicitaire	advertising research
*réclamation,	
à renvoyer en cas de – (souche de contrôle)	return in case of complaint
*réclame f.,	
– de la semaine	this week's special offer, draw
semaine f. (de) –	publicity week
*reconstitution f.,	
– des stocks	restocking, replenishment of stock
– des réserves	rebuilding of reserves
reconversion f. (industrie)	reconversion
reconvertir en ...	to reconvert, to turn over to ...
*recouvrement m. (inf.)	overlap
recyclage m., – (déchets)	recycling
– (formation complémentaire)	retraining, refresher course
rédacteur m. (d'agence de publicité)	copy-writer
redistribution f.	redistribution
redondance f.	redundance, redundancy
réembaucher	to re-engage
*réescompte m.,	
faculté f. de –	rediscount facilities
taux m. de –	rediscount rate
*réévaluation f.,	
– globale	global value adjustment
– individuelle	individual value adjustment
taux m. de –	rate of revaluation
*réexpédier à ...	to send back, to return to ...
*réexpedition f. (à l'expéditeur)	sending back, return
référé m.	summary procedure
ordonnance f. de –	provisional order
président m. en –	judge sitting in chambers
rendre une ordonnance de –	to give a summary judgment
introduire un –	to apply for conditional injunction
regain m. d activité	recrudescence of activity
regardant	near, close, stingy
*région f.	area, region
– agricole	agricultural area
– critique (stat.)	critical region
– sous-développée	development area
*règlement m.,	
– uniforme pour l'encaissement des	uniform rules for the collection of

réglementé / 442

effets de commerce	commercial paper
réglementé,	
marché –	controlled market
prix –	regulated price
***régression** f. (stat.)*	**regression**
– curviligne	curvilinial –
– linéaire	linear –
– multiple	multiple –
analyse f. de –	– analysis
coefficient m. de –	– coefficient
courbe f. de –	– curve
équation f. de –	– equation
ligne f. de –	line of –
surface f. de –	– surface
regroupement m.	**regrouping**
relance f.,	
– de l'économie	economic pump priming
espérer une – économique	to expect an economic revival
lettre de – (*mark.*)	follow-up letter, reminder letter
relancer (*économie*)	**to reactivate, boost, stimulate**
***relation** f.,*	
– bancaire	banker
–s publiques	public relations
***relevé** m.,*	
– de compte journalier	(daily) statement of account
***remboursement** m.,*	
– en 10 tranches annuelles égales	redemption in 10 equal annual instalments
– intégral	full repayment
conditions pl. de –	terms of repayment
date f. de –	date of repayment
droit m. au –	right to repayment
valeur f. de – (*fonds commun*)	redemption price, resale price
remise f.	
– à neuf	renovation
***remise** f.*	
(*effet de commerce*), – simple	clean remittance
lettre f. de –	remittance letter
***remplacement** m.,*	
– en nature (*assur.*)	replacement in kind
achat m. de –	replacement purchase
vente f. de –	replacement sale
***rémunération** f.,*	
– du travail	remuneration of labo(u)r
– en espèces	remuneration in cash
– en nature	payment in kind

443 / rendement

*rendement *m.*,
– effectif, réel — effective yield
– horaire, à l'heure — output per hour, hourly output
– net — net proceeds
amélioration *f.* du – — earnings improvement
diminution *f.* du – — decrease in the yield

renflouer (*entreprise*) — **to set afloat, to put on its feet again**

*rente *f.*,
– de veuve — widow's annuity
– de vieillesse — old-age pension
– d'invalidité — disability annuity
*réparation *f.*,
– du dommage — compensation of damage
*répartition *f.*,
– de l'échantillon — sample distribution
– de marque — brand distribution
– des risques — spreading of risks
– par âge — age distribution
– professionnelle — break-down by occupations, professions

clé *f.* de – — distribution ratio

*répartition *f.* (*titres*)
compte *m.* de – (*fonds de placement*) — distribution account
répercuter sur ... — **to pass on ...**
se – — to have repercussion on ...
répondeur *m.*,
– téléphonique — telephone answerer

*réponse *f.*,
– s.v.pl. sur carte ci-jointe — please reply on enclosed reply form
– par retour du courrier — reply by return of post
– de mémoire provoquée (*mark.*) — aided recall
– de mémoire spontanée — spontaneous recall
– erronée (*mark.*) — answer error
constance *f.* de – (*markt.*) — stability of answers
*représentant *m.*,
– à l'étranger — representative abroad

– du personnel — staff representative
*représentation *f.*,
– à l'étranger — representative office abroad

repris,
emballage – — returnable packing
emballage non – — non returnable packing

,,non –'' — no return
*reprise *f.*,
– saisonnière — seasonal revival

réserve / 444

– (*par le locataire*)	taking over
– (*de voiture*)	trading-in
voiture f. de –	traded-in car
*réserve f.,	
– spéciale (*assur.*)	special reserve
*responsabilité f.,	
– contractuelle	contractual liability
– de l'architecte	architect's liability
– du maître de l'ouvrage	liability of the building owner
– légale	legal liability
– partagée	prorata liability
restockage m.	**restocking, stock rebuilding**
restaurant m.	**restaurant**
– d'entreprise	(industrial) canteen
*restrictions,	
– à l'importation	import restrictions
– au commerce	trade restrictions
– budgétaires	budget cuts
– monétaires	monetary (currency) restriction
allègement m. des ––	easing of restrictions
lever des –	to lift (abrogate) restrictions
*résultat m.,	
– final	final result
– global	total result
– partiel	partial result
– tangible	tangible result
*retenir,	
– à la source	to deduct at source
*rétention f. (*assur.*)	**retention**
retombée f.,	
– (de la crise) sur ...	repercussions on ...
*retraite f.,	
– anticipée	early retirement
atteindre l'âge de la –	to reach the retirement age
rétribuer	**to remunerate**
rétroaction f. (*inf.*)	**feedback**
rétrocédant m. (*assur.*)	**retroceding company**
rétrocéder	**to return, to retrocede**
rétrocessionnaire m.	**retrocessionaire**
*revendeur m.,	
panel m. de –s	dealer panel
*revenu m.,	
– discrétionnaire (*mark.*)	discretionary income
– disponible (*mark.*)	disposable income
– familial	family income
– individuel	individual income
– nominal	nominal income
– salarial	earned income
élasticité f. de –s	income elasticity
équilibre m. du –	income equilibrium

flux *m.* de –s	earnings flow
inégalité *f.* des –s	inequality of income
nivellement *m.* des –s	levelling of income
politique *f.* des –s	incomes policy
tranche *f.* de –s	income bracket
révision *f.* (*remise en état*)	**overhaul**
***révocation** f.* (*chèque*)	**countermanding**
***révoquer** (chèque)*	**to countermand (payment of)**
***risque** m.*,	
– assurable	insurable risk
– constant	constant risk
– couvert	risk covered
– de voisinage	neighbouring risk
– industriel	industrial risk
– nucléaire	nuclear risk
– propre	own risk
– routier	road risk
– variable	variable risk
aggravation *f.* du –	increase of risk
appréciation *f.* du –	risk assessment
couverture *f.* de –	risk covering
division *f.* des –s	spreading of risks
évaluation *f.* du –	risk appraisal
prime *f.* de –	risk premium
rotair *m.* (*le mobile*)	rotair(e)
***rotation** f.*,	
– des postes de travail, – des fonctions	job rotation
rouge (voir aussi *déficitaire*)	
en –	in the red
se solder en –	to go in the red
chiffres –s	red
intérêt –	red interest
nombres –s	red products
***routine** f.* (*inf.*)	**routine**
– d'assemblage (*inf.*)	assembly program (routine)
– d'entrée -sortie	input-output routine
rue *f.*,	
– commerçante	shopping street
***salaire** m.*,	
– de poche	take-home pay
– garanti	guaranteed wage
– indexé	index-linked wage
– mensuel	monthly wage
– plein	full wages
– social	social wages
compte *m.* –	wage account
structure *f.* des –s	wage structure
***salarial**,*	
charges –es, coûts salariaux	wage costs
échelon –	wage bracket, wage group

sauvette / 446

négociations −es | wage talks
poussée −e | upward tendency of wages
appuyer des revendications −es | to support (enforce) wage demands

sauvette, vendeur (marchand) à la − | illicit street vendor
savoir-faire *m.* (know-how *m.*) | **know-how**
*****secret*** *m.* (*coffre*) | **combination**
serrure *f.* à − | combination lock
*****secteur*** *m.*,
 − clé | key sector
 − primaire | primary sector
 − secondaire | secondary sector
 − tertiaire | tertiary sector
sécurité sociale | **social security**
 cotisations à la − | National Insurance contributions
 organisme *m.* de la − | − organization
 prestations de la − | National Insurance benefits
 système *m.* de la − | − system
segmentation *f.* | **segmentation**
 −des marchés | market −
sélection *f.* (*stat.*) | **selection**
 − au hasard | random −
 − systématique | systematic −
*****semaine*** *f.*,
 − du blanc | white sale
 − (de) réclame | publicity week
 réclame *f.* de la − | this week's special offer, draw

séquence *f.* (*inf.*) | **sequence**
*****série*** *f.*,
 − chronologique, temporelle (*stat.*) | time series
 fins *pl.* de − | oddments, remnants
 fabriquer en − | to produce in series
*****serment*** *m.*,
 − déclaratoire, révélatoire | debtor's oath (that he has no further seizable effects)

serpent *m.* (*monétaire*) | **snake, currency snake**
 à l'intérieur du − | within the −
 entrée *f.* dans le − | entry into the −
 sortie *f.* du − | withdrawal (departure) from the −
 réintégrer le − | to reenter into the −
serrure *f.*, − à combinaisons, à secret | combination lock, letter lock

*****service*** *m.*,
 − après vente | after-sale service
seuil *m.* | **threshold**
 − de confiance | confidence level
 − de rentabilité | break-even point

 − de signification | significance level
*****siège*** *m.*,
 transférer le − à... | to transfer the seat (registered office) to...

sigle *m.*	initials
***sinistre** m.,*	
– bénin	minor loss
– en suspens	pending loss
– incendie	fire damage
– partiel	partial loss
cause *f.* du –	cause of loss
déclaration *f.* du –	notice of claim, of loss
description *f.* et estimation *f.* du –	description of claim and estimate of its amount
fréquence *f.* des –s	frequency of losses
probabilité *f.* de –s	probability of loss
service *m.* des –s	claims department
statistique *f.* des –s	loss statistics
***situation** f.,*	
– économique mondiale	world economic situation
***société** f.,*	
– de consommation	consumer society
– de loisirs	leisure society
– de l'opulence	affluent society
– émettrice	issuing company
– immobilière d'investissement	real-estate fund
– étrangère	foreign company
droit *m.* des –s	company law
impôt *m.* sur les –s	corporation tax
software *m.* (logiciel) (*inf.*)	software
***soin** m.,*	
avec un – raisonnable	with reasonable care
sondage *m.* (*stat.*)	sampling
– à plusieurs degrés	multi-stage –
– à plusieurs phases	multi-phase –
– aréolaire	area –
– avec remplacement	– with replacement
– en grappes	cluster –
– par quotas	quota sample
– représentatif	representative –
– sans remplacement	– without replacement
– stratifié	stratified –
enquête *f.* par –	sample survey
plan *m.* de –	– plan
sélection *f.* des unités de –	selection of sample units
taux *m.* (fraction *f.*) de –	– rate
unité *f.* de –	sample unit
sort *m.* (*d'un effet de commerce*)	fate
avis *m.* de –	advice of – (of bill)
demande *f.* de –	tracer
aviser sur le –	to advise the –
sort *m.* (*lotterie*)	lot
tirage *m.* au –	drawing
tirer au –	to draw by lot

sortie / 448

sortie *f. (inf.)* — output
  routine *f.* de – — output routine
sou *m.*, il a des –s — he has tin, brass
  ne pas avoir un – — not to have a penny
  être près de ses –s — to count every penny
  regarder à un – — to look twice at every penny
soudure *f. (fig.)* — **bridging** (of a gap)
  crédit *m.* de – — interim loan
  faire la – — to tide over, to bridge the gap
*****soumission** *f.*,
  – la plus élevée — highest tender
  – la plus basse — lowest tender
sous-agence *f.* — **sub-agency**
sous-compte *m.* — **sub-account**
sous-développement *m.* — **underdevelopment**
sous-échantillon *m. (stat.)* — **sub-sample**
sous-ensemble *m. (stat.)* — fractional population
sous-population *f. (stat.)* — fractional population
sous-programme *m. (inf.)* — **subroutine**
sous-traitance *f.* — **subcontracting**

  industrie *f.* de – — ancillary industrie
sous-traitant *m.* — **subcontractor**

*****soutenir**,
  – une monnaie — to support (back) a currency
souvenir *m.* **aidé** *(mark.)* — **aided recall**

spot-T.V. *m.* — **commercial, spot**
*****stable** *(cours)* — **steady**
stagflation *f.* (stagnation et inflation) — **stagflation**
standardiste *f.* — **(telephone) operator**
*****statistique** *f.* — **statistics**
  – de la mortalité — death –
  – de l'emploi — – of employment
  – démographique — population –
  – descriptive — descriptive –
  – des salaires — wage –
  – du commerce — trade statistics
  – du commerce extérieur — external trade –
  – mathématique — mathematical –
  –s officielles — official –
  –s primaires — primary –
  –s secondaires — secondary –
  – sociale — social –
  – sous forme de tableau — – in tabular form
  institut *m.* des –s — statistical office
  établir des –s — to compile –
*****statistique** *(adj.)* — **statistical**
  enquête *f.* – — – inquiry
  rapport *m.* – — – report
  tableau *m.* – — – table

statistiquement
 enregistrer –
statisticien *m.*
ʘ**stimuler,**
 – l'activité économique

 – la demande
 – la production
 – la vente
stochastique (*stat.*)
 variable –
ʘ**stock** *m.*,
 – au début de l'exercice
 – effectif
 – en fin d'exercice, – final
 – initial
 – permanent (indispensable)
 – minimum
 – obligatoire
 – prévisionnel
 les –s s'épuisent

 les –s se sont dégonflés
 les –s se sont gonflés
 dégonflement *m.* des –s
 excédent *m.* de –s
 gonflement *m.* des –s
 liquidation *f.* de –s
 pénurie *f.* de –s
 réduction *f.* des –s
 écouler des –s
 épuiser les –s
 liquider des –s
 puiser dans les –s

ʘ**stockage** *m.*
 – (*spéculatif*)
 – de l'information
 capacité *f.* de –
 possibilités *pl.* de –
ʘ**stocker,**
 – (*spéculatif*)
 – des informations
subséquent
 endosseur –

subsistance *f.*
 minimum *m.* de –
 moyens *pl.* de –
ʘ**subvention** *f.*,
 accorder des –s
subventionné par l'État

statistically
 to record –
statistician

 to boost business

 to stimulate demand
 to boost (step up) production
 to boost sales
stochastic
 – variable

 opening stock
 actual stock
 closing stock
 initial (opening) stock
 permanent stock
 minimum supply
 compulsory stock
 estimated stock
 stocks are running low, are running
  out
 stocks have been depleted
 stocks are piling up
 decrease in stock
 surplus stock
 inventory accumulation
 liquidation of stocks
 shortage of stocks
 reduction of stocks
 to get rid of old stock
 to exhaust stocks
 to clear stock
 to draw on the stock

stocking
 hoarding
 data storage
 storage capacity
 storage accommodation

 to hoard
 to store data
subsequent
 – endorser

subsistence
 minimum of –
 means of –

 to grant subsidies
 State-subsidized

succession f.,
ouverture f. de la – — opening of a succession
partage m. de – — division of an estate
suffir, qui se suffisent à eux-mêmes — self-contained (industries), self-supporting (countries)
il suffit à toutes les dépenses — he can meet all the expenses
supplément m.,
pour – d'examen — for further consideration
– de travail — additional (extra) work
– de vie chère — (high) cost-of-living bonus
support m. **publicitaire** — **advertising medium**
surassurer — **to over-insure**
surchauffé (*économie*) — **overheated**
surconsommation f. — **overconsumption**
surface f. — **surface**
– de vente — sales space
– financière — financial standing

surgélation f. — **deep-freezing**
surgelé, produits alimentaires –s — deep-frozen foods
surinvestissement m. — **over-investment**
surnombre, en – — **redundant**
surnuméraire m. — **supernumerary**
surplus m.,
– de caisse — cash surplus
– d'exportation — export surplus
sursalaire m. — **extra pay**
surtaxe f.,
– sur les importations — import surcharge

survie f.,
table f. de – — survivorship table
syndicat m. (*émission*)
chef m. de file du – — leading underwriter
membre m. d'un – — member of a syndicate, underwriter
participation f. dans un – — participation in a syndicate

système m.,
analyse f. de – (*inf.*) — system analysis
tambour m. **magnétique** — **magnetic drum**
tarif m.,
– applicable — tariff applicable
appliquer un – — to apply a tariff
établir (fixer) un – — to fix rates
réduire le – — to lower the rates
relever le – — to raise the rates
taux m.,
– de base — basic rate
– de change (voir ce mot)
– de croissance — growth rate
– des salaires — wage rate
– pivot — central (middle) rate
– préférentiel — preferential rate

– progressifs	graduated rates
– usuraire	usurious interest
taux *m.* **de change**	**exchange rate**
– flottant	floating –
– fixes	fixed –s
– officiel	official –
fixation *f.* de nouveaux –	fixing of new –s
marge *f.* de fluctuation du –	fluctuation band (margin) of the –s
réalignement *m.* des –	realignment of –s
laisser flotter le –	to float the –
*****taxe** *f.*,	
– communale	municipal tax
– de péréquation des intérêts	interest equalization tax
– proportionnelle	proportional tax
– sur les opérations de bourse	stock exchange tax
– sur la plus-value	increment tax
télécommunication *f.*	**telecommunication**
réseau *m.* de –	– network
service *m.* de –	– service
*****téléphone** *m.*,	
– intérieur, interphone	housephone, interphone
usagers *pl.* du –	(telephone) subscribers
avoir le –	to be on the phone
par –	on the phone
télétraitement *m.*	**teleprocessing**
télexer	**to telex, to send a telex**
télexiste	**telex operator**
témoins *pl.* (*stat.*)	**controls**
tempérer	**to check, to restrain**
*****temps** *m.*,	
– d'accès (*inf.*)	access time
– d'arrêt (*travail*)	pause
– d'attente (*inf.*)	latency, waiting time
– de panne (*inf.*)	down time
– mort (*inf.*)	idle (dead) time
– partagé, partage de – (*inf.*)	time sharing
(en)-réel (*inf.*)	real time
*****tendance** *f.*,	
– centrale (*stat.*)	central tendency
– curviligne (*stat.*)	curvilinear trend
– de la conjoncture	economic trend
– des prix	price trend
– générale	general tendency
– irrégulière	irregular trend
– linéaire (*stat.*)	linear trend
– saisonnière	seasonal trend
– séculaire (*stat.*)	secular trend
ajustement *m.* de la – (*stat.*)	trend fitting
analyse *f.* de – (*stat.*)	trend analysis

élimination *f.* de la – (*stat.*)	trend elimination
renversement *m.* de la –	trend reversal
tenue *f.* **de compte**	**account keeping**
terminal *m.* (*inf.*)	**terminal**
***terrain** *m.*,	
enquête *f.* sur le –	field-research
enquêteur *m.* sur le –	field-worker
travail *m.* sur le –	field-work
céder (perdre) du –	to lose ground
gagner du –	to gain ground
territoire *m.*	**area**
aménagement *m.* du –	country planning
test *m.*	**test**
– à l'aveugle	blind –
– à posteriori	post test
– ballon	balloon-test
– d'association	association –
– de notoriété de marques	brand-awareness –
– de préférence	preference –
– de produits	product –
– de signification (*stat.*)	significance –
– de texte	copy testing
– d'intelligence	intelligence –
– préalable	pretest
marché *m.* –	– market
période *f.* de –	– period
région *f.* –	– area
ville *f.* –	– town
faire un –	to test
soumettre à un –	to put through a –
subir un –	to undergo a –
subir un – avec succès	to pass a –
***testament** *m.*,	
ouverture *f.* du –	reading of the will
tête *f.* (*inf.*)	**head**
– d'écriture	write (writing) –
– d'effacement	erase (erasing) –
– de lecture	read (reading) –
– magnétique	magnetic –
tirage *m.* (*stat.*)	**drawing**
– avec (sans) remplacement	– with (without) replacement
tiroir-caisse *m.*	**till**
toile *f.* **d'araignée,** théorème *m.* de la –	**cobweb-theorem**
***tolérance** *f.* (*stat.*)	**tolerance**
limite *f.* de –	limit of –
***total**,	
faire le –	to total up, add up
tourniquet *m.*	**turnstile**
traducteur *m.* (*inf.*)	**translator, translating programme)**

*traduire (*montrer*) | to show
se – par... | to result in...
se – par une perte | to show a loss
*trafic *m.*, |
– à grande distance | long-distance traffic
– à petite distance | short-distance traffic
– fluvial | inland water transport
*traite *f.*, |
– à échéance | usance draft
– de cavalerie | accommodation bill
traitement *m.* (*inf.*) | **processing**
– de l'information | data –, information –
– automatique de l'information | automatic data –
– immédiat | on-line –
– intégré | integrated –
– multi-tâches | multi-task operation
– par lots | batch processing
– temps partagé | time-sharing
– en temps réel | real-time –
unité centrale de – | central – unit
*traitement *m.* (*salaire*), |
maintien *m.* du paiement du – | continuation of salary payments
retenue *f.* sur le – | retention on salary
*transbordement *m.*, |
– en cours de route | transhipment en route
*transfert *m.*, |
– fiduciaire | conveyance by way of security
*transformation *f.* (*de produits*) | **processing**
coût *m.* de la – | – costs
industrie *f.* de – | – industry
*transformations *pl.* (*travaux*) | **alterations**
– et réparations | alterations and repairs
faire des – | to make alterations
transiger | to effect a compromise
mieux vaut – que plaider | to come to an arrangement is better than going to law
*transit *m.*, |
autorisation *f.* de – | transit permit
déclaration *f.* de – | transit entry
translatif, acte – de propriété | deed of conveyance of property
*transmission *f.*, |
– de données | data transmission
*transport *m.*, |
– à longue distance | long-distance traffic, (Amér.) long haul
– combiné | combined transport

travail / 454

– de marchandises à petite distance	short-distance goods traffic
– de domicile à domicile	door-to-door transport
– maritime, par mer	ocean (sea) carriage, carriage by sea
– par conteneurs	container transport
*travail *m.*,	
– à l'heure	time-work
– de routine	routine work
– dur	hard work
– malsain	unhealthy work
– salarié	paid labo(u)r
– salissant	dirty (messy) work
spécification *f.* du –	job description
– sur le terrain (*stat.*)	field-work
comité *m.* de –	working party
document *m.* de –	working sheet, working papers
séance *f.* de –	working meeting, working session
*travailler,	
– à mi-temps	to work half-time
– à plein temps, à temps plein	to work full-time
– à temps réduit	to work (on) short-time
*travailleur *m.*,	
– à mi-temps	half-timer, half-time worker
– étranger	foreign worker
*trésorerie *f.* (*banque*)	cashiers' department
état *m.* de la –	liquid position
tri *m.*, – combiné	cross tabulation
analyse *f.* par –s croisés	cross-section analysis
tronqué (*stat.*)	**truncated**
trop-perçu *m.*	**amount overpaid**
trou *m.*, boucher un –	to fill (stop) a gap
faire un – pour en boucher un autre	to rob Peter to pay Paul
trouble *m.*, –s civils (*assur.*)	civil commotions
*unité *f.*,	
– arithmétique	arithmetic unit
– centrale de traitement (*inf.*)	central processing unit, central processor
– de charge	unit (unitized) load
expédié sous forme d'– de charge	shipped as a unitized load
– de consommation	consumption unit
– de coût	cost unit
– de mémoire (*inf.*)	storage unit
– de poids	unit of weight
– du premier degré (*stat.*)	primary (first-stage) unit
– secondaire	secondary (second-stage) unit
univers *m.* (*stat.*)	**universe, population**
urbanisation *f.*	**urbanization**
urbanisme *m.*	**town planning**

urbaniste *m.* — town planner
***usage** *m.*,*
– à – multiple — multi-purpose
– à – unique — one-way

– –s du port — custom of port
– –s locaux — local custom
***usine** *f.*,*
– départ – — ex works
– directeur *m.* d'– — works manager
– fermeture *f.* d'– — closing down of a factory
– ouvrier *m.* d'– — factory-hand
***vague** *f.*,*
– – d'augmentation de prix — wave of price increases
– – de spéculations — wave of speculations
– – de ventes — selling wave
***valeur** *f.*,*
– – à casser, – liquidative — break-up value
– – agréée (*assur.*) — agreed value
– – à neuf (*assur.*) — replacement value
– – d'attente (*stat.*) — expectation value
– – d'attention (*stat.*) — attention value
– – de reconstruction (*assur.*) — reinstatement value
– – extrême — extreme value
– – de réduction (*assur.*) — reduction value
– – de rachat (*fonds commun*) — resale price
– – de réalisation — realization value
– – en argent — cash value
– – estimée — estimated value
– – initiale — initial value
– – limite (*stat.*) — critical value, limit value
– – médiale (*stat.*) — class mark
– – monétaire — value of money
– – moyenne — mean
estimation *f.* au-dessous de la – réelle — undervaluation
estimation *f.* au-dessus de la – réelle — overvaluation, over-estimate
rectification *f.* de – — value adjustment
valeur-travail *f.* — **value of labo(u)r**
théorie *f.* de la – — labo(u)r theory of value
***valeurs** *f. pl.*,*
– – clés, directrices — leaders
– – d'assurances — insurance shares
– – d'automobiles — motor shares, motors
– – cuprifères — coppers
– – textiles — textile shares, textiles
variable (*adj.*) — **variable**
variable *f.* (*stat.*) — **variable**

– – aléatoire — random –
– – continue — continuous –
– – discrète — discrete –

variance / 456

– endogène	endogenous –
– exogène	exogenous –
– stochastique	stochastic –
distribution *f.* à deux –s	bivariate distribution
distribution à plusieurs –s	multivariate distribution
variance *f.* (*stat.*)	**variance**
– interclasse, entre classes	– between classes
– entre groupes	between-group –
– interne, intraclasse	– within classes
– à l'intérieur des groupes	within-group –
– résiduelle	residual –
analyse *f.* de –	analysis of –
variation *f.*	**variation; fluctuation**
–s des prix	price changes
–s saisonnières	seasonal variations
corrigé des –s saisonnières	corrected for seasonal –s, seasonally adjusted
coefficient *m.* de –	– coefficient
venderesse *f.* (*jur.*)	**vendor**
vendeur, personnel *m.* –	sales staff, sales people
vendeuse	**saleswoman, shop assistant**
*vendre,	
– au mieux	to sell at best
– à livraison sur appel	to sell for delivery on call
– en vrac	to sell in bulk
*vente *f.*,	
– à perte	losing sale
– à livraison sur appel	sale for delivery on call
– avec reprise en location (*forme de leasing*)	sale (and) lease back
– couplée, jumelée	tie-in sale
– de panique	panic sale
– de remplacement	replacement sale
– de soldes	clearance sale
– de porte-à-porte	house-to-house selling
– record	record sale
de bonne –	easy to sell
de – difficile	difficult to sell
argument *m.* de –	selling argument, selling point
méthodes *pl.* de –	selling methods, practices
perspectives (prévisions) *pl.* de –	sales prospects
point *m.* de –	point of sale
promesse *f.* de –	undertaking to sell
promotion *f.* des –s	sales promotion
pronostics *pl.* de –	sales forecast
surface *f.* de –	sales space

*ventilation f. | **break-down**
– des coûts | – of costs
– par profession | – by occupations
– par tranches de revenus | – according to income brackets
vie f. | **life**
conditions pl. de – | living conditions

coût m. de la – | living costs
cycle m. de – | life cycle
durée moyenne de – | average life
espérance f. de – | life expectancy
indemnité f. de – chère | cost-of-living bonus
niveau m. de – | living standard, level of living
qualité f. de la – | quality of life

train m. de – | way of life
vieillissement m. **industriel** | **obsolescence**

*virement m., |
– des salaires | payment of wages by transfer
banque centrale de – | central clearing bank
virgule f., – fixe (inf.) | fixed point
– flottante (inf.) | floating point
vivre | **to live**
– de ses rentes | – on one's income
– de ses économies | – on one's savings
voilier m. | **sailing vessel**
transport m. par – | shipment by –
voiture f. |
– de reprise | traded-in car
– d'occasion | used car, second hand vehicle

volonté f. | **will**
dernières –s, acte m. de dernière – | last will and testament
par toute autre cause indépendante de sa – | by any other cause beyond his control
*volume m., |
– des échanges | trade volume
– des exportations | volume of exports
– du crédit | credit volume
– monétaire | volume of money
*voyage m., |
– d'affaires à l'étranger | foreign business trip
en – d'affaires | away on business
*vrac, |
présentation f. en – | bulk display
week-end m. | **weekend**
–prolongé | long –
ventes pl. du – | – sale

INDEX

A

abandon 7
abandonment 7, 102
abatement 7
abbreviation 3
abeyance 354
ability 46
able 46
aboard 40
about 143
above 57
above-mentioned 227
above-named 241, 354
abreast 183
abroad 150
abrogate 7
abrogation 7
absciss(a) 7
absence 7
absenteeism 7
absorption capacity 46
abstract (to) 310, 347
abstract 158
abstraction 347
abundance 7
abundant 7
abuse 7
accelerated 21
acceleration 8, 392
accelerator 392
accept 8, 14, 18
acceptance 8
 – account 8, 67
 – book 213
 – credit 92
 – house 8
 – liability 139
 – market 8
accepting house 8
acceptor 8
access (to) 392
 – time 392
access to... 141
accessory 8
accident 18, 340
accident insurance 26
acclamation 8
accommodating 84
accommodation
 – acceptance 8
 – bill 38, 129, 453

 – paper 255
accompanied 9
accompaniment 9
accompliment 9
accomplished 9
accordance 73
according 336
according to... 74, 352
account 67, 211, 401
 – book 63, 213
 – current 69
 – current book 213
 – s department 337
 – holder 69
 – keeping 452
 – keeping fee 416
 – number 423
 – sales 382
 – s payable 407
accountable 66
 – receipt 66
accountant 67
accounting and auditing firm 165
accounting machine 217
accounting period 166
accredited 9
accumulate 10
accumulation 10
accumulator 392
accuracy 151
accurate 291, 151
accuse 10
achievement 280
acknowledge receipt 10
acknowledgment 10, 50
 – of... 303
acquisition 11
act 11
 – of acknowledgment 12, 302
 – of merchant 63
 – of war 161
acting partner 62
action 14, 287
actuarial 392
actuary 14
add 18
 – to 202
 – up 14, 344
adder 216, 392

adding machine 216
adding-substracting machine 216
addition 14
additional 352
 – percentage 14
 – unit 345
address (to) 15, 399
address 15
 – book 213
 – label 150
 – side 15, 84
addressee 109
addressing machine 216
adjacents parts 361
adjourn 18, 312
adjournment 18, 313
adjudicator 14
adjust 18, 298
adjusted for... 83
adjustment 18, 298, 308, 393
adjuvants 226
administer 14
administration 14
admission 15
 – card 60
 – charge 141
 – free 141
 – ticket 38
admittance 141
adopt 15
advance (to) 30
advance 30
advantage 30
advantageous 30
adverse 101, 259
advertise (to) 294
advertisement 20, 302, 394, 438
 – hoarding 255, 302
 – purposes 302
 – rates 353
advertiser 20
advertising 293, 302, 439
 – agency 17
 – agent 293
 – article 397
 – awareness 429, 439
 – bilboard 302
 – brochure 290

460/Index

- budget 293
- canvasser 104, 294
- charges 294
- competition 293
- consultant 75, 439
- copy 439
- department 337
- design 293
- directory 20
- expenditure 407
- film 293
- gift 293
- material 439
- media 439, 450
- message 439
- page 294
- pillar 16
- reply card 438
- research 441
- slogan 439
- theme 435
- value 293
- van 439

advice 31, 75
advice of fate 447
advise 32
adviser 75
advising commission 243
advisory 77
aerial 15
affected 16, 368
  - by 386
affidavit 177
affix 22
affreightment 17
afloat 167
aforementioned 354
aforesaid 354
after-effects 352
after hours 40
after-sale service 446
again 243
age 398
  - distribution 393
  - group 417
agenda 252, 430
agency 17
  - contract 78, 320
agent 17, 65
aggregate 367
agio 17
agiotage 17
agree 9, 81
  - to... 75
agreed 84
  - upon 81
agreement 9, 81
  - clause 59
agricultural 18
agriculture 18
aim 43
air bill of lading 207
air consignment note 207
aircraft 31
  - industry 419
air fare 258
air hostess 418
air law 121
airline 15
air mail 275
air mail fee 354

air mail letter 207
Air Mail Receipt 15, 300
air mail traffic 155, 368
airplane 31
airport 15, 272
Air Receipt 15, 230
air service 15
  - before 65
air traffic 368
Air Transportation Waybill 74
alarm installation 393
algorithm 393
alienable 18
alienate 18
alienation 184
alimony 262
aliquot 18
allocation 393
allot 29
allotment 14, 318
  - letter 318
  - money 383
allow 19
allowance 19, 39, 214, 280, 313
  - for depreciation 438
  - in kind 395
all risk insurance 27
all risks policy 271
almanac 19
alongside 239
alongside B/L 294
alphabetical 19
alteration 232, 353, 453
although 22
amalgamate 175
amalgamation 17
ambassador 19
amendment 219
amicale 19
amortizable 19
amortization 19
  - loan 19
  - table 19
amortize 19
amount (to) 132
amount 235, 245, 343, 436
  - column 344
analyser 393
analysis 20, 393
analyst 20
anchor (to) 285
anchor 20
anchorage 285
ancillary industry 448
animation 14
annex to... 105
annuity 21, 376
  - insurance 31
annul 21
answer (to) 318
answer 119, 443
answer for (to) 171
  - error 443
antedate 21
antedating 21
anticipate 21
anticipated 21
anticyclical 21
anti-inflation 21
anti-inflationary 21
apiece 266

apologize 152
apology 152
apparent 149
apparent good order 149
apparatus 21
appear 165, 196, 324
  - before 65
appearer 258
applicable 22
applicant 346
application 22, **346**
  - for... 103
  - form 42, 103, 346
  - money 383
  - receipt 300, 304
  - right 284, 346
apply 15, 22, 346
  - for 343
appoint 241
appointment **143**, 241, 315
apportion 318, 383
apportionment 318, 383
appraised 148
appraiser 283, 358
appreciation 269
apprenticed 22
apprenticeship 22
approbation 22
appropriation 16, 190, 318, 393, 423
approval 22
approve 22
approximate 22
approximately 22
approximation 394
arbitrage transactions 16, 23
arbitrageur 23
arbitragist 23
arbitral 23
arbitrate 23
arbitration 23
  - award 98
  - clause 58
  - committee 64
  - proceedings 437
arbitrator 23
arbitrator's award 98
arcade 258
area 441, 452
  - code 419
  - sampling 447
arithmetic 23
arithmetic mean 237
armaments boom 73
arrangement 9, 23, 370
arrear **24**, 325
arrival 24
  - platform 294
  - station 24
article **25**, 256, 394
  - s of apprenticeship 78
  - s of association 342, **349**
  - s of partnership 342
as
  - far as possible 275
  - follows 352
  - from 258
  - loan 365
  - per... 352
  - per advice 32
  - soon as possible 275

– usual 376
– yet 279
ashore 167
assemble 394
assembly program 445
assembly room 327
assert 380
assess 189, 358
assessment 84, 358, 405
assets **12, 22, 32,** 392, 418
– side 12, 392
assign 32
assignee 51
assignment 51, 399
assistant accountant 18
assistant manager 114, 347
assistant secretary 336
associate 26
association 26, 394
– test 452
assort 26
assortment 26
assume 26
assumed 353
assumption 418
assurance 26
assure (to) 28
astonished 150
astonishment 150
at 7
– a discount 254
– all cost 89
– any rate 49
– a premium 259
– a profit 289
– best 229
– buyer's option 180
– cost price 89
– par 254
– seller's option 180
– ship's rail 254
– the least 229
– the suit of 113
– work 14
– your convenience 81
atomic 28
atomistic 395
attach (to) 28
attachable 332
attachment 331
attend 257
– to... 342
attendance fee 202, 279, 377
attendance sheet 164
attended 10
attention 28
attention value 455
attitude 395
– study 395
attract 29
attract away (to) 96
attribute 395
attribute (to) 190
auction 137
auctioneer 64
auction room 94, 383
auction sale 94
audience 395
– research 395
audit (to) 383
audit 64, 329

auditor 383
auditors report 298
austerity 395
– policy 395
– program 395
autarky 29
authenticate 29
authenticity 29
authority 30
– to... 29
authorization 29
authorize 30
authorized signatures 339
auto 29
autocode (to) 395
auto(mobile) industry 29
auto market 29
automobile output 288
autumn fair 167
auxiliaries 226
availability 115, 380
available **115, 377**
average (to) 148
average (subst.) 31, 237
average adj.) 236
– adjustment 115
– adjuster 115
– bond 66
– clause 58
– deposit 31
– statement 115
aviation insurance 394
avoid 323
avoidance clause 59
awaiting 28
away 258
axiomatic 395

B

back (to) 30
back 120, 384
backer 30
backing 30
backlog 62
backlog demand 103
back page 254
backwardation 39, 106
– business 249
– rate 87, 106, 358
backward method 228
bad debts reserve 282
bad delivery 213
bag 331
baggage 32
bagged 331
balance (to) **33,** 145, 343
balance **33, 145,** 311, 324, 342
– book 213
– brought forward 244
– carried forward 244
– depreciation 393
– due 305
– in cash 345
– in hand 342
– method 228
– of trade 63
balance of payments 395
– on current account 395

– deficit 395
– equilibrium 33
– surplus 33
balance sheet 38, 396
– adjustment 304
– data 396
– item 38
– structure 396
– value 378
balast (to) 206
balloon-test 452
ball-point pen 351
band 32
bank 34, 396
– acceptance 8
– account 67
– balance 33, 342
– bills 35
– bookkeeping 34, 66
– charges 172
– cheque 34, 54
– clerk 34, 64, 135
– counters 35
– credit 34, 92
– custom 376
– deposit 34
– director 114
– guarantee 34, 49, 177
– holiday 40, 203
– law 21
– liquidity 212
– manager 34
– messenger 177
– money 234
– note 38
– organization 252
– paper 35
– pass book 34
– place 33
– post bill 35
– references 307
– report 35
– reserve 35
– return 340
– run 35, 182
– sector 395
– share 12, 34, 379
– statement 35, 340
– transfer 385
bankable 33
banker 35, 442
– 's association 26
– 's commission 64
– s' discount 146
banking 34
– account 34, 68
– business 34, 35, 249
– circles 34
– coefficients 401
– commission 34, 64
– company 341
– establishment 148
– failure 205
– hours 184, 430
– house 35, 218
– operation 34, 249
– place 33, 266
– practice 276
– reform 34
– secrecy 336
– syndicate 34, 355

462/Index

- system 395
- transactions 370

bankrupt 35, 160
bankruptcy 35, 161
- petition 161
- proceedings 161

bankrupt's estate 161, 226
banner 45
bar chart 408, 417
bare owner 244
bare ownership 244
bargain (to) 221
bargain 222
- s done 87, 276
- price 285
- sale 302, 382

bargaining 221
barge 262
bar gold 211
barratry 35
barred by limitation 279
barrel 175, 367
barrister 32
barter 62
- arrangement 12

base (to) 36
base 35, 396
- coin 162
- period 396
- rate 332
- year 396

basic
- industry 396
- pay 396
- premium 435
- product 396
- wage 369

basin 36
basis 35
- of assessment 26
- price 284

basket 430, 431
batch 182
- processing 453

bear (to) 273, 353
- down 33
- in mind 325

bear 33, 348
- account 99, 274
- covering 100
- engagement 139
- operation 33, 348
- operator 202
- position 374
- sale 100, 381
- seller 100, 380
- transactions 100, 249

bearer 274
- certificate 365
- clause 58
- debenture 245
- paper 129
- securities 365, 379
- share 12

bearing 362
beef output 437
before
- hours 31, 40
- long 186

beforehand 276
beginner 97

beginning 97
behavio(u)r 66, 72, 403
belong (to) 21, 324
below 57
below-mentioned 227
bend (to) 269
beneficiary 37
- first 396
beneficium 36
benefit (to) 290
benefit
- of discussion 36
- of division 36
- of the doubt 36

berth freighting 17
best 229
better 226, **229**
betterment tax 435
beverage tax 189
beware of imitations 79
bias 396
bias(s)ed 396
bid (to) 137, 231, 248
...bid 247
bid 137, 230
bidder 138, 248
bidding 248
big 171, 179, 181
bill (to) 16
bill *(affiche)* 16
bill *(facture)* 242
bill *(loi)* 215
bill 159, 255, 360
- after date 208, 369
- after sight 208, 369
- discount 413
- of exchange 128, 208
- of exchange law 208
- of health 259
- of lading 74, 271, 402
- s in case 273
- s to order 255

billboard 16
- advertising
bill book 213
bill broker 89
bill case 273, 130
bill diary 125, 213
bill file 266
billing 396, 400, 414
- machine 160

billiott 39, 229
bills account 68
bills department 338
bills payable 68
bills payable account 68
bills payable book 129, 204
bills receivable account 68
bills receivable book 129, 204
billsticking 16
bimetal(l)ism 39
bimonthly 39
binary 396
- code 400
- digit 396
- system 397

bind (to) 140, 210
biquinary 397
birth
- allowance 19
- certificate 12
- rate 357

bit 397
black 240
black-bordered 143
black market 223
black marketeer 368
black market price 285
blank 30
- credit 99
- signature 39

block (to) 39, 397
block 59, 256
- diagram 430

blotting
- book 43
- pad 347
- paper 43, 255

blue chips 365
board *(bord)* 40
- *(comité)* 42
- *(panneau)* 255
- *(planche)* 268

Board of... 230
board of directors 75
boat 36
body 83, 94
- corporate 264

bogus transactions 15
bona fide 167
- holder 274
bond (to) 141
bond 245
- agio 246
- creditor 91, 245
- issue 134
- note 11
- subordinated 429

bonded 142
- goods 141
- terms 214
- warehouse 142, 217

bonder 142
bondholder 274
bonding 141
bonus 40
- share 12

book (to) 261, 325
book 213
book debt 110
booking 214, 321
- office 211

bookkeeper 67, 214, 361
bookkeeping 66, 214
- machine 66
- method 66
- voucher 66

booklet 41, **214**
bookpost 34
- by 412

book transfer 421
book value 66, 377
boom 73
boost 449
booth keeper 221
border 416
- control 416
- crossing point 416
- worker 374

born... 239
borrow (to) 136
borrower 136
bottleneck 179

Index/463

bottling 231
bottom 35, 48
  – price 87
bottomry 181
  – bond 78, 182
  – loan 281
bought book 213
bought note 10, 40
bound 311
bounty on 282
boutique 397
box 39
box office 214
boycott 41
brackets 328, 416
brain work 373
brain worker 374
branch 148, 336, 351
  – bank 35
  – house 218
  – instruction 420
  – manager 119
  – networks 321
  – office 351
brand 225, 425
  – awareness test 425
  – distribution 443
  – image 412, 425
  – loyalty 425
  – preference 425
branded goods 289
brand-new 240
brass 417, 448
breach 331
breach of trust 7
bread winner 414
break (to) 199, 330
break 199
breakage 41, 49
break down (to) 383, 456, 457
breakdown 254, 383
breakdown lorry 105
break-even point 433, 446
breaking 331
breaking off 331
break off (to) 330
breakpoint 433
break-up value 378, 455
brewery 41
bridge 272
bridge (to) 448
bridging 448
brief (to) 403
briefly 235
bring forward 320
bring in 299
brisk 12, 20, 223
briskness 14
broad 206, 223
broadcast news 421
brochure 41
broker 89
  – s' firm 89
  – s' note 15, 40
brokerage 89
brokerage house 89
brother 175
brought forward 320
brush 395
budget (to) 42, 397
budget 42, 397

– cuts 444
– deficit 406
– equilibrium 42
– estimate 42
– expenditure 42
– item 397
– period 432
– speech 42
– surplus 151
– survey 412
budgetary 42, 397
budgeting 397
buffer store 426
building 36, 77
  – activity 36, 392
  – association 392
  – company 77, 341
  – credit 405
  – expenses 77
  – industry 36, 419
  – licence 77, 264
  – line 18
  – line plan 268
  – materials 226
  – owner 219
  – permit 264
  – site 363
  – society 404
  – specifications 44
  – subsidy 435
  – worker 396
bulk 389
  – cargo 48, 53
  – display 435, 457
  – sample 124
  – store 426
bulky 138, 388
bull (to) 100
bull 183, 348
  – engagement 139
  – operation 348
  – operator 183, 203
  – position 11, 183, 274
  – purchase 10, 99
  – purchaser 99
  – transaction 183, 249
bundle 208
bunker (to) 53
burden 272, 273
  – of proof 399
  – of taxation 269
burglar alarm installation 393
burglary insurance 27
burthen 272, 273
business 15
  – address 15
  – administration 392
  – agent 17
  – centre 399
  – circles 229
  – cycle downturn 74
  – day 421
  – done 87
  – economics 126
  – ethics 235
  – expansion 16
  – experience 16
  – game 421
  – hours 43, 184
  – house 63, 218
  – knowledge 16

– language 63
– letter 16, 207
– lunch 407
– man 16
– management 179
– manager 178
– movement 16
– organization 252
– papers 255
– practice 434
– premises 215
– quarter 62
– relations 16, 298
– style 63
– term 63
– tour 16, 388
– transaction 63
– travel 16, 388
– trip 457
– world 16
businesslike 330
busy 278
butter auction 230
butter mart 230
buy 10
  – back 297
  – in 153, 297
  – off 297
  – up 8
buyer 278
  – s' market 11, 222
  – s' option 119, 247, 282
  – s' option to double 160
  – s over 80
  – s' strike 417
  – up 8
buying 10, 392
  – back 296
  – commission 64
  – department 337
  – frequency 416
  – in 18, 153, 296
  – intentions 392
  – manager 174
  – motive 392, 428
  – order 251
  – power 276
  – price 86
  – rate 86
  – up 86
by 353
  – air 387
  – air mail 31
  – bookpost 34
  – call-over 328
  – car 29
  – comparison 65
  – compensation 66
  – land 362
  – law 215
  – means of 237
  – messenger 274
  – order of 252
  – post 275
  – poster 387
  – rail 54, 163
  – regular mail 275
  – return 326
  – roll call 388
  – sea 227
  – sea mail 86

464/Index

- seniority 298
- separate post 86
- that time 186
- the dozen 7
- the good office 248
- the gross 181
- the job 170
- the lump 170
- the piece 266
- train 369
- virtue 25, 385
- way of 365

by-product 341

C

cab 358
cable (to) 44
cable 43
- order 251, 359
- transfer 359, 371

cablegram 43, 44
ca'canny strike 181
cadastral 44
calculate (to) 45, 353
calculating machine 217
calculation 45
calculator 45
calendar 45
calendar day 203
call (to) 21
- *(titres)* 99
- *(nommer)* 241
- *(navire)* 310
- *(visite)* 327
- together 327

call **21**
- *(titres)* **119**, 282
- *(teleph.)* 65, 360
- *(navire)* 310
- of more 121, 160, 249

call deposit 389
call deposit account 67
called subscriber 104
calier 387
calling 82
calling subscriber 104
call money 23, 45, 389
call number 244
call on 394
call option 119, 222, 282
call-over 241
call price 37
call receipt 300
calm 223
cambist 45
campaign 46
cancel (to) 323
cancel 21
cancellation 21, 323
cancelling 21
cancelling clause 59
cancel(ling) stamp 247
candidate 46
candidature 46
canvass (to) 292
canvasser 104, 292
canvassing 292, 337
capacity 14, 295

capacity utilization 46
capital 46
- account 47, 67
- expenditure 187, 420
- gains 269
- goods 37, 237, 288
- investment 201
- levy 47
- loss 398
- market 47, 222
- movements 124, 236
- needs 37
- outlays 201
- requirements 37, 47
- reserve 322
- share 12
- stock 47

capitalism 48
capitalist 48
capitalistic 48
capitalization 48, 398
capitalize 48
capitation 84
- tax 189

capsize 54
captain 46
captain's copy 46
captain's report 298
caption 398
capture 173
car 457
- hiring 214
- industry 419
- number 244
- output 288

carbac 255
carbonized paper 255
carbon paper 255
carcass weight 269
card 48, 161
cardboard 49
card index 42, 164, 318
- system 58, 164

care 113, **342**, 447
career consul 77
careful 342
cargo 48, **53**, 160, 398
- boat 48
- homewards 398
- insurance 27
- list 40

carman 46
carriage 159, **372**
- by sea 454
- forward 272
- paid 272

carriage charge 284
carriage release lever 208
carried forward 320
carrier 372, 387
carry 325
- forward 320
- stock 320

carrying
- capacity 46
- forward 320
- out 231
- over 319

carry-over rate 87, 285, 358
cartage 46, 372
- contractor 142, 372

- service 46

cartel 49, 399
carter 46, 387
cartogram(me) 399
carton 49
case 44, 49
- of need 37

case-law 121
case stydy 49
cash (to) 137
cash 44, 67, 147
- account 45, 67
- advances 30
- assets 147
- balance 33, 136
- bargain 222
- book 45, 213
- certificate 39
- credit 92
- deficit 45
- department 45, 337
- deposit 107
- desk 44, 70
- difficulties 374
- disbursements 45
- discount 46
- distribution 345
- dividend 147
- down 67
- down sale 382
- in hand 23, 32, 136, 324
- indemnity 191
- market 222
- on delivery 311
- on delivery charges 172
- on-delivery sale 382
- order 251
- overs 101
- payment 45, 67, 147, 344
- position 45
- price 67, 284
- purchase 67
- ratio 60
- receipts 45, 301, 317, 398
- register 44, 140
- remittance 144
- requirements 374
- revision 45
- sale 67, 382
- share 12
- shorts 101
- stand 402
- statement 40, 45, 149
- subscriber 346
- surplus 152, 450
- transactions 45, 67, 249
- value 455
- voucher 266

cash-and-carry 422, 431
cashier 45
cashiers' department 454
cashless payments 386
cask 175
cast (to) 71, 202
cast 14
casting 14, 98
- vote 387

casualty 340
catalogue 49
category 49
cattle 37

Index/465

– truck 389
cause 49
cease 51
ceasing 51
ceiling 433
– rate 405, 433
cell 399
– frequency 416
census 300
center, centre 50
certificate 50, **365**
– medical 399
certification 51
certified copy (true) 20, 51, 82, 276
certify 51
cession 51
chain
– rule 307
– store 51, 218
chains 51
chairman 280
chairman's address 280
chairmanship 280
challenge 406
cham 399
– index 419
– printer 419
chamber 51
Chancellor of the Exchequer 230
change (to) 52
change 52
– of residence 118
– of route 108, 111
channel 381
character 392
characteristic 398
charge (to) 53, 273
chargeable 53, 190
charges 53, 172
– forward 311
charging 190
chart of account 433
charter (to) 17, 429
charterer 17
chartering 17, 240
charter party 54
charwoman 163, 204, 427
cheap 39
cheaper 226
cheaply 39
cheap-money policy 271
check (to) 140, 175, 270, 300, 302, **383**, 400, 451
check 54
– bit 397
– clock 80, 185
– digit 408
– interview 404, 420
– list 422
– number 429
– out 398
checking 270
– account 67
– apparatus 80
– copy 205
cheerful 115, 223
chemical 56
chemistry 56
cheque 54

– account 55
– book 48, 55
– card 399
– form 55, 170
– perforator 55
– protector 55
– rate 55
Cheques Act 55
chief 54
– accountant 54
– business 247
– cashier 45
– creditor 283
child labour 373
chi-square 400
choice 56
– brand 225
Christian name 278
Christmas
– bonus 180, 435
– gift 397
– sales 429
– shopping 429
– spending 429
cinema advertising 293
cipher (to) 56
cipher 390
– code 206
– language 56, 359
– telegram 57
circle chart 408
circuit 400
circular 57
circularize (to) 292
circulate 58
circulation 57, 330
– s permitting 335
circumstance 57
civil status 149
claim (to) 154, **302**
– back 318
claim (assur.) 340
claim 302, 327
claimant 302, 340
claims
– book 213
– department 447
class 58, 400
– interval 400
– limits 400
– mark 400, 455
classification 58
classify 58, 318
clause 58
clause not to order 400
clean bill 129
clean draft 313
clean remittance 442
cleaning 429
– business 429
– staff 429
clear (to) 66, 100, 208, 294
– inwards 120, 141
– outwards 120, 154
clearance 100, 258, 416
– inwards 120, 141
– outwards 120, 155
– sale 211, 456
clearing 59, 400
– account 59, 67
– advances 30, 59

– agreement 59
– assets 92
– balance 400
– bank 291, 386, 457
– debts 110
– house 59
– office 247
– payment 59
– sheet 211
– system 59
– transactions 59
clerk **64, 135**
– of the court 180
– 's office 180
client 59
– behaviour 401
climate 60
clipping
– agency 393, 405
– service 405
cloak room 75
clock 185
close (to) 60, 163
– with.. 343
close (stingy) 441
closing 51, 60, 163
– down 455
– price 88
– rate 86
– session 336
– time 163
clothing industry 193
cluster 417
– sample 417
– sampling 447
coal (to) 53
coal 53
– basin 36
– mine 53, 185, 229
– shortage 53
– strike 180
– syndicate 355
coaler 53
coaling 53
coaster 44
coasting 44
– navigation 238
– trade 62
cobweb-theorem 447
code (to) 60
code 60
– language 206
– telegram 259
– word 235
coder 400
coding 400
coefficient 60
coffee 44
– break 431
– house 44
coin (to) 36, 234
coin 234
coinable 234
coinage 174, 234
coiner 234
co-insurance 60
co-insurer 400
collapse 131
collate (to) 61
colleague 61
collect (to) 137, 208, 263, **304**

collectable 136
collectible 136
collecting
 – agency 34
 – banker 137
 – business 304
charges 304
 – clerk 45, 177
 – department 337
 – order 219
collection 61
 – *(poste)* 208
 – *(prise)* 283
 – *(perception)* **136**, 263, **304**
 – advice 31
 – area 137
 – bank 137
 – business 137
 – charge 137, 283
 – department 137
 – rates 137, 304
 – service 283
 – tariff 137, 357
collective 61
collector 137, 301
collector's office 80, 263
collide 7
collier 36
collision 7, 61
 – clause 59, 61
collocation 401
collusion 61
colon 270
colonial produce 105
colony 61
column 61
columnar book 61
combination 446
 – lock 401, 446
combined 210
come 210
come
 – back 327
 – in 317
 – out 344
 – to terms 9
coming into force 141
commerce 62
commercial 40, 63, 439, 448
 – attache 28
 – designer 294
 – in formation 338
 – papers 255
commercialize 63
commissary 64
commission **64**, 313
 – account 64, 68, 243
 – agent 65
 – book 64, 213
 – business 64
 – house 64, 218
commissioner 64
commitment **139, 352**
 – commission 401
committee **61, 218**
commodities 25
 – market 222, 223
common **65**
 – Assembly 25
 – Market 222

– money 234
commotion 454
community 65, 401
commutation 428
commuter 428
commuting 427
company 65, **341**, 447
 – bookkeeping 66
 – law 121, 447
 – 's articles 342, 349
 – 's year 20, 340
compare 61, 66
comparison 65
compartment 65
compensate 66
compensation 66, 192, 419, 443
 – agreement 370
 – duties 358
 – transactions 370
compete with 71
competency 66
competent 66
competition 71, 402
 – clause 59, 71
competitive 66, 71
competitiveness 401
competitor 71
compiler 401
complain (to) 268
complaint 268, 441
 – book 302
complementary goods 66
complete 66
complimentary close 171
compliments of the season 244
comply (to) 73, 314, 323, 361
component 401
composition 24, 70
 – proceedings 70
compound (to) 71
comprehensive policy 271
compromise 370, 401
compulsory 246
computer 398, 430
concealment 441
concentration 70, 402
 – curve 405
concern 70
concerning 70
concession 70
concessionary 70
conciliation board 374
conclude (to) 70
conclusion 70
condemn (to) 71
condition 72
conditional 71
condolence 72
conduct (to) 220
conduct 72, 178, 220
confection 72
conference room 334
confidence 72, 402
 – coefficient 446
 – interval 402, 420
 – leven 402
 – limits 402
confidential 72
 – clerk 168

confidentially 72
configuration 402
confirm 73
confirmation 72
 – commission 64
confiscate 73
confiscation 73
conflict 73
conformity 73
congestion 133, 138
congratulate 163
congratulation 163
congratulatory letter 207
connected 10
 – contract 165
connection *(tel.)* 65
connection **59**, 83, **310**
consensual 75
consent 9, 75
conservancy measures 75
consider as 75
consideration **75**
 – *(couverture)* 293
 – *(rémunération)* 165, 314
 – *(délibération)* 102
 – *(cause)* 49
considering (that) 389
consignee 75, 109, 300
consigner 75
consignment 75, 143
 – account 68
 – invoice 75, 159
consignor 75, 109, 155
console 439
 – operator 439
consolidate 76
consolidation 76
consols 76
consortium 76
constitute 76
constitution 76
construction
 – activity 77
 – market 77
consul 77
 – general 77
consulage 77
consular 77
 – fee 358
consulate 77
 – general 77
consult 77
consultative 77
consumer 76, 403
 – association 403
 – behaviour 401
 – 's choice 403
 – 's credit 76
 – 's demand 76
 – durables 76
 – education 410
 – 's expenditure 76
 – (s') goods 37, 76
 – goods industry 193
 – habits 417
 – panel **403**, 430
 – price index 192
 – protection 438
 – research 441
 – society 403
 – spending 76

– survey 403
consuming habits 76
consumption 76
– function 76
– goods 76
– habits 76
– ratio 403
– tax 76, 189
– unit 403, 454
contact (to) 77, 368
contact 77, 299
contain 77
container 77, 403
– port 403
– service 403
– ship 403
– terminal 403
– transport 403
– vessel 429
containerization 403
contango 319
– business 249, 319
– day 66, 203
– rate 87, 285, 319, 358
contemplated by 386
content 77
– s 361
contentious 77
contest 77, 212
contiguous 77, 361
contingency 151, 403
– fund 169
– reserve 322
– table 403
contingent 151, 210
continuation 319, 352
– sheet 207, 352
continue (to) 319
continuous 403
contra (to) 80, 158
contra account 68, 79
contraband 79
– goods 79
– trade 62, 74
contrabandist 79
contract (to) 78
contract 78
contracting 78
– parties 78
contract note 40
contractor 14, 142
contractor's risk 329
contrat price 170, 284
contractual 78, 81
contract work 143, 373
contra entry 25
contraing 79, 158
contrary 78
contribute (to) 80
contribution 80, 84, 171
contributor 80
control 80, 404
– card 404
– data 404
– desk 439
– group 417
– program 438
– stamp 80
– tape 396
– watch 80
controlled 442

controller 80
controlling apparatus 75
convene (to) 82, 327
convenience 81, 159
convening 82
– notice 82
convention 81
conversation 143
conversion 81, 404
– discount 404
– loan 135
– premium 404
– price 404
– risk 329
– table 81
– terms 404
convert (to) 81, 371
convertibility 81, 234, 404
convertible 81
convey (to) 372
conveyance 79, 291, **372**, 454
conveyor 396
convince 81
cook 221
co-operation 82
co-operative **82**, 404
co-opt (to) 404
co-optation 404
co-ordinates 82
copartner 60
coppers 95, 455
– shares 95
co-property 82
co-proprietor 82
copy **82, 153**, 155
– book 44
– platform 404
– testing 452
– writer 402, 441
copying
– ink 82
– machine 82, 217
– press 82
copyright 321
core store, storage 426
corn exchange 40
corporate
– image 415
– body 264
– tax 189, 447
corporeal 83
correct 83
correcting entry 304, 305
correction 304, 404
correlation 404
– coefficient 401
– diagram 404
– function 404
– surface 404
– table 404
correspond 83
correspondence 83
– clerk 83
– department 337
correspondent 83
co-signatory 83
cost (to) 89, 380
cost **89**, 284, 405
– accounting 284
– center 173
– centre 399

– curve 86
– estimate 89
– factor 159
– of a law suit 105
– of labour 284
– of living 89
– price 284
– unit 454
cost-of-living-bonus 55, 192, 435, 450
cost-of-living index 193
cost-induced inflation 194
costing 89, 284, 405
cost-push inflation 194
cosurety 60
cotenant 60
cotton industry 193
counsel 2, 75
counsel(l)or 75
count (to) 70, 401
counter 70, 182
– business hours 184
– clerk 135, 182
– display
display case
counterclaim 103, 303
counterfeit 79
counterfeiter 234
counterfoil 80, 344, 356
– book 48, 213, 344
– waybill 123, 207
countermand 79, 99, 446
countermanding 445
countermark 79
counterorder 80
counterpart account 80
counterpart funds 79
countersecurity 79
countersign 80
countersignature 80
countersurety 51
countervaluation 79
countervalue 80
country 262, 431
– planning 452
coupon 84, 405
– clerk 85
– date 125
– department 337
– holder 85
– keyed 405
– semi-annual 405
– sheet 85
– tax 85, 189
court 374
co-variance 405
cover (to) 90
cover **89, 224**
covered market 183
cover funds 90
covering letter 9
covering note 271
covering purchase 90
cover note 24, 243
cover ratio 60, 90
craft 25
craftsman 25
cranage 182
crane 182
crash 96, 205
crate 44

create 94
creation 91
credit (to) 94
credit 9, 91
credit *(compt.)* 91, 406
– account debtor 96
– advice 31, 91
– balance 94, 342
– bank 34
– card 399
– ceiling 93, 268
– column 61, 94
– committee 401
– control 93, 404
– co-operative 82
– department 338
– entry 275
– expansion 93
– inflation 194
– institution 93, 148, 196
– insurance 27, 329
– interest 94
– invoice 159
– item 275
– limit 93, 268
– margin 224
– market 223
– note 40, 91, 243
– operations 249
– policy 93, 271
– product 94, 241
– report 316
– risk 93, 329
– side 32, 91
– squeeze 406
– slip 40
– society 375
– stringency 93
– structure 93
– terms 93
– union 93
– volume 457
creditor **91, 94**
– account 94
– nation 94, 262
– position 94, 274
– side 91
– s' ledger 213
– s' meeting 91
creditworthiness 343
crew 145
crew list 330
crier 94
crisis 94
– symptoms 94
critical path 399
crop 302
– estimate 302
– outlook 302
– prospect 282
cross 35, 95, 299
– frontier traffic 416
– section analysis 454
– out 38
– tabulation 454
cross-elasticity 131
crossing 35
– out 297
crowding 138
crowner 399
crumble (to) 131

crumbling 131
cultivation 95, 156
cum
– claim **346**
– coupon 203
– dividend 117
– new 122, 346
– rights 346
curb 406
– market 22, 84, 223
currency **88, 112,** 125, **233**
– account 68
– area 390
– asset 112
– bill 129
– cover 428
– dealings 57, 236
– equalization fund 309
– manipulation 423
– option 135
– problem 233
– reform 233
– regulations 112
– reserves 112
– stabilization 233, 428
– stabilization fund 169
– transfer 371
current **85, 88, 138**
– account 69
curtail (to) 20, 66, 305
curtailment 66, 305
curve 86, 405
– fitting 405
curvilinear 406
cushion 112
custodian bank 407
custody 178
bill of lading 74
custom *(clientèle)* 59
– *(habitude)* 183, **376,** 455
– house broker 17
– house receipt 11
– local 455
– of port 455

customer 59
customs 120, 409
– agency 17
– agent 17, 65, 155
– authorities 120
– barriers 35, 120
– charges 172
– collections 120
– declaration 98, 120
– examination 409
– formalities 120
– inspection 120
– inspector 120
– invoice 409
– manifest 220
– office 120
– officer 17, 120
– official 278
– pass book 48
– permit 264
– receipts 301
– regulations 120, 308
– seal 120
– system 355
– tariffication 409
– tariffs 120

– union 120, 375
– value 378
– walls 35
– warehouse 120
cut down 305, 393
cut in... 305
cybernetics 406
cycle 73
cyclical 73, **74,** 95
cyclically sensitive 74

D

dabble 41
dabbler 41
damage (to) 139
damage 101, **119,** 139, 340
damageable 119
damaged 31
dampen (to) 361
damper 235
darsena 95
data 409
– bank 409
– collection 409
– gathering 409
– input 419
– output 420
– processing 409, 420
– processing centre 449
– storage 449
– transmission 453
date (to) 96
date 95
dater 363
date stamp 96, 363
day 203, 204
– before 380
– bill 208, 369
– labourer 204, 253
– service 337
day-to-day loan 135, 281
day-to-day money 23
dead
– letter 300, 345
– letter office 300
– season 332
deadlock 187
dead-weight capacity 272
deal (to) 63
deal in (to) 361, 370
dealer 116, 221, 416, 446
– interview 408
– panel 408, 444
– survey 411
dealing **249, 370**
dear **55,** 89
dear money policy 271
dearness 55
death 97
– certificate 12
– duty 189
– statistics 448
debasement 15
debenture 245
– bond 365
– capital 47, 246
– debt 245
– holder 245

Index/469

- issue 246
- loan 136, 246
- register 245
debit (to) 96
debit 96
- and credit 32
- advice 31, 96
- balance 38, 96, 259, 342
- column 61
- entry 275
- interest 96
- item 275
- note 96, 159, 243
- products 96, 241
- side 84, 96
debt **90, 110**
- due 90
debtor **96**, 305
- account 97
- nation 96, 261
- position 274
debtors' ledger 97, 213
debt service 339
decartelization 97
deceleration 406
decide 98
decile 406
decimal 98
decipher (to) 98
decision 98, 406
- making 406
- space 406
- table 406
- theory 406
decisive 98
deck 272
- cargo 48, 53
- load 272
declarant 98
declaration **98**
declare (to) 99
declared 99
decline (to) *(baisser)* 33, 263
- *(décliner)* 99, 309
decline **99**, 304, 415
decode (to) 98
decoder matrix 425
deconcentration 97
decrease 309
deduct (to) 99, 100, 273, 277, 296, 444
deductibility 406
deductible 100
deduction 99, 100
deed 11
- of partnership 342
- of propriety 365
deep-freezing 445
deep-frozen 445
default (to) 220
default 100
defect **100, 385**
defective 101
defend 101
defendant 101
defer (to) 113
deferred 112
deficiency 220
deficient 101
deficit **101**, 232, 406
deflation 101

deflationary 101
defray (to) 159
degree 101, 407
delay (to) 322, 325
delay **102**, 325
delayed 325
del credere 123
del credere agent 123
del credere commission 123
delegate (to) 102
delegate 102
delegation 102
delete (to) 299
deletions 299
deliberate (to) 102
deliberation 102
deliver (to) **103, 214**, 273
deliverable 212
deliverer 214
delivery **103**, 212, **313**
- of stock 366
- on request 422
- order 39, 103
- van 46, 214
de luxe 216
demand (to) 104, 154
demand **103**
- curve 86
- deposit 107, 389
- deposit account 67
- pressure 104
- price 284
- pull 280
- rate 86, 357, 389
demand, on 407
- function 407
- model 407, 427
- shifts 407
demand-pull inflation 194
demand-induced inflation 194
demijohn 95
demonetization 105
demonetize 105
demographic 105
demonstration 105
demonstrator 105
demurrage 57, 172, 345, 353
demurrage charge 123
denationalization 105
denationalize 105
denomination **85**, 105, 368
depart from 108
department 299, **337**
departmental chief 299
department(al)store 149, 217
departure 105
departure platform 133, 294
deposit (to) 106
deposit **107**, 402
- *(caution)* 9
- account 68, 107
- bank 34, 107
- book 48, 214
- interest 108
- money 234
- receipt 108 300 304 384
- slip 42 384
depositary 107
deposited 106
depositor 106
- s book 108 214

depreciate 108
depreciation 31 108 232 393
- expense 393
- method 393
- rate 393
depress (to) 108
depressed 223
depression 108
deputy chief clerk 346
deputy guardian 375
depth interview 420
derelict 238
derogate from 108
derogation 108
derogatory 108
description 109 289 294
description column 209
design 194
designate 109
designation 109
designer 393
desk 42
- research 413
despatch 115 **155**
- money 115
- note 155
destination 109
de-stocking 407
detach 109
detail (to) 110
detail 109
detain 120
determination 170
detriment 110
devaluation 111
devaluation rumours 111
devalue 111
develop (to) 111
deviate 111
deviation 111, 407
Dewey decimal system 400
diagram 112
diamond industry 193
dichotomy 408
dictaphone 112
dictate (to) 112
dictating machine 217
dictation 112
dictionary 112
differ (to) 113
difference **112, 113**, 124
different **113**
differential 113
differentiation 113
difficult 113
difficulty 113
digit 408
digital 408
diminish 113
diminution 113
dining car 390
direct (to) 119
direct exchange 50, 51
direct
- exchange 50, 51
- mail 439
directions for use 231
director 14
director's report 298
directory 15, 40
directory enquiry 337

470/Index

dirt cheap 285
dirt money 435
disability 191, 420
 – annuity 443
 – insurance 420
 – pension 420
disablement **191**, 373, 420
disaster 340
disadvantage 108
disadvantageous 109
disagreement 108
disburse (to) 97
disbursement 97, 231
disbursement account 97
discerning 205
discharge (to) 96, 97, 309
discharge 73, **97**, 98, 309
discontinuance 108
discontinuous 408
discount (to) 147
discount 114, **146**, 265, 296, 413
 – bank 34, 146
 – broker 146
 – ceiling 413
 – charges 17, 146, 172
 – credit 92, 146
 – department 337
 – house 146, 423
 – market 146, 222
 – policy 146, 271
 – promise 146
 – rate **146**, 357
 – stamp 363
 – store 423, 427
 – terms 146
discountable 146
discounter 147, 423, 447
discredit 114
discreet 114
discrete 408
discretion 114, **180**
discrimination 114
discuss 114
discussion 114
disease 219
disencumber 102, 109
disequilibrium 109
dishoarding 110
dishonest 103, 219
dishonesty 219
dishonour (to) 185
disinflation 109
disinflationary 109
disinvestment 407
disk (to) 408
 – memory 426
dismiss (to) 73, 210, 312, 317
dismissal 73, 210, 317
dispatch (to) 155
dispatch 113, 115
dispatch department 337
dispatch money 115
dispatch note 42
dispersion 408
displacement 106
display (to) 148
display 149, 435, 439
 – carton 399, 408
 – case 413
disposable 115

disposal 116
dispose 115
dispossession 151
dispute 77
dissaving 109, 412
dissolution 116
dissolve (to) 116
distance freight 175
distant subscriber 104
distinction 116
distortion 408
distrainable 332
distrainee 97
distribute (to) 116, 318
distribution 80, **116, 318**, 408
 – account 402, 443
 – pattern 408
 – ratio 443
 – research 408
distributive trade 408
distributor 116,
district manager 114
distrust (to) 227
distrust 226
distrustful 226
diversification 409
divide (to) 117, 257
dividend **116, 318**
 – announcement 117
 – coupon 117
 – entitled to 421
 – limitation 39, 117
 – policy 271
 – reserve 117
 – tax 117
 – warrant 116
division 257, 318
divisional coin 234
divisor 117
dock (to) 36
dock 36, 45, 117
dockage 122
dock dues 122
docker 96, 117
dock (dockers') strike 180
doctrine 117
document **118**, 266
documentary 118
 – credit 93, 118
 – draft 313
 – evidence 205
dole 56, 191
dollar 118, 409
 – area 390
 – clause 59
 – exchange 118
 – gap 409
 – holdings 409
 – loan 409
 – shortage 263
 – surplus 409
domain 118
domestic product 437
domestic staff 128
domicile **118**
domicile commission 119
domiciled 118
domiciliation 119
dominant tenement 169
donation 119
done in duplicate 161

don't drop 367
door 273
door-to-door transport 454
dossier 120
dot charter 454
dotted line 270
double 120
 – option 249, 282
 – taxation 189
down-payment 384
down time 451
downturn 415
downward trend 361
dowry insurance 27
dowry insurance policy 270
dozen 121
draft (to) 230
draft **116, 290**, 369
 – (minute) 230
 – (poids) 270, 354
 – advice 31
 – articles 290
 – bill 290
 – budget 290
 – contract 79, 290
 – reply 290
 – resolution 323
drain 344
draining off 145
draw (tirer) 115, 171, 364, 446
 – (toucher) 367
 – (prélever) 277
 – (minuter) 230
 – by lot 447
 – up 148, 259, **305**
drawback 120, 121, 123, 311, 324, 330
drawee 364
drawer 364
drawing 111, 208, **277, 364**, 447, 452
 – account 67
 – day 363
 – rights 122, 364
 – rights, special 409
 – up 148, 258, 304
dress 362
 – informal 362
dressing case 388
driver 54
driver's licence 264
droop (to) 167
drooping 167
drop (to) 367
drop 309
drug 330
drum (to) 450
 – memory 426
dud cheque 55
due 112, 123, 154
 – to 190, 328
dues 122
dull 206, 223, 328, 425
duly 123, 251, 309
dummy 132, 281, 437
dumping 123
dunning letter 422
duopoly 123
duplicate 120, 123
duplication machine 123, 217
duplication 120

duplicator 123
durables 76
duration 123
dustbin cheek 404
Dutch auction 296
dutiable 120, 123, 188, 345
duties 122
duty 358
 – deferment 405
duty-free 120, 174, 209
duty-paid 11, 122, 209
 – entry 98
 – sale 381
dwelling house 219

E

early reply 290
earmark 16
earmarking 16
earn (to) 176
earned income 328, 333
earnest 24
earning capacity 316
earnings improvement 443
earnings flow 445
ease (to) 233
easement 339
easiness 18, 159
easing 110
Easter 256
Easter holidays 377
easy 159, 235
econometric 126
econometrics 126
economic 127, 410
 – cycle 73
economical 126, 127
ecnomically 127
economist 127
economy **126**, 144, 410
 – size 411
edition 128
education 410, 416
effect (to) 128
effect 128
effort 131
eight 185
ejection 158
elastic 131
elasticity 131
elect (to) 132
election 131
electrician 131
electricity 131
 – shares 379
electrification 131
electrify 131
electronic 132
elevator 132
eligibility 132
eligible 132
emancipated 132
emancipation 132
embargo 133
embark (to) 133
embarrass (to) 133
embassy 19
embezzle 110
embezzlement 110, 116, 219

embossed **364**
emergency 376
 – meeting 327
emigrate 134
emigration 134
emoluments 134
employ (to) 135
employee 135
 – handbook 41
 – 's contribution 84
 – shareholding 392
employer 135
employer's 259
 – association 26, 135, 259
 – contribution 84, 259
 – federation 355
 – liability 135, 323
 – liability insurance 26
employment 134, 433
 – agency 17, 267
 – improvement 443
empties 132, 175, 385
empty 385
enable (to) 149
enclose (to) 191
enclosed 202
enclosure 20, 266
 – label 150, 385
 – stamp 266
encumber (to) 181
encumbrances 53
end (to) 166
end 165
 – of month maturity 125
 – of month requirements 125
 – month settlement 211
endorsable 139
endorse (to) 139
 – back 80
 – over 139
endorsee 139
endorsement 31, **139,** 271
endorser **139**
endowment 409
 – insurance 26
energy 139, 411
 – crisis 411
 – policy 411
 – resources 411
 – sector 411
 – supply 411
enforceable 153
engage (to) **140**
engaged (tel.) 247
engagements **139**, 246, 352
engaging 193
engineer 195
engineering 77
 – industry 419
engrossment 181
enjoy (to) 203
enjoyment 203
enquiry (v. inquiry)
enter **195**, 273
 – on 347
 – up 259
entering and leaving 344
enterprise 142
 – ,free 412
entertainment allowance 192

entertainment tax 358
entice away (to) 96
entirely 141
entitle 122
entrance 141
 – examination 151
 – fee 433
entrepreneur's
 – income 142, 328
 – profit 142
 – remuneration 142
entrust (to) 72
entry 24, **98,** 127, 195
envelope **143,** 269
environment 412
 – social 400
environmental 412
epoque method 228
equal (to) 431
equal 131
 – cost curve 405
 – pay... 411
 – pay for – work 333
 – product curve 405
equality 131, 411
 – of votes 257
equalization 133, 263
equalization fund 66, 263
equalize 131, 263
equidistant 412
equilibrium 145
equip (to) 145
equipment 145, 253
 – leasing 421
 – spending 407
equities 12
equivalent 145
erase 180
erase (erasing) head 452
eraser 179, 180
erasure 180, 299
ere long 186
erosion 412
errand boy 177
erroneously 145, 146
error 145, 412
 – band 413
escalator (index) clause 419
escape 125
escape clause 59
establish (to) 148
established 168
establishment 148, 418
estate 8, **291**
 – agency 4, 17, 418
 – agent 188, 418
 – duties 123
 – duty 189
esteemed 148, 185
estimate (to) 148
estimate 42, 111, 282, 283, 413
estimation 413
 – method 427
estimator 413
estop (to) 170
estoppage 170
estoppel 170
eurocheque 413
Eurodollar 413
evade (to) 247
evasion 151

472/Index

evening dress 362
evening edition 128
evening mail 86
event 414
eventuality 151
eviction 151, 158
ex
– allotment 151
– claim 151, 346
– coupon 151
– dividend 117
– interest 198
– new 151, 346
– quay 7, 294
– rights 122, 351
– store 218
– works 7, 151
exact 151
examination **151**, 196, **396**, 383
examination paper 151
examine 151, 387
examiner 151, 383, 387
example 153
exceed 105, 152
exceeding 226
except 152, 334
exception 152
exceptional 152
exceptionally 152
excess 105
– application 346
– capacity 46
– demand 103
– freight 152
– luggage 32, 152
– offer 248
– price 354
– profits 36
– profits duty 189
– purchasing power 276
– weight 152, 354
excess of loss reinsurance 440
– treaty 440
exchange (to) 124
exchange **40, 51,** 124
– broker 89
– brokerage 89
– business 249, 370
– circles 229
– committee 40
– contract 78
– control 52, 80
– customs 41
– day 40, 203
– department 338
– equalization fund 52
– gazette 40
– hours 40
– law 121
– line 210
– list 40
– market 424
– office 42
– order 40
– parities 256
– policy 52, 271
– position 340
– premium 17, 282
– profits 36, 52

– quotations 40, 84
– rate 52, 451
– regulation 308
– restrictions 112
– (rate) risk 329
– rules 41
– tax 40
– transactions 40, 249
exchangeable 124
Exchequer 230
excise 8
excise administration 307
excited 223
exclude (to) 152
exclusion 152
exclusive 152
– sale 234
excuse 152
execute (to) **152**
execution **153,** 331
executive officers 398
executives 413
executor 153
executory 153
– deed 365
executrix 153
exempt (to) 153, 154
exempt 153
exemption 153, **174**
exercise (to) 153
exercise 154
exert (to) 153
exhaust (to) 145
exhaustion 145
exhibit 157
exhibition 157
– building 168
– committee 157
– grounds 157
– premises 215
– stand 168
exhibitor 157
exit 344
exodus 151
exonerate 153, 154
exoneration 97, 153
exorbitant 154
expansion 154
expansion rate 154
expectation 28, 413
– of life 413, 430
– value 455
expedite (to) 280
expend 106
expenditure 106, 407
– break-dow 407
– ceiling 407
expenses **53, 106, 172**
– legal 416
expensive 89
experience (to) 351
experience 155
experienced 155, 330
expert 155
– advice 156
– committee 156
expiration 156
expire 156
expired 263
expiry 156
expiry date 95, 156

explanatory statement 157
exploit 157
exploitation 156
explosive 226
export (to) 157
export **157**
– bounty 157, 282
– credit 92, 157
– credit insurance 27
– duties 123, 344
– financing 165
– firm 157
– gold point 270
– goods 157
– licence 157, 210
– multiplier 428
– permit 29, 157, 264
– possibility 157, 275
– quota 403
– restrictions 157
– surplus 152, 157, 450
– trade 62, 157
exportation 157
– voucher 388
exporter 157
exporting 157
– country 262
express (to) 158
express 158
– delivery 158
– letter 158
– packet 144
– parcel 158
– train 369
expressed in 209
expressly 158
expropriate 158
expropriation 158
extend (to) 111, 150, 158, 290, 292
extension 158, 292
extension *(tel.)* 275
extension line 210
extent 150, 228, 257
external 110
– tariff 357
– trade policy 271
extinction 158, 414
extinguish 150
extra
– charge 173, 354, 416
– fare 352
– leave 73
– pay 450
– premium 354
– rebate 296
– work 353
extract 158
extrajudicial 158
extraordinary 158
extrinsic 158

F

face side 31
face value 241, 378
facilitate (to) 159
facsimile 159
fact 161

factor 159
 – analysis 393
 – costs 89, 159
 – in costs 159
factoring 414
 – company 414
 – contract 414
 – fees 414
 – system 414
factory 70, 159, **220**, 376
 – building 36
 – hand 253, 455
fail 126, 161, 220
failing him 100
failure 161
fair 167
 – bill 369
 – management committee 167
faith 167
faithfully 18
fake (to) 46
fall (to) **33**, 367
 – back 304, 327
 – due 125, 126
 – off 304
fall 33
 – in prices 318
falling off 114
false 162
falsification 161
falsify 161, 162
family 161, 414
 – allowance 19, 161
 – budget 42
 – business 142
 – concern 142
 – council 75, 162
 – encumbrance(s) 414
 – income 414
 – partnership 414
 – wage 161, 332
Family Allowance Fund 66
fan 414
fancy goods 216
fare 258, 372
farming 156
farming lease 32
fashion 232
fast goods train 221, 387
fate 447
father's day 421
fault 162
faulty drafting 100
favo(u)r (to) 162
favo(u)r **162**
'favo(u)rable **162**
favo(u)rably 162
fee 185, 305
feedback 444
feel 336
feoffee in trust 164
fertilizers 140
few 266
fictitious 164
fideicommissary 164
fidelity premiun 435
fiduciary 164
field 118
 – research 412, 452
 – work 452

 – worker 452
figure (to) 165
 – out 56
figure 55
file (to) 58
 – one's petition 106
file 58, 120, 415
 – store 426
 – system 58
filing **59**
filing cabinet 49, 58
filing clerk 58
filing one's petition 108
fill 61
 – in 314
 – up 314
fillip 350
filter question 440
final 165
 – distribution 318
 – dividend 318
finally 165
finance (to) 166
finance 165
 – bill 129
 – lease 421, 423
Finance Act 215
·Finance department 230
financial 166
 – circles 229
 – position 171
 – reconstruction 25
 – rehabilitation 25
 – standing 343
 – status 171, 340
 – year 42
financing 165
find no sale 381
fine (to) 174
fine 165
fineness 365
finished goods 289
fire 164
 – damage 447
 – extinguisher 414
 – insurance 27
 – insurance policy 270
 – peril 432
 – prevention 435
 – protection 438
 – risk 329
fireman 54
firm (adj.) **163**, 223
firm undertaking 140
firm (subst.) 166, 297, 415
firm up 305
firmness 163, 362
first 278
 – class 56
 – grade liquidity 212
 – hand 278
 – loss insurance 26, 329
 – mover 258
 – of exchange 278
 – rate 298
 – risk 329
fiscal 166
 – band 32
 – year 166
fiscality 166
fishmonger 221

fit up 19
fitting 393
fix (to) 166
fixed **166**
 – assets 187
 – deposit account 67
 – exchange 50
 – income 328
 – interest bearing 379
 – property 187
 – yield... 379
fixing 166
flag (to) 233
flag 259, 431
 – of convenience 431
flap 259
flat 223, 235
 – rate 358
fleet 167
flexibility 167
flexible 167
flex point 270
flight of capital 175
float (to) 134, 206, 415
floatation 134
floating **167**, 415
 – policy 270
 – rate 51, 415
floor rate 405, 433
florin 167
flotsam 145
flow (to) 17
flow **172**
 – production 288, 373
fluctuate 167, 253
fluctuation **167**
 – band 424
 – margin 424
fluvial 167
fly (to) 36
fold 269
folder 54, 106, 162
foliate 168
foliation 168
folio (to) 254
folio 168
follow 352
follower 207, 352
follow-up 352
following 352
following-up
 – advertising 439
 – letter 442
food
 – basket 430
 – products 437
foods 437
foodstuffs 105, 226
food (stuff) industry 193
foolproof 145
foolscap 255
foot 266
for 276
 – account of 68
 – a consideration 365
 – convenience sake 159
 – form's sake 170
 – further particulars 109
 – future delivery 214
 – health reasons 297
 – instance 153

- lack 162
- off-consumption 135
- regularity's sake 251
- value 365
- want of 162, 267
- your guidance 179

force **169, 385**
force up 353, 354
forced 169
forecast 435
foreign **150**
- currency 112
- currency account 52
- currency control office 52
- currency department 338
- department 338
- exchange **111**
- exchange department **52**
- exchange market 52, 112
- exchange positions 52
- exchange rate 112
- exchange transactions 52
- Office 230
- Secretary 230
- trade 62
- trade agency 62

foreigner 150
foreman 54, 79, 145
forfeit 100, 137
forfeiture 98
forge (to) 79
forger 162
forgery 161, 162
forging 161
form (to) **76, 170**
form **42,** 170
formal 170
formality 170
formally 170
formation 76, 170
formation expenses 172
formula 171
formulary 170
formulate 171
fortnightly 39
fortune 171
forward 212, 320
- delivery 212
- dollars 362
- exchange 111
- exchange market 222
- exchange rate 87
- exchange transactions 249
- method 228
- price 87, 212
- quotation 83
- rate 86
- sale 382
- securities 365
- transactions 222, 249

forwarding 143
- agency 155
- agent 372
- charges 155, 172
- clerk 155
- instructions 155
- station 178

found 148, 168
foundation 168
founder 168
founder's share 12
fountain pen 273
fractile 416
fraction **171,** 330
fractional number 172
fractional population 448
fragile 172
frame 44
framework 44
franc 174
franc account 68
franchise 416
- agreement 416
- clause 59

franchisee 416
franchising 416
franchisor 416
frank (to) 80
franking machine 216
fraud 175, 409
fraudulent 175
free (to) 209, 294
free **174,** 209, 315
- alongside ship 162
- and clear 296
- and unencumbered 296
- of (from) 173
- on... 294
- exchange market 223
- gold market 223
- market economy 126
- market price 223
- port 174
- trade 210
- trade area 210, 390
- trader 210
- tradist 210

freedom 173, 209, 422
- degree of 422

free-hand curve 405
freehold 291
freeing 209
freely 210
free-trade policy 433
freight (to) 175
- out 175
freight **175,** 240
- account 68
- contract 175, 404
- insurance 27, 175
- market 223
- note
- out 175
- rate 175, 357
- ton 367
- traffic 368
- train 368

freighting **17**
frequency 416
- analysis 393
- curve 416
- distribution 408, 416
- moment 428
- of turn-over 330
- polygon 416
- table 416

fringe benefit 30, 395
fringes 30
from
- producer to... 158, 382
- stock 350

frontier 175, 416
- area 416
- station 178
- traffic 368
- worker 374

front page 254
frozen 178
fuels 48
fulfil (to) 159, 247, 314
full **268**
- employment 268
- employment policy 271
- face photo 266
- member 426
- paid stock 365
- power 268, 276
- time 454
- time work 373

fully 141
- paid 422
- paid up 384
- subscribed 347

function 168
fund 168
funded income 328
fundholder 169, 316
funds **169, 293,** 416
fungible 169
furnish (to) 171
furniture 229, 231
furniture removers 104
furniture repository 178
furniture van 104
further 19
- to... 352

fuse 175
fusion 175
future 91
futures 212
futures market 222

G

gainer 176
galloping 194
gamble 202
gambler 18, 202
gambling 17
game 202
gap 205, 454
garage 177
garageholder 177
garnishment 156, 331
gas 178
- consumption 178

gasoline 147
gaussian 417
general **178**
- manager 114

gentleman 235
genuine 383
geography 178
geometrical mean 237
gift 397
- packing 411
- parcel 397
- scheme 439

Index/475

- subscription 397
- system, free 439
- voucher 397
- ware 397

gilt-edged 119
give
- account 315
- change for 315
- for the call 10
- notice 105
- on stock 319, 320
- quittance 296
- the rate 320

giver
- for a call 11
- for a call of more 160, 278
- for a put 381
- for a put and call 278
- for a put of more 160, 278
- of the rate 283
- on stock 320
- to the option 250

glass industry 193
glut 138
go (to) 25
- a bear 202
- a bull 202
- off 96, 127, 381, 383
- out 344
- to law 148
- up 183

going out 344
going to strike 406
gold 250
- bar 211
- block 250
- block countries 250
- bond 246, 250
- bullion standard 149
- clause 59, 250
- coin 250, 266, 430
- cover 250
- currency 233
- exchange standard 149
- export 250
- franc 250
- hoarding 250
- loan 136, 250
- market 250
- mine 229
- movement 236
- parity 250, 256
- point **179**, 270
- premium 250
- reserve 250, 322
- rush 430
- specie standard 149
- standard 250
- trade 250

gondola 417
- shelf 417

gone 14
- away, no address 258

good **39**
- delivery stock 365
- for printing 39
- wine... 140

goods 37, 221, 394
- account 68
- department 338

- flow 415
- in stock 217
- movements 124
- on hand 217
- platform 294
- station 178
- traffic 368, 454
- train 368
- wag(g)on 389

goodwill 59, 169
go slow strike 181
governed by... 307
government 179
- annuity 316
- guarantee 177
- interference 195
- loan 135
- revenue 328
- spending 106

governor 179
graduated 126, 290
grant (to) 9, 247
grant 119
granfee 70
granting 247
grantor 50
graph 180
graphic 417
gratis 180
gratuitous 180
gratuitously 179
gratuity 180
greetings telegram 359
grocer 145
groceries 145
grocer's shop 145
gross *(grosse)* 181
gross *(brut)* **41**
- amount 235
- lease 421
- national income 328
- national product 289
- premium 435

groundless 168
ground rent 305
group (to) 182
group 182, 417
- insurance 394
- interview 420
- policy 433

groupage document 409
grower 156
growing 290
growth 95, 406
- curve 405
- industry 193
- pace 406
- pattern 427
- potential 434
- prospects 406
- rate 95
- ratio 9
- shares 379

guarantee (to) 30, 177
guarantee 30, **177**
- fund 168, 177
- insurance 27

guarantor 9, 30, 49, 177
guaranty 30, **343**
guardian 95, 375

guardianship 95, 375
guidance 179
guide card 182
guilder 167
gummed 179

H

habits 417
haggle 221
haggling 221
hailstorm insurance 26
hairdressing saloon 334
half 104, 232
- day job 427
- dozen 105
- time 427
- time worker 454
- timer 427, 454
- yearly 336

hamper (to) 141
hand (to)
- in 313
- over 313

hand 218
- blotter 43
- luggage 32
- made 218
- written 221

handicraft 25
handicrafts... 25
handing over 313
handle (to) 220, 221
- with care 28

handling 220, 221
- charge 401, 409
- cost 172, 221

handwriting 221
handwriting expert 155
harbo(u)r 272
- authorities 273
- dues 123, 273
- installations 274
- master 46, 273
- police 273
- station 178

hard currency 112
hard ware 417
harden (to) 297, 305
hardening 297
harvest 302
hatching 417
haul, long 453
hawk (to) 61
hawker 221
hawking 61, 62
head 363, 452
- cashier 45
- money 405
- office 42, 283, 339
- side 159
- tax 189

headed note paper 255
heading 61, 275, **331**
headline 61
hear (to) 141
hearing 418
heating 54
heating apparatus 54

476/Index

heating expenses 172
heating surface 54
heave here 345
heaviness 216
heavy 216
hectogram 183
hectolitre 183
hectometer 183
hedge (to) 90
hedging selling 90
hedging transaction 183
height 183
heir 184
 – at law 184
 – on trust 164
heiress 184
held indivisum 193
here 186
hereafter 57
hereby 279
hereinafter 105
hereunder 57
herewith 20, 57, 202, 279
hesitate (to) 184
high 132, 183, 344
 – Authority 183
 – finance 165
highest bidder 345
hinder (to) 141
hindrance 141
hire (to) 216
hire **216**
 – contract 78, 214
 – of services 216
 – purchase 215, 360
 – purchase agreement 360
 – purchase control 360
 – purchase credit 360
 – purchase financing 360
 – purchase restrictions 360
 – purchase system 360
hiring 214, 216
histogram 418
hoard (to) 363, 449
hoard 35
hoarder 363
hoarding 255, 363, 392, 449
hold (to) 110, **361**
 – on lease 361
 – the line (wire) 296
 – with chains 345
hold 45
holder **110**, 274, **367**
holding company 184, 341
holiday 203
holiday allowance 377
holiday period 377
holidays 377
home
 – bill 130
 – consumption 76
 – country 229
 – currency 234
 – demand 103
 – industry 193
 – made 159
 – market 272
 – port 272
 – produce 289
 – trade 63
 – work 373

Home Office 230
Home Secretary 230
homeward freight 175
honest 184
honesty 184
honorary 184, 242
honour (to) 185
honour 184
hoof 266
hope (to) 147
hope **147**
hostess 418
hotel 185
 – bill 429
 – chain 399
 – expenses 172
 – industry 185
hot money 185, 398
hour **184**
hour worked 253
house 218
house bill 129, 255
house coal 53
householder 161
household 426
 – articles 427
 – expenses 427
 – furniture 229
house
 – journal 143
 – number 244
housekeeping 426
 – book 213
 – money 426
housephone 451
house-to-house 408
 – distribution 116, 408
 – selling 456
housing 77, 215
 – allowance 191
 – problem 215
 – shortage 215
hull 82
 – insurance 27
humidity 185
hunger strike 180
husbandry 126
husband's authorization 29, 225
hush money 275
hypermarket 418
hypothecation 237

I

ice 416
idea box 39
identical 187
identification 187
 – words 235
identify 187
identity 187
 – card 48, 187
 – certificate 12
idle 248
if
 – cashed 335
 – necessary 151
 – undelivered 191

 – unsold 248, 335, 382
illegal 187
illegality 187
illegible 187, 339
illicit 187
illness 219
image 418
imitate 79, 187
imitation 187
immediately 187
immigrate 187
immigration 187, 418
 – policy 418
 – quota 418
immobilization 187
immobilize 187
immovable 187
impact on 318
impartial 187
impatience 188
impede 134
impediment 134
import (to) 188
import **188**, 418
 – article 188
 – bounty 188
 – credit 92
 – duties 122, 188
 – firm 188
 – gold point 270
 – licence 188, 210, 264
 – list 188
 – permit 29
 – quota 77, 418
 – trade 62, 188
 – value 188
importance 188
important 188
importation 188
 – voucher 388
importer 188
importing 188
 – country 188, 262
imposition 189
impossibility 189
impossible 189
improvement 19, 39, 229
impulse 418
impulsive 418
in
 – abeyance 354
 – accordance with 73
 – any denomination 368
 – apparent good order 149
 – bad faith 167
 – bond 123, 142
 – bulk 389
 – cash 67
 – cipher 56
 – consideration 297
 – default 100
 – demand 301
 – due course 361, 376
 – due form 112, 170
 – due time 376
 – duplicate 153
 – favour of 289
 – force 385
 – full 141, 197
 – full payment 224
 – full settlement 343

Index/477

- good faith 167
- good repair 143
- good tone 223
- hand 153
- kind 238
- order to 17
- parts 213, 368
- payment 365
- person 291
- process of... 138, 387
- progress of... 138, 153
- proportion as 29, 291
- pursuance **22**, 153, 352 385
- request 104, 301
- respect 131
- rotation 330
- round sum 344
- settlement of 343
- stock 217
- the aggregate 367
- the capacity 295
- the chair 280
- the longer term 389
- the market 223
- this connection 291
- this respect 131, 299
- triplicate 153
- whole 368
- witness whereof 167
- words 206
- writing 127, 207, 221

incalculable 190
incapable **191**
incapacity 191
incentive 350
incidence 191
included 401
inclusive 191, 401
income 316, **328**, 444
- bracket 328, 445
- distribution 328
- elasticity 131, 444
- equilibriun 444
- from 328
- groups 328
- s policy 434
- tax 189, 328, 358
incoming letters 86
incomplete 191
incontestable 191
inconvenient 195
inconvertible 191
incorporate into (to) 191
incorporated 264
incorporation 191, 264, 419
incorporeal 38, '419
increase (to) 29, 219
increase **9, 29,** 219, 353
increment 419
- tax 451
- value tax 189
incur 138
indebted 305
indebtedness 138
indeed 128
indemnification 100, 191
indemnify 100, 191
indemnity 191
index (to) 318
index 192, 419

- bond 192
- card 164
- clause 192
- linking 419
- number 419
indexation 419
indexed 192
index-linked 192, 419
indexnumber 192, 241
index-tied 192, 419
indiarubber 179
indicate 193
indication 192
indifference curve 405
indorse (to) 139
indorsement 139
indorser 139
industrial 194
- disease 289
- press 143
industrialization 193
industrialize 193
industry 193, 419
infancy 235
infant 229
inflate 179
inflation 179, **194,** 419
inflationary 194
- pressure 434
- spiral 194
- tendency 434
- threat 419
inflation spiral 194
inflatory 194
inflexion point 270
inflow 17
influence 194
influx 17
inform 195, 316, **335**
informality 320
information 194, **315,** 419
- processing 453
- slip 316
infrastructure 195
ingot 211
ingot gold 211, 250
inherit 184
inheritance 184
initial (to) 132, 256, 386
initial 195
- expenses 148
initialling 148
initials 256, 447
initiate 206
initiative 195
injection 195
injunction 231
injuries to workmen 8
ink 138
ink eraser 179
inking pad 356
inkpot 138
inkstand 127, 138
inland
- bill 130, 369
- navigation 36, 238
- port 272
- rate 357
- revenue 301
- telegram 359
- water transport 453

- waterway bill of lading 74
- waterway consignment note 300
innovation 195
input (to) 412
- file 415
- output 412
- output instruction 420
- output routine 445
inquire (to) 316
- into 140
- within 316
inquiry 195
inquiry agency 17
inquiry office 43, 316
inscription 195
insert 191, **196**
insertion 196
inset 137
inside broker 89
insist 196
insolvency 196
insolvent 196
inspect 196
inspectation 196
inspection 196
inspection 387
inspector 196
instability 196
instalment 11
instalment agreement 360
instalment buying 360
instalment credit 360
instalment plan 10, 361
instalment sale 360
instalment system 361
instalment transaction 360
instance 196
instead 260
institution 196
instruction **196,** 279, 420
instrument 197
insufficient 197
insufficiently 197
insurable 26
insurance 26, 394
- agent 17, 27, 437
- book 273
- broker 27, 89
- certificate 27, 50
- company 27, 341
- consultant 28
- contract 27
- fund 28, 168
- green card 399
- market 395
- policy 28
- premium 18, 282
- proposal 395
- shares 455
- stamp 28
- taker 28, 278
- value 28
insurant 28
insure 28
insured 28
insurer 28
insurrection 420
intangible 197, 419
integral 197
integration 197, 420
intelligence test 452

478/Index

intention 197
interaction 420
interbank 420
intercompany 403
interdiction 197
interest (to) 197
interest **197, 198,** 451
 – account 68, 199
 – bearing 198, 288
 – coupon 199
 – equalization tax 451
interested 197
interest table 199, 355
interference 195
interim
 – agency 420
 – balance sheet 38
 – dividend 199
 – interest 198
 – loan 405, 448
 – report 298
interlineation 199
intermediary 199
intermediate 199
international 199
interpenetration 199
interphone 451
interpret (to) 199
interpretation 199
interpreter 217, 199
interrupt 199
interruption 199
interval 420
intervene 200
intervening parties 258
intervention 200
 – limit 433
 – point 200
interview 143, 420
inter-war period 263
intrinsic 200
introduce **200,** 280
introduction 200
invalidate 200
invalidity pension 262
invention 200
inventor 200
inventory (to) 200
inventory 200, 350
 – accumulation 350, 449
 – building 350
invest (to) **200, 267**
investment 201, **267,** 420
 – account 201
 – bank 201
 – climate 400
 – credit 201, 406
 – expenditure 201, 407
 – financing 201
 – goods 37, 419
 – goods industry 193
 – multiplier 428
 – opportunity 420
 – outlays 201
 – plan 201
 – policy 201
 – program(me) 201, 438
 – projects 201
 – purposes 201
 – securities 201, 365, 379
 – seeking 47

 – spending 201
 – trust **268,** 341
 – trust certificate 50, 431
 – trust share 50
investor 48, 201
invisible 201
invisibles 188
invitation 201
 – for tenders 14
 – to tender 394, 429
invite 201
invoice (to) 160
invoice **159,** 242
 – amount 160
 – book 160
 – clerk 160
 – discounting 413
 – price 160, 284
 – value 160, 378
invoicing machine 160, 217
inward mail department 338
irrecoverable 201
irredeemable 201, 202, 242, 311
irregular 201, 421
irregularity 201, 421
irresponsible 202
irrevocable 202
island 418
issuance 411
issue (to) 133, 411
issue 134
 – department 134, 338
 – market 222
 – or tap 134
 – price 87, 284, 436
 – prospectus 292
 – syndicate 355
 – terms 134
 – value 378
issuer 133, 436
issuing 133, 411
issuing house 134
italic 202
italicize 202
item 24, 202, **275**

J

jetsam 145
jettison **202,** 227
job
 – description 454
 – evaluation 439
 – rotation 411, 445
 – seeker 411
 – wage 332
 – work 373
joint 73
 – and several 343
 – account 68, 257
 – cargo 182
 – creditor 60
 – debtor 60
 – management 61
 – manager 60
 – owner 82
 – ownership 82
 – undertaking 257

jointly 73
 – and severally 343
journal 204
 – item 204
journalize 204, 273
journey 388
judge (to) 205
judge 205
judgment 205
judicial 204
judicially 205, 421
judicious 205
jumble w397
jurisdiction 205
jurisprudence 205
justification 205
justify 205
just out 256
juxtaposition 205

K

keep 143, 178, 361,
 – dry 185
 – flat 269
 – in repair 143
 – up 143
 – upright 97, 317, 361
keeping in repair 317
key 59, 367
 – currency 428
 – figures 400
 – industry 59, 419
 – sector 446
 – word 235
keyboard 59
kind 178
kindness 246
kiosk 205
kite 59 364
kite 129, 369
 – flying 50
kneehole desk 24
knock down 14
knockdown price 436
knock-out price 285, 385
know 335
know-how 446
knowledge 74

L

lab (oratory) 421
label (to) 150
label 385, 413
 – adhesive 392
labelling 150
labo(u)r **218, 373,** 423
 – agreement 404
 – cheap 423
 – conference 373
 – conflicts 73, 373
 – contract 79, 373
 – creation program 373
 – disputes 73, 373
 – exchange 40, 247, 373
 – force 272
 – foreign 423

- hour 184
- legislation 206, 373
- market 223, 373
- mobility 231
- movement 253
- party 253
- protection 438
- question 253
- shortage 263
- theory of value 455

lack 220
- of.. 263

ladder 125
ladder system 126
lamented 309
land band 34, 168
land carriage 372
land charge 110
land charge deed 111
landed 168
- estate 291
- property 38

land improvement 19
landing
- certificate 50
- charges
- permit 264
- stage 96, 133

landlord 291
Land Registry Office 44
land tax 80, 168, 189
language 206
- lab 421

languid 206
languish 206
languishing 206
large 179, 181
lash 396, 429
last 108
- name 240
- will 457

late *(tard)* 356
- *(ancien)* 219

latency 451
launch 206
launching 290
law 121, 206, 215
- bureau 43
- costs 172
- department 43

lawyer 32
lay (to)
- off 210
- out 97
- up 108

lay days 148, 203, 268, 349
laying
- down 231
- off 210, 265
- up 57

layout 231
laytime 102
leaders 379, 380, 455
leading
- counters 380
- line 25, 302
- shares 379
- underwriter 21

leaf 164, 388
leak 387

leakage 84
learn 328
lease (to) 16, 33
lease **32**, 163, 406, 421
leaseholder 134
leasing 16, 406, 421
- agreement 404, 421
- company 421
- object 421
- operations 421
- technique 421

least 229
leather 95
- industry 419

leave 258, 296, 344
leave 73
- pay 431

lecture 72
ledger 179
ledger account 68
left-hand page 384
left-luggage office 75
legacy 206
- duties 123

legal 206
- department 77
- entity 264
- expenses insurance 394
- portion 322
- status 264
- tender 206

legalization 206
legalize (to) 29, 206
legally 205
legatee 206
legend 206
legislation 206
leisure 215, 423
- industry 423
- society 447
- wear 423

lend 281
- stock 268

lend-lease 435
lender 281
less 232
lessee 214, 421
lessor 33, 421
let 216
letter 206, 269, 422
- book 213
- box 39
- card 49
- clip 266
- lock 446
- of allotment 31, 207
- of apology 207
- of application 103
- of complaint 302
- of condolence 207
- of credit 208
- of hypothecation 186, 206
- of indemnity 207
- of introduction 207
- of lien 375
- of marque *(mart)* 207
- of recommendation 207
- of regret 31, 207
- of reminder 207
- of thanks 207

- opener 217, 253
- paper 255
- scale 265
- telegram 359
- to follow 352

letterhead 141, 207
letting 214, 216
level (to) 240
level 126, **240**, 410, 429, 457
levelling 240
lever 208
levy 208, 277
liabilities 259, 407, 431
- side 431

liability **138**, **323**, **329**
- book 329
- card 329
- ledger 329
- side 259

liable 26, 259, 305, 323
- to.. 345, 352

liberalization 209
liberalize 209
liberty 209
licence, license **210**, **264**
licensee 37, 210, 274
lien 122, 325, 416
- upon 284

lienor 91
life 437
- annuitant 316
- annuity 21, 316, 385
- insurance 27
- (insurance) policy 270
- table 235

lifeless 190
light 164
- dues 122

lightening 18
lighter 18, 262
lighterman 36
lithting 126
- expenses 172

lightning strike 180
limit (to) 211
limit 211, 268
- lower 400
- of classes 422
- of tolerance 452
- upper 400, 433

limitation **211**, **279**
limited, 150, 324
- partnership 341

limitedness 150
linear 422
linearity 422
line 210, 324, 422
- block 400
- chart 417
- limits 433
- of credit 93, 159, 422
- printer 418
- production 399
- spacer 208

liner 239, 256
link 422
liquid 211
- position 454
- resources 237

liquidation 211
liquidation account 211

480/Index

liquidator 211
liquidity 422
 – creation 422
 – difficulties 374
 – preference 212, 435
 – ratio 60, 101, 212
 – requirements 422
list (to) 200, 422
list 40, **212**, 330
 – of correspondents 192
 – of those present 164, 279
listed 84
list price 284
litigation 212
litigious 212
live 457
 – up to 247, 323
 – weight 269
liveliness 20
livestock insurance 27
living
 – conditions 457
 – costs 457
 – expenditure 397
 – standard 457
 – wage 333
load (to) 53
loaded weight 269
loading 17, 53
 – berth 133
 – charges 53, 221
 – gauge 176
 – on board 230, 427
 – port 133
load line 210
loan **135**, 280
 – account 67
 – bank 281
 – certificate 281
 – industrial 405
 – interest 136
 – society 281
 – subscription department 338
lobby 417
local charges 267
locking up 187
lock out 215
lodge (to) 107
lodging allowance 191
log book 40, 204, 213
lombard loan 281
long **215**
long-dated 125, 215, 362
long lease 134
long-run *(period)* 264
long-term **215**, 362
look-after (to) 380
loop (to) 397
Lorenz curve 405
loose-leaf book 313
loose-leaf ledger 179
loro account 68
lorry 46
lose (to) 263, 452
losing sale 456
loss **265**, 340, 432, 447
 – assessment 441
 – in output 288
 – leader 394, 437
 – statistics 447

lost 14, 131
lot (to) 216
lot **215**, 447
lottery 216, 367
lottery bond 379, 380
lottery loan 135
lottery ticket 38, 215
low 35, 240
 –, cyclical 406
 – point 94, 108
lower 7, 33, 296
lower-income groups 127
lowering 296, 305
lowness 232
loyal 216
lubricants 216
lucrative 216
lucre 216
luggage 32
 – insurance 27, 32
 – label 413
 – ticket 32, 42
 – van 389
lull 7
lump sum 170
luxury 216
luxury tax 189, 216, 358

M

machine 216
 – hour 184
 – language 421
 – made 217
 – posting 226
 – tool 217
 – work 373
machinery 21
macroeconomic 423
Madam 217
magnetic
 – disc 423
 – drum 423
 – tape 423
 – tape reader 422
maiden name 239, 240
mail 86
 – credit 92
 – order house 382
 – order selling 382
 – sorting department 338
 – transfer 86
 – transfer order 251
mailing list 15
main
 – establishment 148
 – hall 182
 – point 283
maintain 18, **143**, 218
maintenance 143
 – charges 143
 – leasing 421
majority 219
majority decision 219
majority holding 257

majority interest 257, 219
majority stake 257
make 225
 – a point 361
 – sure 28
maker 364
maker's price 284
make up 352
make-up man 229
making 218
 – over 328
 – up 66
 – up day 66
 – up price 66
mall 417
man and supply 23
man of straw 184, 281
manage 14, 114, 178, 220 307
management 14, **114**, 178 220, 221, 307, 431
 – and labour 431
 – decision 406
 – game 421
 – report 417, 440
 – secretariat 408
 – training 398
manager **114**, 178
manageress 114, 178
managership 114
managing committee 62, 114
managing director 14, 114
mandatary 220
mandate 219
mandator 219
man-hour 184
manifest 220
manifold (to) 271
manipulate (to) 423
manipulation 220
manpower 213
 – potential 434
manufactory 159, **220**
manufacture (to) 159, 221
manufacture 158, 289
manufacturer 158, 194, 221
manufacturers price 284
manufacturing 221
 – cost 159, 172
 – industry 221, 419
 – licence 210
 – process 159
 – secret 159
manure 140
marathon meeting 423
margin (to) 225
margin 224, 424
 – of fluctuation 395, 424
marginal **225**, 424, 425
 – alteration 317
 – note 132, 224
 – stop 224
marine 225
marine (insurance) policy 270
marital 225
maritime 225
mark (to) 225
mark (to) 225
 – up 17
mark 225, 425
 – s awarderd 83

marked 225
- down 196
- up 196
market 222, 424
- analysis 20, 223
- behaviour 424
- condition 73
- day 223, 267
- development 414
- discount 146
- dues 122, 223
- economy 126
- fluctuations 223
- mechanism 425
- place 224
- position 274
- price 224
- price-list 427
- rate **357**
- report 223, 224
- research 223
- segment 424
- segmentation 424, 446
- share 424
- structure 424
- technique 224
- value 41, 221, 378, 383
marketable 239
marketer 425
marketing 424, 425, 427
- audit 425
- consultant 425
- co-operative 404
- department 425
- function 425
- goal 425
- instruments 425
- manager 425
- mindedness 425
- mix 425
- plan 425
- policy 425
- program 425
- research 413
- strategy 425
- technique 425
marking 225
- clerk 34
- ink 225
- thread 225
marriage 226
- certificate 12
- settlement 78, 81
married woman 225
marshalling yard 178
mart 230
mass 226
- advertising 439
- display 413, 425
- production 159, 226, 288
- storage 426
master
- clock 185
- file 415
material 226
materials 226
maternity
- benefit 191
- insurance 394
mate's receipt 38, 133, 226, 304

matrix (to) 425
- storage 425
matter 295
- at issue 212
mature 125
maturity 125
maturity date 125
maturity tickler 48
maxima 425
maxim(iz)ation 226
maximize (to) 226
maximum 226
maximum limit 269
mean 227, 428
means 237, 324, 428
measure 228
measurement 202
measurement freight 138, 175
measurement goods 221
measurement ton 367
measurer 228
mechanical 226
mechanism 425
mechanization 226
mechanize 226
media 426
- evaluation 426
- research 413, 426
median 426
medium 426, 428
- of exchange 124, 428
medium-term 362
meet 327
meeting 25, **327, 335**
meeting room 334
member 227
- country 262
- state 426
membership 294
- card 227
memorandum 227
memorandum pad 39
memory (cfr. storage) 429
- address 392
- capacity 426
- error 412
- protection 427
men's wage 332
mention 227
mercantile 227
- marine 221
mercantilism 228
Merchandise Marks Act 225
merchant 62, **221**
- fleet 167
- man 221
merge (to) 175
merging 175
merit 228
- bonus 282
- rating 228
message 228
messenger 274
messenger boy 117
Messrs.. 235
metal 228
metallic 228
metallurgic 228
metallurgy 228
meter 229
method 228, 427

metre 229
metropolis 229
microeconomic 427
microeconomics 427
microfilm 229
middle 229, 236
middle class 58
mid month settlement 211
migration 427
mileage allowance 419
milliard 39, 229
millinery 229, 232
million 229
mine 229, 427
miner 229
minimum 229
- amount 229
- reserve ratio 401
- supply 449
- weight 230
mining 156, 427
- concession 70, 229
- engineer 427
- industry 193
- shares 13, 379
mini-snake 427
minister 230
ministry **230**
minority 230
- holding 257
- interest 257
- report 230
- stake 257
mintage 234
minter 234
minting 174, 234
mint par 256
minuscule 230
minus sign 232
minutes 287
misappropriate 110
misappropriation 110
miscalculate 226
miscalculation 226
misenter 80
misentry 80
misinvestment 201
mislaid 131
mislead 146
mismanagement 179, 226
misprint 162
Miss 217
miss (to) 220
missing 220, 334
mission 231
mistake **145, 162**
misuse 7
mobility 231
mobilizable 231
mobilization 231
mobilize 231
mode 231
moderate 232
modern 232
modernize 232
modification 232
modify 232
moment (stat.) 428
monetary 233
monetization 233
monetize 233

Index/481

money **23, 233**, 425, 428
- at bankers 35
- changer 35
- circulation 428
- debt 110
- difficulties 133
- lender 33
- market 23, 222, 223
- market paper 223
- of account 234
- order **219**, 261
- rate 23
- value 233
monoculture 428
monometal(l)ism 234
monopolist 234
monopolization 233
monopolize (to) 234
monopoly 234, 428
- position 428
- profits 428
monopsony 428
month 232, 427
monthly 227
- return 310
moor 19
mooring 19
moratorium 235
more
- or less 232
morning dress 362
morning edition 128
morning mail 86
mortality 235
- curve 405
- table 235, 355
mortgage (to) 181
mortgage 186
- bank 34, 185
- bond 186
- certificate 186
- charge 185
- debenture 186
- debt 90, 110, 186
- deed 185, 416
- loan 135, 186
- market 186
- rate 186
- registry 186
mortgageable 185, 186
mortgagee 185, 281
mortgagor 136, 186
most favoured 163
mother country 229
mother's day 421
motivation research 235
motor
- bus 29
- car 29
- car accident 8
- car credit 92
- car fleet 431
- car industry 29
- car insurance 26
- coach 29
- lorry 29
- shares 455
- show 334
- truck 46
- van 29
motors 455

movable 231
movables 38, **229, 231**
movement 57, 235
moving-band production 288
moving belt 396
Mr... 235, 339
Mrs... 217
multi-national 428
multi-phase sampling 447
multiple **317**
- address telegram 359
- firm 218
- rate system 52
- shops 218
- taxation 189
multiplication 237
multiplication table 237, 355
multiplier 237, 428
- effect 428
multiply 237
multiprocessing 428
multiprogramming 428
multi-purpose 455
multi-stage sampling 410, 447
multi-task operation 453
mutual **237**
mutual fund 168

N

naked 244
name 240
named 241
- vessel 407
name day 203
narration 209
narrow 150, 223
nation 238
national
- income 328
- wealth 171
nationality 238
nationalization 150, 238
nationalize 150
nationals 324
natural person 264
nature, by 428
navigability 238
navigable 238
navigation 238
- dues 428
near 279
- money 212, 439
- stingy 441
necessary 239
necessitate 239
necessity 239
need (to) 220
need 37
negative 239
neglect 239
neglected 102
negligence 239, 414
- clause 59
negligent 239
negotiability 239
negotiable 62, **239**
negociate 147, **240**

negotiation 239
neon sign 140
net **340**
- amount 235
- national income 328
- national product 289
- proceeds 443
- register tonnage 202
network 321
neutral money 234
new 240, **243**
- for old 112
new business 437
- expenses 437
new-business department 290
new-issue market 134, 222
news 244
- agent 221
newspaper 204, 421
- office 43
newsstand 205
New Year 244
next 287
night
- charge 357
- safe 60
- service 337
- shift 145
- watchman 380
- work 373
nil 244
no
- admittance 101, 141, 143
- agents wanted 199
- cards 161
- change given 22
- charge is made 180
- funds 293
- goods exchanged 124
- occupation 289
- parking 101, 256
- return 443
- smoking 101
- thouroughfare 197
- wonder that 150
nomenclature 241
nominal 241
nomination 46, 241, 279
non-
- acceptance 241
- arrival 242
- bank place 267, 395
- bank sector 395
- conformity 242
- cumulative 242
- delivery 242
- execution 242
- ferrous 228
- foods 437
- fulfilment 241
- inflammable 195
- liability 242
- member state 426
- payment 242
- performance 194
- profit association 26
- profit seeking 397
- quoted 242
- resident 242
- resident convertibility 81

– sale 242
– shipment 242
– trader 242
noon edition 128
nostro 242
– account 68, 242
– liabilities 242
notarial 429
notary 242
notary's deed 242
notary's fees 242
notary's office 242
notary's residence 242
note (to) **243**
note 39, 40, **242**
– book 48
– issuing bank 134
– of exclamation 270
– of expenses 243
– of hand 252
– printing press 39, 268
notes 429
notice 243, **277**
– of claim 447
– of dismissal 207
– of meeting 31
notification 243
– of crediting 31, 386
– of debiting 31, 386
notify 32, 243
notoriety 243
notorious 243
nought 390
novation 244
novelty 244, 397
now that 279
nuclear 244
– risks insurance 394
null 244
– and void 31, 244
– hypothesis 418
nullity 244
number (to) 245
number 241, **244**
numbering 245
numbering machine 168
numerator 245
numerical 244

O

oath 337
–, debtor's 446
object (to) 245
object 43, 245
objects 429
– of value 379
objection 245
obligation 246
oblige (to) 180, 246
obligor 246
obliterate 247
observation 247, 311, 429
observe 247, 311
obsolescence 429, 457
obstacle 247
obverse 31, 159
occasion 247
occupant 367

occupational 289
occupy 247
ocean
– bill of lading 74
– carriage 454
– freight 175
– navigation 238
odd 187
oddments 415, 446
of
– his own accord 248
– the one part 256
off-consumption 135
offer (to) **248**
– for sale 383
offer 248, 429
offered 247
offer(ing) for subscription 346
office **42**, 53, 168, 247
– buildings 42
– cleaning 429
– expenses 43, 172
– furniture 43, 231
– hours 43, 184
– machine 43, 217
– messenger 177
– paste 61
– premises 43
– requisites 171
– room 43
– staff 43, 264
– work 43, 373
official 168, 248
off-print 364
oil 185
– company 432
– consuming country 432
– crisis 432
– exporting 432
– industry 266
– mill 359
– needs 432
– policy 432
– producing 432
– products 432
– shares 266, 379
– ship 266
– situation 432
– supplies 432
oiler 36, 239, 266
oils 266
old 385
old-age insurance 26
old-age pension 262, 443
oligopolistic 248
oligopoly 248
omnibus
– survey 412
– train 369
on
– account 49, 54, 75, 297
– application 103, 346
– approval 71
– behalf 240
– board B/L 74
– business 16
– credit 362
– delivery 212
– demand 43, 103, 182
– examining 383
– grounds of 49

– hire 214
– holiday 377
– joint account 65
– presentation 279
– production 289
– receipt of 144, 304
– record 227
– request 103
– sale 382
– sale or return 71
– sight of 389
– tap 330
– the hoof 266
– the-job training 437
– the one hand 256
– the spot 267
– vacation 377
– your part 256
once 168
one-man business 142
one-man company 341
– one-price store 217, 285
one-way... 455
– packing 411
onerous 248
ones 376
open (to) **253**
– here 254
open 254
– all the year round 254
– door 271, 273
– market 223
– market policy 271
– working 156
opening 253
– balance 253
– credit 405
– price 87, 285
– rate 253
operating loss 157
operation 430
– research 301
operational 430
operator 156, 360, 429
opinion 430
– leader 430
– research 413, 430
– survey 412, 430
opportunity 247
opposite 57
opposition 249
option 160, 249
– bargain 222, 239, 283
– day 283
– dealings 15, 249, 430
– declaration 283, 319
– declaration day 203, 319
– money 249
– price 87, 283
– rate 283
– to double 121, 160
– to quadruple 160, 222
– to treble 160, 222
or
– better 229, 335
– order 251
– otherwise 30
order (to) 62
order **62, 219, 250, 251**
– at best 229
– book 48, 62, 213

Index/483

- cheque 54
- clause 58
- form 39, 42, 62
- s in hand 273
- number 244
- of magnitude 250
- of the day 252
- paper 129, 252, 255
- to pay 219, 430

orderbook 398
ordinate 250
ordinary 250
oriented 252
organization 252
- chart 430
organize 252
origin **253**, 293
original *(adj.)* 253
original *(subst.)* 230, 253
other side 258
otherwise 30
ounce 248
out
- and home 18
- of date 263
- of-pocket expenses 173
- of print 145
- of stock 350
- of-town bill 106

outbid 137, 314, 353
outbidder 353
outbidding 353
outbuildings 105
outdoor staff 338
outdoor work 373
outfit (to) 145
outfit 145
outgoing letters 86
outlay 97
outlet 97
outlier 429
outline law 215
output 288, 448
- per hour 443
- potential 275, 288
- routine 448

outside
- broker 89
- market 223
- service 338

outstanding 309
outward
- bound 257
- freight 18
- mail department 337

over 39
overboard 202
over-capacity 353
overcapitalization 353
overcapitalize 353
overcharge (to) 70, 354
overconsumption 450
overdraft 99
- commission 64
- facilities 405

overdrawn 99, 108
overdue 24, 325
over-employment 353
overestimate 353, 455
overflow (to) 407
over-full employment 353

overhaul 445
overhauling 313
overheads 173
overheated 450
overheating 402
overinsurance 27, 353
over-insure 450
over-investment 450
overlap 441
overleaf 384
overload 353
overloading 353
overmeasure 152
overpaid 454
overpay 262
overproduction 354
oversea 253
- (s) bank 34, 430
- (s) market 222
- (s) possessions 253
- (s) trade 62

overseer 71
overstaffed 432
oversubscribed 354
oversubscription 346
over the counter market 223
overtime 373
overtime hours 184
overvaluation 353, 455
overvalue 99
overvalued 354
overwhelmed 7, 97
overwork 353, 354, 373
overworking 354
owe 112
owing (to) 112, 297, **352**
own (to) 274
own 291
owner 156, 274, 291, 438
- and charterer 175
- charterer 23

ownership 291

P

pack (to) 133
package 431
packaging 402
- industry 193
- material 411

packet 143
packing **132,** 411
- cardboard 133
- case 133
- charges 133, 172
- cloth 133
- extra 256
- free 174
- included 263
- list 61
- material 226
- paper 133, 255
- returnable 443
- to charge for 402

pad 356
page (to) 254
page 254
- printer 418

paginate 254

pagination 254
paging 254
paid-on charges 97
paid up 209
pallet 254
- board 254

palletization 430
palletize 430
panel 430
- enveloppe 143
- member 430

panic 497
- buying 392

pantechnicon van 104
paper 255
- bound 41
- clip 28
- factory 255
- guide 182
- industry 193
- knife 84
- mill 255
- release lever 208
- securities 255
- standard 149
- weight 280

par 254
parcel 61, 143, 215, 256
- out 216
- to be called for 412

parcelling out 216
parcel post 61, 337
parcels cartage 159
parcels service 228
parent company 341
parent house 219
pari passu 256
parities realignment 440
parity 256, 431
- alterations 431
- bit 397
- change 431
- check 404
- point 256
- price 256
- table 355

park (to) 256
parking 256
part 162, **256, 257**
part with (to) 100
partial 258
partially paid 422
participant 257
participate 257
participating 270
participation 257, 431, 436
particular partnership 257
parties entitled 32
parting visit 386
partly 257
partner **26,** 62, 257
partnership 26, 62
partnership firm 341
part payment 260
part shipments 258
part-time work 373
part-time worker 374
party 32, **258**
- of the first 65
- of the second 65

party wall 231

par value 254
pass (to)
 – for payment 430
 – on... 443
pass 259
 – in transit 372
 – to... 273
passage 258
passage money 258
pass book 48, 214
passenger 258
 – count 401
 – list 212
 – ship 239
 – ticket 258
 – traffic 57, 368
 – train 368
passing 258
passive 259
passport 258
passport office 258
passport photo 258, 266
patent (to) 41
patent 41
 – charges 41
 – office 41
 – rights 194, 291
patended 41
patentee 41
pattern 351
 – book 125
 – parcel 125
patience 259
patronage 259
pause 451
pawn (to) 140, 176
pawnbroker 33
pawnee 176
pawner 176
pay (to) 261
 – in 384
 – off 19, 212, 294, 312, 325
 – to bearer 262
 – to the order 262
 – up 152, 209
payability 154
payable 260
pay day 203, 260
payee 37, 130, 258, 278
payer **262**
paying
 – agent 119, 339, 413, 417
 – by the month 427
 – in 384
 – in slip 40, 384
 – its way 385
 – off 294
 – out 97
payment **260, 384**
 – in full 209
payment commission 64
payments agreement 261
payroll 40
pay schedule 150
pay sheet 132, 260
peak 344
 – hours 184
 – level 240
pecuniary 262
pedlar 221
pegged 284, 347

penalty 100
pencil 90
 – eraser 90, 179
 – sharpener 90
pending 138
penholder 273
pension (to) 262
 – of 262
pension **262**, 326, 432
 – claim 327
 – fund 44, 262
pensionable 327
pensioner 263, 327
pensioning 327
 – off 230
pent-up inflation 194
per
 – capita 363
 – head 363
per cent 276
percentage **276**, 356
 – distribution 356
percentile 432
perforate 263
perforation 270
perforator 263
perform (to) 314
peril 432
perils of the sea 171
period 263, 432
 – of turnover 330
periodical 264
perishable 264
permanent 264
permit (to) 264
permit 264
... permitting 264
person 264
personal **264**
 – drawings 208, 277
 – estate 229, 231, 291
 – property 171, 231
 – security 177
personally 265
personalty 231
personnel 264, 432
 – department 265, 338
 – manager 264
 – office 432
 – (merit) rating 432
 – representative 432
petition 161
petro-dollar 432
petrol 147, 413
 – consumption 413
 – coupon 413
 – pump 147
 – rationing 413
 – tank 147
petroleum 432
petties 227
petty expenses 227
phone (to) 360
photo 266
photocopy 266
photostat (to) 266
photostat 266
pick-up 321
picketing 433
pie-chart 417
piece 266

 – of furniture 229
 – wages 332
 – work 266, 373
 – worker 253, 374
 – work wages 266
pig on pork 129, 230
pigeon-hole cabinet 49
piggyback service 421
pilot 266
 – boat 36, 266
 – fractory 433
 – market 432
 – price 419
 – service 266
 – survey 412
pilotage 266
 – dues 266
pit-head 427
 – stocks 350
placard 16
placarding 16
place (to) 127, **267**
 – on the run 338
place 210, 266
placing 127
 – orders 267
 – shares 267
plaintiff 104, 431
plan **268, 290**
planned economy 126
planning 268, 433
plant 145, 253
plant manager 156
plate glass insurance 26
platform 268, **294**
platform ticket 363
plea 152
please.. 282, 388
 – advise by... 243
 – don't fold 269
 – forward 352
 – note that 243
 – quote 306
 – twin over 368, 384
pleasure 268
pledge (to) 106, 140, 176, 238
pledge **176**, 238
pledged 176
pledgee 91, 176
pledger 176
pledging 176, 238
pledgor 176
plenary 269
plethora 269
plot 408
plus 269
pocket diary 17
pocket money 23
pocket size 170
point 270, 433
 – examination 413
 –, fixed 457
 – of purchase 433
 – of sale 433, 456
 – of view 270
policeman's report 287
police records 49
policy 433
 – (politique) 271
 – (assur.) **270**
 – conditions 433

486/Index

−, cyclical 402
−, easy-money 434
− fee 433
− fiscal 433
− holder 271
−, monetary 433
− number 433
− stamp 271
Poll tax 405
pool 272
pooling 427
population 272, 434
− policy 105
− statistics 105
port
− *(babord)* 32
− *(harbour)* 272
− *(side)*
− bill of lading 74
− equipment 274
− of call 146
− rates 274
− regulations 273, 308
porter 274
porterage 172
portfolio 273, 434
portion 274, 296, 370
portion policy 270
position 274
possess (to) 274
possession 274
− title 365
possessor 274
possibility 275
possible 275
possibly 151
post (to) *(poste)* 106, 275, 434
− *(compt.)* 259, 371
− up 204
post
− *(courrier)* 86
− *(poste)* **275**
− box 275
− office 42, 275
− office box 39
− office order 220
− test 434, 452
postage 172, **272**
− stamp 364
postal **275**
− authorities 275
− cheque account 67
− cheque service 337
− order 275
− receipt 300
− transfer form 219, 386
− zone number 245
postcard 49
postdate (to) 275
poste restante 412
poster 16
− advertising 439
− artist 393
− hoarding 255
− pillar 16
− stamp 364, 385
posting 320
postman 159
postmark 275, 397
postmaster 163
postpone (to) 18, 312, 317

postponement 18, 313, 317
postscript 275
postwar
− price 284
− years 182
potency ratio 392
potential 434
pound 213
− sterling 213
power 276, 434, 439
− consumption 411
− cut 85
− of attorney **287**
− needs 411
− production 139
− station 399
− supply 139, 411
practical 276
practice 276
pratique 434
precaution 282
precedent *(subst.)* 277
pre-emption 277
prefabricated 277
prefer 277
preference **277, 283**
− bond 246, 284
− share 12
− test 452
preferential 277, **284**
preferred 284
prefinancing 277
prejudice 277
prejudicial 277
pre-judicial 277
premises 215
premium 282, 435, 436
− bond 245
− hunter 216
− income 436
− loan 135
− offer 429
− rebate 436
− receipt 440
− reserve 322
prepay 261
prepayment 276, 418
prescribe 279
prescription 279
presence 279
present (to) 279, 435
present 14, 279
presentation 279
presenter 279
preside 280
presided over 280
president 280
press 280, 435
− advertising 439
− campaign 280
− clipping 435
− conference 435
− cutting 85
− news 280
− telegram 359
pressed 247, 278, 362
pressure 280, 362, 435
− groups 280, 457
pretest (to) 435
pretest 435, 452
prevailing 14

prevent 134
previous 276
− deduction 277
previously 276, 277
prewar 31
− price 284
price 86, 284, 436
− agreed 284
− bid 86
− cartel 399
− cash flow ratio 405, 440
− changes 456
− control 80, 286
− control office 286
− determination 286
− difference 286
− discrimination 114
− display 393
− earnings ratio 405, 440
− elasticity 131
− equilibrium 436
− fixing 286
− fluctuation 167
− freezing 39
− index 193
− inflation 194
− inquiry 286
− labelling 425
− level 87
− list 286
− marking 436
− mechanism 426
− movement 286
− offered 87, 255
− policy 271
− quotation 88
− reduction 305
− regulation 286
− scissors 58
− stability 286
− stabilization 88
− stop 39, 286
− structure 286
− support 347, 436
− tag 413
− ticket 413
− to underwriters 283
− trend 451
− upsurge 436
primage 53
Prime Minister 230
prime trade bill 255
principal *(adj.)* 283
principal 63, 119, 219, 259
principal and interest 47, 283
print 72, 190
printed 190
printed-paper rate 357
printer 190, 418
− 's error 162
− 's proof 145
printing 72
− house 190
priority 283
− bond 246
− right 283
private **257, 283**
privilege 284
prize 215, 283
− bond 215, 365
− court 75, 283, 374

– drawing 364
pro
– and con 276
– forma 340
– forma invoice 159
– memoria 276
– memoria figure 276
– memoria item 227
– rata 221, 292
probability 287, 436
– calculus 437
– distribution 436
– sample 410
probable 287
probation 349
probationer 349
probatory force 287
probity 184
procedure 287
proceedings 287
proceeds 289, 403, 437
process 287
– chart 417
process-server 156, 185
processing
– *(transformation)* 453
– costs 453
– enterprise 371
– industry 453
processing *(inf.)* 453
– unit 453, 454
processor 437
procuration 287
– conferred by 39
produce (to) 65, 280, 281, 289
produce **289**, 299
produce broker 89
produce exchange 40
produce trade 62
producer 288
producers' co-operative 82
producer(s') goods 37
producing capacity 288
producing country 262
product 289
– s *(calcul)* **241**
– design 435
– differentiation 113
– diversification 409
– image 418
– manager 437
– method 241
– test 452
production 288, 437
– combination 399
– cost 437
– curve 437
– index 192
– machinery 21, 288
productive 288
productiveness 289, 316
productivity 289, 437
– bonus 437
– measurement 289
profession 289
professional 289, 437
profit (to) 290
profit 36, 177, 289, 396
– after tax 396
– and loss account 68
– balance 37

– margin 424
– maximization 289, 425
– motive 216
– sharing 257
– sharing bond 246
– shrinkage 36
– taking 37, 396
profitable 216, 289, 314
profitableness 316
program 438
– library 438
programmer 438
programming 438
– language 438
progress 138, **147**, 290
– report 440
progressive 290
prohibit (to) 290
prohibited 197
prohibition 197, 290
prohibitive 290
prohibitory 290
prolong 290, 292
prolongation 290, 292
promise 290
promissory note 38, 252, 396
promotion 290
– list 356
– stand 435
prompt 290
promptitude 290
proof 145, 281
– of debt 365
propaganda 290
propelling pencil 272
propensity 290
– to consume 424
– to invest 420
properly 309
properties 275
property 32, **38**, 171, **292**
– acquired 11
– developer 438
– fund unit 399
– joint 396
– levy 277
– shares 380
proportion **291**, 292, 296
proportional 291
proportionally 291
proportionately 292
proposal 291
propose 291
proposition 291
proprietor 291
proprietress 291
prospect (to) 292
prospect 265, 395, 438
prospecting 292
prospective 403
prospectus 292
prosperity 292
prosperous 292
protect 335
protection 292, 438
protectionism 292
protectionist 292
protective 292
protector 268
protest (to) 292
protest 292

– charges 172, 293
– strike 180
protestable 292
protested 292
proved 205
provide (to) 171
provided for 282
province 324
provision 116, 293
provisional 293
proxy 288
– holder 168
prune (to) 305
public 293, 438
– Nuisance Act 215
– policy 251
– prosecutor 230
– utility company 341
– utility concern 142
publication 293
publicity 293, 439
– agency 293
– compaign 294
– department 294
– expenses 439
– man 298
– manager 294
– week 439, 441
publish 294
publisher 128
publishing house 128, 218
pull 364
punch (to) 270
punch 217
punch(ed) card 49, 263
punched tape 396
– reader 422
punching 432
– machine 217, 270
punctual 151, 271
punctuality 151, 271
punctually 271
pupil(l)ary 294
purchase (to) 10
purchase 10
– book 160, 204, 213
– invoice 159
– option 430
– price 10, 284
purchaser 11
–, actual 401
purchasers' association 82
purchasing
– capacity 46
– department 337
– power 276, 434
– power parity 256
pure 294
purse 273
pursuance 22, 25, 385
purveyor 171
push 276
– boat 434
pushing 428, 434
put (to) 99
– out 267
– through 65
put 282
– and call 249, 283, **349**
– and call option 282
– and call price 87

- of more 121, 122, 160
- option 222, 282
- price 87
putting in 310
putting into... 231
putting up 231

Q

qualification share 12
qualified 46, **294**
quality 294, 439
- of life 457
- control 439
- label 413, 439
- standard 439
quantile 439
quantitative 295
quantity 295
- index 193
quarantine 195, 431
- flag 195
- station 195
quarter 375
quarterly 375
quarter's rent 362
quartile 439
quasi public 256
quay 294
quayage 295
question 295
- mark 270
queue (to) 165, 415
quiet 223
quorum 241, 296
quota 77, 296, 403
- sample 447
- share reinsurance 440
- share treaty 440
- system 296
quotation 83
quote (to) 84
quoted 84, 196
quotient 296

R

radio
- advertising 293
- announcement 20
radiotelegram 297
rail 440
railway 54
- carriage 372
- consignment 144
- consignment note 300
- guide 54
- line 210
- shares 12, 379
- sidings 387
- station 178
- stocks 164
- strike 180
- ticket 38
Railway Bill of Lading 207
raise 132, 183, 231, **310**, 314, 345
raising 132, 310

rally (to) 320
rally 321
random 417
- choice 400
- component 401
- distribution 408
- sample 410
- variable 455
randomization 399
range 393, 413, 417
rank (to) 298
rank 298
- correlation 404
rapid 387
rare 299
rarefaction 440
rate 86, 357, 450
- of freight 285
- of revaluation 441
- of turnover 330
- per cent 276
ratepayer 80
ratification 299
ratify 299
ratio 60, 297, 298, 429
rationalization 299
rationalize 299
rationing 299
ratten (to) 331
rattening 331
raw materials 226
re: 70, 245
reach 258, 368
react (to) 299
reaction 299
reactivate 442
read (to) 212
read and confirmed 212
reading as follows 209
read(ing) head 452
reader 422
readership analysis 392
ready-made 72
ready money 67
ready reckoner 35, 70
real 306, 383
- estate 38, 291
- estate company 341
- estate fund 416
- estate leasing 406, 421
- estate market 187, 223
- national income 328
- property 38
- property market 187
- time 451
- time processing 453
realignment 440
realizable 299
realization 299
- value 155
realize **299**
realty 187
re-appointment 306
reason 297
reasonable 298, 440
reasoned 235
rebate 306, 330
rebuild (to) 303
rebuilding (reserves) 441
recall 440
- aided 443, 448

recapitulate 300
recapitulation 300
recash 314
recede 304
receipt (to) 11, 132, 296
receipt **295, 300, 304, 317**
- book 296, 399
- form 296
- for payment 11
- for the balance 343
- s and expenditure 106
- s and payments 344
- stamp 296, 363
receipting 132
receive (to) 9, **301**, 367
received 276, **301**
- from 301
- on account 301
- with thanks 11
receiver (tel.) 127
receiver 300, 301
receiver's office 301
receiving cashier 137
receiving station 178
reception 9
- desk 300
- stamp 181, 300, 363
recession 300
reciprocal 301
reciprocals 301
reciprocally 301
reciprocity 301
- agreement 301, 370
- transactions 370
reckon (to) 70, 353
recognition 302
recommend 303
recommendable 303
recommendation 303
reconcilement 383
reconciliation 22, 383
reconditioning 313
reconditioning expenses 172, 313
reconduction 303
reconsider 327
reconstruction 25, 303
reconversion 441
reconvert 441
recopy 303
record (to) 66
record 303
- figure 303
- level 429
- output 437
- sale 456
records destruction 394
recoup (to) 304
recourse 303
recover (to) 298, 304, 311, 320
recoverable 303, 304
recovery 304, 305, 310, 321, 402
recredit (to) 158
recrudescence 441
recruitment 133
rectification 305
rectify (to) 304, 305
recycling 441
red 445

– , in the 406, 445
– light 164
– , out of the 406
redeem (to) 19, 297
redeemable 19, 297, 311
redemption 19, 311, 326, 442
– loan 135
– premium 282, 311
– price 442
– table 268, 356
– value 378
redhibition 305
redhibitory 305
redirect 306
rediscount (to) 306
rediscount 306, 441
– , elegible for 395, 411
– facilities 441
– rate 357, 441
redistribution 441
redraft 301, 326
redraft charges 301
reduce 7, 20, **113**, 305
reduction 101, **113**, 305
– value 455
redundancy 353, 441
redundant 450
re-elect 306
re-election **306**
re-eligibility 306
re-eligible 306
re-endorsement 79
re-engage (to) 315, 441
re-enter (to) 309
re-equipment 306
re-establishment 25
re-examine 318
re-exchange 301, 326
re-export 306
re-exportation 306
refer (to) 306, 317
referee 306
reference 306
– number 244, 306, **317**
– sample 124, 306, 410
referred to... 386
referring to... 306
refinancing 307
refinancing credits 307
reflation 307
refloat 315
reflux 307
reform 307
reforward 306
reforwarding 306
refrain (to) 134
refresher course 441
refund (to) 330
refund 311, 330
refusal 307
refuse 307
regard 131
region 441
– critical 441
regional 307
register (to) 140, **303**
register 307
registered **303**
– office 339
– stock 366
– trade mark 106

register ton 367
registrar 301
– of mortgages 75
registration 140
registration fees 122, 140, 303
registration office 42
registry 87, 140
registry office 42
regression 442
– analysis 393, 442
– coefficient 442
– curve 442
– equation 442
– surface 442
regret (to) 309
regret 309
regrettable 309
regrouping 442
regular 309
regularity 309
regularization 309
regularize 309
regulate **308**
regulations 308
rehabilitation 25
reimburse 312
reimbursement 311
reimport (to) 309
reimport 309
reimportation 309
reinstate (to) 309
reinstatement value 455
reinsurance 300, 440
– broker 440
– company 440
– premium 440
– treaty 440
reinsure 300
reinsured 440
reinsurer 300
reinvest (to) 309
reinvestment 309
relapse (to) 304, 327
relation **298**, **310**
release (to) 209
release 97
reliable 72, 167
relief 209
relief fund 169
relieve (to) 209, 311
relinquich 321
remainder 311, 324
remark 247
remarks column 247
remedy 367
remember (to) 298
remind (to) 298
reminder 298, 442
– entry 273
– letter 442
remisier 313
remission 313
remit (to) 313
remittance 313
– , clean 442
– letter 442
remitter 312
remitting banker 312
remnants 415
– sale 337 342
removal 104

– contractor 104
– expenses 104, 172
remove 104, 371
remunerate (to) 314, 444
remuneration 314, 327, 442
remunerative 314
render account 315
renew (to) 303, **315**
renewable 315
renewal 303, **315**
– fund 315
– premium 282
renounce (to) **315**, 321
renovation 442
rent (to) 216
rent 163, 214, 216, 316
– insurance 26
– restriction 216
– subsidy 215
– tax 216
renting 214
renunciation 321
reopening 317
reorganization 317
reorganize 25, 317
repack 311
repair (to) 318
repair 143, 317
repairing shop 318
reparcelling out 312
repatriate 298
repatriation 298
repay (to) 312
repayable 311
repayment 311, 442
repawn 315
repeat (to) 309, 318
repeated 309
repercussion 318, 444
– to have-on 443
repetition-paid telegram 359
replace 314
replacement 314, 442
– in kind 442
– purchase 392
– sale 442
– value 455 .
repledge 315
replenishment 440
replevin 218
reply (to) 318
reply 319, 443
– coupon 85, 405
– form 170
– paid 319
– paid postcard 49
– paid telegram 359
report (to) 299
report 298
reporter 299
represent (to) 320
representation 320
representative 320, 443
representing 321
reprint 309
reproach (to) 321
reproach 321
repudiate 321
repudiation 321
repurchase 296
repurchaser 297

490/Index

reputation 321
reputed 321
request (to) 104, 282
request 104, 282
– , on 394
required 321
requirements 63
requisite 321
requisites 331
requisition 321
resale 328
– price 436, 455
resaleable 327
research 301, 441
– cyclical 402
– centre 399
– department 338
– institute 301
– work 301
researcher 55
resell (to) 327
reseller 327
reservation 321
reserve (to) **322**, 325
reserve **297**, **321**, **322**, 444
– account 68, 322
– capital 46, 322
– currency 428
– fund 169, 322
resettlement 306, 309
reship (to) 311
residence 118
– mansion 218
– permit 311
resident 323
residential quarter 323
resign (to) 105
resignation 105
res judicata 205
resolution 323
resort (to) 303
resources 237, 324
respect 131
respectability 185
respectable 185
respite 318
respondentia 182
respondentia loan 281
responsibility 323
responsible 323
rest 324
restaurant 444
restitution 324
restock 300, 315
restocking 315, 350, 441, 444
restrain (to) 175, 451
restrict (to) 324
restricted 324
restriction 324, 444
restrictive 324
– credit policy 271
result 324, 444
resume (to) 320
resumption 321
resurvey 79
retail
– business 218
– dealer 110
– price 284, 285
– price index 192
– sale 382

– trade 62, 109
retailer 110, 221
– survey 411
retention 325, 444
– , own 433
– on salary 453
retire **325**, **326**, **344**
– in rotation 344
retirement 344
retiring 344
retraining 306, 441
retrench 66
retrenchment 66
retrocede 444
retroceding company 444
retrocession 327
retrocessionaire 444
retrospective 128
– effect 327
return (to) **315**, **317**, 324, **326**, 330, 444
return 441
– (revenu) 298, **314**
– (relevé) 310
– (restitution) 327, 330
– (retour) 321
– address 392
– cargo 326
– freight 326
– home 321, 388
– , no 443
– of income 98
– premium 326
– ticket 18, 38, 326
returned article 421
returns 221, 315, 326
– book 204, 214, 326
– inwards 317
revalorization 327
revalorize 327
revaluation 306, 327
revalue (to) 306
revenue 328
– authorities 166
– band 32
– curve 86
– earning 298
– earning house 218
– receipts 317
– stamp 166, 364
Reverend 328
reversal 79, 158
reverse (to) 80
– side 328
reverting to 327
review 329
revise (to) 328
revival 310, 321, 442, 443
revive (to) 311
revocable 329
revocation 329
revoke (to) 329
revolving credit 9, 92
rhythm 331
ribbon 331
rich 329
richess 329
rider
rigging 180
right 121, 160
– subscription 409

right-hand page 304
ring 165
ring up 360
riot 411
rise (to) 29, **235**, 314
rise **29**, 137, 183, 310
risk (to) 330
risk 314, 445
– appraisal 445
– covering 445
– premium 445
risk bearing capital 46
risky 183
river
– insurance 27
– port 272
– transport 372
Rhine
– navigation on the 428
road 331
– accident 8
– building program 438
– map 49
– risk 445
– traffic 368
– transport 331, 372
– up 52
– works 374
rocket (to) 235
roll call 241, 388
rolled 331
rolling 330
– mill 203
– stock 226
roll top desk 42
Rome Treaty 370
room 333
roster 356
rotair(e) 427, 445
rotation 330
– number 245
– roll 331
rough **99**
– book 227
– draft 41
– estimate 179
round 330
round off **24**, 344
route map 333
routine 331, 445
– work 454
royalties 122, 305
rubber 46
– company 46
– estate 46
– shares 46
rubbishy 300
ruin 331
rule (to) 307
rule 307
– of three 307
ruler 307
rules, uniform 441
ruling 14
rumour 41
rump accounting year 414
run (to) **36**, 114, 173
– into debt 138
run on... 331
runner-up 314
running **138**, 338

- as follows 70, 209
- down clause 59
- in 330
- number 245
rush hours 331
rush hours 280
rust and oxidation 330

S

sabotage 331
sack 331
sacrifice (to) 331
sacrifice 331
safe **60**
- arrival 39, 134
- custody 107, **177**, 209
- custody department 337
- deposit 337
- deposit agreement 61
- deposit box 60
- deposit vault 61
- hiring 61
safekeeping department 337
safety 336
safety margin 224, 336
sag 167
sagging 167
sailing 257
- date 105
- list 105, 212
- schedule 212
- telegram 105
- vessel 457
salary 22, 370
- account 402
sale **96, 381**, 406, 456
- contract 12, 79
- invoice 159
- room 334
- value 221, 378
saleable 96, 380
sales
- analysis 20
- book 160, 204, 214
- campaign 46
- department 383
- expectations 435
- figures 382
- forecast 456
- manager 54, 114, 382
- office 43
- people 456
- promotion 290, 456
- prospects 456
- space 456
- staff 456
- tax 358
- woman 456
saloon 334
salvage 335
salvage charges 172, 335
sample (to) 125
sample **124**, 410
- assortment 125
- book 125
- card 48, 124
- distribution 443
- fair 125, 167

- packet 125
- post 125
- room 125
- size 125
- survey 412
- taking 125
- unit 447
sampled 248
sampler 125
sampling 125, 277, 410, 447
- design 410
- distribution 410
- error 412
- plan 410, 447
- point 410, 433
- rate 410, 447
- technique 410
sandwich man 184
satiated 334
satisfaction 334
satisfy 109, 334
saturated 334
saturation 334
saturation point 270, 334
save (to) 126, 144
save… 335
saver 412
saving **144**
- of time 177
saving clause 59, 335
savings 126, 412
- account 144, 401
- bank 44
- bank book 144
- bank deposits 107, 144
- bank stamp 363
- capital 144
- deposits 107
- function 144
- habits 144
- institution 144
- motives 412
- premium 412
- ratio 144
- scheme 412, 433
say 57, 114, 342
scale 35, 125, 410
scalp 41
scalper 41
scarce 299
scarceness 324
scarcity **263,** 299
scatter
- of points 433
- coefficient 408
- diagram 408, 417
schedule tax 189
scissors 58
- movement 58
scrap 163
- metal 231
scratching out 180
scratch paper 255
screen advertising 293
scribbling paper 255
scrip 365
scrip certificate 335
scrupulous 74
sea 227
- carriage 454
- letter 207

- mail 86
- risks 227, 329
- traffic 225
sea-borne 225
sea-damaged 31
seagoing ship 239
seal (to) 335
- up 44
seal 44, **335**
sealing 335
sealing wax 44
seamen 179
seaport 227
season 332
- clearance sale 352
- ticket 7
- ticket holder 7
seasonal 332
seasonally adjusted 83, 407
seat (to) 77
seaworthiness 149, 238
seaworthy 149, 238
second 111
- of exchange 14, 336
- endorser 363
second-hand 247, 306
secrecy 336
secret 336
secretarial office 336
secretariat 336
secretary **336**
- general 336
- of State 230
- of the Treasury 230
- 's office 336
secretary-treasurer 336
secretaryship 336
section 25, 162, 256
sectional market 223
sector 336, 446
secure (to) 50, **238**
securing 50
securities 131, 365, **378**
- clearing bank 396
- department 338
- ledger 180
security **49, 50,** 177
- analyst 20
- dollar 118
- holding 366
- holdings 273
see to… 380
seen 369
seize (to) 332
seizure 75, 183, **331,** 423
selection 446
self
- contained 450
- liquidating premium 435
- liquidator 435
- supporting 450
self-financing 29
self-service 209, 422
- shop 217, 422
- store 422
self-sufficiency 29
sell (to) 281, 456
- a bear 367
- at best 456
- for delivery on call 394
- for future delivery 213

Index/491

492/Index

- forward 213
- off 212
- out 153
- short 367
seller **380**
- 's market 223
- 's option 222, 282, 430
- 's option to double 166
- 's over 88
selling
- agency 346, 382
- agent 346, 417
- agent's commission 64, 182
- argument 394
- at a loss 229
- campaign 46
- group 355
- licence 210
- limit 383
- method 456
- monopoly 383
- off price 284
- office 43, 70, 382
- order 251
- organization 383
- out 153, 328
- point 456
- practices 456
- price 285, 383
- rate 87, 381
- technique 381
- wave 455
semiannually 336
semicolon 320
semifinished goods 339
semimanufactured 105
seminar 337
semiofficial 248, 256
semipublic 256, 431
semi-self-service 422
send (to) 144
- back 441
- out 206
sender 209, 144, 155
sending 143
- back 441
seniority 20, 298
sense 336
separate post 86
separate property 291
separation allowance 192
separation of goods 307
sequence (to) 446
sequester (to) 337
sequestrated 337
sequestration 337
sequestrator 337
serial manufacture 337
series 337
serve (to) 339
- a writ 185
service 337
- instructions 192, 227, 338
- lease 421
- program 443
- regulation 308, 338
- telegram 359
servient tenement 169
set 202
set afloat 443

setback 357
setting free 231
setting up 418
settle 148, **308**
settlement 76, 211, **308**, 343, 413
- bargain 222, 249
- market 222
- of account 24
- price 86
settling day 203
sewn 41
shake before using 130
sham 164
sham dividend 116, 164
sham sale 340
shape 170
share 12, **256**, **296**, **365**, **379**, **392**
- capital 13
- certificate 13, 50, 365
- for share 366
- fraction 330
- index 13, 419
- market 13
- premium 282
- price indices 192
- register 14, 213
- split 392
shareholder 13, 14, 244
- 's register 14
shareholding 434
sharer 257
shatter (to) 71
shed 183
sheet 32
shelf 413, 440
- remain on the 423
shelf-life 402, 409
sheriff's officer 185
shift (to) 108
shift 145
ship (to) 155
ship 238
- broker 89
- chandler 429
- lost or not lost 244
- mortgage bank 281
- 's manifest 220
- 's sweat 45, 397
- yard 52
shipbuilding industry 419
shipment 133
shipowner 175, 438
- 's firm 218
shipper 55
shipping
- agency 225
- agent 65
- charges 133
- clerk 155
- company 238
- documents 48, 133
- exchange 40
- house 218
- instructions 196
- intelligence 236
- line 210
- movement 225, 236
- news 236
- note 133, 264

- port 272
- shares 225, 379
- ton 367
- weight 133, 319
shipwreck 238
shipwrecked 238
shoe industry 193
shoot up 235
shop 96, 217, 397
- assistant 217, 456
- closing 60
- entrance 423
- equipment 423
- exit 423
- girl 218
- premises 215
- rules 308
- window 111, 387, 397
- (working) rules 308
shopping
- arcades 417
- basket 430
- behaviour 392
- cart 399
- center 50
- street 62, 445
- trolley 434
- week 302
shopworn 31
shore rights 145
short (subst.) 266
short (adj.) 88, 219
- bill 89
- deliveries 102
- distant traffic 453
- of... 220
- paper 255
- position 274
- sale 381
- seller 380
shortage (deficit) 101
- (manque) 220
- (penurie) 213
- in the cash 357
short-dated 89, 125, 362
shorthand 350
- machine 217, 350
- note 350
- typist 350
- writer 350
- writing 365
shortly 266
short-term 362
short-time work 373
short-time worker 374
shortweight 220
show (to) 343, 453
show
- case 387
- day 203
- room 157, 334
- window 387
- shutdown 415
sick
- benefit fund 44, 423
- leave 73, 423
sickness 423
- allowance 423
- benefit 142
- insurance 26, 423
side 84

– line 387
siding 387
sight 389
- bill 199, 255, 369, 389
- deposits 107, 389
- draft 116
- quotation 83
- rate 357, 389
- remittance 313
sign (to) **340**
sign **140**
signal 50
signatory 339
signature 339
- book
- card 339
- folder 339
- loan 281
signed 342
signer 339
significance
- level 446
- test 452
signing 339
- clerk 168
silent partner 62
silk mill 220
silo 340
silver 23
- currency 233
- standard 149
sink 19
sinking fund 19, 44, 168
Sir 235
sister company 342
sisters 342
sit-down strike 181
situation **340**
- vacant 135, 248
- wanted 103, 135
size 113, 170, 228, 411
- economy 402
- family 411
skeleton law 215
skilled 155, 294
skim off (to) 7
skimming off 145
skim off 145
slack time 440
slacken 233
slackening 297, 407
slaughter price 331
sleeping car 390
sleeping partner 62
slide rule 308
sliding wage scale 339
slip 256
slogan 340
slum 357
slum-clearance campaign 357
slump 73, 96, 102, 131, 377
- down 102, 131
small 227, **265**
- change 233
- investors 265
- savers 144, 412
- savings 144
smaller 232
smart money 435
smuggle 79

smuggler 79
snake 446
snow ball system 40
soar (to) 235
social 340
- aid 26
- insurance institution 27
- security 336, 446
- standing 274
- worker 26
society 447
soft currency 112
software 423, 447
sold note 40
sole 375
- agent 152
- of exchange 339
solicitor 32
- 's office 150
solvability 343
solvency 343
- coefficient 60
solvent 343
sort (to) 375
sorter 375
sound **331**
source 346
space 49, 134
- bar 147
- salesman 294
spacing 197
spare (to) 144
spare parts 266
special 347
- offer 441, 446
- partnership 341
specialized 347
specie 244
specie consignment 144
specie point 270
specific 348
specification 40, 44, 247, 347
specified 110
specify (to) 347
specimen 232, **339**, 348
- page 254
- signature 334
- true to 410
speculate 348
speculation 348
speculative 348
speculator 348
speed 387
- goods 221
spell 145
spending
- cuts 106
- pattern 427
sphere 349
- of action 51
spinning mill 165
spiral 348
split (to) 172
splitting 172
spoil (to) 176, 178
spot **115**, 448
- exchange rate 87
- goods 115
- market 67, 115, 222
- payment 67
- price 87, 115, 267

– rate 86, 115
- sale 115, 382
- transactions 115
spread (to) 126, 318
spread 34, 348, 349
- over 413
spreading 443
spring fair 167
spring sales 382, 436
sprinkler installation 414
square 399
stability 349
stabilization 348
- loan 131
stabilize 348
stable 349
staff 264, 432
- changes 236
- department 265, 338
- expenditure 432
- female 432
- magazine 143, 204
- manager 54, 264
- pension fund 265
- policy 432
- provident fund 169
- recruitment 265
- reduction 264, 305
- regulations 432
- representative 443
- room 432
- training 432
- transfers 236, 237
stag 216
stagflation 448
staggered strike 417
stagnant 350
stagnation 221, 349
stake 169, 230, 231
stale cheque 55
stall keeper 183, 221
stamp (to) 17, 148, 364
stamp 148, **363**
- act 364
- charges 364
- duty 364, 416
- office 43
stamped 364
stamping 17, 148, 363
stand (to) at... 274
stand 349
standard 149
- deviation 409
- error 413
- money 234
- of life 429
- of living 349
- rate 357
standardization 242, 349
standardize (to) 242, 349
standby credit 92
standing
- (betail) 266
- (récolte) 266
- (permanent) 264
-, financial 450
- order 251
staple (to) 18
staple commodity 289
staple products 25
stapler 18

stapling 18
stapling machine 217
start (to) 259
starting period
state 149
 – guaranteed 177
 – interference 200
 – management 307
 – supervision 149
State Department 230
statement
 – (relevé) 40, **149, 310**
 – (déclaration) 89
 – (extrait) 158
 – analysis 38
 – of account 69, 442
 – of affairs 396
 – of condition 38
 – of loss 399
stating 227
station 178
stationer's shop 255
stationery 25, 349
 – clerk 126
 – department 126, 337
stationmaster 178
statistic 349
statistical 349, 448
 – dues 123
statistician 449
statistics 349, 448
status 340, 343
statute barred 279
statutory **349**
 – declaration 243
stay-in strike 181
steady 223, 347, 349, 448
steel
 – pool 272
 – trust 375
steerage 141
 – passenger 141
stencil (to) 271, 350
stencil 350
stenotypy 350
step 104, 126
step up 449
steps method 126
sterilization 187, 350
sterling 350
sterling area 390
sterling bloc 350
stevedore (to) 24
stevedore 24
stevedoring 24
stick 17
 – no bills 101
sticker 392
stiffen (to) 297
stiffening 297
still 138
stimulate 350, 442, 449
stimulus 350
stingy 441
stipulate 350
stipulation 350
stochastic 449
stock (to) 351
stock **154, 293, 350**
 – account 67, 68, 366
 – arbitrage 23

 – book 213, 217
 – breeder 132
 – breeding 132
 – deposit 107
 – dividend 351, 409
 – market 40, 223
 – market trend 405
 – in trade 217, 350
 – on hand 350
 – order 251
 – price level 429
 – turnover 330, 350
stock exchange 40
 – circles 41
 – operator 41
 – order 251
 – parlance 206
 – regulations 308
 – session 335
 – tax 451
 – tip 375
 – transactions 99
stockbroker 17
stockbuilding 350
stoker 54
stockholder 110, 366
stocking 449
stockjobber 361
stockpile 350
stocktaking 350
 – price 285
 – value 350, 378
stocks **365**
stop (to) 39, 51
stop 24, 276
 – payment 400
 – payment order 261
stop-loss order 251
stopp (to) 97
stoppage 24, 39, 51
 – of work 406
stopped **249**
 – bonds 365
stopper 439
stopping 24
storage 122, 141, 218, 426
 – accommodation 449
 – capacity 398, 426, 449
 – charges 218
 – protection 426
 – unit 454
 – word 426
storage charges 218
store (to) 134, 218, 426, 449
store 217
stored terms 214
storekeeper 217
storing 134
storm and tempest insurance 394
stow 24
stowage 24
stowage plan 268
stower 24
straddle 274, 348
strain 362
stranded goods 145
stranding 126
street
 – dress 362
 – market 22, 222

 – price 86
 – vendor, illicit 446
strength of the staff 265
stride 147
strike (to) 70
 – off 297
 – out 35, 38, 297, 300
strike **180**, 417
 – breaker 181
 – committee 181
 – fund 44, 168, 181
 – movement 236
 – notice 417
 – pay 181
 – picket 181, 435
striker 181
striking off 297
striking out 297
string 165
strong 171, 223
stronger side 61
strong room 333
structure 351
stub 80, 344, 356
study 150
style 105, **297**, 341
sub-account 448
sub-agency 448
sub-book 48, 213
subcontracting 448
subcontractor 347, 448
subdivide 351
subdivision 351
subject 70, 245
subject to... 259, 345, 352
subjoined 57
sublease 346
sublessee 347
sublessor 346
sublet (to) 347
subletting 347
submanager 347
submit 345
subordination 351
sub-participation 347
subrogate 351
subrogation 351
subroutine 448
sub-sample 448
subscribe 7, 347
subscribed 347
subscriber 7, **346**
 – (tel.) 104
subscription (abonnement) 7
 – (cotisation) 84
 – (souscription) 296
 – list 296
subsequent 449
subshare 13, 85
subsidiary 8, 351
subsidies 449
subsidize (to) 351
subsidy 351
subsistence 154, 449
 – level 154
 – minimum 427
substitute 226, 351
substitution 351
 – effect 351
 – product 437
subtitutional goods 351

substract (to) 347
substraction 349
subvention 351
subway 258
succeed 327
success 351
succession 351, 450
successive 351
successively 351
successor 351
sue (to) 148
suffer 351
sufficient 352
sufficiently 352
sugar 351
 – campaign 46, 352
 – cultivation 352
suing and labouring clause 59
sum 235, 343
 – at length 343
 – in words 343
 – total 344
sum up 367
summarily 343
summarize 300
summary 343
 – procedure 441
summer time 184
summit conference 344
summon 344
summons 231, 343
Sunday 113
sundries 116
sundry 116
superannuation
 – contribution 263
 – fund 327
super-boom 354
superette 352
supermarket 352
supernumerary 450
supersaturate 354
supertare 354
supervise (to) 354
supplement 352
supplementary 352
supplier 171
supply (to) 18, 22
supply 22
 – and demand 248
 – curve 86, 248
supplying 22, 171
support (to) 347
support 347
supported 347
supporting purchases 347
suppose (to) 353
supra protest 199
surcharge 353
surety 49, 177, 353
 – bond 11
surface
 – worker 253
surge 147, 434
surname 162, 240
surplus 39, 151, 324, 354
 – dividend 352
 – population 272
 – produce 152, 288
 – profit 37, 352
 – reinsurance 440

 – reinsurance treaty 440
 – stock 449
 – value 269
surprising 150
surrender (to) 297
surrender 297
surrender value 284, 297, 378
surrogate 226
surtax 50
survey 156
survey 156, 184
 – expenses 156
 – report 298
surveyor 196
survival 354
survivor 354
survivors' pension 262, 354
suspense 354
 – account 67
 – entry 127, 128
suspension 355
 – filing 58
swaps 249
swap operation 355
sweating 156
sweepings 33
swell 179
swelling 179
swindle (to) 147
swindler 55, 147
swing 224, 355
switch board 356
switched transaction 355
sworn 26, 205
sympathy 355
syndic 355
syndicate (to) 355
syndicate 355
 – credit 403
 – leader 399
 – participations 257, 355
 – transactions 355
system 307, **355**
 – analysis 450

T

tab 249
tab card 182
table 355, **356**
 – of limits 269
tabular 356
tabulating machine 217
tabulator 217, 356
tacit 356
tackle 254
tail probability 436
take **278**
 – advantage 290
 – delivery 278, 300
 – effect 344
 – firm 278
 – for the call 119
 – for the put 11
 – forward 312
 – home pay 445
 – ill 278
 – in 320
 – in bad part 256

 – in stock 319
 – off 208, 296
 – on hire 216
 – over 320, 392
 – over bid 429
 – part 278
 – samples 278
 – stock 200
 – the rate 320
 – up **208**
 – it upon 171
 – up stock 366
take over (to) 392
taken as a whole 389
taken up (time) 278
taker 278, 320, 430
 – for a call 381
 – for a call of more 160
 – for a put 11
 – for a put and call 119, 381
 – for a put of more 160
 – of an option 249
 – of the rate 283, 301
taking **283**
 – delivery 300
 – firm 283
 – in charge 436
 – off 208
 – of holdings 431
 – over 300, 444
 – possession 141
 – samples 277
 – up 208
tale quale 358
tale quale rate 87
tangible 356
tank car 390
tanker 36
tank vessel 239
tape 396
 – price 87, 359
 – punch 432
 – quotation 83, 359
 – unit 407
tare (to) 356
tare 356
target price 436
tariff (to) 357
tariff 356, 450
 – agreement 357
 – applicable 450
 – nomenclature 409
 – walls 35
 – war 357
tariffing 357
taste 179
 – preference 435
tax (to) 189, 358
tax **80, 189, 358**, 451
 – abatement 392
 – burden 166, 190
 – collector 80, 190, 263, 301
 – collector's office 301
 – consultant 75, 166
 – credit 415
 – cut 190
 – dodging 175
 – evasion 151
 – form 80
 – free 153

496/Index

- liability 166
- , municipal 451
- privileges 166
- proceeds 190
- , proportional 451
- rebate 314, 190, 406
- reform 166, 307
- screw 166
- system 415
- treaty, antidouble 418
- withholding 434
- yield 190, 415

taxable 188, 189
- article 249

taxation 189, 415, 418
- authorities 14, 30, 166
- reform 307

taxi 358
taxpayer 80
tea-room 334
tear-off calendar 45
tear out 109
teaser advertisement 439
telecommunication 451
- network 451
- service 451

telegram 358
telegram form 170
telegraph (to) 359
telegraph 359
- messenger 274
- office 43
- restant 359

telegraphic 359
- key 59
- transfer 44, 260
- transfer order 251

telegraphically 360
telegraphist 360
telegraphy 359
telephone (to) 360
telephone 360
- answerer 443
- booth 43
- call 360
- call box 43
- charges 172
- directory 21, 192, 360
- exchange 360, 399
- interview 420
- line 360
- message 360
- network 360
- number 360
- office 360
- operator 360, 448
- spelling key 235
- subscriber 7, 360, 451
- system 360

telephonic 360
telephonically 360
telephonist 360
telephony 360
teleprinter 360
teleprocessing 451
television advertising 293
telex (to) 451
telex 360, 451
- address 392
- operator 451
- subscriber 360

telexed 360
tenant 214
- 's protection 438
- 's repair 214, 317
- 's risks 214
- 's third party risk 329

tendency 252, 361, 451
tender (to) for... 345
tender 88, 261, 448
- (soumission) 14, 248, 345

tenderer 345
tenement 169
tenor 125
tension 362
-, cyclical 402

term **102, 362**
terminal 212, 452
- market 222
- point 361
- price 87

terminate (to) 165, 323
termination 323
terminus 363
terms **71**, 361, **362**
- of trade 363

testamentary 363
- disposition 116

testator 100, 363
testatrix 363
testimonial 50
test 452
- area 452
- market 424
- number 56
- period 452
- town 452

text 363
textile
- industry 363, 419
- machine 217
- shares 455)

textual 363
thank (to) 312
thanks **312**
- to... 139

thaw (to) 101
theft 388
theft insurance 27, 388
the more as 269
third **363**
- of exchange 375
- party **363**
- party insurance 27

thirty years' possession 274
thoroughfare 197
thousand 229
three-cornered 124, 374
three-course-rotation 374
three-field system 374
three months' bill 129, 208, 254, 369
threshold 446
thriftiness 412
through bill of lading 74
through freight 175
through rate 358
through train 368
throw (to) 202
throwaway packing 411
thumb index 249
tick off (to) 270, 400

ticker **363**
ticket 38, **363**
ticket day 203
ticking off 270
ticklish question 433
tidal dock 36
tide over 448
tie-in sale 456
tie up (to) 187
tight 299
tightness 299, 324
thightning 324
till 44, 205, 243
- further notice 252

timber yard 52
time **102, 168, 361**, 451
- after sight 102
- bargain 15, 249
- bill 369
- charter 17
- dead 451
- deposit 107
- freight 175
- idle 451
- policy 270, 394
- real 451
- series 446
- series chart 408
- sharing 451, 453
- table 185, 214, 338
- wages 332
- work 454

timed 422
tin 417, 448
tin-lined 44
tip (to) 375
tip 375
tip-in 137
tip wag(g)on 390
tissue paper 255
title (account) 420
title deed 76, 291
to
- be called for 43, 178
- be had 382
- be kept dry 90
- be rolled 331
- whom it may concern 21

tobacco
- manufactory 220
- monopoly 234

tobacconist's shop 96
to-day 29
to-day's 204
token 202
- money 234

tolerance 124, 367, 452
- limit 422

to-morrow 103
- week 185

ton 367
tone 115, 362
tonnage **202**, 367
- certificate 367
- duty 367

tontine 367
top 344
- price 87

topside up 109
total (to) 14, 367
total 179, 367

totality 367
totalizator 367
totalize (to) 367
totally 367
top up 14
touch (to) 368
touch 77, 299, **310**
touched 368
touring 368
tourist 368
 – office 43
 – traffic 368
tow (to) 183, 313
towage 313
 – charges 313
town 385
 – and country planning 393
 – cheque 55
 – clerk 336
 – planner 455
 – planning 454
 – traveller 267, 268
trace (to) 45
trace 165
tracer 447
tracing paper 255
track 387
trade (to) 63, 239, 368
 – in(to) 361
trade 62, 228, 239, 368
 – acceptance 8
 – agreement 9
 – association 355
 – balance 33, 395
 – bank 34
 – bills 63, 255
 – charge money order 219
 – channels 408
 – current 85
 – custom 63, 376
 – directory 20
 – discount 146, 296, 327
 – income tax 358
 – margin 224
 – mak 159, 225
 – mission 231
 – paper 255
 – policy 271
 – price 221
 – reference 306
 – register 63, 307
 – restrictions 236, 444
 – statistics 448
 – union... 355
 – unionist 355
 – volume 457
traded 365
 – in car 457
trader 62, 221, 368
 – feme sole 415
tradeswoman 415
tradeunion 355
trading 62, 239
 – account 68
 – company 63, 341
 – in 444
 – profit 156
 – (profit) margin 224
 – results 157, 324
 – stamp 363
 – vessel 221

 – year 154
tradition 368
traffic (to) 368
traffic 368, 453
 – accident 8
 – block 133
 – long distance 453
trafficker 368
trailer 313
train 368
trainee 349
training 170
 – course 437
 – period 349
tramp 370
tramping 370
tramp navigation 238
tramway line 210
transact (to) 370
transactions 222, 249, 370
transcribe (to) 371
transcription error 413
transfer (to) 50, 371, 372, 386, 399, 446
transfer 51, 237, 371, 385
 – account 386
 – agreement 371
 – bank 34
 – business 371
 – deed 164
 – duty 358, 371, 372
 – entry 24, 128
 – of labour 236
 – of manpower 236
 – register 371
 – risk 329
 – ticket 83
transferable 51, 371, 372
transferee 51
transferor 50
transform 371
transformation 371
transhipment (voir trans(s)hipment)
transire 205, 258
transit 371
 – bond 11, 371
 – country 262
 – duties 123, 371
 – entry 99, 453
 – goods 222, 371
 – list 371
 – permit 453
 – port 371
 – trade 62, 371
 – traffic 368, 371
transition period 372
transitory 372
 – items 66, 401
translate (to) 368
translating program 452
translation 368
translator 368, 452
transmission 372
transmit (to) 372
transport (to) 372
transport 372
 – charges 372
 – company 372
 – inland water 453
 – insurance 372

 – risk 329, 372
 – strike 330
transpose (to) 350, 373
transposition 373
trans(s)hipment 371, 453
 – B/L 74
 – charges 172, 371
 – note 11
 – permit 264
trash 300
travel (to) 389
travel agency 17
traveller 389
travel(l)er's cheque 54
travel(l)er's letter of credit 208
travelling allowance 191
travelling exhibition 157
travelling expenses 172, 220, 383
travel requisities 25, 388
treasurer 374
treasury 374
Treasury bill 129
Treasury bond 39, 51
Treasury certificate 374
Treasury Department 230
treatment 370
treaty 370
treble 375
trend 252, **361**, 414, 451
 – analysis 451
 – elimination 452
 – fitting 451
 – reversal 452
trial 147
 – balance 38, 147
 – order 147, 251, 401
 – period 263
triangular 124, 374
trick question 440
triennial 374
trillion 375
trip 388
triple 375
triplicate 375
triptyque 375
trolley 399
trough 94, 240
 – the waves 406
truck 29, 46, **390**
 – leasing 421
 – load 53
trucking bill of lading 207
truncated 454
trunk call 65
trust **164, 375**
 – agreement 375, 404
 – basis 375
 – company 375
 – deed 164
 – indenture 164, 175
 – letter 175
 – receipt 175
 – receipt 175
 – transactions 164
trustee 95, 164, 355, 375
 – as 415
 – in bankruptcy 355
trusteeship 164, 355
trustification 375
trustworthy 72, 167

truth 384
try (to) 147
tug *(boat)* 313
turn 52, 328
 – key 400
 – for the better 52
 – for the worse 52
turning to account 231
turn over (to) 441
turnover 236, **330**, 400
 – commission 64, 69
 – tax 189
turnstile 452
twice 168
two-stage sampling 410
two-third majority 219
two-tier market 424
type (to) 95, 127, 356
type bar 208
type sample 124
typewrite 95, 127, 356
typewriter 217
 – eraser 179
 – room 95, 334
 – table 42
typewriting 95
 – paper 255
 – ribbon 331
typewritten 127, 217
typing 95
typist 95

U

umpire 353
unable 190
unacceptable 241
unaccepted 241
unalienable 190
unanimously 387
unanswered 319
unbankable 242
unbias(s)ed 396
unblock 97
unblocking 97
unbound 311
uncalled 242
uncertain 191
unclaimed 242, 302
uncoined 242
unconfirmed 242
unconvertible 191
uncovered 99
uncustomed 209
undamaged 243
undated 243, 334
undecipherable 191
undeliverable 345
undelivered 191
under
 – advice 32
 – construction 77
 – cover 143, 269
 – separate cover 269
 – ship's tackle 254
 – the style of 297
 – usual reserve 137, 321, **334, 335**
 – reserve 165
underconsumption 346

underdeveloped 262
underdevelopment 448
under-employment 347
underestimate 347
underestimation 347
underground
 – railway advertising 293
 – work 156
 – worker 253
underinsurance 346
underlease 346
underlessee 347
underlessor 346
underlet (to) 347
underletting 347
under-production 347
under-secretary 347
undersign (to) 347
undersigned 347
understaffed 265
understand 141
understanding 141
understood 141
undertake 142
undertaker 142
undertaking 142
 – business 142
 – to buy 438
 – to sell 456
undervaluation 455
undervalue (to) 347
underwrite 177
underwriter 355, 399, 450
underwriting 177
 – account 403
 – agreement 273
 – commission 64, 177, 283
 – syndicate 177, 283
undiscountable 194
undistributed profits 117
undivided 193
undue 193
unduly 193
unemployed 57
unemployment 56
 – benefit 19
 – curve 56
 – fund 168
 – insurance 26, 56
 – ratio 56
unencumbered 209
unestimable 194
uneven 187
unexchangeable 193
unexpired 242
unfavourable 101
unfit 191
unfreeze 101
unified 375
unilateral 375
unimpeachable 188
uninsured 242
union 375
unique 375
unit 375, 454
 – load 375
 – of account loan 375
 – of product 376
 – of production 288
 – of weight 454
 – price 285

universe 412, 454
unjust 195
unknown 191
unlawful 187
unless... 78, 334
unlimited 187
unlisted 84
unload 96, 98
unloaded weight 269
unloading 96, 98
 – berth 96
 – platform 294
unmortgaged 209
unpacked 242
unpaid 188, 242
unprecedented 217
unproductive 190
unprotected 244
unquoted 191, 242
unreservedly 321
unsaleable 200, 242, 421
unseal 97
unsealing 335
unseaworthiness 149, 195
unseaworthy 195, 238
unsecured 56, 243
unsettled 188, 242, 309
unshaken 194
unship 96
unshipment 96
unsigned 242
unsold 200
unstamped 17, 210
unsteadiness 196
unsteady 196, 223
unsurmountable 197
until **205**, 243
 – further advice 31
untransferability
untransferable 191
upkeep 143
upkeep expenses 172
upper deck 272
upset price 230
upsurge 434
up to... 204
up-to-date 183, 204
up-valuation 306
upward
 – movement 25
 – trend 183, 361
urbanization 454
urge 196
urgency 376
urgent 376
urgently 196, 376
usance 376
 – draft 453
use (to) 135
use **376, 377**
 – value 376, 378
used 306
 – car 247
useful 376
useless 200
user 376
usher 185
usual 183, 250, 376
usually 250
usufruct 376
usufructuary 376

usufructuary's repair 317
usurer 376
usurious 376
usury 376
utility 376
– program 438
utilizable 377
utilization 376
utilize 377
utmost 229, 275
utter 259

V

vacancy 134, 377
vacant 377
vacation 377
– pay 431
– period 377
vaccum packing 411
vague 377
valid 377
validity 380
valorization 380
valorize (to) 380
valuable 378
valuables 379, 380
valuation *(estimation)* 148, 151, 283
– *(de la valeur)* 379
valuation clause 59
value 125, **377, 379**, 455
– adjustment 379
– date 95, 141, 379
– global adjustment 441
– individual adjustment 441
– index 193
value added 377
value-added tax 358
– compensated 379
– for collection 137
– given clause 59, 379
– here and there 66, 379
valueless 334, 378
valuer 283, 358
van 389
variable 455
– yield 379
variable 455
variance 456
– component 401
variation 456
– coefficient 456
vaults 61
vehicle leasing 421
veil of money 233, 387
vending machine 408, 423
vendor 280, 456
vendor's share 12
venture 330
verbal 383
verification 383
verify 383
via 369
viable 385
vice chairman 385
vice consul 385
vice president 385

Vienna rules 307
view 386
viewer research 412
viewing habits 417
virtue 385
visa (to) 258, 386
visa 386
vise (to) 258, 386
vise 386
visible 386
visit (to) 387
visit 386
visiting card 48
visiting hours 386
visitor 387
visitor's tax 358
vocational 289
– education 170
– guidance 252
– training 170, 437
vogue 387
voice 387
void 242
volet 238
volume 238
– index 193
– of money 457
voluminous 238
voluntary chains 51
vostro account 68
vote(to) 388
vote **387, 388**
voting 388
– paper 388
vouch (to) 177
voucher 22, 205, **266**
voucher copy 205
voyage 388
– charter 17
– freight 175
– policy 270

W

wage 176, **332**, 445
– account 445
– adjustment 18, 333
– s agreement 332
– s assignment 399
– s book 213, 333
– bracket 445
– (s) claim 333
– s conflict 73
– costs 445
– demands 446
– earner 333, 374
– earning 333
– earning woman 415
– freeze 333
– group 445
– increase 333
– s index 193
– inflation 194
– level 240, 333
– movements 333
– packet 260
– pause 333
– payment 260
– payment of -s by transfer 431
– policy 271, 333
– pressure 435
– price spiral 348
– push 434
– rate 450
– (s) scale 176, 348
– s sheet 40, 260
– statistics 448
– stop 333
– structure 351, 445
– talks 446
– s tax 333
– worker 333
– zone 333
wag(g)on 389
wait 28
waiting
– list 25
– period 398, 407
– room 333
– time 451
waive (to) 315
walk clerk 177
walk out 417
wall advertising 293
want 37
– of .. 263
wanted 104
war 182
– clause 182
– economy 126
– loan 182
– profits 182
– profits tax 182
– risks 177, 329
– risk insurance 27, 182
ward 294
ward's patrimony 294
warehouse (to) 134, 218
warehouse 108, **267**
– book 213
– charges 172
– keeper 142
– receipt 300
– rent 218
– warrant 50, 242
warehousing 134, 218
– charges 172
– entry 98
warehousman 218
warn (to) 177
warning strike 180
warrant 300, **390**
warranted pure 177
waste (to) 228
waste 228
– book 41, 218, 227
– paper basket 82, 254
waste not, want not 412
water
– carriage 372
– damage insurance 394
watering 47
watermark 165
waterway 385
wave 377
wax 58
way **387**
– in 141
– out 141, 344

– s and means 237
waybill 207
weak 160, 223
wear and tear 376
wearing-out 235
weather conditions 71, 361
weather insurance 27
weather permitting 361
weather working day 203
wedding card 161
week 336
weekend 457
  – sale 457
  – white 446
weekly 183
week's return 340
weighbridge 272
weigher 265
  – s and measurers 228
weighing 265
weight (to) 265
weight 269
weighted 272
weighting 271
weighting coefficient 271
weight note 243, 270
weight stamp 148, 181, 265
welcome booklet 41
well-attended 10
well-conditioned 71
well-connected 10
well-equipped 19
well-established 25
well-founded 168
well-informed 195
well-known 74
well off 171
well-situated 340
well-to-do 18
well up in... 85, 274, 354
wet goods 211
wharfage 123, 294, 295
when due 125
whole 141, 367
whole-life insurance 27
wholesale 181
  – dealer 181
  – house 181
  – price 181
  – price index 142
  – trade 62, 181
wholesaler 182, 221
wholly 161
widow's annuity 443
widow's pension 262
wild-cat strike 181
will 363, 452, 457
willing party 258
win 176
wind up 212
winding up 211
  – sale 382
windmill 129, 369
window 148
  – cleaning business 429
  – display material 413
  – dresser 148
  – dressing 375, 423
  – dressing competition 71, 148
  – envelope 143

  – illumination 148
  – pack 411
  – shopping 422
  – soiled 31, 148
wine shop 96
winner 176
winning number 176
wintering 184
wintering port 184
wipe off 23
wire (to) 359
wish (to) 109, 345
wish 345
with
  – attached documents 28
  – care 28, 172
  – coupon 28
  – regard 131
  – respect 131
  – rights 122
withdraw (to) 325
withdrawal 218, 277, **326,** 435
within 102
without **334**
  – notice 32
womanpower 218
woman worker 253
women executives 54, 142
women's labour 373
women's wage 332
woollen industry 193
word (to) 209
word 235
wording 209, 361, 363
work (to) 374
  – out 99, 131
work **373,** 450, 454
  – at piece rates 373
  – at time rates 373
  – week 373
workable 276
worked day 203
worker 253, 374
  – foreign 454
working **156**
  – account 68
  – capacity 46
  – capital 169, 331
  – class 58, 253
  – conditions 373
  – day 204
  – expenses 106, 157, 173
  – group 373, 417
  – hours 184, 373, 418, 433
  – luch 407
  – meeting 454
  – order 430
  – papers 454
  – party 454
  – plant 157
  – session 454
  – sheet 454
  – to rule 180
  – week 336, 373
workman 253
workman's record 214, 373
workmen's dwelling 253
workmen's train 253, 368
works 52, 376
  – council 142
  – ex 455

  – foreman 71
  – manager 54, 156, 455
  – regulation 143, 308
work-to-rule 180
work week 373
world 233
  – consumption 233
  – crisis 233
  – demand 103
  – economy 233
  – famous 233
  – known 233
  – market 223, 233
  – production 233
  – stock 233
  – supply 233
  – trade 233
  – war 233
  – -wide 233
  – -wide policy 271, 433
worthless 242, 334
wrapper 34
wreck 145, 238
wreckage 145
writ 156
  – of execution 153, 332
write 127
  – back 80, 158, 330
  – head 452
  – off 19
  – out 94
writing 127
  – back 79, 330
  – book 44
  – head 452
  – off 19
  – pad 347
  – paper 255
written 127
wrong **162**

Y

year **20, 154,** 394
year book 20
yesterday 184
yield (to) **299,** 315
yield **314,** 443
yours.. 301, 334

Z

zinc-lined 44
zone 390

ADDRESS, SALUTATION, COMPLIMENTARY CLOSE

ADDRESS	SALUTATION
President U.S.A.	
(His Excellency) The President of the United States	*Sir :* (or) *Mr. President,*
King	
His Majesty the King	*Sir,*
Queen	
Her Majesty The Queen	*Madam,*
Prince	
His Royal Highness The Prince	*Sir,*
Princess	
Her Royal Highness The Princess	*Madam,*
Duke	
His Grace The Duke of...	*My Lord Duke,*
Duchess	
Her Grace The Duchess of...	*Madam,*
Marquess	
The Most Hon. The Marquess of...	*My Lord Marquess.*
Marchioness	
The Most Hon. The Marchioness of...	*Madam,*
Earl	
The Right Hon. The Earl of...	*My Lord,*
Countess	
The Right Hon. Countess of...	*Madam,*
Viscount	
The Right Hon. The Viscount of...	*My Lord,*
Viscountess	
The Right Hon. The Viscountess of...	*Madam,*
Baron	
The Right Hon. Lord...	*My Lord,*
Baroness	
The Right Hon. Lady...	*Madam,*
Baronet, Knight	
Sir John D..., Bt.	*Sir,*
His wife	
Lady D...	*Madam,*
Cardinal	
His Eminence *(first name)* Cardinal *(surname)*	*Your Eminence,*
Archbishop	
The Most Reverend *(full name)* Archbishop of...	*Your Excellency,*
Archbishop (Prot. Church)	
His Grace The Lord Archbishop of...	*My Lord Archbishop,*
Bishop	
The Right Reverend *(full name)* Bishop of...	*Your Excellency,*

ADDRESS	SALUTATION
Bishop (Prot. Church)	
The Right Reverend The Lord Bishop of...	*My Lord Bishop,*
The Right Reverend *(full name)* (U.S.A.)	*Right Reverend and Dear Sir :*
Bishop of...	*My Dear Bishop* (last name) :
Dean (Prot. Church)	
The Very Reverend The Dean of...	*Very Reverend Sir,*
Clergyman (Prot. Church)	
The Reverend P. N. Henderson	*Reverend Sir,*
Priest	
The Reverend *(full name)*	*Dear Reverend Father,*
	Dear Father (surname)
Mother superior	
Mother *(name)*	*Dear Mother Superior,*
Sister	
Sister *(name)*	*Dear Sister* (name),
Rabbi	
Rabbi *(full name)*	*My Dear Rabbi* (surname),
Ambassador	
His Excellency *(full name)*	*Excellency,*
	Dear Mr. Ambassador : (U.S.A.)
Consul	
J. B. Davison, Esq.,	*Sir,*
Minister	
The Right Hon. *(full name)*	*Sir,*
Cabinet member	
The Honorable *(full name)*	*Dear Sir,*
Secretary of...	*My dear Mr. Secretary :*
Governor (U.S.A.)	
The Honorable *(full name)*	*Dear Sir :*
Governor of...	*My dear Governor :*
Member of Parliament	
H. B. Lake, Esq., M. P.	*Dear Sir,*
Senator (U.S.A.)	
The Honorable *(full name)*	*Dear Sir :*
	My dear Senator (last name) :
Representative (U.S.A.)	
The Honorable *(full name)*	*Dear Sir :*
	My dear Congressman (last name) :
State representative (U.S.A.)	
The Honorable *(full name)*	*Dear Sir :*
	My dear Representative (last name) :
Chief Justice (U.S.A.)	
The Honorable *(full name)*	*My dear Mr. Chief Justice :*
Chief Justice of the U. S.	
Lord Mayor	
The Right Hon. The Lord Mayor of (London)	*My Lord,*
The Right Hon. The Lord Provost of (Edinburgh)	

ADDRESS	SALUTATION
Mayor (U.S.A.)	
The Honorable *(full name)* Mayor of the City of...	*Dear Sir :* *My dear Mr. Mayor :*
Army officer	
Lieutenant W. G. Davis Captain (Major, etc.) W. G. Davis	*Dear Sir,* *Dear Captain Davis,*
Man	
(Professor Dr.) Robert Smith Robert Smith, Esq. Mr. Robert Smith	*Sir,* (very formal) *Dear Sir,* *Dear Mr. Smith,*
Boy	
Master Robert Smith	*Dear...*
Married woman	
Mrs. (Robert) Smith	*Madam,* (formal) *Dear Mrs. Smith,*
Unmarried woman	
Miss Smith *(eldest daughter)* Miss Jane Smith *(other daughters)*	*Dear Miss Smith,* *Dear Miss Jane,*

BUSINESS

Man

Mr. Walter J. Thomas Walter J. Thomas, Esq.	*Dear Sir,* (U.S.A.) *Dear Sir :* *Dear Mr. Thomas* (more amicable)

Firm

Messrs. Henry Thomas & Son Messrs. Thomas & Wright (Messrs.) Williams & Co, Ltd	*Dear Sirs,* *Gentlemen :* (U.S.A.)
The Secretary The National Trading Co	*Dear Sir,* (U.S.A.) *Dear Sir :*

Address

Messrs. F. J. Jones & Co
37 Harcourt Avenue
LONDON E. C. 4

The Western Fuel Oil Company
1023 Industrial Avenue
DENVER 6, (Colorado)

Date

London 25th March 1964
Chicago March 25

COMPLIMENTARY CLOSE

To persons of rank
I have the honour to be (to remain),

King
   Sir, *Your Majesty's most humble and obedient subject*

Queen
   Madam, *Your Majesty's most humble and obedient servant*

Prince, Princess
   Sir, (Madam) *Your Royal Highness' s most humble and obedient servant*

Duke, Archbishop
   my Lord Duke (Archbishop), *Your Grace's most obedient servant*

Duchess
   Madam, *Your Grace's most obedient servant*

Marquess, Earl, Viscount, Baron, Bishop.
   my Lord, *Your Lordship's obedient servant*

Marchioness, Countess, Viscountess, Baroness.
   Madam, *Your Ladyship's obedient servant*

Baronet, Knight
   Sir, *Your obedient servant*

His wife
   Madam, *Your obedient servant*

Official
Yours respectfully ; (U.S.A.) *Respectfully yours*
Very respectfully ; Yours obediently

Informal
Yours (very) sincerely ; (U.S.A.) *Sincerely (cordially) yours*

Business
Yours faithfully ; Yours very truly
Very truly yours (U.S.A.)

ABBREVIATIONS

A.

a	are	a. m.	ante meridiem
a. a.,	always afloat	a/o	account of
a. a. r.	against all risks	A.P.	accounts payable
a/c	account	A/P	authority to pay, to purchase
A/C	account current		
acct	account	A.R.	accounts receivable
a. d.	after date	a/r	all risks
AEI	Associated Electrical Industries	A/S, A.S.	account sales
		a/s	at sight
A.F.B.	air freight bill	av.	average
AFL	American Federation of Labor	avdp.	avoirdupois
		a/w	actual weight
agt	against	a.w.b.	air waybill
a.h.p.	air horse power		

B.

B.A.I.E.	British Association of Industrial Editors	B.O.	branch office; buyer's option
bal.	balance	B.O.T.	Board of Trade
bar., bbl	barrel	b. p.	by procuration
b/d	brought down	B.P.	bills payable
B/E, b/e	bill of exchange	B.R.	bills receivable
B.E.A.	British European Airways	Bro.	brother
b/f	brought forward	Bros	brothers
B.H.	bill of health	B/S	balance sheet
BIS	Bank for International Settlements	bt	bought
		b. t.	berth terms
Bk	bank	bu	bushel
B/L	bill of lading	B/V	book value
b/o	brought over		

C.

C.	cent; centime; circa	c. i. f. & i.	cost, insurance, freight and interest
C.A.	chartered accountant		
ca	circa; centiare	CIO	Congress of Industrial Organization
C.A.D.	cash against documents		
c.a.f.	cost, assurance, freight	cl	centiliter
C.B.	cash book	c. l.	car load
C.B.D.	cash before delivery	cm	centimeter
c/d	carried down	C/m	call of more
c. d.	cum dividend	C/N	credit note
CED	Committee for Economic Development	c/o	care of
		Co.	company
CEEC	Committee of European Economic Cooperation	C.O.D.	cash on delivery
		cons.	consols
c. & f.	cost and freight	conv.	conversion
c/f	carried forward	Corp., cpn	corporation
cf.	compare (conferatur)	C.O.S.	cash on shipment
cg	centigram	C.P.	carriage paid
C.H.	custom house	C/P	Charter Party
C/H	clearing house	c. p. d.	charters pay duties
ch. fwd	charges forward	cr. ; Cr.	credit; creditor
ch. ppd	charges prepaid	ct	cent
ch. pd	charges paid	C/T	cable transfer
chq.	cheque	c. t. l.	constructive total loss
c. i. f.	cost, insurance, freight	c.t.l.o.	constructive total loss only
c. i. f. & e.	cost, insurance, freight and exchange	cum	cumulative
		cum div.	cum dividend
c. i. f. & c.	cost, insurance, freight and commission	cum. pref.	cumulative preference
		c/w	commercial weight
		cwt	hundredweight

D.

d.	pence; penny; discount	d/d	days after date
D/A	documents against acceptance; deposit account	d. d.	dangerous deck
		deb.	debenture

ABBREVIATIONS

def.	deferred	**dm**	decimeter
Dept	department	**D/N**	debit note
d. f.	dead freight	**D/O**	delivery order
dft/a.	draft attached	**doz.**	dozen
dft/c.	clean draft	**do**	ditto
dft	draft	**D/P**	documents against payment
dg	decigram	**Dr**	debtor; doctor
disc., diset	discount	**dr**	dram
div.	dividend	**d/s, d. s.**	days after sight
dkg	dekagram	**D/W**	dock warrant
dkl	dekaliter	**D.W.I.**	Dutch West Indies
dkm	dekameter	**d.w.**	deadweight
dl	deciliter	**dwt**	pennyweight
DL	dayletter	**dz.**	dozen
DLF	Development Loan Fund		
DLT	daily letter telegram		

E.

ECA	Economic Cooperation Administration	**E. & O. E.**	errors and omissions excepted
ECAFE	Economic Commission for Asia and the Far-East	**e. o. m.**	end of month
ECE	Economic Commission for Europe	**e. o. h. p.**	except otherwise herein provided
EFTA	European Free Trade Association	**EPU**	European Payment Union
		ERP	European Recovery Program
e. g.	exempli gratia	**esp.**	especially
E.I.	East Indies	**Esq.**	Esquire
EMA	European Monetary Agreement	**ex.**	out
		ex cp.	ex coupon
encl.	enclosure	**ex div.**	ex dividend
end.	endorsement	**ex int.**	ex interest

F.

f.	feminine	**FOA**	Foreign Operations Administration
f. a. c.	fast as can		
f. a. a.	free of all average	**f. o. b.**	free on board
FAO	Food and Agriculture Organization	**f. o. c.**	free of charge
		f. o. d.	free of damage
f. a. q.	fair average quality	**fol.**	folio; following
f. a. q.	free alongside quay	**f. o. q.**	free on quay
f. a. s.	free alongside ship	**f. o. r.**	free on rail
fath.	fathom	**f. o. s.**	free on steamer
F.C.A.	Fellow of the Institute of Chartered Accountants	**f. o. t.**	free on trucks free on truck
fco	franco	**f. o. w.**	free on wagons free on wharf
f. c. & s.	free of capture and seizure		
f.c.s.r. & c.c.	free of capture, seizure, riots and civil commotion	**f. p.**	fully paid
		f. p. a.	free of particular average
f. d.	free discharge	**Fr., fr**	franc
F.D.	free delivery to dock	**FRB**	Federal Reserve Board
ff.	following; folios	**frt**	freight
f. g. a.	free of general average	**frt pd**	freight paid
f. i. b.	free in bunker	**frt ppd**	freight prepaid
f. i. o.	free in and out	**frt fwd**	freight forward
f. i. t.	free in truck	**ft**	foot
fo.	folio	**fwd**	forward
F.O.	Foreign Office	**f. x.**	foreign exchange

G.

g.	gram(me)	**GNP**	gross national product
g. a.	general average	**g. o. b.**	good ordinary brand
GATT	General Agreement on Tariffs and Trade	**Govt**	government
		G.P.O.	general post office
g. b. o.	goods in bad order	**gr.**	gross
g. m. b.	good merchantable brand	**gr. wt**	gross weight
g. m. q.	good merchantable qaulity	**G.W.R.**	Great Western Railway

ABBREVIATIONS

H.

ha	hectare	hl	hectoliter
h. c.	home consumption	hm	hectometer
hg	hectogram	H.M.C.	His Majesty's Customs
hgt, ht	height	H.O.	head office
hhd	hogshead	H. P.	hire purchase
H.L.	House of Lords	HP	horse power

I.

IAF	International Aeronautical Federation	i.h.p.	indicated horse power
IATA	International Air Transport Association	ILO	International Labour Organization
IBRD	International Bank for Reconstruction and Development	IMF	International Monetary Fund
		in.	inch
L.B.	in bond	Inc., Incorp.	incorporated
ICAO	International Civil Aviation Organization	incl.	inclusive
		insce	insurance
ICC	International Chamber of Commerce	inst.	instant
		int.	interest
ICFTU	International Confederation of free Trade Unions	inv.	invoice
		I O U	I owe you
ICIE	International Council of Industrial Editors	ITA	International Tourist Association
i. e.	id est (that is)	ITO	International Trade Organization
I/F	insufficient funds		
IFC	International Finance Corporation	ITU	International Telecommunication Union

J.

J.	journal	JEIA	Joint Export-Import Agency
j.a., J/A	joint account	jnr, Jr	junior

K.

kg	kilogram	kw.	kilowatt
km	kilometer		

L.

L., £.	pound	LCO	telegram in the language of the country of origin
lb., lbs	pound, pounds		
£ E.	Egyptian pound	ldg	loading; landing
£ T.	Turkish pound	liq.	liquidation
l. c., L/C	letter of credit	loc. cit.	loco citato
LCD	telegram in the language of the country of destination	l.t., l. tn	long ton
		Ltd	limited
LCF	telegram in French language		

M.

m	meter	M.O.	money order
m.	month	mortg.	mortgage
m. d., M/D	months after date	M.P.	Member of Parliament
masc.	masculine	M/P, m. p.	months after payment
m. D.	memorandum of deposit	M/R	mate's receipt
Messrs	plural of Mr	Mr	Mister
M.E.T.	Mid European Time	Mrs	Mistress
mfr	manufacturer	M/S, m. s.	months' sight
mg	milligram	MSA	Mutual Security Agency
ml	mile	M.T.	metric ton
mm	millimeter		

N.

N/A	no advice	N.B.	nota bene
n/a	no account	n. d.	no date
NAM	National Association of Manufacturers	n. e. s.	not elsewhere specified
		N/F	no funds

ABBREVIATIONS

NL	night letter	Nos, nos	numbers
N/N	no noting	NPV	no par value
N/O	no orders	Nr	number
No., no	number	n.r.t.	net register ton
n.o.e.	no otherwise enumerated	N/S	not sufficient funds
n.o.s.	no otherwise stated	n. wt	net weight

O.

o/a	on account	o. p.	over proof
o/d, O/D	overdraft; on demand		out of print
o.e.	omissions excepted	O. P.	open policy
OEEC	Organization for European Economic Cooperation	O/R, o. r.	owner's risk
		ord.	ordinary; order
OIT	Office of International Trade	o/s, O.S.	out of stock
		oz.	ounce
O/o	order of		

P.

p.	page; per; premium	P.M.G.	Postmaster General
P.A., p. a.	particular average	P/N	promissory note
P/A	private account; power of attorney	P.O.	post office; postal order
		P.O.B.	Post Office Box
p. a.	per annum	P.O.O.	Post Office Order
PAA	Pan American World Airways	p. o. r.	pay on return
		p. p., p. pro.	per procuration
p. c.	price current; per cent	ppd	prepaid
p/c	petty cash	ppt	prompt
pcl	parcel	pref., prf.	preference
pd	paid	prox.	proximo
pf., pfd	preferred	P.S.	postscript
P/L	profit and loss	pt	payment
p. l.	partial loss	P.T.O.,p.t.o.	please turn over
p. m.	post meridiem	ptly pd	partly paid

Q.

qlty	quality	qty	quantity
qt	quart		

R.

r. & c. c.	riot and civil commotions	RFC	Reconstruction and Finance Cooperation
rd	rod		
R/D	refer to drawer	R. O. D.	refused on delivery
R.D.C.	running down clause	RP	reply paid
re	in regard to, relating to	r. p. s.	revolutions per second
rec.	receipt; received	R.S.W.C.	right side up, with care
recd	received	RTAA	Reciprocal Trade Agreements Act
ref.	reference		
reg.	registered	Rt Hon.	Right Honorable
retd	returned	Rt Rev.	Right Reverend
rev.	revenue	Rways	railways
		Ry	railway

S.

s.	shilling; sellers steamer; sailed	S/D, s. d.	sight draft
		S/N	shipping note
$	dollar	s. o.	seller's option
s	stere	S.P.	supra protest
SAS	Scandinavian Airlines System	spt	spot
		sq. ft	square foot
s. d.	without date	sq. in.	square inch
sgd	signed	sq. yd	square yard
sh.	shilling	Sr	senior
S. & h. ex.	Sundays and holidays excepted	S.S., SS.	steamship
		s. t.	short ton
shipt	shipment	St.	street; Saint
sig.	signature	St. Ex	stock exchange
S/L.C.	sue and labour clause	stg	sterling
s. & l. c.	sue and labour clause	s. v.	sub voce

ABBREVIATIONS

T.

t	metric ton; troy	t/q	tale quale
T.A.	telegraphic address	TR, T/R	trust receipt
tel.	telephone	T.R.	tons register
t. l., T.L.	total loss	TT, T.T.	telegraphic (cable) transfer
T.L.O.	total loss only	TM	multiple telegram
tn, tns	ton, tons	TR	telegram to be called for
T.O.	turn over	TWA	Trans World Airlines

U.

U.K.	United Kingdom	U.S.A.	United States of America
ult.	ultimo	U/ws	underwriters
UPU	Universal Postal Union		

V.

v	volt	viz	videlicet (namely)
v., vid.	vide (see)	V.P.	Vice President
val.	value		

W.

w.	watt	W.P.	without prejudice
W.B.	way bill	w. p., W.P.	weather permitting
w. c.	without charge	w. p. a.	with particular average
W.E.T.	West European time	W.R.	war risk
w. g.	weight guaranteed	wr. W/R	warehouse receipt
W.I.	West Indies	W.W.D.	weather working day
w. o. g.	with other goods	wt	weight

X.

x. c.	ex coupon	x. n.	ex new shares
x. d.	ex dividend	Xmas	Christmas
x. i.	ex interest		

Y.

y.	year	yr, yrs	{ year, years
Y.A.R.	York-Antwerp-Rules		your, yours
yb.	year book	yrly	yearly
yd, yds	yard, yards		

POIDS ET MESURES
WEIGHTS AND MEASURES

1. MÉTRIQUES — METRIC

DE LONGUEUR — LINEAR MEASURE

kilomètre	km	1.000 m	0.621	miles
hectomètre	hm	100 m	109.362	yards
décamètre	dam	10 m	10.936	yards
mètre	m	1 m	1.0936	yards
décimètre	dm	1/10 m	3.937	inches
centimètre	cm	1/100 m	0.394	inches
millimètre	mm	1/1.000 m	0.0394	inches

DE SUPERFICIE — SURFACE MEASURE

kilomètre carré	km^2	1.000.000 m^2	0.386	sq. miles
hectomètre (hectare)	hm^2	10.000 m^2	2.471	acres
décamètre carré (are)	dam^2	100 m^2	119.600	sq. yards
mètre carré (centiare)	m^2	1 m^2	1.196	sq. yards
décimètre carré	dm^2	1/100 m^2	15.500	sq. inches
centimètre carré	cm^2	1/10.000 m^2	0.155	sq. inches

DE VOLUME — CUBIC MEASURE

mètre cube	m^3	1 m^3	1.308	cubic yards
décimètre cube	dm^3	1/1.000 m^3	61.024	cubic inches
centimètre cube	cm^3	1/1.000.000 m^3	0.061	cubic inches

DE CAPACITÉ — CAPACITY MEASURE

hectolitre	hl	100 l	2.75 / 21.997	bushels / gallons
décalitre	dal	10 l	2.200	gallons
litre	l	1 l	1.760	pints
décilitre	dl	1/10 l	0.176	pints
centilitre	cl	1/100 l	0.070	gills

POIDS — WEIGHTS

avoirdupois

tonne	t	1.000 kg	0.984	tons
quintal	q	100 kg	220.462	pounds
kilogramme	kg	1 kg	2.205	pounds
hectogramme	hg	100 g	3.527	ounces
décagramme	dag	10 g	5.644	drams
gramme	g	1 g	15.432	grains
décigramme	dg	1/10 g	1.543	grains
centigramme	cg	1/100 g	0.154	grains
milligramme	mg	1/1000 g	0.015	grains

2. ANGLO-SAXONS
BRITISH & U.S.

DE LONGUEUR		LINEAR MEASURE		
inch	in.		2.540	cm
foot	f ft	12 inches	0.30480	m
yard	yd	3 feet	0.91438	m
fathom	fath	6 feet	1.8288	m
pole		5½ yards	5.0292	m
chain		22 yards	20.1168	m
furlong	fur	10 chains	201.168	m
mile	mi	8 furlongs	1.609	km

DE SUPERFICIE		SURFACE MEASURE		
square inch	sq in		6.4516	cm²
square foot	sq f	144 sq. inches	9.2903	dm²
square yard	sq yd	9 sq. feet	0.8361	m²
perch, rod, pole	p	30¼ sq. yards	25.293	m²
rood	r	40 perches	10.117	a
acre	ac	4 roods	40.468	a
sq. mile		640 acres	259	ha

DE VOLUME		CUBIC MEASURE		
cubic inch	cu in		16.387	cm³
cubic foot	cu f	1.728 inches	0.028317	m³
cubic yard	cu yd	27 cubic feet	0.764553	m³

DE CAPACITÉ		CAPACITY MEASURE			
			Brit.	U.S.	
gill	gi		0,142	0,118	l
pint	pt	4 gills	{ 0,568	0,473	l
			0,568	0,56	l (dry)
quart	qt	2 pints	{ 1,136	0,946	l
			1,136	1,12	l (dry)
gallon	gal	4 quarts	4,546	3,787	l
peck	pk	2 gallons	9,092	8,81	l
bushel	bu	8 gallons	36,37	35,24	l
quarter	qr	8 bushels	2,909		hl
barrel	bbl	31½ gallons		119,2	l
barrel	bbl		163,7	119,2	l (dry)
barrel (petrol)		42 gallons		158,8	l

AVOIRDUPOIS		AVOIRDUPOIS		
grain	gr		0.0648	g
dram	dr		1.772	g
ounce	oz	16 drams	28.350	g
pound	lb	16 ounces	453.593	g
stone	st	14 pounds	6.350	g
quarter	qr	28 pounds	12.700	kg
hundredweight	cwt	112 pounds	50.802	kg
ton	t	20 hundredweights	1.016,04	kg

POIDS TROY		TROY WEIGHT		
grain	gr		0.0648	g
pennyweight	dwt	24 grains	1.5552	g
ounce	oz	20 pennyweights	31.1035	g
pound	lb	12 ounces	373.2420	g

POIDS APOTHICAIRES		APOTHECARIES' WEIGHT		
grain	gr		0.0648	g
scruple	's ap	20 grains	1.296	g
drachms	dr ap	3 scruples	3.888	g
ounce	oz	8 drachms	31.1035	g

marabout

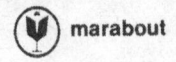

J.V. Servotte

dictionnaire commercial et financier

Betreff: Stellengesuc

als Volontär

Da ich erfahren habe

mir, Ihnen ergebe

Nach vierjähr

Handelsab

français/allemand
allemand/français

Achevé d'imprimer sur les presses de **Scorpion**,
à Verviers pour le compte des nouvelles éditions **marabout**.
D. 1980/0099/183